The
ENCYCLOPEDIA
of
BIRTHDAYS

The
ENCYCLOPEDIA
of
BIRTHDAYS

KNOW YOUR BIRTHDAY
DISCOVER YOUR TRUE PERSONALITY
REVEAL YOUR DESTINY

THERESA CHEUNG

THUNDER BAY
P · R · E · S · S
San Diego, California

Thunder Bay Press
An imprint of Printers Row Publishing Group
9717 Pacific Heights Blvd, San Diego, CA 92121
www.thunderbaybooks.com • mail@thunderbaybooks.com

Thunder Bay Press
Publisher: Peter Norton
Associate Publisher: Ana Parker
Editor: Dan Mansfield

Produced by HarperCollins*Publishers*
Editor: Caitlin Doyle • Designer: e-Digital Design
Author: Theresa Cheung
Illustrator: Andrew Paciorek

Library of Congress Cataloging-in-Publication data available on request.

ISBN: 978-1-6672-0077-4

Printed in Bosnia-Herzegovina

26 25 24 23 22   1 2 3 4 5

Contents

Acknowledgments

Thank you to Katy Carrington for being the inspiration behind this birthday profile book, to Wanda Whitely for her support, and to Carolyn Thorne and HarperCollins for sensing the need for a reissue. I am very grateful to Holly Blood for guiding me skillfully through the editing process of this reissue, to Andy Paciorek (www.batcow.co.uk) for his magical illustrations, and to Nick Fawcett for his superb editing and Lucy Brown and her team for their joyful promotion. Many thanks to Ingrid Court-Jones for her invaluable help during this enormous rewrite. Sincerest gratitude to my agent Jane Graham Maw (www.grahammawchristie.com) for her much-needed wisdom and support. I am also forever in debt to my readers, who have supported me over the many years I've written about New Age topics, and for the inspiration they continue to give me every single day. Special thanks to Lavendaire and to Alexander and to all the other amazing people who championed this book when I thought it had been long forgotten. Last, but by no means least, special thanks to Ray, Robert and Ruthie, for the pure magic and heart they bring into my life and to my soul dog, Arnie, whose loving presence makes every day feel like it's my birthday.

Welcome to a Whole New World of Birthdays!

"No wise man ever wished to be younger."

Jonathan Swift

The day you were born and the day you find out why are often said to be the two most important days of your life! You already know how special your birthday is. But do you know what your purpose is?

Finding meaning in life can prove to be elusive, especially today as the world struggles to reset following the grief, pain and confusion caused by the coronavirus pandemic and the much-needed exposure of global inequality and injustice. Not to mention the relentless rise of materialism, narcissism and fake news. It's not surprising many of us feel directionless and are searching for guidance and comfort in ancient wisdom and New Age insights. That's why I'm over the moon that *The Encyclopedia of Birthdays* has earned itself a much-needed reissue to speak loud and clear to modern times. It will show you that the two most important days of your life are powerfully linked. Harnessing the mystical potential of the day you were born can help you find your meaning and feel like you are born again.

And for those who are skeptical that there is a mystical power associated with the day of your birth, and everything in the cosmos might be linked, I'd like to offer some pause for thought. One of the greatest scientific minds of our generation, physicist Stephen Hawking, died on March 14, which just so happens to be the birthday of another scientific genius, Albert Einstein. And if that poetic synchronicity were not enough, Hawking was born on January 8, the day that another scientific mover and shaker, Galileo, died.

To return the spotlight to actual date of birth: legendary singers Elvis Presley and Shirley Bassey share the same birthday, as do Elton John and Aretha Franklin. Soccer stars Ronaldo and Neymar, actors Emma Thompson and Emma Watson, comedians Spike Milligan and Charlie Chaplin, Stephen Merchant and Billy Connolly, and politicians Margaret Thatcher and Alexandria Ocasio-Cortez are just a few of the countless shared birthdays this book will showcase. Sometimes the personality similarities or driving forces are so strong for people born on the same day of the year it is impossible to dismiss their shared date of birth as just "coincidence." Of course, the expression of a birthday's cosmic potential will be utterly unique to each individual's free choice but, more often than not, when you start to research influential people born on the same day certain common themes, challenges and blessings can be identified. This book will attempt to outline those commonalities in the hope that it will inspire everyone to fulfill their own infinite potential for making a positive impact on the world.

When this book was first published as a weighty hardback in 2007, and a slimmed-down paperback version a few years later, New Age practices were not enjoying the popularity they have today. Despite this, the book struck a familiar chord and over time started to gather a following. I had no idea how cherished it would eventually become but over the years I have received countless messages from people all over the world saying that understanding their birth date potential has helped them understand themselves and their lives better. Some have told me that knowing their profile positively transformed their lives, careers and relationships. As an author there can be nothing more humbling and rewarding than hearing from your readers that the insights you have shared have changed their lives for the better.

Being given the opportunity to update this book close to fifteen years after it was first written, so that it can speak clearly to what is current in our lives today, ensures its relevance. It is also a personal dream come true. I hope this fully updated version will remain a life-changing classic for many, many more birthdays to come.

New Birthday Revelations

This birthday encyclopedia is a resource and guide to personality and finding purpose for people born on each of the 366 days of the year. Simply by knowing birth dates you can discover insightful and accurate, luck-making information about yourself—your strengths, weaknesses, health, relationships, destiny, career and life goals—as well as about your loved ones, family, friends, colleagues, and even people you have just met. Be aware that the emphasis for each profile is on learning. From a spiritual perspective the purpose of life is to evolve. So even if you feel directionless or are going through a tough time, as long as you are learning about yourself you are evolving and living a life of meaning.

You can also use this book for guidance and inspiration every single day of the year. Indeed, this reissue aims to become a wider resource than one for simply looking up your own birthday profile and those of people you know. It is a handbook for daily cosmic guidance. Understanding and harnessing the unique energies and themes associated with each day of the year can maximize your chances of success and happiness on that particular day. This yearbook approach is also beneficial for those who, for some reason or another, are not sure what day of the year their birthday is. If this is the case for you, let this book help you seize your own destiny in your hands. As you review each day of the year, find the profile that speaks most to your personality and declare that day your special birthday.

The Profiles

It is important to point out from the onset that the power of your birthday is determined not just by your sun sign but by a number of other invisible influences and patterns in place the day you were born. This book reaches infinitely beyond popular sun-sign astrology, looking at influences and patterns through the lens of both Western and Chinese astrology, as well as incorporating numerology, Tarot, color theory, characteristics of influential people born on a specific day and, last but by no means least, the very real science linking personality and month of birth that is out there.

To help you understand how your birthday profile and the unique insight into your personality that it offers have been compiled, you'll find the basic principles of these ancient and modern arts, and how they have put their stamp on you, explained in the Introduction (see pages xv–xxvi). But if you want to dive straight into a specific birth profile, whether yours or one of somebody you know, you can always return here another time. Whichever way you decide to read this birthday encyclopedia, be sure to take a moment first to digest the information below about how you can make the very best use of this book. Also, be sure to remember that every

person is born unique and bursting with potential, just as each new day is also unique and bursting with potential.

How to Use This Book

The Encyclopedia of Birthdays is organized as a yearbook, starting on January 1 and ending on December 31, but it is also arranged in parts: the Introduction, Heed Your Signs, 366 Birthday Profiles and Reach for Your Stars.

I have updated the **Introduction** to take into account Chinese astrology, research into personality influenced by month of birth and other influences. It also explains how I compiled each of the 366 birthday personality profiles. You'll see that they are a unique combination of ancient and modern, spiritual and psychological perspectives. You'll also discover how putting all these influences together can help you become an expert on yourself and others. You are strongly advised to read the Introduction (see pages xv–xxvi) *before* reading your individual birthday profile. The information and advice there will inform and enrich what you read in your profile.

Then, after you've read the Introduction, the next step is to refer to pages xxvii–xxviii, **Heed Your Signs**. There, to get you thinking along the right lines about your birthday profile, you will find listed the pages relevant to generic personality traits for your sun sign and its Chinese equivalent. This is helpful information as, whether you feel true to your sun sign or not, the sun is a symbol of your hidden potential and the life lessons you need to learn.

Be sure also to check out **Reach for the Stars** (pages 537–538), the final section of this book, too—preferably *before*

you jump to your individual birthday profile. This will encourage you to see the book not just as a single profile for your birthday or a group of profiles for people you know, but as a **daily** cosmic planner you can dip into every single day of the year for guidance and inspiration. Indeed, you are strongly advised to use this book in this way because, from a spiritual perspective, every night when we gently fade away to the land of sleep, we "die" and are "reborn" again the next morning, therefore making every new day a special "birthday."

The 366 Birthday Profiles (see pages 1–532) are, of course, the main body of the book. They have all been updated to speak to modern times. I could write an entire manuscript on each day of the year because of the wealth of information I could potentially include. But due to space restrictions, I have instead focused on the key information and the most important themes. If you want more insight or want to know more about how to interpret and make the most of your birthday potential, you are welcome to contact me.

How to Contact Me

You can message me via my trusty reader email: angeltalk710@aol.com. But in keeping with this book I have moved with the times and you can now contact me via my Facebook, Instagram and Twitter author pages. You can also message me via: www.theresacheung.com. Do subscribe to my newsletter if you visit my website. It's a way for me to share the latest research and to update you about birthdays and other New Age topics.

Feel free to get in touch if you have any questions, insights or stories you want to share with me and potentially with a wider audience. I endeavor to reply to everyone who reaches out to me. But please bear in mind that sometimes it can take a while to reply if life is super-busy, or I need to take a little time out to celebrate a birthday or two.

And now, without further ado, welcome to a whole new world of birthdays!

Step-by-step guide to getting the best out of this book

1. Read the Introduction (see pages xv–xxvi).

2. Read the pages relevant to you in Heed Your Signs (see pages xxvii–xxviii).

3. Read the closing sections of the book (see pages 533–538).

4. Read and reflect deeply on your individual birthday profile.

5. Read and reflect on the profiles of loved ones and friends, and anyone you care to understand better.

6. Use this book every day as a cosmic yearbook, reading and reflecting on a profile a day to guide and inspire you, and align you with the invisible influences and hidden potential that shapes each day of the year.

Introduction: The Life-changing Power of the Day You Were Born

"There was a star danced, and under that I was born."

William Shakespeare

What exactly is a birthday profile? In short, it's the rebirth of ancient arts—astrology, Chinese astrology, numerology, Tarot, and color theory or chromotherapy—threaded together by a modern psychological interpretation. Every profile also takes into account studies into how the month of a person's birth shapes their personality, along with research into what personality traits highly influential people born on a specific day have in common. This unique combination results in a blend of cosmic and earthly, ancient and modern influences that can significantly affect your personality and destiny, providing you with invaluable insight into yourself as well as the lives, feelings, hopes and fears of loved ones, family, friends, colleagues and everyone else who crosses your path in life.

To help you better understand exactly how each birthday profile has been created, I have included the basic principles of these ancient arts and modern practices. You will see that individually each one can shine a light on the person you are but, when blended altogether, they can provide an exciting road map to your infinite potential.

The Basics of Astrology

Astrology regards personality and destiny as being influenced by the state of the cosmos at the exact moment of birth. The sun, the moon and the planets are seen as basic energies or life forces, and these forces take on different expressions depending on their position in relation to the place and time of a person's birth. A birth or natal chart, also known as a horoscope, records the position of the planets when a person is born. It also looks at how these planets move over the course of their life and the influence such cosmic shifts can potentially have.

Astrology is an ancient practice dating way back in time to Babylonian, Egyptian and Aztec cultures. For centuries in the West, astrology was chiefly used for divination (fortune-telling) purposes by nobles and royalty. It fell out of favor in the seventeenth century and, as science developed, it was dismissed as superstition, but it never completely lost its appeal. In the early twentieth century interest in astrology re-emerged, this time not as a predictive technique but rather as a psychological tool for greater self-knowledge or awareness.

From the 1960s onward the popularity of astrology began to rise, with increasing numbers of people seeking a spiritual perspective on life. Today, astrology is not so much seen as a divination tool but as a self-help or personal-growth aid to finding meaning in life. Another modern development is that astrology is no longer regarded as complicated and requiring professional interpretation. These days anyone can learn about astrology and use its wisdom as a way to help them understand themselves and fulfill their potential.

Most of us know and identify with the characteristics of our sun sign—for example, Aries, Taurus and so on. The sun travels through the 12 signs of the zodiac through the course of the year and so when someone is said to have been born under Pisces, they were born when the sun was passing through the portion of the zodiac named after the constellation of Pisces. Each of the 12 signs has defining personality traits, with the elements of fire, water, earth and air also affecting each sun sign.

The 12 sun or zodiac signs correspond roughly to the 12 months of the year, and each of these sun signs symbolizes archetypes or universal life experiences. In your life you need to journey through the entire zodiac wheel of life and understand the experiences of all the other sun signs, but your sun sign reveals the major personality characteristics you are born to learn and express.

Although two people born under the same sun sign may share general personality traits, the reason they will not be entirely the same personality-wise is that the positions of the other planets will be different, depending on their motion on the day and at the time and place of birth. For example, as the sun travels through the zodiac sign over the course of a month, it passes through three periods of time called decanates, making each decanate approximately ten days long. Each decanate adds the influences of its own associated planet and sign to the basic influences of the sun sign. Therefore, by considering the decanate as well as the sun sign, you can fine-tune the reading for an individual's birthday. Let's look at an example. An Aries born sometime in the second decanate (March 31 to April 9) will be under the additional influence of the second decanate sign of Leo and the star associated with Leo, which is the sun. The ancient Egyptian astrologers considered the decanates to be as important as the sun signs themselves.

Progressions are another important consideration, especially for predictive purposes. The sun takes about thirty years to journey (or progress) through each sign of the zodiac and, in a person's lifetime, it will typically move through three to four zodiac signs, depending on the lifespan of the individual and their date of birth. Each time the sun progresses from one sign to another, this indicates a significant birthday or time in life when there is likely to be a dramatic change in either circumstances or outlook. For example, the progressed sun of a Scorpio born on November 9 will move into Sagittarius at the age of 13, into Capricorn at the age of 43 and then Aquarius at the age of 73. That's why you'll notice that in each of the 366 profiles I have made reference to specific ages.

Fixed stars associated with a particular day of the year also exert additional influences, and other astrological factors come into play, but if decanates and progressions sound confusing, don't worry. You don't need to have your birth chart drawn up or to consult complicated tables to use this book. I have taken all the calculations and relevant interpretations into account when compiling each birthday profile. All you need to do is read your profile and let it inspire you to reach your full potential.

Sun-sign date variations

You may notice variations in the dates given for your sun sign, depending on which source you consult. This is because the zodiac has 360 degrees, whereas a year has 365 days, or 366 if it is a leap year. In addition, the sun does not enter the various sections of the zodiac on exactly the same date each year. The dates in this book try to take into account sun-sign variations from one year to another, but if you are born within two or three days of the dates given for each sign, your birthday lies on what astrologers call the cusp. If you were born on a cusp this is exciting, as you can read and benefit from the sun-sign insight in the Heed Your Signs section (see pages xxvii–xxviii) for two signs—the one your birthday falls in and the sign that follows or precedes it. For example, if you were born on April 19, you will share both Aries and Taurus characteristics. If you were born on September 23, you will share both Libra and Virgo traits. Needless to say, I have taken the characteristics of both signs into account when creating all the cusp birthday profiles. And, if you were born a few hours after or a few hours before midnight, you may want to read the profile for the day before or after your birthday too, as those influences will cross over to your birthday.

The Science of Astrology

For the skeptics who struggle with the concept of "as above, so below," ponder this: Science has shown that the gravitational pull of the moon on the Earth impacts the water in our oceans and tides. And up to 60 percent of the human adult body is made up of water!

Although some studies show that lunar phases can affect a person's mood and behavior, to date there is no proven link between the position of the moon, sun and planets at time of birth and human personality. However, research into the seasons, and even the month in which a person is born, suggests otherwise.

In the early 1970s, researchers from the UK compiled data from the British population census showing clearly that architects tended to be born in the spring, secretaries in the summer, miners in the autumn and electricians in the winter. The researchers asked members of the British Astrological Association (BAA) to indicate which signs were associated with the professions of nurse and labor union official. The astrologers' predictions corresponded with the researchers' own findings that there was a statistical bias toward nurses being born under the signs of Taurus, Cancer, Virgo, Scorpio and Pisces, and labor union officials being born under one or other of the other signs.

Over the years research has focused on the influence of one star in particular—the sun. This is because ultraviolet radiation (UVR), a type of radiation emitted by the sun, is believed to cause genetic changes in the developing baby that may have a shaping effect on their life and personality. This could explain from a scientific perspective why many of us believe that common characteristics and fates are shared by those born at the same time of the year. For example, researchers have found that your chances of living beyond 100 are higher if you are born in November or December. However, it is important to remember that the research on which this is based, on the impact of sun radiation, doesn't necessarily apply to people born in the southern hemisphere, where summer starts in December and finishes at the end of February.

Here's a snapshot of other significant findings by different researchers to date. Bear in mind that new studies come out all the time; now you have this book, you may want to keep track of them.

Happiness: According to a UK study, people born in March, April and May tend to be more optimistic than people born at other times of the year. But those born in winter and spring can also be more prone to mood swings, with January being the month most linked with bipolar disorder and May being the month most linked with depression. Those born in September, October and November have the lowest rates of depression, but can be more prone to irritability. Another study from Austria suggested that happy people are more likely to have been born in June, July and August. Meanwhile, research from Japan found that people born in December, January and February were likely to be more pessimistic than those born at other times of the year.

Personality: Swedish researchers found that women born between February and April were more likely to be novelty seekers than those born in October and November. Men born in spring were more likely to be impulsive, while those born in winter were prone to intro-spection. According to small studies of celebrities, being born in January and February increases the chances of becoming famous, as these months are linked to creativity. In general, many studies show that those born in win-ter are less positive in their outlook on life than those born in the sum-mer. In addition, November- and win-ter-born children may end up being bigger, taller and more academically inclined than those born in summer, according to American psychiatrists, with September-born babies most likely to go to college. Babies born in the fall also tend to perform better at athletics and sports.

Health: British research has shown that those born in winter have a greater risk of developing heart disease and an increased risk of obesity. In gener-al, the latest research into our month of birth and health in the northern hemisphere suggests that being born in January, June, August and December neither increases nor decreases the risk of disease; October and November are associated with increased risk, with September not far behind; February, March, April and July have a decreased risk; and May is the healthiest month of all in which to be born.

None of this research should encour-age prospective parents to try to time the births of their children. There are many academic children born in the spring and many healthy people born in November. Your personality and your health are influenced by so many things other than the month you were born in.

But what all this science of birthdays does show is that there is some scientific correlation between month of birth and personality traits. I have taken this cor-relation into account when creating the 366 profiles.

Highly Influential

You'll notice a "Born today" list of names for each of the birthday profiles. The characteristics these people had or have in common were also taken into account during the creation of each profile. Some of these people are world famous, but others less so. They were selected for inclusion because in my opinion in their different ways they are all people who maximized or are maximizing the mys-tical potential of the day they were born.

The people chosen all tilted or are tilting the world in a more positive or uplifting direction. (You won't find Hitler, born on April 20, listed, for example, or Charles Manson, born on November 12.) In other words, we can admire and learn from them. Knowing you share a birthday with someone influential or inspirational can be educa-tional and motivational.

Details about these individuals have been kept as concise as possible, simply listing their full name and what they are most well known for. This brevity will hopefully encourage you to do your own research about them because their life choices may offer you further inspir-ation about your own life choices. If in your research about people born on your birthday you do stumble across less savory examples, don't let that disheart-en you. Every person is born a complex mix of positive and negative potential. There are saints and sinners born every single day of the year. Your personality is formed and your destiny created not by your potential for positive or negative, but by the choices you make every day and what you actually decide to do with your one precious life.

Potential and Pitfalls

Even though there may be certain similarities for people born on the same day, as mentioned earlier, never ever forget that every person is born unique and full of their own potential, just as every new day is also unique and full of its own potential. Bear in mind, too, that there are going to be both blessings and challenges associated with each birthday in the year.

We all have free will. Each one of us has a **choice**. We can choose to maximize the blessings of the day or allow negative choices to drain our potential. The purpose of our lives is to evolve. It is only by facing and overcoming challenges that we learn and grow. Sometimes growth hurts, but this struggle isn't necessarily a negative thing. It can be the very best thing for your evolution or spiritual awakening. In other words, if your birthday seems to focus more on overcoming challenges, this doesn't put you at a disadvantage. Quite the opposite. It suggests huge potential for personal growth and living a life of deep meaning.

The Basics of Chinese Astrology

Chinese astrology is similar to Western astrology in that it helps its followers understand themselves and others better. It also consists of 12 signs and each of these signs offers profound insight into personality traits. And just as in Western astrology your horoscope consists of more than your sun sign, that's also the case with Chinese astrology. Each sign has an element, a balance of yin and yang and divisions to consider.

However, the similarities end there. The names of the 12 signs in Western astrology derive from constellations, whereas the names of the 12 signs in Chinese astrology derive from animals. The Chinese believe that the animal sign you are born under impacts your personality and destiny, as expressed in the saying, "This animal hides in your heart." According to ancient myth, the Jade Emperor (some variations say it was the Buddha) called all the animals to take part in a race. But only 12 animals came, so these 12 were given the honor of having a year named after them according to their finishing place in the race, with the rat coming in first and the wild boar or pig last.

Perhaps the biggest difference between the two systems is that Chinese astrology determines your zodiac sign by year of birth, while Western astrology determines it by day and month of birth. Also, the Western zodiac year begins at the spring equinox. In the East each Chinese sign is determined by the lunar calendar and begins at Chinese New Year, which is the second new moon after the winter solstice.

So, given these differences, is it possible to find correspondences between Chinese astrology and the Western signs? The answer is yes, because the 12 Chinese signs that make up the 12-year cycle known as Sheng Xiao ("birth likeness") actually correspond to the 12-year

Rat	1924	1936	1948	1960	1972	1984	1996	2008	2020
Ox	1925	1937	1949	1961	1973	1985	1997	2009	2021
Tiger	1926	1938	1950	1962	1974	1986	1998	2010	2022
Rabbit	1927	1939	1951	1963	1975	1987	1999	2011	2023
Dragon	1928	1940	1952	1964	1976	1988	2000	2012	2024
Snake	1929	1941	1953	1965	1977	1989	2001	2013	2025
Horse	1930	1942	1954	1966	1978	1990	2002	2014	2026
Goat	1931	1943	1955	1967	1979	1991	2003	2015	2027
Monkey	1932	1944	1956	1968	1980	1992	2004	2016	2028
Rooster	1933	1945	1957	1969	1981	1993	2005	2017	2029
Dog	1934	1946	1958	1970	1982	1994	2006	2018	2030
Pig	1935	1947	1959	1971	1983	1995	2007	2019	2031

cycle of the planet Jupiter in Western astrology. It is therefore possible to match each Chinese sign to a Western counterpart. I have taken this East-meets-West astrology correspondence into account when creating each birthday profile.

In the Heed Your Signs section of this book (see pages xxvii–xxviii), you will notice that each sun-sign description also includes its Chinese astrology counterpart description. For example, if you are an Aries, your Chinese sign correspondence is the Dragon. You will therefore have a natural affinity with the symbolic qualities of that mythical animal.

In addition to your Chinese astrology sun-sign match, you are also encouraged to read the relevant section for the animal that corresponds with your year of birth (see table above). That animal may well be associated with a different sun sign to your own. For example, if you are a Taurus born in 1996, you should read your corresponding Chinese astrology sign, which is the Snake, but you should also read the section about the Rat, as you will have an affinity with both

Snake and Rat characteristics and can discover much of value about yourself from reading both.

Numerology Basics

What astrology does through sun or animal signs, numerology does through numbers. Like astrology, numerology is an ancient symbolic method that can be incorporated into a birthday profile to help you reach a better understanding of yourself and the meaning of your life. Numerologists assert that the universe is a mathematical construct. God is believed to be the master mathematician and the vibrational energy of people, places and things is expressed through the sacred power of numbers. By reducing birth dates and names to a number, we can allegedly reveal a person's personality and destiny.

Although numerology probably has its origins in ancient Babylonia and among the early Hebrews, and many different systems have been used in different parts of the world, numerology is most often associated with the fifth-century BC Greek mathematician and philosopher Pythagoras. He believed that there were mathematical connections between the cosmos, humanity, music, shapes, colors and numbers. If certain number patterns appeared, they could be used to predict the destiny of a person. According to Pythagoras, numbers were the source of energy in the world and the numbers 1 to 9 represent the nine stages of life. He is quoted as having said, "The world is built upon the power of numbers."

Numerology assigns characteristics to the digits 1 to 9. Any number larger than 9 is reduced to a single digit by adding all the digits together—for example, the number 123 becomes $1 + 2 + 3 = 6$. The qualities of 123 are therefore equivalent to the number 6. Using the single digits as a guide, the patterns of different dates and a person's name (each letter of the alphabet is assigned to a number between 1 and 9 and several letters are therefore attached to the same number) can be examined to define character and future influences. Briefly, the numbers 1 to 9 represent the following characteristics or qualities:

1. Independent, creative, ambitious, extrovert
   Downside: Can be arrogant and selfish, with tunnel vision

2. Sensitive, domestic, imaginative, musical
   Downside: Can be timid and gullible

3. Scientific, powerful, knowledgeable, multitalented
   Downside: Can be superficial and hedonistic

4. Practical, stable, honest, trustworthy
   Downside: Can be stubborn and overly serious

5. Energetic, sensual, daring, flirtatious
   Downside: Can find it hard to commit

6. Perfectionist, creative, artistic, compassionate
   Downside: Can be super-sensitive and overemotional

7. Intellectual, philosophical, imaginative, intuitive
   Downside: Can be impractical and secretive

8. Practical, just, trustworthy, noble, powerful
   Downside: Can be opinionated, impatient and intolerant

9. Spiritual, humanitarian, visionary, a healer
   Downside: Can be self-serving, possessive and volatile

Although in the majority of cases number combinations are reduced to single-digit numbers, it is important to point out that this is not the case for the master numbers, 11, 22 and 33, which are believed to have extra intuitive potential due to the pairing of the same number. Just as astrologers believe no one sign is better than another, numerologists believe no number is better or worse than any other. All the numbers have potential as well as a downside in the same way that every person has a light as well as a dark or shadow side. The downside simply suggests challenges associated with this number; if these challenges can be faced and overcome, they can be a source of incredible personal growth.

In the creation of each profile for this book, the interpretations of numbers in relation to the date of the month in which you were born is taken into consideration. This is called your *birth day* number. It is one of the five core numbers in numerology based on either your birth date or birth name and indicates the skills that come naturally to you as well as any day-to-day challenges you need to face. According to numerologists, your birth day number has a permanent influence on your life and has great significance in helping you understand who you are and where your talents lie.

Tarot Basics

Each day of the year is also associated with a Tarot card.

Although the true origins of Tarot cards are unknown and may date back to ancient Egypt or earlier, the Tarot cards that we know today originated in Italy during the fifteenth century. The Tarot deck consists of 78 cards in total, comprising the 22 major arcana cards, which the nineteenth-century French occultist Eliphas Levi saw as having symbolic links to the 22 letters of the Hebrew alphabet, and the 56 minor arcana cards, which are divided into four suits: wands, representing the element of fire; swords, the element of air; cups, the element of water; and pentacles, the

element of earth. There are several versions of the Tarot deck in use today, but most are based on the Rider-Waite deck designed by Arthur Edward Waite and Pamela Colman Smith in 1910.

Although each minor arcana card has a divinatory meaning, the major arcana cards are of greater significance in this book because they represent universal or archetypal life themes and the quest for self-knowledge and finding purpose—which is what each birthday profile hopes to reveal. Each day of the year is associated with a major arcana card. You may want to meditate further on the profound wisdom of the Tarot card listed in your profile and what insights it can offer you about yourself and your life. Their meanings are briefly summarized below.

The Fool: Represents the divine child, one who is completely trusting and spontaneous. The Fool is beginning a journey and has no idea where it will lead, but he is also content because he listens to his heart.

The Magician: Symbolizes creative power, curiosity and infinite possibilities. Called the Magus in some Tarot decks, the Magician has access to all four elements of the Tarot to manifest the divine work he has come to Earth to achieve.

The High Priestess: Signifies mystery, dreams and the power of intuition. It is spiritual awakening.

The Empress: Represents the ability to adapt and flow according to the needs of the moment. The Empress draws her strength and peace from the natural world.

The Emperor: Is the balance to the Empress and symbolizes work, money, grounding. It is the ability to express your skills and assert your authority in the material world.

The Hierophant: Is a symbol of inner wisdom, also known as your Higher Self. It's also a compilation of the previous four cards, synthesizing and empowering these initial stages of spiritual growth and evolution.

The Lovers: Signifies the awareness of opposites and the relationship between opposites. The Lovers indicates the need to find balance within yourself and in your relationships with others.

The Chariot: Represents your personal will aligning itself with a power greater than yourself. It is the struggle between your ego balancing itself with the needs of others and the world.

Justice: Symbolizes a rebalancing process, so what has been out of harmony in your life can seek resolution. It is also the karma card.

The Hermit: Signifies a period of solitude or the need to walk alone for a while to discover who you truly are. The Hermit card indicates the need to empower yourself rather than looking for validation externally.

The Wheel of Fortune: Represents a period of dramatic change or the need for change. The wheel of fortune often turns unexpectedly and forces you to step outside your comfort zone, the place where all personal growth happens.

Strength: Symbolizes your potential to rise above challenges you are encountering. It suggests that you are far stronger and more capable than you think you are.

The Hanged Man: This card suggests the need to take a different perspective on life. It is also the card of surrender or simply letting things be.

Death: Signifies letting go of the past so that new things can begin. It is the card of rebirth and renewal.

Temperance: Is a card of moderation and patience. It represents acceptance of a situation and the need to balance opposites or open your mind to differing viewpoints.

The Devil: Symbolizes the pleasures of the material world. It is preoccupation with status, money and power and the need to reconnect with what really matters in life.

The Tower: Signifies the shattering of limiting beliefs about yourself and your life. It suggests sudden change, but also liberation.

The Star: Represents spiritual healing and inspiration. This illumination was made possible through the shattering of illusions or beliefs that have been limiting you.

The Moon: Symbolizes great creativity but also illusion. Something in your life may not be all that it seems.

The Sun: Signifies confidence. It is finding the courage to be yourself and loving the person you are.

Judgment: Represents rebirth and awakening. It is the card of judgment but also of second chances and new beginnings. It suggests that you have the power to change your life for the better.

The World: Symbolizes completion and a joyful celebration of the dance of life. The World card incorporates the universal themes of all the previous cards.

Many astrologers and numerologists believe that the major arcana cards are related to astrological and numerological personality tendencies. For example, the Emperor card is ruled by the astrological sign of Aries and the number 5. As such, the symbolic meanings of these major arcana cards, when considered in combination with the meanings offered by astrology and numerology, can offer another layer of insight to each birthday profile.

The Basics of Color Healing

Each astrological sign is associated with a certain color or colors. According to color therapists or chromotherapists, these can have a special significance in a birthday profile because our lives can be enhanced if we surround ourselves with the colors that are most harmonious with our own personal vibrations for that day.

Color analysts assert that every color vibrates with its own energy and, because of this, can have a healing impact on mood and wellbeing. Seven colors in particular—red, orange, yellow, green, blue, indigo and violet, the colors of the rainbow—have carried religious,

occult and mystical significance since ancient times.

In the late nineteenth century, color theory began to receive attention in the West; in 1878 Edwin Babbitt published *The Principles of Light and Color,* highlighting a theory of healing with color. Modern research can offer credible evidence for some of the ancient claims about colors. Studies show that they really can trigger emotional and physical healing. Many psychologists use color to produce beneficial effects in homes, workplaces and hospitals.

Wearing particular colors can also have a similar effect. For example, wearing blue helps create an atmosphere of peace and relaxation. Blue is also the color of communication and truth. Another harmonious and healing color is green. It is believed to promote self-love. Orange is a stimulating and creative color. Wearing or seeing orange can increase energy and focus. Yellow and gold have a re-energizing effect when mood is low. They are also cleansing and purifying colors. Perhaps the most stimulating and potent color for mind and body is red. It is believed to boost confidence and energy. Purple is the color of intuition, self-knowledge, and personal and spiritual growth. As you read your birthday profile you may want to surround yourself with the color purple.

Putting It All Together

As you can see, the basic principles of Western and Chinese astrology, numerology, Tarot and color analysis, and even scientific studies on birth months, are interrelated. But as you read this book, rather than focusing (as you may have done in the past) on the general characteristics associated with your sun or animal sign or whatever Tarot card, color or number represents you, take a fresh new perspective on yourself. Focus on what your date of birth says about you.

There is a world of possibility contained in each date of birth. You were born during a particular season, under a particular sun sign in a particular decanate. Your sun sign corresponds to a Chinese astrology sign. Each day also has a numerical vibration, Tarot association and a color vibration that have a specific meaning and significance. All these invisible energies shape your personality, relationship and career choices and life experiences, and, when combined with the science of birthdays and personality, as well as research into what influential people born on your birthday have in common, this creates the 366 unique and in-depth personality profiles. The hope is that you will refer to this book time and time again, not only to help you understand yourself and others better by referencing your and their date of birth, but also to help you unlock the potential hidden in every day of the year.

The psychological approach for each profile involves you in becoming an expert on yourself and others. Use the insight here to help you develop a deeper understanding of what makes you and other people tick. Use it to help you discover what your strengths are and to find ways to compensate for your weaknesses. Use it to work toward positive growth and change in all aspects of your life. And use it to help you attract luck and success into your life all year round.

Ultimately, this book is a celebration of growth of all types, including personal growth: the process of growth and change that can be seen each year as the seasons melt into one another; growth and change that manifest in all human development and transformation; and growth and change that bring meaning and purpose to all our lives. If you are going through challenging times, remember that diamonds are made under pressure. Growth simply doesn't happen when you are in your comfort zone, and sometimes growth hurts. Meditate on the insight offered in your birthday profile and allow it to guide and inspire you to become a better person than you were yesterday. The purpose of our lives is to constantly learn and grow. As long as you are learning, you are living a meaningful life.

Only by finding ways to challenge yourself and work toward your true potential can you live for today, transform your tomorrows and start discovering all the wonderful gifts the universe has bestowed upon you from the moment of your birth. Your birthday profile is a defining factor that distinguishes you from other people. But never forget that your profile merely highlights *potential* strengths and weaknesses, and that you always have a choice.

You can choose to see the light or hide in the shadows. You can refuse to budge or you can seize the day. You can wait for luck to happen or you can try to make your own luck. You can watch or you can join in. You can sleep or you can dance under your stars.

Isn't it time for you to dance and live as only *you* can?

Heed Your Signs

"Some day you will be old enough to start reading fairy tales again."
C. S. Lewis

Before reading your individual birthday profile and the profiles of people you know or anyone you hope to understand better, be sure to read about the generic personality traits of your sun sign and Chinese sign equivalent, referring to the page numbers listed below. Many other factors make up a birth chart, but more than anything else in astrology, the sun represents your **potential**. It shines an intense light on what motivates you in life, or what will likely bring you the greatest fulfillment. So, even if you don't feel you are entirely true to your sun sign, familiarizing yourself with your sun-sign personality potential and pitfalls can offer you profound life lessons and wisdom.

- Scorpio and the Pig
  (October 23 to November 21),
  see pages 423 to 464

- Sagittarius and the Rat
  (November 22 to December 21),
  see pages 467 to 508

- Capricorn and the Ox
  (December 22 to January 19),
  see pages 511 to 532, 2 to 20

Be aware, too, that the wheel of the zodiac begins with the sun sign Aries and ends with Pisces, and each of the signs symbolizes the wheel of life and the different ages, phases and stages in our lives. Aries and Taurus are the babies of the zodiac, Gemini and Cancer the children, Leo the teenager, and Virgo and Libra the adults. Scorpio and Sagittarius symbolize a mature hunger for knowledge, Capricorn the consolidation of experience and Aquarius and Pisces move toward idealism and a desire to see the bigger picture, which often accompanies life's later stages. This isn't to say that all Aries-born are innocent and childish or that all Pisceans are wise and mature, as many factors make up a birth chart, but seeing the sun signs in this light can help give you an instant sense and understanding of the driving force behind each sun sign.

By contrast, the Chinese zodiac begins with the sign of the Rat, then follows in this order: Ox, Tiger, Rabbit, Dragon, Snake, Horse, Goat, Monkey, Rooster, Dog and Pig. According to legend this is the order they finished in

a race, but this placement also suggests that curiosity, acquiring knowledge, gaining experience, looking beneath the surface of things and confidently setting intentions should perhaps be the foundation stones for building a fulfilling life. In other words, in Chinese astrology there are strong similarities between endings and beginnings, and the end can become the beginning. Do bear in mind, though, that Chinese astrology acknowledges that the year a person is born and Western sun-sign equivalents are not the only considerations, as animal signs can be assigned by month, day and even hour, meaning every person is a unique combination of several different animals.

All Year Round

After reading about the blessings, challenges and wisdom of your sun sign, it's time to dive into the 366 Birthday Profiles (see pages 1–532). And once you've digested and reflected on your individual profile, and those of all the people you know, be sure to read **The Best and Worst of Days** (see pages 533–535) and **Reach for the Stars** (see pages 537–538). These closing sections will help you transform this book into a **cosmic yearbook** that you can use every single day of the year. Simply refer to today's date, and align yourself with the themes and massive potential for personal growth offered for that day. In this way you can harness birthday guidance and inspiration all year round, whether today is your birthday or not!

366 Birthday Profiles: Your Cosmic Yearbook

"It is never too late to be what you might have been."

George Eliot

In the pages that follow you will find a birthday profile for every day of the year. Remember, this profile represents your **potential**. It is not written in stone. I'll risk repeating myself, as this is too important: You are born with free will and the choice is always yours about what you decide to do with your one precious life. Hopefully, what you read about the unique power of the day on which you were born will resonate strongly with you, and inspire you to believe in yourself and live your dreams.

If what you read doesn't completely resonate, this doesn't mean you are born on the wrong day or the profile is flawed. It simply means you are forging a new path, and there can be nothing more exciting than that. Perhaps what you read in your profile will still offer you food for thought or a different perspective. There are infinite possibilities and many different paths to take in life. And every path you take, even if it is a winding one that doesn't lead to any destination in particular, will teach you something valuable that you need in your search for the bigger picture of your life.

It is not so much the arrival at a destination, but the journey of life itself—and what you learned about yourself during those times you felt lost—that ultimately gives your life its meaning. As long as you are learning and living each day of your life to the full, rest assured you are already living a meaningful life.

Birthstones

Birthstones are gemstones that represent each month of the year. Each stone is said to have a unique energy, meaning and significance. It is widely believed that wearing the birthstone of the month on which you were born can attract good fortune your way. You may want to research the meaning of your birthstone and meditate on, wear or use it in your daily life. But don't feel you can't draw on the healing energies of all the other birthstones, too. A birthstone may be aligned to a certain month, but birthstones and the magic they can bring are for everyone regardless of the month they are born.

1. *January:* Garnet (luck)

2. *February:* Amethyst (wisdom)

3. *March:* Aquamarine (peace)

4. *April:* Diamond or quartz (courage)

5. *May:* Emerald (hope)

6. *June:* Pearl (love)

7. *July:* Ruby (vitality)

8. *August:* Peridot (beauty)

9. *September:* Sapphire (truth)

10. *October:* Opal or tourmaline (healing)

11. *November:* Topaz or citrine (happiness)

12. *December:* Tanzanite or turquoise (intuition)

These Are the Days of Your Life

And once you've reflected on your profile, and those of people you know or have yet to get to know, don't allow yourself to waste the potential of any day in your life ever again. Every morning be sure to meditate on the birthday profile for the day ahead. Let the life wisdom there help you tap into the secret potential and power of that day and attract good fortune your way so that you can choose to make every day of the year, and of your life, a very special day.

The
ENCYCLOPEDIA
of
BIRTHDAYS

January 1

The Birthday of Self-improvement

"When one door closes, another always opens for me"

Bursting with enthusiasm, people born on January 1 are instinctive and idealistic trailblazers. They value the lessons they have learned from their past and use this to plan ahead for a better future. Once they settle on a goal, their drive, determination and organizational skills typically ensure success. But when things don't go according to their best-laid plans, they can become impatient, oversensitive and insecure. They need to break through their fear of the unexpected and recognize that their way isn't always the best or only way.

These people are born experts, often rising to leadership roles where their opinions and skills are highly valued. There is a voice inside them urging them to work harder and longer, and to always do better. This quality makes them big achievers, but they can get so caught up in their self-improvement that they lose their sense of humor and the bigger picture along the way. They thrive when self-employed, but are also drawn to careers in teaching, business, the law, finance and education, healthcare, programming, gaming, personal development or any work that allows them to rise to the top and engage and enlighten others through specialization. Burnout is one of their biggest health risks and, because they are so self-critical, they can suffer from bouts of depression. Listening to their intuition rather than their head will help them find inner peace. Breathing in a few drops of lavender essential oil on a handkerchief can ease stress. **For self-care,** rise and shine at the same time each day. Avoid lying in or burning the midnight oil. Successful people retire and rise early.

January 1-born are often kind-hearted and trusting, but can become controlling of others. They need plenty of adventure and intellectual stimulation in their love relationships, otherwise they will get bored. Under the age of 40 they run the risk of becoming workaholics and marginalizing the importance of their personal growth, but fortunately this destructive trend diminishes the older they get. Once they figure out that resilience, open-mindedness and a sprinkling of laughter mixed with optimism are just as important for success as hard work, their destiny is to lead and inspire others to new heights with their dedicated sense of purpose.

Potential: Dedicated, inspirational

Dark side: Manipulative, impatient

Tarot card, lucky numbers, days, colors: The Devil, 1, 2, Saturday, Sunday, blue, orange

Born today: J. D. Salinger (novelist); Christine Lagarde (politician); Chai Jing (broadcaster)

January 2

The Birthday of the Intuitive Leader

The life lesson: is to understand that being different from everyone else isn't a weakness.

The way forward: is to value your uniqueness as a strength.

Luck maker: Focus on your strengths, and see your weaknesses as opportunities to learn and grow.

"I see clearly what others miss"

The motivated and dedicated but also intuitive and highly observant people born on January 2 have a remarkable ability to tune into their surroundings and the feelings of others. Their sensitivity can work against them, making them feel isolated and different rather than unique and natural. But once they can learn to value their intuition, January 2 people can unlock incredible creativity in themselves and others.

Those born on January 2 are natural artists, teachers and healers, but can also thrive in public relations, management, personal development, life-coaching, counseling, photography, art, writing, social media and any career that offers them an opportunity to observe themselves, others or the world in a creative way. Although they are by nature serious and reserved, when their self-confidence is high their intuition works at its best and is the force that helps them excel in any chosen career. Self-critical perfectionists, they can sometimes be their own worst critic and enemy. January 2-born need to ensure they take regular time out to unwind and relax with their loved ones, friends or pets. Carrying a small rose-quartz crystal around with them helps them to attract the energy of self-love. **For self-care**, every morning on waking immediately think of three things in your life to be grateful for.

The potential for rising to the top of their chosen field is there, but if self-belief is lacking, they will waste their talents with self-doubt and not maximize this potential. The same applies to their relationships. Their giving nature can be taken advantage of. Sometimes, their acute sensitivity makes them unpredictable and moody and it is hard for them to know which feelings belong to them and which belong to others. There is a powerful shift toward setting boundaries and personal growth before the age of 50, and after that they really come into their own. Once they love themselves enough, and realize that thinking is not the same as doing, their destiny is to confidently express their uniqueness and, by so doing, encourage others to do the same.

Potential: Intuitive, dedicated

Dark side: Indecisive, moody

Tarot card, lucky numbers, days, colors: The High Priestess, 2, 3, Saturday, Monday, blue, silver

Born today: Isaac Asimov (sci-fi writer); Daisaku Ikeda (Buddhist leader); Christy Turlington (model)

January 3

The Birthday of
Determination

*"The darkness comes before the dawn;
I will shine through"*

Failure is never an option for the appealing and extremely determined people born on January 3. They are at their most inventive when challenged and, even if it looks like they have failed, they will learn and grow from it and stage a comeback. Their admirable persistence means that they can overcome incredible odds. Sometimes, however, their stubbornness can make them appear intolerant. January 3 people can impose unbearable standards, not just on themselves but also on others, and when pushed into a corner they can resort to using their charm to help them get what they want in a manipulative way.

Born innovators, idealists and self-starters, they can achieve outstanding success in self-employment and business, but they can also excel in charity, the law, prison, the police, charity and humanitarian work, as well as politics, education, environmentalism, digital technology, and as creatives, authors, artists, filmmakers and social-media influencers. Prone to personal vanity, any concerns about appearance should ideally be managed not by cosmetic shortcuts but by a healthy diet and lifestyle, and a youthful and optimistic approach to life. They need to constantly remind themselves that appearance matters but inner beauty matters more. **For self-care**, close your eyes and tune into your intuition for a few minutes each day. Reflecting quietly on what your body, mind and, most importantly, your heart are trying to tell you can help you make better decisions.

In relationships January 3-born easily attract admirers and are loyal and trusted companions, but their tendency to constantly seek attention can become draining for the people in their life. However, when they let go of the need to control and allow others to breathe around them, their relationships can be deeply comforting and fulfilling. Around the age of 40 they typically discover that connecting with their intuition rather than seeking identity and attention from others, causes or projects is the path to true fulfillment, and their life transforms. Once they have mastered this "inside-out" approach to life, their destiny is to share their powerful creativity and make the impossible seem possible.

Potential: Charming, inventive

Dark side: Vain, stubborn

Tarot card, lucky numbers, days, colors: The Empress, 3, 4, Saturday, Thursday, purple, gray

Born today: J. R. R. Tolkien (fantasy author); Sergio Leone (film director); Greta Thunberg (climate-change activist)

January 4

The Birthday of the Eclectic

"I am here to learn"

January 4-born are drawn to the eclectic. They gather, sort and then select only the best, and use this sorting approach to solve problems in all aspects of their lives. Their impressive list of contacts and numerous projects all on the go reflect their unlimited powers of imagination. This erratic approach may seem chaotic, but there is always method in their madness. By learning all that can be learned from a variety of sources, they often emerge triumphant with an encyclopedic knowledge of life that can help them solve almost any complication or cope with any challenge they encounter.

They need careers that give them variety, but also allow them to be creative and spontaneous, such as in the media or travel. The unlimited possibility of careers online suits them perfectly. Born investigators, they can also make inspiring educators, entrepreneurs, web designers, publicists, lawyers, writers, detectives, inventors, scientists, artists, technology experts, designers, influencers, activists and journalists. A brain-boosting diet rich in green leafy vegetables, oily fish, berries, nuts and seeds is recommended for the hungry minds born on this day. Regular meditation is also beneficial. **For self-care**, before going to bed compile a "to-do" list of what you hope to achieve the next day. The following day enjoy the satisfaction of ticking off all those items on the list.

Any interaction with these innovative and meticulous people has to have a point, otherwise they quickly lose interest. Their inability to indulge in chitchat and occasional bouts of intolerance can work against them in their personal and professional lives but, more often than not, their bluntness and conviction are welcomed as a breath of fresh air. Like a fine wine, these people become more successful with age and their potential for success is most likely to emerge after the age of 30 and beyond. The same applies to their relationships. Deep down they are caring, but it can take a while for them to find a partner who can keep up with them. Their destiny is to gather as much knowledge as they can and then to present that knowledge in an authoritative way that both informs and inspires others.

Potential: Independent, imaginative

Dark side: Aloof, chaotic

Tarot card, lucky numbers, days, colors: The Emperor, 4, 5, Saturday, Sunday, blue, brown

Born today: Isaac Newton (physicist); Jacob Grimm (folklorist); Tina Knowles (fashion designer)

January 5

The Birthday of Resilience

The life lesson:

is to understand that for your enthusiasm to be effective, it also needs to be realistic.

The way forward: is to motivate others without overly raising expectations or making them feel cornered or controlled.

Luck maker: Sometimes less really is more.

"Self-knowledge is the beginning of my wisdom"

January 5-born are resilient, glass-half-full individuals, but they can also be extremely practical. They recover well from setbacks, intuitively understanding that learning from the past and any mistakes made along the way is all part of life's journey. They are often wise beyond their years and make commanding advisors, guides and leaders, truly coming into their own during times of crisis. Their buoyant approach to life wins them many admirers but, taken to extremes, it can also make them unrealistically confident, bordering on arrogant.

Born mediators, they thrive in careers that allow them to be a communicator, networker, advisor, politician, motivational speaker or whenever a positive spin needs to be put on things. Advertising, politics, publicity, social services, architecture, marketing and the law can appeal, as do careers in teaching, medicine, sports, counseling, entertainment, the performing arts, science and social media. Regular time out to switch off, relax or simply have fun is essential for the charismatic and often in-demand people born on this day. They may think it is a waste of time, but it will help them come back recharged, re-invigorated and with new perspectives. Wearing orange or red can help boost their energy. **For self-care**, every morning ask yourself—as Steve Jobs famously did—if today was the last day of your life would you want to do what you are about to do today. If the answer is "no" for too many days in a row, it's time to make changes.

Love, for these people, starts in the head and they rate intelligence highly in others. This can make them appear emotionally distant at times but, more often than not, this hides a deeply sensitive nature that is simply afraid to give of itself unconditionally. In their mid-forties there is a movement toward greater responsibility and also toward greater sensitivity, which grows stronger with age. Once they learn to listen to both their inner wisdom and the viewpoints of others, and focus their considerable talents on getting organized and creating a plan to help them achieve their goals, their destiny is to bring the best out in people and be the inspirationally self-reliant rock people instinctively turn to in a crisis.

Potential: Inspirational, resilient

Dark side: Unrealistic, arrogant

Tarot card, lucky numbers, days, colors: The Hierophant, 5, 6, Saturday, Wednesday, gray, green

Born today: Umberto Eco (author); Hayao Miyazaki (filmmaker); Diane Keaton (actor)

January 6

The Birthday of the Philosopher

"I can see what truly matters"

People born on January 6 always look beneath the surface for deeper meaning. They try to see goodness in others, but this can come across as child-like or gullible at times and their intelligence can be underestimated. Although they are typically mild-mannered, they can also be ambitious and hard-working, perfectionist at times, tending eventually to get what they want in life. There is a danger of them rejecting alternative viewpoints and being labeled as stubborn.

Work or study is often their savior because it channels their creative energies and helps them discover what their goals and values are. They are born visionaries and may be drawn to spirituality, therapy and personal development. They also make great programmers, gamers, engineers, architects, artists, designers, journalists, writers, investigators and filmmakers, or may decide to go it alone and set up their own business. They are prone to stress and shallow breathing because of their perfectionist tendencies, so deep-breathing techniques can help ease tension. Inhale deeply through the nose from the belly rather than the lungs and let the lungs fill completely with air. Then push all the air out of the lungs through the mouth. Inhaling and exhaling deeply five times every morning is recommended. **For self-care**, "unplug" from your phone for at least one hour a day, preferably first thing in the morning. Use that hour to focus on who you are rather than what you do.

There is a tender side to those born on this day that can get easily hurt and they may respond with rebellion when people don't take them seriously. After the age of 45 they often learn that, although cathartic, rebellion can never be the whole answer. These people can sometimes be self-sacrificing in relationships and more in love with the idea of love than the person themselves. But once they learn the importance of give and take in their relationships and in life, stop spoiling themselves with choice, and make a decision about what they should devote their life to, their destiny is to help others deal with their own fears and prove that there can be light at the end of every tunnel.

Potential: Visionary, insightful

Dark side: Gullible, stubborn

Tarot card, lucky numbers, days, colors: The Chariot, 6, 7, Saturday, Friday, black, pink

Born today: Kahlil Gibran (poet); Rowan Atkinson and Eddie Redmayne (actors)

January 7

The Birthday of the Practical Dreamer

"I sense true magic in the ordinary"

The life lesson:

is to stop worrying about what other people think.

The way forward: is to understand that what others think is solely their own concern.

Luck maker: Seek out the company of people who lift you up rather than drag you down.

Although January 7-born can appear accessible and appealing, they are drawn to the unfamiliar. They have a sense of responsibility but dream of living unconventionally. Unique in their ability to be both logical and intuitive, they are artists with a logical approach or scientists with intuition. They can sense the moods of others and often absorb negativity from others. These people find it hard to switch off from the suffering and injustices of the world, and humanitarian, charity or volunteer work appeal. They don't believe in half-measures and will always push themselves to the limit, giving any project or goal they set their mind on everything they have got.

Born planners, they make great business leaders, educators, writers, architects, athletes, innovators and artists, excelling both individually and when working in a team. They have organizational skills and can do well as programmers, producers, researchers, team leaders and managers, and their caring nature may draw them to work as counselors, healers, therapists, doctors, social workers or vets. Stress and fatigue can be a big problem for people born on this day, so ensuring they have a good night's sleep, get enough energy-boosting nutrients such as iron in their diet, and enjoy plenty of fresh air and exercise is essential. Unusual forms of calming exercise such as tai chi may appeal. **For self-care**, when you get up in the morning, set the right confident tone for the rest of your day by stretching as tall as you can and letting out a battle cry.

Although often surrounded by admirers, those born on this day are dreamers by nature and have a tendency to drift off into a world of their own, which can make them feel lonely, isolated and cut off from everything and everyone around them, even if they are in a fulfilling relationship. Their sense of connection with the natural world and an extraordinary imagination are a refuge for them. Fascination with the mystical, with unexplained phenomena, is common, especially after the age of 45, although fear of being criticized or thought "weird" may prevent them from pursuing their mystical inclinations. It is extremely important for January 7-born to develop resilience and self-confidence, and to accept that the opinions of others, although valuable, are not final. Once they have faith in themselves, their destiny is to lead the way by healing differences, crossing boundaries and uniting opposites.

Potential: Intuitive, original

Dark side: Isolated, insecure

Tarot card, lucky numbers, days, colors: The Chariot, 7, 8, Saturday, Monday, gray, blue

Born today: Lewis Hamilton (Formula 1 driver); Charles Addams (cartoonist); Gerald Durrell (naturalist writer)

January 8

The Birthday of Dynamic Strength

"I rise above the odds"

The life lesson:

is coping with impostor syndrome.

The way forward: is to understand that feeling out of your depth is not a negative thing but a sign you are evolving.

Luck maker: Progress is only made outside your comfort zone.

January 8-born have stunning potential to rise and shine above all obstacles and make their mark on the world. They are ambitious and motivated, and expect to be acknowledged by others, who typically come away impressed. Driven, hard-working, bold and passionate with visionary flair, they have the potential within them to achieve almost everything they want. The problem is that despite their explosive confidence, they have hidden insecurities that can manifest in irrational impatience, arrogance and intolerance.

Born achievers, they are likely to rise to the top in whatever career they choose, whether that be art, entertainment, science, medicine, healthcare, business, humanitarian work or anything else. They make great designers, developers and teachers, and may also be drawn to the world of politics, medicine, philanthropy and spiritual and personal growth. Because of their determined nature, they can sometimes have a tendency to overdo everything, which can impact their wellbeing. They need to avoid becoming too obsessive and serious by making sure they allow plenty of fun and laughter into their lives. Watching their posture is important, especially if they spend a lot of time in front of a computer. **For self-care**, spend a few moments each morning chanting the word "joy" over and over again to help draw positive things into your life through the power of sound.

These people are wonderful communicators and possess great charm and sensitivity, with an ability to put not just loved ones but anyone at ease. Although they are naturally intuitive, it is important that they do not let practicality and worldly ambition, and a desire to control others, obscure this talent, as it will serve them well in all areas of life, in particular their close personal relationships. Obsession with career and making their mark on the world can overshadow their relationships. After their early forties their intuition and emotional sensitivity steadily increase and grow more powerful. If they can stay positive and develop tolerance and humility in their relationships with others, there is nothing to hold back people born on this day. Their destiny is to shine—and shine they will, in the process inspiring others to shine alongside them.

Potential: Brave, commanding

Dark side: Arrogant, impatient

Tarot card, lucky numbers, day, colors: Strength, 8, 9, Saturday, black, red

Born today: Elvis Presley and Shirley Bassey (singers); Stephen Hawking (physicist); Jack Andraka (inventor)

January 9

The Birthday of the Striver

The life lesson:

is not to use other people as stepping stones to success.

The way forward: is always to treat others with honesty and respect.

Luck maker: Have as few enemies as possible.

"I can break through barriers"

January 9-born tend to be fast-acting, thinking and feeling. Bursting with energy, ambitious and dedicated, they want to rise to the top and will do whatever it takes to get there, even if that means occasionally bending the rules. They demand only the best for themselves and others, and detest mediocrity. They place great value on initiative and their personal freedom, and often prefer to work or forge ahead alone rather than in a group. These people are not afraid of challenge and can bounce back from any setback, but they have a tendency to be ruthless and prone to outbursts of anger, making enemies as they go.

Born experimenters, they need careers that offer them variety, progress, freedom, independence and excitement. There may be quite a few career changes along the way. Marketing, advertising, politics, gaming, the media, computer programming, engineering, real estate, travel guide, journalism or any job that offers them plenty of variety, travel and challenge appeals to them. So focused are January 9 people on striving that they rarely take time to savor their achievements or even the present moment; they find it particularly hard to relax or switch off. It is of great importance for them to find time to properly unwind and take themselves less seriously. **For self-care**, spend 5 to 10 minutes a day sitting quietly with your phone on silent and doing nothing in particular but simply observing the present moment. If your thoughts wander to the past or future, or to your to-do list, gently bring them back to the joyful power of now.

These people are passionate lovers and believe in the idea of having a soul mate. Family is everything to them and they will place the material and financial needs of their loved ones above everything else. Sometimes, though, they neglect to give enough of themselves emotionally. Typically, from their mid-forties onward—sometimes sooner—their sensitivity toward others and their inner life become more prominent. If they can learn to strive as hard to maintain inner balance as they strive to attain success, there is nothing to stop them enjoying the liberating benefits of a purposeful professional life and happy personal life. Their destiny is to show others that going the extra mile and always doing your best really can make a difference and help make the world a better place.

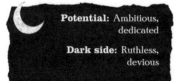

Potential: Ambitious, dedicated

Dark side: Ruthless, devious

Tarot card, lucky numbers, days, colors: The Hermit, 1, 9, Saturday, Tuesday, gray, red

Born today: Kate Middleton (royal family member); Richard Nixon (US president); Simone de Beauvoir (philosopher)

January 10

The Birthday of the Realist

is to take the feelings of others into consideration.

The way forward: is to understand that the truth can be presented in both a realistic and a positive way.

Luck maker: The more you make others feel good about themselves, the better they feel about you.

"I know the best way forward"

People born on January 10 are a force of nature. Individualistic and curious, they tend to speak their mind without subtlety or compromise, and although this can be shocking at times, they are highly valued for their honesty and for their realistic assessments of things. During times of uncertainty people seek them out for their wisdom, which never fails to surprise them. They are also never afraid to support unpopular viewpoints and to champion the underdog. On the downside, their inability to dress up the truth can upset people around them, stopping them advancing as fast in life as more diplomatic peers.

With their ability to see clearly, adapt to change and solve puzzles, these people are born troubleshooters in any career they choose to dedicate their considerable talents to. Bold business ideas are more likely to appeal to them than specialist ideas, and financial return is important. Computer programming, engineering, medicine, accounting, banking, finance, the law, advertising and management all appeal. Their unconventional flair and willingness to take risks may lead them into entertainment, sport entrepreneurship or even to the unknown—these people are highly likely to volunteer for space travel. They need exciting outlets for both their mental and physical energy. **For self-care**, before you talk to, write, text or email someone today, pause for a few moments to consider the impact of your words on the person you are addressing.

In relationships these people can be jealous and controlling, but there is softness beneath their closed-book persona. Likewise, they can appear grumpy and lacking in empathy, but they are not negative or unhappy, just truth-tellers. It isn't until they hit their forties and beyond that they become more empathetic toward those less able to cope with change and the ups and downs of life. Once they begin to understand that not everyone is as clear-sighted as they are, and that a gentler approach can help them achieve their objectives more effectively, people born on this day can earn the loyalty of others and make a lasting impact on the world. Their destiny is to bring both themselves and others closer to the truth, with their revealing assessment of people and situations.

Potential: Honest, original

Dark side: Insensitive, negative

Tarot card, lucky numbers, days, colors: Wheel of Fortune, 1, 2, Saturday, Sunday, brown, orange

Born today: Rod Stewart (singer); George Foreman (boxer); Pat Benatar (singer)

January 11

The Birthday of the Expert Assessor

"I fight injustice and right wrongs"

The life lesson: is feeling powerless to change things.

The way forward: is to understand that you can only change the things you can and, when you can't, you must learn to let go.

Luck maker: Sometimes you need to give others the benefit of the doubt.

January 11-born are insightful and intelligent. They have a natural talent for assessing every situation and person they encounter. They see right to the heart of people and situations, judging them according to their own very high standards. When their formidable powers of evaluation are combined with their discernment and insight, they become outstanding decision makers. Underlying their talent for assessment is a strong sense of justice. They feel compelled to do the right thing in life and to pass judgment, but sometimes this can lean toward critical and controlling behavior and the belief that their word really is the law.

Born helpers, they are drawn to careers where they can use their sharp mind to fight injustice and assist others. Education, journalism, vlogging, campaigning, lobbying, business, counseling, psychology, social work, politics, the law, the police, the military or even the clergy can appeal, as can therapy, music and the arts. These people need to avoid compassion overload by caring for others or fighting for their rights at the expense of their own physical and emotional needs. Self-care is a priority. Surrounding themselves with the color silver can bring inner peace. **For self-care**, every time a voice in your head tells you that you are not doing enough or not doing things correctly, listen to a really upbeat song and hum along or dance to it.

Learning to pronounce their opinions less forcibly and understanding that everybody has a right to a viewpoint empowers both the personal and professional life of those born on this day. They are loyal companions, but it can take an age for them to trust someone enough to really open up to them. Around the age of 40, often sooner, their emotional sensitivity grows stronger and they start to develop a more powerful inner life and greater self-confidence. They have high standards for others but also for themselves, and, because they have the courage and determination to live up to these standards, others will seek them out for advice when they learn to be a little less inflexible. Their destiny is not only to fight injustice but also to help others beat the odds and turn their dreams into reality.

Potential: Fair, compassionate

Dark side: Controlling, perfectionist

Tarot card, lucky numbers, days, colors: Justice, 2, 3, Saturday, Monday, black, white

Born today: Alexander Hamilton (statesman); William James (psychologist); Mary J. Blige (singer)

January 12

The Birthday of
Single-mindedness

The life lesson: is to stop feeling you need to prove yourself to others.

The way forward: is to place more emphasis on who you are than on what you do.

Luck maker: Spend more time listening and networking.

"The work I do makes a difference, it is my calling"

January 12-born are utterly unique in that they somehow manage to be both confident and elusive, occasionally at the same time. Either way, they don't do anything half-heartedly. Once they have settled on a goal, they pursue it with single-minded dedication. Whatever their calling in life, whether it be raising a family, running a newspaper or campaigning for a cause, it becomes their single purpose. They are forever on the lookout for opportunities that can help them achieve their goals, and their sharp wit and uncanny good fortune often mark them out as success stories.

Work is everything and they run the risk of losing themselves to it, so choosing their career wisely is a big deal. Born winners, those born on this day are likely to succeed in any career, but their biggest struggle is choosing what career to pursue. Independent-minded, they can work in teams, often excelling in business, entrepreneurship, sales, marketing, politics, sports, journalism, negotiation, the media and all forms of art. January 12-born have high energy levels, but their intense focus can mean they neglect the most important thing in their life: their health. Self-care and regular exercise are essential, and they would also benefit from meditation to encourage self-awareness. **For self-care**, every morning when you wake up, reflect for a few moments on this question: If you had one year to live, what would your priorities be?

These people often put their emotional life on hold in pursuit of their goals in life. Sometimes they can be so driven that they lose touch not only with loved ones but also with themselves. They are quirky, attention-seeking and critical of others, and being ignored plunges them into a low mood. Carving out a personal life separate from work helps them get their sense of self-worth from within rather than externally. Typically, from around the age of 39 (though hopefully sooner), they place more emphasis on reflecting on what truly matters and inner growth, and this is the key to their happiness. Once they know how to balance their work and their personal life, their destiny is to dedicate themselves to a worthy cause or purpose.

Potential: Dedicated, inspirational

Dark side: Workaholic, attention-seeking

Tarot card, lucky numbers, days, colors: The Hanged Man, 3, 4, Saturday, Thursday, black, purple

Born today: Jack London (author); Jeff Bezos (entrepreneur); Christiane Amanpour (journalist)

January 13

The Birthday of Progression

"I can and will reach my potential"

People born on January 13 rarely pause. Self-improvement, often combined with social or global improvement, is their focus. They are always moving forward, whatever their circumstances. Their ability to adapt to change and overcome obstacles, making even the most difficult tasks seem easy, and keep their cool when all around are losing theirs, gives them a natural charisma. When setbacks occur, they pick themselves up, learn from mistakes and do all it takes to reach their goals—and reach them they will.

People born on this day particularly enjoy initiating new projects and ideas, and they work steadily and in a disciplined way until they have attained what they desire. Born advisors, their calm intelligence suits them to many careers, but they can excel in acting, education, medicine, the military, emergency services, personal relations, counseling, personal transformation, life-coaching, writing and social and humanitarian reform. Instinctively understanding that a healthy body is a healthy mind, these people prioritize self-care. There is a danger of becoming too obsessive about their health. Moderation is important. Spending more time in nature will help keep them balanced and grounded. **For self-care**, every evening set aside a minimum of ten minutes to read a good book, preferably hard copy rather than digital.

These charming people attract admirers, but they want to admire their loved ones in return and this can put intense pressure on their close relationships. They progress faster if they can understand that not everyone has the same drive or need for achievement as they have, and that sometimes the price for always giving 100 percent means they have to stand alone. Of course, they feel disappointment and disillusion at times but, typically after the age of 38 and more often than not sooner, they understand that feelings can help them learn and grow as much as thoughts and logic can. Their destiny is to inspire others to move out of their comfort zone, help resolve disagreements and, in the process, make the world a more harmonious place.

Potential: Charismatic, high-achieving

Dark side: Bossy, unemotional

Tarot card, lucky numbers, days, colors: Death, 4, 5, Saturday, Sunday, black, green

Born today: George Gurdjieff (philosopher); Ruth Wilson, Patrick Dempsey, Liam Hemsworth and Orlando Bloom (actors); Shonda Rhimes (producer)

January 14

The Birthday of
Conviction

"I see how the dots connect to create the bigger picture"

January 14-born are a unique combination of discipline and instinct. They can take in vast amounts of information, weigh it all up, see the vision connecting everything and then work steadily toward their end goals. They are inquisitive and shrewd judges of people and situations. Their panoramic view and strong sense of right and wrong, which they present with absolute conviction, makes them sought-after peacemakers. Once settled on a course of action, they rarely lose sight of the end goal. Even if that means they alone must stubbornly see things through to completion.

Born observers, these people are drawn to work that utilizes their powers of moderation and curiosity or observation. Writing, design, art, photography, social media, broadcast media, publicity, advertising, business, banking and law appeal, but they are determined enough to excel in any career. Despite having a common-sense approach to health, they are often guilty of living on the edge or driving themselves too hard. Prone to stress and insomnia, calming and gentle exercise such as yoga is recommended rather than extreme or high-intensity workouts. Soothing chamomile or warm herbal tea before bedtime help them sleep better. **For self-care**, place your hand over your heart. Breathe deeply, feel your heart beating and hear what it is saying to you. Give your feelings as much consideration as your thoughts.

Personal life often takes second place to work, but this can be for fear of getting hurt. Behind the strong image lies a person who often feels misunderstood; these feelings are heightened if they haven't found a direction in life to which to devote their considerable energies or a person who loves them for who they are rather than what they do. Those born on this day become more emotionally confident and more attuned to the importance of details in their mid- to late thirties and beyond. Once they understand it is not wealth or status they crave, but emotional connection and the ability to make positive change, they can leave their insecurities behind and find their true destiny, which is to introduce positive reform or new ways of doing or looking at things.

Potential: Principled, convincing

Dark side: Obsessive, insecure

Tarot card, lucky numbers, days, colors: Temperance, 5, 6, Saturday, Wednesday, black, green

Born today: Albert Schweitzer (philosopher); Cecil Beaton (photographer); Emily Watson (actor)

January 15

The Birthday of the Protagonist

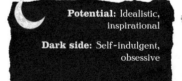

is to learn to cope when there is no recognition or praise.

The way forward: is to do things because you believe in them rather than for show.

Luck maker: Share your success when you can and allow others to take the recognition.

"I am a voice and a force for good"

People born on January 15 can be idealistic, instinctive and ambitious, with a strong desire to lead, innovate and inspire. They passionately want to live a meaningful life and make the world a better place. For them, everything happens for a reason and this spiritual perspective, combined with an uncanny sense of the motivations of others, gives them a talent for seeing life as an exciting ride, with possibilities for great highs and lows, and to learn and grow from both success and failure. They have dramatic flair and others often see them as invincible, with hero-like qualities. Their Achilles' heel is their desire for recognition or credit, and occasional reluctance to share the limelight.

Born campaigners, those born on this day have great empathy for those who are disadvantaged and often find themselves speaking on behalf of others, fighting for human rights or raising awareness of a cause. Whatever career they choose, be it the law, social reform, the military, the police, art, theater, architecture, management, civil rights, healthcare, science or online influencer—they are likely to stand out as decisive innovators. Health-wise, they have a pleasure-seeking tendency that can lead to excess, so it is important for them to follow a healthy diet and exercise plan. Moderation in all things is key. They can also benefit from wearing, meditating on and surrounding themselves with shades of blue and green, to stay balanced. **For self-care**, make a point today of saying "thank you" or praising someone out loud for doing a good job.

These people have a passionate nature. Initially drawn to those who speak to their ego rather than their heart, they do possess a vulnerable side and start to live in an increasingly heart-centered way and to seek out people who speak to their hearts from their mid-thirties onward. This shift toward their inner life and greater sensitivity toward others is an extremely positive thing because, once they find a vocation they believe in and understand that in the drama of their lives other people have parts to play too, their destiny is to become an important and much-needed voice for the good of the people.

Potential: Idealistic, inspirational

Dark side: Self-indulgent, obsessive

Tarot card, lucky numbers, days, colors: The Devil, 6, 7, Saturday, Friday, black, blue

Born today: Molière (playwright); Martin Luther King Jr. (activist); Charo (actor)

January 16

The Birthday of
Satisfaction

"I get things done"

is to manage anxiety about what others think and what will happen to you in the future.

The way forward: is to focus on validation from within and what is good about your life right now.

Luck maker: Fake a smile when you don't feel like smiling to trick your mind into positivity.

People born on January 16 are a delightful mix of empathy and intellectual insight, the mystical and the material, the creative and the logical. They have great organizational skills and it gives them enormous satisfaction to see a job well done. They prefer doing to talking and structure to uncertainty because they believe rules improve their chances of getting things done, but they can become restless if life gets too routine. Although satisfactory completion of tasks is their goal, it is important for them not to become overly negative about themselves or others when results are not as good as expected.

Born managers, these people make excellent organizers, consultants, managers, coaches, advisors, troubleshooters and accountants. Publishing, politics, social reform, charity work, police and the law appeal, as do the caring professions or dealing with people in sales, teaching and personal relations. Music and art offer outlets for emotional expression. **For self-care**, get up as early as you can at the same time each day, even on weekends, and make your bed mindfully. If you need more sleep, go to bed earlier.

Even though they are often highly valued and admired, those born on this day can become over-anxious about where their lives are heading or prone to the belief that they can never live up to their own or other people's expectations. They need to understand that the satisfaction they crave comes not only from their achievements but also from within and from having fulfilling relationships. They prefer to show their love for others by doing things or helping out rather than articulating their feelings. Typically, around the age of 35, though often sooner, they reach a breakthrough point that emphasizes the importance of being more in touch with their emotions and the present moment, which serves them well for the rest of their lives. Once they are able to view mistakes not as failures but as opportunities to learn and grow, they have the potential for an extraordinary life. Their destiny is to communicate to others the importance of doing things the right way and seeing things through, leaving the world not just better organized but a happier place.

Potential: Responsible, insightful

Dark side: Anxious, demanding

Tarot card, lucky numbers, days, colors: The Tower, 7, 8, Saturday, Monday, brown, blue

Born today: Kate Moss (model); Thaddaeus Ropac (gallerist); FKA Twigs (musician)

January 17

The Birthday of the Leader

"I lead and I inspire"

January 17-born love to take the lead, not necessarily because they are egotistical but because, having assessed the situation, it is clear to them that they really are the best person for the job. Despite being respectful of tradition, they can also hold progressive ideas about social reform. They like to help others. A defining characteristic is their tough-minded, self-controlled (sometimes irritable) approach and their belief that the only person upon whom they can really rely is themselves. They know the meaning of the word "struggle," and are a model of inspirational self-made success.

Born disciplinarians, these people are drawn to careers where self-control matters, such as in sport or the military, the law, the police or the clergy. They are superb at managing and inspiring teams, so careers in the civil service, government, banking, teaching and business may appeal. They also have an interest in fashion, hospitality and catering, as well as teaching, writing and humanitarian work. People with this birthday have a tendency to repress their emotions, so they need to find activities such as competitive sport or other forms of vigorous exercise, which can act as an emotional release. **For self-care,** make a point in conversation to ask other people as many questions as you can. You don't have to agree. Simply learn a new perspective and add it to your store of knowledge.

These direct and driven people take the lead in both their working life and relationships. They are loving and generous, but can become controlling of those closest to them and need to give their loved ones freedom as well as intimacy. Fortunately, in their early thirties, there is a shift toward allowing both themselves and others greater freedom, with another powerful shift happening in their early sixties. Once they have learned to get others on their side through cooperation rather than control, and to truly believe there is always a better way, their destiny is to lead by their powerful example and help others to work harmoniously toward the greater good.

Potential: Purposeful, committed

Dark side: Intolerant, domineering

Tarot card, lucky numbers, day, colors: The Star, 8, 9, Saturday, brown, green

Born today: Michelle Obama (US First Lady); Benjamin Franklin (statesman); Muhammad Ali (boxer); Jim Carrey (comedian)

January 18

The Birthday of Fantasy

The life lesson:

is learning to concentrate.

The way forward: is not to stop daydreaming—this is the secret to your creativity—but when your mind wanders to gently bring your thoughts back to the present moment.

Luck maker: Finish what you start, even if that means doing things you find boring.

"I can show you the world"

The creative powers of people born on January 18 can lead them to pure visionary heights. They have a quick wit and boundless energy that often delights others and are often surrounded by admirers. Optimistic, the only things that can bring down these endearing child-like souls are rules. They place a high value on independence and need to find an environment in which their need for freedom and play (fun) is respected because, if they don't, this will lead them to bitterness. They can become bored quickly, losing their concentration and retreating into a world of fantasy or fits of temper if their needs aren't being met, or becoming restless and impatient if they feel too confined.

Born creators, if a career interests them enough, they are likely to excel. Once they learn to combine their creativity with practical application, the fields of advertising, fashion, business, banking, property development and online influencing may appeal. Their idealism draws them to teaching, medicine, science, technology and charity work, and their sense of playful expression to art, film, literature, the media and entertainment. Because they live so much in their heads, they need to make sure they pay attention to their physical wellbeing and avoid mood-altering substances. **For self-care**, when you eat your evening meal, switch off your phone and any distractions. Focus your attention only on the food. Put your life and fork down between bites. Savor the moment.

These people throw themselves deeply into relationships and can be hurt easily if their partner does not respond the same. They often fear they will not find a soul mate who will love them with the intensity they offer and crave, but more often than not they do. They become more emotionally balanced and mature in their thirties, and this empowering trend continues building momentum as they age. Asking them to be more realistic about love and life simply isn't an option or worth forcing on them, as imagination is who they are. Their destiny is to inspire others with their flights of fantasy and encourage them to take a more courageous and imaginative perspective.

Potential: Visionary, stimulating

Dark side: Impractical, undisciplined

Tarot card, lucky numbers, days, colors: The moon, 1, 9, Saturday, Tuesday, red, brown

Born today: Peter Mark Roget (lexicographer); Daniel Hale Williams (surgeon); A. A. Milne (author)

19

January 19

The Birthday of Originality

The life lesson:

is coping with routine and boring details.

The way forward: is to understand that the devil (and the potential for success) is often in the detail.

Luck maker: Find out what you love to do and what you are good at. Then think about how you can use your passion and talents to help others.

"I see the world in a grain of sand"

January 19-born are often honest and direct, with a genuine appreciation of beauty. There is an endearing, sometimes child-like, energy and wonder about them; they are blessed with genuine originality. Independent and free-spirited, they really don't care too much what people think and don't take well to rules and being told what to do, so they often rebel with immature behavior. Even if they appear respectable, they soon show what truly unique individuals they are, as anyone who gets to know them soon appreciates. Destined to shine brightly and to attract others to them like magnets, they become unhappy if they try to repress their originality.

Born movers and shakers, they tend to do better in solitary positions but can work well in groups that allow them to freely use their imagination. The fields of literature, art, engineering and science appeal, and they may be drawn to sports or other physical types of work, as well as careers as experts, advisors and consultants. They can be engaging online experts and video or social media influencers. Bursting with energy, they need to pace themselves; otherwise they risk depression or burning out, so positive thinking and practicing meditation and yoga is strongly advised. **For self-care**, think like a solo mountain climber. Don't underestimate the value of the small and steady steps you need to take to succeed. At the end of each day ask yourself if you gave everything you did that day your very best.

Prone to extremes, these people make intense lovers and need a partner who can keep them balanced and give them the occasional reality check. They are intuitive and can often sense what others miss, but it isn't until their early thirties that the emphasis moves toward nurturing their inner life, and herein lies the secret of their success as they age. Once they learn to listen to rather than repress their intuition, and pay attention to the small as well as the big things, their destiny is to inspire others with their highly original ideas and make an unforgettable and often exceptional impact on the world.

Potential: Visionary, independent

Dark side: Immature, unfocused

Tarot card, lucky numbers, days, colors: The Sun, 1, 2, Saturday, Sunday, brown, orange

Born today: James Watt (engineer); Edgar Allan Poe (author); Janis Joplin (singer)

AQUARIUS

THE WATER CARRIER
(JANUARY 20–FEBRUARY 18)

✳ **Element:** Air

✳ **Ruling planets:** Saturn, the teacher, and Uranus, the visionary

✳ **Tarot card:** The Star (hope)

✳ **Lucky numbers:** 4, 8, 11

✳ **Favorable colors:** Calming and expansive sky blue; yellow, white and lilac

✳ **Driving force:** Innovation

✳ **Personal statement:** I confidently express my original ideas

✳ **Chinese astrology counterpart:** The Tiger

Although they are known for their visionary, frequently rebellious, "off-the-wall" approach to life, Aquarians are often friendly and compassionate. They often have a deep desire to help others and make the world a better place. They are independent and find it very tough to conform to other people's expectations. But even though they love to be totally original and do things their way, their curious minds can be swayed by logical argument.

Personality potential

Aquarians have revolutionary instincts. They often feel that their role is to push for improvements and progressive change. Their instincts are humanitarian and idealistic, and nothing makes them feel more fulfilled than using their insight, intelligence and skills to help and inspire others. It's not surprising that many people born under this sign are drawn to human rights, environmentalism, politics, people management, technology and other areas where they can help create positive and innovative change for others or for the planet. Their inventive and original thinking and approach to life can often earn them a reputation for being eccentric—a reputation they take great pride in.

The Aquarian instinct is to not respect rules and regulations imposed on them by others unless those rules and regulations make sense to them. They are a law unto themselves at times, but they rarely use their inventive ideas in a destructive manner. In the great majority of cases, the secret to their happiness is to find ways to use their intuition and insight to bring benefit, not just to themselves or a close group of people, but to everyone. Aquarians can't think small. They see the bigger picture.

This sign is ruled by Saturn, the planet of self-discipline, and Uranus, the planet of originality, idealism, unpredictability and endless change. This goes some way to explaining **Aquarians don't just cope well with change, they thrive on it.**

They adore finding out about new things and doing things in different ways to what has been done before. You will rarely find an Aquarian who is content living in their comfort zone. These people need to constantly push boundaries in some way to feel truly alive.

Aquarians are often very sociable, tolerant and friend-ly people with the ability to adapt easily to any person or situation. However, despite having an engaging personality, their intellectual approach means they can find it difficult to allow others to get close to them. They have an enviable ability to detach themselves emotionally from others and from situations. This ability to step outside and observe with-out attachment means they can offer much-valued objective insight. Even though there is always going to be an element of untouchable aloofness and a dreamy quality about them, they are capable of giving a lot of themselves to those they care about and will go out of their way to offer help and support to loved ones and friends when needed.

Above all, these pioneers are way ahead of their time. They are the people of the future. If inspired, they are capable of flashes of intuition and insight that can be breathtaking in their scope and originality. Blessed with an innate ability to see the upside or the positives rather than the negatives, they are an uplifting breath of fresh air with their refreshing and quirky approach to life, even when things are not going their way.

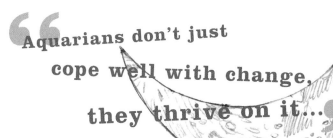

"Aquarians don't just cope well with change, they thrive on it..."

Personality pitfalls

Depending on which planetary ruler—Saturn the teacher or Uranus the visionary—is stronger at the time of their birth, Aquarians can be unpredictable or downright quirky. When

Saturn dominates, they may be prone to serious bouts of stubbornness and impatience; when Uranus dominates, they are likely to have disruptive and rebellious tendencies. They can also possess a streak of perfectionism that can be soul-destroying to both themselves and to others. Fanaticism and bigotry can sometimes find expression in their belief that only they know how to make the world a better place. With a love of change they can rebel simply for the sake of rebelling or follow a set of beliefs blindly without pausing to consider that there could be other approaches.

The objectivity and detachment of people born under this sign may sometimes come across as cold-heartedness. They are idealistic but not always warm-hearted; revolutionary but not always considerate; altruistic but not always sensitive. Indeed, they can be downright tactless and perverse on occasion. They are also prone to so overinvesting in a cause or a set of beliefs that they have little of themselves left over for their family and friends. And sometimes, when the burden of responsibility or expectation is put on Aquarians, it can be in their nature to do exactly the opposite of what is needed or requested, for the simple reason that they like to be perverse. And although they often have large numbers of friends, many of these are in fact merely acquaintances. Aquarians often need to exercise more discretion in their relationships. Fulfilling relationships require both parties to open up and share their feelings—something Aquarians can struggle with, and the reason they tend to have more acquaintances than true friends in their lives.

Darkest secrets

Many Aquarians present a distinct, sometimes eccentric image to the world, but deep down many suffer from impostor syndrome, unsure of who they really are. This uncertainty can drive them to nonconformist behavior in the misguided belief that rebellion will give them the identity and sense of purpose and self-belief they crave.

Symbol

The symbol for Aquarius is the water carrier. Water represents feelings and Aquarians are noted for their ability to offer compassion, but those feelings are carried, which represents the ability of Aquarians to detach themselves if need be. This symbol is also thought to represent the union of feelings and intuition with reason and logic to serve the greater good.

Love

Charismatic, interesting and cheerful, Aquarians rarely lack admirers. They love socializing on their terms and pride themselves on being able to get along with just about anybody. They need a partner who can share their spirit of adventure and zest for life, because someone who is too timid or small-minded will frustrate them.

When it comes to close, intimate relationships Aquarians may struggle because their perfectionist nature finds the inevitable complications that love and emotion can bring difficult to process. With their powerful desire for independence, they may find it the hardest of all the signs to settle into and commit to a relationship in the conventional sense. Allowing another person into their lives is interpreted as an invasion of their freedom—both physically and psychologically—and they may prefer to stay single rather than change or accommodate someone else. The danger here is they can become so set in their ways that it is impossible for them to share, and they end up lonely. Having said this, Aquarians love the excitement and passion of romance, and when they find a quick-witted individual who can match their sense of adventure but who also gives them plenty of space to breathe, they make loyal and loving companions.

Love matches:
Gemini, Leo Sagittarius, Libra

The Aquarian woman

Don't even try to understand an Aquarian woman. She is a beautiful mystery. She is loving but detached. She is friendly but a loner. She is gentle but tough. She is faithful but freedom-loving. She is logical but magical. The only thing predictable about her is her fierce unpredictability.

Conversations with Aquarian women will rarely be dull. She has the charming ability to make anyone feel special. She is genuinely fascinated by and eager to learn about others, and rarely imposes her own opinions on them. It's no surprise that this enchanting creature is often surrounded by admirers, but, when it comes to commitment, she may hesitate and take a few steps back. Emotional closeness can make her feel trapped. It can take an age for a friendship or a casual relationship to move from the superficial to something deep and meaningful.

Aquarian women are many things, but above all they are free spirits. They love their independence. They are averse to friends or potential partners who are jealous and possessive. They also don't take well to criticism or to people who are conventional in their approach to relationships. They are drawn to the eccentric because they are eccentric themselves. It is of the utmost importance that they have plenty of personal space and freedom in all their relationships. Separate bedrooms may be a relationship saver. However, once they do eventually

find someone who is their love match, they can be loyal and tolerant partners. Their unpredictable personality ensures that a love affair with an Aquarian woman always feels like a love affair. It will be many things but it will never be dull.

The Aquarian man

Expect the unexpected from the Aquarian man. He is unconventional and rarely behaves the way other people expect. It can take a long time for him to reveal his true feelings. He will typically be popular and surrounded by friends—everybody is his "friend," even his enemies—but there will be few, if any, people who are really close to him. If he says he does not like someone, the chances are that, in fact, he actually does. Sound confusing? Welcome to the world of Aquarius!

An Aquarian man prefers to keep his real motives, feelings and intentions well hidden. Not because he necessarily has anything to hide, but because he genuinely loves surprising or waking other people up. He also enjoys studying other people and, like a detective, discovering what motivates them. If he can't figure someone out, he will become dedicated to unlocking their mystery. People who are easy to work out or who wear their hearts on their sleeves don't attract him as much as those who are complex and mysterious.

When he does eventually meet someone who interests him enough to make him want to take the relationship to the next stage, the Aquarian male may initially struggle. He is not against marriage or fearful of long-term commitment, but it is not in his nature to share his heart and his life with another person as spontaneously as some other signs. He may even come up with logical reasons to delay or to wait and may therefore marry or commit later in life. This hesitancy is a shame because when the Aquarian man does finally find the courage to take a leap of faith with his heart and share his life with someone else, he can really thrive. He is able to open up and relax and will bring much excitement and joy to a relationship.

Family

Aquarian children are often independent and from an early age may have a rebellious streak. Their parents soon learn that these surprising children tend to do the opposite of what

is expected, so reverse psychology may work with them. They don't tend to thrive in school environments that are overly disciplinarian and traditional, but, if the reasons behind rules and regulations are clearly explained to them, they can be sensible. Children born under this sign often have an insatiable curiosity and need to be allowed to experiment and find things out for themselves. This is the sign of the inventor, after all. They are drawn to art and science in particular. Naturally curious and friendly, these children need to be kept safe by their parents when it comes to interacting with strangers or people they don't know.

Aquarian parents will dive into parenthood with a sense of adventure, and their approach to raising children is likely to be unconventional and sometimes lacking in discipline. This will work out fine if their child loves the freedom of being different, but not so fine if their child prefers fitting in with the crowd and craves structure to feel secure. It really is important for an Aquarian parent to understand that their children may not have the same viewpoints or approach to life as them.

Career

To be fulfilled in their careers, Aquarians must feel they are being original or inventive in some way. They may even become inventors or entrepreneurs. They can do very well in careers involving communication, such as people management, public relations, journalism, the media, television and radio, and can excel on social media, becoming online influencers. Another field they may be attracted to is technology and they can be brilliant with computers. Drawn to humanitarianism, they make fine charity workers, campaigners and even politicians. **Above all, their intention is to help human beings progress in some way**, so it's highly likely they will be attracted to science, medicine, technology, anthropology, archaeology, sociology, ecology, forensics and even space research.

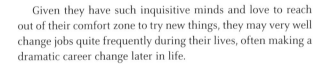

" **Above all, their intention is to help human beings progress in some way** "

Given they have such inquisitive minds and love to reach out of their comfort zone to try new things, they may very well change jobs quite frequently during their lives, often making a dramatic career change later in life.

Health and wellbeing

The average Aquarian—if there is such a person—will thrive best on a diet that is simple, light and nourishing. They should steer clear of fatty and fried foods that will just slow them down mentally and physically, and aim for foods that are as natural as possible. A mainly vegetarian diet rich in fruits, vegetables, oily fish, legumes, nuts and seeds is therefore preferable to a diet rich in animal products and refined, processed food.

Aquarians may feel fitter and more mentally alert when the weather is cooler. They don't tend to enjoy sunbathing as much as those of other signs. They can suffer from circulation problems and should ensure they get plenty of

circulation-boosting exercise, a minimum of 30 minutes a day. Cross-training or creative forms of exercise, such as dancing, will appeal to them more than repetitive exercise. Jogging or brisk walking is highly beneficial, but they should avoid the dullness of the treadmill and head outside to get the energy-boosting benefits of fresh air. Regular stretching before and after exercise is important because Aquarian ankles are vulnerable to injury and they should also make sure they wear supportive footwear.

Aquarians are highly likely to enjoy unusual or eccentric hobbies, from train- and UFO-spotting, to astronomy, to science fiction conventions. They can enjoy team sports, socializing and campaigning for causes they believe in. Mind–body therapies, such as yoga and tai chi, physical therapies such as massage, and even simply thumping a punch bag, can help them unwind when the going gets tough. Although blue is their favored color, wearing, meditating on and surrounding themselves with the color **red** will encourage them to feel less detached and more passionate toward themselves and others.

Born between January 20 and 31

All Aquarians love surprises, but those born between these dates positively thrive on them. They can have stable home or work situations and can be loyal and self-disciplined, but every now and again expect them to shake things up and make everybody rethink their assumptions.

Born between February 1 and 10

Aquarians born between these dates find it tough to maintain relationships with people who are not willing to experiment and evolve in the same way that they do. These people just love to constantly reinvent as a way to motivate themselves and others to change for the better.

Born between February 11 and 18

Aquarians born between these dates are sensitive deep down, but they can appear dreamy, aloof and detached at times. They prefer to mix with people who are as original and as visionary in their approach to life as they are. Unconventional and innovative people, their lives will involve many twists and turns.

Life lessons

Aquarius is perhaps the most forward-thinking and future-orientated sign of the zodiac. Progressive and unconventional, Aquarians are likely to challenge traditional thinking at every opportunity, and have the ability to initiate positive change in the world and ease the suffering of the underprivileged. They need to ensure that their passion for progress does not develop into fanaticism. Although they come across as confident and sociable, emotional intimacy frightens them as they fear it will limit their individuality. Their natural ability to detach can come across as cold, but it often masks lack of self-belief. They try to find a sense of identity in being different, though this approach can only work if eccentricity is an expression of their true identity, rather than a false self they have taken on. They need to understand what it is within them that drives them to always be the square peg in a round hole. Only when they know that, can they establish a genuine identity for themselves. They also need to understand that oneness or agreement does not always diminish their position, it can enhance it.

Aquarians are ahead of their time and always looking to the future for another challenge. This makes them true visionaries, but it also makes them restless, with a tendency to push too hard to make things happen. They often don't know how to relax, let go and savor the present moment, and so they miss out on the inner peace that living mindfully in the now can give them.

Aquarians can truly inspire other Aquarians to visionary heights, but they can also help them understand how they can impact others in a positive or negative way. The other signs of the zodiac can also teach Aquarians valuable life lessons. Geminis and Leos mirror their love for adventure, with Geminis encouraging them to be more analytical and Leos inspiring them to have more fun. Taureans and Capricorns can teach them to value the importance of rules and traditions. Virgos can teach them self-discipline, Librans the value of agreeing to disagree, Cancerians and Pisceans the joys of empathy and heartfelt compassion. Sagittarians can help them focus their original ideas, while Scorpios can teach them not to fear getting to know themselves and others intimately. Arians can show them how energizing time alone can be, as well as the importance of separating rebellion for its own sake from rebellion for a just cause.

Chinese astrology counterpart: The Tiger

Tigers are the courageous adventurers and bold unpredictable animals of the Chinese zodiac. They absolutely love to be challenged and to take risks, so it is easy to see why they correspond with the rebellious instinct of their counterpart, Aquarius. They are extremely friendly and often charismatic, but never ever forget they also have very sharp jaws and claws. They can be irritable, opinionated, arrogant, detached and uncompromising.

Being part of a team or group is something they enjoy, but they are loners at heart, who prefer to hunt alone. They must also feel free to express their originality at all times. Blending in with the crowd is something they rarely, if ever, do. Emotional intimacy is an issue for them and it takes them a long time to really trust someone with their heart. Born leaders who are addicted to constant change and transformation, these people are often progressive innovators searching for new ways to do things. They find contentment only when they are forging their own path and making progress doing things *their* way, however weird or eccentric that way may be.

Note: Aquarians have an affinity with Tiger-sign characteristics, but be sure to check which Chinese sign corresponds to your **year** of birth (see page xxi), and to read about the characteristics associated with it, too.

January 20

The Birthday of the Ad-libber

"I adapt and grow stronger"

January 20 people are expressive and charming improvisers. They may not always be sure where they are going, but they also have no doubt that they will get somewhere. They have a remarkable ability to learn, adapt and constantly improve their skills, and these qualities help them climb the ladder of success, sometimes to the very top. Although they can occasionally appear superficial and flaky—and their flexibility occasionally runs the risk of tipping over into dishonesty and lack of self-discipline—there is always method to their madness. Their flexible and fun but responsible style ensures that they can overcome almost any setback with their sparkling sense of humor intact.

Born healers, those born on this day genuinely care about the wellbeing of others, especially those who are underdogs, so any career that involves dealing with the public appeals. They can achieve much in the world of medicine and science and also make great teachers, counselors and advisors. Their communication and creative skills may draw them to diplomacy, politics, writing, music, the media, blogging, entertainment, and they can thrive in business and as entrepreneurs. Their flexible approach to life extends to their health, so it is important that they don't ignore warning signs of poor health. **For self-care**, at the end of each day, record in a journal things that you are grateful for about yourself or things you did today that you are proud of. At the start of each day list the tasks you want to complete and enjoy ticking them off as the day progresses.

These people can become insecure when deeply involved with someone special and need to apply the same go-with-the-flow approach to life to their close relationships. Although they appear tough, the respect of others is extremely important to them, sometimes too much so. They need to learn to trust their own judgment more, as they are usually right. Fortunately, around the age of 30, they reach a powerful turning point that emphasizes the need for working with their gut instinct, and their intuition grows stronger and stronger with age. Once they find a direction and the sense of self-worth essential to their growth, their destiny is to show others that adaptability is a strength, not a weakness, and a truly healing way to progress and create harmony in the world.

Potential: Intuitive, resilient

Dark side: Insecure, superficial

Tarot card, lucky numbers, days, colors: Judgment, 2, 3, Saturday, Monday, blue, silver

Born today: Buzz Aldrin (astronaut); Federico Fellini (director); Bill Maher (comedian); Gary Barlow (singer)

January 21

The life lesson:

is to distinguish between fear and intuition.

The way forward: is to understand that intuition is not harshly self-critical, but a gentle caring voice.

Luck maker: Connect with your feelings and listen to your heart before you make a decision.

"I see no limitations"

People born on January 21 are charismatic trailblazers. Boldly original and innovative, others tend to want to follow them and listen to their opinions. They seem to be able to get along with just about anyone and when this is combined with their ambition and ability to learn from their mistakes rather than be derailed by them, they have the perfect recipe for success. Freedom of expression is vital for people born on this day. They don't like to be tied down by rules and rarely relish the role of leader because they lack the ruthlessness to impose their will on others. They prefer to be the planners and visionaries, but it is up to others to see things through to the end.

Born artists and free spirits, these people's combination of innovation and sensitivity gives them great potential in the arts, but they will excel in any profession that values their talent for generating ideas, such as design, advertising, the media, technology, commerce, business and all forms of social media. They may also be drawn to charity work, politics, the law and social reform, as they have a desire to help those who are less fortunate than themselves. Innovative, they are likely to create their own successful self-care plan and, as long as they don't go to extremes, others often look to them for lifestyle advice. **For self-care**, set aside some time when you can be completely alone and use that time to reflect and recharge.

These people don't like to be tied down and will experiment in relationships until they find someone who shares their love of variety. They have a tremendous need to be liked, and this can lead to fast talking, nervousness and indecision. It is essential for them to acknowledge the importance of thinking before they speak and to be less swayed by others' criticism. Fortunately, a profound turning point often occurs before their thirtieth birthday, when their sense of self finally matures. Once they have learned to trust their own instincts, and the importance of discipline and staying the course, their destiny is to break boundaries and help improve and fulfill the lives of others by setting new heights for them to aspire to.

Potential: Inventive, optimistic

Dark side: Nervous, chaotic

Tarot card, lucky numbers, days, colors: The World, 3, 4, Saturday, Thursday, blue, purple

Born today: Christian Dior (fashion designer); Jack Nicklaus (golfer); Placido Domingo (singer)

January 22

The Birthday of the Visionary

The life lesson:

is the inability to commit to a person or project.

The way forward: is to find out what is holding you back. If it is fear, you need to be the bold person you know you are deep down and take the risk.

Luck maker: Learn to handle your impatience, because impatience repels good fortune.

"I am bold, brave and beautiful"

January 22-born are unconventional visionaries and often have an electrifying energy. They don't just break the rules; they destroy them and make new ones. Their imaginative powers are often so advanced that the world isn't ready for them. This can create a sense of frustration, but if they direct their energy constructively, the world will eventually notice. Their biggest hates are boredom and routine. They have the ability to be extraordinarily successful in whatever they choose, but they do need to learn the importance of patience and discipline if they are to find stability and satisfaction. If people born on this day don't understand or can't see their way ahead, they are likely to lose their temper, with explosive results.

Born travelers, they don't just like variety; it is their *life force* and they thrive in any career that offers them fast-paced change, plenty of challenge and no set routine. They make superb pilots, airline personnel, travel guides, journalists, chefs, critics, actors and online influencers. Because they live their lives in the fast lane, they need to eat regular meals and snacks to keep their energy levels constant. Wearing, meditating on and surrounding themselves with the colors blue and green will encourage them to exercise healthy moderation in all things. **For self-care**, perform a routine task, such as brushing your teeth, mindfully. Focus all your attention on that task and, if your attention wanders, bring it back to the task.

Relationships can feel restrictive for people born on this day and they need someone who shares their sense of adventure. Their impulsive approach earns them critics and has its dangers. Their lives would be easier if they learned to appreciate the value of differing opinions. By the age of 29 they typically begin to develop a sense of self-discipline, and this gradual shift toward self-empowerment is a feature for the rest of their lives. Once they learn to control their tendency to flip-flop from one project or relationship to the next and value the importance of patience and introspection, their destiny is to amaze those around them, whatever they choose to do.

Potential: Imaginative, ground-breaking

Dark side: Hasty, explosive

Tarot card, lucky numbers, days, colors: The Fool, 4, 5, Saturday, Sunday, sky blue, silver

Born today: Lord Byron (poet); Francis Bacon (statesman); John Hurt (actor)

January 23

The Birthday of the Dissenter

The life lesson:

is to stop feeling insecure about yourself.

The way forward: is to nurture or parent yourself by making sure that every word or action is one that supports and encourages you.

Luck maker: Accept help and listen to advice from others.

"I follow my own path"

People born on January 23 dislike taking orders or even advice from other people and prefer to live according to their own rules, devoting themselves to their own ideals. Although this approach has its risks, more often than not their courageous and buoyant character sees them making, rather than obeying, the rules. Rarely motivated by financial reward alone, they are idealistic. This quality, along with their original thinking and distinctive style, makes them stand out from the crowd in a positive way. They truly are inspirational figures. Despite their can-do attitude and charisma, people born on this day never feel quite worthy of the admiration they attract. Although this adds to their charm, it can sometimes hold them back, but when they are able to believe in themselves, there is nothing to stop them achieving their own dreams.

Born academics, they are drawn to intellectual pursuits and thrive in student and academic settings. As they are analytical, they can make great scientists and mathematicians. Their more practical side may draw them to technology, finance and business, but their rebellious nature may draw them to entrepreneurship and self-employment. Whatever career they choose, originality will lead the way. They need to avoid becoming obsessive about their health and to seek advice from experts rather than self-diagnose. **For self-care,** visualize your life as a work of art—mold it in beautiful and loving detail in your mind's eye. Make it a masterpiece and then express that inspiration in your daily life.

These people are cerebral and this can make them feel emotionally isolated. It is important for them to connect to their feelings and to their bodies, and for their hearts and minds to work in harmony. Typically, around the age of 28 they become more emotionally mature and responsive in relationships, and less distant, and this positive trend continues with age. If they can balance their rebellious streak with practicality, and make sure their fascination with the abstract does not take precedence over their relationships, their destiny is not just to become rebels with an important cause but to encourage others to see things they normally take for granted in an extraordinary new light.

Potential: Principled, courageous

Dark side: Troubled, isolated

Tarot card, lucky numbers, days, colors: The Hierophant, 5, 6, Saturday, Wednesday, aquamarine, green

Born today: John Hancock (statesman); Édouard Manet (painter); Gertrude B. Elion (chemist)

January 24

The Birthday of the Idol

"I joyously give to life and life joyously gives to me"

January 24 people tend to be stunning. Everybody wants a piece of them and they are never short of admirers, but, despite this, few get close enough to know their hearts. This may be because behind their natural ability to excite others with their imaginative flights there is a deep-seated fear of criticism and rejection. They often feel misunderstood, but there is a spark of originality, even genius about them. The greatest danger is that the admiration they so naturally attract can lead to vanity.

Born nature lovers, these people are at their happiest working with nature, animals or children, where they can experience the level of unconditional acceptance they fear others may not give them. They have the intelligence to become a breakthrough talent in any career, but may be drawn to education, religion, philosophy, the law, sociology, writing, modeling, vlogging or the world of entertainment. They need to make sure they don't get fanatical about their health—maintaining a balance in all things, especially diet and lifestyle, is crucial. **For self-care,** when you wake up in the morning speak to yourself the way a loving parent would to a child. Say out loud that you are special and deserve to be loved simply for being you.

It is not hard for these people to attract potential partners, but it is extremely hard for them to let someone get really close to them. They require a partner who respects their need for personal space. They need to move away from fear of emotional closeness to the belief that others will appreciate them just as they are. Typically, around the age of 27 and then again in their late fifties there are turning points, which suggests greater emotional depth and connection. Once they learn to stop pretending to be someone they are not and become the person they really are, they may lose some of their idol status but will gain something far greater in return: self-knowledge. And when they are finally able to understand themselves better, their destiny is to inspire others to work with them to help make the world a kinder and a better place.

Potential: Exciting, glamorous

Dark side: Vain, insecure

Tarot card, lucky numbers, days, colors: The Hierophant, 6, 7, Saturday, Friday, blue, lilac

Born today: Edith Wharton (author); Neil Diamond (singer); Benjamin Lincoln (officer)

January 25

The Birthday of Purpose

is finding your direction or purpose.

The way forward: is to think about what you love to do, find out what you are good at, and then discover how doing what you love and are good at can help others.

Luck maker: Try to make things better, not perfect.

"I love myself more today than yesterday"

January 25-born come into this world with a powerful sense of destiny. They feel as if they have been sent with a purpose and will feel unfulfilled until they find it, but once they discover their mission, their disciplined approach assures their success. They focus all their energy on their goals, but, because they are empathetic, their goals tend to be for the good of others rather than for themselves alone. They are at their happiest when they are totally immersed in a project, but their over-involvement is never at the expense of their individuality. Eccentric by choice, they refuse to conform; personal freedom is extremely important to them.

Born achievers, the greatest danger for these people is to be without direction, drifting from project to project. Choice of career is crucial as, once they have settled on a direction, they can excel in any profession. Social services, healing and the caring professions are a natural fit, but their curious and organized personality suits writing, sociology, counseling, psychology, politics, music, the arts, finance, sales, marketing and technology. They also make fine inventors. Keeping a favorable attitude toward themselves through positive thinking, as well as a healthy diet and lifestyle, helps them avoid a tendency toward feeling insecure about themselves and resulting self-destructive behavior. **For self-care**, give yourself a kiss on the back of one of your wrists as a symbolic reminder of the life-changing importance of self-love.

These people love the idea of finding a soul mate—someone who completes them—but they are unlikely to find a partner until they learn to complete themselves first. It is vitally important for them to come to terms with who they are and to feel comfortable with their personality, because when they do they are an unstoppable force. Turning points for greater emotional identity are the late twenties and then the late fifties. Once they learn to love and trust themselves, their destiny is to share their sense of original and progressive purpose with the world in a way that truly sets them apart.

Potential: Profound, individual

Dark side: Impatient, self-defeating

Tarot card, lucky numbers, days, colors: The Chariot, 7, 8, Saturday, Monday, blue, green

Born today: Virginia Woolf (author); Alicia Keys (singer); Robert Burns (poet)

January 26

The Birthday of the Last Word

The life lesson:

is your inability to cope when your authority or ideas are questioned.

The way forward: is to take on board different viewpoints from your own, because others can sometimes see what you miss.

Luck maker: Learn to listen.

"I light up the way ahead"

People born on January 26 are enterprising individuals with a commanding presence. They love to spearhead new trends and their determination and success-orientated approach give them the potential to turn all their dreams into reality. Their insistence on always having the last word makes them excellent leaders. The one thing they really don't like is having their authority questioned. They are not known for their patience and are prone to making snap decisions without consulting others, which can cause them trouble; their bluntness can also truly upset others. Once they are able to recognize the importance of compromise and considering the impact of their words and actions on others, their down-to-earth resilient approach, dynamic energy and bold originality guarantee their success and the undying loyalty of others.

Born leaders and motivators, these driven people can go far if they avoid power struggles. Their ability to spot opportunities makes them great CEOs, managers, consultants, life coaches, agents, advertisers, financial advisors and managers, but their individuality and natural authority may also find a home in the world of the law, the media, music and entertainment. An early-to-bed, early-to-rise lifestyle that avoids extremes benefits their health the most. **For self-care**, smile warmly at someone today for no other reason than to acknowledge your shared humanity.

Natural flirts, these people need to avoid getting involved with people for the wrong reasons; for example, because they feel they can help them climb the ladder of success. They are usually found where the party or the action is and are great at networking, but to lead a fulfilled life they must nurture their inner life and the quality of their relationships. Fortunately, after the age of 25, and then again at the age of 55, they tend to shift toward becoming more inner-focused and less externally orientated. Once they have learned the importance of compromise, and to motivate people through a spirit of cooperation rather than dictatorship, their destiny is to be right up there at the forefront of inspirational new trends and ideas.

Potential: Enterprising, dynamic

Dark side: Opinionated, domineering

Tarot card, lucky numbers, day, colors: Strength, 8, 9, Saturday, green, purple

Born today: Eddie van Halen (musician); Ellen DeGeneres (comedian); José Mourinho (soccer manager)

January 27

The Birthday of
Quick Starts

The life lesson:

is learning to control your impulses.

The way forward: is to understand that your emotions are not in charge of you; you are in charge of your emotions.

Luck maker: Discipline is an essential ingredient for success.

"My magic is just beginning"

January 27-born are often blessed with outstanding creative talents that are likely to emerge early in their lives. Material gain is unlikely to be the main motivating force—their motivation is more a personal desire to challenge themselves, to create the life of their dreams. They love the journey more than the arrival, the thrill of the chase. Intelligent, they often pick things up very quickly, and their talent for careful planning but also adapting effortlessly along the way to the new can turn them into trendsetters.

Born studious, these people have the potential to rise to public office and power in high places. They love learning and will use their knowledge and creativity to help others. Social welfare, the healing professions, counseling, teaching, childcare and mentoring others appeal to them. They can also be good freelancers and may use their creativity in the arts, theater, social media or music. Their tendency to become self-absorbed can lead to stress, anxiety and sudden outbursts of rage, so it is important they prioritize regular rest and time out. **For self-care**, perform a yoga tree pose or spend time close to a tree. Let your imagination sense the deep roots of the tree. Feel yourself slowing down and becoming grounded and balanced, but with your head still stretching to the skies.

The love life of those born on this day is exciting and never dull. Taking things more calmly in their relationships and learning to slow down in all areas of their lives is beneficial. They need to follow up their quick starts with a disciplined work ethic. This doesn't mean they should repress their generous, open child-like exuberance; it just means they need to get into the habit of finishing what they start if they want to find fulfillment and be taken seriously by others. Fortunately, in their mid-twenties, they reach a turning point that offers them opportunities to become more mature and show the world that their early promise can be fulfilled; this trend continues as they age. Once they learn the importance of patience and seeing things through, their destiny is to both astonish everyone with their utterly unique creativity and help make others feel special at the same time.

Potential: Enthusiastic, intelligent

Dark side: Restless, immature

Tarot card, lucky numbers, days, colors: The Hermit, 1, 9, Saturday, Tuesday, blue, red

Born today: Mozart (composer); Lewis Carroll (author); Samuel Ting (physicist)

January 28

The Birthday of the Star Performer

The life lesson:

is managing a constant need to be admired.

The way forward: is to understand that the happiness and approval you are seeking must come from within.

Luck maker: Stop trying so hard. Learn to relax, trust yourself and notice your luck improve.

"I am in love with my life"

Those born on January 28 project a confident and charming image. They are star performers with terrific creative potential. Impressing others means as much to them as their achievements, but more often than not their achievements are so special that others are impressed. These people must follow their own path; when this rebellious streak is properly channeled it can help them forge ahead. They understand the importance of hard work and have great insight into the motivations of others. This combination of innovation, insight, practicality and discipline makes them pioneers in whatever field they choose. They are also often known for and highly respected for their integrity and willingness to speak truth to power.

Born designers, they have a flair for anything artistic, as well as architecture, property development, dance and music. Careers that involve communication, public relations, video, and writing are also ideal. High achievers with the ability to motivate others and a strong sense of justice, they can also do well in the law, management and business, as well as social, humanitarian and political reform. They tend to be impulsive and over-eager, and would benefit from mind and body techniques, such as meditation and martial arts, that can teach them mental control. **For self-care**, say "I am worthy" out loud, so both your mind and heart can hear and you start to believe it.

These people's love lives tend to be complicated because they want everybody to love them, but they do need to learn to spread themselves a little less thinly. Despite their star quality, those born on this day run the risk of needing to be told over and over again how special they are. They may also make foolish, unrealistic decisions in their attempt to be noticed. Fortunately, around the age of 23 and again around the age of 53, they make a powerful shift toward greater emotional maturity. Once they learn to listen to their intuition, their destiny is to be noticed and to use their undoubted star quality to make a positive impact on the world.

Potential: Progressive, dedicated

Dark side: Unrealistic, attention-seeking

Tarot card, lucky numbers, days, colors: The Magician, 1, 2, Saturday, Sunday, blue, gold

Born today: Mikhail Baryshnikov (dancer); Elijah Wood (actor); Colette (author)

January 29

The Birthday of the Mystic Warrior

The life lesson:

is dealing with confrontation.

The way forward: is to calmly state your opinion and remain true to yourself.

Luck maker: Be proactive. Reactive people are led by impulses and reeds blown in the wind. Proactive people recognize they can't always control what happens, but they can control how they react.

"I see potential for good in everyone and everything"

January 29-born are persuasive. They say what they think and are direct and forceful without being offensive. Their generous nature and strong belief that there is good in everyone earn them the respect and love of all who cross their path. They often use their expressive, quietly rebellious streak to support the rights of others. The keys to their success are their intuitive power, sensitivity to the mood and needs of others, and their desire to work cooperatively rather than independently. They sense what others are feeling, and when the moment is right, when to make a move. They also understand the power of synergy and how a group of people working toward a common goal is the greatest force of all.

Born campaigners and negotiators, these people have a compassionate nature that marks them out for careers in politics, the law, humanitarian work, charity and social reform. They are intellectual and artistic too, and this can lead them to a career in the media and entertainment or to lecturing, teaching or writing. People-related careers, such as sales, marketing, advertising, personal relations, commerce, or as lifestyle gurus, are also a good fit. Sensitive to both others and their environments, they can be prone to unexpected mood swings, so need to learn ways to protect themselves from absorbing negative energies. **For self-care**, visualize a protective bubble around you whenever you feel uncomfortable in an environment or situation.

Those born on this day may occasionally withdraw into unassertive behavior when challenged and can get very hurt if people criticize them. In their relationships they can hold back emotionally and be self-sacrificing. They tend to find love later in life. Around the age of 22 and 52, they reach turning points when they develop a greater degree of emotional resilience. Life gets easier for them in their early thirties and beyond as they become more resilient and start to realize that within them is the power to achieve almost anything. Once they finally believe in themselves, and understand that it is impossible to please everyone, their destiny is to right wrongs and fulfill their role as the mystic warrior—strong-willed and with the ability to inspire others and gather support for their chosen cause.

Potential: Intuitive, generous

Dark side: Indecisive, withdrawn

Tarot card, lucky numbers, days, colors: The High Priestess, 2, 3, Saturday, Monday, blue, white

Born today: Oprah Winfrey (talk-show host); Thomas Paine (political activist); Anton Chekhov (playwright)

January 30

The Birthday of Assurance

is dealing with feeling lonely.

The way forward: is to accept people as they are and not as you expect them to be.

Luck maker: In conversations, ask questions and listen carefully to the answers.

"I do things my way"

People born on January 30 are confident in their convictions and put their personal mark on things. They live according to their own moral code and are always on the side of the underdog. Their strong social conscience, combined with their determination, charm and intelligence, means they are agents of positive change. Everybody will be in no doubt of where they stand on the important issues, but they are prone to worry and making impulsive decisions. They have a talent for bringing like-minded people together; living in a commune would not be unacceptable to them if it meant they could live according to their all-important ideals. Although they arrive at their position of certainty through reasoned judgment, they do also rely heavily on their instincts. This ability to combine intuition with logic marks them out as exceptionally gifted leaders.

Born campaigners, these people succeed in careers that require them to lead, inspire, educate, manage, negotiate and inform, such as politics, the law or police or even military work. They don't suit routine unless the routine matches their ideals, and may be drawn to aviation, navigation, entertainment, the arts or consultancy work of any kind, be it as head of department, doctor, social worker, psychologist, producer or director. As they are energetic 24/7, it is important for them to schedule regular rest and relaxation. Surrounding themselves with shades of blue can induce feelings of inner calm. **For self-care,** write a short letter of forgiveness to someone who has upset you, but don't post it. As you write, remind yourself that forgiving is not forgetting—it is letting go of negativity, which can drag you down.

A vain need to win the approval of others can lead those born on this day to fudge the truth. They can also find it hard to forgive those who upset them. It is important for them to speak truth to themselves and others, and to know when to let go. Around the age of 21 and then again at the age of 51 they experience significant turning points, which make them less anxious and more balanced. Once they have learned to value the viewpoints of others without seeing them as a threat to their convictions, their destiny is to transform their empathy into compassion and take action to make a positive difference.

Potential: Generous, confident

Dark side: Moody, dishonest

Tarot card, lucky numbers, days, colors: The Empress, 3, 4, Saturday, Thursday, blue, purple

Born today: Franklin D. Roosevelt (US president); Gene Hackman (actor); Emilio Segrè (physicist)

January 31

The Birthday of the Bright Spirit

"I have my mission and I choose to accept it"

January 31-born tend to have an overwhelming desire to be noticed and, because they are bright, endearing people, they often achieve this goal with ease. They are adored for their creativity, originality, determination and easy expressiveness. They can also be quite progressive, with a touch of genius about them. Although they can appear absent-minded and chaotic at times, this is only because their thoughts are always on fast-forward, their mind ever overflowing with ingenious ideas. When they feel on the verge of a creative breakthrough they can get over-excited, but others tend to find their enthusiasm and creativity appealing rather than annoying.

Born consultants and communicators, they excel as teachers, healers, writers, researchers, counselors, scientists and instigators of social and humanitarian reform. They may also channel their tremendous creativity into the entertainment world or the arts, poetry and music. They are prone to bouts of low self-esteem and insecurity, and could benefit from counseling. They may also find alternative therapies that highlight the connection between their thoughts and their physical and emotional wellbeing beneficial; for example, meditation. **For self-care**, set aside 10 minutes to meditate on the color blue or simply to mindfully gaze up at the clouds in the sky, to help stabilize your mood and induce deep feelings of inner calm.

These magnetic people are generally well liked, but they do harbor a tendency to be occasionally oversensitive, reading hidden and often wildly inaccurate meanings into the actions and words of others. When they feel upstaged, put upon or let down, they may overreact and either withdraw completely and become depressed, or startle others with their sharp tongue. They need to learn to be a little less intense and sensitive in their relationships and to accept that sharing the limelight does not diminish but enhances their brightness. Around the age of 20 they develop greater self-reliance; at the age of 50 they have another turning point, which highlights emotional resilience and letting go of the fear of being upstaged by others. Once they learn to rely on their own instincts rather than the approval of others, their destiny is to brighten the world with their enchantingly joyful insights and spirits.

Potential: Original, magnetic

Dark side: Insecure, chaotic

Tarot card, lucky numbers, days, colors: The Emperor, 4, 5, Saturday, Sunday, sky blue, silver

Born today: Franz Schubert (composer); Johnny Rotten (singer); Thomas Merton (monk)

February 1

The Birthday of the Spectacular Turnaround

"I always find a way"

F ebruary 1-born tend to be nonconformist and multiskilled. They can sway others with their conviction, but it is not uncommon for them to make a spectacular turnaround. This unique combination of determination and flexibility means they attract success. They are intuitive and make clear decisions, but are also capable of dramatically changing direction to get to the same place. They have the good sense to always keep their options open.

is coping with uncertainty about what to do with your life.

The way forward: is to understand yourself better, reflect on what brings you joy and what you are good at.

Luck maker: Just do something. Sometimes doing the wrong thing is better than procrastination, because at least you will have learned something.

Born firefighters, they are drawn to careers that require quick reactions, such as paramedics, emergency staff, doctors, nurses and pilots. Management or executive positions and sales and promotions in big companies also appeal, as does banking, the stock market and setting up their own business. It's best they avoid routine jobs. Their originality may draw them to politics, the media, writing and the arts, and their intuition toward humanitarian and caring work. Prone to anxiety, they need to find positive ways to work through their emotions and benefit from yoga deep-breathing techniques. **For self-care**, at the end of each day record the small steps you have taken toward making your long-term goals a reality.

These people tend to wear their hearts on their sleeves and, being an appealing mixture of seriousness and fun, they are never short of admirers. The only danger is that by accommodating themselves to others they can lose touch with who they are. Fortunately, from around the age of 19 and heightened after the age of 49, they make powerful shifts toward deeper self-understanding. With their ability to adapt and strike out in any new direction, people born on this day are often lighting the way for others to follow. Once they know where they are heading and who they want to be, their powers of communication, combined with their versatility and charisma, have the potential to attract great success. Their destiny is to break new ground and reach further than any have reached before.

Potential: Original, inspirational

Dark side: Confusing, insecure

Tarot card, lucky numbers, days, colors: The Magician, 1, 3, Saturday, Sunday, aqua, orange

Born today: Muriel Spark (author); Boris Yeltsin (Russian president); Harry Styles (singer)

February 2

The Birthday of Elegance

"I see and serve the bigger picture"

The life lesson:

is to let down your guard.

The way forward: is to understand that trust and intimacy are not weaknesses but strengths.

Luck maker: Learn how your intuition or quiet knowing speaks to you.

People born on February 2 tend to be sophisticated, with their own elegant style. They resist any attempt to impose rules and regulations, but, despite their fierce independence, they are also open-minded. This makes their presence a reassuring force. They also possess formidable determination. Their focus is often the universal, the social, the bigger picture or the group, and they are frequently healers who have suffered themselves. They are the inspirational warriors for justice who have little time for their own family; the therapists who help others work through their traumas but are unable to identify their own; the mystics who see the bigger picture but can't see their own loneliness.

Born designers, they can be attracted to technical careers, such as programming or engineering, or careers in fashion and design. Their charm ensures that they will succeed in jobs dealing with the public, but their curiosity may also draw them to psychology, politics and sociology, and their intuition may attract them to the arts, writing, social media, teaching, healing and spirituality or even psychic growth. They are often very concerned about their body image and need to avoid taking diet and exercise plans to extremes. **For self-care**, every morning, as soon as you wake up, write down your dreams before you forget them, to see if your dreaming mind has sent you any intuitive insights.

Although surrounded by admirers, these people tend to keep close relationships at arm's length. This could be because they can get so absorbed in their ideas or their projects that they place human contact at the bottom of the list. It is crucial for their own psychological growth that they learn to love themselves and allow others to love them. Fortunately, around the age of 18 and then again around the age of 48, they have opportunities to become less controlling and more satisfied with themselves. If they can learn to apply the same level of intuitive understanding to themselves as they apply to others, their destiny is not just to make the world a more refined place but to become truly inspirational individuals.

Potential: Dynamic, sophisticated

Dark side: Aloof, unsatisfied

Tarot card, lucky numbers, days, colors: The High Priestess, 2, 4, Saturday, Sunday, white, purple

Born today: James Joyce (novelist); Shakira (singer); George Halas (football coach)

February 3

The Birthday of New Frontiers

"I learn new things every day"

February 3-born have an inquisitive mind that thrives on variety. They are boundary-breakers and nothing excites them more than a challenge or a new experience. They give every task they commit to their undivided attention. However, once they have worked things out, they move on to something else. The danger is flitting from one subject to another without acquiring anything but superficial knowledge. Challenge is what makes them feel alive and if they are not being challenged, they may make their lives more difficult on purpose. For example, setting themselves impossible deadlines at work or pushing themselves to the limits physically.

Born technicians, they are drawn to careers in technology and science, and their gift for communication makes writing, teaching, selling, counseling, social media and therapy appealing to them. Whether they choose scientific, technical, business, sport or creative careers, their adventurous spirit and determination to learn new skills sets them apart. A routine approach to diet, exercise and sleep can help bring much-needed stability into their lives. **For self-care**, stretch for a few minutes as soon as you wake up in the morning. Don't reach for your phone first thing. Make those delicious waking moments all about yourself.

Boredom and not being able to explore new frontiers are their greatest fears in both life and relationships. This could result in superficiality, but it doesn't mean that these people are incapable of commitment and emotional closeness; they simply need to feel that they haven't had to sacrifice their personal freedom. Between the ages of 17 and 46 they have opportunities to develop emotional confidence; after the age of 47 there is another turning point that helps them lose their fear of emotional closeness. Once they learn to value the personal as much as the impersonal, and not to back off when things get intense, their destiny is to seek out new frontiers and to walk untrodden paths for others to follow.

Potential: Inventive, adventurous

Dark side: Unreliable, superficial

Tarot card, lucky numbers, days, colors: The Empress, 3, 5, Saturday, Thursday, aquamarine, violet

Born today: Felix Mendelssohn (composer); Elizabeth Blackwell (physician); Isla Fisher (actor)

February 4

The Birthday of the Bedazzler

"I am born to innovate"

February 4-born always stand out. They can bedazzle others with their original thoughts and authoritative flashes of brilliance. Their methods may not always be orthodox, but their thoughts are original and their problem-solving techniques effective. Although they are admired for their sincerity and self-discipline, the logic behind their thoughts and actions is often incomprehensible, not just to others but sometimes to themselves. Their speed of thought can be exhausting and others may respond with bewilderment rather than bedazzlement. Feeling like a square peg in a round hole can make them feel insecure and they may try very hard to fit in, but this is a mistake as they shouldn't try to win the admiration of others by limiting their greatest strength: their originality.

Born innovators, these people are drawn toward science, technology, politics, medicine, business, entrepreneurship and entertainment. They may specialize as therapists, psychologists, doctors or natural healers, or be drawn to charity work or social reform. They can make fantastic artists, photographers, designers, architects, sculptors, painters, online influencers and podcasters, as these careers offer outlets for their originality. Innovative in everything they do, they may be drawn to alternative medicine and holistic health practices. **For self-care**, take off your shoes and socks and walk barefoot. Direct physical contact with the earth through "earthing" can bring feelings of calm and balance to mind, body and spirit.

In relationships they are attracted to adventurous and unusual people like themselves. They are capable of intimacy, but acknowledging their feelings is not easy for them. They can be unempathetic and harsher on themselves than anyone else, and can also be impatient and impulsive without thinking through the impact of their actions. Fortunately, inner calm becomes more likely the older they get, and after their mid-forties they really come into their own. If people born on this day can understand that others respect and admire them far more if they are being themselves, and that they need to celebrate rather than curb their originality, their destiny is to amaze others with their honest, if occasionally eccentric, but always brilliantly innovative approach to life.

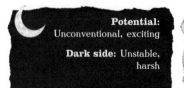

Potential: Unconventional, exciting

Dark side: Unstable, harsh

Tarot card, lucky numbers, days, colors: The Emperor, 4, 7, Saturday, Sunday, silver, blue

Born today: Charles Lindbergh (aviator); Rosa Parks (activist); Betty Friedan (feminist)

February 5

The Birthday of the Smooth Operator

The life lesson:

is to open up about how you feel.

The way forward: is to understand that no emotion should be ignored. Every emotion has something valuable to teach you.

Luck maker: Show your vulnerability. Admitting you have fears too will bring people closer to you.

"I know the secret"

Those born on February 5 are often respected for their quiet charm, razor-sharp wit and confident ability to tackle even the hardest of challenges with charm and grace. Although they come across as graceful and eloquent operators who seem to be extremely capable—sometimes to the point of overconfidence—underneath they are no less insecure than anyone else. They have simply learned to carefully hide their insecurities behind a facade, and the admiration of others means a whole lot more to them that they would care to admit, which is why they often relish the role of caretaker, advisor, supporter or educator of others.

Born guardians, they can excel in medicine, education, law, criminology, counseling, management, politics, finance, consultancy, the clergy, social work and psychology. Their curiosity may lead them to careers in the arts, design, science, writing or research, as well as online influencing. They can be exceptional thinkers as well as speakers, and nothing thrills them more than discovering mysteries to solve. They work well in teams, either in business or sport, and when promoting a cause, but, if they are able to develop their unique ideas and skills, they have remarkable potential to excel in any chosen field. Regular health check-ups are advised, as these people find it hard to admit they are fallible and to ask others for advice, because they consider giving advice to be their own role. **For self-care**, watch a classic heartfelt movie, such as *Titanic* or *Ghost*, to help reconnect you with the transformative power of your heart.

Those born on this day are happiest when surrounded by people as articulate and as intelligent as them, but, if they are starved of intellectual stimulation, they can come across as condescending at times. Fortunately, between the ages of 15 and 44 their sensitivity toward others grows, and after their mid-forties they feel even greater empathy for others. They have a tendency to think more than they feel. But when they are able to correct that head-over-heart imbalance, their destiny is to make the impossible seem possible and to use their smooth operating skills to achieve remarkable things for themselves and others.

Potential: Articulate, versatile

Dark side: Condescending, inconsistent

Tarot card, lucky numbers, days, colors: The Hierophant, 5, 7, Saturday, Wednesday, turquoise, green

Born today: Robert Hofstadter (physicist); Jane Geddes (golfer); Cristiano Ronaldo and Neymar (soccer players)

February 6

The Birthday of the Charmer

"I am in love with my life"

The life lesson: is dealing with a need to be praised.

The way forward: is to understand that people need to like you for who you are and not for being accommodating.

Luck maker: Be loyal and true to who you are.

February 6-born are charmers. Well liked by just about everyone, they have a winning way about them. They are also never wrong-footed by the unexpected, always willing to courageously explore new territory, and this boldness generally earns them universal praise. Approval really matters to them, but this need for affection isn't a one-way street; in many ways, life is one big love affair for them. The only downside to their perpetually love-struck approach is that when people don't warm to them or things don't go their own way, they can get easily hurt. Sometimes disillusionment can make them behave in overly dramatic ways, which can irritate rather than endear.

Born captivators, they can use their people skills to bring them success in public relations, politics, the media, public speaking, sales, marketing, promotion, vlogging and teaching, and may also be drawn to research, humanitarian causes, social reform, the arts and science and, in some instances, the world of sport. They tend to be obsessed with their physical appearance and need reminding that true beauty comes from within. **For self-care**, every time you are tempted to compromise yourself to win approval from others, gently tap your forehead with your fingers as a physical reminder to turn the focus on being true to yourself.

These people make passionate lovers, but they tend to be in love with the idea of love, forever seeking that endorphin high. They need to be careful not to go from lover to lover or to sacrifice who they are to accommodate others, and to understand that companionship is not just about pleasing others but also about trust, respect and having boundaries. There is a turning point in their mid-forties onward when they finally and fully understand that their self-worth needs to be based on more than popularity. Once they make sure their emotional needs are not sacrificed to the altar of people-pleasing, their destiny is to inspire others to follow their example and believe life can be really good, and with that kind of positive expectation, more often than not it is.

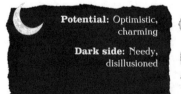

Potential: Optimistic, charming

Dark side: Needy, disillusioned

Tarot card, lucky numbers, days, colors: The Lovers, 6, 8, Saturday, Wednesday, turquoise, pink

Born today: Babe Ruth (baseball player); Ronald Reagan (US president); Mary Leakey (paleoanthropologist)

February 7

The Birthday of the Prophet

"I dream of a better world"

The life lesson:

is to talk less and do more.

The way forward: is to remember that actions speak louder than words.

Luck maker: Don't take everything personally. Not everything is about you.

People born on February 7 are progressive, with a sharp sense of fairness. It is impossible for them to witness injustice without speaking out. They are prophets with a vision and a desire to help others and right wrongs. They have little patience for conformity and, if forced into a corner, may "act up," with disruptive behavior. They have a wonderful imagination and a youthful approach, so when this tendency is combined with their spontaneity and lack of planning, they can come across as child-like. Others may dismiss them as dreamers, but this is a mistake as they do often turn dreams into reality. Although they are natural communicators, when they feel misunderstood or things don't go their way, they can retreat into cynicism. **For self-care**, tap your heart with your hand to remind yourself to always speak with integrity whenever you are tempted to spin the truth.

Born storytellers, these people can present information in a compelling way and often make excellent writers, teachers, actors, journalists, politicians, lecturers, filmmakers, salespeople and social-media influencers. Their analytical mind may draw them to science and medicine or they may become self-employed. Whatever they choose, they need work that offers them stacks of variety and challenge and an opportunity to create positive change. Humanitarian and social causes certainly appeal, as does the world of alternative healthcare. Prone to stress, February 7-born will find that wearing, meditating on or surrounding themselves with soothing shades of blues or greens can produce a calming effect.

In relationships they tend to put loved ones on a pedestal and this can lead to problems when these don't live up to the promise. Those born on this day need to accept people for who they are, not for what they could be. They must also understand that life isn't either right or wrong, and there will always be shades in between and many paths to the greater good. In their early forties they become more open-minded. Their destiny, once they learn to accept that others won't always agree with them, is to be a modern-day prophet who encourages rather than commands others to initiate reforms to make the world a fairer and better place.

Potential: Visionary, spontaneous

Dark side: Cynical, unrealistic

Tarot card, lucky numbers, days, colors: The Chariot, 7, 9, Saturday, Monday, blue, purple

Born today: Charles Dickens (author); Loren Carpenter (scientist and co-founder of Pixar); Chris Rock (comedian)

February 8

The Birthday of the Hypnotist

The life lesson:

is to avoid attraction to the seedier side of life.

The way forward: is to acknowledge rather than repress negative feelings and to understand what these feelings are trying to tell you.

Luck maker: Surround yourself with positive and inspiring people.

"I have a dream"

Those born on February 8 think on a grand scale and are often in touch with the future, shaping it with their progressive ideas. They have an intuitive understanding of people and situations, and are often able to spot future trends. The hypnotic power that they possess gives them astonishing influence over others and they are well aware of that power, sometimes coming across as serious or grave as a result. They have a sense of humor, but don't relish idle conversation and prefer to get to the heart of the matter. Prone to procrastination and indecision because they see so many possibilities, they need to learn to think and talk less and do more.

Born mystics, these people have great intuitive powers and thrive best in careers that allow them to use their powerful imagination and give them plenty of freedom. Their ability to see the bigger picture and look ahead makes them excellent designers, investors, property developers, architects, traders, planners, researchers and forecasters. Their empathy may draw them to education, the media, advertising or the arts, in particular writing, acting and music, and to New Age therapies and the world of personal growth and development. Prone to indulgence and bouts of laziness, they need to understand that too much sleep is as unhealthy as too little. **For self-care**, every day put your headphones on and listen to an upbeat music track that makes you want to get up and dance—for example, "Hey Ya" by Outkast.

The profound sensitivity of those born on this day means that they can effortlessly tune into the moods of others, over-identifying with their problems and minimizing their own. It is important for them to learn where other people end and they begin, as their sensitive nature tends to attract draining, toxic people into their lives. Fortunately, although there are opportunities earlier, in their early forties they start to become more protective of their personal energy. Once they understand their powerful impact on others, and how others affect them, their destiny is to bring peace, along with a much-needed dose of fantasy, into the world.

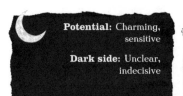

Potential: Charming, sensitive

Dark side: Unclear, indecisive

Tarot card, lucky numbers, day, colors: Strength, 1, 8, Saturday, dark blues and greens

Born today: Emanuel Swedenborg (philosopher); John Williams (composer); John Grisham (author)

February 9

The Birthday of the Winning Attitude

The life lesson:

is to be less self-critical.

The way forward: is to talk to yourself as though you are a child, in a positive, supportive and loving way.

Luck maker: Keep your cool when the going gets tough. Panic doesn't solve anything.

"Nothing can stop me"

February 9-born are independent and generous individuals with a unique and, at times, nonconformist perspective on life. They are shrewd observers and capable of great understanding of others' problems, even if they have not experienced those problems themselves. Above all, they are fighters. When life knocks them down, they bounce right back with resilience, and this winning attitude can lead them to great achievements. Often sought out for their sound advice, they make great teachers and leaders, influencing and inspiring not just with words but with their example—showing others through their own actions how to rise above challenges with a winning attitude. Their inner strength can make them seem unbreakable at times, but they do possess a soft side that takes rejection and criticism to heart. They also have a tendency to act rashly; they need to remain calm under pressure.

Born mentors, these people are perfect for advisory positions and make great educators, carers, counselors, consultants, therapists, politicians, lawyers and psychologists. They are multitalented and often have more than one career. Science, social and humanitarian reform, the arts, design, technology, property development, navigation, aviation, international business, social media or any career that involves plenty of travel and variety is ideal. Blessed with boundless energy, their secret to good health is eating little and often and avoiding alcohol and drugs. **For self-care,** sprinkle a few drops of jasmine oil on a handkerchief to breathe in when you feel overwhelmed. This will help you see the sunnier side of life.

When it comes to relationships, these people need to learn to be as understanding of themselves as they are of others. Before the age of 40 they seek the approval of others, but, after that, the emphasis switches to self-love as well as a need to take the initiative in all areas of their lives. Once they are able to regard themselves more positively—and to be less harsh in their self-criticism—their destiny is to achieve the high goals they set themselves, devote themselves to a positive cause and, in the process, become an inspirational role model to those lucky enough to cross their path.

Potential: Resilient, inspirational

Dark side: Insecure, hasty

Tarot card, lucky numbers, days, colors: The Hermit, 2, 9, Saturday, Tuesday, turquoise, red

Born today: Peggy Whitson (astronaut); Alice Walker (novelist); Tom Hiddleston (actor)

February 10

The Birthday of Achievement

"If I can dream it, I can do it"

People born on February 10 are life's go-getters. The pursuit of their career goals is likely to take precedence over anything else, especially in their early adult years. Their clear-sighted recognition of their aspirations, along with their ability to concentrate fully and adapt if need be, means that they are more than likely to surpass their professional goals. However, they do need to be careful that they don't become perfectionist and obsessive in their drive to succeed. Material success isn't likely to be their motivation, but rather gaining approval for making their mark in the right way. Integrity matters greatly to them and they aren't likely to walk over or take advantage of others to get to where they want to be.

Born achievers and hard workers, these people have the imagination but also the discipline, drive and determination to succeed in any career they choose. They could be a great lawyer, police officer, politician, civil servant, executive, charity worker, entrepreneur, athlete, artist, researcher, pilot, social media influencer and so on. The list of career possibilities is endless, so it might be beneficial for them to try their hand at many different options. Health-wise they would benefit considerably from plenty of fresh air and exercise as well as hobbies and interests outside the workplace. **For self-care**, slow down. Just 10 or 15 minutes of quiet time doing nothing can make a real difference with connecting to the luck-making power of intuition.

For those born on this day, home needs to be their sanctuary, but, without realizing it, they can subordinate the needs of loved ones to their careers and may end up alone for lengthy periods as a result. At 40 they reach a significant turning point, when they become less reliant on achievement for a sense of self-worth and more committed to nurturing close relationships with others and, just as important, nurturing the relationship they have with themselves. As long as they remember that admiration isn't the same as affection, and that periods of solitude can be a source of great creativity and strength, their destiny is to be highly respected for their integrity and to devote themselves to a cause that makes a genuine difference.

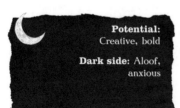

Potential: Creative, bold

Dark side: Aloof, anxious

Tarot card, lucky numbers, days, colors: The Wheel of Fortune, 1, 3, Saturday, Sunday, blue, orange

Born today: Boris Pasternak (novelist); Harold Macmillan (British prime minister); Laura Dern (actor)

February 11

The Birthday of the Upgrader

The life lesson:

is coping when you or others mess up.

The way forward: is understanding that making mistakes is an important learning experience.

Luck maker: Be open to learning from others. Nobody likes a "know-it-all."

"I can always find a new and better way"

People born on February 11 feel they were born to help improve everyone and everything. In their minds, both people and things are always in need of an upgrade. They often have an earnest, engaging quality about them, and a real talent for finding new ways to make life easier. They do this not for material benefit or recognition, but because they believe that the less stress people have, the more they can devote themselves to meaningful pursuits. Although they prefer to motivate by example, people born on this day can be a lot of fun and have a knack for making others feel good about themselves.

Born inventors, these people are attracted to careers in science, technology, education, invention, programming and architecture, as well as personal development. In business they make great consultants and specialists, or they may devote themselves to charity work, psychology, philosophy, the arts or personal transformation. Prone to self-indulgence, understanding the power of moderation and the mind–body link is important for their wellbeing. **For self-care**, meditating on an amethyst crystal or surrounding yourself with the color violet keeps your mood uplifted.

These people tend to let their current projects absorb them, neglecting relationships. In love they need personal freedom and intellectual stimulation, and are drawn to unusual people. Thinking of themselves as improvers and educators, they should understand that not everyone appreciates their help. Sometimes the only way for people to learn is through making their own mistakes and finding their own solutions. They may get resentful if another person tries to point things out, especially if they do so in a blunt manner. It is important for them to develop their sensitivity. Before the age of 40 they are emotionally sensitive, but after that, directness takes center stage and they need to learn to channel this directness positively and sensitively. With their inventive insight into what a situation or a person needs, there is little doubt that those born on this day (as long as they can master the art of diplomacy and be less critical) can break new ground. Their destiny is to experiment with original concepts and upgrade the world in the process.

Potential: Progressive, inventive

Dark side: Tactless, self-indulgent

Tarot card, lucky numbers, days, colors: Justice, 2, 4, Saturday, Monday, blue, silver

Born today: Thomas Edison (inventor); Julia Mossbridge (neuroscientist); Jennifer Aniston (actor)

February 12

The Birthday of the Bold Integrator

The life lesson:

is focusing energy on one project.

The way forward: is to understand that concentration is an essential ingredient for success and, without it, productive energy gets scattered.

Luck maker: Have more fun. Smile and the world smiles back at you.

"I unite and heal and bring peace"

Those born on February 12 have a talent for integration. They gather all the available information and then try to synthesize and unite it to form a bold plan. They love to bring harmony and always see themselves in the role of peacekeeper, pointing others in the right direction; that direction is, of course, the one they believe to be correct. They need to recognize the importance of consensus and to understand that, although their ability to see the bigger picture qualifies them to take the lead, great leadership is not about dictatorship but about motivating others to go in the direction you want them to go.

Born politicians and leaders, these people may consider politics, the military, the law, education or social reform, but, whatever career they choose, they are likely to rise to the top. Other work areas they may be drawn to include the arts, writing, philanthropy, charity work, anthropology, science, management, counseling, publishing, advertising, accountancy, or anything that requires their invention. Creatures of routine, when it comes to their health they might want to experiment with their food and exercise choices now and again. **For self-care**, practice daily meditation to help direct and focus your thoughts.

The detached exterior and fierce devotion to work of those born on this day can make it hard for them to open up, but, when they finally do relax and let go of inhibitions, they make loyal and sensitive companions. Tenacious, confident, original, ethical and creative, these people do need to be careful not to squander their many talents in too many directions. Until their late thirties there are opportunities for them to develop greater self-awareness, but in their forties and beyond there is a focus on personal integration and purpose; in many ways, this is when they really start to shine and can courageously and tenaciously initiate and implement their innovative projects and plans. They have the charisma to lead and inspire others, and, once they have learned to be more open-minded, their destiny is to create harmony in any environment that they find themselves in, making the world a more peaceful place.

Potential: Original, purposeful

Dark side: Intolerant, moody

Tarot card, lucky numbers, days, colors: The Hanged Man, 3, 5, Saturday, Thursday, blue, pink

Born today: Abraham Lincoln (US president); Charles Darwin (scientist); Raymond Kurzweil (inventor)

February 13

The Birthday of the Enigmatic Expert

"I live my life my way"

People born on February 13 are exuberant, original and daring. They see a world of exciting possibilities. Trailblazers, they are at their best when performing, and their unique presentations have the potential for greatness. Although they are often the center of attention, there are parts of themselves they keep private, giving them an enigmatic quality that only serves to intrigue their audience more. Being a little wild, they will almost certainly encounter criticism. It is important for them to hold fast to their individuality and to resist the urge to fit in. They just need to find the right goals to which to devote their considerable energy and their success is assured.

Born entertainers, these people love adventure and acclaim, and their versatility makes them ideally suited to the world of entertainment, music, media and vlogging. Science, education, counseling, astronomy, aviation, politics, social reform, charity work or setting up their own business may also appeal. They need to make sure they don't take reckless risks with their health, and should follow a balanced diet and moderate rather than intense exercise routine. **For self-care**, mind–body exercises, such as yoga, tai chi or meditation, can help bring a sense of inner calm.

February 13-born may flit from one relationship to another, eventually finding love with someone as elusive and dramatic as themselves. They can lead with their hearts rather than their heads, and this spontaneity has heart-breaking risks. Sometimes they can come across as bossy or eccentric; they do need to learn to look before they leap. After the age of 37 there is a turning point, suggesting they will become more aggressive and focused in pursuit of their goals. Once they are able to listen to both their heart and their head, and find a sense of inner security, these elusive but extrovert individuals really come into their own when entertaining and educating others. Their destiny is to express themselves and, by so doing, to influence and inspire their adoring fans to express themselves, too.

February 14

The Birthday of the Vulnerable Wit

"My word is my bond"

Those born on February 14 are charming, intelligent and warm-hearted, but also shrewd observers of human frailties. They think fast, often communicating in brilliant one-liners, but their incisive wit can work both for and against them. They can be wonderfully entertaining yet also blunt, driving others away with wounding comments. Their sarcasm tends to surface most when they feel impatient or frustrated because others aren't responding to their demands. And because others open up to them easily, they need to be careful that they don't become gossips. Their jovial banter can be a way for them to camouflage their true feelings. They are typically the first to cry when a sad song is played or to feel heart-breaking empathy for those who are suffering. This tender vulnerability can often surprise those around them, given their cool exterior.

Born broadcasters and interviewers, these people make great talk-show hosts, editors, podcasters, researchers and networkers. The world of banking, insurance or the stock market may appeal, as might writing, publishing or the art and entertainment worlds. Their empathy may draw them to education or social reform and charity work, and their verbal and analytical skills help them excel in business or science. They often give the appearance of being calm and in control, but underneath they are prone to insecurities. They would benefit from the inner calm that regular meditation can bring them. **For self-care**, if you feel angry or stressed, punch a cushion, scream or write in a journal to help you release rather than repress tension.

In relationships those born on this day can seduce people with their words, humor and spontaneity, but they should apply some of their penetrating insight to themselves as well as others, and understand that their emotions bubble so quickly to the surface because they have been repressed. Fortunately, from their mid-thirties onward, they become more emotionally self-aware. They may appear tough, but there is great emotional depth behind their banter and, with them around, life always seems easier, lighter and much, much happier. Their destiny is to influence and inspire others with the power of their bright words and ideas.

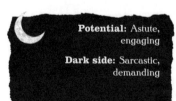

Potential: Astute, engaging

Dark side: Sarcastic, demanding

Tarot card, lucky numbers, days, colors: Temperance, 5, 7, Saturday, Wednesday, blue, green

Born today: Mike Bloomberg (politician); Carl Bernstein (journalist); Gregory Hines (choreographer)

February 15

The Birthday of the Enterprising Adventurer

"My life is an adventure"

February 15-born are live wires. They like to walk on the wild side, both physically and mentally. When faced with a challenge, it is impossible for them to sit on the sidelines; they have to jump in and offer their solution. Charming and energetic, they master new skills fast and use their ingenuity to elevate a project to new heights. They live life in the fast lane with little inclination to slow down. They are a powerful force, but find it hard to know when to stop. Intellectual freedom is important and they want to experience or investigate everyone and everything. This can lead to burnout or information overload and bouts of moodiness.

Born climbers in whatever field of work they choose, their energetic and wild nature suits careers in extreme sports, mountaineering, dancing, skating, the circus, aviation, space travel, nature trekking and stunt work. They may be attracted to jobs that keep them on the edge, such as teaching, journalism, science, the law, technology, the police, the military and banking, but are also drawn to art, writing and psychology. Nature lovers, they may work with animals or in conservation. They are prone to mood swings, so learning to manage their emotions is important for their wellbeing. **For self-care,** spending a few moments sitting quietly with your eyes closed to focus on breathing in and out deeply can bring a sense of inner peace.

The relationships of these people tend to be as adventurous as they are and they can get into tricky situations. In love, as in life, they need to understand that self-discipline has value. Fortunately, they tend to grow more self-disciplined the older they get, with 35 being a turning point for them. As long as they learn the importance of self-discipline and goal-setting, these multitalented individuals have the potential to realize their dreams. They may have a wild streak that often lands them in trouble, but they are genuinely motivated by a desire to make the world a happier and more exciting place. With them around, life can be many things, but it is never dull. Their destiny is to encourage others by their own example to live with a more adventurous, open-minded spirit.

Potential: Bold, curious

Dark side: Reckless, moody

Tarot card, lucky numbers, days, colors: The Devil, 6, 8, Saturday, Friday, blue, pink

Born today: Galileo Galilei (astronomer); John Barrymore (actor); Chris Farley (comedian)

February 16

The Birthday of the Alchemist

The life lesson:

is overcoming low self-esteem.

The way forward: is to become your own best friend and speak to yourself in a loving and gentle way.

Luck maker: Surround yourself with people who have your back.

"I always uncover what is real"

People born on February 16 can transform even the most difficult of experiences into something positive. There is a touch of the alchemist about them in their ability to see the bigger picture, bring together all the relevant information and cut right to the essence or truth of a situation. Even if they sometimes appear quiet on the outside, underneath there is great inner strength earned through learning from setbacks and upheavals in their past. They often have an astute understanding of others and how the world works; rarely, if ever, do they miss a trick. Their capacity to be realistic and intuitive makes them potentially great leaders, admired for their cleverness and ability to know how and what is the most productive thing to say and do. The downside is they can sometimes appear detached, and their impatience with others may come across as rude and arrogant.

Born reviewers, they have a great eye for detail as well as the bigger picture, and this makes them great journalists, editors, advisors, mentors, teachers or life coaches. They may be drawn to leadership roles in business, banking or the stock market, or careers where they can express their creativity with art, social media, entertainment or perhaps charity work and social reform. Regular meditation and time out help them strike that important balance between their inner and outer life. **For self-care**, each time you hear your inner critic, visualize it taking a holiday on a sunny beach. The more you send your inner critic on holiday, the more you start to love and value yourself.

These people can suffer from low self-esteem and they need to start believing they deserve to be loved. In their mid-thirties they reach a turning point when they become more focused and self-appreciative. It is important at this point in their life that they don't mask their feelings with a bossy manner or with detachment. When they believe they deserve good things to happen to them, their destiny is to help others focus on the positives in their lives and to strike gold both personally and professionally, which is after all every true alchemist's dream.

Potential: Confident, calm

Dark side: Arrogant, detached

Tarot card, lucky numbers, days, colors: The Tower, 7, 8, Saturday, Monday, blue, lavender

Born today: Eckhart Tolle (author); Ice T (rapper); John McEnroe (tennis player)

February 17

The Birthday of Self-Discipline

The life lesson:

is to let others in.

The way forward: is to understand that success may earn the admiration of others, but it may not win their love.

Luck maker: Move out of the corner. When you learn other ways of doing things, you can make luck from a vast field of opportunities rather than a narrow corner.

"If there is a will there is a way"

Those born on February 17 often figure out early in their life that the key to success is discipline. They are determined, earnest, ambitious people with a clear idea of where they want to go and what they need to do to get there. These qualities, combined with their remarkable willpower, can give them the appearance of invincibility. They are the athletes who train relentlessly, the entrepreneurs who sacrifice everything, the artists or scientists who devote their lives to their art or research. Underneath their tough exterior they are sensitive and can be easily hurt.

Born detectives who love a mystery, and with a sharp eye for details others might miss, these people may be drawn to careers in the law or the police or programming. They may also be attracted to writing, journalism and education and can make great athletes, artists, singers, influencers and scientists. Indeed, they thrive in any career that requires self-discipline and may be drawn to management, charity work or self-employment. Health-wise, they can be guilty of pushing their bodies and minds too hard, so it is important they strive for balance in holistic wellbeing. **For self-care,** the more you trust yourself, the easier it will be for you to trust others. Be true to yourself with your words and actions every single day.

The downside of their tunnel-vision approach is that those born on this day ignore anything that hinders their quest; all too often this is personal relationships. They should make sure that their emotional happiness does not take a backseat to their professional ambition, especially after the age of 33 when they often become even more determined. The incredible stamina of these people means they are able to achieve a level of self-mastery to which others can only aspire. Once they figure out what they are best at, there is nothing that can stop them achieving remarkable things with their life and improving the world in the process. Their destiny is to inspire others with their fierce vitality and inspirational self-discipline.

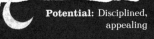

Potential: Disciplined, appealing

Dark side: Inflexible, cold

Tarot card, lucky numbers, day, colors: The Star, 1, 8, Saturday, blue, maroon

Born today: Ed Sheeran (singer); Michael Jordan (basketball player); Paris Hilton (influencer)

February 18

The Birthday of the Eternally Young

The life lesson:

is learning when to stop.

The way forward: is to understand that everything has a tipping point and sometimes less is more.

Luck maker: Try meditating to find the stillness within to connect with the luck-making power of your intuition.

"I look on the bright side of life"

February 18-born never grow old in their minds and hearts. With a charismatic, youthful energy about them, they brighten up their surroundings with their infectious optimism and enthusiasm for new and improved ideas and projects, however impossible they may seem. These people are courageous risk-takers. They will always be the first to volunteer or put themselves forward. They are never happier than when they are pushing things one degree harder, higher or faster, but they do need to ask themselves why they feel the need to live like this. Sometimes deep-seated insecurities are hidden behind their restless impatience.

Born DJs, these people need careers that allow them to express their originality. Multitalented, they can flourish in any career, but may be drawn to business, public relations, social-media influencing, music, publishing, writing, the self-help industry, journalism, the leisure industry, the media, art and entertainment. They are thrill-seekers, but they should avoid over-indulgence as far as their health is concerned, and learn when to stop or say no to anything that is not optimum for their wellbeing. **For self-care,** learning to cook properly would not only benefit your health but also encourage you to slow down and think about what you are ingesting.

Others are often drawn to the youthful spirit of those born on this day and may look to them for leadership in both life and love, but they aren't always happy in that role as it hinders their freedom. Although their life sparkles with heart and adventure, they may find themselves wondering why they lack a sense of real achievement. It is important for them to learn to focus their energies rather than scatter them; fortunately, after the age of 32, they become more assertive and self-disciplined. As long as they avoid looking in the wrong direction for adventure, remain true to themselves and understand that showing off isn't the most fulfilling or grown-up way to gain supporters, they have the potential to win the admiration and respect of others and, most important of all, a sense of pride in themselves and their achievements. Their destiny is to motivate others with their infectious energy.

Potential: Dynamic, innovative

Dark side: Impatient, restless

Tarot card, lucky numbers, days, colors: The Moon, 2, 9, Saturday, Tuesday, sky blue, red

Born today: Yoko Ono (artist); John Travolta (actor); Toni Morrison (novelist)

PISCES

THE FISHES (FEBRUARY 19–MARCH 20)

❋ **Element:** Water

❋ **Ruling planets:** Jupiter, the philosopher, and
Neptune, the speculator

❋ **Tarot card:** The Moon (intuition)

❋ **Lucky numbers:** 3, 7, 12

❋ **Favorable colors:** Green, blue, aquamarine, indigo

❋ **Driving force:** Compassion

❋ **Personal statement:** I uncover hidden truth

❋ **Chinese astrology counterpart:** The Rabbit

People born under the sun sign Pisces typically have a dreamy nature. Visionaries, with the intuitive perception to see the undercurrents beneath the surface of things, they are often highly sensitive, imaginative, creative or artistic. They easily adapt themselves to different people and situations, and have an uncanny ability to sense and feel what others are thinking and feeling.

Personality potential

Pisceans are the last sign, completing the 12 signs of the zodiac, and have a little of each of the other signs in them. They are the everyman and everywoman of the zodiac. This is why they find it so easy to understand and relate to anyone. It also explains why compassion and empathy for others flows through them and they care so deeply about the wellbeing of others. They often work in hospitals, care homes, day-care centers, counseling services or places where the less fortunate in society can be found.

The compassion and tolerance of Pisceans sets them apart as truly generous and caring individuals. They are perhaps the most caring sign of the zodiac. They rarely miss an opportunity to do something positive for others, both people they care about and people they don't even know. The reason for their generosity is that, just as every fish relies on its community for survival, they believe that helping others strengthens not only the people they help but the entire community they are a part of. Their generous spirit and sincere belief that the whole empowers the individual makes them highly respected and valued members of any group or society. Also, they don't help others with an expectation that they will be helped in return, and, thanks to this humility, they often find themselves unexpectedly benefiting when someone remembers their giving nature and helps them.

Pisceans have a vast imagination and a highly intuitive approach to life that helps them see beyond the details to the bigger picture. Ruled by the mystic planet, Neptune, and the philosophical planet, Jupiter, they often feel the need to escape into flights of intellectual fantasy. Despite their idealism, they are not work-shy and are prepared to roll up their sleeves and put in the energy required to transform their beautiful visions into reality. Their discipline and ability to multitask and effortlessly adapt to different people and situations means that they can succeed in whatever they put their mind to. The main reason for their success, though, is that they know how to trust their gut feelings, and their intuition is often spot on. For Pisceans, *feeling* that something is right is the most important ingredient in their lives. The more they listen to their intuition, the happier and more fulfilled they are likely to be.

> **The compassion and tolerance of Pisceans sets them apart as truly generous and caring individuals.**

Personality pitfalls

Highly sensitive and empathetic, Pisceans can often lose themselves in other people or issues. They don't know where they start and someone else begins, and there can be a tendency to become co-dependent in their relationships. Some Pisceans take the soft option of living through their loved ones, rather than finding out who they are and what they want to do with their life. Fading into the life of another person or finding their identity through a group or career means that they don't fulfill their true potential.

Commitment can also be an issue for Pisceans. Their panoramic ability to see all sides of a situation and awareness of all the different choices out there means that they can constantly sit on the fence, making no decisions and doing nothing at all or, like a slippery fish, making themselves impossible to pin down. They can also come across as indecisive and ineffective, promising much but delivering little. Often lacking firm boundaries and the ability to structure and manage their time effectively, they can quickly earn a reputation for being unreliable. In addition, their high sensitivity means that they can slip into the role of victim, and any kind of criticism or boundary-setting can make them feel incredibly negative and insecure. Their confidence can be easily knocked sideways and, instead of learning how to deal with rejection or criticism in a positive way, they may try to numb their feelings through addictive behavior.

The moods of Pisceans are often changeable and sometimes these shifts can go from one wild extreme to another. Other people can have a hard time trying to understand where they are coming from and may feel that they have to walk on eggshells around them in case they upset them. Also, Pisceans can end up resorting to lying or manipulation to avoid being blamed for anything. As they belong to the most impressionable and gullible sign of the zodiac, they can attract toxic people or energy vampires into their lives who don't have their best interests at heart. They can believe in and trust anyone and anything except themselves, and this lack of self-belief is often their biggest roadblock to achieving success and happiness in life.

Darkest secrets

Pisceans can appear easy-going, gentle and lovely, but underneath the surface they are people of extremes. They can suffer from serious mood swings and can overcompensate for their inconsistencies with a fierce temper. Working for the greater good is essential for them to truly thrive, but they won't flourish unless they deal with their self-esteem issues first. They can lose themselves in endless dreaming and planning, and become people who are all talk and no action. Once they learn to recognize their strengths and underused talents, the key to their success is to stop dreaming and start doing.

Symbol

The Pisces symbol is two fishes swimming away from each other, and it is a perfect illustration of the broad vision but also the constant awareness of choice that defines the Piscean personality. Swim apart or stick together? The Piscean considers all options. Their nature is to be fluid and to empathize with both sides, as well as with what is above and beneath them.

Love

Pisceans take to relationships like a fish to water. Romantic and tender rather than passionate in their love-making, they thrive with partners who are dreamy and deep, like them, but who also offer them stability and calm as a counter-balance to their highs and lows. Sometimes they can be shy and introspective and hard to pin down because they lack self-belief. They need to learn to love themselves first, before they can fall in love with others.

Compassionate and self-sacrificing by nature, they can be deeply hurt when others betray or reject them, but sometimes the deep pain of heartbreak can be the making of them. It teaches them that the only path to healing is to discover within themselves what they hope someone else will bestow on them—in other words, to understand that alone they can be enough.

When they do fall in love with someone, they do so deeply and pour all of themselves—mind, body and soul—into the relationship. This can be both wonderfully magical and romantic, but also overwhelming for their partner. Pisceans tend to put their loved ones on pedestals, but over time they can learn to accept reality and realize that it is impossible for every relationship to be sunshine and roses all the time.

Love matches:

Capricorn, Taurus, Cancer, Scorpio.

The Piscean woman

Caring, sensitive, mysterious and with little or no inclination to dominate in a relationship, the Piscean woman is often surrounded by ardent admirers. Delightfully feminine and charming, with the ability to adapt to any social setting and devoted to the wellbeing of others, she has a touching aura of vulnerability.

Even though she can appear fragile, this does not mean that the Piscean woman is a pushover. Indeed, she is much stronger than she often appears to be and more capable of looking after herself than anyone may give her credit for, including herself. If she is hurt or betrayed, she can lash out fiercely with hurtful anger and sarcasm, though being critical or harsh isn't in her nature. She is a compassionate and tolerant person and her first instinct is to trust and support, to heal and help. She is loyal to a fault, but there is often a frustrating, elusive quality about her and an unwillingness to give direct answers. Trying to figure her out can take a lifetime, but it is well worth the effort.

Despite her ability to merge with and give completely of herself to others, there will always be something mysterious and lonely about this woman, however many loved ones she surrounds herself with. At times, it can feel as if she is in sole possession of a truth that is too deep to express with words. People who want to get close to this compassionate and magical creature need to learn to accept her elusive and constantly shifting quality.

The Piscean man

The Piscean man often appears as the answer to your dreams. He is a romantic dreamer and when he falls in love it is deep—so deep it can feel utterly intoxicating. You are swept off your feet. He merges himself with every aspect of your life. Problems can arise, though, if a partner wants to have some space and freedom in the relationship. The Piscean man may take this as a rejection and find it hard to step back. This isn't necessarily because he is needy or co-dependent, but because he identifies himself so much with another person that creating distance can feel like a rejection and trigger deep insecurities. Once he has merged with another person, he can quite literally feel their pain and sense what they are thinking.

The Piscean man will be their partner's biggest fan, encouraging them to live their dreams. However, it is crucial for the success of the relationship that he does not forget about his own dreams and that he is encouraged to transform those dreams into reality, because, more often than not, his ideas have great potential for success. He does not crave material things or need worldly success to feel fulfilled, but he does need to feel loved and encouraged. His sensitivity and mood swings can be alarming at times. His partner can love and support him during the low times, but the only person who can truly save him and help him rise up and feel whole again is himself.

The Piscean man may be sensitive, but relationships with him can be utterly enchanting. Once he learns to trust his instincts and believe in himself, he has the uncanny ability to plunge into the unknown and surface with hidden treasures, renewed optimism and a vision for a better future.

Family

Piscean children are often described as old souls. They seem wise beyond their years. They have a tendency to exaggerate and embellish the truth to please others and also because their dreams feel so real to them. It is important they learn

from an early age the importance of telling the truth. Often imaginative, they should be encouraged to develop their creativity in every way. They can suffer from shyness or lack of self-confidence and don't thrive in a competitive environment, losing motivation if others do better than them. Their parents or carers need to help them understand that there is no such thing as failure if they can learn from it, and the only person they need to compete against is themselves. Piscean children can suffer from separation anxiety, bullying by others and resulting school phobia, so nurturing their self-esteem from an early age is important.

The Piscean dreamy nature can lead to disorganization and lack of concentration. These children would benefit greatly from time management and also from basic meditation skills to help them find focus. As they are impressionable, it is important to monitor and limit their screen time and the company they keep. They need to discover who they are before others impose their identities on them. Science is a field that may intrigue them from an early age, as well as the world of the arts.

Piscean parents are likely to be loving and to always put their children first. They can, however, become over-involved in their children's lives to the point of smothering them. They can also fail to put firm guidelines and boundaries in place with their children, and need to learn that these are necessary for their children to feel secure.

Career

Pisceans are drawn to careers that give them an opportunity to be creative and artistic in some way. The worlds of music, acting, art, dance, photography, writing, fashion, design and so on appeal, as do scientific or technological careers that allow them to find creative solutions and express their far-sighted vision.

> "Pisceans are drawn to careers that give them an opportunity to be creative and artistic in some way."

Being so aware of the suffering of others, the chances are you will find Pisceans excelling as counselors, therapists, teachers, nurses, doctors, psychiatrists, policeman, social workers and prison officers. Drawn to the mystical side of life, they may also work as a priest or a healer, or in mind, body, spirit-related careers. Their love of the sea may encourage them to consider careers related to ships and fishing. Not known for their practicality and organization, Pisceans can come into their own when their job offers them a set daily routine or structure. They don't tend to thrive in careers that require managerial skills, but they are capable of being good managers if they put their minds and hearts to it. They do prefer to work behind the scenes, but can step out from the background to take charge if they believe the cause is a worthwhile one. There may be several career changes during their professional lives and periods when they are working two jobs at the same time.

Health and wellbeing

While they may be excellent at caring for others, Pisceans are often not so great when it comes to taking care of themselves. Self-care is essential for them, as is paying attention to their diet, health and lifestyle, and to the health of their feet—proper footwear is essential. Sensitive to their environment, they can be easily influenced by anything from loud music to bad weather to distressing stories on their news feed. This sensitivity can affect their emotional and physical health. If they become aware of just how much external influences affect their health, this will help them understand that their mood swings and health problems, such as headaches and stomach upsets, can be linked to their emotions and sensitivity.

Pisceans need to learn to distinguish between real hunger and emotional eating, because they are prone to comfort-eat during times of stress. Keeping a mood and food diary will help them recognize unhealthy eating habits and triggers, so they can then take steps to manage or avoid them. Eating in a calm and peaceful environment and chewing their food slowly will also benefit them.

Very susceptible to the aging impacts of nicotine, Pisceans should avoid smoking and passive smoking. Drugs should also be avoided for obvious reasons. They have a tendency to rely too much on over-the-counter medications for their aches and pains. Unless they are advised to take such remedies by their doctor, they should avoid them and experiment with natural therapies instead.

Pisceans need to live their dreams, whether through books, classes, hobbies or in their imagination. Spending time in nature is highly recommended to boost the wellbeing of this water sign, especially beside lakes, rivers and the ocean. Hobbies that interest them may include dance, writing, painting, poetry, skating and sailing, as well as visits to museums and historical sites. With their tendency to take on the problems of others and to feel tense about the injustices of the world, taking regular time out for relaxation is essential. Meditation, mindfulness and yoga are great stress-busters. Wearing the color **purple** will encourage them to look within

themselves for a sense of purpose, identity and fulfillment, rather than trying to find it outside themselves in others.

Born between February 19 and 29

Pisceans born between these dates are idealistic but also sometimes inconsistent and impractical. Age brings them wisdom and they tend to find fulfillment later in life when opportunities to express their exciting vision are more likely to present themselves.

Born between March 1 and 10

Those born between these dates tend to be artistically inclined and to have great creativity. They should be especially careful to avoid toxic people and co-dependent behavior, and should aim to surround themselves with positive and inspiring people.

Born between March 11 and 20

People born between these dates find fulfillment by serving the world in a positive way. They are highly compassionate souls, capable of bringing great happiness wherever they go, but, to find success, they need to live their lives on their own terms.

Life lessons

The biggest challenge for Pisceans is to be able to empathize with others without taking on their pain. It is vital that they learn to set boundaries. Being such compassionate souls, Pisceans all too often end up giving too much of themselves away. This means people take advantage of them, draining their energy and creativity as they listen to and serve others while neglecting their own needs. Pisceans are also vulnerable to co-dependent behavior, becoming too reliant on others for their self-esteem. They need to learn to believe in their own power and find their own identity.

When the world overwhelms Pisceans, they can turn to escapism and fantasy as a coping mechanism. This is positive

if they channel their sensitivity into creative or artistic pursuits, or things that serve the greater good, but can be disastrous if they turn to drugs or other addictions. Their creativity is their "super power," but unless they find ways to use it responsibly, they can waste their fine creative potential in daydreaming. The daily routine and mundanity of daily life can be deadening for a Piscean. Paying the bills, shopping, keeping the house tidy and holding down an uninspiring job can be soul-destroying for these impractical souls. They love their lives to be spontaneous and need to learn to balance their free-flowing lifestyle with the mundane necessities.

Since they have something of every sign of the zodiac in them, Pisceans can get inspiration for the task of grounding themselves in reality from all the other signs, including their own, as they can learn what works and what does not work for other Pisceans. Virgos can encourage them to be more tidy, efficient and organized. Taureans and Capricorns, especially, can show them the benefits of practicality and common sense. Aquarians can encourage them to speak out and push the boundaries more. Geminis and Librans can help them be more cerebral and less emotional in their approach to life. Cancerians can encourage them to ask for help when they need it; Sagittarians can teach them the importance of focusing their idealism and being less influenced by the opinions of others. Scorpios can help them distinguish between people who genuinely admire them and those who are simply using them, while Arians and Leos can help them include more optimism and adventure in their approach to life.

Chinese astrology counterpart: The Rabbit

Those born in the year of the Rabbit are drawn to everything beautiful and imaginative in much the same way that Pisceans are. They are compassionate dreamers but, like Pisces, can also be extremely gullible. Sociable and caring, they will trust others easily, but their trusting and unquestioning nature can also be their downfall, as others do not always have their best interests at heart.

Rabbits love to belong to a group and are highly respectful of others. But, like their Piscean counterparts, they are also highly sensitive and need plenty of time alone. They love to burrow, and will escape from the responsibilities of their daily lives when things get too noisy or overwhelming. Their dislike of being pinned down can earn them the reputation of being fickle but, in general, Rabbits are thought of as creative, kind and lucky people.

Note: Pisceans have an affinity with Rabbit-sign characteristics, but be sure to check which Chinese sign corresponds to your **year** of birth (see page xxi), and to read about the characteristics associated with it, too.

February 19

The Birthday of Wanderlust

"I make a name for myself wherever I go"

The life lesson:

is to finish what you start.

The way forward: is to understand that ideas are the easy part; having the willpower to see them through is what determines success or not.

Luck maker: Be a role model for others. What do you want your loved ones to learn from you?

Those born on February 19 do things only one way: their way. They prize their independence above all else and don't like to be ordered around. They think their own thoughts and make their own way in life and often have a lust for travel, thriving on new situations and people. With their independent spirit and need to make their mark, they can often be found at the cutting edge of their chosen field. Although they perform best alone, they can also make inspirational leaders or enthusiastic team players. Their appetite for life and new situations is huge, and even when settling down in a career or a relationship, their eye is always on the horizon, wondering what else might be out there for them. The danger with this inquisitive approach to life is that they can appear reckless or selfish at times.

Born explorers, they make outstanding campaigners, performers, artists, actors, musicians, dancers, scientists, explorers, travel guides, influencers and designers, but they may also be drawn to sales, promotion, childcare, education and promoting global causes through science, medicine, social and environmental work and the caring professions. They have a free-spirited approach to their health and resist any attempt to impose diet and exercise routines. Self-care and plenty of rest and relaxation are essential. **For self-care**, if you have trouble sleeping, a warm bath, a good book and a glass of chamomile herbal tea can work wonders.

A mix of vulnerability and excitement, these people often have a hypnotic power over others, but their approach to life can prevent them connecting empathetically. At around the age of 31 their ambition heightens. It is particularly important for them, at this stage in life and beyond, not to scatter their energies selfishly. Their lives will always be full of opportunities because they have a knack of finding them. Along the way they may encounter setbacks, but they never let these disillusion them. In their mind and their life, the only way is *their* way and that way is always up. Their destiny is to test the limits and move themselves and others forward.

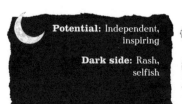

Potential: Independent, inspiring

Dark side: Rash, selfish

Tarot card, lucky numbers, days, colors: The Sun, 1, 2, Saturday, Monday, blue, orange

Born today: Nicolaus Copernicus (astronomer); Millie Bobby Brown (actor); Jeff Daniels (actor)

February 20

The Birthday of the Perceptive Charmer

"I see beauty in everyone and everything"

People born on February 20 tend to be sensitive and able to immediately tune into the energies of those around them, altering their reactions instantly. Highly ambitious with an appealing charm, they are sure to stand out. Sometimes they can appear superficial, but behind their charm there is always great intelligence. They also have great compassion, instinctively dealing with anyone—whatever their background or social status—with great understanding and warmth. They can sometimes be impressionable, unable to separate their own emotions from the emotions of others. There is a danger when they become aware of their ability to instinctively relate to others that they can misuse it. It is important, therefore, for them to learn not to compromise themselves or take advantage of others in the single-minded pursuit of their goals.

Born healers and givers, these people may be drawn to medicine, education, the caring professions or social media or the performing arts, where they give of themselves to an audience. All kinds of public relations also appeal, as does counseling, advising, science and the worlds of beauty and personal development. They have such a giving nature that learning to say no and setting boundaries are crucial for their health and wellbeing. **For self-care**, treat yourself. At least once a week gift yourself something you want: a book, a film or a beauty treatment.

In their relationships, it is vitally important they learn to protect themselves from over-identification with others. Before the age of 30 they can have a self-destructive tendency to merge completely with other people, but after their thirtieth birthday they become more assertive, confident and self-protective. If they can learn to make their receptivity and powerful perception work for and not against them, they have remarkable potential to make a difference and to be highly valued by others. They need to understand that even though they have the drive, intelligence and charisma they need to climb right to the top, simply being true to themselves, their values and their giving nature is their greatest power, because when they are around, people just feel better about themselves.

Potential: Intuitive, appealing

Dark side: Self-sacrificing, oversensitive

Tarot card, lucky numbers, days, colors: Judgment, 2, 4, Thursday, Monday, green, silver

Born today: Rihanna (singer); Ludwig Boltzmann (physicist); Cindy Crawford (model)

February 21

The Birthday of the Dominating Presence

"I prepare the way for others to follow"

February 21-born feel most comfortable when going their own way and least comfortable when required to follow. Their independence may be a result of a tough childhood where expectations often took precedence over emotional connection. They may spend many years trying out various occupations or roles, often feeling that they don't quite fit in and occasionally reacting childishly as a form of rebellion. It is only when they understand that the key to their success is to be themselves that they truly come into their own. Although they may have developed a tough outer shell, they can also be extremely sensitive, even shy. It is important that they do not become too aggressive or cynical if others hurt or take advantage of them, for it is their sensitivity that can give them sudden flashes of inspiration.

Born conductors and composers, any career that allows them to direct, motivate, guide, inspire or lead others appeals—for example, management, science, business, education, research, music, the arts, aviation, entertainment or politics. They may also want to work with their hands in design, architecture, craftsmanship, construction or building. Prone to mood swings, they need to eat a healthy, balanced diet packed with mood-boosting nutrients, such as oily fish, nuts, seeds and green vegetables. **For self-care**, make sure you spend at least 20 minutes out in the fresh air and daylight every day to boost your mood and increase the likelihood of a good night's sleep.

In relationships these people love the thrill of the chase, but a part of them longs for stability and that special someone. Around the age of 29 they tend to become more assertive and self-aware—while this is positive, it is important this doesn't tip into self-absorption. They have big dreams and, once they learn to listen to their hearts as well as their heads, there is little that can prevent them getting exactly what they want out of life. Wherever they go, others look to them for motivation and inspiration. Their destiny is to inspire others to reach their full potential, by their own example.

Potential: Influential, creative

Dark side: Self-absorbed, cynical

Tarot card, lucky numbers, day, colors: The World, 3, 5, Thursday, green, purple

Born today: Scott Kelly (astronaut); Alan Rickman (actor); Nina Simone (singer)

February 22

The Birthday of the Investigator

The life lesson:

is to be less self-critical.

The way forward: is to understand that failure is an essential stepping stone to success, and vulnerabilities bring others closer.

Luck maker: Recognize your own value and others will recognize it too.

"I solve problems"

People born on February 22 love a good mystery. Inspired problem-solvers with inquisitive minds, they have a real talent for unearthing the truth. They often try to do opposing things or express different viewpoints all at once; this can confuse but also fascinate others. They believe it's not what you do but how you do something that matters. Their passion is investigation and the process of problem-solving. Because they tend to be self-reliant individuals, they often expect others to be the same and they can have perfectionist tendencies that make them highly self-critical and pessimistic when others disappoint them.

Born investigators, the chances are they won't have a conventional career or, if they do, their interests reflect their eclectic tastes. They thrive in careers that require strong and steady leadership and problem-solving, making great detectives, scientists, medics, secret agents, consultants, researchers, recruiters, human resources managers, politicians and troubleshooters. Music, art, writing and journalism can also appeal, as can the caring professions, charity work, social reform, the military, health and fitness and alternative healing. Prone to erratic eating habits when passionately engaged in an investigation or case to solve, they need to ensure their diet doesn't lack essential nutrients. **For self-care**, wearing, meditating on or surrounding themselves with the colors pink, orange and green encourages them to be more nurturing and less detached.

In their relationships these people can blow hot and cold and need to place a higher value on commitment and emotional honesty. They may be great at solving problems, but often neglect their own inner life. They benefit from opening up to others and being more understanding of mistakes—both their own and others'. Their tendency to experiment with differing goals, sometimes at the same time, is strong throughout much of their adult life. After the age of 57 they may focus their energies more. But whatever age they are and whatever path they choose, it will be a fascinating one that brings them closer to their ultimate goal of making their own life—and the lives of others—a little simpler. Their destiny is to show the world that diversity is a strength that can help and heal others.

Potential: Dynamic, inquisitive

Dark side: Detached, critical

Tarot card, lucky numbers, days, colors: The Fool, 4, 6, Thursday, Sunday, green, purple

Born today: George Washington (US president); Drew Barrymore (actor); Rajon Rondo (basketball player)

February 23

The Birthday of the Capable Front-runner

"I can show you the way"

Those born on February 23 have an optimistic, methodical approach to life. They are quietly rather than openly confident, believing that their accomplishments speak for themselves. Because they aren't pretentious, other people tend to be drawn to them. They can be incredibly efficient, capable of delivering quality results for any task that they undertake. Indeed, they find great joy in the work itself rather than the reward, often believing, having weighed up the alternatives, that they are the best person to get things done. Their confident certainty can appear uncompromising, but it is also infectious, with others frequently placing great trust in them. They are extremely articulate, yet also excellent listeners, an unusual combination that distinguishes them from other great speakers.

Born analysts, these people make great advisors, counselors, negotiators, planners and consultants in any field. Their communication skills may draw them to success in business, the arts and entertainment, but whatever career they choose, their determination ensures their success. They have a tendency to push themselves far too hard, so regular relaxation, laughter and time out is essential for their well-being. **For self-care**, spend time doing things that you love to do rather than feel you ought to do, even if you think those things don't serve any purpose. Success without happiness is empty and meaningless.

These people tend to be dazzled by looks first, and head and heart second, and need to apply the same analytical approach to their personal life as they do to their professional one. They should use their verbal skills and their empathy for others positively rather than in a manipulative way, especially between the ages of 27 and 56, when they become more confident and ambitious, and are likely to start many new ventures. Much of their life will be spent making everything in their lives, including themselves, the very best that it can be, and, as a result, it often is. As long as they accept that life isn't—and wasn't meant to be—perfect, the destiny of these capable front-runners is to encourage others to do things the right way.

Potential: Capable, confident

Dark side: Manipulative, uncompromising

Tarot card, lucky numbers, days, colors: The Hierophant, 5, 7, Thursday, Wednesday, all shades of green

Born today: Samuel Pepys (diarist); George Frideric Handel (composer); Dakota Fanning (actor)

February 24

The Birthday of the Romantic Bard

"I bring healing, beauty and connection"

February 24-born are creative, intuitive and generous spirits with a genuine desire to help others selflessly. Romantic, they see the world through the eyes of a love-struck poet. Intimacy is important to them—without it they can pine away. Highly sensitive, they are constantly tuning into the moods of others and the situation going on around them. This makes them good peacemakers and valuable members of a team, as they can often spot potential problems and avert them before they happen. They are equally adept at seeing potential opportunities. The danger lies when they concentrate on the emotional needs of others rather than on their own.

Born poets, these people are often drawn to the arts and the entertainment world in general. Sensitive to color and patterns, they may also express themselves through design or technological innovations. Any job that places them in the role of mediator, facilitator, advisor, agent, manager or negotiator suits them, as does humanitarian work, the police, the military, teaching and the caring and health professions. Prone to a sedentary lifestyle, they must ensure they get plenty of regular exercise, preferably in the fresh air. **For self-care**, learn to say no more. Don't let others walk all over you; set boundaries.

The longing for intimacy or emotional connection always rules the professional and personal life in some way of those born on this day. Emotional traumas from their past may be suppressed, but will often manifest themselves in a quest for the perfect partner or in a passionate devotion to a cause. They give too much of themselves in relationships and it is vital for them to set healthy boundaries. Fortunately, between the ages of 26 and 56, they have opportunities to develop their assertiveness and, the older they get, the steadier they become. Once they have learned that love isn't just about easing pain but also about creating joy, and that intimacy is not just about sacrificing but also about receiving, they discover within themselves the tenacity and vision to achieve just about anything. Their destiny is to help, heal and connect others and, by so doing, make the world a more loving and giving place.

Potential: Generous, creative

Dark side: Needy, passive

Tarot card, lucky numbers, days, colors: The Lovers, 6, 8, Thursday, Friday, turquoise, pink

Born today: Steve Jobs (entrepreneur); Floyd Mayweather (boxer); Edward James Olmos (actor)

February 25

The Birthday of the Guru

"I guide and inspire myself and others"

Those born on February 25 have a confident belief that the good of the collective is more important than the personal. They can be radical in their desire to right social wrongs, and selfless in the pursuit of their goals. There is a touch of the inspirational guru about them. Blessed with a simple, unaffected style that can help them relate to people from all walks of life, they impress everyone with their honesty, optimism and genuine desire to make a positive difference. These people are often found working their magic on the sidelines; nothing gives them more satisfaction than engineering success for others.

Born lecturers, gurus, guides, teachers, coaches, advisors, mentors, interviewers and journalists, they excel in any career that involves revealing, inspiring and guiding others. They are the consultants with the winning formula, the brilliant teachers empowering the next generation, the dedicated coaches, the directors with vision. They may be drawn to explore their creative and empathetic potential in the arts or through the worlds of personal growth, healthcare and social reform. With so much focus on the mental aspect of success, it is important that they don't neglect their bodily health. **For self-care,** wearing, meditating on or surrounding yourself with the color red will encourage you to become a person of action and passion.

As far as love is concerned these people often play it too safe, so if opportunities for intimacy arise they should take them. They can come across as detached, but to those who know them well they are capable of making the most helpful observations. They should beware of becoming so lost in the world of thought that they present as negative and unrealistic. Fortunately, between the ages of 25 and 54, they become more assertive and, with age, more content. Above all, they have a team-player mentality, a profound sense of justice and a desire to help the worthy win. This is a potent mix and, once they feel comfortable leaving the sidelines, their destiny is to teach, inspire and guide others to a far better place.

Potential: Inspirational, honest

Dark side: Detached, unrealistic

Tarot card, lucky numbers, days, colors: The Chariot, 7, 9, Thursday, Monday, turquoise, indigo

Born today: Jameela Jamil (presenter); George Harrison (musician); Pierre-Auguste Renoir (painter)

February 26

The Birthday of the Wise Soul

"I bring justice and hope"

People born on February 26 are often described as wise old souls. They have tremendous insight into how things work and the motivations of others, and when this insight is combined with their hypnotic persona, others tend to do what they say or follow their example. It is important for them that they don't abuse this power—fortunately they rarely do as they also have a powerful sense of integrity and social justice, and a desire to improve the world. They like to find something to like in everybody and in every situation, and their unfailing optimism is truly enlightening. Blessed with great wisdom, their ability to inspire others helps them achieve success, but a part of them feels more comfortable as an outsider looking in. They sometimes feel an urge to be alone with their thoughts or to sacrifice themselves to a higher cause.

Born judges, these people make great lawyers but may also be drawn to teaching, counseling, consultancy, social reform or any career where they can advocate for others. They also have an artistic side, which may express itself in design, music, writing or drama. If their need for love is denied, they should make sure they don't seek comfort in food or unhealthy addictions. **For self-care**, wearing, meditating on or surrounding yourself with the color orange can lift your spirits and make you feel warmer and more secure.

Those born on this day struggle to let others get close to them, and to both receive and give love, but when they find someone to open up to emotionally, they make loyal, loving companions. They have a tendency to preach or to be rigid in their opinions, which is emphasized between the ages of 24 and 54, when they should surround themselves with close friends or loved ones who can warn them when they are heading off-track. Fortunately, they respond extremely well to constructive criticism and can change their ways. Once they learn the vital importance of real emotional connections with others, and that needing to be loved is not a weakness but a strength, their destiny is to follow their inner wisdom and right social wrongs.

Potential: Wise, hypnotic

Dark side: Detached, harsh

Tarot card, lucky numbers, days, colors: Strength, 1, 8, Thursday, Saturday, turquoise, violet

Born today: Li Na (tennis player); Johnny Cash (singer); Helen Clark (New Zealand prime minister)

February 27

The Birthday of
Hypnotic Allure

"I am born to shine"

February 27-born have the ability to turn heads and win hearts. They have a magnetic and striking intensity that can hold others spellbound. They like the limelight and seem destined for it. Others admire their easy confidence and sense of purpose. They are both open-minded and analytical. They like to understand exactly how things work and their accumulated knowledge base takes them to the very top. There is one area of their lives, however, that is their Achilles' heel: their emotional life. Despite their charismatic image, they are impulsive and passionate and often have a chaotic personal life, with broken relationships and friendships littered around them.

Born actors, these people seem destined to shine on screen or video and they make great performers. Any career where people can watch or learn from them is ideal. They make amazing teachers and creative writers. In business, they are drawn to sales, publicity, marketing and advertising, but they can also excel in entrepreneurship or setting up their own businesses. High-energy individuals, they need a regular exercise program to keep them toned, but also to ensure they work off their excess energy in a healthy way. **For self-care**, breathing exercises, yoga and meditation can encourage them to manage their emotions and find inner calm.

These people need to apply discipline to their personal relationships and to stop making inconsistent, unreasonable demands on others, especially between the ages of 23 and 52 when they become even more adventurous. If self-love and setting boundaries isn't learned during this period, the result could be personal chaos. At their worst, people born on this day can be social-climbing attention seekers. At their best, they are lovable and spontaneous creatures, who can both intoxicate and inspire. They may be described as a little crazy, but once they invest their energy into a worthwhile cause they can achieve truly great things. Their destiny is to enchant others and enjoy the limelight they seem destined for with their unique brand of magic.

February 28

The Birthday of the Original Charmer

The life lesson:

is to rein in your impulses.

The way forward: is discovering willpower, and understanding that nothing makes you think, say, feel or do anything. You are in charge.

Luck maker: Practice an attitude of gratitude. Appreciate what you have and how far you have come.

"My life is an exciting ride"

Those born on February 28 can light up the world with their energy and originality. Natural performers, they are never short of admirers and are blessed with the ability to charm just about anyone. Articulate and entertaining, they go out of their way to get a laugh or reaction from others, even if this involves exaggerating the truth. They thrive on being noticed, but attention-seeking isn't what drives them. Their motivation is a thirst for adventure. Underlying their restlessness, however, is a deep-seated fear of standing still, and this fear drives them toward sensation-seeking and self-destructive behavior. Underneath their bravado they secretly long to find a real purpose. This won't be possible until they discover that self-esteem is not created by thrill-seeking but by being content with who they are.

Born travelers, these adventurous people thrive in careers that offer them variety and an opportunity to indulge their curiosity, such as gaming, travel, tourism, science, research, modeling, vlogging, sports and teaching, and they can also thrive in management or business. Later in life they may be drawn to the caring or helping professions as well as to the arts, writing and the entertainment industry. They live in the fast lane and setting aside regular time for rest and relaxation helps them avoid burnout. **For self-care**, wearing, meditating on or surrounding yourself with the color purple will encourage you to look within for inspiration, rather than without.

These people need to learn to be more comfortable with being rather than doing, because, until they find inner calm, their life may hurtle chaotically from one situation and one person to another. They should learn to cultivate this inner calm before their early fifties, when there is an emphasis in their life on new directions. They experience life more intensely than others, but it is vital they rein in their compulsion to indulge every whim. They should never suppress their optimism and curiosity, but if they can just look before they leap, they can become far more than original charmers; their destiny is to become life's pioneers, boldly going where none have gone before.

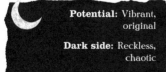

Potential: Vibrant, original

Dark side: Reckless, chaotic

Tarot card, lucky numbers, days, colors: The Sun, 1, 3, Thursday, Sunday, turquoise, orange

Born today: Paul Krugman (economist); Karolina Kurková (model); Linus Pauling (chemist)

February 29

The Birthday of Wistful Vivacity

The life lesson:

is to believe in yourself.

The way forward: is to stop comparing yourself to others and only compare yourself with the person you were yesterday.

Luck maker: People react to a person's self-image. Notice what you are thinking and feeling about yourself and replace negativity with positivity.

"I innovate and improve"

February 29-born sense there is something different about themselves from early in their lives, since they only celebrate a real birthday every four years and have to swiftly learn the art of compromise by celebrating their birthday on other days. They are likable, vivacious, sometimes eccentric characters with an eternally young, wistful quality that can make them appear less resilient and driven than they really are. Although they have remarkable insight into what makes people tick, others are unlikely to understand what motivates them although their motivation is simple: to feel needed and—above all—to feel they have an important part to play in improving the world. They like to inspire or help others, but, being sensitive, they can withdraw into immature behavior if they don't get the response or gratitude they expect.

Born competitors, these people thrive in careers where they can constantly improve and prove themselves. Sport, business, science, banking, the stock market, social media and life-coaching may all appeal, as might writing, art, design and music. Their empathy and ability to compromise may draw them toward the law, humanitarian work, the caring professions or the world of personal growth and transformation. They can be self-indulgent, so they need to stay disciplined as far as their diet and health are concerned. **For self-care**, write the words, 'I am enough' in lipstick or pen on your bathroom mirror so that it is what you read when you see yourself in the morning.

In relationships those born on this day need to ensure they don't become overly dependent on others for validation, and to cultivate their own sense of self-worth. They may feel driven to aggressively validate their differences by working ever harder to achieve their goals—a strategy they may take to self-destructive extremes, especially before the age of 51, when there is an emphasis on being assertive and ambitious. Once they realize their powerful intuition and youthful zest for life are strengths not weaknesses, these special individuals find that others not only accept but highly value their unique contribution. Their destiny is to find outlets for their huge creativity and innovation, and, by so doing, talk directly not just to the minds and hearts of others, but also to their souls.

Potential: Inspirational, original

Dark side: Immature, self-indulgent

Tarot card, lucky numbers, days, colors: The High Priestess, 2, 4, Thursday, Monday, turquoise, silver

Born today: Tony Robbins (life coach); Martin Suter (author); Dean Radin (scientist)

March 1

The Birthday of the Practical Visionary

The life lesson:

is dealing with self-doubt.

The way forward: is to talk to yourself in a reassuring way, as a loving and supportive parent would to a child.

Luck maker: Stop thinking "what if?" Worry achieves absolutely nothing, so use that energy proactively to take small steps toward achieving your goals.

"I believe in miracles"

March 1-born have great originality and intelligence, a talent for inspiring others and for transforming ideas into reality. Sensitive and charming, they have an eye for beauty, seeing the world with the vision of an artist. They can also be extremely practical—anyone who dismisses them as dreamers is making a big mistake. They often feel a deep concern for the wellbeing of others, although it may not be until later in life that they inject practicality into those concerns. When focused they can accomplish miracles through their determination and conviction, but they are also prone to lack of self-confidence, can be easy influenced, and their ideas and talents taken advantage of.

Born creative directors, these people have the skills to succeed in business, but they need careers that enable them to channel their imagination and originality into constructive projects. They are drawn to writing, drama, music, art, design, architecture, social-media content, app creation, programming, gaming or freelance work. Later in life they are attracted to social reform and charity work. They tend to be dreamy and to neglect the importance of exercise, so a regular workout schedule is advised. **For self-care**, walk or jog, preferably in the park or countryside, as you can get fit and daydream at the same time.

Drawn to controlling types and conflict averse, they need to set clear boundaries in their relationships and find people who offer them support but also freedom to express their visionary ideas. They are at their most vulnerable to negative influences or causes that aren't worthy of them before the age of 20. Fortunately, they become more assertive and self-assured as they age, but they should watch that they don't become selfish in the process. After the age of 50 they feel a need to devote themselves fully to family or to a variety of humanitarian or environmental causes. Once they manage self-doubt, they often find themselves in the position of a leader and their destiny is to make a difference by transforming their own original ideas, and the ideas of others, into solid achievements.

Potential: Artistic, ambitious

Dark side: Self-doubting, selfish

Tarot card, lucky numbers, days, colors: The Magician, 1, 4, Thursday, Sunday, turquoise, orange

Born today: Frédéric Chopin (composer); Justin Bieber (singer); Denis Mukwege (doctor)

March 2

The Birthday of Personal Vision

is dealing with conflict.

The way forward: is not to run away but to see it as an opportunity to learn and a catalyst for greater creativity.

Luck maker: Network— having positive professional and personal connections improves your chances of success.

"I am a hundred percent dedicated"

People born on March 2 have strong personal beliefs, which they cling to regardless of the opinions of others or the changing climate around them. They are truly intuitive and independent thinkers with the ability to inspire and occasionally alarm others with their intensity. Once committed to an ideal or decided on a course of action, they hold fast to it come what may. Although others have much to learn from their dedication, their one-track approach can block other opportunities for enriching their lives. Fortunately, the personal vision they dedicate themselves to so passionately is often one that inspires them to make positive changes to their world. They need to ensure their convictions neither exclude the possibility of change nor alienate them from the closeness and security of personal relationships.

Born charity workers, these people need careers they can devote themselves to, mind, body and spirit. The healing, medical, caring and charity professions appeal, as might teaching, writing, politics and social reform. They may also dedicate their intuitive creativity to the world of content creation, the media, promotion, the arts, music, writing and entertainment. There is a tendency to isolate themselves or bury themselves in work, so they need to make sure they get out into the world, absorbing lots of fresh air and engaging with people. **For self-care**, meditating on, wearing and surrounding yourself with the color orange will encourage you to project and seek out warmth and connection with others.

Prone to putting their loved ones on pedestals, March 2-born need to love them for who they really are, not for who they want them to be. The tendency to neglect loved ones in favor of personal convictions, or to become emotionally dependent on those close to them, is strongest before the age of 48, but after that they become more emotionally confident. If these people can identify more with themselves and less with work, and give to others without losing themselves in the process, their destiny is to translate their unwavering dedication to their personal vision into a reality and, by so doing, make the world a more enlightened place.

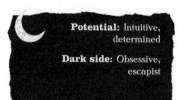

Potential: Intuitive, determined

Dark side: Obsessive, escapist

Tarot card, lucky numbers, days, colors: The High Priestess, 2, 5, Thursday, Monday, turquoise, silver

Born today: Mikhail Gorbachev (Russian president); Karen Carpenter and Jon Bon Jovi (singers); Theodore Geisel (Dr. Seuss)

March 3

The Birthday of Proposals

"I say and I do"

Those born on March 3 may feel from an early age that they were destined for something great. Intelligent, determined and versatile, they unquestionably have great potential. The issue is more about where to begin; they may find themselves taken up with plans and proposals for the best step forward. Pragmatic, these people are quick to recognize any potential problems in their preparation and, although they are aware of the end goal, nothing escapes their attention. In fact, they love the preparation stage, often enjoying it more than the execution of a project. The upside is that they are fully focused on the present. The downside is that they get so absorbed in planning, considering and proposing that things never move forward.

Born script writers, these people have the observational skills and inventive creativity to make great writers, journalists, gamers, content creators and bloggers. They like to engage in work that has a meaningful message and can improve lives, so they may be drawn to teaching, lobbying, social work, politics, humanitarian causes as well as counseling and the arts. They spend a lot of time planning their diet and self-care plan, but need to ensure this doesn't take the joy and spontaneity out of their lives. **For self-care**, like yourself more. Write a list that includes everything that you are proud of about yourself, and keep adding to it every day.

Lack of self-belief can be an issue for these people and they won't have satisfying relationships until they learn to love themselves first. They need to work on their decision-making skills and to stop holding themselves back with an endless succession of "what ifs?" Fortunately, between the ages 18 and 47 there is an emphasis on increasing their assertiveness, and from their fifties onward on calm and stability. Once they do settle on a course, they need to make sure they don't get so lost in it that they lose touch with who they are, because they are remarkable people with the ability to achieve great things. Their destiny is to express their original ideas and talents, uplifting others in the process.

Potential: Determined, visionary

Dark side: Compulsive, insecure

Tarot card, lucky numbers, day, colors: The Empress, 3, 6, Thursday, turquoise, purple

Born today: Alexander Graham Bell (inventor); Perry Ellis (fashion designer); Jessica Biel (actor)

March 4

The Birthday of
Inspired Aloneness

"Self-knowledge is the beginning of my wisdom"

March 4-born tend to be independent, ingenious and highly creative individuals. They are able to work and, if need be, live alone. It's not that they are antisocial or seek to cut themselves off from the outside world; it's just that striking out alone is a trend for them that often leads to their success. For them, solitude is liberating and an opportunity to concentrate and be productive. Comfortable with themselves, they rarely succumb to peer pressure and conformity. This can come across as shyness but misses the point about these gentle people. Although they hate confrontation, they aren't shy but simply at their most productive when doing things alone. The danger is becoming so self-involved that they cut themselves off from reality, and from the joys of close personal relationships.

Born magicians, these intriguing people are often drawn to magic, mind-control techniques, music and art. They can make amazing illusionists, conductors and DJs. They are ideally suited to self-employment and entrepreneurship or setting up their own business. They may also excel in the worlds of education, psychology, academia, security, gaming and computer programming. Although they need personal space as much as they need oxygen, they must ensure that they don't cut themselves off from socializing completely for their emotional wellbeing. **For self-care, see red.** Wearing, meditation on and surrounding yourself with shades of red will encourage you to come out of your shell more.

These people are extremely empathetic in intimate relationships. It truly is better for them to live alone than to be with someone who tries to control them. Before the age of 46 they tend to prioritize new projects, but they need to ensure that others don't take all the credit for their hard work. After the age of 47 they become more self-assured. Once they believe that they have the right to be heard, their destiny is to educate, motivate, entertain and inspire others with their magical ingenuity.

Potential: Independent, ingenious

Dark side: Self-absorbed, aloof

Tarot card, lucky numbers, days, colors: The Emperor, 4, 7, Thursday, Sunday, turquoise, gray

Born today: Antonio Vivaldi (composer); Richard DeVos (businessman); Dav Pilkey (author)

March 5

The Birthday of Agony and Ecstasy

"I feel every thrilling moment of my life"

People born on March 5 come across as charming individuals, but troubled waters lie below. Their smoothness conceals a complex emotional personality that is as fascinating as it is frustrating. One moment they're being witty; the next moment they can dissolve into insecurity. Underneath their confident façade is a highly sensitive soul who desperately needs regular time out in solitary reflection. Inside, they have hidden insecurities and if they don't deal with them, they are at the mercy of their impulses. They can worry that becoming more emotionally stable will result in a loss of intensity, but they need to understand that self-control will only strengthen their creativity.

Born directors, these people are always drawn to the world of movies, where they make great directors, actors, camera people, designers, costume and production staff as well as the world of music, the media and entertainment. Their love of adventure makes careers that involve travel, advertising and marketing appeal. Politics, social reform, charity work, health and healing jobs are also a good fit, but their communication skills serve them well in any career. Prone to mood swings, they need to learn to connect to their inner calm, perhaps by meditation, being in nature or listening to beautiful music. **For self-care**, avoid using screens in the hour before you go to bed. Read a real book before you go to bed to induce feelings of calm and reflection.

Given to emotional extremes, these people often fall deeply in and out of love. They need a partner who offers them both unconditional love and firmness. Given the instability of their emotional life, it is very important for them to learn to balance their emotions, especially before their mid-forties, when they are determined to make their mark. After the age of 47 there is an emphasis on greater stability. Once they learn to work with both their head and their heart and manage their intense emotions, the world will always be a brighter place with these impulsive individuals around. Their destiny is to make their lofty visions for the future a reality.

Potential: Entertaining, insightful

Dark side: Unreliable, insecure

Tarot card, lucky numbers, days, colors: The Hierophant, 5, 8, Thursday, Wednesday, turquoise, green

Born today: Momofuku Ando (inventor); Andy Gibb (singer); Eva Mendes (actor)

March 6

The Birthday of Refinement

"I see the world with angel eyes"

March 6-born are often pulled toward ideals of sensual beauty and refinement and, although they are unlikely to notice it, they also have a strange beauty of their own. Their gift is their ability to open the eyes of others to the beauty of the world and to appreciate every nuance of nature. Above all, these people are motivated by a desire to experience and be uplifted by the ideal of true beauty. Much of their lives will be devoted to a never-ending quest to translate this perfect ideal into reality. They see the world with heavenly eyes and this is one their most endearing qualities. There is a danger, however, that in their idealization of everything and everyone around them, they can lose touch with what or who is actually there. Others may feel that these individuals are more in love with the fantasy than with the reality. When reality does finally bite and their initial intensity fades, disillusionment may be the cruel result.

Born sculptors, they are naturally drawn toward beauty, fashion, art, health, nursing, art, poetry, music, design or sculpture. Politics, social reform, life-coaching and personal transformation also appeal, but, whatever career they choose, they invest their talents to achieve high standards. Health-wise they need to be careful that their love of sensual pleasures does not lead to over-indulgence. **For self-care,** barefoot walking, or "earthing" can help ground you, as can spending more time in nature and surrounding yourself with shades of balancing green or earthy brown.

It is important for people born on this day to learn to be more objective and less demanding of both people and situations, especially before their mid-forties when they are most likely to be very easily disillusioned. Fortunately, after the age of 45 they become more practical. Others may see them as unrealistic or superficial, but there is real depth and originality under their often charming and sensuous exterior. They do need to learn to develop a more realistic approach, accepting that their lofty standards may not always be attained, but in their constant search for beauty and refinement their destiny is to be an inspiration for all those who cross their path.

Potential: Refined, sensual

Dark side: Naïve, disillusioned

Tarot card, lucky numbers, days, colors: The Lovers, 6, 9, Thursday, Friday, pink, lavender

Born today: Michelangelo Buonarroti (artist); Rob Reiner (filmmaker); Elizabeth Barrett Browning (poet)

March 7

The Birthday of Exceptional Vision

"I dream a dream"

Those born on March 7 often have an otherworldly quality about them. This is because they have a tendency to live in an imaginary world. They are blessed with exceptional vision, but they can also be analytical and practical, and can strike an easy rapport with just about anyone. They never forget a name or a personal detail and like to ensure everybody gets a chance to be heard. Although they have many admirers, they can be lonely. They detest conflict and distance themselves whenever things get heated or they are criticized. The more they run away, the more insecure they become about themselves, as well as secretive and suspicious of others.

Born designers, they have a strong need to express their vision and may be drawn to careers in art, film, music, dance, poetry, sculpture, web design, photography, social media, teaching, social and charity work and the healing professions. Whatever career they choose—whether it be business, technology, law, politics or sport, or any other—their determination ensures success. Prone to insecurity, wearing, meditating on or surrounding themselves with the color red will encourage them to assert themselves more. **For self-care**, write in a journal every day. The more comfortable you are with expressing yourself honestly, the more likely you will do the same in your relationships.

People born on this day should find ways to express how they feel other than retreating into their shell, and be more honest in all their relationships. Up until their early forties, they work at becoming more assertive, which is a positive sign. After the age of 44 they are keener to gain greater emotional and financial stability. Because they are so open-minded, these people may take a while to settle on their chosen goal, but once they are able to focus their vision and energy in a worthwhile direction, their intelligent and sensitive approach assures success. A part of them will always remain untouchable, but this doesn't make them appear or feel lonely—it just adds to their magic. Their destiny is to realize their visionary goals.

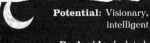

Potential: Visionary, intelligent

Dark side: Isolated, secretive

Tarot card, lucky numbers, days, colors: The Chariot, 1, 7, Thursday, Monday, all shades of blue

Born today: Ivan Lendl (tennis player); Rachel Weisz (actor); Rob Roy (Scottish folk hero)

March 8

The Birthday of the Uncompromising Rebel

"I have the courage of my convictions"

People born on March 8 are fiercely uncompromising. They may sometimes hide their nonconformity behind an agreeable exterior, but anyone who knows them well understands that deep down they are independent thinkers. They distrust authority, believing that everybody deserves the right to think for themselves. Their subversive approach can exhaust others, but their rebellion is not for the sake of it. It is prompted by an ability to easily spot the weaknesses in a situation and to identify a better approach. In fact, these people are outstanding problem-solvers and this marks them out as potentially great reformers in whatever field they choose. They have a vivacious approach to life and a need for constant challenge and change. Although they can sometimes alienate others with their forceful opinions, they are blessed with considerable charm and need to use their hypnotic power over others wisely.

Born reformers, they can excel in business, and scientific or artistic endeavors, and they make excellent academics, researchers, chemists, musicians, painters, writers, designers, programmers, consultants and finance experts. Politics and social reform may also appeal as well as public relations and life-coaching. They tend to be accident prone, so should take special care when exercising or traveling. **For self-care,** let go of resentment. If someone has upset you, write a letter expressing your frustration but don't send it to them. Tear it up and release any feelings of draining resentment you have, reminding yourself that you have forgiven but not forgotten.

These people crave intimacy but also fear it, and they need to be more spontaneous and to open themselves up to others more. They are capable of commitment, but sooner or later the uncompromising aspect of their personality demands progress. These restless tendencies tend to be emphasized before the age of 42, but after that there is a turning point, suggesting a need for more stability. Once they have learned to temper their uncompromising tendencies and they can get people fully on their side, their destiny is to lead others toward new ways of thinking and doing things.

Potential: Independent, magnetic

Dark side: Irresponsible, manipulative

Tarot card, lucky numbers, days, colors: Strength, 2, 8, Thursday, Saturday, electric blue, red

Born today: Anne Bonny (pirate); Anselm Kiefer (painter); James Van Der Beek (actor)

March 9

The Birthday of the Bold Explorer

"I boldly seek out new horizons"

March 9-born are innovative explorers willing to venture boldly into the unknown or to experiment with new ideas. Their courageous, curious nature is admired by others. and because they are so independent, their lives are often packed with excitement. They have a zest for life and often move so fast it can wear themselves and others out. They can flit from one job or relationship to another, as they love variety and challenge. Although others may find them reckless, they are far less impulsive than they appear. From an early age they have learned to trust their intuition because it frequently leads them in the right direction. Despite their independence, they can be oversensitive to others' opinions, easily getting hurt when criticized.

Born campaigners with a sense of justice and empathy for the underdog, they can often be found pushing for social reform. Indeed, whatever career they choose—be it sport, art or charity work—they fight for social and humanitarian concerns. Their ability to solve problems and advise may draw them to teaching, counseling, psychology, writing and management, while their intuitive ability may draw them to healing or the New Age or psychic worlds. Learning to recognize physical signs of stress, such as an upset stomach and insomnia, can help them avoid burnout. **For self-care**, treat yourself to a relaxing warm bath with your favorite essential oil, such as clary sage and juniper, whenever you feel run down.

These people are highly intuitive and for this reason others often seek their advice, becoming dependent on them in the process. Such emotional dependency, however, can cause feelings of frustration. With a tendency to take things too personally, it is important for those born on this day to learn to calm down, especially before the age of 40, when their lives are full of new ventures. After the age of 42 there is greater emotional steadiness. A part of them always longs to escape, but, once they have found a way to be more responsible and committed without losing their sense of adventure, their destiny is to push forward social reforms and make the world a better and fairer place.

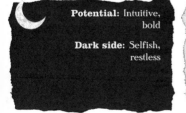

Potential: Intuitive, bold

Dark side: Selfish, restless

Tarot card, lucky numbers, days, colors: The Hermit, 3, 9, Thursday, Tuesday, turquoise, red

Born today: Yuri Gagarin (astronaut); Bobby Fischer (chess player); Brittany Snow (actor)

March 10

The Birthday of Sensitivity

The life lesson:

is building and protecting your self-esteem.

The way forward: is to challenge every self-critical thought you may have.

Luck maker: Enjoy yourself more. The more relaxed and happy you feel, the more likely you are to attract good fortune.

"I see the world from the inside out"

Those born on March 10 have a vulnerable quality about them, however successful they appear. A part of them is always searching for greater self-understanding. They are extremely empathetic toward others, particularly the less fortunate, and because they are so tuned into their feelings, they tend to experience life intensely. They can get deeply hurt by the words or actions of others, but instead of expressing their pain, they withdraw instead. Preoccupied with inner conflicts, there is a danger of becoming self-involved, but if they can learn not to use their sensitivity as a way of escaping confrontation, the emphasis they place on internal rather than external fulfillment marks them out as truly enlightened people.

Born healers, they are well suited to the caring and healing professions, to social and charity work, teaching, counseling and careers that bring happiness and enlightenment to others, such as the arts, music, writing, blogging, dance, drama and social-media influencing. Other work options include careers that utilize people skills, such as advertising, lobbying, politics, medicine, sales and international business or entrepreneurship. Health-wise, they often put the needs of others above their own and it is vital they strengthen themselves emotionally and physically, otherwise they may suffer from compassion overload, burnout and stress. **For self-care**, spend time with people who make you feel good about yourself; avoid those who drag you down.

In relationships these people don't have problems attracting admirers and they are kind and generous to the people in their lives. But they can become self-sacrificing with smothering, jealous behavior. Fortunately, before the age of 40 there is an emphasis on balancing their sensitivity with becoming more assertive. After age 40 they tend to gravitate toward greater emotional stability, and this trend further ensures they become less vulnerable. Caring and contemplative, once they learn to balance their own needs with those of others and direct their insight toward the common good, they can be an inspiration. Their destiny is to dedicate their wisdom to helping others find happiness and fulfillment in life.

Potential: Profound, inspiring

Dark side: Insecure, smothering

Tarot card, lucky numbers, days, colors: The Wheel of Fortune, 1, 4, Thursday, Sunday, turquoise, orange

Born today: Jon Hamm (actor); Kate Sheppard (New Zealand suffragist); Kim Campbell (Canadian prime minister)

March 11

The Birthday of the Magician

"I sense and make progress happen"

People born on March 11 are progressive, with one foot in the present and another firmly placed in the future. The key to their success is their intuition, and when they understand how to make it work productively, they are an unstoppable force. Magician-like, they have an uncanny knack of seeking out opportunities and people who can help them progress. They always seem to be one step ahead, and if they are not the source of a trend, they use their imagination to work with it or move beyond it. They are often at the cutting edge, but can lapse into selfish or manipulative behavior if it will get them what they want.

Born investors, these people make great stock-market traders and planners, as they have an instinct for future trends. They also make excellent art and antique collectors, as well as chefs. They may be drawn to public service, politics, marketing, human resources, education, life-coaching and alternative therapies, as well as music, arts and entertainment. They can be overly concerned about appearance and need to remember that good looks begin with a healthy diet and lifestyle, and not in the mirror. **For self-care**, practice mindfulness techniques—every day choose a simple task, such as brushing your teeth, and give it your full and undivided attention.

These people need relationships that offer them plenty of fun and variety. Routine does not suit them. Once they set out to achieve a goal, they work tirelessly until they reach it. Their emphasis on looking ahead is highlighted until the age of 39; they become more relaxed about their goals after that, focusing more on stability. Once they have settled on a course worthy of them, understanding that there are some things they can never control, and that the present has as much value as the future, they can use their intuition and determination not just to predict the future but also to play a part in creating it. Their destiny is to make whatever they are involved in the best and most effective it can possibly be.

Potential: Intuitive, progressive

Dark side: Selfish, manipulative

Tarot card, lucky numbers, days, colors: Justice, 2, 5, Thursday, Monday, turquoise, silver

Born today: Douglas Adams (author); John Barrowman (entertainer); James Franklin Hyde (inventor)

March 12

The Birthday of the Untamed Spirit

"My life is my adventure"

The life lesson:

is to avoid extreme behavior.

The way forward: is to understand that you are special for being you. You do not need to constantly prove to others how exciting you are.

Luck maker: Write an action plan. When you commit your goals to writing, you tend to take them more seriously.

March 12-born have tremendous spirit and a desire to test themselves in increasingly demanding challenges. Others may warn them to be more responsible, but it's impossible for these untamed spirits to listen to sensible advice. They must challenge themselves. Sometimes their exploits land them in trouble but, more often than not, they have prepared for the risks beforehand. They are resilient enough to learn from setbacks and mistakes and bounce back even stronger. Multitalented, they can find it hard to find focus, but specializing is essential for their success.

Born gamblers, these people thrive in careers that involve an element of risk. In business they are drawn to banking, investment, accountancy, stockbroking or setting up a business. Politics, police and detective or secret agent work appeal, as does work in art, music, comedy, writing, journalism, theater, media, New Age areas, publishing and education. Regular intensive exercise is strongly advised to help them work off some of their manic energy in a way that is beneficial to their health. **For self-care,** for at least ten minutes each day, sit still and be quiet. Do nothing, just be with yourself and focus on your being, rather than on what you are doing.

In relationships these people have an air of danger about them and are attracted to people who are edgy, like them. Lack of direction can be a problem; they need to settle on a life course that is worthy of their courage and resilience. Up until the age of 38, there is an emphasis on change, but after that they tend to slow down and feel a need for both personal and professional stability. Often believers in destiny or spirituality, these people have a profoundly intuitive side, which they would do well to cultivate. Whatever they end up doing, one thing is sure—wherever these creative, courageous spirits are to be found, there will always be an element of excitement or controversy swirling about them. Their destiny is to be untamed and, by so doing, inspire others to challenge themselves and take radical new directions.

Potential: Exciting, courageous

Dark side: Impulsive, irresponsible

Tarot card, lucky numbers, day, colors: The Hanged Man, 3, 6, Thursday, turquoise, apricot

Born today: Anish Kapoor (sculptor); Mitt Romney (US senator); Liza Minnelli (singer)

March 13

The Birthday of
Surreal Potential

"I think and live outside the box"

Those born on March 13 are instinctively drawn to what is unconventional and unexplained. Whether they are religious or not, they often believe in fate or otherworldly realms. These people like to study the world and the people around them, often making uncannily accurate predictions. They have a talent for conversation and others tend to value their insights and advice. From an early age they probably challenged conventional thought and their insatiable curiosity seems to grow stronger as they grow older. They do need to cultivate a more pragmatic approach because they can easily get lost in hypotheticals and never realize their potential.

Born diplomats, those born on this day often excel in debates and public speaking and may be attracted to careers in theater, filmmaking, politics, journalism, broadcasting and the media. Their good communication skills may also lead them to sales, advertising, marketing, digital innovation, publishing and education; science, research, writing, philosophy, religion and metaphysics may also appeal. Cerebral, they need to ensure they don't neglect their physical health. **For self-care**, put on a favorite upbeat song and dance. Let your hair down now and again and be sure to get plenty of energizing fresh air and exercise.

Although they can be sensual and romantic, these people can easily become cynical about love and need to seek out those who are supportive rather than critical. They believe so much in fate they can unwittingly steer events a certain way to make their thoughts come true. This is especially dangerous, because they are prone to cynicism when life disappoints—a tendency that is highlighted after the age of 37 when there is greater inflexibility. It is therefore important, especially as they grow older, to keep the spirit of optimism alive. Fortunately, however tough things get, they always retain their unshakable belief that there is more to life than has yet been discovered, and this gives them both resilience and insight. As long as they aren't sidetracked by self-importance or negative expectation and don't lose touch with reality, these people are capable of truly unique thoughts and achievements. Their destiny is to lead others toward previously unknown insights.

Potential: Original, wise

Dark side: Cynical, unrealistic

Tarot card, lucky numbers, days, colors: Death, 4, 7, Thursday, Sunday, turquoise, silver

Born today: William Macy (actor); Percival Lowell (astronomer); Ozuna (singer)

March 14

The Birthday of Dazzling Inventiveness

"I see potential in everyone and everything"

The life lesson: is making decisions and sticking with them.

The way forward: is to weigh up the pros and cons and then make a decision. Even if the decision is wrong, you will still be moving forward, because you have learned from it.

Luck maker: Step out of your comfort zone—the place of procrastination. It is not the place to go for opportunity.

March 14-born tend to be intelligent, versatile and refreshingly open-minded. They have the curiosity to jump from one idea to another without losing track of the bigger picture. Abhorring intolerance and injustice, they are extremely sensitive to the feelings of others and this earns them their admiration and loyalty. They also have the ability to take what is familiar and transform it into something new by presenting it in an unexpected way. There is a dash of brilliance about them, but they do have problems making decisions. This is because they find it hard to decide on a single course of action that takes into account all viewpoints.

Born lecturers, they are good with words and can explain anything clearly. Education, the law, debating and politics appeal to them, as well as research, writing, science and finance. Their humanitarian concerns may lead them to social reform and the healing professions and they can express their creativity and expansiveness in sports, the arts and music. Too much thinking and talking can make their lifestyles sedentary, so they should ensure they get plenty of fresh air and exercise. **For self-care**, place your hand on your heart, close your eyes and tune into the rhythm of your heartbeat. Listen to what your heart is trying to tell you.

In relationships these people need to listen to their heart more. Until the age of 36 the emphasis is on swift changes of mind and direction, but, fortunately, after the age of 36 they are better able to make a stand; and, after the age of 40, most find their focus and really come into their own. As well as indecisiveness, they also need to overcome their tendency to be self-effacing. They must trust themselves and their decisions more. Once they have learned to be bold, the uncommon intellectual gifts and daring inventiveness they are blessed with ensure that there will be no end to the wonders they can create. Their destiny is to reinvigorate what is familiar by discovering startling new insights.

Potential: Open-minded, intelligent

Dark side: Indecisive, passive

Tarot card, lucky numbers, days, colors: Temperance, 5, 8, Thursday, Wednesday, turquoise, green

Born today: Albert Einstein (physicist); Aamir Khan (actor); Simone Biles (gymnast)

March 15

The Birthday of the Mountain Climber

"I scale new heights"

Those born on March 15 are adventurous, determined, charismatic individuals with the potential to become leaders. They can sometimes be arrogant and overly competitive in their race to get ahead, and should be careful not to make enemies as they climb upward in case they meet these people on their way down. Progress in their chosen line of work tends to be rapid. They are adventurous but not reckless, and have the ability to weigh up positives and negatives, form a plan of action and concentrate on achieving their aims. This is a winning combination, especially when allied to their enthusiasm and energetic personality.

is fear of failure in your chosen field.

The way forward: is to understand that there is no such thing as failure if you learn and grow from it.

Luck maker: Share your success, giving credit to others where credit is due. This makes others more willing to help you.

Born pilots, they are often attracted to careers that quite literally take them higher, such as flying, climbing, building, travel and sport. They also tend to scale the heights in management, advertising, the law, banking, journalism, music, science, entrepreneurship or whatever they choose. In their search for adventure they need to be careful to avoid mood-altering substances or unhealthy addictions that can seriously damage their health and chances of success. **For self-care,** stop regarding everyone as competition—the only person they need to compete with is the person they were yesterday.

In relationships, they need to learn to place as much importance on their personal as their professional life, because without love their achievements feel empty. Before the age of 35 they place greater emphasis on getting ahead than the goal itself. This can impact their personal happiness, but fortunately, after the age of 36, they seek a more meaningful direction and this is when they really come into their own, although they should watch out for a streak of obstinacy. Potential leaders, these people need to learn not to overwhelm themselves with their restless drive to succeed. Once they value the love and support of others, they have all the originality and pioneering power they need to blaze a spectacular trail and reach their destiny—the very top.

Potential: Adventurous, determined

Dark side: Competitive, obstinate

Tarot card, lucky numbers, days, colors: The Devil, 6, 9, Thursday, Friday, turquoise, pink

Born today: Eva Longoria (actor); Andrew Jackson (US president); Ruth Bader Ginsburg (US Supreme Court justice)

March 16

The Birthday of Equilibrium

"I am a champion of peace"

People born on March 16 are wholesome, balanced personalities able to combine their imaginative potential with a practical approach. Their talent for maintaining equilibrium or seeking to balance the scales is the secret of their success. They have a great talent for negotiation and for making people pull together as a team. At work they are ambitious and disciplined, but at home they create an atmosphere of peace and security. They have a dreamy, intuitive side that is sensitive to the needs of others, but they can also use their common sense to make sure everyone feels important. Their living and work places are tidy and elegant, though not obsessively so; as a result, people often feel instantly at home in their space.

Born mediators and diplomats, those born on this day flourish in situations where they can coordinate and inspire, and make great managers, CEOs, counselors, therapists, social workers, critics, journalists, bloggers, lecturers and teachers. Their practical approach to creativity may express itself in design, art dealing, web design and image consultancy. Wearing, meditating on and surrounding themselves with the color red will encourage them to move out of their comfort zone and be more daring with their life choices. **For self-care,** make your own wellbeing a top priority by getting fresh air, eating well, listening to music and having fun every day.

Once these people learn to philosophize less and laugh more, their relationships can be a source of great fulfillment and happiness. Sometimes they don't prepare enough for the potential of unexpected setbacks in their personal and professional lives and they need to ensure their own views don't become so muted that they disappear altogether, especially after the age of 34 where there is an emphasis on stasis. They need to be careful during this time not to let their practical, hedonistic side overshadow their idealistic and intuitive side. Once they are able to acknowledge rather than deny their changeable nature, and take on responsibilities with excitement rather than apprehension, they will not only maintain their precious equilibrium, but discover the exhilarating sense of achievement that goes with it. Their destiny is to put their energy into visionary concepts that can practically improve lives.

Potential: Balanced, imaginative

Dark side: Cautious, passive

Tarot card, lucky numbers, days, colors: The Tower, 1, 7, Thursday, Monday, every shade of blue

Born today: James Madison (US president); Jerry Lewis (comedian); Anna Atkins (botanist)

March 17

The Birthday of
Magical Sparkle

The life lesson:

is to make a commitment and stick to it.

The way forward: is to understand that it is not what you think and say that makes your mark in life but what you do.

Luck maker: Stop self-sabotaging behavior. Running away does not protect you from pain, it just piles on more unhappiness.

"Everything is awesome"

March 17-born have an enchanted quality and often appear to be floating through life. This isn't to say that they are lazy or never experience setbacks, as they experience disasters just the same as everyone else, but, however tough life gets, they always seem able to emerge with a lightness and sparkle. Although they are charismatic, with creative talents, their difficulty lies in drifting from one interest to another; rather than facing a challenge, they prefer to avoid it. There are many possible reasons for this: lack of self-confidence, dislike of confrontation and, above all, a fear of commitment and responsibility.

Born dancers, these people may express their creativity physically through music, drama or dance. They are often drawn to the arts, design or any career where they can delight others with their ability to generate magic. Education, travel, public service, politics, the law, philosophy, spirituality, healing and aviation may also appeal. Meditating on and surrounding themselves with the color blue will encourage them to spend time reflecting on their responsibilities. **For self-care**, do the things you find tedious or dislike first thing in the morning. Successful people get the tough tasks out of the way first.

Blessed with a caring nature, these people love to help others. The responsibility of this may be a struggle for these sparkling souls, but the ability to be patient and reliable in their relationships with others and in their professional life forms a vital part of their gaining the self-confidence needed for success. When properly channeled, their curiosity and positivity can bring great success and gain admiration. Facing up to tedious or difficult situations brings them more satisfaction than drifting aimlessly and irresponsibly. Before the age of 33 there is an emphasis on change, but afterwards they often become less flighty. Once their butterfly nature has learned that touching the ground, becoming more responsible and finishing what they start doesn't mean the death of their creativity and optimism but rather the making of it, their destiny is to live highly creative lives and to lead others toward a more optimistic, magical approach to life.

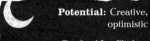

Potential: Creative, optimistic

Dark side: Flighty, unreliable

Tarot card, lucky numbers, days, colors: The Star, 2, 8, Thursday, Saturday, turquoise, maroon

Born today: Nat King Cole (singer); Gottlieb Daimler (inventor); Grimes (singer)

March 18

The Birthday of Spiritual Strength

is to remember what truly matters.

The way forward: is to understand that nobody on their deathbed says they wished they had spent more time at the office.

Luck maker: Help others when they are down on their luck. This will earn you their lifelong gratitude.

"Tomorrow is another day"

Those born on March 18 have the ability to recover from adverse circumstances, not once but time after time. They have remarkable physical, emotional and spiritual resilience, and if they can learn the lessons from setbacks, the potential to become inspirational motivators and leaders. Intelligent and resourceful, they use their willpower to overcome obstacles. They also have a knack of being in the right place at the right time, a great sense of humor and an optimistic outlook. People find them appealing but also exhausting, as they live at a fast pace. Their preoccupation with moving forward can also cause them to neglect important details and others' feelings.

Born motivators and arbitrators, they make great life coaches, motivational speakers and carers, as well as negotiators, mediators, brokers and agents. Careers that utilize their resilience, such as the military, police, prison work, politics, education, social media and the entertainment world, suit them well, as does work involving travel and public interaction, such as advertising, sales, movie-making, invention, design and architecture. They run the risk of becoming self-obsessed, so it is important they spend time thinking about the needs of others as well as their own. **For self-care**, spend more time relaxing in the company of the people you really care about.

In their relationships they relish challenge and excitement, and prefer to be the one doing the chasing. They need to ensure that the emotional needs of those close to them are met. Before the age of 32 they are more assertive, but also more obsessive in their approach to their goals. After the age of 33 they slow down a little and become more secure and settled. Whatever age they are, their recuperative powers are remarkable. They have an unshakable belief that however tough things are now, they will be better tomorrow. More often than not, life rewards this positive attitude and things improve significantly. Once they learn to avoid being ruthless, whatever field they choose to work in they can encourage others to rise above challenges. Their destiny is to change the lives of those they touch by their intensity and bravery.

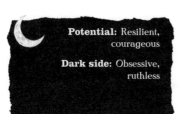

Potential: Resilient, courageous

Dark side: Obsessive, ruthless

Tarot card, lucky numbers, days, colors: The Moon, 1, 9, Thursday, Tuesday, turquoise, scarlet

Born today: Queen Latifah (singer); Rudolf Diesel (engineer); Neville Chamberlain (British prime minister)

March 19

The Birthday of True Grit

"I am unstoppable"

People born on March 19 often possess a youthful vitality and openness. Although they may appear absent-minded sometimes, they are very practical and once they have settled on a goal, they work tirelessly to achieve it. They are a brilliant combination of imagination and action, creating a mental image of what they want and then taking the practical steps to achieve it. In fact, they are virtually unstoppable when they have put their plan in place; however difficult, mundane or repetitive things are, they see it through. This determined approach is a recipe for success and—if directed toward a worthy goal—can take them not just to the top but to new ground. The downside is that too many of their goals are based on material success and recognition, so they need to learn that fulfillment does not just come from outward things but also from inner contentment.

Born movers and shakers, their combination of energy and organization offer the potential for incredible success. Business and management, art and entertainment may appeal, but they are at their happiest working in fields where they can improve lives, such as politics, science, the military, the healing professions, education and social reform. Prone to stress-related conditions, regular time out and walks in the fresh air are key. **For self-care**, treat yourself to regular massages and soothing warm baths with relaxing essential oils.

They tend to sacrifice their personal lives for their professional ones, putting their relationships at risk, but if they do this the fulfillment they hope they will find through their career will always elude them. Only when they are able to look within and understand the importance of both personal and professional satisfaction can they achieve lasting happiness and success. After their mid-thirties they become more relaxed and settled, but they still need to beware of stubbornness, narrow-mindedness and disregarding others' viewpoints. As long as they acquire a degree of self-knowledge, they have both the fantasy and the fire to make their dreams come true. Their destiny is to apply their true-grit approach to initiate social improvements.

Potential: Determined, charming

Dark side: Materialistic, inflexible

Tarot card, lucky numbers, days, colors: The Sun, 1, 4, Thursday, Sunday, orange, green

Born today: Glenn Close and Bruce Willis (actors); David Livingstone (explorer); Wyatt Earp (US marshal)

March 20

The Birthday of the Insightful Wanderer

"Things are really looking up"

March 20-people were born on the last day of the Western zodiac wheel, and are among the most insightful and mature individuals of the year. They possess such a wealth of gifts that it is hard to pinpoint one, but underneath their versatility lies their great compassion for others, a gift that can bring them big rewards, but at a price. Their feelings can overpower them and they may be prone to depression, but they are also optimists who believe in the basic goodness of people. They long to make the world a better place, but they can become confused to the point of indecision when they empathize too strongly with others' emotions.

Born counselors and problem-solvers, they make great advisors, therapists, consultants, coaches, managers, diplomats, researchers, influencers, healers, carers, social workers, psychics and teachers. Their sensitivity may express itself in the world of art, music, drama, dance, writing, photography, social media, design and filmmaking. They tend to live in their head, so it is important they do not neglect their physical needs. **For self-care**, take better care of yourself. Successful people know how important self-care is for their wellbeing, so they integrate it into their daily lifestyle.

In relationships they need to avoid sacrificing their happiness from a sense of duty. Until the age of 30, if they don't strengthen themselves emotionally, others may take advantage of their vulnerability and generosity. After 30 they have the potential for greater emotional stability; this is when they become more effective instruments for good. There may be many changes of direction as they experiment with different roles, but their experiences help them discover who they are and what they want from their lives. Once they settle on a goal, often to improve the lives of others in some way, they do achieve their dreams because they are both practical and idealistic. In their later years they draw on their rich experience of life to become a wise elder with a wealth of invaluable advice to offer the next generation. Their destiny is to inspire others to overcome challenges and reach their full potential.

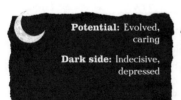

Potential: Evolved, caring

Dark side: Indecisive, depressed

Tarot card, lucky numbers, days, colors: Judgment, 2, 5, Thursday, Monday, scarlet, silver

Born today: Ovid (poet); Spike Lee (director); Holly Hunter (actor)

ARIES

THE RAM (March 21–April 19)

- ✳ **Element:** Fire
- ✳ **Ruling planet:** Mars, the warrior
- ✳ **Tarot card:** The Emperor (authority)
- ✳ **Lucky numbers:** 1, 9
- ✳ **Favorable colors:** Red, orange, pink
- ✳ **Driving force:** Courage
- ✳ **Personal statement:** I am born to lead
- ✳ **Chinese astrology counterpart:** The Dragon

Arians are the pioneers of the zodiac, which isn't surprising as they are the first of the 12 signs, the zodiac year beginning in March. They love to be independent, take the initiative and forge ahead through life's ups and downs. Enthusiastic, courageous and assertive, they don't fear standing out from the crowd and are natural born leaders. Routine and predictability frustrate them and they have a seemingly insatiable appetite for challenge and adventure. No matter what their age, they often have boundless, youthful energy and will propel themselves headfirst into the world every single day without fear or hesitation.

Personality potential

Some Arians come across as loud, while others are subtler and more like lambs than rams in their approach to life, but either way an Arian is typically impossible to ignore. These people live their lives on their own terms. They like to be the ones giving the orders and make inspiring leaders, bosses and motivators. As the first sign of the zodiac, they are often the spark or seed that can ignite enthusiasm in others. Being highly individualistic, they don't find compromise easy, but their rock-solid confidence that obstacles can be overcome is infectious. Their positivity energizes and inspires all those who cross their path.

Arians are ruled by Mars, the planet of the Roman god of war, and their element is fire, which ignites, burns and molds. Key words include: initiative, courage, assertiveness, independence, passion and leadership. There is something incredibly honest and straightforward about people born under this sign. Details aren't important to them. They are only concerned with the bigger picture and can see clearly to the heart of the matter. Their refreshing ability to let go of grudges, learn from setbacks and see every day as a new beginning earns them respect and admiration, sometimes awe, from others.

Determined to succeed, Arians are movers and shakers. They don't patiently wait for things to happen; they *make* them happen. Indeed, nothing excites an Arian more than a challenge to overcome. They are natural risk-takers. Once they have met a challenge, their restless nature will forge ahead to bigger and better tests. Achievement matters greatly to them and they don't want anyone or anything to stand in the way of their goals. Headstrong and driven, they want to win no matter what competition or setbacks stand in their way. **They are independent people—if they can't lead or be in a position of authority, they may prefer to work alone.** However, if things don't work out—which is likely if you consider all the risks that Arians are prone to taking—you won't find them wallowing in self-pity. They will simply pick themselves up, try a new approach and keep moving onward and upward until they reach the top—the place they believe themselves destined to be.

> **They are independent people— if they can't lead or be in a position of authority, they may prefer to work alone.**

Personality pitfalls

The impulsiveness and child-like honesty of Arians can be endearing, but it can also make them vulnerable and gullible. They often have to learn the hard way that honesty is not always the best policy. Less bluntness and more subtlety will help them get their point across more effectively. And although their natural leadership potential makes them invaluable during times of crisis, when there is not a battle to be fought their love of combat and addiction to having an adrenaline rush can make them impatient and bad-tempered. When fired up, the Arian temper can burst explosively and without warning.

Arians tend to be self-centered, at times veering toward narcissistic. They can get so wrapped up in themselves that they fail to notice what is going on around them. If they are made aware of what they are missing they can, however, be extremely noble and will fight tirelessly for the underdog.

It is also common for Arians to be hasty. They rush into relationships or projects firing on all cylinders, but if things are not going their way or they lose interest, they tend to drop the person or project hastily. Prone to being bossy, reckless, arrogant and hot-tempered, Arians can greatly improve their lives by cultivating qualities such as patience, self-discipline and humility, as well as paying greater attention to detail.

Symbol

Aries is symbolized by the ram, and they certainly possess a tendency to ram their ideas down people's throats, pushing and crashing headfirst into things without clearly seeing the way ahead. There is, however, a softer side to them; but, in general, these people are true to their symbol: blunt, forceful and to the point—just like a battering ram.

Darkest secrets

Arians need to win and to follow their own rules, but this desire to lead and stand out as an individual is not because they think they are better than others, but largely because they need to be seen and admired. What other people think about them matters far more to them than they are usually willing to admit, and this can be their Achilles' heel.

Love

Arians are passionate lovers. They love to be in love, and fall in love innocently and swiftly. They are generous partners and demand fireworks from their lovers and partners in return. They panic if they feel that their grand passion is not being returned, and need constant reassurance from other people that they are loved and valued. Sex is important for Arians, perhaps more so for them than for others. Although they expect absolute adoration and loyalty from their partners, be warned: they don't necessarily return that devotion themselves. They adore the honeymoon stage of new relationships and make wonderfully exciting and adventurous lovers, but, just as in all areas of their lives, if things become routine and predictable, they can get restless and may stray. For relationships to become long term with an Aries, there needs to be plenty of excitement and adventure.

Love matches:

Leo, Sagittarius and Libra.

The Arian woman

The Arian woman is energetic and active, and will often have attractive, strong features. She is constantly busy and has that "can-do" attitude about her. She doesn't appear to need anyone to hold a door open for her, but, having said this, she can also be extremely feminine and flirtatious. Resilient and eternally optimistic, she believes that miracles can and do happen. If something doesn't work out, it doesn't set her back for too long. In her mind, there is always another way and tomorrow *is* always another day.

Arian women can be charismatic pioneers and fiercely independent—think Joan of Arc. Sometimes their confidence can batter the egos of potential partners, but an Arian woman does not want someone in her life who is too fragile or overly devoted to her. She wants a partner she can admire, perhaps even look up to. The best way, therefore, to catch the eye of an Arian woman is to be detached and to leave her guessing. Let her think you can easily resist her obvious charms and she will then try to prove to you she is worth it.

Although the Arian woman often has many admirers, she always longs for the man or woman she can't get. She is tough and strong, but can also play the role of the vulnerable female if it suits her. The person who wins her heart will find that beneath her confident "I can fend for myself" exterior, there is a gentle (sometimes fragile) soul full of trust, love and dreams for the future.

The Arian man

The Arian man is likely to be a whirlwind of activity. Dressed for action, with his phone constantly beeping, he is often fiercely competitive and self-assured, at times arrogant. He takes the initiative and expects others to follow his lead. Above all, he is simply bursting with energy and ideas, and loves to win in love and life. Even if he is a more "sheep-like" Aries and doesn't appear to be a leader at first glance, there is always the potential behind his seeming gentleness for him to discover his horns and find some way to forge ahead.

Deeply affectionate and prone to grand and generous gestures, the Aries man doesn't expect the people in his life to hold back. If he falls in love, it will be head over heels. He will put his partner on a pedestal and shower them with attention and gifts, but if his partner needs space from his constant need

for adoration and romance, he may try to look somewhere else. This doesn't necessarily mean he will cheat. More often than not his honesty prevents him from cheating. He is more likely to end his current relationship before embarking on a new one.

Perhaps the best way to attract an Arian man is to be confident and to play it cool. This man loves a challenge and likes to take the initiative in love, but if you do end up in a relationship with him, forget about flirting with other people. He is one of the most possessive and jealous signs of the zodiac and needs to be reassured constantly that he—and only he—comes first in your life.

Family

Arian children thrive on attention and affection. They need constant stimulation and have boundless energy, but their enthusiasm can easily burn out. Parents or carers are advised to hold back on investing in equipment for lessons or activities, to see first if these children's interest in them is more than just a passing fancy. They can be brilliant students, but the attention to detail required for academic success can bore them. They come alive when they need to take exams because testing appeals to their desire to prove themselves and forge ahead. They are adventurous and therefore injury-prone. Highly likely to answer back or challenge authority at every turn, Arian children need clear boundaries put in place so that they do not end up out of control. They don't tend to thrive, though, under endless rules, and the best way to parent or school them is to give them plenty of opportunities to show that they are winners. Telling them that you love them regardless of whether they succeed or fail will bring out the best in them.

Arian parents are warm and affectionate, and typically indulge their children because raising a family reconnects them to their own child-like nature. They have little difficulty understanding and relating to youth. They encourage their family to be as active as possible. This works fine if their children love action and taking risks as much as they do, but not so well if they have a child who is more introverted and happier doing quieter activities, such as reading. It is important for them to see their child as an individual rather than an extension of themselves, and thus to avoid forcing them to do things that don't come naturally to them. Although things can

be noisy and chaotic in their households, Arian parents ensure their children have plenty of love, laughter and magic in their lives. They also encourage them to see the wonder and potential in everyone and everything.

Career

Arians thrive in competitive environments. They are driven and quick to create plans and initiate projects. Routine jobs are not ideal for them, but if they do find themselves in a job that isn't a great match, they can tolerate it as long as they have outside interests and hobbies that absorb their tremendous energy. **Ideal careers for Arians are those that give them plenty of freedom of expression and the opportunity to innovate and lead from the front.**

Motivated and strong-willed, Arians can excel in almost any field they put their mind to, but jobs that particularly suit their energetic and pioneering spirits include: being in the armed forces, firefighting, police work, piloting planes, medicine, psychiatry, politics, public relations, sport, journalism and any business career that involves management opportunities. Entrepreneurs and world leaders are often drawn from Arian ranks, as they can frequently be forceful agents for change. They love to present, and make great salespeople or social media celebrities. Art and music also appeal to them because they can be intensely emotional; they can flourish, then, in the world of entertainment, filmmaking, directing or the performing arts.

> **Ideal careers for Arians are those that give them plenty of freedom of expression and the opportunity to innovate and lead from the front.**

Health and wellbeing

Arians are often busy, energetic people who love to push themselves to the limits and burn the candle at both ends. Regular down time to relax and unwind is essential for them to thrive. Mindful walks in the countryside where they can observe the calm of the natural world are highly beneficial for them. They need plenty of sleep but should avoid sleeping in, as Arians tend to be at their best in the early morning. Being active people, and natural fidgets, they don't tend to put on too much weight, but they should avoid refined and processed foods, rich in sugar, salt and additives, as it overstimulates them. They should eat natural produce rich in whole grains, fruits and vegetables. Spicy ingredients don't tend to agree with them and they should choose meals that are as simple, nutritious and natural as possible.

Regular exercise is a must, not just because it burns off their excess energy but also because it encourages them to take time out. Arians are at their happiest and best when they are physically active, and leisure pursuits that suit them include jogging, cycling, swimming, martial arts and mountain climbing or activities that test their stamina. They are not natural team players, but do enjoy competitive team sports.

Arians are prone to headaches and also to cuts, bruises and minor burns. They should therefore adopt the motto "more haste and less speed." Wearing, meditating or surrounding themselves with the color **green** will help restore calm, balance and natural healing to their lives.

Born between March 21 and 30

Mars is extremely powerful for Arians born between these two dates. March Arians tend to be fairly intolerant of viewpoints different to their own, and demanding of themselves and others. This Martian energy-boost gives them incredible mental and physical stamina. They are never afraid to rush in headfirst where angels fear to tread, but they need to make sure that they are not so focused on their goals that they walk over others while achieving them.

Born between March 31 and April 10

Arians born between these dates have traces of one of the other fire signs in their psychological makeup: sunny Leo. They are humorous, honest, bright spirits who attract people easily to them, but their power to impose their will on others, often without any opposition, needs to be used responsibly.

Born between April 11 and 19

Arians born toward the end of their sun sign often have stronger humanitarian tendencies. They have great courage and optimism and like to get things done their way, but they also tend to be gentler in their approach to life and more willing to champion the underdog and to try to help or take care of others.

Life lessons

Arians have a wonderful energy and zest for life, but there is one thing they could benefit from learning and that is the value of patience. Like the hare in the famous fable "The Tortoise and the Hare," they are often too hasty and impatient, and this can sometimes cause them trouble and cost them the race.

If an Arian wants something, they want it right now. They loathe waiting for anyone and anything (queuing is their pet peeve), but they have to learn that some things in life require time and patience before results can be achieved. Arians are superb at brainstorming, visualizing and starting up new projects, relationships and enterprises; but when things require follow-through, dedication and discipline or begin to become routine, they start looking for other options. This can cost them dearly, and they would do well to stop and think carefully about what they have to lose before they drop out of school or college, change jobs or end a relationship.

Being overly competitive is another Arian life challenge. They make terrible losers. Although they don't lose often, it is important for them to learn how to lose graciously and to allow others to step into the limelight now and again. If they are worried that stepping back will make people forget about them, they should not be: Arians are natural born leaders and, in some cases, stars. The same goes for relationships. **Arians are very good at taking and directing, but not so good at giving and accepting.** They need to learn the pure joy of giving and helping others. They also need to learn that sometimes in life you just have to let go and trust others to do their best.

> ❝ Arians are very good at
> taking and directing,
> but not so good at
> giving and accepting. ❞

As Arians journey through life, they need to work on their impatience, impulsiveness and naivety, as well as respecting the feelings of others around them and improving their attention to detail. Above all, they need to experience the joy of seeing things through to completion. Observing other

Arians can reveal to them how best to channel and achieve positive results from their fiery enthusiasm. The other signs have much of value to teach Arians. Those born under Cancer can encourage them to be more sensitive to the needs of others and to develop empathy and understanding. Scorpios, Pisceans and Aquarians can encourage them to look within, rather than externally, for affirmation. Leos and Sagittarians can inspire them to be less serious and more playful in the pursuit of their goals. Those born under Libra can show them the joys of teamwork and the importance of thinking before they speak and looking before they leap. Geminis can motivate them to listen to viewpoints different to their own. Virgos, Taureans and Capricorns can teach them the value of hard work, dedication and commitment, and the importance of perseverance when things become boring or tedious.

Chinese astrology counterpart: The Dragon

In Chinese culture, Dragon-born children are highly esteemed. Parents even try to plan their pregnancies for the year of the Dragon. Like their Western counterpart, Dragons like to be regarded not only as a strong sign, but as the brightest and the mightiest.

Both Arians and those born in the year of the Dragon are pioneers who tend to rebel against authority. They are trail-blazers who make up and live by their own rules. Natural leaders, they are typically adventurous, optimistic risk-takers. They believe in themselves and their ability to make things happen.

Once Dragons have focused their energy on a goal or a dream, little can stand in their way of achieving it. They can, however, be intolerant, arrogant and destructive in a scorched-earth kind of way, if things don't go the way they feel they should be going or people don't conform to their expectations. Independent, noble and majestic spirits, there is often a touch of magic—star dust even—about them that is both mesmerizing and enchanting.

Note: Arians have an affinity with Dragon-sign characteristics, but be sure to check which Chinese sign corresponds to your **year** of birth (see page xxi), and to read about the characteristics associated with it, too.

March 21

The Birthday of
Clear-Sightedness

The life lesson:

is to work harmoniously with others.

The way forward: is to understand that when people stand together their impact is stronger than one person standing alone.

Luck maker: Be tactful. Softening your approach so you don't alienate others does not mean you have lost any of your passion.

"I do things my way"

March 21-born are powerful, freethinking individuals with an iron will to succeed, in keeping with their elite status as the first born of the Western zodiac year. They are quietly confident and direct in all their dealings and opinions, so other people know where they stand with them. They live according to their own values and if other people don't understand these, they aren't prepared to explain themselves, much preferring to go it alone. Although remarkably clear-sighted and independent, these people can come across as inflexible, blunt and stubborn.

Born commanders, they have terrific leadership potential, which can be put to good use in the military, police, education, business and the law, and their directness sees them succeeding in sales, marketing, lobbying, health, life-coaching, sports and fitness. They have CEO potential but may prefer freelancing or setting up their own business. Self-sufficient, they prefer to take care of themselves when unwell, but do need to ensure they don't shut themselves away entirely from the care of those who love them. **For self-care**, practice mindfulness techniques to help you be present and handle impatience. Each day, give one routine task you do, such as washing your hands, your full and undivided attention.

These people enjoy their own company, but can find great happiness in relationships with those who give them plenty of space. They should learn not to become narrow-minded when pursuing their goals, accepting that success does not always result from following a direct path. Between the ages of 30 and 60 their stubborn tendencies are likely to be highlighted. During these years they need to make sure they work on transforming their way of thinking, so that it takes into account the viewpoints of others. Once they learn to moderate their impatience, they have the energy, intuition and perception to become exceptional leaders. When they find themselves in a position to impress others with their freethinking, all who come into contact with them become more clear-sighted about who they are and what they want. Their destiny is to blaze an inspirational trail with their potent conviction.

Potential: Powerful, perceptive

Dark side: Impatient, tactless

Tarot card, lucky numbers, days, colors: The World, 3, 6, Tuesday, Thursday, red, green

Born today: Gary Oldman (actor); Rosie O'Donnell (comedian); Ayrton Senna (racing driver)

March 22

The Birthday of Frankness

"The truth is out there"

The life lesson: is learning to be tactful.

The way forward: is to understand that sometimes directness comes across as insensitive and arrogant. Being tactful is presenting the truth in a way that considers the feelings of others.

Luck maker: Stop interrupting. Don't immediately jump in with your views when someone is talking. Listen and ask questions to see if you can learn anything helpful.

Those born on March 22 are frank, honorable and reliable. They tend to gain the support and admiration of others. They speak their minds because they value truth above all else. Although this can sometimes offend, more often than not others find themselves listening to their wisdom. The influence they have is an awesome responsibility, and if they can learn to channel it sensitively, they can help others clearly see the facts. They can appear uncompromising, but they are never close-minded. They are forever curious and nothing fascinates them more than new technology and scientific discoveries.

Born lawyers, they see life in black and white and may be drawn to careers in the law, science, medicine, accounting, engineering, programming and technology. Their search for the truth may also lead them to the arts, music and film. With their talent for leadership, management and spotting opportunities, they can succeed in any career and may set up their own business. Health-wise, they can veer toward over-indulgence or being obsessive about their diet and exercise routine, and they need to find a middle way. **For self-care,** spending more time in nature, and wearing, meditating on and surrounding yourself with the color green, will encourage you to find inner and outer balance.

In their relationships these people blow hot and cold. They need to be as honest in love as they are in life. There may be many changes of direction in their twenties, but, from their thirties onward, there is more emphasis on stability and this is when they really come into their own. They can get carried away in the moment, but generally, when they find a worthy goal, their refusal to be diverted from it gives them enormous potential for success. And when they achieve that success, there are few who feel they do not deserve it. Once they have learned the art of compromise, their destiny is to uncover the truth or real nature of a situation and, by their fine example, encourage others to do the same.

Potential: Confident, honest

Dark side: Blunt, uncompromising

Tarot card, lucky numbers, days, colors: The Fool, 4, 7, Tuesday, Sunday, red, silver

Born today: Yayoi Kusama (artist); Andrew Lloyd Webber (composer); Reese Witherspoon (actor)

March 23

The Birthday of the Eternal Student

The life lesson: is to get in touch with your emotions.

The way forward: is to understand that if you don't pay attention to your emotional needs, your self-esteem and self-knowledge will be poor.

Luck maker: It is not so much what you say, but how you make people feel when you say it, that makes the difference.

"I live to learn"

People born on March 23 want to know how and why things work, and what makes people tick. They have insatiable curiosity and getting a sound education is the key to their success. They have great insight into the strengths and weaknesses of others, yet can sometimes be lacking in empathy, relying on knowledge rather than personal experience. Even though they are often surrounded by debaters, they do run the risk of becoming observers rather than participants. Eternal students, the issues that most interest them are those that they could most benefit from applying to themselves. Their information-gathering approach has both strengths and weaknesses; it does not take into account the importance of a person's inner life and how that provides meaning and comfort.

Born surgeons, they have the necessary detachment for careers in medicine, the law, science, engineering, computer-game design, psychology, athletics and teaching. They can also be drawn to publishing, acting and the arts, but whatever career they choose, their ability to be objective helps them succeed. Prone to eye strain due to long working hours on screens, they need to make sure they drink plenty of water and maintain a regular sleep schedule. **For self-care**, get in touch with nature. One of the most effective ways to calm your mind and connect to your heart is to spend more time in natural settings.

Once they learn to search for love with their heart as well as their head, these people can be generous companions. Their scientific tendency to observe and overanalyze is most pronounced before the age of 58, and it is essential they learn to recognize their emotional needs, because they may be prone to bouts of insecurity. Inquisitive, perceptive and exciting to be around, once they have learned to look within as well as outside themselves for stimulation, they have the enthusiasm and determination they need not only to make startling observations but also to act upon them with life-enhancing benefits. Their destiny is to make new discoveries and observations for others to work with.

Potential: Curious, exciting

Dark side: Detached, insecure

Tarot card, lucky numbers, days, colors: The Hierophant, 5, 8, Tuesday, Wednesday, red, blue

Born today: Mo Farah (athlete); Eric Fromm (psychologist); Wernher von Braun (scientist)

March 24

The Birthday of Stormy Tranquility

The life lesson:

is to deal with negative feelings.

The way forward: is to understand that negative feelings, such as anger, fear, insecurity and jealousy, are simply messengers to alert you to a need for change.

Luck maker: Like seeks like. If you feel good about yourself, you increase your chances of attracting positive people and things into your life.

"Life is simple, no need to complicate"

March 24-born take great pleasure in the simple things of life, but there can be a dark cloud underneath their innocent wonder. They prefer simple solutions to complicated alternatives and are at their happiest when their private life is steady, but, despite this, their lives are often far from tranquil. Challenges seem to be attracted to them and continue to test them until they come to terms with their own inner conflicts. They should never ignore or suppress their dark feelings, but must learn to face them head-on. When they are able to do this, they find there is far less to fear than they thought.

Born motivators, their ability to elevate the moods of others suits them to teaching, counseling, healing, life-coaching, influencing and social work. Their strong communication skills may draw them to the law, writing and entertainment, and their leadership potential and ability to find the simplest, happiest and speediest solution serves them well in business or any career they pursue. Prone to mood swings, they need to take plenty of time out to relax and unwind and to laugh with friends and loved ones. **For self-care**, take a deep breath. Deep breathing and regular meditation will help you find the inner peace to deal with feelings of frustration.

Other people may find it hard to understand why these lovely people with an army of admirers so often seem vulnerable and moody. As such, they present an enigma. It is important for them to listen to the messages that their emotions, both positive and negative, convey, especially between the ages of 27 and 57, during which there is an emphasis on external success. As well as learning to face their inner demons, they do need to take a more realistic approach to life that takes into account complications. This should not, however, be at the expense of their simplicity and sweetness, since their most powerful strength is the noble art of lighting up the lives of others. Their destiny is to make even the most cynical among us smile.

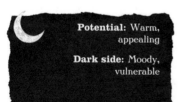

Potential: Warm, appealing

Dark side: Moody, vulnerable

Tarot card, lucky numbers, days, colors: The Lovers, 6, 9, Tuesday, Friday, pink, green

Born today: Harry Houdini (magician); Steve McQueen (actor); Alan Sugar (entrepreneur)

March 25

The Birthday of Electric Energy

The life lesson:

is self-control.

The way forward: is to understand that when you lash out at others it is often because your inner equilibrium is disturbed.

Luck maker: Give others the benefit of the doubt more. Most of the time people do have good intentions.

"I am a creative vortex"

Those born on March 25 like to be where the action is, and that is where they are often found. Their dynamism marks them out as natural leaders, because others tend to follow when they show the way, but their natural preference is often to go it alone. They may have developed a tough skin to protect themselves from life's knocks, but they have a sense of natural justice and compassion for the vulnerable. Quirky and imaginative, what really distinguishes them is their boundless energy. Daring, with stacks of bright ideas, these people's spontaneity can sometimes get them into trouble through hasty decisions. Adopting a more mature, reflective attitude helps them make smoother progress.

Born propagandists and fighters for a cause, they may be drawn to careers in education, sales, writing, promotion, public relations, lobbying, social work, stock market, the law, music, acting and the arts. Their enthusiasm and high creativity ensure they succeed in whatever career they choose. With their boundless energy, it is essential for their wellbeing that they have regular periods of rest and solitude to recharge their batteries. **For self-care**, when decisions need to be made, press pause and give yourself time. Most of the things that you think are urgent, truly aren't.

Although much of the electric energy of those born on this day is externally directed, they do need plenty of time out for quiet reflection, as this will help them avoid mood swings. This need for time to daydream alone can confuse those who regard them as whirlwinds of constant energy, but people need to understand that it is vital for them. Until the age of 25 they tend to be daring and carefree, but after the age of 25 there is greater emphasis on the need for direction, consistency, security and stability. In their thirties, forties and beyond, they really come into their own. If they keep a lid on their temper and give themselves those regular times out, the electric and highly creative energy and imagination of these people will help them surge right to the front of their chosen field. Their destiny is to inspire others to highlight and reverse social wrongs.

Potential: Dynamic, compassionate

Dark side: Moody, hasty

Tarot card, lucky numbers, days, colors: The Chariot, 1, 7, Tuesday, Monday, red, sea green

Born today: Elton John and Aretha Franklin (singers); Sarah Jessica Parker (actor)

March 26

The Birthday of Honesty

"I see the honest truth"

People born on March 26 have the boldness to achieve much in life. They appear laid-back, but they love to cut to the chase, not wishing to make things more complicated than they are. They don't have time for small talk or spin; directness, both intellectual and emotional, is their goal. A desire for honesty dominates their personality, encouraging them to explore situations others might avoid. It also helps them get things done efficiently and they can make even the hardest of tasks seem easy. The only problem with their straightforward approach is becoming too detached and lagging behind those who are more passionate. Easily dissatisfied when relying on the efforts and opinions of others, they are the best judge of what does or does not work for them.

Born managers, they may be drawn to careers that highlight discipline and organization, such as the military, the police, the law, politics, accounting and technology. They are never happy being told what to do, so their independent spirit may draw them to the world of art and entertainment or to going freelance and setting up their own business. As far as health is concerned, they value simplicity as they do in all areas of their lives, and thrive when following a disciplined, healthy diet and regular exercise schedule. **For self-care**, lose yourself in a feel-good movie every now and again. It will help you connect to your heart—the place where all true magic begins.

In relationships they need to learn that they can't always have things their own way. They also tend to close their minds and need to understand that the less-is-more approach to life isn't always appropriate. Until the age of 24 they are adventurous, but after that, they become more interested in stability, and these are the years to express their creativity. As long as they stay open-minded and don't lose touch with their spontaneity and wry humor, they are capable of producing quality work of incredible depth. Their destiny is to simplify what is complicated and to help others cut right to the heart of the issue.

Potential: Bold, easy-going

Dark side: Inflexible, detached

Tarot card, lucky numbers, days, colors: Strength, 2, 8, Tuesday, Saturday, red, green

Born today: Keira Knightley (actor); Kenny Chesney (musician); Robert Frost (poet)

March 27

The Birthday of the Individual

"I am ready for action"

March 27-born tend to be endearing individuals with their own inimitable style of dress and behavior, attracting attention wherever they go. They don't just have star quality; they have something far more special—the likability factor. Despite always being in demand, achieving their goals matters more to them than gathering admirers. Their work is all-consuming for them, and they will push themselves single-mindedly. Their determination and refusal to fit in often results from youthful struggles, and, while it gives them resilience, it can also sometimes make them unsympathetic to the feelings of others. However, they have tremendous courage and take control in times of crisis, typically saving or helping others before themselves. Ironically, it is during periods of stability that they struggle most to find meaning and purpose, and they may lapse into bouts of inaction.

Born paramedics, firefighters and emergency staff, these people may be drawn to careers in medicine, the police, prisons and the helping professions. They have fine communication skills and make great broadcasters and public relations officers; they excel anywhere they are placed in front of the storm. Their individualism may suit them to design, music, writing, art, drama and film, and they may also be attracted to research, politics, the law and science. Prone to relying on fast food and takeouts, their health would benefit if they learned to cook their food from scratch. **For self-care,** carrying a small rose-quartz crystal encourages them to love themselves more than their work.

Their driven personality can make those born on this day appear aloof. They need to step outside themselves every now and again, and realize there is a whole world out there. This tendency toward self-absorption is highlighted before they hit their mid-fifties. During these years they need to make sure they get in touch with the feelings and concerns of others. It is important for these multitalented, charismatic individuals to understand that they don't need to wait for a crisis to make their mark. Once they learn not to neglect their own emotional needs or to isolate themselves, their destiny is to be a pioneer and blaze their own unique trail.

Potential: Dynamic, individualistic

Dark side: Obsessive, self-absorbed

Tarot card, lucky numbers, day, colors: Strength, 3, 9, Tuesday, all shades of red

Born today: Quentin Tarantino (director); Wilhelm Rontgen (physicist); Mariah Carey (singer)

March 28

The Birthday of Magnificent Remoteness

"I walk alone"

Those born on March 28 tend to be independent loners, but somehow find themselves incredibly popular because of their warm, common-sense approach to life, as well as their morality and generosity. They remain calm and can be detached towers of strength during troubled times when, whether they like it or not, they find themselves offering advice to others. They often have a burning desire to create something special in their chosen field. Despite their serenity, drive and obvious intellectual talents, a lack of self-confidence can prevent them from advancing as high as they deserve.

Born police officers because of their ability to stay calm in a crisis, these people make ideal emergency workers, negotiators, lawyers, and are suited to careers in the military, the police and prisons, as well as in medicine, science, sport, education, social work, business, building and commerce trades. Their creativity may draw them to the arts, architecture, design, photography, music and filmmaking. Prone to reactive depression, they need to identify less with what they do and more with who they are. **For self-care**, every morning when you get ready for work or your day, smile at yourself in the mirror.

Charming, inspirational and popular, these people need privacy, and others should not try to invade or place limits on this, as their remoteness is in many ways the key to their success. They need regular solitude to gather their strength and protect themselves from feeling vulnerable. Although their self-effacing nature is endearing, they should find ways to build their self-esteem. Until they do so, they will doubt their abilities and move forward with difficulty. The best years to build their self-confidence are before their mid-fifties, when they should not settle for second best, sacrificing their personal fulfillment in the process. After the age of 53 the emphasis is on achieving even greater self-expression. They do need regular time away, but whenever they feel ready to rejoin the world, they bring their utterly unique brand of creativity. Their destiny is to motivate others by presenting their magnificent, can-do, highly innovative face to the world.

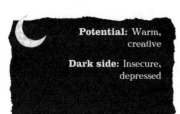

Potential: Warm, creative

Dark side: Insecure, depressed

Tarot card, lucky numbers, days, colors: The Magician, 1, 4, Tuesday, Sunday, red, gold

Born today: Lady Gaga (singer); Julia Stiles (actor); Rick Barry (basketball player)

March 29

The Birthday of the Discerning Presence

"I am a bringer of peace"

is asserting yourself.

The way forward: is to understand that asserting yourself is not rude, but simply ensuring that your valuable contribution is recognized.

Luck maker: Know with absolute certainty that you can succeed, even when things don't go to plan. We tend to get what we expect.

People born on March 29 are highly intuitive and observant. They notice everything going on around them, carefully considering all aspects of a situation before making a decision. This controlled approach to life often proves highly successful. Others may criticize them for being too cautious or for lacking passion, but they have a knack of winning in the end. Polite and sincere, these sensitive, wise and honest people are not driven by personal ambition but by a desire to make a positive difference and to bring harmony. The danger is that their caution can lead to negativity or pessimism; it is important for them not to spiral into depression if people let them down.

Born producers and leaders, these positive and multitalented people are likely to be successful in whatever they choose, but the law, business, education, publishing, computing, engineering, medicine and social reform appeal. If they develop their creative side, they may be drawn to music, dance, photography, art and film production. Being sensitive, they need to eat a healthy diet and avoid foods and drinks high in sugar, salt, additives and preservatives. **For self-care**, wearing, meditating on or surrounding themselves with the color orange will encourage them to be more optimistic.

Those born on this day must understand that human beings are complex and it is better to believe the best of people. Before the age of 51 they need to be especially careful not to sink into cynicism and inflexibility, as there is an emphasis in their life on establishing stability. They like to keep to themselves, but when in the company of others their discerning detached presence has a calming influence, and this quality can thrust them unexpectedly into the limelight. These gentle, loyal and fiercely intelligent individuals, with their own enigmatic purity and beauty, are more than qualified to tightly control the reins of power and assume leadership roles when put in positions of authority. Once they ensure that others do not take them for granted or assume credit for their achievements, their destiny is to inspire, comfort and profoundly influence others with their calmness, courage and deep wisdom.

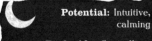

Potential: Intuitive, calming

Dark side: Controlling, cautious

Tarot card, lucky numbers, days, colors: The High Priestess, 2, 5, Tuesday, Monday, red, silver

Born today: John Tyler (US president); Ian Cheng (artist); Elle Macpherson (model)

133

March 30

The Birthday of Irresistible Conviction

is learning to be patient.

The way forward: is to understand that sometimes the best course of action is inaction and biding your time.

Luck maker: Sleep on it. What you can't solve today, you may have a fresh perspective on tomorrow.

"My heart leads the way"

March 30-born are an irresistible combination of dynamic confidence and courage, and touching earnestness and vulnerability. Although they are resilient, they find it hard to hide their disappointment when things don't go to plan, and this contradiction can both antagonize and endear them to people. They are at their happiest when allowed to lose themselves in their personal goals. Others may think them self-absorbed, but there is something sensual and irresistible about them, and, because they are so upbeat, passionate and focused, they often have more than their fair share of admirers and good luck. They can, however, sometimes surrender their natural optimism, so it's important for them to keep positive.

Born designers, these people have the determination and creative potential to achieve success in art, music, design and the entertainment world. Their enjoyment of mental tasks may inspire them to work in teaching, research and writing, while their confidence may lead them to sales, advertising, business and public affairs, and their independence to freelancing or setting up their own business. Stress is their biggest health risk, so they need to ensure that they eat a healthy diet, get plenty of fresh air and exercise, and spend time with loved ones. **For self-care**, wearing, meditating on and surrounding themselves with calming shades of blue and purple will help quell their exuberant fires.

Those born on this day should take the time to unwind, otherwise they run the risk of becoming obsessive at work and isolated in their personal life. They should not neglect their emotional needs between the ages of 20 and 50, during which time they typically focus on acquiring wealth and status. After the age of 50 they may feel a need to exchange ideas; this is when their talents are more likely to gain recognition. As long as they don't allow themselves to become buried by their ambitions or their perfectionist tendencies—and others allow them the freedom to pursue their highly creative vision—they have the potential not just to achieve outstanding success but to provoke feelings of adoration in others. Their destiny is to inspire strong emotions and motivate others with their fearless energy and passion.

Potential: Dynamic, sensual

Dark side: Impatient, perfectionist

Tarot card, lucky numbers, days, colors: The Empress, 3, 6, Tuesday, Thursday, red, purple

Born today: Celine Dion (singer); Vincent van Gogh (painter); Richard Sherman (football player)

March 31

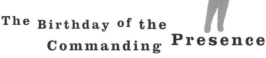

The Birthday of the Commanding Presence

"I set the pace"

Those born on March 31 have a commanding presence, their authority unquestioned. They have little time for small talk but plenty of time for action. There's a calm balance about them that makes them highly valued professionally and personally. They are pragmatic and capable of compromise if life demands it, but if they feel others are overcomplicating things they can be ruthless. They are natural leaders, though feel most comfortable within a team where their contagious energy motivates others. Emotional control is important to them. When they feel overwhelmed by emotions, they may lapse into cynicism or sudden outbursts of temper rather than facing them.

Born business people, they have the determination and flexibility to achieve success in business, politics, education, the military, the police and public service, but their commanding presence serves them well in any field. In their career they should look out for opportunities to travel and make changes and avoid getting into a rut. Health-wise, they should ensure they don't repress their feelings so much that they suffer from stress and depression. **For self-care**, writing down your feelings every day in a journal or diary will encourage you to face and understand rather than avoid your emotions.

Life has a way of forcing these people to get in touch with their feelings, through either the people they meet or the situations they experience. They aren't great risk-takers, as they prefer security to gambling, but it's important for them not to let opportunities to express their talents pass them by. They are most likely to favor a steady approach before the age of 50; during this time they should get out of their comfort zone every now and again. After the age of 50 they become more experimental. Once they learn to listen to their emotions as much as their common sense, these resourceful, realistic, energetic and remarkably influential people are destined for a rare combination of success in every aspect of their lives. Their destiny is to motivate others to work alongside them and follow their energetic example.

Potential: Commanding, determined

Dark side: Ruthless, cynical

Tarot card, lucky numbers, days, colors: The Emperor, 4, 7, Tuesday, Sunday, red, silver

Born today: René Descartes (philosopher); Johann Sebastian Bach (composer); Al Gore (US politician)

April 1

The Birthday of Calm Confidence

"I work with integrity"

April 1-born are far from being April Fools. From an early age they have a mature wisdom and confidence about them. They are dependable, the ones who show up punctually, always giving one hundred percent. Although they have a reputation for being responsible, they are rarely dull, as they have a youthful appeal. Their honesty, calm and earnestness gain them many admirers, but being by nature reserved, they also have a great need for personal reflection and time alone to conjure up their highly original plans. They make excellent leaders, but their motive is never based on ego, as it is the work itself that inspires and fulfills them.

Born teachers with incredible organizational skills, these people make outstanding teachers, managers and guides. They may also be drawn to politics, programming, merchandising, administration, criminology, troubleshooting, and have the creativity to thrive in the media and entertainment worlds, but their outstanding ability to focus on their work assures their success in virtually any field. Regular exercise is essential, as they have a tendency to prefer work that focuses on the mental rather than the physical. **For self-care**, take a few moments to consciously slow down your breathing and find inner calm. Remind yourself when you feel overwhelmed that you are a human being, not a human doing. Learn to simply *be*.

Relationship-wise those born on this day do need to be careful that they don't become isolated workaholics, especially between the ages of 19 and 49, which are the years when they seek security and routine. After the age of 50 they move toward new interests, learning and communication. Their responsible and quietly confident approach to life, and lack of desire to promote themselves—unless thought necessary for the task in hand—is a true joy to behold. Once they have learned to trust and speak their mind, their destiny is to solve problems and see others benefit from their innovative solutions.

April 2

The Birthday of
Utopia

"The future looks awesome"

is to listen to differing viewpoints.

The way forward: is to understand that one of the best ways to win the respect and support of others is to listen to them and make them feel included.

Luck maker: Don't set yourself up for failure by setting unrealistic goals. Accept your limitations and those of others, and value what you know you can realistically achieve.

Those born on April 2 have a youthful, utopian view of the world. They are also compassionate toward those who are suffering and love to debate their visions of a better, kinder future. Their idealism tests the patience of those with a more realistic mindset and they may become so passionate in their convictions that they verge on the fanatical. Their motives can be misunderstood and criticized as naïve, but this is unlikely to deter them. What matters isn't what others think, but their personal vision and being true to their beliefs.

Born movie directors, they have the potential to be excellent designers, artists, filmmakers, actors, writers, or to thrive in any kind of work that gives them a medium to project their idealism or personal vision to others. People-related careers, such as lobbying, public relations, counseling, social reform and charity work, may also appeal. Health-wise, those born on this day need to pay attention to any bodily signs their bodies are sending them, as they tend to live in their daydreams rather than the real world. **For self-care**, make sure your bedroom is a place of peace and calm, and that you avoid screen time at least an hour before bed, as this will help you have the refreshing sleep you need to function at your best.

In relationships these people need to avoid putting potential partners on an unrealistic pedestal. Before the age of 48 their tendency to be uncompromising is heightened, so they should learn to accept differences of opinion, tempering their idealism with realism. After 48 they become more willing to entertain different viewpoints. Once they have learned to use their undoubted power to energize others positively, and to direct their passion to goals that are worthy of them, they have enormous potential to overcome almost any obstacle. Their endearing honesty and determination to see the best in everybody can help even the most cynical believe in undreamed-of possibilities. Their destiny is to inspire and encourage others to realize their full potential, by their example.

Potential: Idealistic, compassionate

Dark side: Fanatical, naïve

Tarot card, lucky numbers, days, colors: The High Priestess, 2, 6, Tuesday, Monday, scarlet, silver

Born today: Émile Zola (author); Marvin Gaye (singer); Michael Fassbender (actor)

April 3

The Birthday of the Keynote Speaker

is to work independently.

The way forward: is to understand that teamwork brings great rewards, but the most fulfilling adventures happen when you strike out on your own.

Luck maker: See rejection not as something to fight or get depressed about but as information you can use to move forward.

"I inspire others"

People born on April 3 are at their happiest and best when they can occupy the key position in their personal and professional lives. It gives them enormous satisfaction to feel indispensable; and with their remarkable creativity and energy, they often are. They like to be where the action is, and life is seldom dull for these people. Warm and generous with excellent communication skills, they thrive on change but can become moody if they are left out of the action. Fortunately, this doesn't happen often, since people usually depend on them. The only danger is that they become too dependent on them, which can create frustrations when they want to change direction.

Born promoters, they have the persuasive powers to make great salespeople, politicians, advertisers, promoters, motivational speakers and actors, but they have the potential to achieve success in any field. Careers that involve travel, variety and adventure, such as journalism, aviation, business, research, archaeology and tourism may also appeal. They need to make sure they don't take their own health for granted in their concern for the wellbeing of others. **For self-care**, schedule regular quiet time, when you switch off your phone and are alone. Read a good book, daydream or relax in a bath. Doesn't matter what you do, just spend time in solitude.

In love, these people need to make sure they retain their sense of independence. Highly intuitive, if a little unrealistic at times, they have change as a constant theme in their lives, especially from their mid-forties onward, when the emphasis is on forging new directions. The challenge offered by change is essential for their personal growth because staying in one role limits the development of their vision. They make great team leaders because they like to feel needed, and as long as they learn to respect the viewpoints of others and not to become oversensitive when they encounter criticism, their ability to energize others toward a common goal is second to none. Their destiny is to promote a worthy cause.

Potential: Warm, generous

Dark side: Unrealistic, moody

Tarot card, lucky numbers, days, colors: The Empress, 3, 7, Tuesday, Thursday, scarlet, green

Born today: Jane Goodall (primatologist); Charles Wilkes (explorer); Eddie Murphy (actor)

April 4

The Birthday of the Catalyst

"The best is yet to come"

April 4-born are catalysts—impacting the lives of others in a profound and often positive way as they have strong humanitarian leanings. Their creative energy is explosive, and both personally and professionally they have little trouble initiating projects and inspiring others to join their cause, hurling their considerable energy and self-confidence into a project. Initiators, they have great courage and think nothing of striking out in a new direction. This flexible approach gives them huge potential for success. They do tend to leap onto the next project before the previous one has been completed, and, to find true fulfillment, they need to see things through to the end. If they don't slow down, they risk burnout and the loss of their exceptional energy.

Born initiators, once they have tapped into their natural organizational skills, they have great potential for success in business, entrepreneurship, management, promotion, design, production, architecture and finance, as well as the literary and performing arts, and social reform. Their impulsiveness is the greatest risk to their emotional and physical health and they need to consider the consequences of their actions before leaping right in. **For self-care**, mind–body techniques, such as deep breathing, meditation, mindfulness, as well as tai chi and yoga, all help you slow down and find inner calm.

Others admire those born on this day, but may have trouble keeping up with their constant shifts of direction. These people, then, may end up alone if their impulsive tendencies become too unreliable, and they should surround themselves with supportive people who can gently warn them when they are heading off course. Until the age of 46 there is a positive emphasis on stability, which they should capitalize on, and after that they become more interested in new ideas. It's important that they have established sufficient financial security before exploring any new interests.

Once they have learned that perseverance and self-discipline, along with a realistic approach, are the keys to their success, the energy of these people is spellbinding. The world would be a less colorful place without them. Their destiny is to fight for the rights and the wellbeing of others.

Potential: Exciting, enthusiastic

Dark side: Impulsive, unreliable

Tarot card, lucky numbers, days, colors: The Emperor, 4, 8, Tuesday, Sunday, scarlet, blue

Born today: Robert Downey Jr. (actor); Maya Angelou (poet); Muddy Waters (musician)

April 5

The Birthday of the Athlete

The life lesson:

is learning to unwind.

The way forward: is to understand that time out isn't time wasted but time gained, as you will return refreshed.

Luck maker: Learn the art of compromise to help get others on your side.

"Only the best will do"

Those born on April 5 don't tend to seek out success, but success often finds them anyway. Like athletes totally dedicated to their sport, their goal is to constantly strive for their personal best. They tend to value work above all else, but, because they are highly principled, their success is never at the expense of others. They need to feel that they deserve their success, and given the fact that they are blessed with both the creativity to inspire others and the determination to see things through, they have great potential to succeed. They dislike and try to avoid conflict, but are not pushovers. Others may be surprised at their stubborn bluntness, when criticized.

Born pioneers and sports stars, these people excel in careers that test them, such as sports, music, dance, art, theater, social-media influencing, and entertainment. They may also set up their own business or be drawn to the law, civil service, politics, life-coaching or education, but they have the organizational skills to succeed in any career. Since they tend to give so much of themselves to work, they need to make sure they don't take their health for granted. **For self-care**, put a piece of your favorite relaxing music on, close your eyes and listen to whatever whispers from your intuition come to mind.

Learning to open up in their relationships is a challenge for those born on this day. Their stubbornness is highlighted before their mid-forties, during which time there is an emphasis in their life on security, but, after that, they become more interested in change and this can be an extremely positive period. Natural leaders, because they set high standards, they should be careful that they don't become too perfectionist and demanding of themselves and others. They have the determination to overcome even the most frustrating of obstacles and, even though they don't seek or even realize it, they utilize their willpower to take them all the way to the top. Once they learn to be more flexible in their goals and opinions, their destiny is to motivate and inspire others, by their own example, to be the best that they can be.

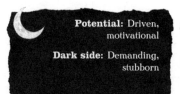

Potential: Driven, motivational

Dark side: Demanding, stubborn

Tarot card, lucky numbers, day, colors: The Hierophant, 5, 9, Tuesday, scarlet, orange

Born today: Joseph Lister (surgeon); Pharrell Williams (musician); Spencer Tracy (actor)

April 6

The Birthday of Irresistible Curiosity

"My curiosity is my courage"

The life lesson: is trusting yourself.

The way forward: is to understand that unless you trust yourself, you can't expect others to trust you either.

Luck maker: The importance of being earnest. Centering your life around anything but positive values eventually backfires and leads to unhappiness.

People born on April 6 have charisma and a wild-eyed excitement about them. They are ruled by an irresistible curiosity about everyone and everything, their minds forever open to new and better ways of doing things. They have limitless energy and the ability to visualize undreamed-of possibilities. Multitalented, flexible and with an ability to laugh at themselves, it's easy to see why they seem destined for great success, but also why some fail to realize their full potential. Lack of discrimination is their problem and their openness may lead them down many wrong paths, attracting those who haven't got their best interests at heart.

Born investigators, these gifted people have a knack for finding innovative solutions and make great troubleshooters, home-improvement experts, planners and organizers at work, and event organizers. They are also drawn to science, detective work, research, education, philosophy, the law, sales, diplomacy, negotiation, public relations, charity work, politics, acting, music and any career with plenty of opportunity to learn. They need to make sure that their love of experimenting does not extend to addictive foods or substances. **For self-care**, protect your eyes and posture. When spending long hours reading or learning, be sure to check your posture and give your eyes regular breaks from screens.

Those born on this day enjoy sexual adventures and it may take a while for them to avoid superficial relationships and commit emotionally. It is important for them to learn to trust their intuition more and to beware of giving too much of themselves too soon. Before their mid-forties they may search for stability, and this is the ideal time to develop their self-confidence and sense of direction so that they are not too easily led astray. After the age of 45 they may concentrate on expanding their interests. As long as they can get in touch with their own feelings and become more discriminating, they have the potential to be great innovators and to lead others to previously uncharted areas. Their destiny is to discover as yet unknown truths.

Potential: Charismatic, original

Dark side: Gullible, superficial

Tarot card, lucky numbers, days, colors: The Lovers, 1, 6, Tuesday, Friday, scarlet, green

Born today: Raphael (painter); James Watson (biologist); Paul Rudd (actor)

April 7

The Birthday of Intensity

"My life has purpose"

April 7-born are bold idealists and when they commit to someone or something they burn with an extreme intensity. They feel there must be a deeper or spiritual meaning to their lives, but they can rush into what they believe is their destiny only to find that they lose interest or it wasn't really for them. Their vibrant, creative personality inspires them to progress, but when things don't go their way they can suddenly erupt into bouts of rage and rebellion, alienating others in the process.

Born interviewers, with a talent for initiating progress, they have great communication skills that suit the law, teaching, writing, journalism, acting, directing and online influencing, but they may also be drawn to humanitarian reforms or the world of business, preferably working for themselves. They have great potential for success in any career they choose as long as they learn to stay calm in a crisis. Since they lack the patience for being unwell, prevention through self-care really is their best medicine. **For self-care**, wearing, meditating on and surrounding yourself with calming shades of blue will help when you need to cool down and do some logical thinking.

These people struggle to adjust when the early intensity of relationships needs to evolve to commitment. To have the ability and drive to get where they want to in life, they must learn to adopt a more considered and calmer approach in all areas of their lives. Rebellion is likely a feature of their youth, but before the age of 43 they have opportunities to adopt a calmer approach. After 44 they have a greater desire to learn new skills. If by this age they have learned the importance of finding the middle way, they are likely to come into their own. Their positive expectations of happiness are often rewarded, and although it may take a while for them to find their one true purpose, when they do find it they discover that the waiting was worthwhile. Their destiny is to make their bold dreams and the dreams of others a reality.

Potential: Visionary, vibrant

Dark side: Rebellious, impatient

Tarot card, lucky numbers, days, colors: The Chariot, 2, 7, Tuesday, Monday, scarlet, sea green

Born today: William Wordsworth (poet); Russell Crowe (actor); Billie Holiday (singer)

April 8

The Birthday of Noble Intention

"I am here to help"

Those born on April 8 have a passionate sense of right and wrong. Their intentions are noble and motivated by a concern for those who haven't been given a chance to develop their potential. The admiration of others is not their main concern; what matters to them is the wellbeing of others. Despite their warmth and compassion, they see things in black and white, and run the risk of becoming intolerant. They need to control their impulses and find more effective ways of getting their point across. They can appear detached, but are a tower of strength in a crisis. Beneath their noble exterior lie fears of inadequacy that can manifest in self-sacrificing behavior, but if they can overcome these fears, their enormous determination and sharp intelligence can help them achieve almost anything.

Born reformers, they are daring and original and well suited to careers in the law, the military, politics, sports, and humanitarian and social reform. As natural psychologists they may be drawn to healing, counseling, life-coaching, writing, journalism, drama, music and art. Often more concerned about the health of others than their own, they need to put their health and wellbeing first, otherwise they are prone to stress. **For self-care**, carry a small rose-quartz crystal to encourage yourself to take better care of your heart.

These people easily attract admirers, but there is something untouchable about them. When in relationships they need to be less insecure and let those they love have their freedom. Before the age of 42 they are keen on establishing stability, but after that their focus is on new interests and this is when their self-confidence blooms. Their passion to succeed is strong but, typically, not selfish, as they express their uniqueness through helping others in some way. This is what gives these enigmatic but lovely people the potential to bring harmony to the world. Once they have learned to become neither too intolerant of others nor too self-sacrificing, their destiny is to turn their noble intentions into reality and become righters of wrongs.

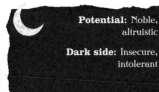

Potential: Noble, altruistic

Dark side: Insecure, intolerant

Tarot card, lucky numbers, days, colors: Strength, 3, 8, Tuesday, Saturday, dark blue and red

Born today: Barbara Kingsolver (author); Katee Sackhoff and Robin Wright (actors)

April 9

The Birthday of the Whirlwind

The life lesson:

is knowing when to stop.

The way forward: is to understand that stopping when you still want more keeps desire and motivation alive; over-indulgence kills it.

Luck maker: Surround yourself with people who challenge rather than agree with you, because alternative viewpoints increase the chances of success.

"I am riding high"

People born on April 9 live and love like a whirlwind, possessing an insatiable appetite for both work and the pleasures of life. Blessed with terrific stamina, originality and single-mindedness, they have great potential to achieve their ambitions. Professionally, they prefer to take the lead and can be accurate predictors of social trends with the talent to turn their ideas into reality and, by so doing, enrich the lives of others as well as their own. They are charming, but can also be outspoken and blunt with the need to win every argument. They also don't take kindly to criticism, regarding any such comment as a form of betrayal.

Born freedom fighters, they have the pioneering spirit, courage and leadership skills to excel in any career. They are drawn to business, the military, engineering, politics, social reform, management, online influencing and entrepreneurship, as well as music, art, drama and retail. Their fondness for pushing the limits can lead to physical over-indulgences and excess, and they need to learn the importance of moderation in all things. **For self-care**, find balance. If you are not feeling your best, ask yourself if you have taken good care of your body, mind, heart and soul today.

These people can be erratic and extreme, but their drive and passion can carry others along in a whirlwind of enthusiasm. There's little time for quiet reflection in their relationships, though there will be plenty of excitement. Until the age of 41 they may concentrate on material stability and it is important they base their lives around positive, rather than negative, values. After the age of 41 they may broaden their horizons, becoming more interested in psychological growth. At any age, life doesn't pause for them—it's an action-packed adventure with many surprises and opportunities. If they can put these opportunities to good use and temper their impulses, their destiny is to organize their original ideas and put them to progressive and good use.

Potential: Progressive, energetic

Dark side: Intolerant, excessive

Tarot card, lucky numbers, day, colors: The Hermit, 4, 9, Tuesday, scarlet, orange

Born today: Isambard Kingdom Brunel (engineer); Gregory Pincus (biologist); Cynthia Nixon (actor)

April 10

The Birthday of the Shrewd Hero or Heroine

"Life is my rollercoaster"

The life lesson:

is patience.

The way forward: is to understand that the only power that is real is in the now, and fully experiencing the present is the most fulfilling way to live.

Luck maker: Discuss your problems with those you trust. Without the emotional fulfillment of close relationships, external achievements lose their magic.

April 10-born tend to be dazzling individuals who love to take risks. Their life tends to be a rollercoaster, but they are not reckless. They are shrewd action heroes and heroines. Those who don't know them well may be alarmed by their confidently radical approach, but behind the scenes they always consider everything. This combination of pragmatism and adventure, combined with intelligence and intense energy, bodes well for success. Restless and action-orientated, they tend to race through life as if they are afraid of missing out on something.

Born stunts people, they excel in careers that involve an element of risk, such as banking, stock-market trading, forecasting, advertising, sales, marketing, the law, acting and the entertainment world, but they may also choose to strike out on their own and set up their own business. Health-wise it is essential they learn to unwind more because they are prone to workaholism and, if they don't know how to relax, they may be prone to mood swings, stress and depression. **For self-care**, mind–body therapies such as meditation, mindfulness, yoga and tai chi, and spending more time in nature, encourage inner calm and restraint.

Naturally charming, the nonconformist perspective of these people often attracts admirers. They can be detached and have anxiety issues in their relationships, which indicates a fear of rejection, and they need to learn to connect with their feelings, experiencing the joys of intimacy with others. Until the age of 40 they may concentrate on establishing stability, but after this age they want to learn new skills. Since they find it easier to compete than to cooperate, they are amazing self-starters with real leadership potential. Once they are able to balance their restlessness with patience, there is no doubt that these warriors, with their ability to plan and complete a project, will go far. Their destiny is to encourage others to step outside their comfort zone—the place where all the most exciting action happens.

Potential: Daring, dedicated

Dark side: Restless, detached

Tarot card, lucky numbers, days, colors: The Wheel of Fortune, 1, 5, Tuesday, Sunday, scarlet, yellows

Born today: Steven Seagal and Daisy Ridley (actors); John Madden (sports commentator)

April 11

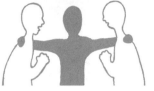

The Birthday of the Mediator

"I see the connecting thread"

is responding to
the needs of loved
ones.

*The way
forward:* is
to understand
that shirking
emotional
responsibilities
for work or more
stimulating
pursuits does not
bring you the
fulfillment you
crave.

Luck maker:
Don't over-
commit: being
selective in what
you choose to do
will bring clarity
of mind and
increased energy
and focus.

Those born on April 11 are warm-hearted, assertive individuals able to see and solve problems from both an emotional and a practical viewpoint, which makes them great diplomats. They can bring even the most opposing opinions into line with great tact. Optimistic, these people are often the first to volunteer to help a just cause and devote their formidable interpersonal skills and tenacity to creating a progressive plan that more often than not succeeds. They have leadership potential, but prefer to be a part rather than a focus of the action. Ideas rather than image matter more to them, as does finding common ground.

Born judges, they are suited to careers that serve the common good such as the law, politics, administration, negotiation, translation, diplomacy, influencing, lobbying, research, technology, science and the clergy, and they also make great teachers, counselors, psychologists and social workers. They have the superior communication skills to succeed in business, sales, music, media, social reform, marketing and management. They have a perfectionist tendency to push themselves too hard, especially mentally, so learning to switch off regularly and think about nothing in particular is key. **For self-care**, you would benefit enormously from regular walks in nature or green spaces to bring you inner peace and connect with the magical workings of the natural world.

These people are sociable and never short of admirers but, unfortunately, aren't always diplomatic in their private lives, so they can be unresponsive to the needs of those closest to them. Around the age of 40 they are likely to focus their energies less on financial security and popularity, and more on loved ones. Once they have learned greater flexibility and emotional openness, they can use their powers of persuasion, tenacity and clear-sightedness to champion justice and teamwork, creating a more harmonious world. Their destiny is to enlist the support of others for their progressive ideals.

Potential: Diplomatic, intelligent

Dark side: Perfectionist, impersonal

Tarot card, lucky numbers, days, colors: Justice, 2, 6, Tuesday, Monday, scarlet, silver

Born today: Percy Lavon Julian (chemist); Ethel Kennedy (human rights campaigner); Joss Stone (singer)

April 12

The Birthday of the Enigmatic Interviewer

"I learn and I learn"

People born on April 12 find that others love to listen to them. They have the wit and the ability to get others to open up to them, and even laugh at their own insecurities. Their inquisitive minds are forever on the alert, looking out for the latest news or research to inform or entertain. Keen observers, they prize knowledge above all else and love to share publicly what they have learned. There is a danger that they can become critical in the process or heavily influenced by the opinions of others; it is important for them to stay open-minded, and not become dogmatic.

Born investigative journalists, they have super communication skills and excel in careers involving reporting, research, presentation, politics, engineering and the arts. Their progressive humanitarianism may draw them to public relations, social reform, online influencing, gaming, science, healing, business and the law. Regular exercise, along with sufficient sleep, is essential; although their health is generally sound, they should never take it for granted. **For self-care**, spending time alone is essential, not with a book or screen but just with yourself, so you can check in with the wisdom of your intuition.

These people find it hard to share their feelings, being more comfortable in the role of interviewer. To avoid loneliness, they need to open up more about themselves to loved ones. They may spend a great deal of their early adult life wandering from experience to experience, place to place, in search of a satisfying profession, but, fortunately, this trial-and-error approach works because they regard every experience—even a disappointing one—as a learning opportunity. Then, in their forties, they typically find a purpose that fully utilizes their vast store of knowledge and experience. Getting to know who they are and what they, not others, think about things is central to their success. When they are in touch with their own feelings, they can better relate to, inform and motivate others. Their destiny is to invigorate and inspire others with their originality and sparkling optimism.

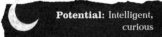

Potential: Intelligent, curious

Dark side: Judgmental, elusive

Tarot card, lucky numbers, days, colors: The Hanged Man, 3, 7, Tuesday, Thursday, red, purple

Born today: Herbie Hancock (musician); David Letterman (TV host); Saoirse Ronan (actor)

April 13

The Birthday of the Reformer

"There is always room for improvement"

April 13-born are natural reformers, tirelessly making improvements. They have stacks of brilliant ideas and, although some might think them eccentric, their unusual approach to problem-solving is inspired. They excel at this and coming up with better ways of doing things. Mental stimulation is essential and they get easily bored and restless, with a tendency to fidget if they are not challenged. Their greatest satisfaction comes from moving humanity forward, or from being involved in projects that benefit others. They can be prone to insecurity about themselves, often feeling the need to withdraw from scrutiny, especially when working on a project, and, as a result, can be labeled reclusive or, in extreme cases, odd.

Born politicians, they are attracted to careers that can translate their reforming vision into reality, such as politics, the law, the military, medicine, healing, science and psychology, as well as music, writing and art. Careers that offer them opportunities to manage, lead or pioneer in some way also suit. They need to resist the tendency to withdraw into escapism when their feelings overwhelm them. Regular exercise is a great way for them to become more externally focused. **For self-care**, wearing, meditating on and surrounding themselves with the color orange will encourage them to feel more optimistic and outgoing.

These people don't actively seek out the company of others, because they are essentially private, preferring to make their mark through their work, but they do derive great satisfaction from the support of a few close and supportive companions. Their drive to seek new challenges is further highlighted after the age of 37, when their focus changes from that of material stability to intellectual curiosity. Although sensitive, with a need for privacy, when the time feels right they can overcome any fear or hesitation and step out with boldness, often breaking new ground in the process. Once they learn to turn rejection and criticism into resolve and learning, their destiny is to turn their pioneering and progressive vision into reality.

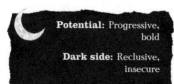

Potential: Progressive, bold

Dark side: Reclusive, insecure

Tarot card, lucky numbers, days, colors: Death, 4, 8, Tuesday, Sunday, scarlet, violet

Born today: Garry Kasparov (chess champion); Thomas Jefferson (US president); Samuel Beckett (playwright)

April 14

The Birthday of Respect

"My honor is my life"

Those born on April 14 have fantastic communication skills. Whatever situation or line of work they find themselves in, others tend to listen to and respect them. Indeed, the respect of others matters greatly to these people, as they themselves have great respect for others and especially for tradition and the past. They often prefer conservative methods to more radical ones. They like to take the lead but, despite this autocratic tendency, they are intuitive, often quick to adjust their behavior accordingly. Their respectful attitude toward others serves them well, their success rarely being resented.

Born writers, these people excel in all careers that utilize their superior communication skills, such as writing, social media, journalism, the media, teaching, academia, entertainment, politics, advertising, the law, acting and the arts. Their great people skills may draw them to tourism, public relations, museum work, marketing, the leisure industry and all kinds of business. They can be overly concerned with their appearance and need to understand that the best beauty treatment is to avoid yo-yo dieting by eating healthily and exercising regularly. **For self-care**, learn something new. Make a point of researching something or someone you know nothing about. This will add to your store of knowledge and open your mind to new possibilities.

Sensitive souls, those born on this day are at their happiest when they feel supported in their personal life. It is therefore important for them not to ignore the needs of those closest to them. Until the age of 36 they concentrate on material security, but after that they enter a period of increased productivity during which they may use their communication talents to become a voice for an organization. Even though they suffer from bouts of uncertainty—manifested in their perfectionist obsession with details and tendency to play it safe—they have what it takes to achieve remarkable things. Once they have learned to acknowledge the contributions of others and take the odd risk or two, their destiny is to follow in the honorable footsteps of the greats before them.

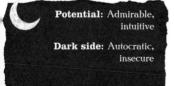

Potential: Admirable, intuitive

Dark side: Autocratic, insecure

Tarot card, lucky numbers, days, colors: Temperance, 5, 9, Tuesday, Wednesday, scarlet, sky blue

Born today: Arnold Toynbee (historian); John Gielgud and Julie Christie (actors)

April 15

The Birthday of the Sharp Intellect

"My life is a work of art"

People born on April 15 are sensitive and charismatic, but also ambitious and powerful. The key to understanding their apparent contradictions is their sharp intellect and ability to respond insightfully to almost any argument. Their insight can also make them super-sensitive to what is going on around them and they may take their skills of observation to extremes. This can cause friction in their interactions with others, and also personal insecurity, because they may observe something out of context and draw the incorrect conclusions. They may also take themselves and everyone else a little too seriously, forgetting the importance of simply having fun. On the plus side, these are observant people who can detect hidden insights and their compassion means others often turn to them for support and advice.

Born designers, they are multitalented and may have several career changes. Their creativity makes them great artists, gardeners, beauticians, decorators and chefs. They may also be drawn to teaching, acting, the law and research, but, whatever career they choose, they will pioneer projects. Health-wise, laughter is their best medicine and they need to give themselves plenty of opportunities to have fun, to avoid being overly serious in all aspects of their lives. **For self-care**, wearing, meditating on and surrounding yourself with shades of orange will increase feelings of spontaneity, warmth and enjoyment.

In relationships they need to make sure there is a balance between giving and taking, because they tend to give too much of their power away to others. Their ability to see life in broad rather than specific terms may be regarded by others as unrealistic and, until the age of 35, they concentrate more on practical considerations. After that they communicate more effectively and enjoy mental exploration—these are the years when they really come into their own. If they can learn to channel their rare and brilliant combination of intense creativity and intellectual tenacity into a direction that others find acceptable, they can make their unique mark on the world. Their destiny is to become truly inspirational figures.

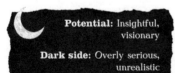

Potential: Insightful, visionary

Dark side: Overly serious, unrealistic

Tarot card, lucky numbers, days, colors: The Devil, 1, 6, Tuesday, Friday, scarlet, lime

Born today: Emma Thompson and Emma Watson (actors); Leonhard Euler (mathematician); Leonardo da Vinci (artist and inventor)

April 16

The Birthday of the Truth Seeker

"Always look on the bright side"

April 16-born seek the truth to life's mysteries. They are visionaries who have the determination to turn dreams into reality. Relentlessly charming, they know how to make people smile and want to make the world a happier place. Even though they search for the truth through humor, they are not superficial. They have a deep awareness of life's darkness but also the insight to understand that humor is often the most cathartic response. This can make their contribution invaluable, as it helps lighten the load, but it can also work against them. Instead of facing situations that need to be resolved, they sidestep conflict with levity, and this can lead to hidden tension.

Born comedians, they bring a lightness of touch wherever they go and make intriguing entertainers, tour guides, actors, clowns, writers, artists, designers, pilots and architects. Their organizational ability may draw them to science, technology, the law, medicine, gaming and research, and their love of action to travel and sport. Health-wise, they tend to overindulge in everything they enjoy, easily slipping into irresponsible behavior, so they need to practice moderation. **For self-care**, practice meditation to help you turn your gaze from externals and other people, and realize that happiness comes from within.

In relationships those born on this day can be overly idealistic and generous, others often taking advantage of them, so they need to set boundaries. Until the age of 34 they focus on building secure foundations, but after that age they have a greater interest in strengthening relationships. This is positive, as becoming more aware of the dreams of others—and not just their own—aids their personal growth. Once they strike a healthy balance between their inner and outer selves, others will admire them not only for their lightness of spirit but also for their absolute conviction that it really is a wonderful life. Their destiny is to realize their dreams in a way that engages as well as motivates others to similarly look on the bright side of life.

April 17

The Birthday of Willpower

"I mean business"

The life lesson:

is opening up to others.

The way forward: is to understand that everyone, even those with the strongest self-control, has times when they feel vulnerable and in need of support.

Luck maker: Replace self-judgment with self-acceptance. The next time you judge yourself negatively, stop and forgive yourself.

Those born on April 17 are ambitious, opportunistic individuals with the willpower and resilience to bounce right back from setbacks. They know their own mind, having a clear idea of where they are going and how to get there, and have a talent for spotting opportunities, not just for themselves, but for others. Their quiet, forceful intensity and conviction gives them an air of importance and the ability to get others on their side. Although it can seem as if they were born to be successful, they work extremely hard and do whatever it takes to make their mark. They thrive on challenge and, in the process, make either loyal friends or resentful enemies.

Born politicians with a desire to see justice done, they will find that careers in the law, the military, the police and humanitarian fields appeal, but their organization and discipline may draw them to administration, business, accounting and banking. Some may prefer to be self-employed or to express their ideals in music, design or the arts. They can often feel lonely and misunderstood, and need to avoid seeking comfort in either selfish materialistic addictions or obsessive behavior. **For self-care**, regular exercise, in particular brisk walking or dancing, encourages them to be more sociable and spontaneous, and helps release emotional tension.

These people are prone to mood swings and like to be alone when dark moments are upon them. This strategy benefits them professionally though not personally, as not sharing limits the depth of close bonds. They have a tendency to see everyone and everything as either good or bad and need to appreciate the complexity of life and relationships. Until the age of 33 they strive for security and certainty, but after that age they do move toward embracing a more flexible worldview. It is important for them to ensure that their amazing willpower does not make them too judgmental or serious. Once they inject a little light-heartedness into their lives, they discover that their authority isn't weakened but strengthened, and that wherever their dreams take them, others gladly follow. Their destiny is to become a fine leader.

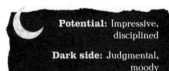

Potential: Impressive, disciplined

Dark side: Judgmental, moody

Tarot card, lucky numbers, days, colors: The Star, 3, 8, Tuesday, Saturday, scarlet, green

Born today: Sirimavo Bandaranaike (Sri Lankan prime minister); Jennifer Garner (actor); J. P. Morgan (banker)

April 18

The Birthday of Dignity

"Things can only get better"

People born on April 18 are influential people with boundless energy and conviction. Often taking the lead in conversations or projects, and with sympathy for the underdog, they come across as bold, hard-working and dignified. Sometimes their standards are so high they set themselves up for frustration, which may erupt in sudden outbursts of temper or, even worse, disdain. They are concerned about how they appear to others, and, craving the recognition and praise of others, they don't take criticism well.

Born philanthropists, they thrive in careers that involve justice or bringing improvements to people's lives, such as social reform, charity work, humanitarian concerns, the law, the military, politics, the police, public services or the healing and caring professions. They may also share their progressive ideas in the arts, tourism, writing, commenting and online influencing. They are at their healthiest and happiest when their lifestyle is structured, and need to make sure their daily routines are regular, and that they go to bed and rise early at the same times each day. **For self-care**, make your bed when you get up every morning. This sets the right tone of self-discipline and order for the rest of the day.

In their relationships those born on this day enjoy the thrill of the chase and are not excited by people who don't challenge them intellectually. They need to be careful that they don't become extreme, fanatical or strongly influenced by authority figures, especially before the age of 32. After the age of 33 they become flexible and independent. Around the age of 62 there is another important shift, which accentuates their emotional needs, home and friends. Despite the seriousness of their ideals, they can be deliberately provocative at times and should never seek to repress that lighter spirit. When they become more spontaneous in their words and deeds, they have the potential to earn the respect, loyalty and affection of others. Their destination is to raise standards and achieve both their personal and humanitarian ambitions.

Potential: Influential, compassionate

Dark side: Extreme, unpredictable

Tarot card, lucky numbers, day, colors: The Moon, 4, 9, Tuesday, scarlet, orange

Born today: Ardito Desio (explorer); David Tennant (actor); Conan O'Brien (TV host)

April 19

The Birthday of Magnetic Self-sufficiency

"I alone can do this"

is accepting help from others.

The way forward: is to understand that no person is an island, and personal and professional relationships thrive when there is a balance between giving and taking.

Luck maker: Network and delegate more. Keep connections with others alive as luck often comes through other people.

April 19-born often possess faith in themselves. Much of their confidence is gained through their experience of victory and lessons learned from defeat. Strongly competitive, they are not interested in anything that doesn't seriously challenge them, and because they have the ability to turn weaknesses into strengths, they can rise to the very top. Nothing gives them more satisfaction than knowing that they have made their own success happen, and their poise makes them natural leaders. Although career-focused, they are rarely materialistic. Their goal is not wealth or status but to be self-sufficient, as for them dependency is weakness. Learning to accept any type of support is difficult, but reaching out to others helps their personal development.

Born freelancers, their people and persuasive skills suit them to careers in public relations, advertising, the law, politics and management, while their creativity may also draw them to journalism, technology, programming, entertainment, fashion, art and design. Self-starters, working for themselves is ideal. Their idealism yearns to benefit others, so they may thrive in medicine, teaching, charity work or work that serves the greater good. Regular exercise and participating in sports provide a healthy outlet for their competitive instinct. **For self-care**, give both yourself and someone you care about a heart-shaped crystal or stone as a reminder of the importance of the loving bonds in your lives.

These people often have irresistible sex appeal, and once they decide they want someone (or something), they tend to get their way. They need to learn to step back now and again, and let others take the lead. Until the age of 31 there is an emphasis on routine in their life and they need to be careful not to be over-controlling or to ignore the feelings of others. After the age of 32, however, they may widen their interests, placing more emphasis on spontaneity, and this period is extremely productive. Once they have learned to listen more and control less, their stamina, intelligence and personal magnetism can help them succeed in virtually anything. Their destiny is to introduce self-sufficient, smooth-running methods and systems that truly improve the lives of others.

Potential: Magnetic, independent

Dark side: Isolated, controlling

Tarot card, lucky numbers, days, colors: The Sun, 1, 5, Tuesday, Sunday, scarlet, gold

Born today: Kate Hudson (actor); Maria Sharapova (tennis player); Roger Sherman (US founding father)

TAURUS

THE BULL (APRIL 20–MAY 20)

❋ **Element:** Earth

❋ **Ruling planet:** Venus, the lover

❋ **Tarot card:** The Hierophant (determination)

❋ **Lucky numbers:** 2, 6

❋ **Favorable colors:** Green, pink, pale blue

❋ **Driving force:** Security

❋ **Personal statement:** I have what I need

❋ **Chinese astrology counterpart:** The Snake

Taureans tend to be reliable, hard-working and determined people, but if they are to reach their considerable potential for success in life, they need personal security. They must feel emotionally and financially secure before anything else. They are blessed with considerable practical skills and common sense, but this can sometimes be coupled with lack of flexibility and a change- and risk-averse approach to life. They often love to surround themselves with beautiful things, not only to remind themselves and others that they are progressing in the world, but also to draw attention to their softer, gentler, more creative and sensual side.

Personality potential

People born under the sun sign Taurus are typically strong, resilient and determined. On a surface level these may at first appear to be traditional masculine qualities, but it is important to point out that Taurus is ruled by Venus, the planet of harmony, love and beauty. This means that Taureans can be a delightful combination of strength and softness, dynamism and compassion, who work long and hard but who also know how to enjoy the fruits of their success. A Taurean will give his or her all to a project, but when necessary they really know how to switch off, unwind and take pleasure in what they have achieved.

The Taurean mind is methodical, careful and decisive, and they use their powerful minds to quietly and carefully build themselves both a fulfilling career and a meaningful life. **For a Taurean, if something is worth doing, it's worth doing properly. Shortcuts are never their style.** They like to think things through carefully, take their time to make decisions and pay very close attention to the details; as a result, the solutions they come up with are often practical and creative. Their most irresistible characteristic is perhaps their natural charm, which they express in different ways. Taureans often have deeply calming and reassuring speaking voices and will always find time to encourage those in need of support. They are especially good at offering practical and common-sense advice, and will work hard to make sure their living and working environments are harmonious. Being surrounded by loving family, close friends and good food is one of their favorite things. They also have a side to them that appreciates the arts and beauty, and the finer things in life.

> **For a Taurean, if something is worth doing, it's worth doing properly. Shortcuts are never their style.**

Personal integrity matters a great deal to the resilient people born under this sun sign. They can be relied upon to do the right thing and to see things through to the end, no matter what obstacles or setbacks they encounter along the way. Although they are loyal, trustworthy and reliable people, this does not mean they are dull. Once you get to know them you will find that, complementing their tenacity, perseverance and dependability, there is an endearing, earthy charm and a surprising creativity; these qualities can attract countless admirers and success into their life.

Personality pitfalls

Taurus is the first earth sign of the zodiac and, like the Earth herself, these people can be stubborn, unforgiving and harsh.

A more flexible approach to life would certainly benefit them. They possess a distinct reluctance to take risks or try anything new, and they can also be guilty of self-indulgence and superficiality in their relentless pursuit of earthly pleasures.

Although Taureans often have an air of calm and a certain authority about them, they sometimes lack confidence in themselves; this can make them appear indecisive and lazy. Perhaps the most unattractive aspect of the Taurean character, however, is their possessiveness. Their loved ones are cherished and admired, but they are often regarded as possessions or property without free will of their own. Add to this an incredibly stubborn streak that makes it hard for Taureans to forget and virtually impossible for them to forgive, and you have a person with selfish, at times bullish, immovable tendencies.

Their bouts of low self-esteem, possessiveness and jealousy often stem from their overwhelming need to feel secure. If their sense of ownership—whether this be of a person, friend, lover, possession or project—is threatened, their fury may explode in a blind rage. Just as this fury has taken a long time to build up, it will also take a long time to subside, and, like an erupting volcano, it will leave a trail of devastation in its wake.

Symbol

The Taurean symbol is the bull. Conjure up in your mind an image of a bull in a rage and you will recognize that this is an alarming sight. The bull can put up with or turn a blind eye to a lot of goading and tormenting—perhaps more than any other sign can stand—but there will come a time when this strong animal stops, turns around and wreaks indiscriminate devastation and destruction on anyone or anything in its path.

Darkest secret

The greatest fear of the Taurean is not having enough funds in the bank to keep up appearances. This is not necessarily because money is their only motivation in life, but because so much of their personal identity is tied up with being able to surround (protect) themselves with material possessions. External or outward signs of success matter a great deal to Taureans.

Love

Those born under the warm sun of Taurus are among the most sensual lovers of the zodiac; they adore cuddling, love-making and physical signs of affection. They can be wonderfully passionate, loyal and romantic lovers. However, when it comes to the choice of a long-term partner, they tend to be methodical in their approach. There may often be a lengthy engagement period, for example, during which they test the waters. The reason for their hesitation is that a long-term successful relationship is the greatest deal to them and they want to do all they can to make sure they make the right choice. To thrive they need to have harmony in their relationships.

Emotional security is vital, and if that is threatened in any way their possessiveness and jealously will kick in and gradually build up until they explode in sudden flashes of temper that can shake the foundations of any relationship. However, Taureans will do everything in their power to avoid getting to this point, and in the great majority of circumstances they are loving, kind, respectful and generous with their affections and their finances.

Once Taureans have committed themselves to a relationship, there can be no doubt of their loyalty and devotion, but they do need to be careful that this devotion does not turn into complacency, and that routine, and their extreme desire to possess their partner—body, mind and soul—does not stifle their tremendous potential for happiness in their relationships.

Love matches:
Cancer, Virgo, Capricorn and Pisces.

The Taurean woman

The Taurean woman is typically fiercely protective and supportive of those she loves. She's also one of the most courageous women of the zodiac, both morally and emotionally. And because she appreciates people for who they are, she also has the remarkable ability to get on with just about everyone from doctor to dog walker.

It is a rare Taurean woman who doesn't try to make her home look clean, even beautiful. She is very intolerant of untidiness and sloppy habits. Many Taurean women have a marked talent for or appreciation of the creative arts, in particular music. Although she can be sensual and passionate in the bedroom, in everyday life she is self-contained and likes to do things her own way. If you try to rush or push her into doing anything that she hasn't made her own mind up about, she may become irritable. It isn't wise to get her angry because, if she is goaded, she can suddenly burst into a violent temper that will take a long, long time for you and her to forget.

When it comes to choosing a partner, she looks for someone who is strong and determined, like herself, and who is willing to contribute as much as she does to the relationship.

Once she has committed to a relationship, she is a fiercely loyal partner and stands by the person or people she loves, even when all others have deserted them. She also never fails to inspire her partner with her resilience. Those lucky enough to have a Taurus woman fall in love with them find that her dependable strength and practicality can quite literally move mountains.

The Taurean man

As the image of a bull suggests, the Taurean man tends to be strong, determined and hard-working. At first glance he may appear conservative in his appearance, but if you take a closer look, you'll notice how expensive his clothes and personal items are. He may appear unassuming and sensible, quietly and practically working behind the scenes, but, give him a few years, and you will find that he has transformed himself into someone running the entire place. In a nutshell, don't ever underestimate the potential of the male Taurean. When he sets his mind on something or someone, he almost always gets what he wants somehow. He can wear people down with his dogged persistence.

When it comes to choosing a partner, the Taurean male prefers someone with grace and intelligence who can balance his mature approach to life. He needs his freedom and doesn't want someone who is co-dependent, but he also wants a person whom he feels needs his considerable support. He isn't prone to making wild romantic gestures, but you can be sure he will keep his word and treat you with the utmost respect. He does not enjoy mind games. If he says he values you, he means it and you can have no doubt of his intentions.

Once he is in a committed relationship the Taurean man will work tirelessly to build a secure home and future for the two of you, and this future will include a beautiful home, plenty of vacations and luxuries, and, perhaps most welcome of all, strong and supportive yet gentle and loving arms to protect you from life's ups and downs.

Family

Taurean children are often content and passive, and their stoic and happy approach to life earns them the label of being a well-behaved child early in life. It may take a while, however,

for them to learn to walk, as they enjoy crawling, but parents should not worry about delayed development. When they are ready, they will confidently take their own first steps, and when they do, their legs will be strong and steady and they will naturally and easily find their balance.

These children are also quick learners, and when they learn something, they don't easily forget it. Discipline is comforting for them because if they don't have boundaries set, they feel insecure. Once they know what is or is not expected, they grow in confidence. They can be greedy and selfish, and do have a fiercely stubborn side. The only way to get through to them when they are being obstinate is to appeal to their morality by asking them to consider what the right thing to do is.

Taurean parents provide their children with secure and loving homes. Discipline is strong, which is fine for children who respond to this kind of approach, but to children who are dreamier and more artistic it can be stifling and might lead to rebellion, so a more flexible approach is encouraged. Providing their children with security is important to Taurean parents, but ironically they may work so long and hard to achieve this goal that they end up missing out on quality time with their children while they are growing up. The danger then is that their children grow up with their material needs met but their emotional needs neglected. As with everything in life, striking a balance is crucial.

Career

The ideal career for a Taurean is one in which there aren't too many distractions or changes from routine, meaning that they can work steadily toward a goal. They don't tend to do well in jobs that require rapid-fire, on-the-spot decisions, as they prefer to take their time making any kind of decision. Their ideal workplace would be calm, low key and well ordered.

Areas that may suit them best include technology—both on- and off-line—banking, insurance, investment, architecture, building, interior design, farming or caring for the land, art, filmmaking, theater, music, singing or voice-coaching, the jewelry trade, dealing in antiques and art, or any job that requires hard work, stability and reliability. Work that gives respectability in established institutions also appeals, and Taureans' gourmet tastes make them excellent chefs and restaurateurs.

Health and wellbeing

Taureans love good food so they do need to watch that their diet doesn't become too indulgent. It is important for them to make sure they eat a balanced diet rich in whole grains, fruits, vegetables, legumes, nuts, seeds and oily fish, but this can sometimes be difficult to achieve because they tend to work long hours. Avoiding large meals in the evening is recommended for their digestive health, as is making sure they eat breakfast and take a proper break at lunchtime to eat a nutritious meal. Regular exercise is also essential, and most Taureans enjoy team games and exercise classes. Because they have a propensity to move fairly slowly, they benefit from aerobics, brisk walking, jogging, wrestling, judo and dancing to help speed them up. Colds, sore throats and bronchial problems may plague Taureans from time to time, and they can be prone to neck strain, but good posture and regular exercise helps to sort out any shoulder and neck tension.

Most Taureans enjoy socializing. They love nothing better than entertaining or spending quality time with friends and family. They can be extremely generous with their time and

their money. Pleasure-seeking—including plenty of good food, sex and retail therapy—can be high on their list of priorities. To avoid bouts of lethargy, especially during retirement, they are advised to take up new and interesting hobbies; travel and working for a charity are especially beneficial. Patience and attention to detail are their strengths, so hobbies they may particularly enjoy include gardening, painting, golf and embroidery. Their love of their home can manifest itself in an interest in interior decoration and upholstery, and collecting art. Reading, and meditating on or wearing the color **orange,** will encourage them to be more flexible and creative in their approach to themselves, others and life.

Born between April 20 and 29

The influence of the plant Venus is particularly strong here, and people born between these dates are likely to be incredibly sensual and loving. They do possess a tendency to crave the biggest and best of everything, and learning the art of simple contentment may be one of their biggest life challenges.

Born between April 30 and May 10

People born between these dates tend to be highly creative, but they can also be extremely and unjustly critical of themselves. Their path to happiness lies in their ability to trust their intuition as much as in analyzing every detail.

Born between May 11 and 20

These people have sound financial sense and are also highly practical and success-orientated. They need to ensure they don't become workaholics in their pursuit of financial security. Getting in touch with their Taurean sensuality will remind them of the importance of finding a healthy balance between work, rest and play.

Life lessons

Taureans may be delightfully sensual and tactile, but along with this pleasure-orientated approach to life they often have a propensity for laziness and self-indulgence. Taureans see absolutely no reason why they can't have every material thing they want in life, and this reasoning can sometimes lead them into greed. They need to learn how to distinguish between what they need and what they want, because underneath their love of luxury and pleasures lies the misleading and self-destructive idea that others respect them for what they have, not for who they are.

The major life lesson for Taureans is therefore to learn that their self-worth is not tied up with their job, their house or what they own, but with who they are. Self-worth is an internal state that can't be bought by money or material things, or obtained from other people. Taureans also need to work on their possessive nature and learn that if you truly love someone, you set them free.

Prone to being quite stubborn and aggressive—even combative—when they get angry, Taureans need to understand that no one can control the way they feel but themselves. Their intense desire to stick to the status quo and prevent change can also hold them back, so they need to recognize that not all change is bad; in fact, sometimes it can be the best approach. Change means growth because it opens the door to new choices and points of view that can lead to great improvement. The secret for success is for Taureans to learn to have more belief in themselves and their ability to cope with inevitable periods of uncertainty and change. For steady, predictable Taureans uncertainty can be terrifying, but what they need to understand is that it's only terrifying because they think it is. If Taureans can change their mind about change and uncertainty, they will almost certainly change their lives for the better. Last, but by no means least, Taureans are stoic people, but this can tip over into intolerance and they need to understand the transformative power of forgiveness.

Witnessing other Taureans can teach them about what is and what is not the most effective approach for their sign. The other signs of the zodiac can help Taureans to learn important life lessons. Scorpios can teach Taureans to be subtle rather than stubborn in their approach when things aren't going to plan, and Cancerians can encourage them to be more forgiving. Leos can teach them self-confidence and the ability to thrive on the challenges change offers. Arians can help them to step out of their comfort zone and Sagittarians can encourage them to be more adventurous. Taureans can also draw inspiration from Pisceans and Aquarians and their ability to place ideals above material gain. And, along with the other two

air signs, Gemini and Libra, Taureans may be encouraged to value and perhaps even enjoy change. Virgoans can help them fight their tendency to laziness and Capricorns can motivate them to make their minds up and move forward rather than constantly sit on the fence.

Chinese astrology counterpart: The Snake

The Chinese Snake sign shares the patience, strength of purpose and determination of its Western counterpart, Taurus. Snakes are typically faithful companions with a sensual or pleasure-focused approach to love and life. They can be extremely creative and artistic, but they are also one of the most materialistic signs. A high value is placed on personal security, money, career, and gathering more than enough material possessions for themselves and their loved ones. These creatures know how to get and, more importantly, how to enjoy the good things in life.

Snakes are strong, silent and calm creatures, but when threatened in any way they can be deadly. They can surprise everyone around them with a sudden and unexpected attack or change of direction. At times they come across as vain, aloof, self-serving, indulgent and apathetic, but there is also a seductive power about them which, when combined with their drive, quiet focus and persistence toward achieving their relationship and life goals, ensures their popularity and success.

Note: Taureans have an affinity with Snake-sign characteristics, but be sure to check which Chinese sign corresponds to your **year** of birth (see page xxi), and to read about the characteristics associated with it, too.

April 20

The Birthday of
Hypnotic Personality

"Let me lead the way"

Those born on April 20 tend to be hypnotic individuals with an enviable ability to inspire others to follow their lead. They are fiercely determined and energetic, and eager for the admiration of others, but as they have personal integrity, they rarely use their charisma for personal gain or unworthy causes. Once they find a cause or goal to inspire them, they identify strongly with it, but there is also a part of them that remains independent. Their unique combination of ambition and sensitivity can make them moody and insecure, but it also gives them an enigmatic, compelling quality. They struggle to deal with the inevitable criticism their intensity and perfectionism inspires, preferring to block out alternative viewpoints, often dominating others. They can also retreat into a dream world far removed from reality. It is important they keep an open mind, stay in touch with reality and accept that they can sometimes be wrong.

Born managers, they have the focus, determination and natural leadership skills to become excellent negotiators, agents, consultants, team managers, executives, entrepreneurs and advisors. Their desire to improve the lives of others may lead them to humanitarian concerns and their creativity may draw them to the world of art, acting, social media and entertainment, perhaps freelancing or setting up their own business. It is essential they pay careful attention to their diet and the impact it can have on their mood, as there is a tendency for them to comfort-eat when feeling low. **For self-care**, carry an agate in your pocket. Green agates can help balance and restore energies, ease stress and soothe body, mind and soul.

Sensual and loving, those born on this day find that physical touch is their fuel, and they are often the first to kiss, hug or hold hands. Their tendency to be inflexible is highlighted in their first 30 years, but after that they become more interested in learning and communication. If they can also become more open-minded, there is absolutely nothing to stop them achieving the idealistic goals and ambitions that inspire them and the success they deserve. Their destiny is to lead and inspire others toward implementing their original and progressive ideals.

Potential: Magnetic, sensual

Dark side: Unrealistic, dominating

Tarot card, lucky numbers, days, colors: Judgment, 2, 6, Tuesday, Monday, scarlet, silver

Born today: George Takei and Jessica Lange (actors); Luther Vandross (singer); Killer Mike (activist and rapper)

April 21

The Birthday of Graciousness

The life lesson:

is to graciously accept help from others.

The way forward: is to understand that other people have just as much of a need to help and guide as you do.

Luck maker: Sometimes good enough is enough. Perfectionism can be the enemy of luck and success.

"I strive to always give my very best"

People born on April 21 impress others with their majestic and self-sufficient graciousness. Their professional reputation is everything to them, and because they have such fierce self-discipline, they often end up way ahead of others. Financial reward and getting ahead do not motivate them—their true motivation is a desire to excel at what they do. Their tenacity, integrity and sensitivity to alternative viewpoints earn them the respect of others. They give their opinions, however controversial, in a positive, constructive way. Although they are driven, they know how to relax and make people laugh, and in keeping with their regal inclinations, have a love for the good things in life. They can be very generous, but need to avoid becoming too controlling and to give those in their charge the chance to make and learn from their own mistakes.

Born motivators, they are attracted to careers that allow them to mentor or encourage others, such as teaching, coaching, counseling, consultancy, online influencing or management. They also have an affinity with writing and other artistic endeavors, and may be drawn to the law and social reform. Their love of "pleasurable" pastimes can lead to addiction or over-indulgence. They need to learn the importance of moderation in all things. **For self-care**, meditating on, wearing and surrounding yourself with the color purple will encourage you to focus less on external pleasures and more on inner fulfillment.

In relationships these people are self-sacrificing and need to take as well as give. After 30 they put greater emphasis on opening their mind than on acquiring stuff, and these are the years they become more resilient, less at risk from losing themselves in work and material things. There may be some changing around career-wise, but when they do find their feet, their single-mindedness and earnest desire to see others progress will help them realize their ambitions and, gracious nobles that they are, earn them the respect of others. Once they learn to avoid perfectionism, and look within rather than outside themselves for satisfaction, their destiny is to encourage and inspire others to reach their full potential.

Potential: Dignified, driven

Dark side: Perfectionist, controlling

Tarot card, lucky numbers, days, colors: The World, 3, 7, Friday, Thursday, lavender, pale blue

Born today: HRH Queen Elizabeth II; Charlotte Brontë (novelist); Iggy Pop (rock singer)

April 22

The Birthday of Quality

"I expect only the best"

April 22-born believe they are born to create something of quality. They are ambitious in an understated way and have the hypnotic ability to make others follow their lead. Their talents express themselves best in their superior organizational skills and ability to motivate others to work toward a common goal. Their co-workers respect their down-to-earth approach and ability to offer positive encouragement. Confident and charming, their Achilles' heel is their urgent need for power, and they can become overbearing and, sometimes, unkindly critical of others. Looking within for satisfaction helps them to become more aware of their own power without the constant need for external validation.

Born executives, they crave material reward and the recognition of others for their efforts, and can find this in management, finance, banking and commerce or setting up their own business. Their communication skills may lead them to the law, teaching, acting, music and politics, and their creative talents may attract them to the arts. Health- and lifestyle-wise, they expect and seek out quality, enjoying searching for the best diet, gym, vacation and so on, but they need to ease up on their high expectations now and again. **For self-care**, practice an attitude of gratitude. Focus on what you have to be grateful for in your life.

Prone to suspicion in their relationships, those born on this day can take a while to truly open up to others. Until the age of 28 they are likely to be concerned with power and money, but after the age of 28 they develop an interest in education and learning new skills. This continues until their fifties, when there is a shift toward their feelings, and a growing importance of friends and family. Once they find a goal their charisma helps them make their own very special mark on the world. Their destiny is to direct their considerable energy toward helping and inspiring others to achieve real progress in the world.

Potential: Charismatic, ambitious

Dark side: Controlling, unkind

Tarot card, lucky numbers, days, colors: The Fool, 4, 8, Friday, Sunday, pale blue, silver

Born today: Immanuel Kant (philosopher); Jack Nicholson (actor); Robert Oppenheimer (physicist)

April 23

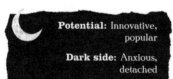

The Birthday of the Elusive Guide

"I light up the way"

Those born on April 23 possess an elusive quality. Few really get to know these nonconformist people well. Being misunderstood does not bother them as they aren't too concerned about what others think about them. From an early age they have a powerful desire to establish their individuality and would rather guide than follow others. Natural innovators, their progressive and fair outlook has the potential to put them way ahead, but they do have a strange tendency to become set in their ways and there can be an anxious streak to their nature.

Born writers, they thrive in careers where they can express their talent for innovation and communication, such as teaching, drama, journalism, art, movie-making, blogging, online influencing, music, and photography. They may also be drawn to counseling, promotion, mediation, advertising, management, business, sales, marketing, real estate, politics, the healing professions and public relations. Health-wise, they need to be less stuck in their ways and understand that their diet and lifestyle needs to adapt as they age. **For self-care,** stay flexible by incorporating yoga or a daily stretching routine into your life.

Although popular, these people can set their hearts on someone unattainable and when in a relationship need to be less possessive. They should try to overcome reservations, especially regarding close relationships, because they tend to be at their happiest and best in the security of one loving union. Until the age of 27 they may cling to the safety of routine, but after that they are more receptive to new ideas, ways of thinking and doing things. Blessed with great insight, originality and tenacity, they have the potential to achieve great things. Once they can become more spontaneous, step outside their comfort zone and allow themselves to become the innovators that they really are, they can act as a guide and source of hope to others. Their destiny is to make their unique mark on the world in an uncontroversial, harmonious and healing way.

Potential: Innovative, popular

Dark side: Anxious, detached

Tarot card, lucky numbers, days, colors: The Hierophant, 5, 9, Friday, Wednesday, all shades of blue

Born today: Max Planck (physicist); Michael Moore (director); Chloe Kim (snowboarder)

April 24

The Birthday of Devotion

"My heart is my guide"

The life lesson: is resisting the urge to respond to every request.

The way forward: is to understand the difference between generosity and gullibility. Don't give to people who are taking advantage and perfectly capable of helping themselves.

Luck maker: Say "no" more to others and "yes" more to yourself. If you spread yourself too thinly you lose your power.

People born on April 24 love to inspire and guide. They are magnetic with enormously kind hearts and believe in universal love and equality. They have a strong protective instinct, but the parental role they like to assume with others can be alternately endearing and exasperating. They should learn to allow others the chance to follow their own hearts and, if need be, make their own mistakes. As well as being devoted to close relationships, they can become utterly dedicated to their career, often fully identifying with it, and may endlessly fret over keeping a healthy balance between their personal and professional life. They give their heart to everything they do and need to understand that sometimes less is more.

Born educators, they have the communication skills and nurturing instinct to mentor others, which make them excellent teachers, coaches, doctors, counselors, writers and online influencers, and they may also be attracted to public life and become involved in politics, acting, music, media, sport and entertainment. Environmental concerns, philosophy and spirituality may also appeal. One of the biggest threats to their wellbeing is their inability to say no to the constant demands of others. They need to put themselves first more regularly. **For self-care,** wearing, meditating on and surrounding yourself with the color pink will boost your energy and encourage you to focus more on yourself.

In relationships they can feel let down when those they nurture fall from the lofty pedestal on which they've placed them by not following their guidance. Until 26 their lives are often centered on a need for security; after the age of 26 there are opportunities for them to develop more interests. Throughout their lives, learning to confidently use the word "no" helps them feel less torn between career and personal life. It also allows them to make their unique mark on the world and to put their organizational capabilities, compassionate, creative energies and single-mindedness to their best possible use. Their destiny is to guide, motivate and inspire not just their loved ones but everyone lucky enough to cross their path.

Potential: Inspirational, nurturing

Dark side: Smothering, over-accommodating

Tarot card, lucky numbers, day, colors: The Lovers, 1, 6, Friday, blue, pink

Born today: Barbra Streisand (singer); Anthony Trollope and Sue Grafton (novelists)

April 25

The Birthday of
Imposing Vigor

The life lesson:

is to value life beyond the material.

The way forward: is to remember that when you forget to take care of your soul, you are more likely to become dependent, stressed and directionless.

Luck maker: Balance being with doing—stop doing all the time and just be more of the time.

"I am what I do"

April 25-born are hard to ignore, with their imposing presence and dynamic energy. Doers rather than thinkers, their intelligence and undaunted drive to succeed fill those who are less self-assured with awe. They can, however, self-sabotage by making hasty decisions and taking unnecessary risks. Their direct, practical and realistic approach with little time for reflection doesn't take into account the subtler aspects of things. These people are anything but vague, but the danger of their lack of interest in the abstract is that when things don't go to plan, they haven't built up the spiritual resources to find comfort within.

Born lawyers, their sense of purpose and focus serve them well in any career, but they may be drawn to the police, business, finance, science, engineering, construction, technology and design. Their compassion may also lead to them to politics or social and charity work, and their creative side to drama, music, writing and art. There is an earthy sensuality about them and they tend to relish testing themselves physically. Wellbeing issues tend to be emotional and related to low self-esteem, rather than physical. **For self-care**, carrying a small moonstone crystal around encourages you to connect more with your intuition or inner wisdom.

Those born on this day can become anxious in close relationships, fearing that people will leave them, but once they become more self-confident, they can have deeply rewarding relationships. After the age of 26 there are opportunities for them to open their mind to new ideas and study, and they should ensure their emphasis is not just on the practical but also on the theoretical or spiritual. From their mid-fifties their focus shifts toward nurturing close relationships, where previously their energies are likely to have been on their career. Above all, they have a presence that effortlessly commands respect, and as long as they remember to check their impulsiveness and nurture their spiritual self, there is little that these capable people cannot accomplish. Their destiny is to take practical and positive steps in the direction of progress.

Potential: Dynamic, focused

Dark side: Materialistic, impulsive

Tarot card, lucky numbers, days, colors: The Chariot, 2, 7, Friday, Monday, pale blue, sea green

Born today: Renée Zellweger and Al Pacino (actors); Guglielmo Marconi (inventor); Oliver Cromwell (statesman)

April 26

The Birthday of Beautiful Logic

"Heaven is in the details"

is to learn that perfectionism is not the path to fulfillment.

The way forward: is to understand that people are not statistics or geometry. In human terms perfection is often found in the imperfections.

Luck maker: Put yourself in someone else's shoes. Considering alternative viewpoints can offer fresh and perhaps better perspectives that you have not taken into consideration.

Those born on April 26 can be visionary, but it's their painstaking attention to detail that marks them out. They understand that logical planning is essential for success. Given this methodical approach, they can often be found running slick projects. Self-starters, they are often admired for their efficiency and reliability. There is always the risk that they can become rigid with a controlling tendency that can be damaging, and they need to respect diversity of opinion. Their love of logic, order and detail should never be allowed to estrange them from their heart. The sooner they can start getting in touch with their feelings and those of others, the sooner they can enjoy a more balanced and healthier life.

Born landscapers, they like to nurture projects and are drawn to careers that require them to constantly oversee and check the efficiency of progress, such as gardening, farming, education, manufacturing, administration, the civil service, accounting, real estate, business, banking, medicine, research, technology, programming and science. Their creativity may express itself in design, writing, painting, music, filmmaking and online influencing. They tend to get stuck in a rut and would benefit from more flexibility in their food and lifestyle choices. **For self-care**, practice heart-opening yoga poses, such as the fish, cat, sphinx or camel poses, as this will encourage you to open your heart emotionally and spiritually.

In their dedication to perfection these people can become isolated from others. Learning to embrace and enjoy the inconsistencies of others helps them feel less lonely. Until the age of 25 their stubbornness is likely to dominate, but after the age of 25 they may become more flexible in their approach by studying and communicating. After the age of 56 they feel the need to draw closer to those they love and care for. Once they understand that human beings aren't perfect or logical, there is no reason why their inspired and productive strategies can't help them achieve and even exceed their goals. Their destiny is to become champions of quality, produced by close attention to those all-important details.

Potential: Meticulous, independent

Dark side: Perfectionist, inflexible

Tarot card, lucky numbers, days, colors: Strength, 3, 8, Friday, Saturday, pale blue, burgundy

Born today: David Hume (philosopher); Leoh Ming Pei (architect); Jet Li (actor)

April 27

The Birthday of
Charming Self-reliance

The life lesson:

is not to isolate yourself.

The way forward: is to understand that while you can be highly productive alone, it is important for your personal growth also to share your time with others.

Luck maker: Answer the phone—luck is always knocking and you just need to open the door and let the good things in.

"Let me think about it"

People born on April 27 are deep thinkers. They favor the world of their own reflection over everything and everyone else. Self-sufficient, they rarely seek approval or validation from others. Their sensitivity is often coupled with a strong sense of realism, giving them great potential for creativity and innovation. Despite their natural reserve, others often find them charming and fascinating. Indeed, they can come really into their own in a group setting; inspiring others with their compassion, generosity and surprising sense of humor. They can get frustrated at times when others don't offer as much support as they do, but it is important that they don't become bitter and isolate themselves from the psychological benefits of interacting with others.

Born researchers, they can excel in the law, education, business, invention and journalism. Their technical skills may lead them to careers in computing, technology and engineering or they may find that medicine, psychology, humanitarian or social work appeal. Whatever career they choose, they need the autonomy to plunder the treasure trove of their own original ideas. Reflective and drawn to study on screens, they need to ensure they get plenty of fresh air, so they reap all the mood-boosting benefits of exercise and daylight. **For self-care**, watch a comedy show or visit a theme park. You need to focus more on scheduling time to have more fun in your life.

These people may spend periods self-partnered, but, once they meet someone who returns their devotion and understands their need for solitude, they can make loyal, loving companions. There is a risk of temptation toward extremist ideas that will limit their psychological growth, but, fortunately, between the ages of 24 and 54, they experience an increased need to communicate and exchange new ideas. This can be an extremely positive and productive time for them. As long as they make sure they remain emotionally open and live in the present and not some distant future, they can achieve considerable success. Their destiny is to improve and inspire the lives of others by sharing their encyclopedic knowledge and bold ideas.

Potential: Independent, charming

Dark side: Withdrawn, rigid

Tarot card, lucky numbers, days, colors: The Hermit, 4, 9, Friday, Tuesday, pale blue, lilac

Born today: Mary Wollstonecraft (feminist); Samuel Morse (inventor); Sheila Scott (aviator)

April 28

The Birthday of the Conductor

The life lesson:

is learning to let go.

The way forward: is to understand that great leadership is about encouraging others to take charge of themselves, not making them dependent.

Luck maker: Taking responsibility for everything and everyone leads to burnout. To improve your luck, master the art of delegation.

"There is light at the end of every tunnel"

April 28-born tend to be energetic, radiant individuals with a wonderful ability to guide and motivate others. Life is a dance or an orchestra and they like to cast themselves in the essential role of creative choreographer or conductor. Highly resilient and focused, their strength and leadership cause others to rely heavily on them. Some may find their honesty too blunt, but they would rather risk offending than be involved in deception. Their sensitivity helps them guide others with empathy and respect. Occasionally they can be guilty of over-controlling behavior, but this is often due to fears of not being needed. Learning to take themselves less seriously helps them develop the psychological strength to let others take control of their own lives.

Born directors, they have a great understanding of human nature and may be drawn to teaching, therapy, counseling, advising, management, advertising, negotiation, media, publishing, broadcasting, movie-making and online influencing. Their natural flair for creativity may draw them to design, theater, music and the arts, and their need to be needed may draw them to medicine, the law and the caring professions. Extremely energetic, they need to find outlets for their energy through regular exercise, to help them release any pent-up tension. **For self-care**, declutter. Devote some time every day to tidying up and throwing out or giving away to charity what you don't need or use anymore.

In relationships—as in their professional life—they must learn to take as well as give direction. From the ages of 23 to 53 they explore new interests and skills, and if they can take advantage of these opportunities for growth and diversification, they can successfully work toward the fulfillment of their goals and their dreams. Once they are able to listen to alternative viewpoints, take on the advice of others, and let go of things and people who are dragging them down, their destiny is to direct and inspire others with their dedication, focus, honesty, dependability and glimpses of pure creative magic.

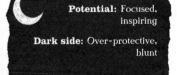

Potential: Focused, inspiring

Dark side: Over-protective, blunt

Tarot card, lucky numbers, days, colors: The Magician, 1, 5, Friday, Sunday, pale blue, orange

Born today: Oskar Schindler (industrialist); Harper Lee (author); Penélope Cruz (actor)

April 29

The Birthday of Impeccable Manners

The life lesson:

is learning to have fun.

The way forward: is to understand that if you are not enjoying your life, you are not a success.

Luck maker: Try cloud-watching. Gazing at the moving clouds can provide the calming state of mind that helps your luck-making intuition surface.

"I am poised for success"

Those born on April 29 are dignified, and often have impeccable manners and appreciation of the finer things in life, preferring the company of equally poised people. But they are not snobs and can modify their behavior according to the company they keep. This doesn't mean they are superficial, just that the positive opinion of others, from whatever walk of life, matters greatly to them. Rarely unprepared, they will always perform to the best of their ability. Reliable, they are often found in positions of leadership, but the downside of their self-assurance is that maintaining their poise can be exhausting. It is vital they make time to have fun, as always being counted on by others can go to their heads.

Born image consultants, they understand the importance of presentation and can excel in fashion, design, marketing, promotion, advertising, public relations, social-media influencing and business. Those who are artistically gifted may gravitate toward writing, journalism, acting, music and art, while their desire to help may draw them to teaching, humanitarian concerns, beauty, sport, the healing professions and the study of spirituality. They understand the importance of a healthy lifestyle for their body image, but need to make sure they don't become too obsessive with their food and exercise choices. **For self-care**, meditating on, wearing and surrounding yourself with all shades of purple can help you connect with your intuition or inner wisdom.

In relationships these people tend to be givers rather than takers, but there are times when they might feel deeply lonely for no apparent reason; this is usually because they aren't paying attention to their own feelings. Before their early fifties they have many opportunities to explore new interests and develop new skills. Around the age of 52 they may concentrate on emotional security. If they can understand that how they feel from the inside is more important than how they look on the outside, they will unlock outstanding potential for success and happiness. Once they connect with their powerful intuition, their destiny is to help make the world a more harmonious place by bringing out the kinder, politer instincts in others.

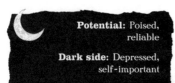

Potential: Poised, reliable

Dark side: Depressed, self-important

Tarot card, lucky numbers, days, colors: The High Priestess, 2, 8, Friday, Monday, all shades of blue

Born today: Daniel Day-Lewis, Jerry Seinfeld, Michelle Pfeiffer and Uma Thurman (actors); Andre Agassi (tennis player)

April 30

The Birthday of
Commitment

The life lesson: is celebrating yourself.

The way forward: is to understand the vital importance of concentrating on establishing and celebrating your own identity, independent of who you are with or what you do.

Luck maker: Let go of guilt and focus your luck-making energy on what you have achieved, how far you have come and can still go.

"I dedicate myself"

People born on April 30 tend to appear calm and collected. Despite their relaxed, light-hearted exterior, they have incredible drive and only feel truly fulfilled if they are devoted to their work, a cause, a group or a person. Commitment, responsibility, duty and respect for society's rules are valued above all else. They often feel inclined to take up a charitable cause or generally do good deeds in the neighborhood. However, there is a danger that their commitment to others becomes unquestioning and their dedication to a goal turns into obstinacy when viable alternatives are presented.

Born officers and highly valued for their reliability, practicality and intelligence, they have the potential to thrive in any career they choose. They may be drawn to education, law enforcement, the military, commerce, promotions and business. They may also be attracted to the caring professions or humanitarian or social work, and, if they are creative, to the worlds of arts and entertainment, especially design and production. Prone to prioritizing the needs of others over their own, they need to make regular time to be alone and to focus on themselves. **For self-care**, meditating on the color pink or carrying a rose-quartz crystal will encourage you to fall in love with yourself and put your own heart first.

In relationships those born on this day can be loyal and devoted, but any criticism is likely to be met with anger; they need to learn to take it for what it is: someone else's opinion. There are many opportunities before they reach their fifties to treat criticism as a learning experience and, after that, their focus is more on emotional stability. Multitalented, they have the potential to make their mark on whatever project or goal interests them, and when they do focus their disciplined energy on a worthwhile cause, they can surprise everyone with their spontaneity and ability to bring about genuine progress. Once they commit to the development of their own talents, their destiny is to move the world forward by demonstrating the importance of dedication and respect for others.

Potential: Reliable, intelligent

Dark side: Obstinate, reactive

Tarot card, lucky numbers, days, colors: The Empress, 3, 7, Friday, Thursday, pale blue, purple

Born today: Carl Friedrich Gauss (mathematician); John Peters Humphrey (human rights advocate); Kirsten Dunst (actor)

May 1

The Birthday of Astuteness

"I rise above"

The life lesson:

is seizing opportunities.

The way forward: is to understand that excessive caution can be as dangerous to personal growth as excessive risk.

Luck maker: Always be prepared to leap into the unknown. Stay alert, because at any moment you could meet a person or have an experience that could change your life for the better.

May 1-born are often blessed with wit and highly astute insight. Calm and reflective, they choose their words wisely. Empathetic and kind but also strongly intuitive, they notice what is both seen and unseen and then calmly rise above themselves, others and the situation so that they can apply reason and establish an effective plan of action. This considered approach means others rely on them for a much-needed sense of perspective, but it can also mean they downplay their own abilities and opinions. They need to have more faith in themselves, as they are capable of achieving far more than they realize.

Born counselors, they are drawn to careers that utilize their powerful skills of observations in a caring or healing way, such as medicine, psychiatry, law enforcement and criminology. They may also be attracted to sales, marketing, real estate, banking, catering and the health and leisure industries. The more creative may excel in writing, design, art and music. They have a tendency to become too sedentary, so regular exercise, a minimum of 30 minutes of brisk walking a day, is essential. **For self-care**, wearing, meditating on or surrounding yourself with the color red is both physically and emotionally stimulating and will encourage you to be more spontaneous.

They prefer their relationships to be slow and steady rather than intense and complex. The familiar and firm comforts them, and changes or new situations can alarm them greatly, even though they rarely show their fears on the surface. It is important for them to learn to embrace change, because once they do, nothing can stop them. There are opportunities between the ages of 20 and 50 to diversify, experiment and step out of their comfort zone. After 50 they focus on emotional stability. Once they wake up to their huge potential, acknowledge their emotional needs and use their insight to their own advantage, they surprise themselves and others with their fierce creativity and passion. Their destiny is to be bringers of harmony and, by so doing, to help make the world a happier and more productive place.

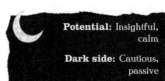

Potential: Insightful, calm

Dark side: Cautious, passive

Tarot card, lucky numbers, days, colors: The Magician, 1, 6, Friday, Sunday, pale blue, gold

Born today: Calamity Jane (frontierswoman); Joseph Heller (writer); Joanna Lumley (actor)

May 2

The Birthday of Inquisitive Honesty

The life lesson:

is being more sensitive to the feelings of others.

The way forward: is to understand that people sometimes find it hard to cope with the truth so you need to find a gentler way of presenting it to them.

Luck maker: Always make time for kindness because there's no telling when you could need help.

"Practice makes perfect"

People born on May 2 are no-nonsense and want results, not theories. Fiercely intelligent and honest to the point of tactlessness, they don't intend to upset others, as they are naturally inclined toward harmony; they simply believe the best way to effect improvement is to say it like it is. Blessed with tremendous insight into human nature and respected by others, their blunt insights may come across as insensitive. Perfectionists, they shine in whatever task is set them and motivate others to emulate their fantastic self-discipline and organizational skills. They can work well in a team but prefer to work solo.

Born surgeons, they have great potential for success in the caring professions, medicine and scientific research, as well as technology, advertising, the media, writing and acting. Social reform, building, architecture and management may also appeal, as does sport or any career that is also a vocation, but whatever field they choose they tend to succeed. As important as their career is to them, they are more productive if they identify less with work and seek to discover other interests. **For self-care**, text less and talk more. Whenever possible, try to talk to someone instead of texting them or, better still, meet them in person instead.

The private life of those born on this day is exactly that—private—but, despite their reticence and tendency to be controlling in relationships, they are at their happiest when there is a balance between give and take. Their insatiable curiosity can earn them a reputation as a gossip, so respecting the privacy of others is paramount, especially between the ages of 19 and 49, when there is an emphasis on communication. After the age of 49 they may feel the growing importance of nurturing their own feelings as well as those of others. If they can listen to the honest and caring advice they give others and apply it to themselves, they have the potential to achieve outstanding success. Once they have become more aware of the hugely powerful impact of their words and deeds on others, their destiny is to work for the common good.

Potential: Authoritative, insightful

Dark side: Perfectionist, tactless

Tarot card, lucky numbers, days, colors: The High Priestess, 2, 7, Friday, Monday, pale blue, silver

Born today: Catherine the Great (Russian empress); David Beckham (soccer player); Dwayne Johnson (actor)

May 3

The Birthday of Sensational Efficiency

"To everything there is a season"

Those born on May 3 are not just well organized, they are sensationally efficient. Their living and work spaces tend to be tidy and others count on them to ensure things run smoothly. Their natural charm earns them admirers, and steady improvement is a feature of their lives rather than sudden change for the better. Strong-willed and insightful, they can judge people and events harshly and need to avoid becoming inflexible. They tend to worry too much and work too hard to prove themselves, but, fortunately, they are perceptive and usually able to take an honest look at themselves and their motivations.

Born psychologists, they have the emotional detachment to make great counselors, psychologists, therapists, mediators and psychiatrists, and are well equipped for careers in the military, the law, politics, science, business, advertising, marketing, real estate and banking. Affinity with nature may lead them to farming, gardening, agriculture and horticulture, and their creativity shines in writing, acting, music and interior design. They have an indulgent side, which can have a negative impact on their physical health, and they are also prone to worrying, which can lead to stress. **For self-care,** when anxiety strikes, go for a brisk walk or jog to release tension and calm your mind, or try the soothing therapy of yoga and meditation.

Commitment to one person can be an issue, as those born on this day judge others by their accomplishments rather than through their hearts. In their teenage years they may feel restricted, but any setbacks they experience pave the way for two good things: determination and patience. As long as they keep pushing steadily forward, life rewards them with success. Before the age of 50 communication is the main driver but, after 50, emotional security becomes dominant. At any age, they have much to offer others, and as long as they remember to curb their tendency to overanalyze and detach emotionally and to listen to their heart as well as their head, their destiny is to help others to reach their full potential and, at the same time, make their own big dreams of progress a reality.

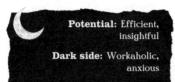

Potential: Efficient, insightful

Dark side: Workaholic, anxious

Tarot card, lucky numbers, days, colors: The Empress, 3, 8, Friday, Thursday, lilac, green

Born today: Niccolò Machiavelli (strategist); Bing Crosby, James Brown (singers); Golda Meir (Israeli prime minister)

May 4

The Birthday of
Sparkling Goodness

"Keep calm and carry on"

is not wearing yourself out on behalf of others.

The way forward: is to understand that sacrificing yourself on the altar of altruism drains your energy and optimism.

Luck maker: Understand that before you take care of others, you need to take care of and empower yourself.

May 4-born are perceptive, non-judgmental people with a gentle, hypnotic sparkle that draws those who seek guidance. They prefer to help others through deeds and the example of dependability and compassion, rather than through words or theories. Whatever situation they are in, they frequently end up as a mentor and a guide, and rightly so, as others have much to learn from them. Warm-hearted, they are quick to see the potential for goodness in everyone. Because they appear so calm and in control, and others naturally seek them out for support, they often give a lot of themselves to others, so it is important for them not to put their own dreams on hold.

Born advisors and counselors, their advice and guidance are sought regardless of their career choice. Charity work, politics, teaching, medicine and the caring professions, public relations, the emergency services and sport may appeal, or they may develop their creativity in music, singing, acting, influencing and design. They expend a lot of energy and time nurturing others, so it is crucial for their health and wellbeing that they prioritize their own needs and self-care. **For self-care**, place a pen and notepad beside your bed before you go to sleep. On waking, record your dreams. What is your dreaming mind trying to tell you?

The calm and common-sense approach to life of these people earns them much respect from others, and in relationships what a person thinks and feels matters more to them than what they look like or do. They should take risks and make big changes, typically before the age of 50, when there is an emphasis on new directions. This will not damage their sparkling reputation; it will enhance it, because to feel truly fulfilled, they need to live their dreams and ideals, not just think about them. After the age of 50, making changes becomes easier, as they pay more attention to their personal needs. Once they nurture their own dreams as much as they nurture those of others, their destiny is to reach for their dreams and, by so doing, inspire others with their steadiness, empathy and refreshing optimism.

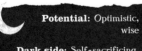

Potential: Optimistic, wise

Dark side: Self-sacrificing, unfulfilled

Tarot card, lucky numbers, days, colors: The Emperor, 4, 9, Friday, Sunday, lilac, copper

Born today: Bartolomeo Cristofori (instrument maker); Audrey Hepburn (actor); Horace Mann (educator)

May 5

The Birthday of Motivating Energy

"Let's do this"

The life lesson:

is to avoid becoming controlling in your dealings with others.

The way forward: is to understand that others need to learn life's lessons by themselves; the best guidance is to encourage others to be more independent.

Luck maker: Listen more—other people may have valuable information and insights to share.

People born on May 5 are a rich resource of innovative ideas and solutions, and know the best way to implement them. Others rely on them to inject their unique brand of motivating energy when things have ground to a halt, and unless they feel undermined, they never seem to tire. They have superb communication skills and love to motivate and inspire others to take action. They get right to the heart of things, sometimes highlighting uncomfortable truths along the way, to help others progress. They naturally assume the role of motivator or mentor and take this role very seriously, becoming manipulative and jealous if they feel this is threatened. Hidden beneath their serious but practical exterior there is a highly idealistic and sensitive individual.

Born politicians, they have the motivational energy to excel in sales, promotion, advertising, lobbying, politics, business, marketing and online influencing. Education, philosophy, the law, medicine and life-coaching also appeal, as do music, the arts, catering and the retail and beauty industries, because these people have hidden sensual and creative depths. Health-wise they need to learn the art of moderation in all things, as they tend to go overboard in one area of their lives, be it diet, exercise, sex or work. **For self-care**, learn to meditate—this will help you to quieten your mind, so that you can hear the voice of your inner wisdom or intuition more clearly.

In all their relationships, those born on this day should learn to listen more, be less possessive and allow others to make and learn from their own mistakes, especially before the age of 46 when the emphasis is on communication. After that they become more sensitive toward their own feelings and those of others. Using their unusual sense of humor and trusting their intuition more will give them the self-confidence they need to focus their energy not just on guiding others but on motivating themselves to develop and express their own creative potential. Once they have learned to influence without being authoritarian, their destiny is to motivate and inspire others with their tremendous knowledge and energy.

Potential: Inspiring, knowledgeable

Dark side: Domineering, jealous

Tarot card, lucky numbers, days, colors: The Hierophant, 1, 5, Friday, Wednesday, lilac, cobalt blue

Born today: Karl Marx and Søren Kierkegaard (philosophers); Craig David and Adele (singers)

May 6

The Birthday of the Sensitive Star

"I know it when I see it"

The life lesson: is coping with extreme sensitivity.

The way forward: is to see your sensitivity as a strength rather than a weakness and be sure to take regular time out alone when you feel overwhelmed.

Luck maker: Distinguish between intuition and fear. The voice of intuition tends to be calmer, kinder and less wordy than fear. So, an inner voice that is self-critical, indecisive, harsh and judgmental is fear speaking.

Those born on May 6 are sensitive to the feeling of others, especially those less fortunate. Curious to learn about everyone and everything, they love to mentor and help others cope with challenges. If they can't help others directly, they inspire them by living the kind of magical life most of us can only dream of. They have a deep desire to do something meaningful in the world and may subscribe to humanitarian causes. Being super-sensitive, they can get easily hurt, and more objectivity would help them avoid mood swings and also feelings of insecurity, which can push them into a secondary role. They need to turn their astute understanding of what motivates others toward themselves to cure their lack of self-belief.

Born doctors, these people can find career fulfillment in science, medicine, the caring professions and psychiatry, and may also be suited to politics and the arts, where they can use their sensitivity to inspire and help others. Whatever career they choose, be it programming, research or public affairs, their natural psychological skills aid them greatly. Building up their self-esteem is essential for their holistic health and wellbeing. **For self-care**, mind-training therapies, such as cognitive behavioral therapy, help you feel more positive and provide tools to challenge negative thinking.

It may take those born on this day a while to settle into a relationship, but when they do, they often find that giving and receiving love (and sex) is a strong motivational force in their lives. Before the age of 45 there is an emphasis on communication, and it is essential they learn not to take everything so personally. After that the focus is more on emotional closeness, family and security. They should remember that every step they take toward fulfilling their ambitions and dreams works to inspire and motivate others. Once they believe in themselves, their destiny is to inspire others with their prodigious energy, be that in a practical or motivational way.

Potential: Intuitive, astute

Dark side: Insecure, moody

Tarot card, lucky numbers, day, colors: The Lovers, 2, 6, Friday, lilac, pink

Born today: Sigmund Freud (psychiatrist); James Turrell (artist); George Clooney (actor)

May 7

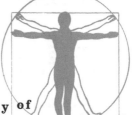

The Birthday of Absolute Perfection

"I don't want to miss a thing"

May 7-born know that the most important values are spiritual, but they are also keen to succeed materially and gain recognition from others, and this combination of inner and outer expectation is in keeping with their dedicated quest for perfection in all areas of their lives. They are fine communicators and completely devoted to their goals and ideals. Sometimes they give too much of themselves and can neglect both their own needs and the needs of loved ones. There is always a danger that their desire to "have it all" manifests in unrealistic fantasies and they need to focus on making their inspirational goals a workable reality. Their intelligence and drive help them succeed materially, and making money is not generally a problem, although—because they enjoy sharing the good things in life—keeping it sometimes is.

Born composers, they have superb communication skills and excel in journalism as well as the arts, particularly as writers and musicians. Advertising, lobbying, business, art, education, humanitarian reform, spirituality, New Age ideas and therapies, and the world of personal growth may also appeal. Health-wise they put self-care behind the demands of their ideals, so it is essential they have regular rest and relaxation. **For self-care**, daily mindfulness techniques, such as concentrating all your attention on simple activities like washing your hands, help you evolve spiritually and find fulfillment in the everyday.

In their relationships these people long for spiritual union and run the risk of becoming lonely because of impossible expectations of others. Before their early forties they concentrate on change, communication and learning new skills. After 40 their focus is self-awareness, as these are the years when relationships come to the fore. Connecting to their intuition and searching for spiritual meaning beneath the surface of things is their lifelong mission and source of greatest fulfillment. Once they understand their inner conflicts better, their destiny is to put their high ideals to positive and productive use, and, by so doing, make the world a more beautiful place.

Potential: Refined, dedicated

Dark side: Unrealistic, lonely

Tarot card, lucky numbers, days, colors: The Chariot, 3, 7, Friday, Monday, lilac, blue

Born today: Robert Browning and Rabindranath Tagore (poets); Piotr Ilyich Tchaikovsky (composer); Eva Perón (actor and politician)

May 8

The Birthday of the Irresistible Messenger

"Willpower is the key to success"

People born on May 8 rarely back down. Iron-willed and armed with tremendous conviction, they are dedicated to their ideals. Diplomacy isn't one of their strengths and they can appear judgmental and harsh, but once they understand the value of converting rather than alienating others using the art of gentle persuasion, they are an irresistible force. Underneath their formidable exterior lies a caring and generous side, which—as they tend to regard any kind of vulnerability as a weakness—they only reveal to their nearest and dearest. It is important for them to understand that the source of their strength and power is found both in their conviction *and* in their gentleness.

Born conservationists, they have an innate appreciation of nature, history and community life and may therefore devote themselves to farming, conservation and environmental concerns or to preserving buildings. They can excel in promotion, negotiation, sales, publishing, advertising, the law, politics, real estate and management, and their creativity may draw them to music, writing, social-media influencing, podcasts, design, architecture and filmmaking. Health-wise they prefer to self-medicate and do need to remain open to the advice of their doctor, as willpower is not always the cure-all they believe it to be. **For self-care**, smile more, even if you have to fake it. Your brain can't tell the difference between a real and a fake smile, so smile with your teeth until your heart chimes in.

In their relationships these people need to learn that love can be both a serious and a laughing matter. Before their early forties the emphasis is on communication and after that they are more likely to focus on fostering emotional connections. At any age, if they can learn to take themselves less seriously, happiness and success are within easy reach. Wherever they decide to devote their energies, becoming more diplomatic makes it easier for them to realize their ambitions. Once they have learned to be gentler to both themselves and others, their destiny is to be the charismatic voice for their generation, community or cause.

Potential: Persuasive, caring

Dark side: Judgmental, harsh

Tarot card, lucky numbers, days, colors: Strength, 4, 8, Friday, Saturday, lavender, green

Born today: Edward Gibbon (historian); David Attenborough (naturalist); Enrique Iglesias (singer)

May 9

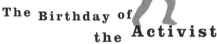

The Birthday of the Activist

The life lesson:

is dealing with anger.

The way forward: is to understand what triggers the anger and have a positive plan to release it, such as punching a cushion or challenging negative thoughts.

Luck maker: Transform any disappointments into opportunities to learn, do things better and make a positive difference.

"There is a better way"

Those born on May 9 often appear cool and collected but, underneath, they pulsate with hidden yet powerful energy and drive. They value integrity and fair play highly and can often be found in the role of reformer, protester or activist if they witness any kind of injustice. Their desire to champion those who are less fortunate or to support a just cause is intense. They may have struggled to overcome hardships in their past and this has given them compassion and inner courage to draw upon. Because they are so committed to progress and justice, they can be unrealistic at times and also unforgiving when others fail to live up to their high standards. They need to manage their anger, because all the respect their earnest desire for progress may have gathered can vanish in an instant.

Born politicians, they have the qualities needed to excel in the law, acting, politics, teaching, lobbying, social work, humanitarian concerns and the caring professions. Their charm can draw them toward the arts and people-orientated careers such as promotions, sales and marketing, and their business sense and leadership potential suggests success in management or self-employment. Non-competitive activities such as walking and dancing or mind–body therapies such as yoga and tai chi can help them release tension. **For self-care**, wearing, meditating on or surrounding themselves with calming shades of blue will encourage them to be more objective and to stay cool, calm and in control.

Fiercely possessive in relationships, those born on this day need to make sure they give the people in their lives room to breathe. Until the age of 42 there is an emphasis on sudden changes of direction and learning through challenges, but after the age of 42 life tends to get easier for them and they can concentrate on security, both emotional and financial. Once they learn to be more flexible and to respond in more constructive ways when upset, their success, and more important to them the success of the progressive ideals they believe in, are virtually guaranteed. Their destiny is to inspire others to improve things for the better with their passion and commitment.

Potential: Honorable, charismatic

Dark side: Temperamental, unrealistic

Tarot card, lucky numbers, days, colors: The Hermit, 5, 9, Friday, Tuesday, lavender, green

Born today: Billy Joel (singer); Howard Carter (archaeologist); Sophie Scholl (activist)

May 10

The Birthday of Natural Rhythm

The life lesson:

is finding time and energy for others.

The way forward: is to understand that close relationships are not incompatible with single-minded dedication to a goal or project. Finding balance is the key.

Luck maker: Focus on what you can give, not on what you can get from others.

"I go with the flow"

People born on May 10 follow their own natural rhythm and give the appearance of floating through life, intuitively knowing when to make the right move. This effortlessly intuitive approach is often highly effective. They like to go their own way and tend to work best as an individual rather than as part of a team, becoming wholly absorbed in projects that fuel their imagination. They have the communication skills to inspire others to follow their lead, but also have an impulsive, thoughtless and occasionally self-indulgent side that can make them enemies. With an imagination that is highly developed, they are visionary innovators who enjoy looking at the world with a perspective that is often way ahead of their time.

Born dancers, they can excel in design, the arts, music and dance, and may also be drawn to sports, education, science, medicine, alternative health, business, politics, programming, web design or working for themselves, as all these fields offer them scope for their ambitious imagination to express itself. Movement, activity and socializing are important for their wellbeing and they may even get depressed if they don't set aside enough time to dance. **For self-care**, practice gratitude. Every night before sleep think of three people, and three things, you are grateful for.

Those born on this day are sensual and flirtatious, tending to go for looks over personality, and need to be less superficial in their choice of companions. They should learn to look before they leap, avoid people who lead them astray, and devote their tenacity and energy to a worthy cause. Before the age of 42 they risk getting involved in questionable or directionless pursuits, but after that the focus shifts to security and they should embrace this opportunity to connect deeply with their own and others' feelings because it is the path to their fulfillment. Once they are able to develop their empathy, their destiny is to lead and inspire others toward progress, by encouraging them to look at things from a fresh perspective.

Potential: Intuitive, independent

Dark side: Thoughtless, self-indulgent

Tarot card, lucky numbers, days, colors: The Wheel of Fortune, 1, 6, Friday, Sunday, lavender, orange

Born today: Bono (singer); Miuccia Prada (designer); Fred Astaire (dancer)

May 11

The Birthday of Distinctive Flair

The life lesson:

is not losing sight of what is real.

The way forward: is to tell it like it is, keep the facts in mind and don't try to exaggerate the truth. Being authentic earns the respect and support of others.

Luck maker: Listen to what others have to say now and again. It might be a revelation.

"I can see a rainbow"

May 11-born have an independent spirit that rarely answers to anyone or anything. They live in a world of their own creation and enjoy adding their distinctive, fun-loving flair to any situation they are in. Highly creative, they excel at making what is seemingly mundane appear entertaining or new. With a stubborn need to discover for themselves, their imaginative, insightful and original approach causes them to constantly challenge conventional thinking. Their greatest gift is their ability to make life feel more colorful and exciting, though they can come across as intelligent but ineffective when they get so immersed in their unusual thoughts that they lose touch with reality. They need to understand that with a little self-mastery they have the potential to achieve something better than the admiration of others: their respect and loyalty.

Born entrepreneurs, they may find ways of making a success of their original ideas in business, travel or self-employment. They may also excel in musical, creative or dramatic arts, or their interest in the human condition may draw them to research, the law and politics. They are prone to worrying, and if they have any health concerns, it is important that they discuss them with a doctor rather than getting anxious. **For self-care,** declutter. Regularly tidying up your home and work space encourages you to streamline your thought processes and adds a much-needed dose of organization and self-discipline, too.

These people have the ability to bring a magical sparkle to all their relationships and love being around children or those who are young at heart. Until the age of 40 they focus on study and experimentation, and they need to be careful not to lose themselves in exaggeration or fantasy. After the age of 40 they place more emphasis on stability and security. Once they are able to stay more objective and not lose sight of what is real and practical, their destiny is to make their mark on the world through innovating in a way that entertains, informs and inspires.

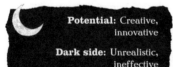

Potential: Creative, innovative

Dark side: Unrealistic, ineffective

Tarot card, lucky numbers, days, colors: Justice, 2, 7, Friday, Monday, lavender, silver

Born today: Irving Berlin (composer); Salvador Dalí (artist); Natasha Richardson (actor)

May 12

The Birthday of Lucidity

The life lesson:

is to learn the importance of tact.

The way forward: is to understand people are more willing to listen when you aren't on the offensive.

Luck maker: Sincere compliments (not flattery) make other people feel good and more likely to help or support you.

"True discovery is to see with new eyes"

Those born on May 12 appear serene, but, on closer acquaintance, surprisingly independent, witty, engaging people with a wealth of startling ideas emerge. They have tremendous willpower and self-discipline, and, although they don't seek out leadership positions often, they find that others choose them to lead because they inspire confidence. Highly observant, they use humor to challenge conventional thinking, but they need to watch this doesn't turn into sarcasm. They tend to become reticent to reveal their own feelings and dreams, and a part of them always remains a mystery. Despite their need for privacy, when they do share their unique, optimistic and expansive perspective, they have tremendous potential to motivate others.

Born film critics, with their powers of observation and ability to get right to the point they thrive in careers such as consultants, advisors, journalists, broadcasters, podcasters, comedians or critics. Their caring side can express itself in education, counseling, charity or healing work, and their creativity in design, sports, music and the arts. They need regular exercise, as well as to eat breakfast, regular meals and snacks during the day to fuel their naturally high energy levels. **For self-care**, regular meditation can help them be more objective and focus more attention on the positive rather than the negative.

Those born on this day tend to hold back emotionally in their relationships and they need to learn that feelings, however trivial, are worth sharing. Until the age of 39 there is an emphasis on study and developing their communication skills, and this is the time to soften their sharp tongue. After 39 the focus turns to home and taking care of themselves and others emotionally, and they need to focus on others' strengths rather than weaknesses, praising as much as they criticize. Once they understand that the more they give, the more they get back, and to focus on the positives as well as the negatives in a situation, there is nothing to stop them reaching for their dreams. Their destiny is to offer the world their fresh and innovative perspective.

Potential: Expansive, observant

Dark side: Sarcastic, distant

Tarot card, lucky numbers, days, colors: The Hanged Man, 3, 8, Friday, Thursday, lilac, green

Born today: Florence Nightingale (nurse); Tony Hancock (comedian); Katharine Hepburn (actor)

May 13

The Birthday of the Wild Child

The life lesson:

is learning to control impulses.

The way forward: is to understand that self-control is the key to success, because without it you are like a reed blowing in the wind.

Luck maker: Think before you act—considering the pros and cons before making decisions can make all the difference.

"I am born to be wild"

People born on May 13 have a magnetic and playful charm. Untamed and often self-taught spirits, they follow their instincts and often clash with social conventions, but their wild-child presence has an electrifying effect. They should be aware of the effect their popularity and success can have on others and modify their light-hearted approach because it can foster envy and resentment. They love movement and variety, and find routine boring and practical concerns unfulfilling. Although their butterfly approach makes them fascinating to be around, if they can learn to delve more deeply into subjects or situations, they will discover how enriching more intense knowledge or serious commitment can be. These people appear to glide through life, but it's likely that at some point a significant event, generally one with painful consequences, will give them the impetus to look within rather than outside themselves for true fulfillment.

Born designers, they have the impulsive, energetic creativity and independence to make great writers, artists, musicians, athletes and entrepreneurs. Their natural charm may also draw them to people-focused careers, such as public relations, human resources, teaching, the law and social-media influencing, but whatever career they choose, their chances of success are high. Lots of fresh air and exercise, preferably every day, is absolutely essential for their health and wellbeing.

For self-care, the best therapy is to commit to a course of study in one specific area to avoid spreading yourself too thinly.

Attracting admirers comes easily to those born on this day, but for relationships to be fulfilling, they need to have as much concern for the welfare of others as they have for themselves. Before the age of 37 they are likely to experiment and should aim to deepen their approach and outlook; after the age of 37 they may be more concerned with emotional commitment. When this newfound earnestness and sense of purpose is combined with their characteristic zest for life, not even the sky is the limit for them. Once they can look within themselves for insight, their destiny is to invigorate, inspire and, if necessary, shock others into progressive ways of thinking and doing things.

Potential: Energetic, fascinating

Dark side: Superficial, flighty

Tarot card, lucky numbers, days, colors: Death, 4, 9, Friday, Sunday, lilac, light blue

Born today: Stevie Wonder (singer); Daphne du Maurier (author); Dennis Rodman (basketball player)

May 14

The Birthday of the Progressive Outlook

is to be kind to yourself.

The way forward: is to understand that driving yourself too hard decreases, rather than increases, your chances of success.

Luck maker: Seize the power of the moment. The only, and best, way to create a better future is to live fully in the present.

"Higher and farther than ever before"

May 14-born are intellectually ahead of their peers. Their progressive outlook allows them to see potential that others who are less curious and imaginative may miss. Self-starters, they are unlikely to seek help, but, such is the power of their vision, others are often willing to support them. With the ability to lift whatever enterprise they undertake to the next level, they can only feel more fulfilled by innovating and making progress in some way. As indefatigable workers they usually achieve success, but there is a risk of burnout if they don't recognize their limits. Sometimes their progressive outlook is ridiculed, but more often than not they just need to wait, because sooner or later others come around to their visionary thinking.

Born social scientists, they have the vision and problem-solving skills to excel in politics, travel, science, research, space, information technology as well as advertising and investments. Artistic and creative pursuits such as music, drama, art, filmmaking and writing may appeal. With their love of variety, they need a career that avoids routine, so social media, journalism or working for themselves are all good choices. Taking regular time out to relax, have fun and unwind is absolutely essential for their holistic wellbeing. **For self-care,** say thank you more to everyone and everything. An attitude of gratitude is a prerequisite for a happy and fulfilling life.

In their relationships those born on this day need to stop trying so hard to gain admiration, and, instead, seek those who love them for who they are, not who they pretend to be. Their tendency to drive themselves too hard or be extremely self-critical is a theme throughout their lives, but is especially strong before the age of 36. At the age of 37 they may concentrate on the growing importance of their personal life, becoming more self-confident with each increasing year. And once they learn to be less critical of themselves and more patient with others, and to focus their energy on the present as well as the future, their destiny is to predict ground-breaking future trends capable of changing the world.

Potential: Innovative, energetic

Dark side: Perfectionist, restless

Tarot card, lucky numbers, days, colors: Temperance, 1, 5, Friday, Wednesday, lilac, blue

Born today: Mark Zuckerberg (entrepreneur); George Lucas (director); Cate Blanchett (actor)

May 15

The Birthday of Delightful Introspection

The life lesson:

is coming out of your shell.

The way forward: is to concentrate more on others than on yourself when you enter a new situation.

Luck maker: Open up—people who are enthusiastic and excited about life help others feel excited, too.

"Somewhere over the rainbow"

Those born on May 15 are often intelligent and highly imaginative. Truly young at heart, they have the ability to touch the souls of all those lucky enough to cross their path. Their creativity marks them out as the ones with the brightest solutions or magical ideas, and when they are around the world seems a fresher, more colorful place. The downside is that their dreams don't always translate into action because they tend to withdraw into self-imposed isolation and expect others to follow through. It really is important for them to put themselves forward and take responsibility for their creativity, since this is the only way they can reach their potential and fulfill their dreams. Others see them as living in a world of their own, which is often correct as they have an irresistible urge to acquire knowledge.

Born webmasters, they have the potential to inspire others and succeed in any career, from scientific research to business to something more artistic and creative. They may devote themselves to programming, web design, sports, finance or accounting, but whatever they choose, they should seek work or outside interests that engross and fulfill them. It is important for their wellbeing that they don't isolate themselves, so spending more time with loved ones and friends is advised. **For self-care**, wearing, meditating on and surrounding yourself with the color orange will encourage you to feel warmer and more spontaneous, and secure in the company of others.

In their personal life they may expect others to make the first move, and need to take the initiative and show more affection. Until the age of 36 they focus on education and new interests, and they may opt to stay in school or train longer than others. After 36 home and family life present opportunities for them to shake off their passivity and become more confident. Despite the dreamy image they present, when they learn to take responsibility for their talents and act as well as dream, others are drawn to the inspirational fruits of their vision. Their destiny is to share their innovative ideas and, by so doing, bring great happiness and illumination to the world.

Potential: Intelligent, enchanting

Dark side: Passive, detached

Tarot card, lucky numbers, day, colors: The Devil, 2, 6, Friday, lilac, pink

Born today: Andy Murray (tennis player); Madeleine Albright (politician); L. Frank Baum (author)

May 16

The Birthday of Bright Color

"I see the world in wonder"

is being more considerate to yourself and others.

The way forward: is to spend more quiet time alone, as this will give you greater insight into your motivations and more empathy for the feelings of others.

Luck maker: Keep your cool. Staying calm in a crisis shows others your inner strength, inspiring confidence.

People born on May 16 have expressive energy that often reveals itself in diverse, hidden or outrageous ways. They feel compelled to fly in the face of convention or rebel in their own distinctive way. Colorful and expressive, they make life unpredictable but never boring. Whether introvert or extrovert, they can be volatile and prone to extremes when their passions are triggered, and others learn to tread carefully around them. If they can't control their wildness, they run the risk of wasting their energy, but if they can harness their energy, their potential for success—especially for creative ventures—is infinite. It is important that they manage their emotions, learning to be less reactive, so that during bad times they have better coping mechanisms.

Born performers, they have a flair for the dramatic and excel in the world of entertainment, both on- and off-line, and the arts. Sporting careers or jobs involving banking, property, speculation, design or management may also appeal. Their compassion may draw them toward humanitarian or charity work. Eating a healthy, balanced diet, as well as retiring and rising early, help keep their emotions, weight and health more in balance. **For self-care**, take regular exercise, especially brisk walking and jogging, to release pent-up stress and tension in a positive way.

Sensual creatures, these people's relationships can be strained by their volatility and controlling tendencies. Until the age of 35 there is an emphasis on learning, and this is the ideal time for them to learn to manage their emotions better and consider the feelings of others. After 35 the focus is on emotional security, and growing in self-discipline is absolutely crucial. Although self-mastery is the key to their success, this should never be at the expense of their colorful personality. It is through their dynamic style of expression and passionately held convictions that they can impress others and add a touch of the exotic to the world around them. Once they get that essential sense of balance and objectivity, their destiny is to direct their prodigious energy to influencing, inspiring and entertaining others.

Potential: Exciting, expressive

Dark side: Moody, unpredictable

Tarot card, lucky numbers, days, colors: The Tower, 3, 7, Friday, Monday, lilac, sea green

Born today: David Hughes (inventor); Liberace (pianist); Janet Jackson (singer)

May 17

The Birthday of Profound Clarity

"I mean what I say"

Those born on May 17 are often straightforward and to the point. There is a touch of the mystic about them as they say clearly what they mean and mean what they say, and they are often an inspiring example of personal integrity. However, this clear-cut and deeply profound approach can win them as many enemies as supporters, and they might benefit from learning more tact. Their refusal to be diverted from their chosen course would appear to be a recipe for success, but sometimes they overestimate the power of what can be achieved through solo determination and they would benefit from recognizing the power of teamwork.

Born musicians, they have the creativity to excel in the world of art. Education, science, research, medicine and the law may also appeal, along with entrepreneurship. Once they learn the importance of teamwork, they may be drawn to public relations, lobbying, promotion, marketing, social work and banking. Prone to headaches and taking themselves too seriously, they should take plenty of time out to relax and laugh with loved ones and friends. **For self-care**, consider pet ownership, in particular training and owning a dog. If that isn't possible, spend time in nature for the stress-relieving benefits.

These people are extremely sensual, but would rather be alone than with someone they can't respect. Until their mid-thirties their emphasis is on learning; after the age of 34, they may focus more on emotional intimacy. If they can learn to get in touch with their own feelings and those of others, it promises great fulfillment. Their fixed views on things can hold them back, as life is not black and white. However, if they learn to develop a more tolerant approach, it will help them achieve their aims and attract a following, and also open up their compassion and determination to improve the lives of others. Once they learn the power of synergy, their destiny is to inspire others with their creative and organizational talents.

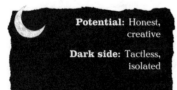

Potential: Honest, creative

Dark side: Tactless, isolated

Tarot card, lucky numbers, days, colors: The Star, 4, 8, Friday, Saturday, lilac, green

Born today: Enya (musician); Cool Papa Bell (baseball player); Alan Kay (computer scientist)

May 18

The Birthday of the Brave Warrior

"My mind is my greatest weapon"

May 18-born are deeply compassionate. Their greatest desire is often to alleviate the suffering of others and to right social wrongs. When they believe in the justice of their cause, they do not flinch from taking a courageous position to defend it. As well as being progressive, they are also practical and present a logical approach to situations, making their guidance much sought after, although their black-and-white stance can sometimes make them seem stern and insensitive. They should learn that not everyone is as practical or capable as they are, and that humility and wonder have their special place in life.

Born martial artists, they enjoy initiating projects and taking the lead, and can excel in life and sports coaching, the law, government, promotion, marketing, negotiation, charity work and humanitarian causes, fundraising or working with animals and nature. They may also express their creativity in philosophy, psychology, arts, music or dance. Getting in touch with their feelings, and spending time with loved ones, is extremely important to release tension. **For self-care**, regular massages help you relax and unwind and indulge your sensual, loving side.

Those born on this day are likely to have an interest of some kind and prefer to mix with those who share their passion. Yet they would benefit from meeting people from other walks of life, as they may give too much of themselves to their passion. Until the age of 33 they may focus on learning and study but still lack direction. Typically, by the age of 34 they settle on a direction, as they want more security and stability, and at this stage, they need to guard against becoming over-zealous promoting their chosen cause. Whatever path they choose, they are energetic campaigners for human progress. They have tremendous courage and steadfastness, and this, combined with their considerable compassion, sets them apart as true movers and shakers. Once they can recognize the merit of conflicting viewpoints and become more tolerant, their destiny is to truly inspire with their ability to take direct action to right wrongs.

Potential: Progressive, compassionate

Dark side: Fanatical, stern

Tarot card, lucky numbers, days, colors: The Moon, 5, 9, Friday, Tuesday, lilac, rose

Born today: Bertrand Russell (philosopher); Frank Capra (director); Yun-Fat Chow (actor)

May 19

The Birthday of the Convincing Candidate

"Everything great begins with a dream"

Those born on May 19 are articulate individuals with a clear sense of fair play. They speak out eloquently when they notice injustice and act decisively to ensure positive changes happen. They have a natural ability to convince others that changes need to be made and action taken. Such is their persuasive power that people often find themselves feeling energized after spending time with them. There is a danger, however, that those born today can use their magnetic communicative skills for unworthy causes or descend into dishonesty, and they should avoid this dark path at all costs.

Born songwriters, these people thrive in careers in which they can motivate, inform and inspire others such as in education, politics, medicine, science, research, social work and reform, counseling, religion, spirituality, the caring professions and philosophy. Their way with words makes them natural broadcasters, writers, journalists, speakers, singers and entertainers. They have a wild streak, so need to limit their caffeine intake and make sure they don't take unnecessary risks with their health. **For self-care**, chant: whenever stress starts to bite, say "Aum" out loud several times to induce feelings of peace and balance.

In their relationships, those born on this day should not let concerns about social status override their true feelings. Until the age of 32 they concentrate on learning and developing their talent for communication. Indeed, a sound education is vital to bring out their potential. After the age of 32 they become more focused on emotional intimacy and security; these years can be highly fulfilling. Inventive and original, their ideas are always worth listening to, whatever they choose to expend their energies on. Once they learn to strike a balance between standing up for their own ideas and being receptive to ideas that are not their own, not only are they able to persuade others of the importance of their ideals, they can also champion the needs of those less fortunate than themselves. Their destiny is to become a progressive voice for their peers and perhaps their generation.

Potential: Inspiring, fair

Dark side: Dishonest, materialistic

Tarot card, lucky numbers, days, colors: The Sun, 1, 6, Friday, Sunday, lavender, orange

Born today: Nancy Astor (politician); Florence Chadwick (swimmer); Pete Townshend (musician)

May 20

The Birthday of
Continuous Momentum

The life lesson:

is learning to pace yourself.

The way forward: is to understand that your desire to always seek the novel leads you to poorly planned behavior that repels rather than attracts success.

Luck maker: Finish what you start and understand the importance of patience, attention to detail and self-discipline.

"There is always more to see, know and do"

People born on May 20 are often communicative, and when one of their highly original impulses strikes, not only do they talk about it a lot, they act on it. However serene they may appear, underneath they crave freedom and find it impossible to keep anything to themselves, provoking in others excitement and confusion because of the speed at which they think, talk and act. They can be accused of superficiality, but though there is never enough time in the day for these people to do everything they want, they throw themselves wholeheartedly into all that they do. Often feeling as if they simply can't switch off, for their personal growth they must learn to look within themselves to find the excitement they crave.

Born firefighters, they may be drawn to careers in the emergency services, travel, rally driving, rescue, extreme sports, broadcasting or the media, and their humanitarian, philosophical and artistic side may also manifest through careers in social work, education, counseling, politics, science, research, the arts, music, songwriting and the healing professions. Constantly on the go, they must not neglect their health and should establish a regular sleep schedule, aiming to be sound asleep by midnight. **For self-care**, meditate, find inner calm and take time out to be still and observe yourself, to add a much-needed dose of objectivity to your life.

In their relationships (as in their work and all areas of their life), those born on this day need to learn that all that glitters is not gold. Until the age of 31 they focus on study and communication; after that they concentrate more on emotional depth and security, making this the ideal time for them to commit to a project, person or place. Once they learn to strike a balance between being and doing, these pioneering and stylish adventurers have the potential to be both an energetic jack-of-all-trades *and* an accomplished master of one; and this is a very rare combination indeed. When they can maintain a balance in all areas of their lives, their destiny is to energize others with their sparkling, original perspective.

Potential: Exciting, expressive

Dark side: Undisciplined, superficial

Tarot card, lucky numbers, days, colors: The Moon, 2, 7, Friday, Monday, lavender, silver

Born today: Cher and Joe Cocker (singers); John Stuart Mill (philosopher); James Stewart (actor)

199

GEMINI

THE TWINS (MAY 21–JUNE 20)

* **Element:** Air
* **Ruling planet:** Mercury, the messenger
* **Tarot card:** The Lovers (choices)
* **Lucky numbers:** 3, 5
* **Favorable colors:** Yellow, green, blue, white
* **Driving force:** Thoughtful communication
* **Personal statement:** Variety is the spice of my life
* **Chinese astrology counterpart:** The Horse

Geminis are extraordinarily versatile people. As the first dual sign of the zodiac, they have no problem doing different things at the same time—in fact, they often prefer it that way. Their need to constantly communicate with others is strong, and a life without phones, texts, social media and messaging is often inconceivable for them. Highly creative but impossible to pin down, people born under the sun sign Gemini can be both frustrating and delightful at exactly the same moment.

Personality potential

Gemini's ruler is Mercury, the witty and light-footed messenger of the gods in ancient Greek mythology, who traveled across the heavens delivering messages to humans. This explains why people born under this sun sign are often on the move, eager to gather new knowledge and experience new things. They take great pleasure in knowing a little about a lot, although not a lot about any one subject in particular, and live by their motto: Variety is the spice of life.

Geminis learn through imitation. They are highly versatile and anyone who makes an impression on them becomes their role model or mentor. They are natural communicators and can often dazzle others with their charm, wit, intelligence and humor. They pick things up amazingly fast. If you put a Gemini in a new group of people or a new situation, they will blend in and adapt quickly without any trouble. One of the reasons they are so readily accepted into new situations is that they simply love to talk. **They are genuinely curious about other people and seem to always know the right thing to say.** As well as being great talkers they are also charming and seem to have more than their fair share of good luck. One of the reasons they are luck magnets is their cheerful demeanor, willingness to experiment and firm belief that if one door closes other doors will open; if they can't find a door, they will try to enter through a window! Their quest is always for new

perspectives or alternatives, and can oscillate from genius one day to scatterbrain the next—hence the duality that defines the symbol of twins.

Staying with the theme of duality, Geminis can do two or more things at once with the greatest of ease; so, if you see one with a phone in each hand, don't be surprised. But it's not just multitasking and communicating at which these people excel. They are also natural negotiators, psychologists and experts in human relationships, which makes them excellent teachers, motivators, politicians and therapists. A Gemini knows how to talk even the most stubborn person round. In short, people born under the Gemini sun sign can have a touch of the magician about them.

> "They are genuinely curious about other people and seem to always know the right thing to say."

Personality pitfalls

Although Geminis are creative thinkers, when they have a new idea they have a tendency to rush in without first developing a strategy for success. Their ability to adapt can sometimes help them overcome their lack of planning and organization, but more often than not this can get them into trouble. However, perhaps their biggest personality pitfall is their superficiality. Their ability to assimilate knowledge quickly means that they often know a lot about many things, but not enough about what really interests them. This character trait can also have a negative impact on their relationships, resulting in them having a lot of acquaintances but few genuine friends.

Silver-tongued Geminis are not incapable of bending the truth if it serves their purposes. They also have a tendency to gossip, and their inability to keep secrets can upset those who have confided in them. There is no doubt that Geminis can be superb communicators and masters of language, but they often use words as a way of talking themselves out of genuine emotions. They tend to live in the realm of thoughts and ideas, and real feelings, such as love and sorrow, can deeply unsettle them. Inconsistency may be another problem. They may start one project with great enthusiasm but find it hard to sustain this to the end; this means that unfinished projects litter their path in life. This lack of focus hampers their chances of success and happiness, and, since fulfillment is what they are ultimately searching for and the reason why they flit around so much, the result can be mood swings and despondency.

Symbol

The symbol of the twins perfectly expresses the dual Gemini mind and personality. They have a sharp intellect that can see both sides of an argument but, instead of taking their time to decide where they stand, they tend to flit from one idea to another. Even though they usually believe what they say at the time they say it, it's not unusual for Geminis to change their minds, and hearts, from one day to the next.

Darkest secret

Geminis may appear to be the life and soul of the party, but their charisma and apparent self-confidence can sometimes hide a deep-seated emptiness. It could be said that the Gemini's restless quest for new perspectives is really a search for a part of themselves that they feel they have lost—the missing twin.

The more popular and in demand a Gemini is, the more they are likely to feel desperately alone until they realize the feeling of completeness they seek can only be found within.

Love

Love is a blissful romantic ideal and the ultimate high for Geminis. They long for a soul mate and may have many relationships and affairs in their quest to find him or her.

Geminis don't really trust their emotions and, if they find themselves overwhelmed by feelings, they will try to rationalize and explain them logically. This can make them appear distant and, at times, untouchable. It can also stop their relationships moving forward from initial attraction to a deeper and more intense connection.

People born under the Gemini sun sign tend to do well with partners who are more cautious, level-headed and serious than they are, because this complements their restlessness. Even though both Gemini men and women are born flirts, they demand complete faithfulness and devotion from their partner. They want their partners to be the dependable rocks they themselves find it hard to be. Shared interests are important, and they also want their partner to be sharp and well informed, to add spice to the relationship.

Love matches:
Sagittarius,
Libra
and
Aquarius.

The Gemini woman

Gemini women have a reputation for being playful and fickle, especially when it comes to affairs of the heart. Their mind and their moods are constantly changing, but hidden underneath their detached exterior is a woman who is capable of deep passion. In other words, the Gemini woman is complex and to win her heart you need to get all aspects of her personality to fall in love with you.

Gemini women find it hard to commit themselves to one person at a time, and that's why they don't typically settle down in a relationship until later in life when they have become more mature and self-aware. Until then they will present a different face to almost everyone they meet, but few, if any, of the people they get close to will know them really well.

When the Gemini woman does finally come to a deeper understanding of her own restless nature and settle down, her partner will never know quite what to expect. She'll be distant one day, cheerful the next, thoughtful the day after, sociable the day after that; flighty one day, and loving and devoted the following day, and so on. On the one hand, all this sounds exhausting, but, on the other, it's exciting. This just about sums up the Gemini woman. Her partner needs to be able to keep up with her thoughts and speedy personality changes, but in return she will offer her partner companionship, loyalty, love, romance and—perhaps most important of all—hopes and dreams to last a lifetime.

The Gemini man

Men born under the sign of Gemini love to socialize and may dress in an unusual way that makes them stand out. Typically, they won't talk that much about their own feelings, but they will be witty and well informed. They can also be persuasive and there are few people who don't succumb to their charms.

True to his sign, the Gemini man is often restless and unpredictable, and you'll never be quite sure which personality he is going to be on any particular day. There is one thing, however, you can be sure of if you fall in love with a Gemini man—life will never be boring. He brings excitement and a sense of romance. If you can survive his mood swings from being the most amazing, upbeat man in the world to becoming the most morose and sullen, you'll find yourself absolutely

mesmerized by his incredible and wide-ranging knowledge. He will always remain an enigma and there will be a part of him you can't reach or get close to, but, despite this, being in a relationship with a Gemini man is inexplicably one of the most natural, fun and thrilling rides in the world.

While it's true that the Gemini man has a tendency to flirt, this doesn't mean he will cheat. What he needs is a partner who can offer him plenty of variety and romance, and, although sex matters to him, he needs more from a partner than just the physical. He wants love, warmth, loyalty, conversation and, above all, companionship.

Family

The typical Gemini child—if there is such a thing, given their constantly changing personality—will often walk and talk at an early age. Their parents need to be fast, alert and ready not just to walk but to run and occasionally fly beside them. A young Gemini's mind is always active and they will want to know everything about everything. Patience is something they lack and they will need plenty to keep their active minds busy; this is because if boredom sets in, they can become rebellious and difficult to deal with. It's extremely important that they are encouraged to finish tasks they have started, but don't automatically assume that because they can have so many projects on the go they are scatterbrained. Gemini children have eclectic minds and work best when multitasking. They thrive in a schoolroom environment that is spontaneous, but they don't tend to do so well in schools with a strong disciplinarian ethic.

Young Geminis are also very sociable at school, and as soon as they get their hands on their own phone it never stops pinging. When it comes to examinations and interviews, they know how to talk the talk and walk the walk, but there is a tendency for their work to be opinion- rather than fact-based.

The Gemini parent is often very lively and open-minded, so there is a danger that they will try to fill their child's hours with a range of different activities and interests. This is fine if their child enjoys versatility as much as they do, but not so great if the child is more a creature of routine. On the other hand, the Gemini parent may swing the other way and impose on their own child the very discipline and structure against which they themselves rebelled. They need to be careful that their tongue does not become overly critical, and to understand that while the harsh words of a parent can scar a child for the rest of their life, carefully chosen and loving words can help build their self-esteem for a lifetime.

Health and wellbeing

Geminis seem to grow younger rather than older and they certainly aren't into that growing-old-gracefully thing. If health problems arise, they are more often than not caused by stress and tension rather than physical reasons. Geminis can be very highly strung, possessing vast amounts of mental and physical energy that they need to use up. Sometimes, however, they can go overboard and, like a delicate butterfly, burn themselves out with restlessness. It's extremely important that they learn to listen to their body more and recognize the early signs of exhaustion.

Anxiety and nervous tension are areas of concern if they can't find ways to relax and wind down. Gemini rules the nervous system, which includes arms, lungs, hands and fingers, so those born under this sign also need to watch carefully for breathing problems, asthma and colds that linger.

It's absolutely essential that they avoid smoking, which is bad news health-wise for anyone but particularly so for Geminis, with their tendency for breathing problems. Fresh air, plenty of gentle exercise, and regular periods of rest and relaxation are recommended. As far as diet is concerned, these people need to eat a light diet rich in fruits and vegetables, oily fish, legumes, nuts and seeds, and other foods that support the health of their nervous system.

Geminis love to move and they tend to move fast, but when it comes to exercise, they can get easily bored with a weekly routine. Their best option is to cross-train either individually or via a health club, and to combine a number of different forms of exercise from brisk walking, jogging, cycling and swimming to vigorous sports like squash. Activities such as yoga, which encourage them to relax and unwind both mentally and physically, are also recommended. Mental challenge is just as important as physical challenge for these lively individuals, so quizzes, crosswords and other exercises to stimulate their brain are all beneficial. Wearing, meditating on or surrounding themselves with the color **green** will encourage them to feel more harmonious and balanced.

Career

Geminis are so versatile and multitalented, and have such great communication skills, that they could do well in any career. Having said that, they tend to gravitate toward and excel in the media, social media, journalism, writing, advertising, entertainment, politics, photography, hairdressing and fashion. Being "people-people," they are also natural salespeople, and in business they can do very well as long as they can develop enough self-discipline and patience to see a task through to the very end. **Solitary professions don't typically suit these sociable souls** and they tend to do better when working with other people around them. They also need plenty of variety

> **Solitary professions don't typically suit these sociable souls.**

and challenge, and so flourish in jobs in which there is plenty of conversation, travel, action and feedback.

Born between May 21 and 31

People born between these dates are heavily under the influence of the planet Mercury, so they tend to be highly sociable and communicative. Several steps ahead of their time, their mental brilliance can be fascinating, controversial and—at times—exceptional.

Born between June 1 and 11

These Geminis tend to be more objective, with the clear vision needed to skip the details and get to the heart of the matter quickly or see the bigger picture. Their greatest joy is to see other people happy and, as a result, they may well devote themselves to a social cause.

Born between June 12 and 20

Geminis born between these dates can be more resilient and level-headed. Highly creative, they never fail to impress others with their wit, knowledge, insight and ability to understand what is going on around them.

Life lessons

Geminis are typically intelligent and well informed, but with their gift for words comes a tendency to talk too much and at all the wrong times. They would do well to learn the value of listening, silence and choosing the right moment to speak. They would also do well to understand the harm that reckless gossip can cause. Their fickleness may also alienate friends and loved ones, as they have a tendency to say one thing and do another, or make a date and then cancel at the last moment. Being flirty with everyone can make those who really love them feel as if they aren't special enough.

Although their free spirit is one of their most appealing characteristics, it can also be one of the most infuriating when they refuse to respect authority or restrictions of any kind.

When this nonconformity is combined with their notorious tendency to drop projects as soon as things get routine, the result can be indecisiveness and gaining a reputation for being unreliable. In fact, commitment is something most Geminis struggle with, whether it's commitment to a person, education, job or family—and this flightiness can lead others to think that they aren't dependable or genuine. Some may accuse Geminis of superficiality, but this isn't, strictly speaking, true. At the time, Geminis are one hundred percent genuine, but as they simply want to experience everything that life has to offer, they find it hard to linger long on any one thing or with one person when there are so many other things for them to learn, think about and do. The price they pay for their awareness of everyone and everything is that they can lose sight of their own feelings and personal identity.

Aside from learning to be more tactful, valuing the importance of rules, regulations and honesty, avoiding superficial people and connecting more with their hearts, the greatest lesson for a Gemini to learn is that commitment doesn't have to mean restriction. In fact, focus can be the most liberating thing for a Gemini because with commitment comes true understanding and insight—the missing link Geminis spend their life seeking.

Geminis would do well to repeat daily to themselves the mantra that it's quality not quantity that counts, and they can learn this kind of focus and commitment from witnessing those born under their own sign flounder when they talk and do too much. Virgos, Capricorns and Librans can teach them to be more disciplined and organized; Taureans can show them how to be self-sufficient; Sagittarians, Scorpios and Aquarians can inspire them to go beyond the superficial; Aries can encourage them to throw themselves wholeheartedly into one thing at a time, rather than several. Geminis could also learn the value of an emotional rather than an intellectual approach to life from Cancerians and Pisceans, while Leo can help them discover the feel-good importance of taking regular time out.

Chinese astrology counterpart: The Horse

Those born under the Chinese Horse sign share the superior communication skills and fast-moving, free-spirited approach to life of the Western Gemini. These swift and noble animals live each day of their lives enthusiastically in search of the next adventure or discovery.

Blessed with a curious mind and a lively, independent spirit, Horses' enthusiasm for everyone and everything is infectious. They can be extremely charming, knowledgeable and well-spoken, but their knowledge can often remain surface-level only. These restless creatures don't like to stay in one place for long. They are forever looking for new horizons to explore, not just intellectually but in all areas of their lives. However, once a Horse matures and is able to concentrate their tremendous energy and discover within themselves the focus, self-discipline and commitment needed to succeed, there really is no stopping them. The sky is their limit.

Note: Geminis have an affinity with Horse-sign characteristics, but be sure to check which Chinese sign corresponds to your **year** of birth (see page xxi), and to read about the characteristics associated with it, too.

May 21

The Birthday of the Can-do Attitude

"Bring it on!"

May 21-born show great courage in the face of opposition and are defined by their can-do attitude. Their natural confidence may inspire jealousy, but it gives them the head start they need to achieve their goals. Their approach to life is refreshingly upbeat and no challenge seems to be too much because not only do they have wonderful ideas and talents, they also have self-discipline. They are not just dreamers, but also doers, obsessively doing whatever it takes to get the job done. They are at their best when they are battling their way forward and progressing solo in some way. They must be in the driving seat of their lives, and when they act, their chances of success are significant.

Born inventors, their visionary and practical tendencies bode well for finance careers, social reform and technological invention. Their sensitivity may draw them to humanitarian work, politics, the law, science, engineering and educational research, while their creativity may express itself in the arts, music, writing, journalism and blogging. Being human dynamos, they need to recharge their seemingly limitless energy with healthy food, moderate exercise and plenty of sleep. **For self-care,** mind–body therapies such as yoga, tai chi and aromatherapy massages are beneficial, as is surrounding yourself with or meditating on the color purple.

These people tend to expect others to fall in line with their demands, and they need to learn the importance of give and take in relationships. Until the age of 30 they focus on learning, study and communication. They are typically quick learners, often feeling restless or bored with formal education or training that does not stimulate their ingenious turn of mind. After 30 they shift toward emotional security and stability, and the older they get, the more likely they are to come into their own. As long as they ensure their confidence doesn't turn into conceit, there is very little that can stand in the way of their success. Once they are able to pace themselves and take stock of their motivations and behavior, their destiny is to investigate, develop and implement their stunning ideas.

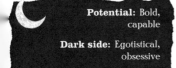

May 22

The Birthday of the Inventor

"I need to focus"

The life lesson:

is avoiding obsessive and/or controlling behavior.

The way forward: is to understand that the more you try to control people or situations, the more they want to break free.

Luck maker: Focus on what matters. Sounds morbid, but writing your obituary can help you organize your thoughts about what you want from life.

Those born on May 22 are both inquisitive and productive. They focus on the details but not to the point that it limits their ability to invent, discover or create something unique. Their biggest challenge is deciding what they want to do and they may spend many years experimenting. When they do eventually settle on a chosen course, it will take over their lives to the point where they get extremely unsettled if their flow is interrupted. Others may regard them as obsessive, but their ability to focus gives them the drive and resilience needed to realize their ambitions. With a tendency to overreach themselves and to hang on to obsolete people or projects, they should never tone down their vision or ambition. But the secret of their success lies in self-awareness and letting go of what is not empowering them anymore, playing to their strengths and minimizing their weaknesses.

Born innovators, they have the potential to be great creatives, inventors and explorers in whatever field they choose. They may find creative fulfillment in business as a CEO, manager, consultant, analyst or trouble-shooter, or in journalism, blogging, advertising, politics, humanitarian work and sports, or in teaching, research, science and the arts. As long as they don't go overboard, they could channel their fierce energy into physical fitness, as they have the willpower to get their body into athletic shape. **For self-care**, meditate by finding somewhere quiet to sit and breathing deeply. If thoughts interfere, gently pull attention back to the breath.

These people have controlling tendencies in relationships and need to give others the freedom they need themselves. It is also extremely important others give them space to explore, especially before the age of 30 when total devotion to one project is essential for their psychological and intellectual growth. After 30 they tend to be calmer and this is when they are likely to find a much-needed balance in their lives. Once they understand themselves better, their destiny is to pioneer progressive and potentially life-changing, but also soundly researched, ideas and methods in a leadership or advisory role.

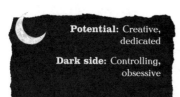

Potential: Creative, dedicated

Dark side: Controlling, obsessive

Tarot card, lucky numbers, days, colors: The Fool, 4, 9, Wednesday, Sunday, yellow, silver

Born today: Novak Djokovic (tennis player); Arthur Conan Doyle (writer); Naomi Campbell (model)

May 23

The Birthday of the Seductive Solution

The life lesson:

is learning to say no.

The way forward: is to understand that people respect you more if you set clear boundaries and let them know what their limits are.

Luck maker: If there is something you long to do, you should face your fears and find ways to give it a go.

"Eureka!"

People born on May 23 exude a radiant, sensual energy that others find impossible to ignore. Their defining feature, however, is their ingenuity. Gifted problem-solvers and natural communicators, they generously give their energy to help others resolve their problems in both practical and emotional ways. When faced with a dilemma, they may find that they have brilliant eureka moments when the answer just pops into their mind. They are highly creative but it is in activity rather than discussion that these intuitive individuals can truly reveal their inventiveness. They are not typically motivated by a desire for attention or leadership but by a genuine desire to help. The downside is that they often neglect their own affairs and others may take advantage of them. It is vital that they speak up for their own needs and interests; if they don't, this can lead to frustration.

Born mentors, they are often drawn to the healing, advising, counseling, psychology, teaching and caring professions, but their communication skills may find expression in the law, diplomacy, business, performing arts, sports, music, dance, writing, blogging and journalism. People-orientated careers suit them best, but they need to make sure they don't neglect their own health and wellbeing for the sake of others. **For self-care,** read about self-care and schedule regular activities, such as a walk in the park, home cooking or a warm, relaxing bath, into your daily schedule.

Those born on this day need to avoid co-dependent relationships where they do all the giving. Until the age of 29 they focus on communication and learning; after 29 they are likely to become more sensitive and security conscious. It is important then that they learn to say "no" to the demands of others and avoid sacrificing their own needs for others. They must accept that people can and do value them for the energetic, innovative and inspiring person they are, and not for how they can help others to progress. Once they have learned to be more self-nurturing, their destiny is to use their prodigious talent and energy to help both themselves and others evolve and move forward.

Potential: Sensual, ingenious

Dark side: Self-sacrificing, passive

Tarot card, lucky numbers, day, colors: The Hierophant, 1, 5, Wednesday, orange, violet

Born today: Carolus Linnaeus (taxonomist); Margaret Wise Brown (author); Jewel (singer-songwriter)

May 24

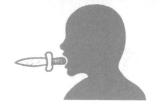

The Birthday of the Incisive Communicator

The life lesson:

is to avoid gossip.

The way forward: is to understand that although gossip gets the attention of others, it does not win their respect. You should only talk about people in a positive way.

Luck maker: Become an apprentice. Nobody likes a know-it-all, so learn from other people.

"This is how I see it"

May 24-born have a real gift for getting to the heart of the matter. With their love of observing and commenting on human nature and the world around them, others enjoy their company and colorful conversation. Although they will always champion the underdog, they do need to be careful that their witty insights do not descend into gossip, negative criticism or sarcasm. Despite being eloquent about everyone and everything, they are often strangely reticent about discussing their own lives. They can also close their minds to conflicting opinions, so it is important for them to learn the art of diplomacy and to respect the opinions of others. As long as these clever people keep their minds positive and inquisitive, their natural vitality, drive, creativity and ability to clarify the most complicated of situations ensures their popularity and success.

Born journalists, their ability to persuade and inspire others makes them great writers, bloggers, columnists, broadcasters and podcasters, and also marks them out for exciting careers in sales, marketing, acting, singing, composing and filmmaking, as well as in the law, teaching, the arts and the media. They should give in to the frequent urge to take time out from their busy social life, as time alone can help them relax and connect to their intuition. **For self-care**, unplug by setting aside at least half an hour a day, preferably first thing in the morning or before sleep, and switch your phone to silent.

In relationships these people need to be less controlling and more open and honest about their feelings. Until the age of 28 they focus on learning and communication, but around the age of 29 they may look for emotional and professional security, and the years that follow are when they are likely to come into their own, with another turning point toward self-confidence in their late fifties. They see possibilities and connections others might miss and these stunning insights can take them very far. Once they learn to be more accepting of differences of opinions, their destiny is to use their fascinating conversational skills to inform, positively influence and guide others.

Potential: Insightful, eloquent

Dark side: Caustic, untrustworthy

Tarot card, lucky numbers, days, colors: The Lovers, 2, 6, Wednesday, Friday, orange, pink

Born today: Queen Victoria (British queen); Daniel Fahrenheit (physicist); Bob Dylan (singer-songwriter)

May 25

The Birthday of the Caring Soldier

"I make a difference with the work I do"

Those born on May 25 are imaginative, inquisitive, compassionate, sensitive, honorable, tenacious and driven. But with so much going for them, they are often as much a puzzle to themselves as they are to others. Despite their desire and willingness to fight to improve and protect the lives of others, they are also deep, reflective thinkers with high expectations. They must become more tolerant because, if they don't, however successful they are they may feel repressed and unfulfilled.

Born humanitarians with a bold agenda for social reform, they have strong leadership potential and can gain great fulfillment by forging a new path in psychology, politics, humanitarian work and the military. The healing professions appeal and their communication skills may help them shine in sales, the law, music, art, acting, journalism and blogging. Sports, computers, engineering, science, research and philosophy are other key areas. They can appear distant and need to ensure they don't isolate themselves and have plenty of companionship, flexibility and fun in their lifestyle. **For self-care**, wearing, meditating on and surrounding yourself with shades of orange and yellow will encourage you to feel more connected to others, more willing to smile.

In close relationships they can be too serious for their own good and need to make sure they incorporate plenty of fun. Their early life may have been isolating or tough, but fortunately after the age of 27 the focus is on nurturing their emotional life. Once they are able to ground themselves emotionally and become more self-aware, they feel less frustrated in the decades ahead. They also discover that their courage in the face of opposition and their compassion for others are not contradictions but highly compatible energies, and the key to their outstanding potential for making a difference and improving human life—be it in the global or personal sense. Once they learn to be more accepting of themselves and others, their destiny is to implement their high ideals with their abundant energy and determination.

Potential: Honorable, caring

Dark side: Cold, repressed

Tarot card, lucky numbers, days, colors: The Chariot, 3, 7, Wednesday, Monday, orange, sapphire blue

Born today: Ralph Waldo Emerson (essayist); Bill Robinson (tap dancer); Igor Sikorsky (aircraft designer)

May 26

The Birthday of the Solicitous Adventurer

"The darkness is before the dawn"

People born on May 26 are often in demand and admired by others, but, deep down, they may dream of running away. Publicly, they promote social values and express serious concern for others, but personally they rebel against restrictions of all kinds. They can be incredibly progressive and compassionate to those less fortunate, but can also be prone to bouts of impulsive behavior when their private feelings conflict with their public dealings. Their dynamic energy is inspirational, though it can manifest in self-destructive or controversial behavior. Conflict is a theme for these complicated but utterly compelling people, yet this is exactly what they want, believing that fulfillment can't be found in their comfort zone. They should understand that self-knowledge can be gained during times of peace as well as times of danger.

Born politicians, they love to talk about their views and make excellent teachers, debaters, lawyers, sales persons, explorers, travelers, critics and performers. Once they are able to discipline themselves enough and concentrate so their energy is not scattered, their sharp mind gives them the ability to succeed in any career. Vigorous exercise is recommended to help them release tension in a positive, healthy and waist-whittling way. **For self-care,** spend less time in buildings and more time alone in nature, where inner peace can be found among the trees, grass and birds.

People born on this day may skip from one relationship to another, but showing their vulnerability gives them greater strength. After the age of 26 there are powerful opportunities to get in touch with their feelings. They need to make the most of these as, contrary to their beliefs, feeling happy and fulfilled is a distinct possibility for them. Once they are able to gain a more profound level of self-knowledge, and their talk matches their walk, their destiny is to rise to positions of leadership and to influence and inspire others through their charismatic and persistent words and deeds.

Potential: Charismatic, concerned

Dark side: Hypocritical, escapist

Tarot card, lucky numbers, days, colors: Strength, 4, 8, Wednesday, Saturday, orange, navy blue

Born today: John Wayne, Peter Cushing and Helena Bonham Carter (actors); Miles Davis, Lenny Kravitz and Lauryn Hill (musicians)

May 27

The Birthday of Progressive Action

"I find the courage to care"

May 27-born are perceptive but not as interested in ideas as in finding practical ways to benefit others. Blessed with self-confidence, they are compassionate yet can also be impersonal during the most difficult circumstances. Their steadiness is matched by their positivity and there is an elegance about them that brightens every situation. Their self-belief draws success and opportunities to them; if self-belief is lacking, this is because they have chosen a career or path in life not aligned to their talents. They find it hard to accept any criticism, so their personal growth depends on becoming more willing to take on board alternative viewpoints.

Born doctors, they have the skills to excel in medical, technical, legal, teaching, programming or government careers, as well as sporting or artistic fields. They may change careers several times, but whatever they settle on, the opportunity to guide and care for others in some way is essential for their fulfillment. They need to make sure they don't lose themselves in their work and neglect their diet and health. Regular exercise is a health-boosting and stress-busting must. **For self-care,** keep a mood journal. When your heart speaks, listen and write down your feelings. The most profound and empowering things in the world are not done, seen or heard but *felt.*

Seductive and affectionate, these people can prioritize work over relationships and have a tendency to be domineering and blank out what they don't want to hear. There are several key times in their lives that offer them opportunities to rethink their life; these will occur at age 25, 30, 40 and 55. Although their greatest wish is to serve others, they should take advantage of these opportunities to understand themselves and what motivates them better. Once they are more flexible in their approach and can accept they have personal failings just like everyone else, the enterprising energy of these clever and passionate people ensures their fulfillment. Their destiny is to help, inspire and guide others to achieve tangible results.

May 28

The Birthday of Rejuvenation

"Catch me if you can"

The life lesson:

is coping with boredom.

The way forward: is to understand that feeling bored can be a positive experience as it can teach you essential life skills, like patience, gratitude and self-sufficiency.

Luck maker: Set aside five to fifteen minutes every day to do nothing but daydream. Tuning into your thoughts can help you connect with the superpower that is your intuition.

Those born on May 28 are often innovative, versatile and think and act with lightning speed. They love to create original schemes and are eager to see them produce results, before rushing onto the next. Novelty, adventure and the excitement of the new are their fuel, and they will constantly seek to reinvent themselves through traveling, visiting new places, meeting new people and trying new things. Others find their silver-tongued charm hard to resist. Competitive by nature, with a perfectionist streak, they are well positioned for success. They like to share their ideas, but they can grow impatient when others seem slow to catch on. They need to seek the right specialist audience that appreciates their originality. It may take a while before they find their feet, perhaps moving from job to job or even from country to country, but when they do achieve this, they usually succeed in spectacular style.

Born performers and doers, they can make great artists, writers, actors, directors, athletes and online celebrities or entrepreneurs. Careers in sales, promotion, commerce, publishing and human resources may appeal, as might the law and charity work, or they may specialize as an advisor or counselor or in psychology or philosophy. **For self-care**, spending time alone with your phone switched to silent can encourage you to focus less on external stimulation for a sense of self and more on slowing down and tuning into your intuition.

Rushing into relationships tends to be an issue for them and they need to slow down. Before 54 they have opportunities to experiment and after 55 they become more confident and powerful in public positions. However, they will always crave new knowledge and experiences and feel a need to renew themselves. They will eventually find that the greatest success comes when they slow down. In fact, reflection and learning to savor their success and be true to themselves might be the most rejuvenating change of all. Once they learn the importance of patience and discipline, their destiny is to inspire others with their progressive, innovative perspectives.

Potential: Original, exciting

Dark side: Restless, hasty

Tarot card, lucky numbers, days, colors: The Magician, 1, 6, Wednesday, Sunday, orange, yellow

Born today: Gladys Knight, Kylie Minogue (singers); Ian Fleming (author); Carey Mulligan (actor)

May 29

The Birthday of the Plate Spinner

"Never enough"

People born on May 29 are charmers but not superficial ones, as they are determined to find a cause that fulfills them. So determined are they to have it and do it all that they may find themselves with dozens of projects on the go, but, remarkably, they have the creativity and determination to keep them all running smoothly, and others constantly wonder how they do it. They are not necessarily motivated by status, ego or wealth, but they do need an audience. If they don't have a following of some kind, they can become frustrated. Unfortunately, their people-pleasing tendency can lead to mood swings. They should learn to deal with their feelings rather than repressing them.

Born influencers, they thrive in people-orientated careers that allow them to be a mouthpiece or instrument to encourage progress or reform. Politics, the law, writing, the arts and social media all appeal, and their easy way with words may draw them to writing, education and sales. If they are attracted to business they may succeed in travel, technology or tourism. In their personal life, they need to slow down and take proactive measures to protect their health. **For self-care**, become your own best friend. When you feel sad or frustrated, offer the love, support, optimism and guidance you generously give to others to yourself.

In relationships these people can blow hot and cold and be interested in several people at once until they find a partner sensitive and strong enough to understand them. It will also take time to settle on a fulfilling career, but before 53 there are opportunities to find a clear direction, as their focus is on emotional security, and after that age they just grow in self-confidence. Wherever they decide to direct their energies to, their greatest wish is to assist others. Once they find a way to make this a reality, they possess the charisma and leadership skills to really help make the world a better place. Their destiny is to improve and inspire the planet through their words, deeds or legacy.

Potential: Inspirational, vibrant

Dark side: Frustrated, restless

Tarot card, lucky numbers, days, colors: The High Priestess, 2, 7, Wednesday, Monday, orange, blue

Born today: John F. Kennedy (US president); Dorothy Hodgkin (chemist); Noel Gallagher (singer)

May 30

The Birthday of
Mercurial Sparkle

is learning to focus your energy.

The way forward: is to understand that scattering your energy is equivalent to scattering your potential for success.

Luck maker: Improve your concentration by removing distractions and switching off your phone. A focused objective mind is a powerful mind.

"A change is as good as a rest"

May 30-born tend to be versatile, talkative, speedy and expressive. With their thirst for knowledge and eye for opportunities, they have the talent and astute mind to succeed in a variety of fields, but need to guard against scattering their energies with diverse interests. Their challenge is to pick only one field and to commit themselves to it for the long haul. As gifted as they are, their insatiable hunger for change can lead them to neglect their commitments and let others down. They can also change their moods rapidly, and although this adds to their mystery and appeal, it can also work against them by unnerving those who may doubt their reliability. The greatest lesson for them to learn is the commitment that is essential for success.

Born traders, they need careers that offer them stacks of variety and challenge, and may be drawn to stockbroking, banking, commerce and trade, as well as sports and arts. Their communication skills may connect them to writing, teaching, journalism, promotion, lobbying, commerce, negotiating and the media. As natural psychologists, they may also thrive in science, counseling, therapy and healthcare. Prone to poor concentration and overload, they benefit from regular scheduled windows of quiet with minimal stimulation to allow their nervous system to reboot. **For self-care**, meditate daily. Find somewhere quiet, sit down, close your eyes and breathe deeply. If thoughts appear, notice but don't interact with them.

These people can effortlessly charm others with their mercurial sparkle, but also unsettle them with their restlessness and ability to be delightful and difficult at the same time, so they need to become more balanced in their approach. Before their early fifties their focus is on emotional security and finding a secure home base, giving them many opportunities to become more responsible and understanding in their relationships. When staying power is combined with their great communication skills, limitless imagination and refusal to be bound by convention, these people are blessed with great innovatory power. Their destiny is to influence, inspire and motivate others with their enthusiasm, energy and magical vision.

Potential: Gifted, expansive

Dark side: Scattered, moody

Tarot card, lucky numbers, days, colors: The Empress, 3, 8, Wednesday, Thursday, orange, purple

Born today: Alexei Leonov (cosmonaut); Brian Kobilka (physiologist); Idina Menzel (singer)

May 31

The Birthday of Clarity

"Let me be clear"

The life lesson: is coping with rejection.

The way forward: is to understand there is no such thing as failure if you learn from it.

Luck maker: Turn rejection into resolve by growing stronger, not weaker, when you experience setbacks. Learn from them and use that new knowledge to adapt your approach and improve your chances of success next time.

Those born on May 31 are known for their minimal-fuss approach to life. Although they appear tough, their greatest desire isn't to be feared or even admired, but for their intentions to be clearly understood. The downside of leaving no room for misinterpretation is that they can become overbearing and intolerant. They can also underestimate the importance of reflection when things don't go as planned, believing that failure is not an option and that being constantly on the go is the best answer to everything. Above all, they have an air of authority and seriousness about them, and although they benefit from letting their hair down occasionally, if they can direct their mind to being expansive rather than single-minded they have the potential to achieve great success and possibly fame.

Born writers, they are attracted to all the arts, be it music, dance, singing, drama, design, painting, poetry or writing. They also find fulfillment in humanitarian work, teaching and people-related careers such as promotions, marketing, hospitality and public relations. They tend to neglect having down time to rest and reflect or deal with insecurities hidden behind their tough exterior. **For self-care**, bring beautiful pot plants and flowers into your home and workspace. Spend time nurturing them and watch them grow or bloom. Let them be a daily reminder of the importance of slowing down, reflecting and smiling more.

In relationships these people abhor game-playing, valuing honesty, loyalty and physical affection above all else. Until their early fifties they may have an ever-growing need for personal intimacy and emotional security. This can be a challenging time for them because they view any personal vulnerability as a weakness. After the age of 52 there is a turning point, suggesting a move toward great creativity and personal confidence. Once they have learned to be less black and white, their destiny is to find inner peace by informing and inspiring others with their insatiable enthusiasm for knowledge-gathering.

Potential: Determined, clear

Dark side: Dogmatic, insecure

Tarot card, lucky numbers, days, colors: The Emperor, 4, 9, Wednesday, Sunday, orange, silver

Born today: Clint Eastwood, Brooke Shields and Colin Farrell (actors); Walt Whitman (poet)

June 1

The Birthday of the Enigmatic Student

"I need to understand"

June 1-born are fun and even those who are less entertaining have a mischievous sparkle in their eyes. They are insatiably curious, rarely concentrating on one subject alone, because details stifle them. They focus their energy on studying and imitating the styles of successful people to learn the best way to achieve their own success. This approach does work, but it means they never get to fully know themselves or what their own talents are, and their low boredom threshold means they rarely see things through. Often surrounded by admirers, they can be vain and may flit from one person to another depending on who flatters them the most.

Born detectives, they can achieve success in careers that utilize their superb observation and communication skills, such as police work, psychology, lobbying, marketing, commerce, advertising, the media, politics, sales, commerce, journalism, writing, blogging, social media, music and theater. They need careers that offer them lots of variety. They find illness frustrating, so the best health advice is to practice preventative medicine by eating a healthy diet and getting plenty of fresh air and exercise. **For self-care**, keep a daily diary to record feelings, goals and dreams, and help you understand yourself better.

Despite their compulsive interest in others, those born on this day are paradoxically also private and don't reveal their deeper thoughts or feelings to others. They do need to get in touch with their own feelings and find what they want out of life to achieve their creative potential. Before the age of 50 they have many opportunities to establish their own individuality; it is crucial that they don't scatter their energies on causes and people unworthy of them. After 50 they become more self-assured. If they find the courage to trust their intuition, they will be able to unite the enigmatic, private aspects of their personality with their charismatic parts. This inner–outer integration gives them the focus they need to realize their own unique potential. Once they have looked within and found out who they are and what they want, their destiny is to bring an inspiring sensual flair to every enterprise they are involved in.

Potential: Inquisitive, entertaining

Dark side: Vain, restless

Tarot card, lucky numbers, days, colors: The Magician, 1, 7, Wednesday, Sunday, orange, gold

Born today: Marilyn Monroe and Morgan Freeman (actors); Lucy Kurien (NGO founder)

June 2

The Birthday of Ingenuity

"My life is exciting"

Those born on June 2 are quick-witted with a talent for analyzing and resolving difficult situations. Their lives are rarely problem-free, but they thrive on testing their ingenuity. If life won't present them with problems to overcome, their natural response is to seek them out. They can be the lifesavers who restore order, but their addiction to crisis can work against them, especially when they develop habits, such as lateness or disorganization, that unnecessarily create an adrenaline rush when things are going smoothly. Also, their enthusiasm to solve problems can attract them to people and causes unworthy of them. They need to remember that the greatest challenge is not found externally but in getting to know themselves better. If they can focus more on their own talents and less on external stimuli, their potential for success is limitless because they have highly developed intuitive powers.

Born troubleshooters, they need careers that offer them independence and allow them to use their ingenuity, such as in science, research, sports, music, design, the arts or consultancy work. They also make great negotiators, agents and lawyers, and their humanitarian streak may draw them to counseling and the caring professions. Intense and exciting people, they may often be prone to stress and need to schedule regular periods of rest and relaxation. **For self-care**, seek magic in the everyday by focusing on the present moment and paying closer attention to the details.

In relationships those born on this day find greater fulfillment when they stop seeking out complicated people for a false sense of excitement and learn that they cannot change others, they can only change themselves. Before the age of 50 they have many opportunities to develop self-awareness, which they should take advantage of, as they offer the key to their fulfillment. After 50 they enter a period of even greater self-confidence. When directed to a worthy cause, and fully understanding that change begins from the inside out, their destiny is to influence, motivate and inspire others with their talent for injecting ingenuity and highly creative flair into problem-solving.

Potential: Inventive, exciting

Dark side: Restless, difficult

Tarot card, lucky numbers, days, colors: The High Priestess, 2, 8, Wednesday, Monday, orange, pearl

Born today: Edward Elgar (composer); Charlie Watts (drummer); Abby Wambach (soccer player)

June 3

The Birthday of Original Wit

"I speak my progressive truth"

People born on June 3 are blessed with charming communication skills, which are the key to their success, both personally and professionally. Persuasive, passionate and witty, their ideas are progressive to the point that others may sometimes struggle to understand them. Not feeling understood is hugely frustrating, because these people have profoundly important things to say. Being free spirits, they need to express their individuality. They are compassionate and believe in equality for all, but are not afraid of using biting sarcasm to make their point when disputes arise. Sometimes they are unaware that their comments can be insensitive and greatly hurt others. This may cause some to avoid them, which upsets them, as silent treatment is what they fear the most.

Born lecturers, they can excel in teaching, research, the performing arts, music, sales, writing, journalism, podcasting, broadcasting, publishing, commerce and business, but whatever career they choose it must involve intellectual challenge. They can be reluctant to visit the doctor, preferring to self-medicate or take the natural approach. Generally, their health is robust, but they should listen to their doctor's advice if health gives them a reason to do so. **For self-care**, mix with sincere people and make sure you avoid toxic, insincere people who drain your sparkle, and choose companions wisely.

Before the age of 48 those born on this day can become more sensitive to the feelings of others, as there is an accent on personal relationships. After the age of 49 the focus switches to greater self-expression and assertiveness. Once they have learned to be more aware of the impact their words have on others, there is little to stop them reaching for the top. They will always be slightly eccentric or unconventional in their approach, but this originality is their driving force. Deep down they know that when they are true to themselves, life is infinitely more rewarding and fulfilling. Their destiny is to inspire others with their original ideas and, by so doing, make their unique mark on the world.

Potential: Expressive, witty

Dark side: Incomprehensible, sarcastic

Tarot card, lucky numbers, days, colors: The Empress, 3, 9, Wednesday, Thursday, orange, purple

Born today: Rafael Nadal (tennis player); Suzi Quatro and Josephine Baker (singers); Anderson Cooper (journalist)

June 4

The Birthday of the Apprentice

"I breathe to learn"

June 4-born have verbal dexterity and spectacular intellectual potential. The key to their success is an education or apprenticeship that can help nurture their quick minds. With an intense desire to learn and improve themselves, they are always hungry for novel information. Their natural curiosity is their greatest strength, but it can also be a weakness if they neglect their own emotional development. They are charismatic, with great leadership potential, but, until they grow in self-awareness, they are happiest working under direction or in a team, to which they are an asset given their intellectual and organizational skills.

Born researchers, they have an aptitude for study and make excellent teachers, programmers, engineers, writers, journalists and inventors. Once they get in touch with their creative side, they may be drawn to acting and the arts. They enjoy inspiring and helping others, so may thrive in sales, advertising, journalism, blogging, social media, social work, counseling and the caring professions. They can be extremely intense about their work and life, so laughter is the best holistic therapy for them. **For self-care**, recall your dreams. Get into the habit of writing them down as soon as you wake up, to see what messages your intuition is sending you.

Intellectual stimulation matters greatly to these people in relationships and they may struggle to commit to one person. They need to understand that relationships are a meeting of hearts as well as minds and bodies. Before the age of age 47 they have plenty of opportunities to focus on their feelings. After 48 they are likely to become more self-aware and able to realize their vision. When they finally tune into their own feelings, they discover a confidence in their own creative potential that may have been dormant. They should develop that potential, as not only will it help them become more powerful in their own right, it is the key to their fulfillment. Once they are in touch with their powerful intuition, their destiny is to achieve progress by sharing their great knowledge with the world.

June 5

The Birthday of the Intellectual Juggler

"I see infinite potential"

Those born on June 5 are superb multitaskers who can successfully juggle many ideas and projects. They have the inspiring ability to generate such innovative ideas that others either admire or fail to understand them. Born to stimulate others to think, they are always seeking to unearth some great discovery or mystery and share their knowledge, but, if they are misunderstood, it is likely to wound them deeply and cause flashes of irritation. Learning to be more patient and focused, and listening to what others say, helps them get their point across more effectively. Prone to worry, they also need to learn to manage their negativity.

Born comics, they have a talent for using their verbal skills and original thoughts to make great poets, entertainers, writers, directors, artists and lyricists. The world of science, engineering and technology appeal, as do the law, diplomacy, business, advertising, merchandising and art dealership, while their compassionate nature may draw them to the caring professions. They tend to be always on the go and need to avoid relying on caffeine or other stimulants to fuel their limitless energy. **For self-care**, recharge your batteries by regularly spending time in nature, listening to beautiful music or interacting with loved ones and friends.

Although those born on this day often have many admirers, few if any really know them well. It takes a while for them to open up. Before the age of 46 the focus is on emotional security and home life. After 47 they reach a turning point, signaling a period of growing self-confidence and allowing them to become more outgoing and measured in their approach. They have boundless energy and creativity and should never lose their vitality, but they do need to learn how to channel it effectively. Once they can find balance between their intellect and their instincts, and learn to worry less and live more, they have the imaginative gifts, technical aptitude and focus needed to develop their novel ideas and share them successfully with others. Their destiny is to inspire and even shock others with their highly innovative ideas and approach.

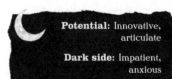

Potential: Innovative, articulate

Dark side: Impatient, anxious

Tarot card, lucky numbers, day, colors: The Hierophant, 2, 5, Wednesday, orange, cobalt blue

Born today: John Maynard Keynes (economist); Dennis Gabor (physicist); Kathleen Kennedy (film producer)

June 6

The Birthday of Anticipation

The life lesson: is feeling misunderstood.

The way forward: is to put yourself in the audience's shoes and tailor your vision to the interests of them.

Luck maker: Be flexible—lucky people are driven and focused, but also know when to adapt.

People born on June 6 bring an aura of excitement and anticipation with them. They are the people who make things happen and others sense this. They have progressive ideals and work steadfastly to make them a reality, often gaining a following with their commitment to improve lives. They love to share, inspire and inform, and are movers and shakers, but they can take their ideals or vision to an extreme, disorientating more conventional people with their behavior. Learning to express themselves with greater simplicity helps them get their point across.

Born event organizers, they are likely to excel in careers that celebrate their unusual ideas and may be drawn to design, the arts, advertising, sales, journalism, education, online influencing and entertainment, as well as careers that involve travel and the outdoors. If they can develop their rational side, they make great scientists and technologists. The greatest threat to their health is their tendency to push themselves to the limits, so exercise and hobbies that help them feel calmer are recommended. **For self-care**, sit down and listen to calming music with eyes closed whenever tension is rising.

Love and relationships come to people born on this day, and although they should never rein in their wonderful impulsive energy, they should find a balance so that their more bizarre tendencies do not alienate others and isolate themselves. Fortunately, before their mid-forties, they are likely to be more restrained, with a strong focus on their home and personal life. At the age of 46 they have an increased need for self-expression and leadership, and they are likely to become more assertive, taking more of a public role. It is important at this time that they understand how their actions serve as a role model for others. Once they have found an audience they can relate to and who relates to them, they more than live up to the anticipation that their progressive visions have created. The relief they feel in finally being understood encourages them to express their caring nature and determination to change the world for the better. Their destiny is to influence and inspire others with their independence of thought and spirit.

Potential: Exciting, idealistic

Dark side: Extreme, misunderstood

Tarot card, lucky numbers, days, colors: The Lovers, 3, 6, Wednesday, Friday, orange, pink

Born today: Nathan Hale (patriot); Thomas Mann (novelist); Björn Borg (tennis player)

June 7

The Birthday of Seduction

"I bring the magic"

June 7-born have a rich inner life full of great ideas and potential. Their enchanting style captivates the imagination and more often than not they are trendsetters. Whatever they decide to do, it is slightly ahead of its time. They understand the power of appearance and typically take great care over how they look, often letting their clothes, body language and eyes do the talking for them—sometimes too much talking, as they are not afraid of being sensational. They are also a lot of fun to be around, instinctively grasping the seductive powers of both surprise and humor. However, if they don't get in touch with their intuition and inner feelings, they run the risk of living life on a superficial level.

Born performers, they love to enchant and entertain an audience. They also make terrific party planners, salespeople, promoters and publishers. Teaching, lecturing, writing, marketing, social media, advertising, commerce and the law may also appeal, but, whatever career they choose, they will bring their seductive flair. Personal grooming matters to them and they need to make sure they don't take their concern with appearance to unhealthy, obsessive extremes. **For self-care,** someone who radiates love for self and others, and kindness and generosity, radiates true beauty from the inside out.

Loving the thrill of the chase and also possessing an instinct to run away, they need to learn the value of commitment in relationships. Before the age of 44 they have significant opportunities to focus on their values and inner life, and after that age, there is a turning point that encourages greater assertiveness; as long as they guard against self-absorption, they can really come into their own during these years. They need to make sure they don't subordinate their individuality to material concerns or repress it for fear others might think them odd. They aren't odd—they're just full of unique creative potential. Once they are able to look within themselves for a sense of fulfillment, their destiny is to enchant the world with their own special brand of charisma and magic.

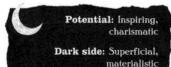

Potential: Inspiring, charismatic

Dark side: Superficial, materialistic

Tarot card, lucky numbers, days, colors: The Chariot, 4, 7, Wednesday, Monday, orange, sky blue

Born today: Tom Jones, Iggy Azalea and Prince (singers); Paul Gauguin (painter)

June 8

The Birthday of Expectation

"I get things done"

Those born on June 8 are honest and direct. They speak their mind and, because they have such high expectations of themselves and others, despise laziness or injustice in any form. Although highly independent and quite happy to work alone, they often find themselves in the position of leader because they have a sense of fair play and understand the importance of adhering to rules—as long as these rules are their own. They also set an inspiring example in their dedication to the task in hand, but they can sometimes tip over into workaholism.

Born architects, they have the inventiveness for vocational careers such as research, science, design, building, landscaping and planning. The law, education, programming, banking and accounting may appeal, as might show business, art and music or self-employment. Exercise is a vital stress-release for people born on this day and it is essential for their holistic wellbeing that they have a workout schedule in place. **For self-care**, cultivate a hobby or interest outside work, such as walking in nature, dancing, singing, reading or listening to podcasts. Doesn't matter what it is as long as it takes your mind off work.

The commitment to work of those born on this day can impact their relationships and they need to set aside enough time to nurture their personal life. Until the age of 43 they should not let their sense of fun and spontaneity disappear and become harsh or judgmental. After 44 they become more self-expressive and assertive, but need to make sure that they do not become overly zealous in their attitude to work. The key to their success is to balance their emotional needs with their strong sense of responsibility. Their curiosity, integrity, industriousness and devotion to progress enable them to blaze a pioneering trail and build a wide social circle. Once they can develop empathy and a greater tolerance for vulnerabilities, their high expectation of fulfillment is realized in their own success and happiness. Their destiny is to influence and inspire others with their innovations and incisive perceptive powers.

Potential: Dedicated, honest

Dark side: Workaholic, judgmental

Tarot card, lucky numbers, days, colors: Strength, 5, 8, Wednesday, Saturday, orange, hunter green

Born today: Tim Berners-Lee (inventor of the World Wide Web); Frank Lloyd Wright (architect); Joan Rivers (comedian)

June 9

The Birthday of Unexpected Opportunity

"I want it all"

People born on June 9 have a wonderful zest and others may find it hard to keep up with their ever-changing thoughts, feelings and emotions. Everything about them is unexpected. Externally, they can be strong-willed, but in personal relationships they can be surprisingly passive. They are unconventional but respectful toward authority. They are generous to those less fortunate, but sometimes insensitive to their loved ones. Action is key for them and they thrive on challenges and variety, often rushing from one thing to another with little spare time. It is important for them occasionally to slow down and catch their breath. They should aim to find focus and direction and to control their impulses.

Born rock-climbers, they prefer active roles that test them physically and mentally rather than administrative roles, and excel in a multitude of professions ranging from sports, journalism, media, writing, music and drama to research, politics and computing. Careers that involve fresh air and activity, such as farming, climbing, building and tourism, may appeal, as does working with children or being self-employed. If they no longer exercise, it is important that they bring it back, as it is an endless source of enjoyment and stress-release for them. **For self-care**, bring health-boosting green plants and flowers into your home and workspace and nurture them mindfully every day to discover the joys of patiently caring for something and watching it grow.

Those born on this day need to understand that relationships are like flowers: they need tender loving care to bloom. Until 42 they focus on security and family, taking a while to leave the nest, unwilling to branch out independently. Around the age of 42, they reach a turning point, which emphasizes power, self-confidence and really coming into their own. These people are colorful and versatile and if they can learn to channel their energies into mature goals, they find that life offers them a series of unexpected but well deserved opportunities for happiness, success and fulfillment. Once they get to know themselves better, their destiny is to be young at heart and inspire others never to forget their dreams.

Potential: Energetic, fascinating

Dark side: Changeable, tactless

Tarot card, lucky numbers, days, colors: The Hermit, 6, 9, Tuesday, Wednesday, orange, crimson

Born today: Peter the Great (Russian emperor); Johnny Depp, Michael Fox and Natalie Portman (actors)

June 10

The Birthday of Paradox

The life lesson:

is being authentic.

The way forward: is to understand that you can't make your unique mark on the world until you understand what makes you unique and who you truly are.

Luck maker: Buy a lucky charm. Charms don't have any special magic—they work because people expect them to.

"Let's be happy"

June 10-born are gifted and hard-working individuals with strongly held views they are not afraid to express. Everything about them exudes vitality, confidence and magnetic charisma, but, behind the scenes, they can be highly strung and overemotional, suffering from bouts of crippling self-doubt. This intriguing paradox defines their personality and the key to success is finding an inner balance. They find it hard to acknowledge their insecurities to both themselves and others, and prefer to lose themselves in either the confident persona they have created or in escapist behavior, but only when they have faced their inner demons can they truly find inner peace. Through it all, they should never underestimate their ability to not just cope but to shine, because they are capable of remarkable things.

Born entertainers, they have great energy and charisma and can excel in stand-up, live theater, music, entertainment, fashion, broadcasting and the arts, as well as in the military, police, public relations, diplomacy, sales, education, journalism, photography or any career that involves variety, as they abhor routine. They have self-destructive tendencies and should avoid alcohol, drugs and other addictive substances. **For self-care**, surround yourself with optimistic and positive people, not those who flatter you insincerely and ultimately drag you down.

Commitment for those born on this day can be an issue in their relationships and they would benefit from a more serious attitude to love. Until the age of 41 they may focus on emotional security and family life; they should take advantage and get in touch with their feelings and also build a network of close friends to whom they can open up. After 41 they enter a period of increasing confidence and self-expression, and, if they make sure they don't avoid problems or let others take advantage of them, this is when they are most likely to develop their talents successfully and come into their own. Once they find the courage to confront their inner fears, they discover within themselves a powerhouse of creativity to achieve their amazing dreams. Their destiny is to first discover and then develop their innovative and inspirational potential.

Potential: Gifted, daring

Dark side: Erratic, self-destructive

Tarot card, lucky numbers, days, colors: The Wheel of Fortune, 1, 7, Wednesday, Sunday, orange, silver

Born today: Hattie McDaniel (actor); Judy Garland (singer); Bill Burr (comedian)

June 11

The Birthday of Expansion

"I am going farther than ever before"

is sustaining close relationships.

The way forward: is to understand that, regardless of career success, your true fulfillment can only be found when personal relationships are equally fulfilling.

Luck maker: Diversify your life goals— studies show that happiness is greater among those who are positive about many areas of their lives.

Those born on June 11 are ambitious. They love to push themselves to the max and often forge ahead toward their goals with surprising force, tearing down any obstacles in their path. They lose themselves wholly in their work, achieving specialist status with pioneering breakthroughs. They are hard workers with a sense of fair play, and work well in teams, but are more suited to being leaders or self-starters. Less evolved individuals may lack supporters because they have slipped into narcissism, and they need to learn empathy and humility to get people on their side. Their zest for life means they have little time for those with less energy or enthusiasm. They avoid negative or depressed people because they instinctively understand that a positive attitude increases their chances of success. But sheer success isn't always enough for them. They crave outstanding, never-heard-of-before success. Although this attitude can take them to the very top, it can lead also to emotional isolation when others find their constant pushing exhausting.

Born runners, they are attracted to research, science, social work, politics, business, the law, art, film, acting, music and sport, but being so hard-working and having superb communication skills, they can thrive in any career. They tend to live to work, not work to live, and this can lead to obsessive behavior and burnout if they don't establish a healthy work–life balance. **For self-care**, wearing, meditating on and surrounding yourself with the color orange will increase feelings of much-needed emotional warmth, spontaneity and security.

Relationships for those born on this day tend to take second place to work, and, for their happiness, they need to nurture their close personal relationships as much as their careers. Before the age of 41 they have opportunities to develop their emotional life and build a sense of security, but after 41 they become more confident and aggressive. If they have learned by then of the damaging effects of their workaholic tendencies, this is when they have the potential to find great fulfillment. Their destiny is to push boundaries and achieve great breakthroughs, not just in their careers but also in their lives.

Potential: Progressive, positive

Dark side: Workaholic, narcissistic

Tarot card, lucky numbers, days, colors: Justice, 2, 8, Wednesday, Monday, orange, buttermilk

Born today: Garret Yount (scientist); Peter Dinklage (actor); Jacques Cousteau (explorer)

June 12

The Birthday of Realistic Positivity

"Things can be better"

People born on June 12 are independent and optimistic. Their strong belief in the power of hope and goodness to cure all has an uplifting effect, helping other people change for the better. Generous and supportive, they only support what they know is achievable, their positivity being tempered by realism. Their aim is to make things better, not perfect, and to encourage others to help themselves. Occasionally, this can manifest in judgmental words, but their tough-love approach generally works. Their self-contained, sunny disposition helps them not only to achieve great things, but also to be pioneers. They can't abide laziness, excuses or procrastination. The downside is they can bury inner conflicts behind a superficial exterior and this approach leads to unhappiness.

is facing your inner demons.

The way forward: is to understand that acknowledging hidden fears reduces their power.

Luck maker: Ignite your intuition by asking it questions, and expect to receive answers that improve your chances of success.

Born motivators, they make great life coaches, speakers, writers and bloggers, and have the organizational skills to excel in a variety of careers, from sports, to medicine, to administration. Travel and tourism may suit, and their love of action may attract them to health, beauty and leisure, while discovering their sensitivity may draw them to drama and music. Health-wise, they need to recognize that, despite their positive attitude, they are not invincible and they need to pay attention to looking after themselves and ensure they have regular health check-ups. **For self-care**, spend time alone on a regular basis to give yourself time to reflect, connect to your intuition and become more self-aware. People who take the time to get to know and love themselves are never lonely or unfulfilled because they know they are enough.

Those born on this day need to understand that loving someone else is impossible until they learn to love themselves. Until the age of 39 the focus is on feelings and learning about themselves. After 39 they become more self-aware and confident, and need to ensure they surround themselves with people who are sincere and encourage them to focus on happiness from the inside out. Once they have learned to understand themselves and connect with their amazing intuition, their infectious dynamism can be validated by remarkable achievements. Their destiny is to lead, motivate and inspire others by their words or by their upbeat example.

Potential: Upbeat, generous

Dark side: Superficial, judgmental

Tarot card, lucky numbers, days, colors: The Hanged Man, 3, 9, Wednesday, Thursday, orange, mauve

Born today: George H.W. Bush (US president); Ervin László (philosopher); Anne Frank (diarist)

June 13

The Birthday of the Wild Dreamer

"Life is infinite possibility"

June 13-born are independent-minded and often ahead of their time. They tire easily of the everyday and their adventurous spirit takes them to places no one else dares to visit. Although following their vivid imagination can sometimes lead them into real danger, it can also make them great innovators. They love to travel and explore, both externally and internally; their thirst for adventure can take them all over the world to exotic places or it can manifest itself in total absorption in their intellectual discoveries. They truly believe the world is theirs for the taking and that they can achieve anything they set their sights on. Many realize their dreams and become highly successful, but the less evolved may struggle to translate their dreams into reality. It is important for them to get in touch with their intuition, as this will tell them what is achievable.

Born meteorologists, they have the curiosity and determination to thrive in any career, but work best in professions involving study, travel, action, progressive ideals and lots of change. Science, research, tourism, forecasting, journalism, writing, sales, sports, social media, personal transformation, spirituality and the world of entertainment may all suit. They are prone to depression when they can't find ways to live out their fantasies, so need to take extra care of their emotional wellbeing. **For self-care**, taking a few minutes of quiet time each day when you are not doing anything in particular can make it easier to connect to your intuition.

Those born on this day need unusual but positive people around them who encourage them to dream, but who provide a healthy dose of realism and objectivity. Until 38 they focus on building emotional security and should take advantage of opportunities to develop greater self-awareness. After that they grow further in self-confidence and need to ensure their appetite for adventure doesn't endanger them. They should never allow routine to dampen their energy and creativity, but if they are to actually realize the impossible, they should study what is possible, and what is not, *before* they leap in at the deep end. Their destiny is to explore and uncover progressive new insights.

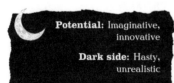

Potential: Imaginative, innovative

Dark side: Hasty, unrealistic

Tarot card, lucky numbers, days, colors: Death, 1, 4, Wednesday, Sunday, orange, amber

Born today: James Maxwell (physicist); William Butler Yeats (poet); Tim Allen (actor)

June 14

The Birthday of the Supervisor

is to resist the urge to always take charge.

The way forward: is to understand that sometimes the only way to empower people is for them to learn from their own mistakes.

Luck maker: Treat all people, whatever their status, as important—a less important person today might one day hold the key to your good fortune.

"I am living the dream"

Those born on June 14 often have a desire to take the lead. They have the ability to observe what is going on around them, and sum up quickly what needs to be done and who should do it. Their self-confidence means they find it impossible to stand on the sidelines. With strong personal opinions and a compulsion to take action to reach their goals, they are capable of outstanding success. They make charismatic leaders, but their actions can be perceived as bossy and abrupt, and, whenever challenged, they can become confrontational. It is important they make a concerted effort to become aware of the damaging impact their blunt force can arouse in others.

Born CEOs, they love all things to do with the media and can excel in publishing, music, film, journalism, videos and influencing. They make gifted business leaders and their competitive nature draws them to sport, sales, the military, education, politics, social-media influencing, commerce, entrepreneurship and business. They should ensure they allow themselves plenty of time to relax and switch off and that they take vacations instead of working through them. **For self-care**, wearing, meditating on and surrounding yourself with shades of green will encourage you to find a balance between your own feelings and the feelings of others.

The lives of these people are busy and full of admirers, and their loved ones often feel they have no time for them. Until the age of 37 the focus is on emotional security, and they try to develop a greater awareness of and consideration for the feelings of others. After 37 they have even greater self-confidence and need to ensure their directness does not tip over into arrogance, as this alienates others. Once they learn to respect the sensitivities of others, they have the potential to be outstanding supervisors, leaders and contributors to whatever field they choose to devote their forthright opinions and common-sense intellect to. Once they have learned the difference between opinion and fact, their destiny is to do what they do best: lead, motivate and inspire others.

Potential: Authoritative, courageous

Dark side: Narcissistic, abrupt

Tarot card, lucky numbers, day, colors: Temperance, 2, 5, Wednesday, orange, emerald green

Born today: Lang Lang (pianist); Nikolaus Otto (engineer); Boy George (singer)

June 15

The Birthday of Irresistible Charm

The life lesson:

is to believe in your own desirability.

The way forward: is to understand that however much you flatter others, the only way to feel truly desirable and fulfilled is to believe in yourself first.

Luck maker: Change begins within— transformation doesn't start with wardrobe, partner, money, status or career changes, but with the way you think and feel about yourself.

"Let me entertain you"

People born on June 15 have natural charm. They use their magnetic, persuasive power to win over everyone they encounter—even the most cynical find it hard to resist them. What makes them so charming is they have a real interest in others and the intuitive ability to know exactly the right thing to say and do to help them feel good. Their outstanding people skills mean they can often be found in influential positions. It is important they devote their persuasive skills to a worthy cause and ensure they don't give others the wrong impression. In all their dealings they should observe a strict code of ethics and be as honest as they can be.

Born advertisers, they can find fulfillment in artistic careers, art, music, drama, influencing or wherever they can gather a following. Marketing, public relations, real estate, promotion, consultancy, social work and the leisure, health, medical and beauty industries may also appeal. As far as their own health is concerned, they need to learn that true beauty comes from within and not from fad diets, creams and relentless exercise programs. **For self-care**, wearing, meditating on and surrounding yourself with shades of purple will encourage you to focus on higher things.

These people should ensure they don't place a higher value on outer over inner beauty in their relationships and should avoid people-pleasing behavior. Until the age of 36 they focus on emotional security and should refrain from putting status and popularity above a sense of personal achievement. After 36 they become more confident and assertive, and, again, they need to make sure they use their seductive energy in productive, positive ways. As long as they truly believe in the cause they are promoting and mean what they say when flattering others, their ambition and personal charm virtually guarantee their popularity, happiness and success. Their destiny is to use their considerable powers of intuition to uplift, inspire and motivate others.

Potential: Seductive, intelligent

Dark side: Calculating, misleading

Tarot card, lucky numbers, days, colors: The Devil, 3, 6, Wednesday, Friday, orange, cerise

Born today: Ice Cube (rapper); Helen Hunt and Courteney Cox (actors); Erroll Garner (pianist)

June 16

The Birthday of Far-sighted Astuteness

"The journey of a thousand miles begins with a single step"

June 16-born are a smooth blend of creativity and patience. They are visionary but also astute enough to understand the importance of working hard to achieve their goals. Although they have an ability to predict future trends, they rarely throw caution to the winds, preferring to plot their course carefully with clear, well-thought-out, one-step-at-a-time plans. Both visionary and realistic, they are at their least productive when they lack balance in life, repress their creative instincts and play things too safe.

Born doctors, their natural communication skills could lead them to teaching, medicine, science, the media, journalism, commerce, sales, business and offering sound financial advice, but they are deeply compassionate people and are more likely to lean toward humanitarian, healing or charitable organizations where they can champion those less fortunate. They may also express their creativity in the arts, filmmaking and design. With a tendency to be overly serious, they would benefit from injecting more relaxation and fun into their lives. **For self-care**, listen to great music when doing chores, working or traveling. It will help boost your mood, concentration and creativity.

These people tend to swing between being detached and over-involved in relationships and need to strike a balance, although they derive the greatest fulfillment from time spent with loved ones. Until the age of 35 emotional security is key and they need to remember to include laughter in their structured life plan. After 35 they often become more assertive, and it's important they don't block their incredible enthusiasm and intuition with indecision, because this period in their lives is the time when they tend to have the power to make their ideas a reality. When they have learned to be neither too impulsive nor too cautious, their desire for progress can be a remarkable force for good, not just for themselves but for all whose lives they touch. Their destiny is to influence and inspire others with their compassion and far-sighted vision.

Potential: Visionary, dedicated

Dark side: Indecisive, overcautious

Tarot card, lucky numbers, days, colors: The Tower, 4, 7, Wednesday, Monday, orange, blue

Born today: Tupac Shakur (rapper); Geronimo (Apache leader); Adam Smith (economist)

June 17

The Birthday of the Influential Example

The life lesson:

is explaining how you feel.

The way forward: is understanding that opening up to others does not weaken but strengthen your position, because others find you easier to relate to.

Luck maker: Forgive yourself and others—no human is perfect, including you, so don't let negativity drain your energy.

"Living the dream"

Those born on June 17 are walking, talking influencers. They believe everyone can follow their dreams. They know how to work hard, but also have a rich creativity that they want to explore and profit from. Demanding a lot of themselves and others, they are an intensely forceful presence. They set a great example to others, who are drawn to their vitality, but they don't feel comfortable in the role of mentor. This is because their own goals matter so much to them that they don't have the patience to support others. They tend to stretch the truth if it makes their arguments more plausible. But even if their exaggeration is uncovered, such is their persuasive influence that others are likely to continue to believe and follow them.

Born conductors, they have the ability to lead, and this offers them many career opportunities or they may work for themselves. They are well suited to the law, research, writing, or humanitarian or social reform, or the healing, personal growth, life-coaching or New Age industries. Their creativity may express itself in the arts, music, design, social-media influencing and all forms of media. Prone to addictive behavior, it is important they apply the same willpower that they display in their professional life to their personal life and health-care. **For self-care**, keep a mood diary to help identify when you are turning to food or addictive behavior for comfort or to ease boredom.

Those born on this day tend to be detached in their dealings with others and would benefit from getting in touch with their own feelings and what really matters in life by finding a healthy work–life balance. Until the age of 34 they may focus on emotional relations, security and family. After 34 they enter a period of growing self-confidence and these are the years when they really come into their own as inspirational leaders or pioneers. They are driven by their progressive ideals, and once they understand the intense impact they have, and the accompanying ethical responsibility, they discover their destiny to inspire others with their courageous example, and fight for what really matters to them.

Potential: Influential, creative

Dark side: Dishonest, detached

Tarot card, lucky numbers, days, colors: The Star, 5, 8, Wednesday, Saturday, orange, coffee

Born today: Venus Williams (tennis player); Igor Stravinsky (composer); Barry Manilow and Lemar (singers)

June 18

The Birthday of Unforgettable Congeniality

"I make a lasting impression"

is to look within.

The way forward: is to understand that the answer to boredom does not lie in externals but in the excitement generated by inner change.

Luck maker: Gratitude is the foundation of a happy life so, instead of looking over the horizon for happiness, focus on all that is good about your life right now.

People born on June 18 have a likeable vitality that uplifts everyone they meet, but behind this there lie insightful and serious minds. They place as high a priority on meeting their personal, financial and professional goals as they do on being liked. Whether they realize it or not, their personality has a lasting effect on others, and even if they are not physically present, their influence is felt in some way. They are highly intuitive and can get their point across effectively without causing offense. This makes it hard for others to forget them. Their ability to leave a lasting legacy makes them potential leaders, although they need to be careful they don't become manipulative. They are indefatigable fighters for the rights of others, but, despite their compassion and intelligence, they can easily get bored. They need constant change and challenge, and this can make them behave erratically and selfishly.

Born lyricists, they can make their mark in the world of the arts, music, poetry and writing and may also blaze a trail as researchers, financiers and entrepreneurs. The law, education, business and the media appeal, as do politics, counseling, charity and social and humanitarian work. Being spiritually inclined, they may be attracted to mind–body therapies such as yoga, tai chi and meditation, which can all help them find the inner peace they need to thrive. **For self-care**, carry a small green crystal, such as agate, to encourage you to be more consistent and balanced in your approach to life.

These people are a lot of fun, but can be hugely unpredictable in their relationships and need to learn to be more consistent and disciplined toward people and situations. Until the age of 32 they may focus on emotional security, but after that they become significantly more expressive and assertive. Once they learn to be grateful for what they already have, they discover that most of what they seek already lies within. Their destiny is to inspire significant progress and leave a lasting legacy created by their presence and humanitarian concerns.

Potential: Charming, intuitive

Dark side: Erratic, manipulative

Tarot card, lucky numbers, days, colors: The Moon, 6, 9, Wednesday, Tuesday, orange, red

Born today: Paul McCartney (singer); George Mallory (mountaineer); Richard Madden and Isabella Rossellini (actors)

June 19

The Birthday of the Activator

is diplomacy.

The way forward: is to understand that being direct doesn't always work and you need to understand the value of gentle tact.

Luck maker: The more special you make a person feel by listening to them and sincerely complimenting them, the more likely that person is to listen to and support you.

"I believe in me"

June 19-born are blessed with the ability to stimulate and uplift others. Their courage, along with their patience, tolerance and generally good intentions, serve as an inspiring example. Whether they realize it or not, they are catalysts spurring others into action. They may choose to fight or to quietly stand their ground, but whatever strategy they choose they rarely crumble under pressure. Their defining characteristic is their tremendous self-belief, keen analytical skills, intellectual curiosity and deep intuition, and this series of blessings can inspire respect, but sometimes trigger insecurities among those who feel less confident. When frustrated, they can tip over into controlling behavior, but more often than not, they see the merits of a less confrontational approach. Above all, they empower others with their compassion and youthful vitality.

Born teachers, they have the ability to inspire and motivate, and may be drawn to careers in education, consultancy, counseling and lecturing. Sales, commerce, promotion, negotiation, life-coaching, training, research, writing, social reform and politics can also appeal, and their need for creative self-expression may connect them to art, design, advertising and social-media influencing. They tend to push themselves too hard and need to make time for rest and relaxation. **For self-care,** to help you slow down and be more reflective, stress-management techniques such as deep breathing, meditation, mindfulness or simply taking a long soak in an aromatherapy bath need to become a permanent fixture.

Sociable and popular, those born on this day can be passionate and committed in relationships but also argumentative. Until the age of 31 their focus is on establishing emotional security and, after that, growing into even greater creativity and assertiveness, and mastering the art of diplomacy as they mature, because these are their golden years. They have the potential to make their mark on the world by guiding and helping others reach their full potential. Once they have learned to be more tolerant and diplomatic, their destiny is to share their sense of purpose and vision of progress to motivate and empower everyone who is lucky enough to cross their path.

Potential: Courageous, energizing

Dark side: Controlling, tactless

Tarot card, lucky numbers, days, colors: The Sun, 1, 7, Wednesday, Sunday, orange, red

Born today: Blaise Pascal (mathematician); Aung San Suu Kyi and Boris Johnson (politicians); Salman Rushdie (author)

June 20

The Birthday of
Excitement

"I feel my way"

The life lesson:

is avoiding extremes of emotion.

The way forward: is to understand that the only way you can find true fulfillment is to be in control of your emotions.

Luck maker: Stop exaggerating—earn the respect and trust of others, because they keep things real and don't dramatize them.

Those born on June 20 are often warm and spontaneous. Indifference is something they simply don't understand, since they live, love and thrive on excitement. Life is never dull when these popular and passionate people are around. They are charismatic and often the natural center of attention. Excellent communication skills, wit, great intuition and an innovative mind make them vibrant conversationalists. However, if they don't get the praise or attention they crave, they may respond with attention-seeking or irrational behavior. They lighten atmospheres and bring out either the best or the repressed emotions of others.

Born journalists, they can think swiftly and sense potential drama or opportunities, making them great writers, problem-solvers, investigators, politicians, teachers and researchers. Their charm means they succeed in people-orientated careers, whether in business or public service and their creativity may manifest through social media, movies and music, as well as psychic potential. Their energy can attract toxic individuals into their lives and they would benefit from becoming more self-aware by practicing mind-control therapies such as yoga and meditation. **For self-care,** have a little quiet time alone each day to think or daydream, and try to simply enjoy the present moment.

Being so popular, those born on this day can find it hard to make time for someone special. It is important for them to surround themselves with warm-hearted but level-headed people who can give them the balance they need. Until the age of 30 there is an emphasis on home, family and emotional security, and they should take opportunities to find a sense of inner balance. After the age of 30, however, they become more assertive and adventurous, and more aware of the impact their passionate responses have on others.

If they can find a worthy cause and moderate their thirst for excitement with self-discipline and a dose of realism, they can transform their magical dreams into reality. Their destiny is to draw people to them and encourage them to be more open, creative, passionate and spontaneous themselves.

Potential: Exciting, charismatic

Dark side: Needy, boundaryless

Tarot card, lucky numbers, days, colors: Judgment, 2, 8, Wednesday, Monday, orange, yellow

Born today: Lionel Richie (singer); Nicole Kidman (actor); Roberto Rodriguez (filmmaker)

CANCER

THE CRAB (JUNE 21–JULY 22)

* **Element:** Water
* **Ruling planet:** The Moon (Intuition)
* **Tarot card:** The Chariot (Transformation and drive)
* **Lucky numbers:** 2, 4
* **Favorable colors:** Indigo, white, gray, silver, cream
* **Driving force:** Feelings
* **Personal statement:** When I feel safe, I come out of my shell
* **Chinese sign counterpart:** The Goat

Cancer is the first water sign and—like the unpredictable sea herself—Cancerians can be gentle and soothing one moment and stormy and snappy the next. They are perhaps the most sensitive of all the signs in the zodiac, and the need to protect themselves and those they love from threat or danger is powerful. Although they may appear enigmatic and can be defensive at times, beneath the surface and an often-tenacious attitude to life there lurks a person who is highly intuitive, and truly caring and compassionate.

Personality potential

Cancerians tend to be compassionate and nurturing by nature. They genuinely care about the feelings of others, and nothing matters more to them than giving and receiving love. Their motivation in life is the pursuit of happiness because they believe that the happier people are, the more productive and fulfilled they will be. Easy-going most, but not all, of the time, they often have a very distinctive laugh and will try to create a harmonious and welcoming atmosphere wherever they go.

Sensitive, caring, intuitive, imaginative and empathetic are all key words associated with Cancerians, whether male or female. They are very protective of those they love and, if their compassion and intuition can flow harmoniously with their practical sense, it makes for a wonderful combination. The ruling planet for Cancer is the moon, the planet of emotions and intuition, and there is a strong tendency for them to let feelings be their guide through life. They will, however, make instinctive rather than impulsive decisions because their impulses are tempered by their practicality.

Home is of utmost importance to Cancerians and any disruption there will cause emotional distress. They are also prone to bouts of nostalgia and will cling to everything from the past. More often than not they will surround themselves

with photographs of loved ones or objects that have very little material value but high sentimental value, either because they were gifts from friends or family, or because they are associated with an especially important personal memory. What others see as clutter, Cancerians will hold onto tightly because these things help give them the emotional security they crave.

Perhaps one of the greatest strengths of people born under this sun sign is that they are highly intuitive when it comes to the needs of others. A Cancerian will instinctively sense what another person wants or needs before any words are even spoken. When this is combined with their nurturing nature, it's easy to see why, in times of crisis, these people are often the lynchpin upon which everyone will depend or seek counsel from. Like a safe harbor where boats can take shelter, Cancerians provide a secure and calm place for people both to escape and to rest, and also to draw strength and inspiration from.

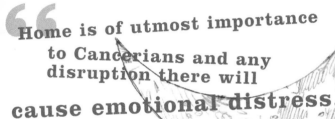

" Home is of utmost importance to Cancerians and any disruption there will cause emotional distress. "

Personality pitfalls

Those born under the sign of the crab can be incredibly moody and argumentative at times, and when they don't get their own way they can behave like martyrs. The problem with this approach to life is that often the person who suffers the most is themselves. They are also the chief worriers of the zodiac, never content unless they are anxious about someone or something.

Although the Cancerian nature is compassionate and caring, it's important not to forget that the crab, their symbol, is covered by a tough outer shell. Make no mistake that those born under this sign are fiercely ambitious. Success in life matters a great deal to them and, if need be, they will fight tough and hard for what they want. More often than not, however, this fighting instinct doesn't express itself enough. This is because they are so tuned into others' feelings and what is going on around them that it's hard for them to take a step back and define not just what they want, but who they are. Cancerians often suffer confusion and mood swings as a result of their sensitivity; with their feelings so dependent on those of others, their emotional landscape is constantly shifting. Then, when the misunderstandings and expectations become too great, Cancerians typically withdraw into their shell to process and make sense of things. This withdrawal can be particularly confusing and painful for friends and loved ones who may have grown to depend on a Cancerian's loving and nurturing presence in their lives.

Personality pitfalls for Cancerians therefore arise out of both their emotional sensibility and their inability to distinguish between their own feelings and those of others. They often don't know if their feelings are their own or ones they have absorbed from other people or the environments they have been in. When feeling threatened or vulnerable, they become self-defensive and possessive, grabbing onto what represents security to them and retreating into their shells.

Symbol

If you want a key to the personality of those born under Cancer, look no further than the symbol of the crab, with its soft, vulnerable interior and its hard, tough outer shell. The crab is a sensitive creature, but the only way it can survive in a dangerous world is by surrounding itself with a hard shell. This can lead to both misunderstandings and vulnerability. For example, Cancerians may decide to remain aloof for fear of getting hurt, but this can make them feel alone and rejected by others. Similarly, they may absorb so much from other people that it is tough for anyone to find out anything about them, and this, too, can lead to feelings of loneliness and isolation.

Darkest secret

Cancerians are prone to constant fretting, and this fear of "what ifs" or nameless dangers can shatter their hopes and dreams. Nothing scares a Cancerian more than change or the unknown, and it's this fear of change that drives them to invest a huge amount of energy and time into relationships or projects that they believe will give them the feelings of security they crave. The problem is that the more they try to control others or their environment, the more insecure and vulnerable they tend to feel, because the only thing that never changes in life is change itself.

Love

Cancerians have seemingly endless supplies of love and nurturing to give others and, although they can live by themselves, they are far more fulfilled and happy in a relationship. If they do live alone, however, they will typically surround themselves with close friends or bond closely with a pet. They make wonderfully caring and support-ive partners, but all this love and emotion can sometimes come across as smothering. Emotional independence in others or not being needed anymore scares them and there could be issues of co-dependence in relationships if they don't learn to let their loved ones breathe.

Cancerians respond best to warmth and affection and, when they fall in love, they fall body, mind and soul. Romantic at heart, they will always put their loved ones first. All this is fine if their affection and dedication are reciprocated, but if not, they can retreat, deeply hurt and vulnerable, into their shell. Fear of rejection may also keep them in that shell for far longer than is healthy for them. Although they will tend to cling tightly to a relationship that shows signs of disintegrating, they are also capable of wandering off if they don't feel loved or appreciated, in order to find someone else who is willing to give them the love and understanding they feel they deserve.

Love matches: Taurus, Cancer, Scorpio and Pisces.

The Cancer woman

Like the waxing and waning moon that rules her sign, the Cancer woman can be magical and illuminating—and occasionally a little crazy when the moon is full. She may appear shy and sweet at first but, over time, she can flower into a fascinating companion with a wealth of hidden talents and a passionate sexuality.

If a Cancer woman falls in love, there tend to be two different sides to her: one is gentle and feminine, while the other is deeply affectionate, at times clingy. The latter can be wonderful if the affection is welcomed, but suffocating if it isn't. Rejection and ridicule are a Cancer woman's greatest fears, and this is why she will rarely make the first move in a relationship. She may also suffer from bouts of low self-esteem when she doesn't feel good enough. If her partner can reassure her during these vulnerable moments, she is theirs for life. Material comfort and security are important for this woman, but she will not expect her partner to provide everything for her; she is more than willing to put in her fair share of hard work to give her family comfort and security.

Above all, there is nothing shallow or superficial about a Cancer woman, and when she falls in love, it's generally for keeps. There is also no end to the heroic sacrifices this woman

will make for those she loves. Her serenity and patience in the face of obstacles and setbacks—both her own and those of her loved ones—will never fail to heal, comfort and inspire.

The Cancer man

Cancer men can be flirtatious, so it will take time and patience to get to know them really well. They may appear aloof, but then, without warning, their defenses may come down and a tender warm smile and endearing laughter may break through. It is important to remember that, however moody, cautious, pessimistic or arrogant Cancerian men may appear, their true nature is this softer, affectionate and caring side. It's just that they often feel too vulnerable to show it.

This man isn't a mama's boy, but the mother figure will be an important one in his life. He'll put his mother on a pedestal or have an image of what a mother should be like in his mind. Cancerians (both male and female) are either very close to their mothers or completely alienated and disappointed with them; either way, the relationship is never casual. So, if you fall in love with a Cancer male, you will have to understand the importance of the mother figure in his life. He will never, ever admit it, but a part of him adores being petted and mothered by females.

With his sensitive and caring awareness of what others feel, and his practical side—which ensures he won't be lacking in cash—this guy is never short of admirers, but it may take a while before he really falls in love. This is because he sets very high standards and rarely compromises; so, in the great majority of cases, if a Cancerian asks a person out more than a few times it's a sign he is genuinely interested.

Family

Cancerian babies often appear very sensitive and intuitive. As babies, when their mother feels tense they will sense that and cry and scream for no reason, and when she feels relaxed they will babble gently and smile. Other changes in the home atmosphere are immediately sensed and that is why Cancerian babies' moods are so unpredictable. They are also often picky and slow eaters as infants, and will need coaxing to eat their fruit and vegetables. It's important, however, for parents not to be too authoritarian or to try to rush them when they eat, because the Cancerian digestion can be highly sensitive.

When they first start school Cancerian children may be shy and withdrawn, and it will typically take them a while to settle and deal with homesickness. Parents can help by encouraging them not to withdraw into their shells but to make new friends and join in activities and clubs that are school-based. The worst advice you can give Cancerians is to "toughen up," because they are easily hurt and can't toughen up. Being sensitive is who they are. They need to learn to acknowledge their emotions and understand what their emotions are trying to tell them, so they see their sensitivity as a gift, rather than a curse.

The best way to discipline a Cancerian child when they have broken a rule is not to send them to their room or withhold their pocket money, but to say they have upset or disappointed someone. This approach will speak to their sensitivity. Parents of young Cancerians should also encourage their children from an early age to tidy up after themselves, as people born under this sign have a tendency to be untidy and to hoard.

As parents, Cancerians often come into their own. Their need to nurture is instinctive, and they make loving and supportive parents. They do, however, need to make sure that they don't overprotect their children and fill them with unnecessary fears. As long as there are no clear signs of danger and threat, the Cancerian parent should learn to bite their tongue every time they want to say "be careful," because children need to learn to take risks at school and in the playground. There is a danger that Cancerian parents might become so involved in their children's lives that they lose a sense of their own identity. They may particularly suffer when their children leave home, so it's important for them to keep their own interests going when they are raising their children.

Career

Cancerians are ambitious and driven, and enjoy challenges at work, but it's important also that their work has some kind of continuity, because security is very important for them. Tenacious, determined and often shrewd, they have a talent for business, where their powerful intuition can serve them well. The caring professions obviously attract them, given their powerful urge to nurture, and they make excellent doctors, nurses and social workers as well as teachers and human resource workers. Work involving the past, in museums, antiques or as a historian may also suit, as will careers involved with boating and aquatic or ocean life. Cancerians love to cook, so they may gravitate toward careers in catering; they may also often have a creative and artistic side to them that seeks expression in music or the expressive arts.

Fulfillment matters more to these people than making money, but having said that, they are often fairly good at making and keeping money. Other careers that might work for them include gardening, animal welfare, counseling, psychotherapy, politics, journalism, advertising and the media.

> **Fulfillment matters more to these people than making money**

Health and wellbeing

Being so sensitive to the feelings of others, Cancerians need to watch their health. Cancer rules the breasts and stomach—breasts feed babies and stomachs are where we take

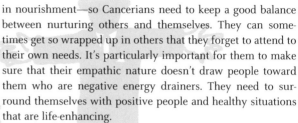

in nourishment—so Cancerians need to keep a good balance between nurturing others and themselves. They can sometimes get so wrapped up in others that they forget to attend to their own needs. It's particularly important for them to make sure that their empathic nature doesn't draw people toward them who are negative energy drainers. They need to surround themselves with positive people and healthy situations that are life-enhancing.

Rhythmical exercise—such as dancing, swimming and aerobics—is highly recommended to help keep Cancerians' sensitive nature balanced. As far as diet is concerned, they need to watch out for trigger foods that can upset their delicate digestion. A diet rich in oily fish, legumes, whole grains, fruits and vegetables normally works best for them. Fad diets should be avoided completely, as should any kind of dependence on recreational drugs, cigarettes and alcohol.

It's extremely important, given their vulnerable inner core, that Cancerians devote plenty of time to self-development, challenging negative thinking and building self-esteem. They need to understand that emotions such as fear, anger and guilt should not be ignored but listened to, because they have something important to teach them. Getting in touch with their emotions is therefore crucial; if they can't do this they may benefit from counseling or therapy. Meditation, yoga and cognitive behavioral therapy can be helpful, as can spending time with positive people. Wearing, meditating on or surrounding themselves with the colors **orange** and **yellow** will enhance feelings of warmth, security, enjoyment and self-confidence.

Born between June 21 and July 3

Cancerians born between these dates are under the full illumination of the moon and all its changing moods. They tend to be highly creative individuals who are deeply emotional, intuitive and loving, but they can also be extremely changeable and sentimental.

Born between July 4 and 13

These people often have deep and penetrating minds. This can make them brilliant, but also rather intense in their approach to people and situations, so they need to learn when to back off and let go. They make very loyal and devoted friends.

Born between July 14 and 22

Extremely compassionate and forgiving, these are the idealistic dreamers of the zodiac and people tend to gravitate toward them in search of illumination. This is fine as long as they learn to self-regulate, ensuring that they take care of their own needs and self-development as well.

Life lessons

One of the Cancerian's greatest strengths—but also their greatest challenge—is their sensitivity, which can sometimes translate into oversensitivity. When a person they are close to is upset or moody, Cancerians tend to be upset and moody, too. Therefore, it's absolutely vital for Cancerians to learn to protect their sensitive nature and to distinguish between their own feelings and those of others. If they don't, the result will be misunderstandings and despondency. But if they can learn to get a grip on their sensitivity and derive their feelings of emotional security from themselves rather than others, their reputation for being moody and unpredictable will disappear.

Being emotionally manipulative is another Cancerian trait that can drag them and everybody else around them down. A Cancerian can cling to a grudge longer than anyone else in the zodiac, and they need to understand that this is incredibly damaging for them and achieves nothing. If they want to move forward, they need to learn to forgive but not forget, and then let go.

Possessiveness, whether it's financial or romantic, can be limiting for those born under this sign, since possessiveness is just another waste of their valuable energy. There will always be a degree of unpredictability in any relationship, so the sooner Cancerians learn that material things can't make them happy, clinging to a partner possessively can't assure them of affection, and true love means freeing others rather than restricting or controlling them, the happier and more fulfilled they will be.

Witnessing another Cancerian lose themselves in empathy or a desire to control others can be a cautionary tale. The other signs of the zodiac can teach Cancerians how to let go of their desire to control everyone and everything. Scorpios can encourage them to look deeper into things and consider the hidden motivations below rather than only seeing what swims on the surface. Aquarians can help them find the courage to embrace their uniqueness. Arians and Sagittarians have the bold and adventurous approach to life that Cancerians may lack. Pisces can also encourage them to let go of grudges and move on. Leos can inspire Cancerians to work on their self-esteem. Librans can help Cancerians balance their fluctuating emotions. Geminis, Virgos and Capricorns can help them become more objective, so that their emotions don't get in the way of achieving their goals, while Taureans can encourage them to put their own emotional needs first.

Chinese astrology counterpart: The Goat

The Chinese Goat sign shares the highly emotional, intuitive and artistic traits of its Western Cancer counterpart. Although they present an aloof or tough exterior, Goats can be extremely sensitive and easily hurt. Resistant to change, they can also be overly negative and downright moody. Progress is only made when they find their sense of self-worth and emotional reassurance and security from within themselves, rather than expecting it to be bestowed upon them by others.

Both Goat and Cancer place a high value on their home and family life. They need to have a safe place to hide and recover whenever the world overwhelms them. Material things matter greatly to them. This is because feeling financially secure helps them feel safe. These gentle, mild and kind creatures can have great resilience and perseverance and, once they learn to believe in themselves and trust rather than fear their feelings, they can climb right to the top of any mountain.

Note: Cancerians have an affinity with Goat-sign characteristics, but be sure to check which Chinese sign corresponds to your **year** of birth (see page xxi), and to read about the characteristics associated with it, too.

June 21

The Birthday of Delighted Awe

"So little time, so much to do"

People born on June 21 approach each day with delighted awe, which isn't surprising as they are born on the longest and arguably most magical day. They often wish there were more hours in each day to do all they want to do. Fiercely individualistic, they don't like to be labeled as anyone or anything, believing they can be and do many different things at once. They run the risk of exhaustion, but they would not want it any other way, so determined are they to live their life to the max. They have terrific enthusiasm and determination, and grow stronger rather than weaker when they face challenges. The big danger is that they can go to extremes, losing themselves in a world of obsession, so they need to learn greater self-control.

Born reformers, they need careers that allow them to express their creativity and offer them variety, travel and human contact. Idealistic and humanitarian, they may be drawn to education, counseling, healing or social work, and their curiosity may draw them to the law, design, religion and philosophy. Their communication skills can make them great writers, advertisers, speakers, artists, salespeople, politicians and promoters. Addictive behavior is a concern and they should avoid this by spending more time with loved ones or reflecting in nature to help them find essential balance. **For self-care**, cognitive therapy or meditation can help increase self-awareness and give you a much-needed sense of perspective.

Often surrounded by admirers, those born on this day may focus, until the age of 30, on emotional security, and they need to ensure they don't become too bossy and impatient. After 30 they become more creative and assertive, and if they can learn to keep a sense of balance and focus, this is when they realize they can have it all—just not all at once. Once they connect with their gift of empathy and avoid becoming obsessive, their innovative thoughts have extraordinary potential to light up the world. Their destiny is to make their mark by sharing their intensely bright vision with others.

June 22

The Birthday of Breathless Anticipation

"It's a new dawn, I'm feeling good"

The life lesson:

is dealing with disillusionment.

The way forward: is to understand that disillusionment happens when you set expectations too high.

Luck maker: Your power is within, not in other people or things. Once you realize this, you become a luck magnet.

June 22-born are romantics. They greet each day, however ordinary, with breathless anticipation. Every new day is an optimistic beginning where anything could happen and they infuse every situation with excitement. They are forever seeking their personal bliss, and although they can be practical and achieve great things in their career, it is rarely at the expense of their personal happiness.

Born designers, they are suited for careers in the arts, such as writing, music and film where they can live out their fantasies, but may also be drawn to interior design, architecture, photography, programming, game design, counseling, education, social work, the law, life-coaching, social reform and the healing professions. They need to establish a healthy sleeping schedule and make sure they don't burn the candle at both ends. **For self-care**, burn incense, such as lavender, frankincense or vanilla, to induce feelings of mental, emotional and spiritual calm.

Heart takes the lead for these people. If they feel they are loved they can achieve virtually anything, so finding true love is of tremendous importance to them. They need to ensure they don't have naïve, unrealistic expectations or put others on a pedestal and become disillusioned when they inevitably fall off. Until 30 the focus is on creating emotional security, and they may stay at home if they don't marry young or build a network of close friends. After 30 they grow in confidence and successfully build their skill set in a chosen field, typically coming into their own in their forties and beyond. They can get lost in a lonely fantasy world, but such is their enthusiasm for life they do not stay there for long. Their belief that today may just be the day when something or someone wonderful enters their lives is a truly fulfilling way to live. Once they learn to consider viewpoints other than their own, and be more realistic in their assessment of people, their destiny is to bring enlightenment to those around them, perhaps the world too.

Potential: Imaginative, grateful

Dark side: Detached, unrealistic

Tarot card, lucky numbers, days, colors: The Fool, 1, 4, Monday, Sunday, silver, white

Born today: Meryl Streep (actor); Dan Brown (author); Erin Brockovich (activist)

June 23

The Birthday of the Improver

The life lesson:

is avoiding gossip.

The way forward: is to understand that if someone tells you something in confidence, you should resist the urge to share it.

Luck maker: Respect the feelings of others even if they are not present and you will gain the respect and trust of all.

"I'd like to teach the world to sing"

Those born on June 23 tend to be sensitive. They long to make the world a kinder place and devote their considerable energy and intelligence to studying it and trying to improve it for the better. Some of their ideas may be eccentric, but such is their insight, charm and ability to just listen that others often feel better after spending time with them. Eager to help other people, they go out of their way to offer support when needed. They place great value on relationships, treating both loved ones and strangers with equal respect, consideration and warmth. However, they can become interfering and repeat confidences. This is not done maliciously, but it can make them appear untrustworthy, which they are not.

Born psychotherapists, they are drawn to the helping and caring professions such as counseling, social work, medicine and healthcare, as well as the law and politics. The arts, writing, music and architecture may appeal, as might technology, education, research, catering, beauty and commerce. All forms of exercise are recommended for these people, especially when they need to boost their mood. **For self-care**, learn to be happy in your own company—this is the key to your personal growth and fulfillment.

Prone to falling in love swiftly, those born on this day may put their loved ones on pedestals they can't live up to and need to love people for who they are, not who they could be. Until 29 they are concerned with home, family and their own emotional security, but after 29 they are likely to be drawn into public situations that require them to be confident. These are the years when they are most likely to realize their dreams of making the world a better place, by enriching it with their creative endeavors, or bringing greater harmony and compassion wherever they go. Once they learn to be more discreet and objective, they have the creative potential and the practical skills to implement beneficial and healing changes. Their destiny is to influence, inspire and improve the lives of others.

Potential: Altruistic, enchanting

Dark side: Unrealistic, interfering

Tarot card, lucky numbers, days, colors: The Hierophant, 2, 5, Monday, Wednesday, cream, white

Born today: Edward VII (British king); Alan Turing (computer scientist); Frances McDormand (actor)

June 24

The Birthday of Inspired Proficiency

The life lesson:

is trusting others.

The way forward: is to understand that a totally independent state is impossible because no one is an island.

Luck maker: Don't be afraid to ask for help—you increase your chances of success when others help or support you.

"Practice makes perfect"

People born on June 24 are ambitious, independent, innovative and driven leaders rather than followers. They choose their own path and are often so accomplished that others follow them. Wherever they choose to devote their energies, be it work or a cause or a passion of theirs, they tend to be extraordinarily proficient. Visionary but also patient and capable problem-solvers, they find that others rely on their detailed approach. They have tremendous concentration, too, adding to their success equation. Despite their motivating impact on others, they perform best when totally immersed in the technical details of their work. This can be at the expense of their personal life. They can be insensitive to the emotional needs of others and need to watch this tendency, as it will hinder their chances of happiness.

Born consultants, they may be drawn to careers as scientists, technical researchers and managers, and those in which they can combine their talent for analysis with their visions may also appeal. Sport and art are highlighted and their interest in mental pursuits can draw them to teaching, research, writing, business, sales and promotion, while their humanitarian instinct may lead them to spiritual or personal growth-and-development careers. Mind–body therapies, such as meditation and yoga, are highly recommended to remind them of the importance of work–life balance. **For self-care**, every now and again switch off from work entirely and spend time with loved ones or pets, or do some forest-bathing.

These people need lots of solitude, which can be difficult for those in their lives to process. Up to the age of 28, issues relating to financial and emotional security tend to take center stage; after 28 they become more daring and creative. Crucial to their success at any age is avoiding unworthy causes and workaholic tendencies, and being empathetic toward others. If they feel they are making a valuable contribution to the world, not only do they get the recognition they need and deserve from others, they also achieve real personal fulfillment. Once they become more self-aware and work on their interpersonal skills, their destiny is to achieve their progressive and reforming visions.

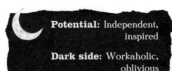

Potential: Independent, inspired

Dark side: Workaholic, oblivious

Tarot card, lucky numbers, days, colors: The Lovers, 3, 6, Monday, Thursday, cream, pink

Born today: Lionel Messi (soccer player); Mick Fleetwood (drummer); Solange Knowles (singer)

June 25

The Birthday of
Original Sensitivity

"I feel you"

People born on June 25 tend to be sensitive, communicative, intuitive and creative souls. They tune into other people's moods and are strongly affected by their environment. Others value them for their problem-solving skills, as well as their insightful, original ideas and approach to life. Their sensitivity makes them valuable team players able to sense what others need without having to ask. If they learn to find a balance between their head and heart, they have all the skills needed to become progressive movers and shakers. If, however, their minds and hearts are unbalanced, the result is insecurity and chaos.

Born artists, they have a natural affinity with creative work and can find great success as designers, writers and artists. A need to express their individuality attracts them to the worlds of entertainment, journalism, architecture, art and music. They need a career that avoids routine and offers them variety, as well as opportunities to learn and nurture others, so the healing and caring professions may also appeal. To avoid the risk of depression, they need to pour less of themselves into others and more into protecting themselves. **For self-care**, whenever you feel overwhelmed, visualize a protective bubble of white or purple light around yourself to block out toxic people and negative situations.

Those born on this day have a people-pleasing tendency and must strive to put their own emotional needs first. After the age of 27 they become less sensitive and more self-assured, and they should seize this opportunity to build self-esteem and rely less on the approval of others, because they can make outstanding contributions to the world. After 57 they are likely to become more practical and to fine-tune their skills. It is crucial they find a cause that fires both their mind and heart, and keeps them focused so that they don't risk scattering their energies. Once they learn self-discipline and to be more objective and realistic, they discover that, along with their creativity and powerful intuition, they are also capable of producing not just great, but truly inspirational work. Their destiny is to become a compassionate, efficient force for good.

June 26

The Birthday of Energetic Fortitude

The life lesson:

is to let others be.

The way forward: is to understand that sometimes the best way to help people grow is to let them learn from their own mistakes.

Luck maker: If you have problems receiving from others, you need to ask yourself why you are blocking good things from happening and why you always prefer to be the giver.

"How can I help?"

June 26-born often have a resilient approach. They bounce back from misfortune and enjoy the feeling of being relied on by others. Warm and sensual, with a love of creature comforts and the finer things in life, they have great compassion. Their emotional resilience is often matched by tremendous physical energy and they enjoy lots of physical challenge, but their greatest passion is guiding the people closest to them. They are truly empathetic individuals whose intuitive response to the feelings of others arouses within them an urge to protect, guide and nurture. Whether they have children or not, they will assume a mentoring role for loved ones and colleagues and thrive when part of a close-knit team or community. Their strong social orientation can bring great fulfillment, but also conflict, as others may find them too controlling.

Born governors, they may be drawn to careers where they can make a practical contribution to helping others, such as social and charity work, education, economics, politics, journalism, writing, science, self-help and counseling, but they can also flourish in diverse occupations such as sports, health, research, technology, the performing arts, sales, marketing, social-media influencing and catering. Wearing dramatic, bright colors such as red helps increase their self-confidence and rightfully turn the spotlight away from others onto them. **For self-care**, it is absolutely crucial that you learn to place self-care at the top of your list of priorities, so schedule regular soothing massages.

Those born on this day need to ensure they don't become over-protective and smothering in their close relationships. If they neglect their emotional development, this can manifest in unsure or compulsive behavior, such as an obsession with order and cleanliness. After the age of 26 they have greater opportunities to become more self-aware and gain self-confidence. Once they have learned to be as protective and nurturing of their own needs as those of others, their destiny is to make a truly inspired and valuable contribution toward helping people fulfill their potential and making the world a better place.

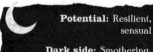

Potential: Resilient, sensual

Dark side: Smothering, compulsive

Tarot card, lucky numbers, days, colors: Strength, 5, 8, Monday, Saturday, cream, burgundy

Born today: Colin Wilson (author); William Thomson (physicist); Ariana Grande (singer)

June 27

The Birthday of Progressive Conviction

"I know the best way"

Those born on June 27 often give the appearance of being watchful and vigilant, ready to defend themselves and their loved ones. Competitive, driven and persuasive, they feel they have a duty to guide and, if necessary, lead others to the moral high ground they comfortably inhabit. They have deep empathy for those who are less fortunate and a burning desire to effect social improvement. There is a tendency to become defensive and to cautiously withdraw into their protective shell when others try to offer their opinions or criticize them. The single-mindedness of these intense, live wires can also mean that they miss out on opportunities. Remaining inquisitive and open-minded is the key to their happiness and success in life.

Born life coaches, they may express their humanitarian urges in a range of caring and helping careers such as medicine, nursing, teaching, therapy, religion, spirituality, self-help, the law, social and charity work. They may choose to spread their message more overtly online or in the arts, music, acting, blogging, broadcasting or writing, or even sales, politics and the performing arts. They should avoid getting stuck in a rut and include plenty of healthy variety in their food and exercise choices. For self-care, all forms of stretching, such as yoga and dance, or any form of exercise that encourages flexibility is beneficial, along with a curious, open mindset.

These people can be quick to take offense and suffer from mood swings, so emotional management is important. Keeping their minds and hearts open and not becoming defensive or inflexible helps them avoid unnecessary rifts in relationships and problems in their working life. Emotions and family matters are the key focus in their mid-twenties, and although they can appear self-assured, they may find that they lack confidence until after the age of 25. Becoming more open-minded and accommodating helps unlock their powerful intuition and give them the inspiration they need to bring about real and significant improvements in their own lives, the lives of those around them and beyond. Their destiny is to devote their considerable energy to helping and inspiring others.

Potential: Driven, compassionate

Dark side: Inflexible, defensive

Tarot card, lucky numbers, days, colors: The Hermit, 6, 9, Monday, Tuesday, cream, red

Born today: Helen Keller (activist); J. J. Abrams (filmmaker); Tobey McGuire (actor)

June 28

The Birthday of the Sprite

"I believe I can fly"

is not always to feel you have to entertain or deliver for others.

The way forward: is to understand that you alone teach other people what to expect from you, so you should teach others to treat you with respect.

Luck maker: Unwavering belief in your own worth generates the ability and enthusiasm to attract luck your way.

People born on June 28 are focused and driven, but there is also a lightness of spirit about them. They don't take themselves seriously and often break tension with their sharp wit that wins them admirers. Occasionally, they can offend their targets, but generally they have the ability to surprise and delight. Underneath their fun-loving exterior there is the iron will to turn their visions into reality. Sometimes they may be accused of disorganization because they like to be on the go. But the quality of the work they produce is anything but chaotic. They can make the toughest tasks seem easy, yet what others don't see or hear about (as these people rarely complain) is the hard work they put in. They also like to be the center of attention, and their mischievous good humor suits the spotlight well.

Born entrepreneurs, they have humanitarian leanings and may be drawn to science, philosophy, innovation and the caring and healing professions. They are natural psychologists, so people-orientated careers, such as promotions, public relations, sales and counseling, as well as teaching and coaching, may appeal. A desire to be creative may draw them to design, acting, music, the media, social media, the world of entertainment or self-employment. They need to avoid becoming over-involved in their friends' problems, as this drains the lightness and energy out of them. **For self-care**, meditate for at least 10 minutes a day by sitting quietly alone and focusing inward, for a sense of fulfillment.

Often surrounded by admirers, those born on this day can overshadow others with their bright energy. Their longing to be noticed may be the result of hidden insecurities and in their early life they may be shy. However, after the age of 23, they gain much-needed self-confidence. Once they understand that people can and do love them for who they are and not for their ability to entertain or deliver, their destiny is to share their happiness and inspiration with those around them and light up the world in the process.

Potential: Delightful, energetic

Dark side: Chaotic, self-conscious

Tarot card, lucky numbers, days, colors: The Magician, 1, 7, Monday, Sunday, cream, orange

Born today: Rupert Sheldrake (parapsychologist); Elon Musk and Muhammad Yunus (entrepreneurs); Jean-Jacques Rousseau (philosopher)

June 29

The Birthday of the Altruistic Visionary

"I dream the impossible dream"

June 29-born are intuitive, imaginative and sensitive, with a talent for anticipating other people's words, actions and reactions. They have the rare ability to put themselves in another's shoes, and have the practical and technical skills to transform their progressive visions into reality. With their compassionate intuition these people give much and genuinely love to share their success. They often support people who are lonely or insecure to boost their self-esteem. They present an innocent, youthful and charming face to the world and rarely complain or drag things down with negativity. Their aim is always to uplift and help others, and, while they may be accused of superficiality, they have the drive needed to achieve their altruistic goals.

Born teachers, they are well suited to careers in education, and the caring and healing professions. Fashion, leisure, design, beauty and charity work may also appeal. Their imagination and intellect excel in science, medicine, aviation or business, and their need for creative expression in writing and the performing arts. They often have a talent for making money, although their business success is typically motivated by a desire to share their happiness rather than gain personal success. They tend to put the needs of others before their own and need to remember to take care of themselves. **For self-care**, ensure you do more things that make you feel good, such as regularly treating yourself to a massage, a new outfit or a film.

In relationships these people can be incredibly generous, but if their behavior becomes too self-sacrificing, they may suffer from bouts of indecision and anxiety about their own focus and motivation. Before 20 they may be reserved but, after 23, they develop self-esteem and creativity. The older and more confident they become, the more likely it is that they can make their own dreams a practical reality. Once they learn to find a balance between their own needs and those of others, their destiny is to influence and inspire others with their generosity and ability to make the impossible seem possible.

Potential: Generous, intuitive

Dark side: Self-sacrificing, indecisive

Tarot card, lucky numbers, day, colors: The High Priestess, 2, 8, Monday, cream, silver

Born today: Nicole Scherzinger and Little Eva (singers); Lily Rabe (actor); Antoine de Saint-Exupéry (poet)

June 30

The Birthday of Mystery

"I am complex and that's okay"

Those born on June 30 have an air of mystery about them. They appear highly motivated with a quirky sense of humor and willingness to take great risks, but they also keep to themselves, which makes them fascinating but complicated individuals, difficult for both themselves and others to understand. They can work tremendously hard, but can also succumb to bouts of extreme idleness that can surprise others. This time out is important to them, and they should use it to recharge their batteries and do some much-needed self-examination. There is a tendency to absorb the needs of others above their own and, by so doing, lose their identity. They must learn to love themselves more and understand that their needs matter as much as others'.

Born trainers, they have a flair for the dramatic and may excel in art, theater, music, film, writing and design, but they also make great teachers, athletes, agents, performers and promoters. Their intelligence may draw them to accounting, finance, science, medicine and alternative healing, and their humanitarianism to counseling and charity work. Prone to bouts of depression and worry, it is important they give themselves plenty of time to unwind and examine their motivations. **For self-care**, action makes you feel better. When your mood is low, take moderate exercise, such as a brisk walk, which can lift your mood and boost your energy and concentration.

Although these people dislike public displays of affection, they are extremely giving and loving to their close ones. Their early life inclines toward introversion, but around the age of 22 they may undergo a transformation of their power, creativity and confidence. These are the years when they are likely to achieve their personal and professional ambitions; in later life they often find practical ways to be of inspirational service to others. When they are able to reconcile their inner conflicts, and become more self-aware, and find the emotional courage to open up more, they have the potential for outstanding success. Their destiny is to motivate and empower others with the truly authentic example they set of genuine compassion and commitment.

July 1

The Birthday of Delicate Equilibrium

The life lesson:

is to be consistent.

The way forward: is to understand that when you are ruled by impulses, you lose control of yourself and your life.

Luck maker: Stop destroying your own chances of success with self-sabotaging behavior. Observe yourself and notice when you are saying and doing things that are not positive.

"I have the courage to care"

July 1-born are adventurous and imaginative spirits with a remarkable memory, and are capable of great humanitarianism on behalf of others and their community. They appear friendly but also crave solitude, and balancing their sensitive and gregarious energies is a lifelong balancing act. They have tremendous empathy for both sexes and are often sought out for their opinions. They love to give advice and offer support, especially if it's for those less fortunate, and others love their spontaneous generosity. Their volatile, artistic temperament can, however, cause them to act on impulse, and they can alienate others by saying or doing things they come to regret. Prone to self-doubt, they need to reconcile their inner and outer selves so that they don't get trapped in insecurity and negativity.

Born counselors, they can excel in therapy and the caring professions, as well as teaching, social work, childcare and politics. They can succeed in management positions but may prefer to fly solo and work for themselves. Sport and leisure, filmmaking, acting, fashion, directing, the media and performing arts may also appeal. Body conscious, they need to understand that until they feel happy on the inside, neither diet nor exercise is going to make them feel good about their bodies. **For self-care**, before making decisions, you should press pause and take some deep breaths to help center yourself and rationally weigh up the pros and cons.

Until the age of 21 those born on this day may lack self-confidence but, after that, there are many opportunities for them to develop this and they need to take advantage of them, because if they don't they can torture themselves with self-doubt. Once they reach a delicate balance and learn to both give and receive, they can tap into a deep inner magic that can not only inspire and be of service to others, but also enhance their own potential for happiness. Their destiny is to turn the spotlight on injustices and help alleviate suffering in the world.

Potential: Ambitious, compassionate

Dark side: Impulsive, self-doubting

Tarot card, lucky numbers, days, colors: Magician, 1, 8, Monday, Sunday, cream, gold

Born today: Diana Spencer (British princess); Amy Johnson (pilot); Debbie Harry and Missy Elliott (singers)

July 2

The Birthday of Emotional Intensity

"I am feeling my way"

The life lesson:

is self-love.

The way forward: is to understand that, while the love of others can temper feelings of insecurity, the only way to feel truly confident is to love yourself first.

Luck maker: Ditch self-doubt—it blocks luck and attracts toxic people who drain rather than boost your chances of good fortune and happiness.

People born on July 2 are intuitive and an exciting combination of emotional intensity and fierce determination. At times their emotions can overwhelm them and others, leading either to introversion or to over-the-top exuberance, and the key to their success is learning to step outside themselves, observe and manage their emotions. Extraordinarily sensitive, they empathize easily with others, particularly those who are less fortunate, and have the magical ability to make other people feel like family. Their public persona is colorful and capable, but they can be plagued by private insecurities. Prone to self-sabotaging behavior, these people need to understand their inner insecurities; building their self-esteem is a crucial requirement for their psychological growth.

Born psychiatrists, they are well suited to careers in therapy, counseling and medicine, as well as the arts—in particular, writing and drama, which can give them a creative outlet for their emotions. They may also have a talent for business, particularly in management positions, real estate, the media or advertising. Susceptible to stress because of their feeling-based approach to life, they would benefit from soothing mind–body therapies such as yoga and meditation. For self-care, spending more time in nature and surrounding yourself with the color green will help you find inner calm.

Those born on this day attract people into their lives effortlessly, and constantly support and uplift others, but often find it hard to accept the support and praise they richly deserve themselves. Until the age of 20 they may be reserved, but after this they have opportunities to become more self-assured, and over the next three decades their confidence grows, helping them achieve the positions of authority for which they are well qualified. They should also seek to find positive ways to learn from, channel and balance their negative emotions. If they devote energy to personal development and understand that just because they feel something, it does not mean it defines them, they will find great fulfillment. Their destiny is to use their formidable determination and magical imagination to inform, motivate and radically inspire others.

Potential: Intuitive, exciting

Dark side: Insecure, uncertain

Tarot card, lucky numbers, day, colors: High Priestess, 2, 9, Monday, silver, rose

Born today: Hermann Hesse (author); Lindsay Lohan, Margot Robbie (actors)

July 3

The Birthday of the Surveyor

"I don't want to miss a thing"

Those born on July 3 are astute observers and always seem to be vigilant in a philosophical rather than judgmental way, keenly studying what life has to offer them. They are often rational at heart and have an enviable ability to manage their emotions. Although endlessly fascinated by others and the world, they tend to keep themselves detached, as without emotions to cloud their judgment they think they can be more effective. Their calm and smooth, charming manner is utterly irresistible, and because they long to make the world a better place when they believe in a cause, their progress is virtually unstoppable. Their curiosity can sometimes earn them the reputation of being interfering or cynical, or lead them to questionable people or causes, but their rationality usually helps them steer clear of any wrongdoing.

Born psychologists, they are well suited to careers in medicine, science, research, education and detective work. They have the imagination to excel in the arts and entertainment and can make excellent managers and administrators. Other careers that suit include charity work, the law, catering, art and antiques. They have a tendency to observe rather than participate in life, so it is important for them to ensure they spend plenty of time with loved ones. For **self-care,** socially orientated activities, such as dancing, team sports or joining a gym, are excellent for wellbeing.

Those born on this day often have a thoughtful approach to relationships, but they need to ensure they don't love people for who they want them to be rather than for who they are. Until the age of 19 they may focus on security and family, but after this they may be offered exciting opportunities to develop confidence and strengthen their performance in their chosen field. After the age of 49, although service to others is highlighted, they should make sure they don't become cynical or superior. Once they find the crucial balance between detachment and involvement, and can engage intellectually and emotionally with the world around them, they find that their talents combine to endow them with outstanding potential to become effective reformers and fighters for justice. Their destiny is to influence and inspire others and help the world evolve through their vision.

Potential: Calm, insightful

Dark side: Detached, superior

Tarot card, lucky numbers, days, colors: The Empress, 1, 3, Monday, Thursday, cream, lavender

Born today: Franz Kafka (author); Tom Stoppard (playwright); Tom Cruise (actor)

July 4

The Birthday of Dedication

"One for all and all for one"

July 4-born identify strongly with causes, groups and organizations, whether family, co-workers, local community, country or even humanity as a whole. Shared human bonds and goals are extremely important to them, and they often dedicate themselves to defending people's wider interests. Whatever path they choose, they are at their happiest when they are working toward a common goal. Ironically, they are also quite private individuals, preferring to keep their own feelings to themselves. Despite their reserve, it's no coincidence that these people were born on Independence Day, as their dedication and loyalty are matched only by their courageous spirit and desire to defend and protect those less fortunate. They are also extremely intuitive, but because this gift can make them feel different, they may choose to reveal it only to those who know them well.

Born firefighters, they thrive in any job that involves helping people and has an element of risk. They make great paramedics, emergency workers, police, military and doctors. They can also be drawn to promotion, lobbying, the law, publishing, banking and politics. Any job that involves food or caring for others also appeals, and their love of the dramatic may draw them to art, sport and entertainment. They tend to neglect their health and wellbeing for others, so they need to prioritize their own. **For self-care,** anything that encourages you to get in touch with your intuition, such as meditation, mindfulness and dream recall, is beneficial.

Opening up to others isn't easy for these people. After the age of 19 they are increasingly drawn into public positions that require strength and confidence, and during these years they should guard against inflexibility. After 48 they are likely to become more practical, analytical, observant and methodical. If they devote themselves to a cause worthy of them, they have the potential to rise to the top, taking others with them. The opposite is true if they make the wrong choice, so learning to make the right decisions is their major challenge. They can make the right choice with ease, however, if they learn to work with their intuition, investing time and energy to listening to their inner voice. Once they understand that the answers they are seeking lie within, their destiny is to devote their considerable talents to furthering the common good.

Potential: Courageous, generous

Dark side: Self-sacrificing, reserved

Tarot card, lucky numbers, days, colors: The Emperor, 2, 4, Monday, Sunday, cream, lavender

Born today: Nathaniel Hawthorne (author); Giuseppe Garibaldi (general); Post Malone (singer)

July 5

The Birthday of Fireworks

"Sparks will fly"

People born on July 5 have a flair for injecting sparkle, energy and excitement into any situation or atmosphere. Everything about them is colorful, and their vitality and charm light up the workplace and social gatherings. Thriving on constant variety and stimulation, their life never seems to stand still, and even if they are in a routine because of work or family commitments, they ensure they have an outside interest to absorb them. Their boundless energy and enthusiasm can exhaust others, and their wild shifts in mood may also confuse people. The key to their success is education and constant learning, as this helps them develop the self-discipline they need to reach their true potential. Their restless nature makes it hard for them to concentrate for long periods or conform to a schedule, and their vivid imagination often makes them feel different, but they should cherish rather than repress their creativity as it can be an endless source of inspiration.

Born inventors, their creative flair draws them to careers in design, architecture, technology, art, music, filmmaking and dance. Multitalented, they also excel in sales, promotion, counseling and entertainment. Despite being rebels at heart, they can often be found in positions of authority, and their love of variety draws them to entrepreneurship. Their need to constantly push boundaries and experiment may cause them to risk their health, so it is important that they slow down, and focus their minds. **For self-care**, cognitive therapy, hypnotherapy and meditation are highly recommended to help you find inner calm.

Those born on this day would benefit from associating with people who are calm and gentle. After the age of 18 their confidence increases and this is when they are most likely to be adventurous and creative. It is important they do not fritter away their energy in too many directions. After 47 they may become more discriminating. Their desire to keep busy is a key characteristic, but when combined with a more centered existence, their explosive ideas finally transform from dreams into progressive and lasting achievements. Once they become more grounded and disciplined, their destiny is to innovate and, by so doing, light up the world with their visions of reform.

July 6

The Birthday of Passionate Attachment

"I'm all in"

The life lesson:

is avoiding tunnel vision.

The way forward: is to understand that alternative viewpoints are not a threat but an exciting opportunity to learn more.

Luck maker: Don't rely on one thing. Human beings have complex needs and fulfillment can never be found from one source, one person or one thing alone.

July 6-born are blessed with an infectious energy, vibrant optimism and focused enthusiasm about every aspect of their lives. It is impossible for them to be anything but passionate and intense about their relationships, responsibilities and career. Compromise makes no sense to them and this can sometimes cause them problems, as they can become completely single-minded in their pursuit of their dreams. It is extremely important, therefore, that they learn to be less obsessive, broadening their interests and horizons to include not just one, but several potential sources of fulfillment.

Born image consultants. they have the insight and focus to succeed in any career, but they may be drawn to teaching and self-employment, as well as banking, business, trading stocks, promotion, advertising, public relations, show business, the arts, journalism, charity and humanitarian work, the healing professions and work in the community. They should avoid any dependency on toxic substances, such as alcohol, and maintain a well-balanced diet and moderate exercise program for wellbeing. **For self-care**, wearing, meditating on or surrounding yourself with shades of yellow will encourage you to feel lighter and be more open-minded.

These people tend to jump into relationships and need to avoid becoming needy and to allow those they love to have room to breathe. Until the age of 46 they have opportunities to become more self-assured; they need to take advantage of these to broaden their perspective. After the age of 46 they are likely to become more health conscious and discriminating; during these years it is important for them to manage their financial assets, as their passionate nature means they may spend money faster than they make it. Above all, they need to learn not to devote all their energy and enthusiasm to one area of their life. When they cultivate a more well-rounded approach, they find that they have all the talent and personal magnetism they need to transform their passionate dreams into reality. Once they learn to be more open-minded and -hearted (and more realistic), their destiny is to use their remarkable charisma to raise standards everywhere they go.

Potential: Passionate, exciting

Dark side: Needy, narrow-minded

Tarot card, lucky numbers, days, colors: Lovers, 4, 6, Monday, Friday, cream, pink

Born today: Nancy Reagan (US first lady); Bill Haley (musician); Kevin Hart (comedian)

July 7

The Birthday of the Beautiful Dreamer

"I can paint a rainbow"

People born on July 7 have the imaginations to support projects deemed unfeasible and then surprise others by showing that they are indeed feasible. The key to their ability to achieve the impossible is their rare combination of visionary imagination and strong determination. They are beautiful dreamers, blessed with the creativity and idealism others often lose when they become adults. They can appear naïve at times, and although their honesty is touching and endearing, it may limit their rise professionally and socially. This is unlikely to bother them, however, because for them a life that lacks honesty or creativity is a life not worth living. They do not react well to criticism and may retreat into a shell of resentment, self-pity and defeatism that is not conducive to their psychological growth.

Born painters, they are often drawn to the arts, music and acting, but can also use their energy and intuition in the world of business, entrepreneurship, influencing, science, technology, the law, banking and publishing. They have a low stress threshold, so they must ensure they give themselves plenty of time to unwind, rest and relax. **For self-care**, music and spending time close to water are healing for you in mind, body and soul. You also benefit from regular massage and meditation.

Although those born on this day can appear reserved, they also tend to fall in and out of love quickly and they need to be less demanding of their loved ones. After the age of 16 they often become more assertive. After 45 they are likely to become more analytical and discriminating. They do not lose their remarkable imagination, but these are the mature years when they fine-tune their creative talents in a more practical way, using their creative approach to life to lift others out of the mundane. Crucial to their success or failure, however, is their willingness to step away from their dreams occasionally, and be more realistic. Once they develop the emotional maturity to be more objective, they have all the potential and passion they need not only to generate ambitious plans and see them realized, but to earn the support, belief and admiration of others. Their destiny is to touch lives and hearts with their ingeniousness and creativity.

Potential: Creative, determined

Dark side: Demanding, resentful

Tarot card, lucky numbers, day, colors: Chariot, 5, 7, Monday, cream, emerald

Born today: Tiny Grimes and Ringo Starr (musicians); Robert A. Heinlein (author)

July 8

The Birthday of Mysterious Reality

"Nothing is going to stop me now"

Those born on July 8 are admired for their efficiency and dynamic energy, but the admiration is more respectful than loving. Such is their willpower they stop at nothing to achieve their goals. They can devote themselves to one single purpose and stick with it. If they practice due diligence and invest their time and energy wisely, their one-track approach leads to success. Their sense of purpose is so strong it can override right and wrong, so it is crucial they decide on their values and stick to them. Their intense motivation may be connected to never feeling quite good enough, and although this can fuel their success, it can also make them prone to perfectionism or controlling behavior. It is important they get in touch with their emotions and learn to love themselves for who they are, not for who they could or should be.

Born scientists, they have the imagination and tenacity to excel in scientific, commercial or technology-based careers, as well as in artistic jobs that involve research, practical skills and goal-setting. They may be drawn to management, finance, teaching, counseling, the law, advertising, marketing, the media or community work. Tending to be sedentary, these people prefer to sit on the sidelines guiding others rather than participating, so it is important they do regular exercise. **For self-care,** regular brisk walks or jogs in natural settings, especially when stressed, boosts your physical, mental and emotional wellbeing.

Those born on this day are anything but an open book and will often remain a mystery, even to those closest to them. They need to avoid treating their partners as children and let them breathe. Until the age of 44 they have opportunities to develop their skills, and after 45 practical considerations become more important—this is when they are capable of achieving great things professionally and personally. If they become more sensitive to the feelings of others, they can earn not just the respect but also the loyalty and love of those they live and work with. Once they understand that their priorities may be different from everyone else's, and they place equal value on the concerns of others, their destiny is to implement their progressive ideas and dramatically improve lives.

July 9

The Birthday of the Lovable Innovator

"Anything is possible"

Those born on July 9 are powerhouses of energy and enthusiasm. They put their heart and soul into everything they do, whether it is work or a relationship. Endearingly curious, their wide-eyed wonder and out-of-the-box originality has a motivating effect on everyone they deal with. They have tremendous innovative potential and their absolute conviction that anything is possible and that mysteries can be solved may lead them to explore concepts that others may dismiss as totally impossible. Despite their fierce originality, they understand the importance of being realistic, and when their innate optimism and charisma are added to this combination, it's no surprise that they are often fascinating and admired by others. Prone to stress when criticized, they can withdraw into bitterness and disillusionment, so it is vital that they find constructive ways to cope with disappointment, using it as an incentive or a learning experience.

Born pioneers, they often present new theories in science and art, as well as in mysticism and spirituality. Their gift for working with people makes them natural for any people-focused job, and their interest in humanitarianism may lead them to the healing professions, the law, social work and counseling. Other careers include writing, blogging, public speaking, sales, promotion, publishing, design and the performing arts. Prone to energy dips because they throw themselves into things so completely, they need to make sure they have plenty of relaxation time, preferably alone. **For self-care**, every morning or evening you should unplug your phone and focus on your own needs and opinions rather than those of others or on your newsfeed.

These people have high expectations in their relationships and need to make sure there is an equal balance of giving and receiving. Until the age of 43 they should take advantage of any opportunity to develop more self-confidence. After 43 they are likely to become more discriminating, practical and perfectionist. If they can just learn to try another approach if the first fails, their enduring interest in investigating, exploring and pushing the boundaries gives them outstanding potential to create and implement their visions. Once they have learned to deal with life's challenges, their destiny is to forge innovative new directions.

Potential: Vital, imaginative

Dark side: Insecure, bitter

Tarot card, lucky numbers, days, colors: Hermit, 7, 9, Monday, Tuesday, cream, cherry red

Born today: Elias Howe (inventor); Michael Graves (architect); Tom Hanks (actor)

July 10

The Birthday of the Dark Horse

The life lesson:

is to express your feelings.

The way forward: is to understand that revealing your passion does not suggest loss of control but shows others that you are committed.

Luck maker: Listen to your impulsive heart more often—it is usually right.

"Timing is everything"

July 10-born observe and learn from others' successes and defeats and then carefully plan their actions accordingly. Others may regard them as passive, but they're not; they're steady and purposeful, only making a move when certain it will be successful or well received. Quick learners, they can be flexible and adaptive in their approach. Sensitive to everything going on around them, once they have the information they need for the best chance of success, they move toward achieving their goals with determination, utilizing their intellectual and practical skills. They may appear steady, but when people get to know them better, everything about them is constantly surprising. They only step into the limelight if it serves a purpose. Underneath their sensitive persona is a steely determination to succeed that reveals itself when the time is right. Problems arise, however, when they plan and procrastinate for too long and miss their chance for success.

Born forensic experts, they may be drawn to careers in psychiatry, science, psychology, counseling and law enforcement, but they may also excel as performers, journalists, writers, painters and athletes, and may also consider photography, tourism and self-employment. Although they are quick to observe the importance of good health in others, they can be casual about their own physical wellbeing. **For self-care**, regular exercise and massages help you feel more connected to your body.

In relationships these people can take a long time to make a move or declare what they are thinking and feeling, often remaining a mystery to their loved ones. At certain points in their lives—their mid-fifties, especially—they can astonish people with a total change of lifestyle or direction, but even though the change may shock others, it is likely well planned. When they finally decide to invest their energy into a worthy cause, everyone wonders how they could have underestimated the creative energy of this dark horse hiding behind a mild-mannered exterior. Once they learn to participate in life more, and sometimes let their heart rule their head, their destiny is to surprise and delight others with their progressive vision.

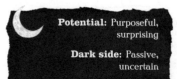

Potential: Purposeful, surprising

Dark side: Passive, uncertain

Tarot card, lucky numbers, days, colors: Wheel of Fortune, 1, 8, Monday, Sunday, cream, orange

Born today: Nikola Tesla (physicist); Arthur Ashe and Virginia Wade (tennis players); Marcel Proust (author)

July 11

The Birthday of the Innovative Chameleon

"I do understand"

People born on July 11 have an easy-going charm that puts everyone at ease. They can blend in no matter where they are or who they're with, and often find themselves in situations where their charm gives them access to key information. Their diplomatic skills are extraordinary and they are excellent at working around problems and sidestepping confrontations. This doesn't mean they are lazy or evasive. Although they are amiable and sensitive, they can be fiercely innovative and ambitious. Their personality is defined by an intense interest in creating successful relationships and a need to be liked.

Born journalists, they have an affinity for work involving communication and may make performing, influencing, blogging, writing, drama, art or music their career, but they may also excel in commercial enterprise, politics or sport. Other careers include banking, the law, sales, public relations, carpentry, cooking and design. They tend to stay fit and healthy when they work out with other people or join a sports team, but it is important they can also do so when alone. **For self-care**, wearing, meditating on or surrounding yourself with the color blue will encourage you to be objective, clear and truthful in your self-expression.

Those born on this day have much love to give and thrive in close relationships, but may become restless when things get routine. Before the age of 40, if they are discreet, they earn respect and support, but if they choose to break confidences, they earn a reputation for unreliability. After the age of 40 they have opportunities to become more discriminating and be of practical service for others. They need to take advantage of such opportunities to find emotional fulfillment through honesty, discretion and compassion. As long as they center their lives on positive values and steer clear of people-pleasing, these multitalented individuals have the potential and versatility to produce excellent work, whatever they decide to do. Once they find the courage to base their lives on love and integrity, and stand out as well as blend in, their destiny is to use their empathy and optimism to motivate, uplift and inspire all those lucky enough to cross their path.

July 12

The Birthday of the Insightful Initiator

"Trust me, I know how to help"

The life lesson:

is to accept you may be wrong.

The way forward: is to understand that truly great leaders and people adjust their opinions and directions if life gives them a reason to do so.

Luck maker: Be a mirror. Sometimes people don't want help or advice, they just want to be heard; mirroring their words back to them makes them feel heard and understood.

July 12-born are defined by their altruism. Their desire to help others succeed makes them empathetic and insightful, but it also compels them to initiate and take charge. It's a mistake to dismiss these seemingly gentle people as a pushover. They hold strong convictions and have a powerful influence over others, and the key to their success is whether they employ this in a positive way that encourages others to grow independently, or in a negative way that fosters dependence. If they can practice non-interference and understand that others need to learn by making their own mistakes, they find that their chances of success increase. This isn't to say they should hide their talents. It's just that they are such capable, persuasive individuals that others tend to be guided rather than inspired by them.

Born advisors, they don't follow the herd, so may prefer to work solo. Apart from politics, science and social work, other career choices include counseling, education, the law, writing and all forms of advice giving, including sales, negotiation and promotion. Their excellent communication skills give them tremendous potential to succeed in the arts and in any career they choose. They tend to lose themselves in work and need to make sure they do not neglect their health. **For self-care**, schedule regular periods of peace and solitude to focus on your own feelings and what is best for you, rather than for others.

In their relationships these people need to strive for equality, and not always take the lead. Until the age of 40 they have many opportunities to demonstrate their creativity and strong convictions. After the age of 40 they may become more pragmatic and discerning. As long as they ensure that they nurture others without smothering them, this is the period when these empathetic but progressive individuals can do what they do best—initiate action that changes the lives of others for the better—and, by so doing, make their own special mark on the world. Their destiny is to lead, guide, advise and inspire others.

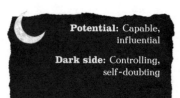

Potential: Capable, influential

Dark side: Controlling, self-doubting

Tarot card, lucky numbers, days, colors: Hanged Man, 1, 3, Monday, Thursday, white, purple

Born today: Henry David Thoreau (naturalist); Malala Yousafzai (activist); Milton Berle (comedian)

July 13

The Birthday of the Action Person

The life lesson:

is believing in yourself.

The way forward: is to understand that like seeks like and, if you doubt yourself, others will doubt you. So, you need to change the way you think about yourself.

Luck maker: Do something every day that you fear. The best way to overcome fear is to get out of your comfort zone and, whatever the outcome, grow in confidence from the experience.

"I am what I do"

People born on July 13 are daring and resilient risk-takers with the enviable ability to bounce back stronger, typically with a new approach or strategy, whenever life knocks them down. Fearless and focused, there is little that can intimidate them, except perhaps when it comes to affairs of the heart where they can be a little awkward. Their approach to life is action-orientated and results-driven, and, when you add to this their keen intelligence, inventiveness and explosive energy, this results in an amazing potential to seize the moment and act incisively. Sometimes their self-confidence is dented when a risk backfires, and it is vital during this time that they do not slump into negative thinking. Taking decisive action and avoiding procrastination is their strength, but to be true to themselves they first need to believe in themselves.

Born entrepreneurs, they may be drawn toward careers where they can work for the wellbeing or education of others, such as social work or teaching, although they are equally well suited to self-employment, sports, science, art, the media and entertainment. Other possible careers might include public relations, lobbying, sales, landscaping, building and real estate. As they love to make sudden diet and lifestyle changes, they need to give themselves plenty of time for rest and relaxation. **For self-care**, wearing, meditating on and surrounding yourself with shades of blue will help you approach situations in a calm, controlled and confident way.

These people are so action-orientated that they need to understand the importance of subtle words and gestures in fulfilling relationships. Around the age of 39 they are most likely to be plagued by self-doubt, but if they can make this turning point work for rather than against them by becoming more disciplined and thoughtful in their approach, they will find that their creativity and optimism bounce back. Once they have learned to trust their judgment, weigh up the pros and cons before taking a risk and believe in themselves, their destiny is to surprise and inspire others with their daring and originality.

Potential: Daring, resilient

Dark side: Reckless, self-doubting

Tarot card, lucky numbers, days, colors: Death, 2, 4, Monday, Sunday, cream, pale blue

Born today: Julius Caesar (Roman emperor); Patrick Stewart and Harrison Ford (actors); Wole Soyinka (playwright)

July 14

The Birthday of the Illusionist

The life lesson:

is reliability.

The way forward: is to understand that however great your ability to charm, the best way to earn admiration is to let your actions do the talking.

Luck maker: Avoid people-pleasing behavior. Making the approval of others your first priority minimizes your own goals and chases luck out of your life.

"Look into my eyes"

Those born on July 14 are magnetic and intelligent people with the ability to cast a spell over others through their seductive intensity and superb communication skills. Their charm can be subtle or bold, but it always matches the occasion perfectly. Whoever they are talking to, they know exactly how to convince and inspire confidence. Masters of the art of illusion, their talent for developing believable and fascinating theories is awesome. Although they have considerable gifts and tremendous drive, they can get bouts of melancholy for no apparent reason. As they have such a powerful impact on others, it is crucial they devote their thoughts and talents to worthy causes and avoid any unscrupulous activity.

Born campaigners, they can often be found in careers with altruistic or humanitarian aims, such as politics, the law or charity work, but may also devote their talents to writing and artistic pursuits. Commerce, finance, business, teaching, therapy, the world of magic and entertainment or working for themselves may also appeal. Prone to sudden dark moods, they should not deny these but treat them as an opportunity to connect with their feelings and understand themselves better. **For self-care**, writing down feelings is both cathartic and educational. You should keep a mood diary to record both events and feelings.

Winning the hearts of others by sensing their hidden motivations and promising to fulfill their desires earns those born on this day popularity. But if they also want to be admired, they need to balance their seductive gift with solid results and prioritize their own needs over those of others. Until the age of 38 they are likely to grow steadily in confidence and creativity. After 38 they will develop a more methodical attitude, together with a desire to be of service to others; this is when they have the best opportunities to turn the illusions they create into reality. When they use their personal magnetism to achieve rather than talk about their ideals, they are a force to be reckoned with. Once they find a cause to believe in and their own truth, their destiny is to dramatically influence, inspire and improve the lives of others.

Potential: Charming, persuasive

Dark side: Misleading, gloomy

Tarot card, lucky numbers, days, colors: Temperance, 3, 5, Monday, Wednesday, cream, sky blue

Born today: William Hanna (animator); Ingmar Bergman (director); Gertrude Bell (archaeologist)

July 15

The Birthday of

Stimulus

"Let's do this"

The life lesson:

is to avoid selfishness.

The way forward: is to understand that selfishness only brings short-term satisfaction. Consideration for the needs of others brings both short- and long-term satisfaction.

Luck maker: Learn to read people better by studying body language. Lucky people are always sensitive to how others perceive them because they want to come across honestly and positively.

July 15-born have a rare ability to stimulate others. They do not feel envious of the success of those they live and work with and generously offer praise, which only serves to increase their popularity. Their game-changing insight and creativity blesses them with the ability to implement progressive change and enrich the lives of others in the process. Their determination to make a positive difference is utterly compelling and inspirational. If, however, they become materialistic or selfish and use their influence to manipulate others, they can be ruthless. It is crucial they become aware of the hugely influential impact their exciting and imaginative personality tends to have on others.

Born business people, they have the ruthless streak needed in business or commerce, but may prefer to reach out to the world through creative and expressive endeavors, such as acting, music, art, writing or speaking. They may also be attracted to teaching, journalism, research, science and the caring professions, but, whatever career they choose, education or training is key to help them realize their potential. Prone to excess, their love of life's material pleasures may lead to gambling or addictive behavior. Finding a higher meaning to life in spirituality is healing for them. **For self-care**, you will benefit greatly from meditation as well as quiet time alone reading, thinking and daydreaming.

Those born on this day have the ability to attract admirers effortlessly, but they also tend to take advantage of the vulnerabilities in others and need to ensure they are emotionally honest. Until the age of 37 they are likely to confidently express and use their magnetic charm, but at around this time they reach a turning point and move away from selfishness. Their desire to be of service to others becomes more intense and they really come into their own. To utilize their leadership potential they need to understand themselves and their magnetic influence over others better. Their destiny is to positively enrich the minds and hearts of all those lucky enough to cross their path.

Potential: Influential, motivational

Dark side: Materialistic, ruthless

Tarot card, lucky numbers, days, colors: Devil, 4, 6, Monday, Friday, cream, pink

Born today: Rembrandt van Rijn (painter); Emmeline Pankhurst (suffragette); Jocelyn Bell Burnell (astrophysicist); Forest Whitaker (actor)

July 16

The Birthday of
Passionate Logic

The life lesson:

is resisting the tendency to be didactic.

The way forward: is to understand that forcing others to listen to your viewpoint is likely to cause resentment and backfire.

Luck maker: Listening more and speaking less helps you learn what you need to succeed.

"If I can dream it, I can do it."

People born on July 16 have an impulsive, passionate nature. They have adventurous and exciting dreams and, more often than not, these come true. Once they are inspired, their energy is without equal, but they have another side, their logical side. This unusual combination of passion and logic makes them unusual and exceptional. Whatever life path they choose, they will always have a conflict between their logic and their impulses, and this will come across in words that are rational but presented passionately or behavior that is impulsive but explained logically. When their logic and passion are perfectly balanced, they feel at their happiest, but when one is more dominant than the other, it can lead to unhappiness and obsessive or confusing behavior.

Born speakers, these people are well suited to the arts, where their innovations inspire, inform or entertain others, but they may also choose to help others by becoming social or religious campaigners, charity workers or life coaches. Education, counseling, writing or any job that involves communicating or acting for others, such as politics and the law, may also appeal, as does social-media influencing. These strong-willed individuals are unlikely to take any advice when it comes to diet and health. They must do plenty of research to find what works best for them. **For self-care**, wearing, meditating on or surrounding yourself with the color green will encourage you to find balance, and think and feel more positively.

Those born on this day tend to pursue and succeed in capturing romantic partners others might think are unsuitable and out of their league. Emotion is likely to take the lead in the first 35 years of their lives, but after the age of 35 they shift toward logic and reason, and are likely to have a more practical and discriminating attitude, with service to others becoming more important. The key to their success is to allow neither their rational nor their impulsive side to take the lead. Once they find that perfect balance, they have within them outstanding potential not just to achieve their own dreams but also to bring excitement into the lives of others. Their destiny is to make a positive and transformative contribution to the world.

Potential: Passionate, devoted

Dark side: Obsessive, confusing

Tarot card, lucky numbers, day, colors: Tower, 5, 7, Monday, cream, lagoon blue

Born today: Will Ferrell (comedian); Roald Amundsen (explorer); Michael Flatley (dancer)

July 17

The Birthday of Mastery

"I have whatever it takes"

Those born on July 17 are often acknowledged for their mastery in their chosen field. Their independence, confidence and self-discipline make them extremely capable and impressive. Although they frequently present a serious face, they are passionate and creative, and, to those who know them well, possess a crazy sense of humor. They are great at working their way patiently up to the top, but sometimes their progress is so slow it is detrimental to their creativity. It is important not to waste their creative potential, so choice of career is vital as they will not find fulfillment until they devote themselves to something that inspires them or speaks to their principles.

Born podcasters, they are multitalented, with huge potential in whatever career they choose. They may be drawn to finance, accounting, management, the law, politics, science, promotion, advertising and sales, or may develop their creativity with the spoken or written word in journalism, broadcasting, lecturing, entertainment or the media, or working for themselves. They are likely to take great care of their physical health, but need to pay greater attention to their emotional health. **For self-care**, do more of what you love to do and less of what you feel you ought to do.

Those born on this day tend to be traditional when it comes to affairs of the heart, but, paradoxically, may also be tempted to have secret emotional affairs. Until the age of 36 their cool efficiency wins the respect of others. After the age of 36, when they have opportunities to become even more practical and discriminating, it is important that they direct their efforts toward gaining recognition also for their creativity. If they make sure that their self-sufficiency does not cause them to seem unapproachable, they will be well on track to achieving success without forfeiting the goodwill of others. They may also find that although their wish to have others acknowledge their mastery is granted, they find greater happiness from their ability to touch others with their generosity and creativity. Once they stop trying so hard to win people's respect, their destiny is to inform, entertain and inspire others.

Potential: Self-sufficient, capable

Dark side: Procrastinating, isolated

Tarot card, lucky numbers, days, colors: The Star, 6, 8, Monday, Saturday, cream, maroon

Born today: David Hasselhoff and James Cagney (actors); Gordon Gould (physicist); Angela Merkel (German chancellor)

July 18

The Birthday of the Better Way

"I am the change I want to see"

July 18-born often throw their energetic hearts, minds and souls into whatever they do. Admired for their dedication, conviction, self-discipline and determination, they are unlikely to follow the conventional path in their personal or professional lives, and always aim to find a better way, often speaking out boldly to let others know about it. Although they can give the appearance of being extreme, there is real method in their madness. Independent and innovative, they identify with a group or the common good because they are empathetic souls, but also because they gain confidence from the support and recognition of others.

Born politicians, they may be attracted to politics, the military, music, art, religion or sport. They can also excel in team roles in business, education, research, science, public relations, charity, humanitarian and social work and the caring professions. Whatever career they choose, they are best suited to management and leadership positions. They also need to find time to develop their own identity and interests apart from the group. **For self-care**, getting in touch with your emotions is crucial—feelings should be listened to because they have something important to say.

These people tend to neglect affairs of the heart for their career or cause, so they do need to focus on loved ones more often. Until the age of 34 they are likely to align their talents with shared aims, so it is important they don't become extreme or inflexible. After the age of 34 they may become more discriminating. The need to work with and serve others is as strong as ever, but the emphasis is on supplying creative and progressive solutions, making these powerful years for them. They will always be gifted problem-solvers able to find a better way for others, but their best approach is to trust their highly developed intuition, as it will attract countless opportunities to them. Once they learn to think independently and not always to identify with others, their destiny is to be an inspirational force for justice and progress in their community and beyond.

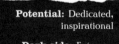

Potential: Dedicated, inspirational

Dark side: Extreme, insecure

Tarot card, lucky numbers, days, colors: The Moon, 7, 9, Monday, Tuesday, white, crimson

Born today: Nelson Mandela (activist); Richard Branson (entrepreneur); Nick Faldo (golfer)

July 19

The Birthday of Energetic Self-awareness

"Every day is an opportunity to improve myself"

is challenging negative thinking.

The way forward: is to understand that negative thinking is just as unrealistic as positive thinking. The aim is more realistic thinking.

Luck maker: Believe in your own value and think and act as if you have already achieved success.

People born on July 19 set themselves extremely high standards. Self-improvement is a key life theme. They expect a great deal from themselves and others, but most especially themselves. Energetic and charming, they love to keep their bodies and minds active and often push themselves incredibly hard or jump from activity to activity. They need to keep moving and, above all, to feel that they are learning, growing and improving in all areas of their lives. They are incredibly self-aware, and when they make a mistake, they immediately acknowledge it, trying to find ways of improving their performance in the future. Others love them for their ability to learn and change, but their self-awareness does come at a price: a painful awareness of their own inadequacies. They can be prone to relentless self-criticism, accompanied by insecurity, mood swings and impatience.

Born sprinters, their high energy levels may draw them to sports or the mastery of technical and artistic pursuits. Other fulfilling careers include politics, education, the caring professions, design, the law, business, lobbying and the performing arts. They love to move so are likely to get plenty of exercise, but equally important for their wellbeing is building their self-esteem, and they might benefit from mind-control techniques, such as cognitive behavioral therapy, which can help them challenge negative thinking. **For self-care**, spending more time simply *being* instead of doing helps boost self-esteem, giving you the objectivity and distance needed to manage your emotions effectively.

Those born on this day have a strong need for emotional security and often seek intense and close relationships. After the age of 34 they are likely to become even more perfectionist. It is important that they learn to be less subjective and more patient with themselves, because then they can really make the most of their wonderful potential to become the highly creative and charismatic person they are meant to be. Once they start building self-esteem, their destiny is to help humanity evolve along with them.

Potential: Self-aware, charming

Dark side: Negative, moody

Tarot card, lucky numbers, days, colors: The Sun, 1, 8, Monday, Sunday, orange, gold

Born today: Benedict Cumberbatch, Anthony Edwards and Jared Padalecki (actors); Edgar Degas (artist)

July 20

The Birthday of Evolution

"The journey is better than the arrival"

The life lesson:

is to live in the now.

The way forward: is to understand that the fulfillment you seek is not external but within.

Luck maker: Showing gratitude for the things you take for granted increases your chance of success and happiness.

Those born on July 20 thrive on the challenge of the new, feeling exhilarated rather than daunted by fresh horizons. No matter how comfortable or secure they are, routine is deadly for them and their restless spirit constantly seeks to move forward and evolve. These people rarely remain static for long, and their energy and intensity are boundless, both physically and intellectually, as they are inquisitive and constantly searching for knowledge and novel experiences. Given the constant process of evolution that defines their lives, they run the risk of being unreliable. Popular and courageous risk-takers, nothing really unsettles them except boredom, and they are far more likely to be anxious when their lives are too easy or stuck in a rut. Others may find their constant need for challenge tough to understand, but these people really are at their happiest and best when they are striving.

Born gamers, they succeed in learning-based careers such as education, the law, counseling, medicine, life-coaching, personal growth, sport, technology, science, travel and event-planning, and they also accomplish much in research and business. Alternatively, careers in filmmaking, art, music, drama, web or game design, or entertainment may appeal. They tend to put their bodies and minds under tremendous pressure, so regular rest and relaxation are essential. **For self-care**, wearing, meditating on and surrounding yourself with calming shades of blue can help you find a balance between being and doing.

Often attracted to restless types like themselves, those born on this day thrive better with people who are more stable. Until the age of 32 they may be lacking in concentration and it may take them longer than normal to find their direction. There is a change of emphasis after 32, when they become more orderly. During these years, if they can find goals that provide them with enough adventure, they can focus their energy toward increasing their knowledge and enriching the lives of others. Once they find a balance between being and doing, and understand that the most exciting adventure lies within rather than without, their destiny is to evolve into superbly creative and motivational individuals.

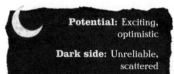

Potential: Exciting, optimistic

Dark side: Unreliable, scattered

Tarot card, lucky numbers, day, colors: The Moon, 2, 9, Monday, cream, silver

Born today: Jacinda Ardern (New Zealand prime minister); Gregor Mendel (geneticist); Sandra Oh (actor)

July 21

The Birthday of Daring

"I boldly go where no one has gone before"

July 21-born are dynamic and curious with an innate understanding of what motivates others. They are superb at analyzing and getting right to the heart of the matter, and this unique combination of shrewdness and daring draws success their way. They love to be on the cutting edge of innovative projects, preferring to be in battle rather than on the sidelines, and have the creativity and ambition needed to succeed. They always aim high, even if that aim is unrealistic. Their melodramatic sense of humor gives them resilience. Drama of any kind excites them and they make great conversationalists because they can see both sides of the argument. They crave excitement and are likely to be attracted to gaming, racing, theme parks, diving or any adrenaline-fueled situation that provides drama and demands courage.

Born emergency workers, they are suited to careers in the military, aviation, fire- and crime-fighting, security, and the caring and counseling professions, but can also thrive as scientists and teachers. Their debating skills may draw them to writing, politics, sales, business, philosophy, psychology, filmmaking, journalism and the media, and cooking may appeal to their flamboyant side. Their thrill-seeking urge may make them vulnerable to drugs, alcohol and addictions, so it is vital for them to find activities and friends to keep their feet on the ground. **For self-care**, get as much fresh air and exercise every day as you can.

Those born on this day are attracted to creative, independent, hard-working people who know their own minds, and need challenge in their relationships as much as they need it in their lives. After 30 their focus changes to a more pragmatic, rational approach, but they never lose their desire for life to be fast-moving. Their greatest strengths are their daring and courage, and when this combines with their empathy, the result is a rare and fascinating individual who is both understanding and dynamic. Once they learn the importance of self-discipline and humility (and of surrounding themselves with people who support rather than drain them), their destiny is to inspire and encourage others to think independently and, by so doing, turn a fresh and bright spotlight on human progress.

Potential: Exciting, interesting

Dark side: Restless, reckless

Tarot card, lucky numbers, days, colors: The World, 1, 3, Monday, Thursday, gold, green

Born today: Ernest Hemingway (author); Robin Williams and Josh Hartnett (actors); Sui Wen-ti (Chinese emperor)

July 22

The Birthday of Brave Compulsion

The life lesson:

is learning from mistakes.

The way forward: is to understand that making mistakes is an essential ingredient for success, helping you learn, grow and fine-tune your approach.

Luck maker: Pay attention to the details— this can make the difference between something being average and outstanding.

"My life is a work in progress"

People born on July 22 want to take action, not talk about it. Progress is their middle name. While their compulsion to act can lead them into difficulties, it can also make them remarkable innovators. They have tremendous physical and creative energy. When disaster strikes, they are brilliant at coping. It's likely they have learned the importance of self-sufficiency from an early age and have become resilient as a result. Impulsive and action-orientated, their lives feature great highs but also great lows, though they rarely lose their self-belief or give up. While such self-belief is admirable, in their impatience to get things done, they don't take into account their vulnerabilities and any potential red flags.

Born chefs, their varied gifts give these people potential to succeed in many careers, but they are particularly well suited to creative, artistic and technical pursuits in which they take leadership positions. Sales, diplomacy, politics, education, writing, fashion, design, catering, cooking, engineering, entrepreneurship, invention and counseling also appeal. Lack of self-awareness is a potential problem for them, as they may push themselves too hard. They would benefit from regular periods of rest and quiet. **For self-care**, list your likes and dislikes and do more of what you like, because if what you are doing frustrates you, you should make changes.

Although charming, these people can have problems handling frustration, and this can manifest in controlling behavior or mood swings. Until the age of 29 there is an emphasis on creativity and sociability, and they need to learn from both their failures and successes. After 29 there are opportunities for them to become more methodical and orderly, which is ideal as attention to detail is the key to their success. Above all, these people are natural optimists and, even though their actions can sometimes wear others out, their compulsion to re-energize and challenge themselves marks them out as inspirational leaders and survivors. Once they learn to turn their weaknesses into strengths and practice more haste and less speed, their destiny is to show others that they can achieve great things when patience and discipline are combined with courage and creativity.

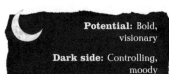

Potential: Bold, visionary

Dark side: Controlling, moody

Tarot card, lucky numbers, days, colors: The Fool, 2, 4, Monday, Sunday, gold, purple

Born today: Selena Gomez and Danny Glover (actors); Emma Lazarus (poet); Alexander Calder (sculptor)

LEO

THE LION (JULY 23–AUGUST 22)

* **Element:** Fire
* **Ruling planet:** Sun, the individual
* **Tarot card:** Strength (passion)
* **Lucky numbers:** 1, 5
* **Favorable colors:** Yellow, gold and orange
* **Driving force:** Flamboyance
* **Personal statement:** I live every moment to the fullest
* **Chinese astrology counterpart:** The Monkey

Warm-hearted and vital, Leos are eternal optimists who like to live every waking moment of their lives to the fullest. They often have larger-than-life charismatic personalities and the ability to light up everyone they meet. Leos can be generous, outgoing, humorous and creative, but they can also have a vain and attention-seeking streak, and their high expectations of everyone and everything can sometimes make them appear arrogant or dismissive of others.

Personality potential

It's not often that you see a sad or gloomy Leo. These energetic and driven individuals are ruled by the sun, the giver of life, and under normal circumstances Leos can be found bringing laugher and activity to everyone and everything they touch. They hate being miserable, and there is always a "buzz" of excitement and spontaneity when they are around. All the other zodiac symbols revolve around the sun, and Leos, since they are ruled by the sun, therefore believe they are the center of the universe. With their knack of convincing others that they are very important people indeed, it's no surprise that plenty of Leos shine on social media or gravitate to the worlds of entertainment and politics.

Without doubt, **Leos like to be the center of attention, and this is typically the place where you will find them.** Key words associated with Leos include creativity, bravery, generosity, energy and enthusiasm. They can also be unusually resourceful people. Far-sighted and efficient, they can work their way toward a bright future, overcoming any obstacles they meet on the way. Their positive, upbeat attitude enables them to create opportunities out of rejection or disappointment. They aren't possessive of their success, however, and will generously share it with others. Other people need lots of energy and stamina to keep up with Leos, but lions are always willing to share their sunshine with those they love and admire.

People born under the sun sign Leo are attracted to anything extraordinary or shiny and new. They love novelty and thrive on change. In addition, they can also be blessed with endless enthusiasm, energy and imagination, and all these qualities gather other people to them like moths to a flame. Leos are particularly good at seeing the big picture and, when this visionary ability is combined with their creativity, drive and charisma, they can often be found in positions of leadership and authority.

> **Leos like to be the center of attention, and this is typically the place where you will find them.**

Above all, Leos live every waking moment to the fullest. They have an inner sunshine that is truly energizing and inspiring. The generous, warm-hearted nature of these creative souls has the potential to light up not just any room they are in, but the world.

Personality pitfalls

Leos like to be center stage and tend to expect and demand adoration from others as a right. In many instances they do this in such a charming way that no one takes offense, but they do need to be careful that their exuberant, ego-led approach to life does not turn into domineering bossiness. Ego problems, which can veer into narcissism, are common for sun-sign Leos. If you tell a Leo you agree with them or they are amazing, you will see them grow an inch with pride and almost purr with contentment, but if you tell them you disagree with them or that you don't think they are going about things in the right way, you will see them quickly deflate like a balloon. They are very sensitive to criticism of any kind and will take personally every negative thing that people say about them. If you challenge them you can expect their sunny warmth toward you to evaporate. This sounds contradictory considering that self-confidence is a key phrase for Leos, but often this self-confidence is more bluffing than reality. They are notorious for over-selling themselves, and their pride and boasting can often mask a lack of confidence or impostor syndrome.

Leos, like a lion dozing in the sunshine, can also be extremely lazy, but, more often than not, their laziness is down to insecurity. If they are not sure that they can do something or be the brightest and the best at what they do, they would rather not do it at all and will feign apathy or indifference. Leos also can put more emphasis on looking the part rather than being the real deal. This desire to look good can make them extremely vulnerable to false praise and false criticism. Snobbery, arrogance, selfishness and a tendency not to match their words with their actions can dim the brilliant light of this sun sign. Perhaps their worst personality pitfall, however, is their misguided belief that they are always right. Leos can be exceedingly dogmatic and they need to cultivate a more open-minded approach, as well as respect for the opinions of others.

Symbol

To get a picture of Leos at their best, imagine a playful lion cub and then a fully grown majestic king of the jungle. Like the lion that is their symbol, Leos have a noble but playful air about them that commands respect wherever they go or whatever situation they are in. But again, like the lions they are, they can also be overpowering, vicious and lethal if they are going in for the kill.

Darkest secret

Few would guess that underneath the noble, sunny exterior Leos display to the world is a vulnerable soul who seriously undervalues themselves, and craves love and recognition above all else. They need others to validate them and struggle to validate themselves. Without love, adoration and recognition, the characteristic brightness of a Leo will fade. Winning is important to them, but more important than that is being the one who everyone loves, respects and admires, and they will try to be that person at whatever cost.

Love

Being in love is pure ecstasy for the Leo. They want that loving feeling to continue forever. They will treat their partner like a king or queen and be generous, passionate and romantic lovers. When a relationship shows signs of slipping into a routine, they will do all they can to bring the magic back.

They never tire of being told how wonderful they are and are very susceptible to flattery. They can also be surprisingly vulnerable and sensitive when they share their hearts, and are easily hurt because they are so idealistic when it comes to affairs of the heart. They don't want to be won over hastily. They adore the art of seduction with good food, fine wine, great conversation and, of course, lashings of flattery.

Unfortunately, and especially when they are younger, Leos have a tendency to fall for the wrong type of person for them, but when they do eventually find the right person they don't tend to stray, but are steadfast and loyal. They prefer partners who are quieter than themselves, as they definitely like to be in charge in a relationship. But this isn't necessarily the best thing for them. They are often happier with the challenge of someone who isn't intimidated by their posturing and attention-seeking and who maintains their own opinions and independence.

Love matches:
Aries, Gemini, Libra and Sagittarius.

The Leo woman

Vivacious, intelligent, clever and sexy, the Leo woman rarely goes unnoticed. She is warm, friendly and generous and will often be a natural leader. It can be quite daunting for a potential partner to know how to approach the Leo woman, as her self-confidence and popularity seem to know no bounds. The secret is to flatter her, as flattery is her secret weakness. It's also important that her partner does not stifle her. This woman cannot bear confinement. She needs to make her own decisions and lead her own life.

The Leo woman is many things, but above all she is a proud lioness—vain at times but also magnificent. Despite all her airs and graces, though, deep down a Leo woman is vulnerable. If a partner criticizes her, is unfaithful or leaves her, she can be wounded and it can take a great deal of time for her to rebuild her self-esteem and recover from the deep hurt. She may become very wary of risking her heart again.

Anyone in a relationship with a Leo woman has to learn not to be jealous when she is lighting up a room and surrounded by a group of admirers. Her flirting does not mean that she is tempted to stray; it's simply who she is. In her mind it's only natural for other people to admire and respect her, but, paradoxically, she also needs and constantly seeks reassurance that she is desirable.

The Leo man

The Leo man will typically be surrounded by followers or admirers of some sort. The secret to getting his attention and winning his heart is simple—admire him. Even if he is one of the quieter types born under this sign, he will still respond to adoration and flattery.

Whether or not the Leo man is truly the king of the jungle or the greatest showman is open to debate, but there is no doubt that he was born to command and to be respected by those who follow his rules. He's also capable of magnificent strength, devotion and courage on behalf of the people he loves or a cause he believes in.

The Leo man needs love to feel happy and fulfilled, and if it is missing from his life he will slump into despondency and even depression. He needs to be worshipped in a relationship, and when he does find the partner of his dreams, he will make a passionate and generous lover. But there is a drawback, and that is his jealousy and possessiveness. He expects his partner to belong to him body, mind and soul, and their life to revolve around his life, but, ironically, he'll grow restless if his partner is totally subservient. Another drawback is that the Leo man is a born flirt. Even if he is deeply in love, this won't stop him from appreciating beauty and his eyes will frequently wander. But as long as his partner is keeping him content with plenty of romance and attention, and offering enough challenge to keep him on his toes, he is unlikely to stray.

Family

Leo babies and children tend to have delightfully sunny, optimistic dispositions. They can also be playful and, at times, mischievous. From an early age the classic Leo trait of attention-seeking appears. Their natural leadership potential also shines through fairly early in their lives when they are with other groups of children, but parents should be alert to signs of bossiness and egotism, as these will alienate them from their peer group. The same applies to their siblings or place in the family if they have no siblings. Leo children are likely to try

to take charge or manage the family dynamic. It is important to remember, however, that this apparent self-confidence isn't really as powerful or strong as it may appear, and it is actually quite easy to discipline a Leo child. Adults who need to reprimand them should do so in a positive and loving way; otherwise the child's self-confidence could be dented. The best way to parent a Leo child is not through criticism or anger, but through gentle guidance and loving reassurance.

Parents of Leo children should try to encourage them to listen more, as this will help them keep an open mind and make them less likely to become inflexible in their opinions when they grow up. Leo children also have a very stubborn streak, which should be discouraged. They need to understand that there is always more than one way to achieve a goal.

It's not unusual for Leo parents to be more like friends and playmates to their children than anything else. This is fine to a certain extent, but children need parents who can set firm boundaries for them. Leo parents can also become extremely demanding, pushing their children toward unobtainable perfection, which isn't healthy for their child's development.

Career

Leos can excel in many careers but are well suited to those in which they can use their imaginative, creative abilities and their sense of drama. The world of media and entertainment is an obvious choice, but they may also be drawn to the world of fashion and advertising, or jobs in which there is an element of glamour or luxury, or that require them to be center stage in some way. They may be fine surgeons or lawyers, for example. Other career choices could include politics, public relations, social-media influencer, journalism, building, architecture or new product development.

Leos make great managers and bosses, but they do need to subdue any autocratic tendencies if they are to retain the loyalty and respect of their employees. **Their ideal working environment will have an air of luxury about it** and, as well as being convenient and comfortable, it will be a place that inspires creativity. Leos often take up causes, playing the role of savior or hero and putting great plans for the future in place. They can also shine as entrepreneurs, picking trends before others do and pioneering the way for others to follow. During times of crisis or uncertainty at work Leos really come into their own, displaying the courage, optimism and strength that is needed to help them and others overcome setbacks.

> "Their ideal working environment will have an air of luxury about it"

Health and wellbeing

Leo rules the heart, so a heart-healthy, low-cholesterol diet is advised, as is lots of exercise. Although Leos don't tend to get ill often, if they do, their need for attention and affection from friends and loved ones can be overwhelming. Being incredibly independent, they often find it hard to accept the advice of a doctor, but it's important for them to understand that occasionally they need to relinquish control and give it to someone with greater knowledge than themselves. Their backs are also vulnerable and they should pay attention to their posture to prevent inflexibility. Exercise with a creative element, such as dancing, skating or martial arts, is rewarding.

As far as leisure activities are concerned, Leos may struggle. They detest the word amateur and if they take up a leisure interest, more often than not it will be pursued to professional standards. Their dedication is admirable, but they need to learn that you don't have to be great at something to enjoy it.

Leos do have a love for the good life and a great weakness for fine food and wine. This can lead to weight problems if they aren't careful, so moderation is advised. As well as healthy eating and regular exercise, it's also extremely important for them to make sure they set aside time each day for rest and relaxation. Otherwise, they are in danger of burning themselves out. They need to be aware that they can only experience health and happiness when all aspects of their lives—heart, mind and spirit—are in balance, so finding ways to regularly renew and strengthen these four key areas of their lives is extremely beneficial. Getting plenty of fresh air, spending time with friends and loved ones, and sticking to a regular sleep, exercise and meal routine helps them feel more secure, especially during times of stress. Wearing, meditating on and surrounding themselves with calming colors like **blue** and **green** will encourage them to seek this balance.

Born between July 23 and August 3

The sun-kissed people born between these dates are natural leaders and everyone tends to look to them for illumination, guidance and security. There is a danger they can become autocratic and too harsh on themselves and others, demanding nothing less than perfection, which is, of course, impossible.

Born between August 4 and 14

These Leos tend to be more adventurous. They love to travel and long to explore the world and other cultures. Mostly easy-going, they have a lucky streak, and if they can keep their ego at bay, they seem to attract friends and good fortune wherever they go.

Born between August 15 and 22

The fighting spirit of these people is admirable and there is little doubt that once they set their sights on something, nothing will stand in their way. They are inspirational, but do need to be careful that their fierce ambition does not encourage them to walk over the feelings of others as they climb the ladder of success.

Life lessons

While Leos have no problem claiming and expressing power, they can have problems understanding the responsibility that goes with that power. One of their greatest challenges in life is to get fulfillment and energy from their own personal empowerment rather than through exerting power over others.

Leos should try to understand why they so long to be the center of attention; the answer is that they rely far too much on outward approval for their feelings of self-worth and personal identity.

If they can just accept that they don't need to be amazing to be loved and appreciated, and that being a loving, content human being is enough, Leos can find the fulfillment and happiness their warm and open hearts deserve. They also need to understand that to be human is to make mistakes; and we learn and grow most from our mistakes. Being fallible doesn't disappoint other people—it helps form a connection with them. And finally, Leos need to spend less time looking in the mirror and more time looking within. Good looks eventually fade, but inner strength and beauty just get better and stronger with age. While it is true that appearances matter, there are far more important indications of character than the clothes a person is wearing, the amount of money in their wallet or the number of followers on their social media. And really Leos have no need to get so hung up on outward show, because they possess incredible strength of character, kindness, dignity and compassion. Developing these traits brings them a great deal more happiness than looks, followers and fashion.

Leos can light each other up, but only if both lions are willing to share the spotlight. If such unlikely humility between lions happens, it can be a rare and magical opportunity for personal growth. Other signs of the zodiac can help Leos learn these life lessons. Virgos, Capricorns and Taureans can teach

Leos about the huge benefits of quiet discipline, patience and hard work behind the scenes. Scorpios can show Leos how to look beneath the surface for hidden treasures and true fulfillment, and Leos can learn from Aquarians about working tirelessly to make the world a better place without the need for outward show or recognition. Geminis can encourage them to see different perspectives from their own and Librans can help them find a healthy balance between rest and work. Arians and Sagittarians can show them that every adventure does not need an audience, and Cancerians and Pisceans can help them understand that true love involves humility and empathy.

Chinese astrology counterpart: The Monkey

Both the Chinese Monkey sign and Leos are flamboyant and playful characters. Everything is larger than life and there is a big emphasis on having fun. The Monkeys are curious, energetic, creative and adventurous animals, willing to go outside their comfort zone time and time again to achieve their goals.

Both Monkey and Leo are born performers. The world is their stage. Others can easily get swept away with the engaging show they present. Their warm self-confidence can sometimes tip over into arrogance and their lively nature can sometimes lend itself to impatience and irritability if things aren't going to their plan. But, more often than not, they have such charisma and optimism that others find it very easy to forgive them.

Note: Leos have an affinity with Monkey-sign characteristics, but be sure to check which Chinese sign corresponds to your **year** of birth (see page xxi), and to read about the characteristics associated with it, too.

July 23

The Birthday of the Liberator

The life lesson:

is to avoid being taken advantage of.

The way forward: is to understand that there is a difference between compassion and gullibility, and you should only be there for those who appreciate you.

Luck maker: Give to others by all means, but not to the point that you neglect yourself.

"A problem shared is a problem halved"

Those born on July 23 tend to be the warm pair of shoulders others choose to cry or lean on for support. They have a gift for helping others in any way they can. Their selfless wish is to see others liberated from fears, insecurities and misfortunes. But as well as being compassionate, they have a sharp mind. They can be a little conservative, but underneath they are bursting with curiosity and creativity. Ironically, for someone who is always there to listen to others, when it comes to their own feelings, they can be a closed book. They need to pay as much attention to their emotions as they do to others', because their feelings have important messages for them.

Born carers, they need to feel wanted and thrive in the caring professions, medicine, teaching, the law, social and charity work. They may also be successful in the military and police and in management positions. Their love of freedom may encourage them to work for themselves or express their creative side through the performing arts. They tend to put their own physical and emotional needs last, so need to take better care of themselves. **For self-care**, meditation is highly beneficial, as it helps you become less uncertain about yourself and more self-aware.

Those born on this day are often popular but do need to make sure they avoid toxic individuals who take advantage of their instinct to help and give. After the age of 30 they reach a turning point when they are likely to become more practical, analytical and discerning in their approach to life. From then on, their lives can be fulfilling and powerful if they grow in emotional confidence. Once they stop trying to be everyone's liberator and liberate themselves, their conviction, creativity and passion for the common good indicate potential for outstanding success both personally and professionally. Their destiny is to support and deeply influence the opinions and lives of others.

Potential: Compassionate, creative

Dark side: Self-sacrificing, gullible

Tarot card, lucky numbers, days, colors: The Hierophant, 3, 5, Sunday, Wednesday, gold, blue

Born today: Woody Harrelson, Daniel Radcliffe (actors); Alison Krauss, Slash (musicians)

July 24

The Birthday of Charismatic (Un)certainty

The life lesson:

is feeling happy alone.

The way forward: is to celebrate solitude because of the freedom it offers you from the opinions and expectations of others.

Luck maker: The best way to attract popularity and good fortune is to find ways to be of service to others.

"Buckle up, it's going to be a bumpy ride"

July 24-born are highly original and exciting. Their charisma draws others to them, in the hope of catching some of their surprising magic. Sometimes they may be reckless in their thirst for adventure, but they much prefer to put themselves on the line than take the safe route because they thrive on challenge. The excitement of the journey is more important than the arrival for these adventurous spirits. They appear fearless, but what they fear most of all is routine, the mundane and not moving forward. They need to learn that some of the greatest adventures lie within, and that getting to know themselves better is an endless source of excitement and discovery. Whatever they devote their dynamic creativity to, they are invariably attracted to the unusual, and their actions always attract the admiration of others.

Born entertainers and entrepreneurs, their passion and creativity suit many careers as long as they are in a leadership position or can make their own decisions. They are good organizers and can thrive in business, as well as promotion, advertising, online influencing, education, psychology, humanitarian work, politics, acting, music and writing. Their compulsion to seek adventure may lead them to experiment with activities detrimental to their wellbeing, so they need to ensure they have plenty of healthy interests to stave off boredom. **For self-care**, wearing, meditating on and surrounding yourself with the color purple can encourage you to be more reflective and focus on spiritual growth.

Settling down can be a problem for these restless and easily bored souls, and they need to become more self-sufficient. After the age of 30 opportunities arise to be of service to others and they need to take advantage of these opportunities for fulfillment. Once they have learned to think through the consequences of their actions and discover that others notice them just as much, if not more, when they demonstrate their gifts of sensitivity and creativity, they have the potential not just to lead but to truly amaze. Their destiny is to motivate and inspire others to believe anything is possible.

Potential: Inspirational, hypnotic

Dark side: Selfish, fickle

Tarot card, lucky numbers, days, colors: The Lovers, 4, 6, Sunday, Friday, gold, pink

Born today: Alexandre Dumas (author); Amelia Earhart (aviator); Jennifer Lopez (singer); Simón Bolívar (liberator)

July 25

The Birthday of Pure Intention

"I do the right thing"

People born on July 25 have progressive beliefs. They strive to do the right thing, their actions governed by a personal code of conduct that forbids them from doing anything that disadvantages others. Their sense of honor gives them purpose and is more important to them than success. They are more interested in the reasons for a person's behavior than the outcome, and winning or losing matters less to them than sincerity. This is why they often appear enlightened or carefree—because they know that no experience is ever wasted. With much to teach people, they have the potential to be an example of maturity and integrity, but their belief that everyone has the same level of sincerity as they do can be naïve and mean that others often let them down.

Born officers, these multitalented people can thrive in any profession, but to ensure success they need to believe in their own abilities. Their charm may draw them to activism, charity work, public relations, politics and lobbying, though they may also be drawn to careers where integrity is key such as accounting, the law, police work and the military. They are good with words, so teaching, writing, journalism and acting may also appeal, as may art and music. Prone to pushing themselves too hard, they must never ignore signs of fatigue, and should take time out or a vacation to recover. **For self-care**, meditation and mindfulness techniques are highly beneficial to keep you grounded.

Often surrounded by admirers, those born on this day need to avoid too many "yes" companions and should seek out people who challenge them. After the age of 28 they are likely to become more worldly-wise and discerning, and during these years they need to ensure perfectionism does not block their creativity. In fact, throughout their lives they should be a little less harsh on themselves, because if they learn to be more accepting of themselves, they will find that it isn't just their honesty that makes others smile with appreciation, it is also their creativity, charm and unwavering devotion to their progressive vision. Their destiny is to inspire and motivate others with their integrity and infectious enthusiasm for every aspect of life.

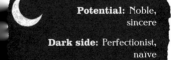

Potential: Noble, sincere

Dark side: Perfectionist, naïve

Tarot card, lucky numbers, days, colors: The Chariot, 5, 7, Sunday, Monday, gold, sea green

Born today: Rosalind Franklin (chemist); Matt LeBlanc (actor); Iman (model)

July 26

The Birthday of
Self-assurance

"Let me make this clear"

is to not become overconfident.

The way forward: is to understand that, for confidence to work, it needs to be appealing and not overwhelming. Others need to feel motivated, not cornered or embarrassed.

Luck maker: Demonstrate a willingness to learn—nobody likes a know-all.

Those born on July 26 tend to be charming and confident. They will offer their opinions unstintingly as fact, expecting others to agree and acknowledge them as authorities. As a result, others tend to listen because they have an air of authority and experience about them that people automatically respect and admire. They also don't speculate widely but focus their energies on one particular field of interest in which they have immersed themselves and earned the right to speak with authority. They don't believe in fabricating and others can be sure that what they are saying is the honest and blunt truth, however painful it may be to hear. Such is the wit and insight of their pronouncements that people can put them on a pedestal, but this elevated status can isolate them from those whose admiration, affection and respect they crave.

Born performers and directors, they are well suited to careers on stage, filmmaking, the arts or in creative areas such as social-media influencing, the media and advertising. Their communication skills may draw them to promotion, sales, writing, psychology, counseling, public relations and business. These people tend to be dynamos and it is essential that they participate in regular exercise to burn off excess energy in a healthy way. **For self-care**, physically, mentally and emotionally calming forms of exercise such as yoga, swimming and tai chi, or simply talking a walk in the park, are recommended.

Those born on this day enjoy sharing and need people in their lives who are not intimidated by their self-assurance. From the age of 27 they have an increasing desire for more order and efficiency, and in the years that follow they need to become more sensitive, not just to their own feelings but to those of others. Once they can get in touch with their humanity and humility, and accept that others have feelings just like themselves, they can use their formidable insight and passion to implement impressive strategies for success in all aspects of their lives. Their destiny is to arouse strong and potentially life-changing responses in others.

Potential: Impressive, honest

Dark side: Overconfident, uncompromising

Tarot card, lucky numbers, days, colors: Strength, 6, 8, Sunday, Saturday, gold, maroon

Born today: Carl Jung (psychiatrist); Mick Jagger (singer); Helen Mirren and Sandra Bullock (actors); Stanley Kubrick (director)

July 27

The Birthday of the Director

"It's all or nothing for me"

July 27-born are blessed with energy, passion and natural authority, as well as fantastic organizational skills—a formidable combination that often sees them playing a key role in projects they are involved in. These human dynamos can often be found successfully managing or directing others. Fueled by the desire to see real progress, they rarely do things by halves, and throw themselves into the pursuit of their visionary goals with dedication. Their style is often so authoritative that it can mislead others into assuming that they are invincible, but the truth is they are not. Underneath, they can be vulnerable. While they are superb at managing what is best for others, when it comes to their own concerns, they can be uncertain and indecisive.

Born executives, these people have the talent to succeed in business, but their creativity and love of color and beauty may draw them to the arts, public relations, sales, education, administration and management. The law, counseling and design may also appeal, as do publishing, sport, leisure and all forms of technology. Ensuring they schedule regular meals and time for exercise in their busy day helps them feel more in control. **For self-care**, spending more time in nature, hanging nature pictures on walls and using them as screensavers can ease stress.

Those born on this day tend to be possessive in their relationships, which they need to work at. After the age of 26 they often become more efficient; it is important to ensure they channel this practical emphasis positively and don't procrastinate in a career or lifestyle that does not utilize their full creative potential. They are natural leaders but, for their own growth and fulfillment, it is vital that they focus their energies on making the right decisions for themselves. With a little more self-awareness, these creative and determined thinkers can produce original ideas that can become a tangible reality, virtually guaranteeing success. Their destiny is to marshal their formidable energy and talent and not just immerse themselves in but realize their progressive visions.

Potential: Authoritative, generous

Dark side: Insecure, procrastinating

Tarot card, lucky numbers, days, colors: The Hermit, 7, 9, Sunday, Tuesday, yellow, orange

Born today: Hans Fischer (chemist); Max Scherzer (baseball player); Peggy Fleming (skater); Boyan Slat (investor)

July 28

The Birthday of the Independent Spirit

People born on July 28 are fiercely independent and competitive. They have superb communication skills, but prefer to lead by active example rather than by words. They relish testing themselves against challenges and can find it almost impossible to admit defeat. Throughout their lives they always value self-reliance above all else. Others are in awe of this self-assurance, and although it can lead them to considerable achievements, it can also cause loneliness and disappointment because they really crave affection, not admiration. Their combative approach can often be perceived as selfish and inconsiderate, which is unfair as they can be warm, intuitive and kind. Yet until they learn tact and can create strong emotional connections with others, their creativity and potential may be misunderstood.

Born fighters, they are well equipped for professions requiring confrontational tactics, such as the military, politics, commerce and sport, and even design, fashion and art. They excel in the theater as both actors and directors, as well as in writing, publishing, sales, social reform, health and charity work. Their leadership potential ensures they rise to positions of power swiftly. Regular exercise is beneficial, though not the competitive kind as they are competitive enough already. **For self-care**, watch the clouds by day and gaze at the stars by night to help appreciate the expanse of the universe and your connection to everyone and everything in it.

Often surrounded by friends and admirers, those born on this day may be reluctant to open up and share their feelings in relationships. From the age of 25, they have opportunities to become more thoughtful with their time and energy, and to recognize there is more to learn from losing than winning. If they can let others see how generous and earnest they are, they can enjoy the affectionate recognition they need to truly celebrate their seemingly endless winning streak. Once they learn to reach out and share the spotlight, and understand that trusting others does not weaken but increase their strength, their destiny is to inspire others by being among the first, the best and most beautiful at everything they do.

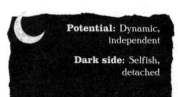

Potential: Dynamic, independent

Dark side: Selfish, detached

Tarot card, lucky numbers, day, colors: The Magician, 1, 8, Sunday, gold, yellow

Born today: Beatrix Potter and Jim Davis (illustrated authors); Marcel Duchamp (painter); Karl Popper (philosopher)

July 29

The Birthday of the Good Leader

"I work for a great cause, not applause"

is deciding for yourself.

The way forward: is to understand that using your own judgment and expressing originality is liberating, whereas subordinating your individuality to the needs of the group leads to resentment.

Luck maker: Let the past go. Lucky people understand they are utterly unique and free to choose and create their own ideas and lives.

Those born on July 29 are vital, optimistic individuals dedicated to fostering community or some kind of shared vision. Their motivation is not to benefit themselves but the good of the group or the cause they are committed to, be this their family, community, work, country, belief system or the planet. Within their social group, they gravitate toward leadership positions, and because they are strong-willed with clear-cut goals and the organizational talents to motivate others, they can be truly inspirational. Their desire to support those around them, combined with their generosity and loyalty, generally earns them a great deal of affection, gratitude and respect.

Born charity workers, they make excellent teachers, soldiers, activists, civil servants, social workers and political party workers, but they can be drawn to the world of team sports, entertainment, broadcasting, journalism or writing. Their leadership skills also make them great business leaders and directors. They don't thrive in subservient positions and are at their finest when dedicated to a cause or group they believe in and in which they are able to express their inventiveness. Health-wise, they would benefit from freeing themselves from culturally accepted ideas about aging, and focusing instead on feeling youthful at any age. **For self-care**, carrying a small rose-quartz crystal around with you can act as a visual reminder to focus on caring for your own emotional needs.

The intense communal bias of these people does not leave much room for those closest to them to develop independent interests, which is ironic considering they love to encourage self-reliance in others, usually within a framework of community awareness. It's vital they make time for themselves for their own psychological development, especially before the age of 54, when the desire to be of service really takes center stage. They may make outstanding contributions to their community or even humanity as a whole in their lives. Once they are able to serve their community or cause without losing themselves in it, their destiny is to become a living, inspiring example of how dedication to the common good can nurture and inspire true individuality.

Potential: Generous, inspirational

Dark side: Conformist, repressed

Tarot card, lucky numbers, days, colors: The High Priestess, 2, 9, Sunday, Monday, gold, silver

Born today: Walter Hunt and Vladimir K. Zworykin (inventors); George Bradshaw (publisher); Martina McBride (singer)

July 30

The Birthday of the Robust Explorer

The life lesson:

is moving beyond the material.

The way forward: is to understand if happiness doesn't come from within, unhappiness will follow, no matter how rich and successful you are.

Luck maker: Learn about spirituality, recall dreams and notice coincidences. Look for the deeper meaning in life.

"I want it all"

July 30-born set ambitious material goals for themselves. Practical and down to earth but also sensual and robust, they are often comfortable in their skins and their forceful, self-confident manner usually takes them to the top in their careers. Money and status, and all the privilege and pleasure they can bring, matter greatly to them. They hate playing games of any kind and can be extremely generous. One of the reasons they devote so much energy to increasing their earning power is that they enjoy being able to offer material support to others. Despite their morality, reliability and generosity, their target-orientated ambitions tend to exclude personal growth. Unless they learn to cultivate an interest in their psychological growth, any victories in the material world seem frustratingly hollow.

Born dealers, their goal-orientated approach makes them suited to careers in finance, business, accounting and commerce, as well as sports. Their sensuality may equip them for the beauty, health and leisure industries, as well as the media, arts, acting, painting and writing. Their biggest health risk is neglecting their emotional needs and their intuition. **For self-care,** pay equal attention to caring for mind, body, heart and soul—only when all four are in balance can you experience fulfillment and happiness.

These people make warm and supportive companions, but loved ones often take second place to material goals. Before the age of 53 their emphasis is firmly on practicality, and, given their material bias, it is crucial they try to see beyond this. After the age of 54 they have a growing need for intimacy, creativity and harmony and to look within for fulfillment. These highly robust individuals are motivated by a desire to achieve concrete progress, and they have all the determination and star quality they need to succeed. Their journey toward success, however, is considerably happier and more rewarding if they can learn to appreciate and value the things that money can't buy. Once they have opened themselves up to emotional and spiritual growth, their destiny is to find ways to both support and enrich the lives of others.

Potential: Ambitious, sensual

Dark side: Materialistic, unfulfilled

Tarot card, lucky numbers, days, colors: The High Priestess, 2, 9, Sunday, Monday, gold, silver

Born today: Emily Brontë (author); Christopher Nolan (director); Daley Thompson (athlete); Arnold Schwarzenegger (actor)

July 31

The Birthday of the Descriptive Artist

"Beauty is in the eye of the beholder"

is not being cynical.

The way forward: is to understand that the negative approach to life is just as unrealistic as the optimistic, as it means there is too much focus on one perspective.

Luck maker: Self-love and self-belief are crucial, especially when things are not working out, because these qualities give you the resilience you need to bounce back.

Those born on July 31 are eloquent observers, always curious and uncovering information that they love to share or describe to others with remarkable accuracy, insight and a dash of humor. Nothing seems to escape their attention. Their communication skills are superb. Those less comfortable with social interaction may prefer to use the medium of writing, music, art or painting to make their contribution, but whether they become artists or not, they often have a well-developed aesthetic sense, loving to surround themselves with beautiful people and things. Their thirst for exploring, describing and occasionally idolizing aspects of humanity and life, combined with their logic and determination, suggest they can make intellectual breakthroughs in whatever area they devote themselves to.

Born researchers, their keen observation and descriptive powers may draw them to journalism, broadcasting, forensics, detective work, crime, journalism, the law or science. Teaching may appeal, as does management, administration, politics, charity work, medicine, writing and visual art. They tend to worry and need to learn that this achieves nothing—they should change what they can and let go of the things they can't. **For self-care**, social interaction and generosity to others helps your psychological growth, so you need to make sure you don't neglect loved ones and friends.

Work matters greatly to these charming and interesting people, and they may neglect their loved ones as a result. If they are to be happy, they should strike a better work–life balance and pay as much attention to their heart as to their body and mind. Their observations of the harsh realities of life may lead them toward bouts of negativity, especially before the age of 52 when they focus on practicality and realism. If they can keep their generous spirit alive with uplifting thoughts and compassion, and the emotional connection it needs to thrive, they have the potential to turn their dreams of beauty into reality. Their destiny is to make or describe great discoveries and to utilize their profound knowledge to inform and inspire others.

Potential: Articulate, determined

Dark side: Workaholic, anxious

Tarot card, lucky numbers, day, colors: The Emperor, 2, 4, Sunday, gold, mauve

Born today: J. K. Rowling (author); Milton Friedman (economist); Wesley Snipes (actor)

August 1

The Birthday of Independence

"Born free"

People born on August 1 are independent-minded and often speak out passionately when confronted with criticism. They don't thrive in subordinate positions and are best suited to roles where they can lead or act as a free agent. Self-reliant, they hope others see the wisdom of their ideas, but they never force them to accept their point of view, believing wisely that people need to be ready for the truth to hear it. They will, however, subtly try to influence others with their delicious humor, which is often laced with brutally accurate insights. Their self-sufficiency is both their blessing and their curse, as it means their originality and organizational skills can help them make tremendous progress, but it can bring unhappiness and make them feel emotionally isolated. They can also become inflexible, narrow-minded or fanatical in their beliefs, which can block their psychological growth and chances of achieving success.

Born scientists, they are best suited to careers such as science, journalism, directing or teaching, where their work or research can be transformed into results or products. They may also be drawn to social reform and the healing professions, while their leadership skills make them suited to business and management, their creativity pulls them toward art, music, drama and filmmaking, and their independence to self-employment. They tend only to listen to their own advice regarding diet and exercise, but they should also heed the advice of qualified scientists and health experts. **For self-care**, mindfulness techniques can help you experience the wonder of the present moment.

Everyone wants a piece of these capable, fun people, but their craving for solitude means few people really know them well. Before the age of 51 they focus on practical problem-solving and efficiency, but, whatever their age, they need to become more sensitive to the feelings of others. Once they find a balance between their wish for privacy and independence and their need for cooperation, these strong and independent individualists can surprise themselves and others with flashes of outstanding and truly inspired creativity. Their destiny is to showcase their talents to a wider audience.

Potential: Influential, insightful

Dark side: Detached, inflexible

Tarot card, lucky numbers, day, colors: The Magician, 1, 9, Sunday, gold, orange

Born today: Herman Melville (author); Sam Mendes (director); Coolio (rapper); Jason Momoa (actor)

August 2

The Birthday of Clear Sight

The life lesson: is to fall in love, first with yourself, then with others and then with life itself.

The way forward: is to stop confusing love with admiration.

Luck maker: Spend less time obsessing about what you do not have and more time being grateful for what you already do.

"Without vision there is no hope"

August 2-born tend to be straightforward. Their clarity of vision identifies material goals and they direct their prodigious energy, determination and self-discipline to their realization. Developing their talents and being admired for their status, wealth and power is more important to them than being liked. They are often confident of reaching their professional goals and are rarely thrown off-track because they know exactly what their strengths and weaknesses are, and don't set themselves impossible goals. On their journey to success they may appear to change course, earning themselves a reputation for inconsistency, but they have not lost sight of their ultimate aim and are simply experimenting with different ways to get there.

Born inventors, their originality and vision promise success as entrepreneurs, content creators and scientists. They can work well in business, banking and the law, but prefer to set up their own businesses and may also be attracted to promotion, sales, the media, education, counseling, advertising, publishing, personal relations and event-planning. Their creativity may find expression in the arts or theater as a composer, actor or playwright. They tend to live action-packed lives and are prone to stress and burnout, so it is important they make time for relaxation and their loved ones. **For self**-care, spending time in nature and meditating on the color purple helps you look beyond the surface of things for much-needed deeper meaning.

Despite their toughness, these people can be deeply hurt by criticism, but are unlikely to show it and often hide it in unexpected harshness and selfishness. Before the age of 52 they focus on efficiency and logic; they also feel an urge to become more introspective, which they should nurture at any age because getting in touch with their feelings and being more sensitive significantly improves their quality of life. Nonconformist and highly original, they have outstanding potential, and as long as they keep in touch with their intuition and accept help from others when needed, their success and happiness are often assured. Their destiny is to use their imaginative powers and clear vision to influence and inspire the world.

Potential: Original, adaptable

Dark side: Harsh, selfish

Tarot card, lucky numbers, days, colors: The High Priestess, 1, 2, Sunday, Monday, gold, red

Born today: Frédéric Auguste Bartholdi (sculptor); Isabel Allende, James Baldwin and Rose Tremain (authors)

August 3

The **Birthday** of the **Courageous** **Rescuer**

The life lesson:

is learning caution.

The way forward: is to understand that you don't need to live on the edge to feel alive. The journey within is the most exciting and fulfilling exploration you can ever undertake.

Luck maker: Rather than instinctively jumping in, slow down and consider the implications of what you are about to say or do.

"I am a hero"

Those born on August 3 are bursting with energy and have a constant need for excitement and a desire to test themselves against challenges. They love to be admired and respected and their greatest wish is to be seen as the heroic rescuer. Their courageous instinct to protect and rescue can lead them to act impulsively and recklessly, but also help them save the day when others procrastinate. Their adventurous spirit often means they get involved in other people's problems and offer help, but they need to learn to back off, allowing others to make and learn from their own mistakes.

Born lifeguards, their bravery and determination make them superb emergency workers, firefighters, doctors, healers, counselors, life coaches and influencers. They may also excel as entrepreneurs and athletes, or in any career where courage is needed and the culture is competitive. Sales, promotion, negotiation, acting, directing and scriptwriting may appeal, but they have the energy and courage to reach the top in any career. The one thing they hate is being unwell, so they need to practice preventive healthcare, given they are not prone to caution. **For self-care**, wearing, meditating on or surrounding yourself with the color blue will encourage you to be more objective, calm and cool.

Those born on this day are vulnerable to flattery and, if they surround themselves with insecure or co-dependent people, their ego can get inflated, isolating them from reality. Their adrenaline-fueled approach to life eases the older they get, and from the age of 49, their focus on relationships and creativity is likely to satisfy their need for excitement. They always fantasize about rescuing or inspiring others in some way. If they can find a balance between their fantasies and reality, their sudden flashes of insight and outstanding displays of courage can impress and inspire others. Once they can subordinate their ego to the needs of the person or situation they are dealing with, their destiny is to be courageous, selfless and truly motivational pioneers.

Potential: Adventurous, idealistic

Dark side: Interfering, reckless

Tarot card, lucky numbers, days, colors: The Empress, 2, 3, Sunday, Thursday, gold, pale green

Born today: Tom Brady (football player); Elisha Otis (inventor); Ryan Lochte (swimmer); Martin Sheen (actor)

August 4

The Birthday of the Responsible Rebel

"I ask the questions"

People born on August 4 are rebels—free spirits who prefer the road less traveled, even if there is nothing wrong with the path everyone else is taking. Their intense dislike of restraint in any way, combined with their hatred of complacency, often lead them to behave unpredictably or to defend unconventional opinions. Intelligent, compassionate and determined when they channel their energies positively, they can bring great enlightenment. Others should be careful not to challenge their need for independence because autonomy of thought is of the utmost importance to them. So averse are they to submitting to the authority or directions of others that, from an early age, they may reject all attempts to help them. Taken to an extreme, this can make them hot-headed, independent but lonely figures.

Born artists, they are suited to artistic, sporting or educational careers where they can guide and inspire others. They prefer to give rather than take orders and, if working in a group, need plenty of autonomy. Good evaluators, they may be drawn to real estate, banking and the stock market, while their humanitarian instincts may draw them to politics, the law, the healing professions, social and community work. Prone to hiding their feelings to appear strong, they must find positive ways to open up and share them with others. **For self-care**, carrying a turquoise crystal will help you to express yourself with warmth and sensitivity, as will meditating on the color orange.

Those born on this day can have love–hate relationships with people they care about, resisting but craving their love and support. Until the age of 48 they need to take opportunities to learn the art of diplomacy and compromise, as this will make life much easier. After 48 the emphasis is on creativity and relationships. If, throughout their lives, they can learn to distinguish between independence and self-sabotaging behavior, and learn the value of tact instead of becoming misunderstood loners, their destiny is to become responsible rebels whom others learn to depend on for inspiration, guidance and radical, always exceptional, insight.

August 5

The Birthday of Steely Determination

"My dreams really do come true"

August 5-born often have intense focus and steely determination. Their ability to keep their cool when others around them are losing theirs inspires awe, as does their striking originality and incredible energy. They tend to dream big and give everything they have to make their dreams happen. At their happiest and best they are natural optimists, and although their lack of caution can lead them into trouble, they have no problems taking calculated risks. Their inflexible sense of purpose can antagonize others, but criticism rarely deters them. In fact, it renews their determination to prove everybody wrong. They have great potential for success, but underneath their impressive self-discipline they have intense and powerful emotions, which can explode in dramatic outbursts of temper.

Born innovators, their need to act autonomously draws them to freelancing careers in music and directing as well as in science, technology, engineering and academic innovation. The law, sales, business and entrepreneurship may also appeal. Their image matters to them, so they may be attracted to the media, journalism, entertainment, fashion and design. Health-wise they need to focus as much on their inner beauty as on their physical health. **For self-care**, meditation and breathing exercises, listening to music, writing in a journal, and competitive sports are recommended whenever you feel inner tension.

The fiery and domineering tendency of these people can be unsettling in relationships, and it is important for them to be gentler with both themselves and others. Until the age of 47 they lean toward practicality; after that the emphasis is on relationships, creativity and harmony. Throughout their lives it is important for them to learn to trust rather than repress their feelings, because working with their intuition helps them build up the confidence to achieve their dreams. Once they have learned to ease up on themselves and others, to let go of the drive toward perfectionism, and to value the importance of compromise, tact and kindness, their destiny is to use their fierce determination to become truly impressive and inspired agents of positive change.

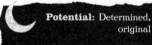

Potential: Determined, original

Dark side: Volatile, reckless

Tarot card, lucky numbers, days, colors: The Hierophant, 4, 5, Sunday, Wednesday, yellow, sapphire blue

Born today: Neil Armstrong (astronaut); Mark Strong (actor); Reid Hoffman (entrepreneur)

August 6

The Birthday of High Expectations

"I dream and live outside the box"

Those born on August 6 gravitate toward what is unusual and exciting. Their fascination with originality leads them to seek out the extraordinary. They work hard and play hard, and big projects and grand schemes are their hallmark. If they are allowed to be the decision-maker and to operate independently, their insight and determination bode well for professional success. Their need for excitement can make it hard to cope with routine, and when life does not live up to their high expectations, they can become moody and restless. They need to find ways to combine their passion for the unique with the routine of daily life.

Born creators, they thrive in careers that offer them plenty of variety, travel, networking and challenge, and may excel in business, sports, merchandising, the travel industry, technology, teaching, coding, manufacturing and banking. They are highly creative and may be drawn to design, art, theater, film, music and entertainment, or they may utilize their compassionate instincts in healing, counseling, childcare and community work. Their lifestyles tend to be chaotic and they would benefit from more emphasis on routine. **For self-care**, embrace moderation in diet and exercise, and make time to have more fun.

These people understand the importance of secure bonds with loved ones, but their commitment to work may make it hard for them to live up to their ideal of devoting equal time to both work and home. They can also be overly serious and neglect the importance of laughter in their relationships. Until the age of 46 they lean toward practical problem-solving and establishing order, but after that age they focus more on relationships and developing their creativity. These can be rewarding years because the realm of creative expression can show them that the extraordinary can be found in the most ordinary things. Once they learn that they don't need to constantly seek out new and exciting experiences to feel fulfilled, their destiny is to help others evolve by not just dreaming but living outside the box.

Potential: Exciting, creative

Dark side: Overly serious, easily bored

Tarot card, lucky numbers, days, colors: The Lovers, 5, 6, Sunday, Friday, gold, pink

Born Today: Alexander Fleming (biologist); Stefan Sagmeister (designer); Alfred Tennyson (poet); Andy Warhol (artist)

August 7

The Birthday of the Undercover Visionary

The life lesson:

is expressing how you really feel.

The way forward: is to understand that most people are not mind readers and sometimes things need to be spelled out to make your intentions clear.

Luck maker: Being true to yourself and acknowledging both your strengths and your weaknesses helps others relax and trust you.

"I can show you the universe"

August 7-born tend to be many-faceted people with hidden talents they are reluctant to reveal. Their secretive nature allows them to surprise and amaze with unexpected flashes of insight or outstanding contributions. They are attracted to the secret, mysterious and unknown, and they are enigmatic; even their loved ones may find it hard to really know them. Although they are sociable and charming, they dwell in a realm of private fantasies that they seldom share. They can become reclusive, but they are more likely to compromise and assume an extroverted personality, while feeling more alive in their hidden fantasy life.

Born planners, they are well suited to careers where they can freely express their vision without limitations, such as technology, trading, sports, acting, painting, music or anything online. Business, the law, life-coaching, personal and spiritual development, crime-fighting, spy work, charity and social reform also appeal. They inhabit a secret world, showing one face to their loved ones and countless different faces to the world, and until they find a way to integrate all aspects of their personalities, they may suffer acute anxiety. **For self-care,** wearing or meditating on the color orange will promote much-needed feelings of warmth and security, as will giving and receiving hugs from loved ones.

Although often surrounded by admirers, when they get serious about someone they can be slow to declare their feelings. Until the age of 45 the emphasis is on looking for ways to restructure and improve their lives, and they should avoid settling into a routine that does not challenge them. After the age of 45 they reach a significant turning point, which sees them recognizing the importance of emotional honesty, creativity and harmony. This is when they are likely to open up, but the sooner they can reveal who they truly are, the better, because their outstanding originality, creativity and intellect should never ever be underestimated. Once they are finally able to be honest, their destiny is to promote their stunning vision and, in the process, help light up the world.

Potential: Charming, visionary

Dark side: Insecure, untrustworthy

Tarot card, lucky numbers, days, colors: The Chariot, 6, 7, Sunday, Monday, gold, sea blue

Born today: Charlize Theron and David Duchovny (actors); Louis Leakey (archaeologist); Mike Trout (baseball player)

August 8

The Birthday of Versatility

The life lesson: is setting realistic goals.

The way forward: is to understand that boldness is admirable, but you set yourself up for certain failure if those goals are not achievable or within your skill-set.

Luck maker: Sometimes getting most of what you want rather than all that you want is good enough.

"Let's make this look simple because simple is beautiful"

People born on August 8 make their success appear effortless, but it is the result of their sharp insight, adaptability, willingness to learn new skills and powerhouse work ethic. They likely sample many careers, but when they are engaged in a project, their focus and discipline are an inspiration. However, once they feel they have learned all they can, they are eager to progress to the next challenge, even if it is totally unrelated to what they have done before. This ability to change direction confuses and surprises others, especially when they veer off at the height of their success.

Born explorers, their inquisitive nature has an affinity with journalism, the travel industry, sports, arts, broadcasting, the media, entertainment, advertising, business, lobbying and tourism. Multitalented, they are likely to move through several jobs and be happiest in roles that offer flexibility and the opportunity to progress and learn. They tend to be perfectionists, so need to make sure they take a step back and unwind every so often. **For self-care**, when you are going through one of your life transitions, sticking to a regular sleep, exercise and meal routine helps you feel more secure.

The super-capable persona of these individuals can be intimidating and they need to show their vulnerable side in long-term relationships. Until the age of 44 they focus on order, problem-solving and being more discriminating, which they should take full advantage of to help them avoid unsuitable career or life choices. After the age of 44 the emphasis shifts to a need for balance and harmony and the importance of partnerships. The key to their fulfillment is to become more self-aware and find ways to stamp their uniqueness on the world. Having said that, they should not try to suppress their characteristic versatility, because their love of diversity and challenge is what makes them exceptionally high achievers. Once they are able to make their goals realistic and attainable, their destiny is to challenge convention and help humanity progress with their enviable ability to make even the hardest of challenges appear natural and simple.

Potential: Versatile, talented

Dark side: Unrealistic, perfectionist

Tarot card, lucky numbers, days, colors: Strength, 7, 8, Sunday, Saturday, yellow, orange

Born today: Paul Dirac (physicist); Dustin Hoffman (actor); Roger Federer (tennis player)

August 9

The Birthday of the Mentor

The life lesson:

is to let others make their own decisions.

The way forward: is to understand that sometimes the best way to help others is to allow them to make and learn from their own mistakes.

Luck maker: Listen more—we have two ears and one mouth for a reason.

"Let me light the way"

Those born on August 9 are dynamic and determined achievers. Their presence is authoritative, and others tend to look to them for guidance as they are ambitious, but they can also be patient, generous and inspiring. They are at their most fulfilled when in the role of mentor, because they understand psychology and what motivates or demotivates others, as well as having countless insights and ideas about how people can improve their lives. They love to be consulted when important decisions need to be made, but can get upset if their advice is not heeded. They need to ensure their concern for others does not deteriorate into an arrogant desire to control them.

Born advisors, they are well suited to careers in which they can guide, educate or be of service to others, such as teaching, counseling, social work, human resources, politics, broadcasting, science, medicine, healing, life-coaching and public relations. The world of entertainment may also appeal. They are great at giving health advice to others, but need to put their own lifestyle in the spotlight, too, as they don't always practice what they preach. **For self-care**, writing in a journal every day and recalling and interpreting your dreams encourages you to be less domineering and to focus on your own emotional needs.

In their relationships those born on this day can be controlling. Learning to listen and understanding the points of view of other people will help them both professionally and personally. Until the age of 43 they have many opportunities to make their mark professionally and they need to be especially careful not to take over the lives of others. After 43 there is a stronger emphasis on relationships and partnerships. Whatever age they are, these wise and generous individuals need to pay less attention to influencing others and more attention to their own inner guidance. Once they understand that a vital part of the personal development of other people is their freedom to choose, and their own amazing intuition is their best guide, their destiny is to be not just a mentor but an inspiring role model, too.

Potential: Influential, insightful

Dark side: Controlling, arrogant

Tarot card, lucky numbers, days, colors: The Hermit, 8, 9, Sunday, Tuesday, yellow, red

Born today: Whitney Houston (singer); Amedeo Avogadro (scientist); Philip Larkin (poet); Gillian Anderson (actor)

August 10

The Birthday of Expressive Charm

The life lesson:

is coping with rejection.

The way forward: is to understand you can use rejection to improve your chances of success—the heart is a muscle and when broken it becomes stronger.

Luck maker: You should visualize yourself as a winner, and instead of hoping for luck, expect it.

"Words have power"

August 10-born are typically appreciated and admired, and they love to help others or to win their approval. They understand the value of strong communication and use their eloquence and charm to persuade and influence. Their greatest desire is to benefit others and their original ideas are often progressive. They have stacks of focus and determination and their smooth voice is heard loud and clear. Although their happy and confident persona makes them popular, it can be tough for others to get to know them. They don't even know themselves and what they want out of life, and this lack of self-awareness is their Achilles' heel. Discovering what their strengths and weaknesses are helps them gain confidence and resilience, and to attract the success they deserve.

Born orators, their sense of justice and desire to help others may draw them to the law, politics, activism, campaigning, lobbying, life-coaching, customer service, and charity and humanitarian work. Their superior creativity and communication skills may thrive in social-media influencing, the media, art, writing, acting, podcasting, public speaking and music, but whatever career they choose, their people skills, charisma and capacity for hard work gives them huge potential to succeed. Health-wise they need to pay attention to their inner beauty and power rather than their external appearance. **For self-care**, when you wake up and before you fall asleep, you should repeat out loud the affirmation: "I am enough."

In relationships, the eagerness of those born on this day to people-please can make them lose touch with who they are, so they should strike a balance between giving and taking. Until the age of 42 they place great emphasis on order, work and efficiency. This is when they are likely to focus on being appreciated and they may suffer greatly if they encounter rejection. After 42 there is more emphasis on relationships and creativity, and if they can open up, these are the years to develop the self-confidence and conviction needed to ensure they become instruments of progress. Their destiny is to make their voice and its progressive message heard in a big way.

Potential: Charming, creative

Dark side: Needy, unaware

Tarot card, lucky numbers, day, colors: Wheel of Fortune, 1, 9, Sunday, yellow, orange

Born today: Antonio Banderas, Patricia Arquette (actors); Jimmy Dean (singer); Suzanne Collins (author)

August 11

The Birthday of the Commentator

"The truth can set us free"

People born on August 11 have the ability to get directly to the point whatever situation they are in. They need and seek greater clarity at all times. They are quick to detect contradictions or manipulative behavior in others and are not shy about confronting them, even if their version of the truth hurts. In fact, they love to reveal insights to others and enjoy being in front of an audience. They can be judgmental, but are also keen to point out the good in people, winning themselves many admirers in the process. Their sharp observation, when combined with their profound insight and strong communication skill, resourcefulness and determination, augurs well for success, but their refreshing love of exposing hypocrisy can work against them.

Born consultants, they may be drawn to careers in academic research, science and education or they may be found working as journalists, law-enforcement agents or in media and broadcasting. They have a flair for writing, blogging and music, as well as sales, promotion and negotiation, and may also excel as business consultants and financial advisors. Their nature is impulsive, so to protect their holistic wellbeing they need to learn to think before they act, speak, eat or drink. **For self-care**, carrying a small green agate crystal can help you resolve inner tension, as can spending more time in nature or natural settings.

An inability to open up emotionally and accept others at face value can lead to relationship tension. Until the age of 41 these people tend to focus on practicality and efficiency, and they need to be careful that they don't become too judgmental during these years. After 41 they reach a turning point when they may become less practical and more creative. Throughout their lives, if they can learn to moderate their brutal honesty and develop greater tolerance of others' imperfections, they can gain the attention, affection and respect of both those close to them and the wider audience. Their destiny is to uncover and present to others essential, sometimes life-changing, insights in a positive way.

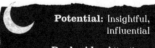

Potential: Insightful, influential

Dark side: Attention-seeking, hurtful

Tarot card, lucky numbers, days, colors: Justice, 1, 2, Sunday, Monday, yellow, silver

Born today: Enid Blyton and Alex Haley (authors); Steve Wozniak (entrepreneur); Chris Hemsworth (actor)

August 12

The Birthday of the Influential Gatherer

The life lesson:

is learning to unwind.

The way forward: is to understand that time out is not time wasted but time gained.

Luck maker: Learn to share and understand the power of synergy—a team of motivated people doing what they are good at is a success magnet.

"Insufficient facts are a risk"

Those born on August 12 love to gather information, believing that no fact is irrelevant. They logically check their facts and the sources and make a well-researched and authoritative decision or evaluation. When their intelligence and focus are combined with determination, they seriously impress with their knowledge and abilities. Often considered experts or virtuosos in their field, they draw on both the latest research and what is tried and tested to create spectacular and innovative results. Their potential for success is vast, but they risk sabotaging their chances by being too critical. Although they should not compromise on their self-belief, learning to be more sensitive to others can stand them in good stead.

Born scientists, they are drawn to careers where logic and fact-gathering are essential, such as education and academia. Business and the art world, writing, podcasting and entertainment may also appeal. Whatever they choose, they need the freedom to work in their own unique way, and a dislike of taking orders may encourage them to be entrepreneurs or seek leadership positions. They need to understand that laughter and positive connections are a source of holistic wellbeing and should ensure they spend time with loved ones and friends, simply having fun. **For self-care**, wearing, meditating on or surrounding yourself with the color orange will encourage you to feel warmer and to fall in love with life.

The tendency of these people to be controlling and to prioritize work over relationships can limit their chances of happiness. Until the age of 40 they are drawn to efficiency and practicality, and they need to be especially careful not to become too strict or emotionally detached. After 40 they focus on quality relationships and bring more creativity and balance into their lives. If they can learn to soften the impact of their forceful approach on others and develop greater tolerance and patience, they can achieve their aims. Their destiny is to unite the calm wisdom of tradition with the creative excitement of innovation and, by so doing, benefit not just themselves and those closest to them but humanity as a whole.

Potential: Knowledgeable, confident

Dark side: Judgmental, workaholic

Tarot card, lucky numbers, days, colors: The Hanged Man, 2, 3, Sunday, Thursday, gold, green

Born today: Cecil B. DeMille (filmmaker); Erwin Schrödinger (physicist); George Soros (philanthropist); Pete Sampras (tennis player)

August 13

The Birthday of the Sharpshooter

is coping with impatience.

The way forward: is to remind yourself when you feel restless that you are in charge of your feelings and actions.

Luck maker: Listen to the voice of your intuition speaking through dreams, coincidences and hunches.

"Not enough hours in the day"

People born on August 13 are comfortable with controversy. They are sharpshooters who always aim high, and their affinity with the outlier or what is odd or strange, coupled with their urge to break with convention, compels them to take challenges or make waves, whatever situation they are in. Their unusual vision and resilience can earn them both admiration and disapproval, but if life doesn't go their way, they are resilient and refuse to be crushed by disappointment. And, as their imagination is grounded in practical skills, many of those who disagree or disapprove of them end up admiring their courage, even if not agreeing with them. As risk-takers, they have the bravery and discipline to attract success, but what they sometimes lack is perfect timing. They need to learn when to cut their losses and move on, when to be patient, and when to pounce. The only way for them to learn the art of great timing is to develop their intuition and trust their gut instincts more.

Born lawyers, they long to make significant contributions to society and may be drawn to careers in the law, politics, science, technology, education, publishing, the media and all areas of humanitarian reform. Whatever career they choose, their sharp intellect and perseverance help them excel. Regular time spent quietly alone is not a luxury but essential for their wellbeing. **For self-care**, stop and smell the roses and spend more time in nature.

Although often surrounded by friends, these people can sometimes have deep insecurities lurking beneath their bravado. Until 39 the emphasis is on order and efficiency, and they need to keep their authoritarian tendencies in check. After 39 they are likely to become more amiable and collaborative. Whatever age they are, they need to understand that aiming true and breaking rules may make them a force to be reckoned with, but these do not guarantee success. Once they are able to recognize and connect with their intuition, they will be able not only to take aim, but to shoot with great accuracy. When they find a cause worthy of their dedication and talent, their destination is to make revolutionary contributions to society.

Potential: Courageous, resilient

Dark side: Brash, restless

Tarot card, lucky numbers, day, colors: Death, 3, 4, Sunday, yellow, purple

Born today: Annie Oakley (entertainer); Alfred Hitchcock (director); Betsy King (golfer); Sridevi Kapoor (actor)

August 14

The Birthday of
Reflection

"It is what it is"

Those born on August 14 are perceptive individuals blessed with clarity of purpose. Nothing escapes their penetrating gaze, and because they understand what motivates people so well and point this out, others can see themselves as they really are. They express their thoughts and observations in a direct, sometimes brutally honest manner, so it is unsurprising when they end up in deep water. Their saving grace is their sense of humor, which softens the impact of their sharp observations, but they need to be aware of the powerful influence their words have and use it wisely. They can motivate others to think more deeply about who they are, but they are surprisingly out of tune themselves and benefit enormously from reflection to discover their own strengths and weaknesses. If they are able to do this, they realize that they have a talent for entertaining and informing the world with the biting accuracy of their comments.

Born commentators and observers, these people love to reflect on society and help progress human behavior. They may be drawn to journalism, writing, filmmaking, psychology, science, statistics, technology, broadcasting, self-help, teaching, counseling, life-coaching and social work. They may also be attracted to commerce, the law, banking, writing, music, the theater and sport. These people tend to compare themselves unfavorably with others and need to ensure they mix with those who support them and make them feel comfortable with who they are and not who they could be. **For self-care**, spend more quality time alone with your phone switched to silent.

The tendency of those born on this day to observe rather than participate can make them feel emotionally isolated and causes much of their unhappiness and confusion. Fortunately, around the age of 38, their interest shifts to relationships and creativity. Yet, if they can remember that communication is not just about watching and responding to others but also about giving of themselves, their strong sense of purpose and creativity will ensure that they can achieve their tremendous potential. Once they are able to turn their perception inward and become more self-aware, their destiny is to inform and enlighten others to become the best possible version of themselves.

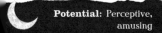

Potential: Perceptive, amusing

Dark side: Critical, unaware

Tarot card, lucky numbers, day, colors: Temperance, 4, 5, Sunday, Wednesday, yellow, blue

Born today: John Logie Baird (inventor); Halle Berry, Mila Kunis and Steve Martin (actors); Magic Johnson (basketball player)

August 15

The Birthday of the Regal Presence

is coping with coming second.

The way forward: is to understand that however much you feel you may deserve it, you can't come first every time, and you learn more from your "failures" than from your "successes."

Luck maker: Avoid overconfidence—nobody likes or wants to help a know-it-all or someone who thinks their way is the only way.

"My way or the highway"

August 15-born are often blessed with a heavy dose of ambition, self-confidence and courage, giving them a commanding, almost regal presence that others enjoy basking in. Even when they are out of their depth, their optimistic self-belief is so strong that they will convince people they are the right person for the role. They are powerful role models, but sometimes others may feel that they are losing their identity in the mighty shadow of these people.

Born leaders and performers, they flourish in careers that allow them to make their own decisions and take charge of others. Sales, marketing, promotion, education, acting, the law, online influencing, writing, sports and self-employment may appeal, and their humanitarian instincts may draw them to counseling and social work. Despite their extrovert persona, they have a tendency to take themselves too seriously, and they need to find time for fun and laughter. **For self-care**, schedule regular periods of relaxation and socializing into your busy schedule.

Those born on this day are generous with their time and money in relationships, but can be controlling, and it is important for them to grant other people a moment in the spotlight. Until the age of 37 they place an emphasis on practical order and efficiency, and they need to make sure that their need for adoration does not lead to an inflated ego. After 38 relationships and creativity are highlighted; they may develop latent artistic talents. Throughout their lives the key to their success is their ability to empathize and allow others to make their own decisions too. Once they are able to develop this awareness, not only are they able to realize their ambitious and progressive visions, but they discover their destiny is to both lead and inspire others at the same time.

Potential: Imposing, generous

Dark side: Egotistical, controlling

Tarot card, lucky numbers, day, colors: The Devil, 5, 6, Sunday, Friday, yellow, pink

Born today: Ben Affleck and Jennifer Lawrence (actors); Napoleon Bonaparte (French emperor); Stieg Larsson (author)

August 16

The Birthday of the Powerhouse

"I express myself"

People born on August 16 are charismatic and love to showcase their unconventional convictions and unique style to a large audience. Their priority is to be noticed and, because they are such a powerhouse of energy, ambition, creativity and enthusiasm, they are often impossible to ignore. Once they have decided on their sphere of influence, they seek to triumph over obstacles or people who stand in their way. Their drive to achieve recognition is so strong that they can be destructive and vengeful toward those who oppose them. Although their behavior appears to be geared toward material success, their more profound motivation is finding happiness.

Born chairpersons, they suit any career where they can direct others. They can find great success in the arts, show business, production, broadcasting or in politics and motivational teaching. The media and big business may also appeal or they may devote themselves to humanitarian causes. Whatever they choose, they don't stay long in subordinate positions and may work for themselves if they cannot lead. They need to understand that family and friends are as important to their wellbeing as a healthy diet and exercise. **For self-care**, meditating on the color blue or walking beside the sea, lakes and rivers can bring objectivity and inner calm.

Fiercely loyal to loved ones, these people value their private life highly because this is where they can relax and be themselves rather than what their admirers expect them to be. Until they reach 36 they focus on being practical, and this is when they tend to be most ruthless—they need to be careful that their creativity does not transform into exhibitionism. After 36 they may place more importance on relationships and creative quality rather than quantity. If they can listen to their powerful conscience and make sure they don't act in hurtful ways, they have the potential not just to seduce others with their charismatic style, but to surprise them with their extraordinary achievements. Once they have learned to avoid extremes and excesses and find a balance, their destiny is to lead and empower others.

Potential: Seductive, ambitious

Dark side: Ruthless, excessive

Tarot card, lucky numbers, days, colors: The Tower, 6, 7, Sunday, Monday, yellow, rose

Born today: Madonna (singer); Steve Carell (actor); T. E. Lawrence (author); James Cameron (director)

August 17

The Birthday of the Dormant Volcano

"Never underestimate me"

Those born on August 17 may present a calm, composed exterior, but, like a dormant volcano, underneath fiery emotions smolder. Strong-willed, intense, independent, resilient and fiercely success-orientated, they attract attention and either win a loyal following or create enemies. They are unconventional and creative, but also have the ability to focus on progressive ideals. These people are a force and make fine leaders, but their Achilles' heel is their argumentative, stubborn nature. They can be extremely defensive, and their occasional rages and desire for revenge can really make people anxious. Learning to think before they speak and act, and listening more, helps them gain the control they need to earn the respect of others that they deserve.

Born leaders, they thrive in careers where they set the tone and influence others, and whatever career they choose they are likely to climb to the top, but they may be drawn to politics, the military, business, the entertainment world, online influencing as well as writing, the law, the police, charity work and education. The biggest threat to their emotional wellbeing is their inability to control their anger. **For self-care**, let go of anger and bitterness, and learn to forgive but not forget.

These people are passionate, loyal companions and often have many friends and admirers, but can be volatile. Until the age of 35 they focus on practicality and creating an effective working environment; these are the years when their untamed energy can be at its most explosive and wild. After 35 they reach a turning point, which highlights creativity, relationships and partnerships; and this is the period during which they can really come into their own. Throughout their lives the key to their success is putting the emphasis on self-control. If they can find ways to harness and direct their incredible energy and talent toward a worthy cause, when their volcanic creativity erupts it will not cause chaos and destruction but instead enlighten, inspire and guide others. Once they have learned to manage their emotions, their destiny is to make a strong impression on others with their dynamic originality.

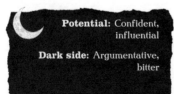

Potential: Confident, influential

Dark side: Argumentative, bitter

Tarot card, lucky numbers, day, colors: The Star, 7, 8, Sunday, Saturday, gold, brown

Born today: Robert De Niro, Sean Penn (actors); Davy Crockett (adventurer); Samuel Goldwyn (producer)

August 18

The Birthday of the Deep Heart

The life lesson:

is setting boundaries.

The way forward: is understanding that over-involvement in the lives of others limits their (and others') personal growth.

Luck maker: Expect luck and see the positive potential in everyone and everything.

"What a feeling!"

August 18-born are among the most sensitive and tolerant of the year. They feel things more deeply than others, but they would not have it any other way, as they believe that feelings hold the key to their fulfillment. They are sensitive not only to their own emotions, but to those of others, many of whom seek them out for advice and support. They feel a pronounced sense of responsibility toward them as well as a strong urge to guide and protect them. Although this generosity of spirit wins them many supporters, it can also cause confusion about their own needs and feelings. Once they gain the self-confidence to connect with their own feelings and be more objective with others, they discover an innovative mindset and a resilience that propels them toward considerable professional and personal success.

Born dancers, they have an affinity with artistic disciplines, but may also be drawn to the caring professions, social work, education, politics, the law and business, as well as design and manufacturing. Their sensitivity may also attract them to the medical or alternative health fields. When feeling overwhelmed, they can turn to food or other substances for comfort, and should find healthier ways to ease their anxiety, such as going for a walk, playing an instrument or soaking in an aromatherapy bath. **For self-care**, wearing, meditating on or surrounding yourself with shades of blue can encourage you to be more realistic and objective.

Generous and warm, these people need to guard against escapism and either emotional over-indulgence or avoidance in their relationships. Until the age of 34 they focus increasingly on order in their lives, and it is important they find ways to connect with other people without losing themselves in them. After 34, relationships and artistic creativity are heightened. If they can find a way to protect their high sensitivity and vivid imagination, this is when they are most likely to inspire others with their idealism and progressive vision. Once they understand that they can only be effective at helping others when they take care of their own needs, their destiny is to arouse great loyalty, affection and a sense of purpose in others.

Potential: Creative, generous

Dark side: Oversensitive, unaware

Tarot card, lucky numbers, days, colors: The Moon, 8, 9, Sunday, Tuesday, gold, orange

Born today: Robert Redford, Patrick Swayze and Christian Slater (actors); Brian Aldiss (author)

August 19

The Birthday of the Editor

The life lesson:

is revealing who you truly are.

The way forward: is to understand that people relate to vulnerability, so appearing too smooth can work against you.

Luck maker: When you don't know what to do, sometimes it is better to do something rather than nothing, because if it doesn't work out, at least you can learn from it.

"The truth is in the details"

People born on August 19 present a smooth face to the world, but, underneath, they have a clear agenda. They appear likable but always remain a closed book, carefully editing what they reveal to others. Image is extremely important to them—sometimes more important than performance. With such attention to detail, preparation and presentation, their work is often exceptional. There is a risk, though, that the emphasis on image means they lose touch with their real feelings and develop delusions of grandeur. They know their own value, but try to hide any weakness with procrastination, preferring to do nothing at all rather than make mistakes.

Born designers, they have the originality, dedication and resourcefulness to succeed in any career, but are often drawn to fashion, modeling, architecture, technology, surgery, publishing, filmmaking or any field where attention to details matters. They may also excel in sales, advertising, publicity, influencing or the entertainment world. Whatever career they choose, they likely end up in charge, directing and editing all the action. Health-wise, it is important that they pay equal attention to their emotional health as they do to their looks. **For self-care**, wearing, meditating on or surrounding yourself with the color orange can inspire you to be more spontaneous and open toward others.

Charismatic, these people attract many admirers, but they can push loved ones away if they don't allow them to see their real personality. Until the age of 33 attention to detail takes center stage and they should be more open with their feelings, because this helps others relate to them better. After 33 they generally become sociable and creative. If they can remind themselves that to err is human, these dynamic individuals can find ways to combine their courage, unconventional originality and endearing complexity to achieve brilliant results. Once they understand that people are not meant to be perfect, their destiny is to motivate and inspire others to pay attention to the crucial details that can make the difference between an average or outstanding finished product or end result.

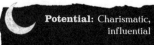

Potential: Charismatic, influential

Dark side: Secretive, indecisive

Tarot card, lucky numbers, day, colors: The Sun, 1, 9, Sunday, gold, orange

Born today: Orville Wright (aviator); Coco Chanel (designer); Bill Clinton (US president); Gene Roddenberry (producer)

August 20

The Birthday of Thoughtful Mystery

"I learn and I grow"

Those born on August 20 are self-contained individuals, whom others find hard to understand. They often have an air of thoughtful complexity around them. Though they spend time alone, they are not lonely people. Quite the opposite, they are genuinely compassionate and concerned for the wellbeing of others, and have an intelligent humor that quickly breaks the ice. It's just that even when they are smiling, their thoughtfulness can be interpreted as sadness or as struggling with secrets. Battling to balance emotional highs and lows is a key theme for these melancholic but beautiful people. Sometimes the intensity of the struggle drives them to seek solace in addictive pursuits or by losing themselves in their work, but neither brings relief. Although they understand their past is compelling, learning to focus their energies on the here and now is key.

Born detectives and researchers, they love to uncover information about themselves and others, and they make gifted journalists, scientists, counselors, accountants, writers, artists and musicians. Progressive with humanitarian leanings, they also choose politics, lobbying, activism, diplomacy, the media, public relations, publishing and self-employment. They often place so much emphasis on their emotional and mental wellbeing that they neglect the importance of their physical health. **For self-care**, regular alone time to get to know yourself is essential and you should ensure that the people in your life are supportive and positive rather than demanding or co-dependent.

In relationships those born on this day long for excitement and romance, but they need to learn that being practical and supportive are also important. Until the age of 31 they concentrate on order, practicality and analyzing to improve their chances of happiness. After 31 the spotlight is on relationships, and if they can find ways to express their dynamic imagination and practicality, and be present in the moment, not only do they solve their personal mystery but they also discover a magical way to live. Once they have learned to look forward rather than back, and to be grateful for what they have, their destiny is to initiate and direct practical plans to improve the holistic wellbeing of others.

August 21

The Birthday of the Attention Magnet

is celebrating your uniqueness.

The way forward: is to understand that self-belief and standing out rather than blending in is the foundation of a successful life.

Luck maker: Forge your own path and don't follow the crowd, because the crowd doesn't really know where it is going.

"I start and then finish strong"

August 21-born have such an intense and bright appeal that they always get noticed, however hard they try to fit in. They stand out because there is something incredibly appealing about them, which may be in their looks, personality, intelligence or natural talent, but the curious thing is that a part of them longs to hide. As long as they are unable to embrace their uniqueness, they find that opportunities for success are limited. However, when they do celebrate who they are, they can use and direct their natural appeal in any direction. Above all, they are extraordinarily imaginative, resourceful and practical, and this personality combination gives them trail-blazing potential.

Born publishers, they may be drawn to writing or education, but whatever career they choose, they are spurred by a desire to make a positive difference, and can be found working in politics, science or the arts, and their love of variety may draw them to tourism, the entertainment world, coaching, medicine and sports. Their desire to prove themselves may lead to the quest for the perfect body and life, but this can increase stress and anxiety. **For self-care**, moderation in everything is key to a healthy life and it is fine to allow yourself the occasional indulgence.

These people are never short of admirers and often have a hectic social schedule, but they are at their happiest when in a committed relationship. Until the age of 30 they focus on perfectionism, and this is when they are most likely to deny or repress their individuality. After 30 the theme is growing self-awareness and creativity, when they can feel more comfortable with themselves and their exceptional talents. Their Achilles' heel is repressing creativity and originality, but when they realize that they can gain more satisfaction from expression and involvement than from detachment and distance, and that people love their originality, they have a world of opportunities at their feet. Once they can focus less on proving themselves to others and more on accepting themselves, their destiny is to become an inspiring role model for anyone who has ever felt different in some way.

Potential: Appealing, talented

Dark side: Flighty, perfectionist

Tarot card, lucky numbers, days, colors: The World, 2, 3, Sunday, Thursday, gold, green

Born today: Usain Bolt (sprinter); Kenny Rogers (singer); Kim Cattrall (actor); Sergey Brin (entrepreneur)

August 22

The Birthday of the Commander

"With self-discipline, anything is possible"

People born on August 22 utilize whatever talents they are blessed with to the max. They believe discipline and hard work are the secrets of success, and they like to be the only commander of their own lives. They also prefer telling others what to do. Their wonderful imagination is expansive and their charisma powerful enough to inspire others to work alongside them. They bring flair and a touch of excitement to even the most mundane chores. Their presence is authoritative and they can be stubborn when challenged, but behind this tough exterior there is a gentle side, although they are unlikely to allow others to see it.

is being open to suggestions.

The way forward: is to understand that listening to the viewpoints of others does not weaken but strengthens your position, as people are more likely to support you if they feel heard.

Luck maker: Be flexible—there are many paths to the same destination.

Born managers, they often find themselves in leadership positions whatever career they choose. In business they may be happier working for themselves, but they can be drawn to accounting, sales, promotion or advertising. Professions that use their mind and creativity may also appeal, such as education, writing, the law, music, writing, blogging, journalism, technology and entertainment. They are excellent at time management but need to make sure they are not so organized that they live in the future rather than the present. **For self-care,** meditation and mindfulness techniques or spending more time in nature help you connect to the present with feelings of gratitude.

Relationships are therapeutic for those born on this day as they help them develop their ability to be more open to compromise. Until the age of 30 they prioritize practical order and lay the foundation stones for realizing their ambitions. Remaining open to advice and suggestion is key. After the age of 30 their natural talent for leadership comes to the fore and the urge to do things their way—sometimes regardless of the potential cost—dominates, but fortunately they also focus on relationships and creativity. If they can find ways to combine their creativity with their commanding presence, they have outstanding potential, not just for leadership positions but for fulfillment in all areas of their lives. Once they learn that there is never only one way to approach a situation, their destiny is to inspire others with their self-discipline, ambition and creativity.

Potential: Influential, disciplined

Dark side: Inflexible, controlling

Tarot card, lucky numbers, day, colors: The Fool, 3, 4, Sunday, gold, lavender

Born today: James Corden (comedian); Claude Debussy (composer); Dorothy Parker and Ray Bradbury (writers)

VIRGO

THE VIRGIN
(AUGUST 23–SEPTEMBER 22)

* ✳ **Element:** Earth
* ✳ **Ruling planet:** Mercury, the communicator
* ✳ **Tarot card:** The Hermit (inner strength)
* ✳ **Lucky numbers:** 5, 6
* ✳ **Favorable colors:** Yellow, green, white, brown
* ✳ **Driving force:** Productivity
* ✳ **Personal statement:** Busy is better than bored
* ✳ **Chinese sign counterpart:** The Rooster

Virgos are perhaps the most misunderstood sign of
the zodiac. They have a reputation for being detailed,
sensible, organized, meticulous, practical, efficient,
busy and analytical. While this reputation is well
deserved, it's important to point out that they also
have razor-sharp perception, probing minds and an
innate creativity. The Virgo drive to create perfection
reflects their desire for beauty and keen sense of
aesthetic order, but there is always a danger that
this perfectionism can breed self-criticism,
narrow-mindedness and fussiness.

Personality potential

Virgos tend to be reliable, intelligent, hard-working, systematic
and considerate. One of their greatest talents is their innate
ability to get to the bottom of problems, find the missing link
or to keep working at something until they eventually achieve
a breakthrough. There's also something incredibly refined
and elegant about their approach to life—these people are the
fine-tuners of the zodiac, giving attention to the important
details that other, more hasty signs often forget.

The Virgo love affair with detail can often be reflected in
their living or working environment, through their choice of
design and décor, or through their clothing—they are typically
impeccably dressed and fragrant smelling. Personal hygiene
matters a great deal to them. They wouldn't dream of turning
up anywhere looking anything less than their best. Although
**they are one of the few signs who have the potential to be
multitalented** because they can use both sides of their brain at
the same time—the creative and the analytical—they tend to
be extremely modest and feel uncomfortable in the limelight.

They are quite happy to work quietly in the background or be the second in command. To them the approval or admiration of others means far less than the joy and satisfaction they get in creating order and making sure that a job is well done or a mission accomplished.

Virgos are ruled by the planet Mercury, so stimulating and intelligent conversation is very important to them—they often make great writers, teachers, researchers, lecturers, counselors, journalists, interviewers and debaters. From an early age they are also often interested in the visual and decorative arts and crafts, antiques and music, opera and ballet.

> **They are one of the few signs who have the potential to be multitalented**

Above all, Virgos are efficient and, because they can be relied on to get a job done, other signs of the zodiac tend to rely on them. Graced with integrity, practical creativity, discipline, common sense, refinement and an eye for the important details, this sign rarely lets other people down. Virgos never shirk responsibility or an opportunity to be of service, because their instinct to serve, help others and make sure everything runs smoothly is strong. It's often the case that these quiet, modest souls have far more power and influence than they themselves would believe possible.

Personality pitfalls

As admirable as their drive for perfection may be, their need for every detail to be in place can make many Virgos highly critical of themselves and others. They can be as hard on themselves as they are on others, and all too easily set impossibly high standards that de-motivate rather than inspire. And, although they are talkative and able to express their ideas clearly, they can at times overelaborate and give painstaking attention to unnecessary details, meaning that they lose sight of the bigger picture. Their perfectionism also leads to a lack of confidence, so they will often look to others for approval. But even if they get that approval, they are so self-critical that they will doubt any praise or love they are given. In fact, the Virgo craving for constant approval can place them among the more needy sun signs of the zodiac.

Virgos may avoid trying something new because they fear making mistakes, and this will limit their range of experience, earning them a reputation for being narrow-minded. They also have a rather unpleasant self-righteous and relentless air about them, and carping criticism of others can be one of their worst faults. Coupled with their tendency to believe they are always right and that nobody can do things as well as they can, there may also be a tendency toward prudishness. They will condemn anything that does not meet their exacting standards of wholesomeness. But ironically, on rare occasions, these may be double standards, since some Virgos find themselves secretly attracted to the darker things in life.

Symbol

The symbol for Virgo is the virgin, but don't make the mistake of thinking that those born under this sun sign are innocent. Although there is often an untouchable, pure quality about Virgos, they are no strangers to the ways of the world. Virgin, in this instance, means perfect, and that can relate to sex and passion too. In other words, these people set themselves the very highest standards. It's quality rather than quantity they desire, and their approach to love and to life is refined and meticulous.

Darkest secret

People born under this sign have a reputation for being critical, and others in their lives may fear that they can never live up to their high standards. But what they don't know is that the Virgo tendency to nag often masks a secret terror that they themselves are simply not good enough, attractive enough or likable enough.

Love

Love is a pure and splendid thing for Virgos, but lack of confidence in themselves can be the biggest barrier to happiness in their relationships. They can even question why others would want to spend time with them. Their humility can be endearing but, over time, if the problem isn't dealt with it can become damaging. It is crucial for every sign to fall in love with themselves, but especially so for Virgos because, if they can't do this, no amount of love, compliments and affection from a partner will convince them they are lovable.

The Virgo tendency to be critical of their partners is one that they could do well to monitor. When it comes to the physical aspect of love, partners may often feel that those born under this sun sign are holding something back. There is always a part of them that remains untouchable and this mysterious quality can give them great sex appeal, but it can also stop them from fully expressing themselves and feeling fulfilled emotionally and sexually. Learning to relax with their partner and allowing themselves to be loved for who they are, warts and all, is the key to their happiness in love and, indeed, life.

Love matches:
Capricorn, Scorpio, Cancer and Taurus.

The Virgo woman

The Virgo woman may appear fragile and vulnerable, but underneath her fluttering, shy exterior is a woman made of steel. She may be pure-minded, but she is not naïve, and her practicality and common sense make her extremely independent. Virgoan females may be many things, but they are not clinging vines and are more than capable of opening their own doors. This lady may not be given to outward displays of affection or spontaneous romantic gestures, but her heart is far warmer than most people suspect. If she appears aloof or cold, it's important to remember that her emotions are controlled, not non-existent.

Although she can be painstakingly meticulous about details and good manners—and presentation matters a great deal to her—she can also be the kindest, most generous and, if she is truly in love, the most affectionate woman in the world. Her perfectionism can be irritating, but there's something very endearing about this woman's modest manners; her organized approach has a positive effect on all those who cross her path. When people get to know her better, they also discover a sharp wit and a lovely sense of humor—her laugh really is music to the ears.

Virgo women value honesty and truth highly in a relationship and they are the souls of discretion. People can trust them, not just with their hearts but with their secrets and their dreams. If these dreams fade over time, the Virgo woman can help you rediscover your belief in them and yourself again. In short, this woman is a rare treasure whose presence graces and enriches the hearts and lives of all those she touches.

The Virgo man

The Virgo man is often a fidget, both physically and mentally. He never sits still and his mind is brimming with ideas. It's vital that his abundant energy finds a positive outlet, otherwise it's likely to be wasted in restlessness. When it comes to affairs of the heart, this man may not sweep you off your feet. He lives on a practical level and he certainly won't give himself over to extravagant promises and sentimentality. This doesn't mean, however, that love isn't important to him. Love matters a great deal, but the way he chooses to express his love is in his unselfish devotion, rather than through grand romantic gestures.

He may present a detached and icy exterior to the world, but there are ways to win over his heart. In love—as with everything in life—he seeks quality rather than quantity, setting his sights on an accomplished and intelligent partner with a subtle rather than a blatant attractiveness. He'll probably have very few real love affairs and, if a relationship doesn't work out, he buries himself in hard work and an organized lifestyle, and is very cautious about committing his heart again. In fact, many Virgo men can live alone far more easily than other people. They are single by choice.

Although his displays of affection are never overt and he will take his time finding the right partner, because he is highly critical and enormously particular, he can also be powerfully seductive. Then, once he has decided he has found "the one," he will declare his love with touching honesty and do everything in his power to ensure that his love is returned. He is capable of enormous sacrifice for the person he loves, and his love can burn constantly and dependably over the years.

Family

Keen to please and often popular with their teachers at school, Virgo children are typically tidy, well organized and disciplined. They tend to have abundant energy and their hands and their brains need to be given lots to do to keep them occupied and challenged. "Busy is better than bored" is their

motto. When they start a new school, it might be a good idea to familiarize them with the restrooms first, as knowing there is a place for them to go and wash their hands and tidy up matters a great deal to them. School playtimes may be daunting for them and they may at times prefer to stand apart from the crowd. They are extremely sensitive to being made fun of. Parents should try to encourage them to develop their self-esteem through praise and with repeated reassurances that it's okay to make mistakes because that's the best way to learn. It may also be helpful for them to develop hobbies, activities and interests that they can share with other children. Examination time may be particularly stressful for Virgo teens, given their tendency to worry; so, as soon as examinations appear on the horizon, parents should encourage them to master study and revision skills.

As parents, Virgos are often extremely hard-working. They will devote long hours at work to give their family the very best, and then, when they are at home, they will work long hours to make sure their home runs efficiently. Sometimes there may be an obsession with hygiene and cleanliness; this can be detrimental because children need to be exposed to a certain level of germs and infections as they grow up to help build up their immune system. Many Virgo parents bring too much of their work home with them and miss out on spending quality time with the people that matter most to them. Striking a work–life balance is important.

Career

Virgos love details and can be apprehensive about taking the lead, so they can thrive under supervision. When given instructions they will follow them to the letter and to the best of their abilities, which makes them superb assistants and team players. They often take great pride in being the real backbone of any organization or commercial venture. Many also make brilliant and inspirational teachers and linguists, and others do themselves proud in the armed services and the caring and medical professions. Their eye for detail may draw them to careers in publishing, science, pharmacy or the arts.

Other possible career choices include crafts, design, charity work, administration, law, research, accounting and any occupation that enables them to handle complicated details. The ideal working environment for a Virgo is calm, organized, tidy and quiet, decorated in neutral but tasteful colors and with the most up-to-date equipment. As employees they are typically courteous, reliable and thorough, with a quick, analytical mind, but **they do need to watch their tendency to be overcritical and overcautious.** They are an asset to any organization because they love to work hard, but they are not overly ambitious and getting to the top is not their main consideration.

> **They do need to watch their tendency to be overcritical and overcautious**

Health and wellbeing

Virgo rules the intestines, digestive system and hands, and Virgos can have beautiful and elegant hands. They often look younger than their years and their fastidious approach to life means that unhealthy habits are kept to a minimum. Their

343

drive toward perfection, however, can cause physical tension, digestive problems, allergies and perhaps even compulsive behavior. It's therefore crucial for Virgos to learn how to relax and unwind. The more relaxed a Virgo is, the healthier they tend to be.

When it comes to diet, from an early age Virgos tend to be fussy eaters. The phrase "You are what you eat" is ingrained in their psyche, and they are likely to be extremely well informed and conscientious about what they choose to put into their mouths. Having said that, they are also prone to bouts of comfort eating, which can cause digestive problems. If they were less strict in their approach to food in the first place, they might find that they don't get as many food cravings. They should go for mainly whole foods and for foods that are high in fiber, as these will boost their digestion. They should also follow the 80/20 rule, which means that as long as they eat healthily 80 percent of the time, they can allow themselves the occasional indulgence—when an indulgence is not forbidden, food cravings are less likely. Virgos also need to learn to distinguish between real hunger and the hunger that is caused by loneliness, anger and fear. Waiting 15 minutes before eating when they get a craving will help, as will distracting themselves with a walk around the block or chatting to a friend. If the craving is not food-related, it tends to pass.

Fresh air and regular exercise are essential for Virgos, as these will boost their mood and their spirits. Unfortunately, being such hard workers, Virgos often tend to sacrifice these healthy pursuits, but it's important for them to ensure that exercise and regular "me time" is scheduled into their life along with everything else. Meditation, yoga or activities such as gardening, which have a meditative quality about them, are especially good for those Virgos who are prone to worry. Wearing, meditating on and surrounding themselves with the color **orange** will encourage them to work on building their self-confidence.

Born between August 23 and September 3

People born on these days can really hate to be in the spotlight and may well cringe with embarrassment if singled out in the crowd. They prefer to be the quiet achievers who remain in the background, but they are the lynchpin that keeps everyone and everything running smoothly without fuss.

Born between September 4 and 14

These Virgos can bring a clear and concise viewpoint to any situation. They have a quick mind, but although they are extremely practical and logical, they also have brilliant flashes of intuition from time to time.

Born between September 15 and 22

There is something touchingly youthful, pure and innocent about these people. They tend to remain young and active, both physically and mentally, and give the best of themselves every single day of their productive lives.

Life lessons

With their love of helping others and their efficient and organized approach, Virgos are among the most unselfish signs of the zodiac, but it's important for them to make sure that they do not become too servile. They also need to be careful that the high standards they apply to themselves and to others do not make them overly critical and pedantic. Perfection is their ideal, but they will never be truly happy until they learn that it is an impossible ideal, and that only by making mistakes and being imperfect can people learn and grow.

Virgos pay excessive attention to detail and are prone to bouts of intense anxiety about crossing the t's and dotting the i's, but all this may be drawing their focus away from the bigger picture and from what really matters. Their analytical mind is both a blessing and a curse, and they need to learn to distinguish between what does merit close scrutiny and hyper-criticism (for example, a criticism that is unfair or a partner not pulling their weight in a relationship) and what doesn't (such as the color used on a presentation folder or the way a person loads the dishwasher).

Being born worriers, Virgos are in real danger of worrying themselves to an early death. They are often hypochondriacs and their fear of falling ill can increase their risk of poor health. Given the strong link between what a person thinks and the reality they create for themselves, the situations or worries they dread can tend to manifest in their lives. And even if the worst doesn't happen, there isn't much fun in worrying more about life than living it. Virgos really do need

to relax more and let go of their need for perfection. They also should learn that love isn't something to aspire to or work toward but something fulfilling that happens naturally and spontaneously.

Fellow Virgos can showcase to each other the benefits and limitations of an analytical approach to life. All the other signs of the zodiac can offer Virgos help and inspiration as they journey toward greater self-love. For instance, Arians can help them see the bigger picture or meaning of their lives, and Sagittarians can help Virgos see the deeper truths that they often miss or simply do not comprehend. Pisceans and Geminis can encourage Virgos to be less self-critical; Scorpios can help them understand better the reasons why people make mistakes, Cancers can motivate them to open their hearts and Leos can encourage them to use their sharp, incisive mind for more fun and creativity. Capricorns can inspire them to enjoy material things, while Taureans can teach them the importance of self-care. Librans are there to help them find work–life balance, and Aquarians can assist them to be more original and follow their own highly capable path rather than one laid down by others.

Chinese astrology counterpart: The Rooster

The Chinese Rooster and Western Virgo are both organized, disciplined and highly professional in their approach to work and life. Without fail, and like clockwork, the Rooster kick-starts every single day with its morning call that wakes people up and encourages them to rise and shine and get busy living. The most important thing for this sign is productivity and doing the best job.

Both these signs have analytical minds. They sweat the small stuff because they know that the devil is always in the details. They make great mentors and teachers. Although their drive for perfection can make them fly a little too close to fanaticism at times, they are fiercely capable and are the people in the world who get things done—and done to a high standard. Their strong work ethic and logical, determined and endearingly earnest approach means that these people really can achieve just about anything they set their minds to.

Note: Virgos have an affinity with Rooster-sign characteristics, but be sure to check which Chinese sign corresponds to your **year** of birth (see page xxi), and to read about the characteristics associated with it, too.

August 23

The Birthday of Sparkling Accuracy

The life lesson:

is to be sensitive to others.

The way forward: is to understand that focusing solely on your work can bring success, but that success will be hollow if you have alienated and neglected those you care about.

Luck maker: Perform random acts of kindness for others.

"My work matters"

Those born on August 23 have remarkable energy, and when it is directed with commitment their intensity sparkles like magic. Both the process and the product matter to them and they have a keen eye for detail. They are often the person others rely on to make sure everything is organized and running to plan. Their fierce commitment to accuracy can mean they lose sight of the bigger picture sometimes, so it is important for them to keep their goals in mind, because they have everything needed to realize their ambitious visions. Another danger is that they can become so intense about their work that if there is a setback, they can explode in rage. Others may perceive this as aggressive and selfish, but what they do matters greatly to them and they can happily lose themselves in it. However, although this makes them winners in life, it can also mean they unintentionally upset others.

Born coders, they are multitalented and thrive in careers that require problem-solving and a determined and focused attention to detail. They may be drawn to technology, design, teaching, research, academia, publishing, science, engineering, art, sports, information technology, banking, trading, accounting or finance. Whatever career they choose, they are likely to be perfectionists. They do need to remind themselves that however much money or status they have, they can't buy self-esteem or happiness, and they need to appreciate that self-worth only comes from within and not from outside. **For self-care**, every morning when you wake up, you should repeat the following mantra: "I am enough and I have enough."

Those born on this day tend to put their professional life first, making their personal life complicated. After the age of 30 their focus is less on efficiency, and opportunities arise to concentrate more on relationships and explore their creativity. They must take advantage of these and not feel confused by them, because it is complexity that holds the key to their happiness. Once they have learned to find a balance between their own needs and others', their destiny is to act as highly skilled agents of improvement.

Potential: Focused, capable

Dark side: Obsessive, selfish

Tarot card, lucky numbers, days, colors: The Hierophant, 4, 5, Sunday, Wednesday, gold, blue

Born today: Georges Cuvier (naturalist); Gene Kelly and Vera Miles (actors); Kobe Bryant (basketball player)

August 24

The Birthday of the Curious Discoverer

The life lesson:

is to listen to intuition, not worry.

The way forward: is to understand that worry serves no function, and information and knowledge only take you so far, so the only way to progress is to trust your instincts.

Luck maker: Pay more attention to gut instinct, the language of your feelings, and dreams and coincidences.

"I say it as I see it"

August 24-born have a sharp, questioning mind that loves to problem-solve and explore new frontiers. They don't like to take anything at face value, and even the opinions of experts do not stop them from searching through evidence to catch what others might have missed and to discover their version of the truth. Their insatiable curiosity makes them hard to manipulate, and others trust and often ask for their approval and insight. They doubt anyone or anything simple or straightforward, such is their belief that hidden complexities lie beneath the surface, but what they may not realize is that they are hugely complex themselves. They can sometimes miss out on what is subtle or unspoken, and their accuracy and creativity would be enhanced if they learned to develop their intuition.

Born discoverers, they are naturally drawn to philosophy, writing, journalism, blogging, broadcasting, podcasting, the arts and music, but they are also gifted psychologists, therapists and commentators of human behavior and the natural world. Teaching, commerce, science, research and healthcare may also appeal. They need to make sure they don't become over-absorbed in their work and neglect their health and relationships. **For self-care**, wearing, meditating on and surrounding yourself with the color orange can encourage you to love life as much as you love studying it.

Loving the excitement of a new connection made, these people may struggle with routine in their relationships. Until the age of 29 they prioritize practicality and efficiency, but after 29 they may focus more on relationships and developing their latent creative potential. They need to take advantage of these opportunities, as they significantly boost their chances of success professionally and personally. Throughout their lives, they may alternate between extremes of uncertainty and a sense of entitlement. If they can cultivate positive thinking and trust their intuition, they have the potential to enrich the lives of others with their discoveries. Once they learn to observe less and live more, their destiny is to educate, enlighten and enrich the lives of others with their surprising, and at times life-changing, insights.

Potential: Insightful, influential

Dark side: Suspicious, workaholic

Tarot card, lucky numbers, days, colors: The Lovers, 5, 6, Sunday, Friday, yellow, rose

Born today: Stephen Fry (author); Cal Ripken Jr. (baseball player); Marlee Matlin and Rupert Grint (actors)

August 25

The Birthday of the Live Wire

The life lesson:

is resisting the urge to hog the spotlight.

The way forward: is to understand that the only person who can give you a sense of self-worth is yourself.

Luck maker: Stop comparing yourself with others, just measure yourself against the person you were yesterday.

"Look at me"

People born on August 25 are difficult to ignore. Their superior social skills get them noticed and seem to attract success. Others often see them as charming and accomplished. They are live wires and life always seems more exciting when they are around. Although confident on the outside, they seldom feel that way on the inside, and drive themselves hard to prove to others that they are really confident and accomplished. They rarely let down their guard and if they feel insecure in any way they may over-emphasize their opinion with alienating arrogance. It is vital they focus less on trying to win the attention and approval of others and more on challenging their inner fears and building their self-worth.

Born promoters, they may be attracted to the law, medicine, lobbying, politics, event organization, and humanitarian, social, charity or caring work, where they can help or support others. They may also make great managers, teachers and trainers, and may be interested in research, science, engineering or possess musical or artistic talent and a love of the media, acting or writing. Health-wise they need to ensure they place as much emphasis on their emotional and mental fitness as they do on physical fitness and appearance. **For self-care**, cognitive behavioral therapy would help you challenge your tendency to think negatively.

Highly sexual, those born on this day have no problem attracting admirers or making the first move in relationships, but may struggle to relate on a deeper level. Before the age of 28, cultivating their image means a great deal to them, but after that they gradually become more aware of the importance of relationships and what lies within. After 58 they further concentrate on increasing self-awareness and, whatever age they are, when the focus is on their individuality and less on courting others, they are at their best. If they can find the courage to discover and develop their talents and use their sharp intellect, they find that the accomplished and attractive image that the world sees isn't a mask anymore but a reality. Their destiny is to inspire others, by their example, to develop their own unique creativity.

Potential: Charismatic, exciting

Dark side: Insecure, superficial

Tarot card, lucky numbers, days, colors: The Chariot, 6, 7, Wednesday, Monday, yellow, jade

Born today: Sean Connery (actor); Tim Burton (director); Billy Ray Cyrus (singer); Claudia Schiffer (model)

August 26

The Birthday of the Star Potential

is asserting yourself.

The way forward: is to understand the difference between being assertive and aggressive.

Luck maker: Saying no to others and yes to yourself when the situation demands it puts your luck-making focus where it belongs—with you.

"I am the wind beneath the wings"

Those born on August 26 love to be the real power behind the scenes. Although they have undoubted star potential, they often choose to be second in command or an advisor, gaining satisfaction from the knowledge that others' success is largely down to them. They have high standards and their work is often of an exceptionally high level. Yet they can feel uncomfortable in the spotlight, and may underplay their talents. This is because the satisfaction and happiness of others matters most to them and they fear that if their own profile gets too high, it may de-motivate them.

Born executives and team players, they thrive in business settings and any situation where teamwork is required. Their fine communication skills draw them to education, writing, music, performance and the law, and their love of detail to science, engineering and technology. Their sympathy toward others may find an outlet in the healing or caring professions, as well as lobbying and charity work. Compassionate at heart, they must not neglect their own health for the sake of others. Wearing, meditating on and surrounding themselves with the color red can encourage them to be more assertive, as can carrying a small tiger's eye crystal.

Tending to put the needs of loved ones above their own, they should constantly remind themselves that their own happiness matters too. Until the age of 27 their selfless tendencies dominate, and they need to ensure this does not cause them unhappiness and resentment. After 28 they focus on diplomacy and relationships; this is when they are most likely to step into the role of supportive advisor. If they are content with this role, they can feel incredibly fulfilled, but if they are not, it is essential they develop their own creativity and strike out on their own. If they can learn to stand up for themselves, their undeniable star potential and capacity for original thought can finally and rightfully be revealed. Their destiny is either to guide and inspire others in a supportive role, or to enlighten and surprise others as a leader.

Potential: Inspiring, resourceful

Dark side: Unassertive, frustrated

Tarot card, lucky numbers, days, colors: Strength, 7, 8, Wednesday, Saturday, blue, hunter green

Born today: Antoine Lavoisier (chemist); Robert Walpole (British prime minister); Mother Teresa (missionary); Thalia (singer)

August 27

The Birthday of the Humanitarian Spirit

"How can I help?"

is to overcome negative thinking.

The way forward: is to realize that focusing on the negative does not help the common good.

Luck maker: Tilt thoughts toward optimism. Adopt an attitude of gratitude for what you have in the present and expect positive things in the future.

August 27-born have much to offer and may often be found helping others or doing good deeds. Their spirit is humanitarian and from an early age they may have felt called to heal the world. The key to their happiness is letting the world give back to them—they are so generous they define themselves by their ability to help, serve or improve the lives of others. Self-sacrificing, they drive themselves incredibly hard and expect others to offer the same commitment. They are admired and respected, but can get easily disillusioned, seeing only negativity. Developing optimism and positive thinking helps them balance giving and receiving, and turn their life from a struggle into an adventure. They are superb communicators but can be blunt and tactless.

Born charity workers and volunteers, they have the potential to excel in medicine, humanitarian, social and charity work, as well as education, counseling and the healing and caring professions. They may also be attracted to science, journalism, accounting, design and the law. Intuitive and creative, they tend to be drawn to practical or intellectual careers where they can make a visible difference. They need to make sure they don't neglect their physical health, given their strong preference for intellectual pursuits. **For self-care**, spending quality time alone and pampering yourself with massages is beneficial, as is meditation to counter negativity.

Learning to receive as well as give in relationships is vital for these passionate and altruistic people. Until the age of 25 they can help themselves by worrying less about the world and taking positive action. After 25 they have an increased need for partnership or relationships with others. However, their approach to life is always focused on the common good, and if they can find an outlet for their humanitarian spirit, they can not only find fulfillment but might also find that their generosity and kindness are repaid many times over. Once they are able to cultivate an attitude of positive expectancy, their destiny is to set an inspiring example of a fulfilling life and, by so doing, make the world a better place.

Potential: Altruistic, dedicated

Dark side: Negative, tactless

Tarot card, lucky numbers, days, colors: The Hermit, 8, 9, Wednesday, Tuesday, blue, scarlet

Born today: Tom Ford (designer); Lyndon Johnson (US president); Aaron Paul (actor)

August 28

The Birthday of the Debater

is becoming more flexible.

The way forward: is to understand that stubbornness blocks your personal growth but compromise can enhance it.

Luck maker: Have an open mind and listen to other people's viewpoints, because these may offer you useful information.

"What can I say?"

People born on August 28 are superb communicators. They know exactly how to make others listen and, even if they don't agree with them, admire them. They are also practical, with superior organizational abilities, but their convincing debating skills set them apart. Their comments are likely to be informed and backed up with research or experience. This is why others learn to rely on their pronouncements and expect them to comment about everything. They are principled but do tend to become so convinced by their arguments that they start to believe they alone have the answer. It is vital they don't abuse their superior intellect by shutting out alternative viewpoints or by manipulating others with their strong convictions.

Born literary agents, they are suited to careers in publishing, research, education and science where they can combine their creative and analytical abilities, as well as their impressive communication skills. Politics, counseling, sales, show business, music, art, podcasting, public relations, design, sales and promotion may also appeal. They often take great care of their health, but may need reminding that an overlooked component of good health is the quality of relationships with loved ones and friends. **For self-care**, walking is an ideal form of exercise, as it gives you time to think.

People love to hear those born on this day talk, but they need to learn that conversations are a two-way street. After the age of 25 they enter a period of increased emphasis on partnerships, both personal and professional. It is important they keep their active minds stimulated with constant challenges; settling into a mundane routine in which no questions are asked is damaging for them. After 55 they are likely to seek deeper meaning in their lives, becoming more reflective. Whatever age they are, as soon as they can accept that there should always be more questions than answers, they have the potential not just to become influential debaters, but to be brilliant advisors with innovative contributions to offer the world. Once they learn to listen more and speak less, their destiny is to inform, benefit and inspire others with their articulacy.

Potential: Articulate, respected

Dark side: Inflexible, arrogant

Tarot card, lucky numbers, days, colors: The Magician, 1, 9, Wednesday, Sunday, blue, yellow

Born today: Ai Weiwei (artist); Jack Black (actor); Shania Twain (singer); Leo Tolstoy (author)

August 29

The Birthday of the Reinterpreter

"I'll find a new and better way"

is to let go.

The way forward: is to understand that life can't be controlled. Sometimes you have to relax, let go and trust that something good will come your way.

Luck maker: You should have patience and think of your life as a giant jigsaw—sometimes nothing makes sense until all the pieces come together.

Those born on August 29 are highly imaginative people. Reluctant to be confined by convention, they love to problem-solve and make the old seem new, preferring to study what is known, add their blend of unique creativity and then present their findings in a wonderfully refreshing new way. They are the great reinterpreters or reimaginers of the year. Although they are wonderfully creative, they also thrive on routine and often try to impose structure upon every situation. As such they are not just positive thinkers but also positive doers, with the self-discipline and practicality to make their ambitious goals happen. But there is one area of their lives where they find it hard to impose structure and that is their emotional life, which is often subordinated to their professional life.

Born entrepreneurs, they may devote their considerable energy and talent to technology, gaming, computing, design or other fields in which they can operate unhindered and impose a sense of structure. Management, self-employment, the caring professions, education, the law, science, writing, politics, manufacturing, music and entertainment may also appeal. Prone to impatience and stress, they should make sure they avoid comfort eating or other addictive and unhealthy attempts to ease tension. **For self-care**, scheduling more time to have fun and meditating on the color orange can encourage you to be more spontaneous in your interactions.

Others often have a hard time competing with the professional priorities of these driven people and they may be accused of avoiding intimacy. After the age of 24 they have opportunities to focus on creativity and nurturing their relationships, and they should take advantage of these opportunities, as their need for a fulfilling personal life is strong, however much they try to escape it. Whatever age they are, if they can learn that sometimes the best solution to a problem is to stop trying so hard to solve or understand it and to simply let things be, their destiny is to benefit others around them, and perhaps the world, with their innovative and inspiring reinterpretations.

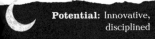

Potential: Innovative, disciplined

Dark side: Impatient, lonely

Tarot card, lucky numbers, days, colors: The High Priestess, 1, 2, Wednesday, Monday, pale blue, silver

Born today: John Locke (philosopher); Richard Attenborough (director); John McCain (politician); Brian Chesky (entrepreneur)

August 30

The Birthday of Brilliant Stability

The life lesson:

is to outgrow your tendency to be controlling.

The way forward: is to understand that the best way to help people is to help them help themselves.

Luck maker: Delegate— understand that empowering others helps you get the job done faster and attracts luck.

"Lean on me"

August 30-born often play a guiding and protective role in all areas of their lives. Others look up to them for guidance, support and direction, and because they are often extremely astute and grounded, these brilliant people are well qualified to assume this responsibility. Self-reliant and strongly focused on their goals, they seem destined for success and recognition wherever they go, but, being so capable, they run the risk of becoming a magnet for needy people. It is important for them to understand the difference between those who genuinely need help and those who are lazy. They must also ensure that others don't become dependent on them.

Born landscapers, their progressive inclinations augur well for any career, but they may be drawn to sport, science, medicine, education and research. The caring professions, writing, acting, social reform, counseling, management, event organization and music may appeal, and because they have a feel for the natural world, farming, agriculture, working with animals or gardening. They are highly sensual and need to beware of over-indulgence when it comes to their health and wellbeing. **For self-care,** wearing, meditating on or surrounding yourself with shades of green—or spending time in natural settings—can promote emotional healing and help connect you to the power of your intuition.

In all their relationships they need to avoid becoming controlling and to make room for freedom as well as intimacy. After the age of 23 they focus increasingly on partnerships and developing their creativity. They need to ensure they don't place too much emphasis on money-making, practical problem-solving, directing and organizing at the expense of their emotional and spiritual needs. This is because, whatever age they are, the more they get in touch with their feelings and the feelings of others, and the more they can connect with and use their intuitive wisdom, the happier and more fulfilled they can be. Once they learn how to let go so that others can learn independence and cultivate their remarkable intuition, their destiny is to profoundly support and inspire all those lucky enough to cross their path.

Potential: Astute, capable

Dark side: Controlling, materialistic

Tarot card, lucky numbers, days, colors: The Empress, 2, 3, Wednesday, Thursday, blue, hunter green

Born today: Ernest Rutherford (physicist); Mary Shelley (author); Warren Buffett (investor); Cameron Diaz (actor)

August 31

The Birthday of Dynamic Attraction

"Bless me"

People born on August 31 have an attractive and appealing energy that draws others to them effortlessly, and they typically climb the ladder of success with ease. Although extremely astute when it comes to understanding others, they are often in the dark when it comes to themselves. Unaware of their real needs, they may rely heavily on the approval of others for self-worth, which puts control of their happiness in the hands of others. It's only when they are able to lessen their need for approval that they can grow psychologically. They are dynamic achievers, but their success feels empty unless they understand their own self-worth.

Born jugglers, they have a fantastic ability to multitask and can succeed in a variety of careers if they are allowed to take center stage. Their people skills and understanding of trends makes them excel in sales, the media and business; their analytical abilities may draw them to science, research, publishing, property development and engineering. Their creativity may express itself in entrepreneurship, the performing arts, sport and social-media influencing, while their humanitarian spirit may lead them to activism and charity work. They should avoid processed and refined foods as they may suffer from diet-related disorders. **For self-care**, you will benefit from meditation and mind–body therapies such as yoga and meditation to help you find inner peace.

These people love to be the center of attention, but can become caustic if attention fades away. After the age of 22 they focus increasingly on relationships and it is crucial they don't lose themselves in work or others, as their fulfillment depends on looking within for guidance and approval. They need to take the many opportunities life presents them to think and act more independently. After 52 they shift toward greater self-reliance and control. At whatever age, the sooner they learn to depend less on others' approval and more on their intuition, the greater their chances of finding true happiness and lasting fulfillment. Once they are able to stay in touch with their internal guide, their destiny is to inspire, motivate and energize others with their magnetic zest for life.

Potential: Dynamic, attractive

Dark side: Needy, stressed

Tarot card, lucky numbers, days, colors: The Emperor, 3, 4, Wednesday, Sunday, blue, caramel

Born today: Maria Montessori (educator); Richard Gere and Chris Tucker (actors); Edwin Moses (athlete)

September 1

The Birthday of the "Thriver"

"I will survive"

The life lesson:

is knowing that sometimes less is more.

The way forward: is to understand that it can be beneficial to hold back or stop while you are ahead.

Luck maker: Train your intuition by paying attention to feelings, dreams, coincidences and sudden insights.

Those born on September 1 are often ambitious and their work gives them great fulfillment, but they are not boring, because they carry out their tasks with an infectious enthusiasm. They like nothing more than to be challenged, and are open to suggestions for improvement. In fact, they have the emotional and physical resilience to survive even the most taxing of circumstances. This makes them not just the survivors, but the true "thrivers" of the year. They take their work and themselves seriously and would benefit from having more fun, although their industriousness and insatiable curiosity for everyone and everything can often compensate. Many excel in their careers, but sometimes their refusal to give up can work against them. They can swing between modesty and confidence, but they have a real ability to motivate and energize others.

Born marketers, their ability to influence others with words augurs well for success in advertising, sales, writing, broadcasting, journalism, influencing, education and performing arts. They may also be drawn to business, management, self-employment, research and promotion, and their resilience helps them shine in physically and mentally demanding careers such as sports and the military. These people have strong physical and mental appetites and need to keep both their bodies and minds constantly active and challenged. **For self-care**, carrying a small quartz crystal around with you and daily meditation can improve your connection to your intuition.

The curiosity of those born on this day when meeting new people can earn them a reputation as a flirt but, once in a relationship, they are likely to remain true. After the age of 21 they have opportunities to develop close relationships; and to strengthen their intuition, which can improve their timing, so they improve their chances of success by knowing when to hang on and when to quit. Whatever age they are, their extraordinary resilience and determination in the pursuit of their goals endow them with potential for inspiring accomplishments. Once they have developed better timing, their destiny is to act as agents of assistance and advancement, not just in their jobs but to all who are fortunate enough to encounter them.

Potential: Courageous, enthusiastic

Dark side: Overly serious, overly persistent

Tarot card, lucky number, days, colors: The Magician, 1, Wednesday, Sunday, blue, orange

Born today: Tarsila do Amaral (artist); Rocky Marciano (boxer); Gloria Estefan, Barry Gibb (singers)

September 2

The Birthday of the Enlightened Non-partisan

"We are in this together"

is putting yourself first.

The way forward: is to understand that letting yourself shine sets an inspiring example of self-confidence and the right to be noticed for everyone.

Luck maker: Throw caution to the wind and get carried away with excitement for what you want to do, because passion motivates others to follow or help you.

September 2-born are idealistic and lively individuals with a non-partisan view of the world. They are the first to defend human rights, and ensure they communicate clearly with everyone, no matter what their background or education. They cannot abide pretension or exaggeration and place a high value on simplicity of language, behavior and action. Others know exactly where they stand with them and that they are fair. In fact, these enlightened people value justice and equality so highly that they sometimes downplay their own talents, allowing others who are less qualified or suitable than themselves to overtake them. They need to know that pushing ahead when their talents merit it does not mean they are egocentric or selfish, but that they are valuing themselves.

Born judges, their egalitarian spirit may draw them to the law, education, healthcare, writing and science. As team players, they can be attracted to the media, sport, public relations, banking, stock trading, accounting, the civil service and business. They often have stacks of energy and their greatest health risk is pushing themselves too hard, making them prone to stress-related problems, such as insomnia. **For self-care**, carrying a small rose-quartz crystal and meditating on the color pink encourages you to love yourself more.

Once these people learn to value themselves, their relationships can be as wonderful a source of fulfillment as their work. After the age of 20 they have an increased need for partnership and relating to others, and it is important they have equality and reciprocal respect in their relationships. There are opportunities during this time for them to develop their creativity. After 51 they are more likely to discover their personal power. The sooner they realize that they don't live to work but work to live, the more fulfilling their lives will be, and the greater their chances of discovering their outstanding potential for influencing others positively. Once they understand that being fair does not mean being overlooked or stepping aside, their destiny is to exert a powerful, positive influence on others and help make the world a fairer place.

Potential: Fair, inspiring

Dark side: Workaholic, self-sacrificing

Tarot card, lucky numbers, days, colors: High Priestess, 2, 9, Wednesday, Monday, blue, silver

Born today: Andrew Grove (Intel founder); Keanu Reeves, Salma Hayek (actors); Lennox Lewis (boxer)

September 3

The Birthday of the Iron Butterfly

The life lesson:

is coping with failure.

The way forward: is to turn rejection into resolve and understand that failure is a vital ingredient of success because it shows you what works and what doesn't.

Luck maker: Focus on the best, not the worst of yourself.

"Only the best will do"

People born on September 3 are fiercely determined, but they prefer to showcase a gentler approach to the world. They are convinced that communication, appealing to reason and a dash of humor are far better for getting their point across than thumping the table. This can move mountains but can also cause others to underestimate their iron will. They have a sharp, original mind and fine organizational or practical skills. They strive for excellence in all areas of their lives, but their easy-going approach makes it hard for others to resent them. Unfortunately, they are not always good at demystifying their progressive ideals, but taking the time to simplify and explain their thoughts or methods to others makes all the difference.

Born lawyers, they are committed to finding workable methods that can benefit others and may be drawn to careers such as the law, crime-fighting, politics, education, writing, science, research, engineering, health and sports or the arts. They also make great managers and executives. They tend to lose themselves in work, and if their job is desk-bound, this can have a negative impact on their mood and well-being. **For self-care,** plenty of fresh air, exercise and regular time out are strongly advised, as is cultivating an interest outside work.

These people set high standards in their relationships, just as they do in their professional lives, and can be unwilling to compromise. After the age of 19 they become more aware of the importance of relationships and opening up to others. Their creative abilities evolve, with some producing truly futuristic work. After 49 they reach a turning point, which brings a deep need for personal transformation and power. Throughout their lives, if they can develop self-confidence and understand that no failure is a failure if they can learn from it, they may find their novel ideas—combined with their iron will hidden behind their easy-going charm—not only outshine others but make them influential agents of progress. Once they find the self-confidence to take risks, put themselves on the line and make their intentions clear, their destiny is to inspire others to work alongside them to make tangible progress.

Potential: Original, determined

Dark side: Controlling, self-doubting

Tarot card, lucky number, days, colors: The Empress, 3, Wednesday, Thursday, blue, jade

Born today: Louis Sullivan (architect); Steve Jones (musician); Shaun White (snowboarder)

September 4

The Birthday of the Master Planner

The life lesson:

is valuing tradition.

The way forward: is to understand that the past does not always have to be banished—it is something to be understood, valued and learned from.

Luck maker: Cultivate an attitude of gratitude by focusing on what you have rather than on what you have not, to attract good fortune and happiness.

"Out with the old, in with the new"

Those born on September 4 are the master planners of the year. They bring due process and precision to everything and are usually organizing, designing or putting more productive systems in place. Others rely on them to be the first and last word on both process and planning. With these people having a natural understanding of how things work, efficiency is important to them and they are superb at finding better ways of doing things. They have an instinct for discovering the flaw in a project, and love exposing and replacing it, but need to avoid becoming caustic in their criticism. Their instincts are so accurate, it is important they choose to focus on worthy causes, otherwise they risk taking advantage of people.

Born architects and planners, these people thrive in many careers but may be best suited to management, diplomacy, education, research, detective work, building and construction, counseling, sales, commerce, manufacturing, engineering, medicine and science, as well as digital influencing and the performing arts. With their tendency to work and play hard, they should take regular time out to avoid burnout. **For self-care,** regular aromatherapy baths, using essential oils such as lavender, can help you unwind, while wearing the color orange can help you feel more spontaneous.

These charming people can captivate others, but they take their relationships seriously—sometimes too seriously. After the age of 18 they have a strong need for a committed partnership, and their sense of harmony and beauty is enhanced. As they age, it is important their focus on future planning does not preclude happiness in the present. After 49 they prioritize personal growth and joint business activity. Their key to happiness and success does not necessarily lie in material gain but in developing their inner world—a goal that may confuse or frighten them. Once they understand that spiritual growth also requires dedication and passion, they can achieve their goals for the future in the most powerful way possible: in the present. Their destiny is to realize their constructive and progressive plans to benefit both themselves and others.

Potential: Charming, constructive

Dark side: Disrespectful, demanding

Tarot card, lucky number, days, colors: The Emperor, 4, Wednesday, Sunday, blue, white

Born today: Beyoncé (singer); Clive Granger (economist); Tom Watson (golfer); Shinya Yamanaka (researcher)

September 5

The Birthday of the Extraordinary Mind

The life lesson:

is avoiding self-sabotage.

The way forward: is to remind yourself that you are in charge of your thoughts and actions and you can change them from negative to positive ones.

Luck maker: Surround yourself with positive and supportive people, and remove toxic people from your life.

"A touch of magic"

September 5-born are extraordinarily creative, magnetic, fast-moving and fast-thinking, with an infectious enthusiasm and a desire to realize their innovative ideas, not just for themselves but for the benefit of others. However, despite their charisma and generous desire to help others, they are prone to needless mistakes that would not have happened if they had taken the time to assess what is realistically attainable and what is simply fantasy. If they can keep their feet on the ground and strive to make things better, not perfect, they are likely to succeed in most of what they put their minds to.

Born designers, they may be drawn to careers in science, computing, landscaping, property development, interior design and technology, but their creative communication skills may see them thrive in the law, sales, promotion, publishing, life-coaching, blogging, education, composition, performing arts, acting, speaking and fashion design. These people think, move and live fast, and it is important for their health that they occasionally slow down and unwind. **For self-care**, wearing, meditating and surrounding yourself with the color blue and practicing mindfulness techniques help you feel calmer and in control.

Often surrounded by admirers, those born on this day should exercise discretion in their relationships, as it is possible to be too popular. Following a rather solitary or rebellious youth, from the age of 17 they become more socially aware, with a strong need to be popular and appreciated. As they age, professional and personal relationships play key roles and their extraordinarily creative potential comes to the fore. If they can learn to harness that creativity so that it is grounded in reality rather than in fantasy, and avoid self-sabotaging habits, their potential for success and recognition is outstanding. They are blessed with a magical sparkle and—with a bit of good judgment added to the mix—they are likely to get most, if not all, of what they most desire. Once they have learned to improve their judgment, their destiny is to showcase their innovative strategies and bring a touch of their unique magic to the world.

Potential: Creative, exciting

Dark side: Irresponsible, self-destructive

Tarot card, lucky number, day, colors: The Hierophant, 5, Wednesday, blue, chrome

Born today: Louis IV (French king); Freddie Mercury (singer); Raquel Welch, Michael Keaton (actors)

September 6

The Birthday of Destiny

"It's meant to be"

The life lesson:

is planning ahead.

The way forward: is to understand that your chances of success increase dramatically if there is a flexible plan in place.

Luck maker: Visualizing yourself achieving your goals helps you believe in your ability to create a positive future.

People born on September 6 seem destined to live by the law of the unexpected. Nothing appears to settle into a comfortable routine, and although this can make them feel anxious, deep down they would have it no other way. As they mature, they are likely to believe that destiny plays a hand in shaping their lives. With their energy focused on the present and their belief that no person, word, action or situation is trivial or unimportant, these people are deeply compassionate and accepting of whatever life brings. The upside is that they know how to savor the present moment, which is the recipe for a happy life. They can also be incredibly supportive and appreciative of the people in their lives, making those around them feel good about themselves. The downside is that they are not putting enough thought or energy into preparing for what might lie ahead.

Born doctors, they excel in medicine, the law, science and psychology, and their analytical skills draw them to image-making, graphics, media and advertising. Other careers that may appeal include sport, leisure, lobbying, the caring professions and social campaigning. They often have a youthful quality about them, but their focus on instant gratification may set them up for diet and health problems. **For self-care**, meal plans and an exercise schedule are key, as is wearing or meditating on the color blue to encourage you to enjoy today but also plan for tomorrow.

These people are at their happiest and best when they are giving, but need to understand that a successful relationship is based on both give and take. Until the age of 46 they feel a strong need for partnership. After the age of 46 they reach a turning point when they evaluate their own personal power, and this is when they feel more self-confident. As long as they make sure their negativity doesn't attract misfortune, and their giving nature is not exploited, they have the potential to become highly expressive, inspirational souls. Once they overcome self-doubt and choose to be proactive rather than reactive, their destiny is to inspire and invigorate others with their empathy, creativity and zest for life.

Potential: Compassionate, passionate

Dark side: Passive, self-doubting

Tarot card, lucky number, days, colors: The Lovers, 6, Wednesday, Friday, blue, pink

Born today: Idris Elba (actor); Cassandra Vieten (scientist); John Dalton (chemist); Macy Gray (singer)

September 7

The Birthday of Tenacity

"Nothing's going to stop me"

The life lesson:

is being kind to yourself and others.

The way forward: is to understand that until you can ease up on yourself and others, your success will not bring you contentment.

Luck maker: Avoid making enemies because everyone can be a potential source of good fortune for you at some point.

Those born on September 7 are determined to the extreme. When they decide on a course of action, nothing can stand in their way. Their ambitious goals matter more than anything else; however many obstacles stand in their way, they do not give up until they have achieved their objectives, even if this means making enemies. They can be ruthless in their determination to succeed, but can also be fiercely loyal and protective of loved ones. Those few people who get close to them respect their determination to succeed, their passion for helping those less fortunate and their inner strength, but they may be a little fearful of getting on the wrong side of them.

Born directors, these people are drawn to careers where they can be progressive and act independently, such as business, management, teaching, writing, programming and industry, and, because they identify so strongly with their work, crime-fighting, activism, sports, artistic or musical careers. Prone to neglecting their health, they need to understand that their work performance and mood can be improved by eating healthily, exercising regularly and getting plenty of fresh air and sleep. **For self-care**, wearing, meditating on and surrounding yourself with the color purple encourages you to look within for deeper meaning.

Powerfully seductive, those born on this day find that few can resist them, but they can be prone to mood swings and need a lot of space in their relationships. Before the age of 45 the emphasis is on relationships, both personal and professional, as well as a desire to develop their creative potential. They should take these opportunities by being a little more flexible and recognizing that professional success is hollow without love in their lives. After 45 there is a turning point, which encourages them to seek deeper meaning, personal transformation and inner harmony. If they can learn to look within to find fulfillment rather than to other people or to work, they can find the contentment they long for. They also find that their courage in the face of adversity can break new ground so that everyone, themselves included, can benefit.

Potential: Courageous, determined

Dark side: Ruthless, unkind

Tarot card, lucky number, days, colors: The Chariot, 7, Wednesday, Monday, sky blue, indigo

Born today: Elizabeth I (English queen); Grandma Moses (painter); Buddy Holly (musician); Chrissie Hynde (musician)

September 8

The Birthday of the Enigmatic Director

The life lesson:

is being yourself.

The way forward: is to understand that you are human and, like everyone else, have many contradictions.

Luck maker: Demonstrating an openness to learning and listening, even if you think you already know the answers, draws others to you.

"Time now to listen"

September 8-born have a clear sense of right and wrong, but they often still come across as complicated or enigmatic individuals. This is because they choose not to show their true selves, preferring to be the authoritative mouthpiece for others, typically a worthy group, organization, team or cause they believe in. They are fiercely ambitious and use their terrific communication and practical skills to help set others on what they believe to be the right path. This earns them respect but not always loyalty, as they are often so convinced of the superior merits of their position that they dismiss conflicting viewpoints, making enemies. They need to be more sensitive and tactful, and to appreciate the negative effect their superior attitude can have on others.

Born generals and directors, these people identify strongly with their careers and may be drawn to politics, the military, the law and education, as well as science, commerce, journalism, the arts and entertainment. Prone to inflexibility both mentally and physically, they benefit from daily stretching or yoga exercises. **For self-care,** you should keep a mood diary or journal to express and try to understand your feelings, and the messages those feelings send you.

Those born on this day are not always easy to get close to and can come across as self-sufficient, but they are happiest when their relationships are close and supportive. Before the age of 45 they gradually realize the importance of social relationships and their creative abilities develop; these years can be dynamic if they can be more sensitive toward others. After 45 they become more self-aware, as the emphasis shifts to personal trans-formation. At some point they are likely to have assumed leadership positions, and nothing is more important to their psychological growth than learning to show tolerance toward others. Although these advanced souls do often know what is best for others and for the world, they must understand that they may not yet be ready to listen. Once they can let others make their own mistakes and find the courage to be themselves, their destiny is to point other souls in the direction of true progress.

Potential: Influential, progressive

Dark side: Proud, inflexible

Tarot card, lucky number, days, colors: Strength, 8, Wednesday, Saturday, blue, brown

Born today: Richard I (English king); Frédéric Mistral (poet); Patsy Cline, Pink (singers)

September 9

The Birthday of the Missing Link

The life lesson:

is coping with worry.

The way forward: is to understand that worry achieves nothing and the only way to change a situation is to take action or let go and move on.

Luck maker: Raise your vibration by using positive thoughts and words to attract success your way.

"The truth is out there"

People born on September 9 are inquisitive and original. They can come across as serious and responsible, and a part of them feels drawn to what is complicated, but this may be because they often feel something is absent from their lives, regardless of how successful they seem. Searching for that elusive something to fulfill them defines much of their lives. They need to understand that the missing link they are seeking can't be found externally but by looking within, as this introspection is the only way for them to understand that the only person holding them back from their huge potential for success and fulfillment is themselves.

Born authors, they love to observe people and can make great writers, bloggers and journalists, but they may also be drawn to education, politics, social, humanitarian and charity work. Public relations, negotiation, research, art and music, as well as self-employment, also appeal. Prone to anxiety and insomnia, they need to make sure their bedroom is a comfortable and peaceful refuge to encourage a good night's sleep. **For self-care**, stress-management techniques, such as meditation, massage and aromatherapy, are beneficial, as is cognitive behavioral therapy to combat negative thinking.

Although people find it easy to confide in them, those born on this day can take a long time to open up and trust others. Before the age of 43 they focus on relating to others, and these are the years when they are most likely to find themselves drawn toward complicated or destructive situations or relationships. After 43 there is a growing emphasis on emotional and spiritual regeneration. This can spur them to new heights because, when driven by self-belief, these curious people not only find what they have always been looking for, but they are able to achieve miracles. Once they have learned to banish their inner critic, their destiny is to inspire others, perhaps even the world, with their compassionate, tenacious and hugely original approach.

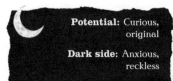

Potential: Curious, original

Dark side: Anxious, reckless

Tarot card, lucky number, days, colors: The Hermit, 9, Wednesday, Tuesday, blue, red

Born today: Adam Sandler, Hugh Grant (actors); Aurelian (Roman emperor); Otis Redding (singer)

September 10

The Birthday of Inspiring Responsibility

"With great power comes great responsibility"

Those born on September 10 are feisty individuals, concerned about the wellbeing of others. Their ability to notice and value tiny but important details means that their aura is one of inspired responsibility. Gifted with resilience, versatility and powerful inner strength, they take responsibilities very seriously, but a part of them also longs to be free; the challenge they face is balancing these two drives. They learn early in life the importance of diplomacy and of accepting other people's weaknesses. Others come to rely on them for a sense of stability—sometimes to the point of dependency. Key to their psychological growth is their ability to develop their own creativity and individuality.

Born captains, they make excellent managers, entrepreneurs and leaders in whatever career they choose. They excel in analytical jobs, such as accounting, administration, research, technology and commerce, and their latent creativity and communication skills may express themselves in education, charity work, art, drama and music. Prone to stress and digestive upsets, they need to avoid fast foods and focus on fresh, natural produce and small meals and snacks. **For self-care**, ensuring you get to sleep before midnight boosts your concentration during the day, while daily exercise, preferably outdoors, enhances mood and wellbeing.

In relationships, these people are often relied on to be the sensible one, but they need to let their hair down sometimes. Before the age of 42 they concentrate on others' needs to be appreciated and relied upon. After 42 their personal power grows and they become more self-reliant. Putting the needs of others before their own, they must learn that their own needs and talents are just as important. The sooner these innovative, occasionally revolutionary thinkers discover a sense of self-worth, the better. When they listen to their hearts as well as their heads, a dash of glamour is added to the stability and responsibility they exude, and others notice and want to hear every inspired word they say. Once they can be both creative and compassionate, their destiny is to make significant changes that can benefit others.

Potential: Influential, capable

Dark side: Uninspired, passive

Tarot card, lucky number, days, colors: The Wheel of Fortune, 1, Wednesday, Sunday, indigo, yellow

Born today: Stephen Jay Gould (paleontologist); Colin Firth (actor); Jack Ma (entrepreneur); Misty Copeland (dancer)

September 11

The Birthday of the Radical Idealist

The life lesson:

is moderation or finding the middle way.

The way forward: is to understand that a balanced approach to everything is the most effective, rewarding and healthy way to live.

Luck maker: Train your intuition by paying greater attention to dreams, coincidences, gut feelings and sudden inspirations.

September 11-born think for themselves. They are usually fiercely moral but love to shock or surprise others with their unconventional views, and, as well as being opinionated, they are incredibly compassionate. Their urge to help others may be so strong that it takes a radical form: either by passionately defending traditional views or by defiantly rebelling against them. They can sometimes appear extremely critical, but this can be caused by a part of them that fears failure and longs for stability. They may also be battling between a desire to be revolutionary and a need to adhere to convention that manifests itself in inappropriate behavior or sudden mood swings.

Born campaigners, they often gravitate to politics, causes, social reform or the law, but may exert their influence through writing or blogging. Finance, statistics, administration, economics, science, technology, teaching and therapy may also appeal. They need to realize the connection between their diet and exercise routine and their mood and health, and should not neglect their wellbeing. **For self-care**, meditation, and recalling and interpreting your dreams, encourages you to connect with your intuition.

These people tend to live through others, yet they need to address an insensitivity to others' feelings. Before the age of 41 they focus on relationships, and opportunities to explore their creativity. They should seize these because successful relationships can give them a sense of perspective they lack, and developing creative interests helps them connect with their intuition, the key to their psychological growth. After 41 they become more self-reliant and in control. If they can listen to their intuition rather than their conviction, become more tolerant and find a worthy cause, they will no longer wish to shock others with radical words and deeds or be drawn to outlandish people and projects for excitement. They want to realize their full potential and, by so doing, encourage others to do the same. In this way these determined and imaginative individuals make their own extraordinary mark on the world. Their destiny is to become the progressive revolutionaries of their age, or, in keeping with their contradictory but fascinating traits, passionate defenders of tradition.

Potential: Original, passionate

Dark side: Critical, irresponsible

Tarot card, lucky number, days, colors: Justice, 2, Wednesday, Monday, indigo, turquoise

Born today: D. H. Lawrence (author); Tom Dreesen (comedian); Taraji P. Henson (actor); Harry Connick Jr. (singer)

September 12

The Birthday of the Motivator

The life lesson:

is cope with stress, because stress is a natural part of life.

The way forward: is to understand the importance of regular time out and time alone to focus on your own needs.

Luck maker: Only take on what you know you can achieve, and understand that taking on too much drains your energy and blocks your chances of success.

"Look up at the stars and not down at your feet"

People born on September 12 have incredible charisma, energy and strong ideals. They are blessed with a strong desire to share their knowledge with those less fortunate to encourage them to be the best that they can be. Driven by a desire to motivate, serve and educate others, they can fight hard for a cause they believe in. They rarely lack courage and others look to them for encouragement and support. At some point, however, they need to determine whether their desire to boost others is a deep-seated need to control rather than inspire, though their potential to positively influence people is truly remarkable.

Born trainers, they are well suited to careers involving motivational speaking, education, teaching, self-help and life-coaching, and they may be drawn to research, science, technology, media, writing, the law and publishing. They make great advertisers, promoters, bankers and accountants, and their humanitarian side pulls them toward politics or social work, while their creativity attracts them to design, music and acting. They have such a lively mind it is essential they constantly learn new skills. **For self-care,** committing to a regular exercise routine may not appeal, so you should incorporate lots of movement into your day. Gardening, cleaning, dancing, walking, swimming and cycling are all beneficial.

These people can be cautious and detached emotionally, but their friendly, witty personality means they are never short of admirers. Until the age of 40 they may chase popularity; as a result, they may overload themselves with commitments they can't fulfill. After 40 they reach a turning point that makes them evaluate their unique contribution to the world. Listening to their inner voice and picking to whom and what they devote their considerable talents is the secret of their success. Once they have learned to say no when they are feeling overwhelmed, and to balance personal time with responsibilities to others, their destiny is to motivate and inspire others. If they can do this, they will make a real and positive difference, not just to the lives of others, but to the world around them.

Potential: Optimistic, courageous

Dark side: Controlling, unreliable

Tarot card, lucky number, days, colors: The Hanged Man, 3, Wednesday, Thursday, blue, purple

Born today: Henry Hudson (explorer); Hans Zimmer (composer); Jesse Owens (athlete); Jennifer Hudson (actor)

September 13

The Birthday of Ardent Concentration

is opening up emotionally.

The way forward: is to understand that emotions are not meant to be suppressed or denied, but felt, listened to and managed.

Luck maker: Listening to feelings does not mean you have to follow them—you are in charge of your feelings and can choose how you respond to your heart.

"Focus is the secret of success"

September 13-born tend to have extraordinary powers of concentration. Their intense determination and resilience are out of this world when they are passionate about someone or something. They have powerful self-belief regardless of what current trends or other people suggest. Their intense focus and highly idiosyncratic approach can win them many admirers, but can also make them appear distant or eccentric at times, although what others think is unlikely to deter them. They have great potential for sensitivity and creativity but tend to run from them, risking controlling and ruthless behavior. However, only when they have learned to acknowledge and manage their emotions can they grow psychologically.

Born managers, they have fine problem-solving skills and thrive in science, analysis, business and technology, although their originality may draw them to design, research, writing and art. They make great team leaders in sales, promotion, public relations, politics, accounting, real estate and banking. Sport and the military are great outlets for their energy and discipline, and their love of education may draw them to teaching, the law and social reform. It is essential they eat healthily and exercise regularly to avoid stress-related health issues. They would benefit greatly from cultivating hobbies. **For self-care,** spending more time talking on the phone or in person helps your relationships blossom.

Prone to periods of intense passion and great secrecy, they need to aim for consistency, be more sensitive to others' feelings and have more fun in their close relationships. Until the age of 39 they have opportunities to open up emotionally. After 39 they seek deeper meaning to their life and place more focus on personal growth. The sooner they learn to listen to their heart as passionately as they do to their heads, the sooner they can devote their considerable talents to a worthy cause, lead by example and make the world a better place. Once their hearts are more open, their destiny is to use their laser-like focus and discipline to achieve pioneering breakthroughs.

Potential: Dedicated, resilient

Dark side: Cold, controlling

Tarot card, lucky number, days, colors: Death, 4, Wednesday, Sunday, blue, silver

Born today: Daniel Defoe, Roald Dahl (authors); Tyler Perry (director); Milton Hershey (tycoon)

September 14

The Birthday of the Problem-solver

"Every problem is an opportunity to do your best"

Those born on September 14 tend to be the first person that others reach out to when they want to understand a situation better. Their creativity and problem-solving skills are exceptional, and because they are not afraid to tell it like it is, they have a reputation for being innovative and progressive. Compromises or halfway solutions are not in their vocabulary and their goal is always to work for improvement. The only skill they need to really fine-tune is tact. They don't mean to offend, as they often have the best interests of others at heart, but they don't understand that sometimes people aren't ready to hear the unadorned truth.

Born architects and builders, they are drawn to any career that requires problem-solving and planning, as well as the law, design, technology, event-planning, management, research, psychology and education. Being multitalented, they need to ensure that they feel genuinely enthusiastic about whatever they choose, because they can't fake interest in things they are not passionate about. They use up a lot of energy, so benefit from going to bed before midnight and rising early. **For self-care**, laugh more to ease stress—sometimes the best way to feel happier is to bring happiness into the lives of others.

Charming and interesting, these people are never short of admirers but need to avoid becoming controlling. Until the age of 38 they have numerous opportunities to become more diplomatic and develop their creativity, which they should take because successful relationships and a flexible approach are the keys to their success. After 38 they become more self-confident and need to understand the powerful influence their words and actions have on others. Once these energetic and constructive individuals find a worthy cause, they have the potential not just to turn things upside down but to make sure everyone flies high and lands the right side up. When they do find a way to influence others without offending them, their destiny is to make a truly original and substantial mark on the world.

Potential: Influential, constructive

Dark side: Controlling, tactless

Tarot card, lucky number, day, colors: Temperance, 5, Wednesday, blue, green

Born today: Margaret Sanger (activist); Sam Neill (actor); Amy Winehouse (singer)

September 15

The Birthday of the Specialist

"Better to be a master of one"

September 15-born are drawn to specialization. Their ability to master and break new ground sets them apart. Others admire them for their technical skills and depth of knowledge about their chosen field. Such is their devotion to their work that they can appear isolated at times, but their potential to excel professionally is outstanding. The secret to success is not so much their technical skills but their ability to wait for the right opportunity. If they jump too soon, they may find that this robs them of success, but if they bide their time, they can reach the heights for which they seem destined. They equate status with financial reward, which can be damaging to their creativity and integrity, so it is important to resist the urge to compromise or take shortcuts to the top.

Born researchers, they are both imaginative and organized, which bodes well for a variety of professions, from science to the arts. They may be drawn to medicine, education, the law and accounting, and their latent creativity and fine communication skills may express themselves in writing, acting, blogging, design, architecture, psychology and finance, while their humanitarian spirit may inspire them to charity work. Working long hours increases the physical symptoms of stress such as headaches and eye strain, so it is important they schedule regular time for themselves to exercise, stretch and relax. **For self-care**, wearing, meditating on and surrounding yourself with the color purple encourages you to be less materialistic and think of the deeper meaning behind things.

Although they are sensual people, those born on this day lose themselves in their work, so they need to value their close relationships and other things money can't buy. Until the age of 37 they are prone to self-indulgence, but they have opportunities to nurture loving relationships. After 37 they focus on personal growth and transformation. If they have learned to get a grip on their materialism, this is when they can really come into their own and step into their perfect role: that of the respected and, possibly, world-renowned specialist. Their destiny is to increase awareness of their special field of knowledge.

Potential: Ambitious, highly skilled

Dark side: Materialistic, isolated

Tarot card, lucky number, days, colors: The Devil, 6, Wednesday, Friday, indigo, green

Born today: Chimamanda Ngozi Adichie, Agatha Christie (authors); Renzo Rosso (designer); Prince Harry (British royal)

September 16

The Birthday of Vitality

The life lesson:

is compromise.

The way forward: is to understand that a win–win scenario where everybody benefits is far more likely to succeed and gain popular support than a win–lose scenario.

Luck maker: Set goals and know when to tone things down. People are unlikely to support you if there are no set plans or they feel backed into a corner.

"On a clear day you can see forever"

People born on September 16 are vibrant and optimistic individuals, with an enviable ability to light up any conversation or situation. Although they are lively and passionate, they are not impulsive; they have great discipline and are motivated by a powerful desire to learn and break new ground in discoveries and achievements. They thrive on challenge and competition, and stand up for their beliefs or the underdog. Fiercely independent, they may find it hard to work with others, but in time they learn to compromise, realizing that giving their opinion gently yields better results than bluntness.

Born consultants and educators, they help others learn and thrive in teaching, counseling, medicine, charity work and advisory services. They may also be drawn to design, building, financial planning, science, manufacturing, business and technology, and their creativity may express itself in the performing arts. They like to live life in the fast lane but can be prone to stress and information overload. It is important for them to slow down and to eat slowly to ensure they digest their food properly. **For self-care**, mindfulness techniques, such as meditation, yoga and tai chi, can encourage you to savor and feel gratitude for the present moment.

These people are passionate and warm companions, but can become moody if there are attempts to change them or restrict their freedom. Until the age of 36 relationships are important, but their desire for popularity may prove elusive until they can control their impulsive candor. From 36 the emphasis is on personal transformation. They should take advantage of opportunities to control their tremendous energy because, once they learn to channel their passion in the right direction, these big-hearted individuals can not only make a name for themselves, but also find true happiness by passing on their discoveries and joy. Once they have learned to work toward a shared vision, their destiny is to inspire others with their infectious enthusiasm and make a positive contribution to humanity.

Potential: Engaging, optimistic

Dark side: Rebellious, moody

Tarot card, lucky number, days, colors: The Tower, 7, Wednesday, Monday, indigo, green

Born today: Lee Kuan Yew (Singaporean prime minister); B. B. King (guitarist); David Copperfield (magician); Nick Jonas (singer)

September 17

The Birthday of Honest Determination

is being spontaneous.

The way forward: is to understand that sometimes your thinking gets in the way of living.

Luck maker: Show your enthusiasm—the more alive and passionate you are, the more people want to help you.

"I do the right thing"

Those born on September 17 are strongly determined and disciplined, with a clear sense of right and wrong. They have stamina and courage and don't fear hard work, often effortlessly taking on routine tasks that others avoid. Control is important for them and, in anything they do, their steady discipline and commitment shine through. They can be imaginative but prefer to be logical and doggedly stick with the facts. Tradition, fair play and maintaining the status quo matter greatly to them. They have a fun side, but it takes a lot to reveal it, and they can come across as serious. When they do open up, others can be assured of their absolute sincerity.

Born lawyers, they have a strong sense of justice and are suited to careers in the law, accounting and law enforcement, as well as science, research, writing, economics, education and the media. The healing professions, technology and engineering may also appeal. They have workaholic tendencies and may be prone to a sedentary lifestyle and accompanying stress if they spend long hours at a desk or computer. It is important they schedule breaks and exercise into their day. **For self-care**, regular massage suits your sensual nature, and wearing and meditating on the color purple encourages you to focus on higher things.

Outwardly reserved, those born on this day take a while to reveal their passionate side in relationships. Until the age of 35 they have opportunities to develop their creativity and nurture relationships, to become less self-contained and more expressive. After 35 they seek a deeper meaning to their life. They tend to prosper and enjoy a good standard of living, but to reach their full potential they should prioritize their spiritual and emotional needs; money alone cannot satisfy them. Above all, they are determined, so when they realize the true value of things that money can't buy, they can inspire others to follow their example and take a more disciplined, compassionate and honest approach to life. Once they are able to open up emotionally and tap into their latent creativity, their destiny is to bring about concrete progress that both inspires and benefits others.

Potential: Persistent, honest

Dark side: Controlling, workaholic

Tarot card, lucky number, days, colors: The Star, 8, Wednesday, Saturday, indigo, brown

Born today: Edgar Mitchell (astronaut); Stirling Moss (racing driver); Anne Bancroft (actor); Frederick Ashton (choreographer)

September 18

The Birthday of Elusive Devotion

The life lesson:

is dealing with conflict.

The way forward: is assertion without aggression. Assertiveness is a skill that can be learned.

Luck maker: Go outside your comfort zone. Success can only be found when you challenge yourself, take calculated risks, and learn and grow from your mistakes.

"Solitude is strength"

September 18-born are highly creative and sensual. There is a touch of the feline about them—they can be devoted and available one moment, independent and elusive the next. Although they can be sociable, few get to know them very well and even getting close to them is no guarantee of commitment. So strong is their need for absolute freedom, they often change their minds at the last minute, causing confusion. Although this unpredictability adds to their seductive mystery, they isolate from time to time to avoid conflict and reflect in private. Problems, however, arise when the need to withdraw and regroup becomes a cover for hiding or escaping; they need to learn that conflict, though unpleasant, is essential for their psychological growth.

Born directors, they have an affinity with filmmaking, writing, music and art. Science, the law, law enforcement, psychology, publishing, education and work that can advance or benefit humanity also appeals. Other attractive fields may include research, statistics, accounting, business, management, administration and psychology. Prone to negativity, these people may benefit from cognitive behavioral therapy or other therapies that help transform their thinking. **For self-care**, wearing red helps you feel more self-confident, and carrying a small rose-quartz crystal encourages you to love yourself.

Being sensitive when hurt, those born on this day seek solace in books, solitude or their work and they may benefit from reaching out to others for emotional support. Until the age of 34 they have many opportunities to develop their sociable side, which they should take because, left to their own devices, they run the risk of being over-serious. After 34 they reach a turning point that brings an emphasis on personal power, and this is when their powers of concentration are likely to be exceptional—once they find a worthy cause, they can attract considerable success. As long as they don't become so absorbed in their work that they lose direction or their own identity, these highly unusual and advanced souls make their mark on the world. Once they have found a way to face rather than run away from challenges, their destiny is to contribute new knowledge that benefits or inspires humanity.

Potential: Creative, dedicated

Dark side: Aloof, negative

Tarot card, lucky number, days, colors: The Moon, 9, Wednesday, Tuesday, indigo, orange

Born today: Samuel Johnson (scholar); Greta Garbo (actor); Ben Carson (politician); James Marsden (actor)

September 19

The Birthday of the Immaculate Presentation

The life lesson:

is to see beyond the material.

The way forward: is to understand that true beauty, meaning and fulfillment can only be found from the inside out and not from the outside in.

Luck maker: Believe that there is an infinite amount of luck to go around, and that luck is heading your way.

"All that glitters is gold"

People born on September 19 are acutely aware of the image they present to the world and how others form an impression of them. They have a unique style and, more often than not, they are elegant or sophisticated. Others may find their preoccupation with outward show superficial, but generally they are fully aware that inner beauty is just as important as outer beauty. They simply believe that presenting a polished image of themselves shows the world their true self. If they haven't allowed themselves to get lost in material concerns, that true self is often deeply wise and profound.

Born influencers, they are multitalented and can thrive in any career they choose, but can make considerable impact online or in writing, the law, teaching, research, counseling, coaching and business. Science and the arts may also appeal, but their restless and inquisitive mind may lead them to change professions many times. Prone to burning the midnight oil, they may find it hard to get going in the morning and benefit from going to bed early and rising early too. **For self-care,** wearing, meditating on and surrounding yourself with the color purple encourages you to think of higher things.

These people are charming and rarely short of admirers, but tend to rush into relationships without making sure there is real compatibility. Until the age of 32 they prioritize socializing, so they need to ensure they don't forget who and what really matters to them. After 32 personal power is more prominent, and they may focus on personal growth. They have opportunities to give their lives more meaning and to connect with their intuition. Successfully overcoming both personal and professional challenges gives them the confidence to step into the role of the resilient and profound sage who others seek out for advice and help. Once they can clearly look beyond the material to find something deeper and more meaningful, their destiny is to draw on their rich experience to advise and inspire others with their life wisdom.

Potential: Wise, sophisticated

Dark side: Superficial, changeable

Tarot card, lucky number, days, colors: The Sun, 1, Wednesday, Sunday, indigo, orange

Born today: William Golding (author); Twiggy (model); Jeremy Irons (actor); Jimmy Fallon (comedian)

374

September 20

The Birthday of the Charming Guide

The life lesson:

is looking before you leap.

The way forward: is to understand that calculated, not impulsive, risk-taking is the key to success.

Luck maker: Don't gloss over mistakes; learn from them to increase your chances of success next time.

"Take my hand"

Those born on September 20 are utterly charming and their engaging persona tends to attract those in need of guidance. They are natural leaders, at their happiest when leading others in a well-thought-out project. Their organizational skills are in great demand, but because they can have problems saying "no," they sometimes take on more than they should. They are capable, independent and resourceful, and pride themselves on finding the best way to manage a situation. However, it is how they cope with setbacks or "failures" that is the key to their psychological growth. If they can learn from mistakes and move forward with increased awareness, their potential for success is outstanding, but if they continue repeating the same mistakes, these will block their progress.

Born planners and managers, they have the potential to achieve success in many careers, but are often drawn to art, music, sport, health and leisure, writing, performing arts or social-media influencing. Sales, public relations, promotion, advertising, statistics, research, education, social reform, politics and psychology also appeal. Curious and intelligent, they need to keep their minds and bodies active, because if they are not constantly learning new things they may become despondent. Learning a language and all kinds of moderate aerobic activity, such as brisk walking, are beneficial. **For self-care**, set boundaries and say "no" to the constant draining demands of others.

These people are passionate and nurturing, but tend to be controlling in relationships. Until the age of 31 they often feel a deep need to be popular and admired, and they may try to overpower others with their opinions. After 31 their sense of personal power increases and they can become more self-reliant. During these years, caution and patience are important as they can be impulsive. Although they should never lose their passion and energy, their chances of happiness increase once they learn to take a step back before making a decision. When they learn that the best way to make their innovative contribution to the world is to advise, organize and inspire, their destiny is to lead others to new areas of interest and, more often than not, new heights.

Potential: Intelligent, engaging

Dark side: Controlling, superficial

Tarot card, lucky number, days, colors: Judgment, 2, Wednesday, Monday, blue, silver

Born today: George R. R. Martin (author); Red Auerbach (basketball coach); Sophia Loren, Gary Coleman (actors)

September 21

The Birthday of the Sensation Seeker

"Mystery is the beating heart of life"

September 21-born are fascinated by all things unexplained, mysterious and, sometimes, dark. They have the ability to inject an air of suspense into even the most mundane of occasions. Because they are so imaginative and creative, they are often hungry to learn or experience the unusual or strange. Highly sensual, they seek out new sensations and love to share their discoveries to enlighten others. Their messages are often profound but misinterpreted, and this can make them feel lonely and frustrated. One reason people don't understand them is that they tend to lose themselves in their current obsession, leaving others with no sense of who they are and what they believe. It is therefore extremely important for them to keep a sense of personal identity.

Born lyricists, they are drawn to careers in music, art, filmmaking and the media, as well as technical work such as computing, technology, administration and accounting. Writing, sales, acting, politics, publishing, commerce, counseling and education also appeal. They need to ensure their love of the strange and unusual does not alienate loved ones, and if they find it hard to open up, they can benefit from therapy or counseling. **For self-care,** recalling your dreams and learning to interpret them shows that the real magic starts within.

Witty and fun to be around, these people attract admirers easily, but they can be unpredictable and blow hot and cold in their relationships. Until the age of 31 they gain much self-esteem from others, and they therefore need to trust their own judgment more. They also should ensure that their sensation-seeking impulses do not lead them into dubious activities. After 31 they have opportunities to feel in control of their life. It is vital for their psychological growth that they move from the passenger seat to the driving seat of their lives. Once they are able to discover within themselves the mystery that excites them externally, their attraction to the unconventional gives them the potential to become truly inspired instruments of human progress. Their destiny is to share and develop their original and progressive ideas with others.

Potential: Interesting, progressive

Dark side: Unaware, bizarre

Tarot card, lucky number, days, colors: The World, 3, Wednesday, Thursday, blue, red

Born today: Trent Shelton (speaker); Stephen King, H. G. Wells (authors); Liam Gallagher (singer); Bill Murray (actor)

September 22

The Birthday of the Architect

The life lesson: is learning to relax.

The way forward: is to understand that down time is not wasted time but an opportunity to rest and recharge.

Luck maker: Don't have enemies—they can block your chances of success.

"I was born to create and make a difference"

People born on September 22 are often multitalented, hard-working and intelligent individuals with excellent communication skills and their own eccentric style. They are at their happiest when they are creating, designing or building, and such is their love of challenge that no sooner have they completed one project than they speed to the next. They feel born for an important reason, which explains their restless urge to constantly challenge themselves and push. They often clash with authority and this can limit their chances of success. Learning to compromise and play the game is difficult for them, but necessary.

Born architects, they are suited to careers in design, construction and commerce, but may be drawn to science, technology, computing, public service, research, writing or humanitarian work, the emergency services or the healing or caring professions. Education, sales, promotion, lobbying, public relations, as well as the performing arts, also appeal. They have workaholic tendencies, so they need to ensure they have clear cut-off points to stop working. **For self-care**, carrying a small citrine crystal encourages you to deal with stress, while meditating on the color green and spending more time in nature helps you find a work–life balance.

Work comes first with these people and they don't enjoy socializing. They take a long time to trust others and risk becoming isolated. Until they reach the age of 30 they need harmony in their professional and personal lives, so relationships take center stage. After 30 they gradually become more self-reliant. If they can learn to be more flexible in their thinking, this is when they come into their own. Once they have learned to balance their restlessness and drive with quality time recharging and connecting with their intuition, amazing opportunities for a life of unique and often brilliant creativity come their way. When they can find a balance between their need to create, work and build, and their desire to be a happy human being, their destiny is to make a genuine difference to society by creating progressive structures that others can either learn or benefit from.

Potential: Progressive, creative

Dark side: Workaholic, isolated

Tarot card, lucky number, days, colors: The Fool, 4, Wednesday, Sunday, blue, pink

Born today: Michael Faraday (scientist); Nick Cave, Joan Jett, Andrea Bocelli (singers); Billie Piper (actor)

377

LIBRA

THE SCALES
(SEPTEMBER 23–OCTOBER 22)

❋ **Element:** Air

❋ **Ruling planet:** Venus, the lover

❋ **Tarot card:** Justice (discernment)

❋ **Lucky numbers:** 6, 7

❋ **Favorable colors:** Pink, pale green, soft blue

❋ **Driving force:** Harmony

❋ **Personal statement:** I make decisions that are fair

❋ **Chinese sign counterpart:** The Dog

Peace, justice and harmony are top priorities for a Libran. They strive to create balance in the world around them and sometimes make great personal sacrifices to achieve it. They have the amazing ability to see every side of an argument, and their open-mindedness and appreciation of beauty wins them much respect. However, when forced to make a decision, the chances are they will sit on the fence until the problem goes away by itself, rather than commit themselves to one side or the other.

Personality potential

Charming, cooperative, sociable, idealistic and brilliantly diplomatic, whether they are conventionally attractive or not, Librans often have an air of grace and beauty about them. In arguments they won't typically confront others; their preference is always to play peacemaker or negotiator. They have a deep dislike of hurting other people, and this compassionate side of their personality may make some people think of them as a pushover. This couldn't be further from the truth. They may adapt, adjust and compromise to keep the peace but, underneath, their character is tough. If you push them too far, they will slowly but surely fade out of your life; their withdrawal will be so cleverly subtle that you will barely notice it until it's too late to take things up with them again.

The Libran unwillingness to get off the fence is not because they don't have a point of view, but because they have too much dignity and maturity to ram their viewpoint down everybody else's throats. They truly believe that negotiation is always the answer and that it's always possible to find a compromise between opposing viewpoints so that both sides feel satisfied. Small wonder they make great diplomats, negotiators and mediators, or flourish in any line of work in which their role is to keep the balance or maintain the status quo

Their powers of mediation and negotiation are beyond compare. Tactful and diplomatic, they can smooth everything and everyone down to find balance and a middle ground.

Librans are often blessed with impeccable good taste, possessing the ability to create harmony and bring beauty to any place or situation. They like to see everything looking beautiful and everyone being happy, and will often cast themselves in the role of mediator or peacemaker.

Above all, Librans are ruled by the harmony-loving planet Venus. They strive for balance in all things and much of the secret of their success in life is through their keen eye for moderation in all things. Librans not only have a knack for making life seem simple and fair; they also have a facility for attracting happiness their way.

> "Their powers of mediation and negotiation are beyond compare."

Personality pitfalls

It really is one of the hardest things in the world for a Libran to make a decision or to decide where they stand regarding a particular debate or situation. And it's not just the big decisions that Librans struggle with—it can be any decision. Afraid of limiting their options, their mind keeps changing this way and that, resulting in indecisiveness and inaction. What they don't realize is that, ironically, not making their mind up is the very reason they lose those opportunities and limit their choices.

Librans are at their happiest and their best when in a close, loving relationship, and if this is denied, they suffer more than any other sign of the zodiac. Dependency is another issue for them, because their need to be in a relationship can sometimes be so strong that they make too many compromises. Complete happiness for them means sharing their lives, but until they can learn to be happy and fulfilled by their own company, the completeness they seek in a relationship will remain elusive.

Laziness and self-indulgence are two negative character traits associated with this sign; the more they refuse to step out of their comfort zone and take a risk by making a decision, the more they are likely to slip into laziness. For such a peace-loving sign, it's surprising that they can sometimes be rather selfish and self-absorbed; if need be, they are also capable of manipulating the truth and the facts to get what they want.

Symbol

Libra is the only sign in the zodiac that has a symbol that is an inanimate object. This isn't to say that Librans are emotionally cold, but they do have a remarkable ability to cast aside their own feelings, see every side of the argument and strive for balance in all things—hence the symbol of the scales, which represent justice in life. The Libran journey is a constant search for peace, balance and harmony, not just for themselves but for everyone.

Darkest secret

They may often look calm and collected and as if they are able to cope with just about anything, but the Achilles' heel of any Libran is their fear of being abandoned and alone. They will therefore often rely on the approval of others for a sense of self-worth. Intelligent and gullible, easy-going and petulant, cautious and reckless, Librans will tip their behavior one way and then another to get the attention, approval and companionship they crave.

Love

Librans rarely have problems attracting partners or friends, and are usually popular. Generous by nature, they love to share and are also excellent listeners. Their talent for friendship means they often have friends from all walks of life, but, as generous and warm-hearted as they are, they can sometimes lack one thing: a sense of humor.

When it comes to affairs of the heart, Librans only feel truly fulfilled when they are in a rewarding relationship. Their usual indecision does not always express itself in their relationships; they can be impulsive and romantic and know exactly who they want to invite into their lives. Curiously, in a close relationship they may be quick to provoke arguments, which is surprising given their love of peace. All this is designed to test their partner's affections and it is a dangerous strategy that can sometimes backfire.

Love for a Libran is a beautiful experience and one that gives their lives true meaning and fulfillment. They can be in love with the idea of love, but, as long as they don't allow their high expectations of others to tip into intolerance and impatience, and avoid any co-dependent tendencies, a match with a peaceful Libran can be a match made in heaven.

Love matches:
Gemini, Leo
Aquarius
and
Sagittarius.

The Libran woman

The typical Libran woman—if there is such a creature, as she is so multifaceted—is often very seductive. She loves luxurious clothes and perfumes, and in many cases is very aware of her good looks. But with all her sweet grace there is plenty of the masculine about her. You're unlikely to see the tougher side of her personality when you first get to know her, but in time it will be impossible for her to hide forever her sharp mind and self-sufficient spirit. This soft but strong woman is perhaps one of the most capable women of the zodiac. She can cope with just about anything and is more than a match for any man or woman.

Above all, the Libran woman is fair, and her commitment to finding a solution that is agreeable to everyone makes her invaluable during challenging and uncertain times. Indeed, she will often come into her own during crises and be the one who keeps everything from collapsing. She loves to talk and discuss everyone and everything, but won't ever believe that her opinion is the correct or only one—she has too much respect for the opinions of others. And when she is in a close relationship, she will typically insist on contributing her fair share both emotionally and financially. She's an amazing combination of sweetness and strength, fragility and toughness, and, whenever she walks into a person's life or heart, the chances are high that they won't ever want her to leave.

The Libran man

A Libran man can give advice and answers for just about everything. His logical, intelligent arguments never fail to impress, and his charm and smile are heart-melting. On the face of it this man seems perfect, but there are also times when his indecision becomes massively frustrating. Making up his mind is tough for him, and even when he does appear to make a decision, he may change it immediately afterward and then change it again after that. All this can drive his friends and loved ones to distraction, but such is his power that when they try to confront him with his inconsistencies, he wins them over with his genuine regret and beautiful words.

When it comes to romance the Libran man comes into his own. He could write books about romance and the art of seduction. He'll use his easy charm and charisma to win over even the most resistant of potential partners. Then, when he

has won them over, he may not be sure what to do and there may be a lengthy decision period during which he weighs up his options. When he finally decides to commit, he will be a devoted, passionate and loving partner, but since the art of romance comes so easily to him, he will always remain a flirt. His partner just has to learn to live with this, as asking a Libran man not to flirt is like telling him not to breathe. Even if he is happily married, he will always be a lover of gathering possibilities, despite knowing he won't ever act on them.

Friendship and love can often get extremely confused for Libran men. They frequently have many friends of the opposite sex because they are so good at understanding what women think and feel. Fortunately, the Libran male loves harmony, so he is unlikely to stray if his current relationship gives him what he needs—intelligent conversation, loyal companionship and plenty of loving affection.

Family

Libran children are often charming and lovable, but parents should keep their eyes open for any tendency toward laziness and procrastination, because this will hold them back later in life. The greatest thing a parent can do with a Libran child is encourage them to be decisive and, when faced with a decision, find the courage to make their mind up. Parents should also help them understand that if they do make the wrong decision, it's not a tragedy or a character flaw but a learning experience. No mistake is ever a mistake if you learn from it. Above all, Libran children need to find the confidence to think and make decisions for themselves.

Librans tend to enjoy their schooldays as long as they feel they are being fairly treated by their teachers and their friends. Logical and analytical, they may lean toward mathematics and science, but they also have great creative and artistic potential, and encouraging this early in life will help them trust and believe in it later on. Parents need to be especially careful that their Libran child does not try to talk them into spoiling them. They need to set firm boundaries because, when a Libran child knows what they can or cannot do, arguments are less likely and they can avoid the discord that upsets Librans so much.

Libran parents are typically gentle and loving, but their tendency to dither over important decisions concerning their child's upbringing—for example, their choice of school—may be detrimental. In addition, their tendency to hesitate when facing less important decisions, such as what to have for lunch, can infuriate their child. They also need to make sure they don't settle for the easiest option and the path of least resistance when parenting. Tough love won't come easily to them, but sometimes tough love is an essential ingredient for good parenting.

Career

Librans love to be surrounded by comfort, so they will often go into careers that give them the kind of money that can finance a luxurious lifestyle. Any profession that calls for diplomacy, negotiation and tact will suit them, and the fashion, beauty and cosmetics industries will also appeal. They are ambitious and hate being ordered about, so they often aspire to be in charge or to run their own businesses. They may not, however, be suited to top jobs where they have to work in isolation, as they work better when surrounded by a team of people. They also thrive in an organized, neat and tidy working environment.

Other occupations that may suit them include the legal professions, diplomacy, management consultancy, civil rights campaigning, banking, publicity, veterinary science, counseling, teaching or any kind of partnership. The Libran love of aesthetics may also point toward a career as a graphic artist, image consultant, artist or art dealer or anything involving music. Whatever career they choose, **they can be a hard-working and highly valued force for harmony and justice in their workplace**.

> **They can be a hard-working and highly valued force for harmony and justice in their workplace.**

Health and wellbeing

Librans are ruled by the planet Venus and this gives them a taste for all the good things in life. They would feel much fitter eating a healthy, balanced diet rich in simple, nutritious foods, such as whole grains, fruits and vegetables. They would also benefit from cooking their meals from scratch and from chewing their food slowly to boost their digestive health. The hips and kidneys are linked to the sign Libra, so they need to eat plenty of fiber to prevent constipation and bloating.

The classic Libran indecisiveness can make them prone to tension headaches and migraines, so learning to relax and unwind—and how to make decisions—is crucial for their peace of mind as well as their health and wellbeing. Quiet time spent alone will help them get in touch with their feelings and figure out where they think their life should be heading, but if headaches and other symptoms of stress persist, they should visit their doctor.

Looking good matters greatly to people born under this sun sign, and if they drink and/or smoke they need to question why they indulge in activities that damage their health as well as their looks. Although they may have exercised when they were at school, once they leave school or college, they may ease or completely give up on physical activity. When this sedentary lifestyle is coupled with their love of good food and wine it can lead to weight gain. It's important therefore for Librans

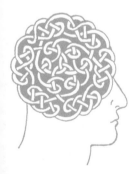

to increase their activity levels to help them lose weight and reduce the increased risk of heart disease and diabetes associated with weight gain, especially around the middle. Regular exercise is important, especially long walks in the fresh air during which they can organize their thoughts.

Retirement can be a challenge for most Librans, as the working life is so rewarding for them. It's therefore vital for them to ensure they have plenty of hobbies and interests outside work, so that they aren't completely defined by their job. Learning techniques taught by cognitive therapy will help them challenge any tendency toward negative thinking. **Yellow** is the color of optimism and self-confidence, and meditating on it will encourage them to have more faith in making their own decisions.

Born between September 23 and October 3

Librans born between these dates have all the sensuous qualities of Venus enriching their lives. They tend to be beautiful, artistic, caring and full of generosity and warmth. They are never short of admirers—indeed, they sometimes may have too many to cope with.

Born between October 4 and 13

There is a touch of the lovable eccentric about these Librans. They are often spontaneous and fun, and anyone who knows them needs to expect the unexpected from them.

Born between October 14 and 22

These people often have a sprightly and youthful approach to life, and are forever on the hunt for new knowledge and information. Their inquisitive minds make them the eternal students of the zodiac and they never tire of learning something they didn't know before.

Life lessons

Librans are quick to grasp ideas and possess an innate creativity that yearns to express itself in producing works of art o unusual or original things. Unfortunately, their indecisiveness can limit the expression of this creativity, so it's important that they try to incorporate their creativity into their lives because, if they do, they will be richly rewarded.

Justice and equality matter for Librans, but partnerships and friendships matter more to them. This makes them delightful hosts—as well as social butterflies—and they are rarely without a lover, but it can also make being on their own extremely hard for them, even if it's only for a few hours. This stands as one of the greatest challenges in their lives. To find true happiness and fulfillment they need to learn to stop looking to other people for completeness. Although Librans are right in assuming that companionship and team efforts are incredibly rewarding, they are wrong in concluding that time spent alone is time wasted or that if their efforts are not being acknowledged and praised by others, they are not worth doing. A social-media detox now and again is strongly advised for this sun sign.

Librans first of all need to learn to be happy and after that they should learn that they don't have to rely on the support of others—they are complete as themselves. Furthermore, the approval of others is fickle and not to be relied on. The truth is that the only person they can count on and need approval from is themselves.

Indecisiveness and a relaxed relationship with the truth are key areas Librans need to work on. They have a tendency to bend and twist to please people or suit the opinions or needs of others, and will sometimes resort to manipulation just to keep things running smoothly. In the end, this always back-fires on them and the vital balance they were trying so hard to achieve is upset. If only Librans would learn that it's impos-sible to make everyone happy all of the time and be liked by everyone. Sometimes it's important to take a stand and risk being disliked because of that stand.

Fellow Librans can delight but more likely frustrate each other with their search for balance and justice in all things. Fortunately, Librans can look to the other signs of the zodiac for more help and inspiration. Taureans can show them the importance of self-care, Virgos and Capricorns can encour-age them to stop second-guessing themselves all the time. Arians can also teach them to be bolder with their decision-making and to place less importance on the opinions of others. Cancerians, Pisceans and Scorpios can inspire them to notice and listen to their feelings, even when these feelings are dark and uncomfortable, while Aquarians and Geminis can help them express their creativity and stick to their viewpoint with courage. And Leos and Sagittarians can teach them not to be afraid of striking out alone, but to enjoy the rewards that going solo offers.

Chinese astrology counterpart: The Dog

The Chinese Dog and Western Libra are both sociable signs. They make the most devoted and loyal companions and don't tend to thrive in solitude. They are talented team players and their path to success often lies in their ability to network, negotiate or work in a team or a partnership.

Justice and fairness matter greatly to them. They will tirelessly champion the underdog and those who can't take care of themselves. Peace-loving in their quest for fairness, when challenged they make formidable opponents. They are typically honest and upbeat in their approach to relationships, work and life, and always look for the simplest and most efficient solution to solve problems. Their concern is also for the well-being of everyone involved and they are the ones others tend to seek out for objectivity and the best advice. Observant with a strong moral code, they can be prone to bouts of indecision and stubbornness at times, but their beautiful charm ensures these people are typically highly popular.

Note: Librans have an affinity with Dog-sign characteristics, but be sure to check which Chinese sign corresponds to your **year** of birth (see page xxi), and to read about the characteristics associated with it, too.

September 23

The Birthday of the Unassuming Warrior

The life lesson:

is communicating the strength of your convictions.

The way forward: is to understand that abandoning your beliefs if they might create conflict is counterproductive because it causes inner conflict.

Luck maker: Be creative with the rules—you don't always start at the beginning or follow the correct process; you use the rules creatively.

"Do what is right, not what is easy"

Those born on September 23 are charming, polite and often unassuming, with an appreciation of what is refined and elegant, yet underneath they are resilient, reliable and have great integrity. They may appear quiet but from early in life they may have faced and overcome challenges, and gained personal strength from this. Many will be unaware of how evolved they are and may underplay their talents; their genuine concern for others may encourage some to take advantage. They approach life with almost child-like simplicity, and if something captivates their attention, their enthusiasm can become infectious. However, if they don't feel enthusiasm, they are honest and direct, as they can't fake it. The key to their happiness is to find a vocation, lifestyle or relationship that genuinely interests and inspires them.

Born musicians, these people may share their eye for beauty as an artist, musician, writer, designer or filmmaker. Other career choices include accounting, finance, education, journalism, the law, law enforcement, civil service, medicine, the healing professions and charity work. They are generally athletic but their lack of competitiveness may prevent them from collecting trophies. They need to steer clear of alcohol, nicotine and other addictive substances. **For self-care**, mind–body therapies, such as meditation and yoga, and mind-control programs such as cognitive therapy or hypnotherapy, help them reframe negative perceptions and become more assertive.

It is not easy to get close to these people, but in a committed relationship, they are likely to be loyal. Before the age of 30 they are concerned with relationship issues, but after 30 they reach a turning point, highlighting emotional maturity and joint finances. After 60 they may become more adventurous. Once they figure out what makes their heart sing, they have the inquisitiveness, determination and fighting spirit to realize their personal and professional goals and command the respect of all those they come into contact with. When they finally find their voice and stop underselling themselves, their destiny is to share with and inspire others with their truly rare blend of creativity, dedication, integrity and dependability.

Potential: Charming, honest

Dark side: Unassertive, unmotivated

Tarot card, lucky number, days, colors: The Hierophant, 5, Friday, Wednesday, sky blue, lavender

Born today: Mickey Rooney (actor); Bruce Springsteen, Ray Charles (singers); Victoria Woodhull (activist)

September 24

The Birthday of the Restless Humanitarian

"Things are calling me away"

September 24-born are often tough to pin down because they are travelers at heart. If their restlessness doesn't manifest externally it will manifest internally; they are travelers in their minds, constantly reading and thinking. Their desire to seek out the new is a dominant theme, alongside their deep need to love and feel loved and a powerful urge to help others. Considerate and empathetic, they have the almost psychic ability to detect unhappiness in others, even if that unhappiness is unspoken. Despite their concern for the wellbeing of others, they often find it hard to commit to routine. A part of them longs to feel secure, but another part wonders whether the grass is greener on the other side. As a result, they vacillate a great deal. The key to their psychological growth is being able not only to choose goals that inspire them, but to stay with them.

Born networkers, they are drawn to social, political, philosophical or humanitarian causes, but may also excel in artistic endeavors. Events organization, diplomacy, networking, fundraising, the law, social reform, writing, drama, music, photography, social-media influencing or broadcasting may appeal. When bored, instead of comfort eating, they need to find healthier ways to satisfy their "hunger," such as phoning a friend, writing in a journal or exercising. Counseling or therapy may help them understand their fear of commitment. **For self-care**, finding a creative outlet for your imagination, such as art, writing or dancing is extremely therapeutic, and meditating on the color gold encourages you to persevere with your dreams.

Although those born on this day are much sought after, they often have a fear of commitment and intimacy. Before the age of 28 they experiment in their social life, forming relationships with people from many different backgrounds. They may also experience career changes or professional uncertainty. After 28 there is a strong desire to find deeper meaning. When they learn that discipline, perseverance and commitment can be liberating rather than restrictive, these multitalented, warm-hearted people discover the potential for tremendous power, which can both move and inspire others. Their destiny is to realize their progressive and humanitarian ideals with action rather than just words.

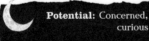

Potential: Concerned, curious

Dark side: Unfocused, detached

Tarot card, lucky number, day, colors: The Lovers, 6, Friday, pink, blue

Born today: F. Scott Fitzgerald (author); Howard Florey (pathologist); Jim Henson (puppeteer)

September  25

The Birthday of Complexity

"I rise above"

People born on September 25 are among the most complex individuals of the year. Deeply empathetic and compassionate, they are also fiercely independent and critical. Engaging and involved but also, in their minds, separate, they can see the bigger picture. They often have a black-and-white approach to everything, yet equally long to live in a world of color. Professional success is often theirs, because they work hard to achieve it, and expect others to do the same, becoming resentful of those who seem to attain success without deserving it. It is important that they learn to manage their tendency to criticize, because their sharp tongues can wound others deeply.

Born journalists, campaigners and broadcasters, they present the cold, hard facts. They may be drawn to the arts, politics, advertising, publishing, museums, antiques, the healing and caring professions and education. Highly sensual, their appetite for physical pleasure is strong. They won't relish a regular exercise program, but undertaking one boosts their mood and manages their energy levels. **For self-care**, spending time in nature and meditating on the color green encourages you to balance conflicting aspects of your personality.

Once these people can value others for who they are and not for who they want them to be, they are warm and loyal companions. Until the age of 27 they focus on their social skills and creative talents, and there are opportunities for financial success. After 27 their emphasis shifts to personal transformation. The older they get, the more adventurous and freedom-loving they become. Behind their soberness these people possess an amazing imagination, dynamic creativity and an ability to stand out from the crowd. The key to their psychological growth is to embrace their wonderful complexity. When they learn to trust their intuition and think universally, they have the potential to be among the most progressive and visionary individuals of the year. Once they can be as honest with themselves as they are with others, their destiny is to evolve personally and, by so doing, point the way toward progress.

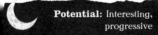

Potential: Interesting, progressive

Dark side: Critical, resentful

Tarot card, lucky number, days, colors: The Chariot, 7, Friday, Monday, lavender, sea green

Born today: William Faulkner (author); Michael Douglas, Mark Hamill, Will Smith, Catherine Zeta-Jones (actors)

September 26

The Birthday of the Perfection Seeker

"Lead into gold"

Those born on September 26 are among the most disciplined, determined and perfectionist souls of the year. Nothing short of excellence from everyone is their expectation and they try, learn and practice until they excel. Their career is of supreme importance and their dedication often takes them to the top. They typically take on far too much, but cope because they thrive under pressure, earning admiration when they achieve the impossible. The downside is that their absorption in work can become damaging to their psychological growth because it makes them ignore their emotional needs and those of their loved ones.

Born academics, they are attracted to science, research, psychology or academia, but the arts—in particular drama, literature, media and music—also appeal to their creativity. Other options include sports, sales, public relations, catering and corporate business, while their desire to improve and mold others may draw them to teaching, charity work and social reform. Prone to stress-related disorders, they need to lower their expectations and stop beating themselves up when they make mistakes. Relaxing and taking regular vacations is essential, as is spending time with loved ones and cultivating an interest outside work. **For self-care,** chamomile tea is good for easing stress at the end of a busy day, as is relaxing in a rose oil aromatherapy bath.

Although these people are attractive and popular, their intensity may cause power struggles in their close relationships. Before the age of 26 finance takes center stage, but they also have opportunities to develop strong relationships with others, which helps them keep a much-needed sense of perspective. After 26 the focus shifts and they are likely to become committed to their careers. During these years their potential for success is outstanding. These remarkable people are driven, focused and occasionally bossy, and when they are able to moderate their obsession with work, their superior concentration and drive yield results that can benefit others considerably. Once they have learned that perfection is neither desirable nor attainable, their destiny is to help and inspire others by exemplifying the self-discipline they need to achieve greatness.

Potential: Influential, disciplined

Dark side: Perfectionist, workaholic

Tarot card, lucky number, days, colors: Strength, 8, Friday, Saturday, lavender, burgundy

Born today: Francis of Assisi (saint); Serena Williams (tennis player); T. S. Eliot (poet); George Gershwin (composer)

September 27

The Birthday of the Enigma

"Forget me not"

September 27-born don't often recognize it, but they leave a lasting and positive impression on everyone they meet. This is because they are sensitive to the feelings of others and like to bring harmony to any situation. However, underneath their pleasant calm persona they are often riddled with hidden fears and this contradiction makes them an enigma. Learning to develop faith in their considerable abilities is crucial. They are far deeper and more complex than anyone realizes. They set incredibly high standards for themselves—failure simply isn't an option—and career success takes priority in their lives. While they believe that professional success is their only option for happiness, fulfillment remains elusive.

Born freelancers, they may be drawn toward lobbying or work in politics and social reform, or freelance technical or design projects, that can enhance or benefit others. Other possible careers include the arts, management, self-employment, entertainment, education, science, writing, music, and the health and caring professions. Regular exercise is highly recommended to help manage weight and boost mood and immunity. **For self-care**, cognitive therapy and hypnotherapy techniques can help you challenge negative thinking.

Although these people are charismatic and exciting, when it comes to affairs of the heart they lack confidence and need to fall in love with themselves first. Before the age of 26, carving out career success takes center stage. After 26 emotional change and transformation come to the fore; this is when they need to notice the way their career choice and interactions with colleagues shape their character. When they learn that hidden feelings and insecurities lead them to a fuller awareness of their potential, there is nothing these multitalented and highly creative individuals cannot achieve. Once they learn to believe in themselves and realize that to be human is to be complex, their destiny is to point the way toward progress in the most enigmatic or unforeseen ways.

Potential: Charismatic, compassionate

Dark side: Insecure, conflicted

Tarot card, lucky number, days, colors: The Hermit, 9, Friday, Tuesday, lavender, red

Born today: Gwyneth Paltrow (actor); Anand Giridharadas (author); Avril Lavigne (singer); Samuel Adams (revolutionary)

September 28

The Birthday of Seduction

"What does the heart say?"

The life lesson:

is to tolerate boredom.

The way forward: is to understand that boredom is not always something to avoid, because the need for constant stimulation can also hold back personal development.

Luck maker: Stop making excuses—inaction and procrastination are the enemies of luck, so you should start doing the things you have always wanted to, now.

People born on September 28 are seductive. Whether they are attractive or not, they have the ability to wrap almost anyone around their little finger. Many of them seek and find fulfillment through the pursuit of love, peace and beauty. They are also highly imaginative and sensitive, with a strong desire to bring harmony. However, they run the risk of believing that their ability to seduce others is enough to bring them good fortune. They should understand that, in order to succeed, they need discipline, insight and hard work. They should respond to any opportunities to back up their charm with substance, and if they can move away from complacency toward hard work, they have huge potential for success.

Born opera singers, they flourish in careers where they can indulge their passions and inspire others, such as writing, art, acting, music, social-media influencing, design, fashion and sports. Other work choices include advertising, broadcasting, publishing, promotions, marketing, the leisure and beauty industries and public relations. Physical appearance is important to them, and if they drink and smoke, they need to question why they are damaging their looks as well as their health. **For self-care**, wearing, meditating on and surrounding yourself with cooling shades of blue helps you feel more in control of your emotions and your life.

These people are master flirts and never short of admirers, but they can be manipulative and flighty in relationships. Until the age of 24 relationships take center stage but after 24 their emphasis is personal growth. They have the ability to charm anyone, but the key to their success and happiness is not their seductive warmth but their willpower. When they take charge and steer their energies in a clear direction, not only can they continue to seduce everyone who crosses their path, but they are also able to realize their dreams of beauty and harmony. Once they learn to manage their emotions rather than allow their emotions to manage them, and get into the driving seat of their lives, their destiny is to entertain and inspire others with their unique aspirations.

Potential: Magnetic, sensual

Dark side: Manipulative, lazy

Tarot card, lucky number, days, colors: The Magician, 1, Friday, Sunday, pink, orange

Born today: Glenn Lowry (art historian); Confucius (philosopher); Brigitte Bardot, Hilary Duff (actors)

September 29

The Birthday of the Maverick

"I'm on the edge"

Those born on September 29 are mavericks at heart. At every opportunity they question authority and convention, and they are not afraid to spark a rebellion. Life is never dull when these live-wires are around. They are rebellious, not because they lack discipline or self-control but because, despite their intelligence and talents, they are unpredictable. This is often due to self-esteem issues or a feeling of not belonging, which can make them swing between extroversion and introversion with confusing speed. Learning not to take things so personally and cultivating an attitude of positive expectancy helps them deal with feelings of rejection and bouts of negativity.

Born dramatists, they are attracted to creative or artistic careers, such as art, design, acting, writing, music, dance and painting. Other choices include technology, social reform, social media, entertainment, business, self-employment, education, teaching and lecturing. Regular exercise is something they enjoy and should be part of their daily routine to boost mood and wellbeing. **For self-care**, meditation or quiet time to think helps you get in touch with your feelings and figure out where you want your life to go. Meditating on the color purple can encourage you to celebrate your brilliant uniqueness.

The constant need of those born on this day to challenge, question and stand out can frustrate those close to them. Until the age of 23 their priority is relationships, and during these years their incessant need to be at the cutting edge of things may earn them more enemies than friends. Their desire to be of service to others can make them subordinate their personal needs and they must strive for greater balance. After 23 they reach a turning point and focus on emotional growth, which highlights the fact that, even though they can work productively with others, they are not team players. The sooner they celebrate their uniqueness as a strength rather than a weakness and learn to listen to their intuition, the sooner they can realize their remarkable potential for success. Armed with self-confidence, their destiny is to inject a sense of possibility and excitement everywhere they go.

Potential: Exciting, courageous

Dark side: Insecure, disruptive

Tarot card, lucky number, days, colors: The High Priestess, 2, Friday, Monday, pink, silver

Born today: Enrico Fermi (physicist); Horatio Nelson (admiral); Michelle Bachelet (Chilean president); Miguel de Cervantes (author)

September 30

The Birthday of Revelation

The life lesson:

is accepting that you might be wrong.

The way forward: is to understand that without an awareness of your own fallibility, you can never uncover the real truth.

Luck maker: When you open your mind and believe that what may appear impossible really is possible, you open the door to luck.

"Justice is conscience"

September 30-born are often intense, with a desire to champion or reveal the truth. They have an uncanny ability for identifying rights and wrongs and suggesting progressive changes to bring about improvement. They are driven by their conscience and an urge to reveal injustice or unfairness in any form, and because they understand that baring the truth can expose them, they create a tough persona. This persona inspires both respect—because of their star power—and fear, because of their eagerness to expose those who do not live up to their high standards, and they can easily become judgmental and critical.

Born arbitrators, they are suited to careers in the law, law enforcement, politics, analysis, accounting and social and humanitarian causes, but they may also have a natural affinity for the arts and provide inspiration through writing, music, painting or song. Other careers that may appeal include medicine, health and personal transformation, publishing, journalism, education, and the healing and caring industries. These people's love of food and drink may lead to a sedentary lifestyle and they need to ensure they take plenty of exercise. **For self-care**, rose or jasmine essential oils are beneficial if you feel lethargic, and meditating on and surrounding yourself with the color orange encourages you to be warmer and more accepting.

Those born on this day demand absolute openness from the people in their lives and need to offer the same in return. After the age of 23 emotional transformation and growth become priorities, but their challenge is to express as much interest in discovering the truth in their own lives as they do in others'. When they can be honest about their own vulnerabilities, they can move beyond self-righteousness to greater tolerance of human weaknesses. And when their tolerance is combined with their remarkable courage and resourcefulness, not only can they ensure that justice is done, but they can also discover their ability to motivate others to work alongside them to create progressive solutions for a fairer and better world. Their destiny is to be a truly dynamic force for progress, justice and much-needed reform.

Potential: Fair, influential

Dark side: Self-righteous, critical

Tarot card, lucky number, days, colors: The Empress, 3, Friday, Thursday, blue, royal blue, purple

Born today: Buddy Rich (musician); Elie Wiesel (author); Marion Cotillard (actor); Rumi (poet)

October 1

The Birthday of Unusual Capability

The life lesson:

is mastering the art of delegation.

The way forward: is to empower others and understand that trying to do everything makes you lose sight of the bigger picture, limiting your potential for success.

Luck maker: Resist the urge to qualify and apologize when someone congratulates you—say "thank you" and own your accomplishments.

"Every journey begins with a single step"

People born on October 1 are sharp and remarkably capable individuals. There is usually something distinctive about them that makes them stand out. They aim high and set lofty standards for themselves, and their strength is their capability and utter dedication to a purpose or goal. At first glance, they can appear stern, but to those who know them well they are open-hearted. Their cool front is a form of defense to help protect them and keep them on track when setbacks threaten to derail them. They often rise to the top, but sadly some find that it isn't as rewarding as they had hoped.

Born supervisors, they have a strong affinity with the scientific, engineering, building and technical professions, but may also be drawn toward politics and social reform or art, music, drama and dance. Business, the law, financial advice and education can also appeal. Prone to stress and anxiety because they tend to do too much, these people should avoid alcohol and other addictive substances and take time out to unwind. **For self-care,** you can release pent-up energy through regular exercise, while doing yoga and regular stretching exercises can encourage you to be more flexible in body, mind and heart.

Those born on this day can take a while to open up in their relationships, but they can be incredibly loyal and loving. Before the age of 21 they concentrate on relationships and social skills, but after 21 personal growth becomes more important. It is crucial they don't take themselves and their careers too seriously, and that they keep a sense of perspective. As long as they don't isolate themselves, with their perfectionist tendencies they can not only make a positive contribution to the world by transforming potential into efficient and progressive systems, but they can also discover within themselves a large capacity for real happiness. Once they have learned to nurture themselves and to balance their professional and personal life, their destiny is to effect positive change, leaving behind a legacy that lasts, benefiting and inspiring their loved ones and the wider community.

Potential: Dedicated, original

Dark side: Obsessive, aloof

Tarot card, lucky numbers, days, colors: The Magician, 1, 2, Friday, Sunday, purple, orange

Born today: William Boeing (industrialist); Julie Andrews, Brie Larson (actors); Jimmy Carter (US president)

October 2

The Birthday of the Graceful Conversationalist

"Everything starts with an idea"

Those born on October 2 tend to talk, think and act quickly and decisively, and the graceful ease and certainty with which they go about their lives endow them with tremendous potential. They let people know exactly where they stand, but what impresses others most is that they are compelling conversationalists with considerable knowledge on a wide variety of subjects. Although they enjoy talking, they also understand the importance of listening and are always hungry for new information and ideas. In fact, they tend to be more at home in the world of ideas and words than of feelings and emotions. Although their inquisitive and candid approach is refreshing, they can sometimes come across as unfeeling. They need to express disagreement in ways that are not overly negative or confrontational.

Born mediators, they may be drawn to careers in public relations, the media, social work and reform. They may also excel as teachers, psychologists and counselors, artists or designers, or in sales, advertising, life-coaching, sports training, negotiation or arbitration. Although they keep their minds very active with study, travel and conversation, they neglect their bodies and need to incorporate activity into their daily lives. **For self-care**, spending more time in nature helps connect you to your feelings, and meditating on and surrounding yourself with the color orange encourages you to be spontaneous and warm.

These people can be extremely sociable on a superficial level but need to feel secure in a relationship to reveal their true feelings. At the age of 20, they have an ever-growing drive toward personal growth and transformation. In the years that follow they are likely to become more committed and decisive, and need to be more sensitive to the feelings of others. When they lean toward the positive rather than the negative, and can encourage rather than discourage others with their sharp insights, these charming conversationalists have the potential not just to entertain and enlighten, but to enlist and direct others' support. Their destiny is to encourage people to express themselves and their beliefs honestly, clearly and with conviction.

Potential: Interesting, insightful

Dark side: Cutting, unfeeling

Tarot card, lucky numbers, days, colors: The High Priestess, 2, 3, Friday, Monday, pink, white

Born today: Mahatma Gandhi (activist); Groucho Marx (comedian); Graham Greene (author); Annie Leibovitz (photographer)

October 3

The Birthday of the Cutting Edge

"All shiny and new"

October 3-born thrive on the brand-new, the innovative and the original. They are eager to explore the latest fashions, ideas, causes and technologies and even to set the trends as well. They are enthusiastic and visionary, so are always right at the cutting edge. Often well-presented, they love to look the part, typically adding their own unique twist to new trends. They have a strong (sometimes perfectionist) drive to be one step ahead of everyone else, leading the way for others to follow. They feel comfortable in the limelight and their greatest fear is to be ignored or, worse still, left out. Fortunately, with their originality and charisma, this rarely occurs. Although they can be the life and soul of their set, a part of them is reluctant to reveal their true feelings. They need to listen carefully to what their emotions are telling them, because they tend to gravitate toward superficiality and materialism, neither of which brings lasting happiness.

Born innovators, they have the potential to be remarkable scientists, engineers, artists, researchers, speakers, healers or pioneering figures for humanitarian change in politics and social reform. Commerce, advertising, sales, the law, education and catering, as well as the performing arts, theater, fashion, online influencing or the film and music industries, may also appeal. Always in demand, they need to focus on quality rather than quantity in their social life. **For self-care**, interpreting your dreams and wearing, meditating on and surrounding yourself with the color purple encourages you to focus on your personal growth and development.

These people can be loving and giving but need to ensure they make strong rather than superficial connections. From the age of 20 onward they have opportunities to find deeper meaning in their lives. When they realize that their emotional development matters far more than being seen, their originality can take them to the only cutting edge where true happiness and success are found: personal fulfillment. Once they discover that the greatest treasure lies within, their destiny is to sense the future and be ground-breaking pioneers.

Potential: Original, exciting

Dark side: Superficial, materialistic

Tarot card, lucky numbers, days, colors: The Empress, 3, 4, Friday, Monday, pink, silver

Born today: Timothy Thomas Fortune, Al Sharpton (activists); James Herriot (veterinarian); Gwen Stefani (singer)

October 4

The Birthday of Edgy Congeniality

"Great heights can be achieved with the pursuit of harmony"

The life lesson: is overcoming complacency.

The way forward: is to understand that until you start testing yourself, you won't learn what makes you happy.

Luck maker: Your confidence and happiness can increase significantly when you set targets and a timetable in which to achieve them.

People born on October 4 love harmony and are among the most popular people of the year. They are deliciously sensual and love to surround themselves with pleasant people and beautiful things. Whatever the situation, they generally come across as elegant and calm because of their nonconfrontational personality and their gift for smoothly getting along with anybody. This doesn't mean they don't have strong opinions—they can be passionate and often have edgy opinions, but prefer to present their ideals with humor, humility and tact, believing that this is more likely to get people on their side. They are also incredibly astute, and know what is worth arguing and fighting for and what is not.

Born counselors, they are attracted to the helping and caring careers such as social work, medicine, the law, engineering, education, therapy or science. Their well-developed visual sense may draw them toward image-making, photography, the media, graphics and design, and their creativity and idealism to the arts, writing and performance. Prone to pleasure-seeking, they should not lose themselves in indulgence and superficiality; if they do, they can succumb to stress and depression. **For self-care**, brisk walking is particularly beneficial, as it gives you time alone to reflect on where your life is heading. Wearing red encourages you to be more assertive.

Popular, tactile and affectionate, those born on this day should stand up for themselves more and understand that conflict does not always destroy relationships—it can sometimes help keep them alive. After the age of 19 they develop a growing need for personal transformation alongside their desire for a life of pleasure and harmony. However, they also find themselves either inexplicably drawn to danger or facing many challenges. Responding with courage and resilience is key to their success and happiness. If they can discover a fighting spirit, these peace-loving but erotic people find not only that they remain popular but that others look to them for guidance and inspiration for creating harmony. Once they become more assertive and set themselves clear targets, their destiny is to make the world a more beautiful place by their presence in it.

Potential: Agreeable, elegant

Dark side: Superficial, complacent

Tarot card, lucky numbers, days, colors: The Emperor, 4, 5, Friday, Sunday, lavender, silver

Born today: Charlton Heston, Susan Sarandon (actors); Amika George (activist); Anne Rice (author)

October 5

The Birthday of Dignified Altruism

The life lesson:

is keeping a sense of perspective.

The way forward: is to understand that getting carried away in your devotion to a cause is counter-productive.

Luck maker: Keep your cool when things are not going well so that others see you as a force to be reckoned with.

"Together we have the power to imagine and do better"

Those born on October 5 tend to put others or the cause they are promoting first and themselves second. They can't do enough to help, and so powerful is their conviction that others often follow their example to do good deeds. They have a well-developed sense of fair play and are concerned for the less fortunate. As a result, they often come across as unusually dignified and altruistic souls. Their willingness to take action earns them respect and loyalty. However, they can lose perspective and get so wrapped up in their own righteousness that they can become angry and intolerant.

Born humanitarians, they make successful social campaigners, politicians, activists, lobbyists and charity workers, and excel in careers in which they can dedicate themselves to a vocation, such as acting, dance, art, music, spiritual growth, sport, education, the healing and caring professions, the performing arts or writing. They must not sacrifice their emotional and physical health for others, because until they can look after themselves properly, they cannot help others effectively. **For self-care**, carrying around a malachite crystal brings emotional calm, and wearing the color green encourages you to keep a sense of balance and perspective.

Those born on this day are sensual and warm companions, but their devotion to good deeds can make the people in their lives feel undervalued. After the age of 19 they have a growing need for personal growth and many opportunities to make their mark. If they are serious about being instruments of progress, they must learn to keep their cool, listen to others and not get carried away with their own power. After 49 they focus on expanding their mind through study and travel. Whatever age they are, these people are always shining examples of dedication to fairness and putting others first. And once they learn to direct their altruism, and set themselves clear boundaries and goals, they have the potential to become leading figures in humanitarian, spiritual or social reform. Their destiny is to expose injustices and devote themselves to a worthy cause that benefits others, and perhaps even the planet, considerably.

Potential: Compassionate, gracious

Dark side: Intolerant, extreme

Tarot card, lucky numbers, days, colors: The Hierophant, 5, 6, Friday, Wednesday, lavender, green

Born on this day: Kate Winslet (actor); Denis Diderot (philosopher); Bob Geldof (singer); Imran Khan (Pakistani prime minister)

October 6

The Birthday of the Romantic Explorer

The life lesson:

is being more realistic.

The way forward: is to understand that relentless positivity can be as damaging as constant negativity, because there is good and bad in every situation and person.

Luck maker: Do some future goal-setting. Lucky people live in the present but plan ahead for their success.

"Tomorrow is not another day"

October 6-born live each day as if it were their last and are among the most alive and spontaneous of the year. Every day is a thrilling ride and an opportunity to fall in and out of love with anyone or anything. Romantic explorers at heart, they are driven by an irresistible urge to savor as many stimulations and sensations as life has to offer. They absolutely adore what is fresh and new, but they are not selfish, because their need to identify with and help others is equally strong.

Born educators, they are multitalented with pioneering potential and may be drawn toward teaching, coaching, travel, social campaigning, engineering, technology, architecture or science, but the worlds of art, design, fashion, beauty, catering, cooking, social media, theater, art, writing, music, dance, promotion and production also offer them opportunities to fully express their creativity. Although their upbeat approach and emphasis on having fun in the moment is commendable, they must ensure they don't become over-indulgent or place value on looks over substance. Counseling, therapy or mind–body therapies, such as yoga and interpreting dreams, are recommended to get to know themselves. **For self-care**, wearing, surrounding yourself with and meditating on the color yellow encourages you to unlock and express your latent imagination.

These people can be wonderfully loyal as well as frustratingly unpredictable in their relationships. After the age of 17 they have an increasing need for personal growth and transformation, and they need to deepen their emotional commitment to others because people can tire of their inability to consider the deeper aspects of life. After 47 they are likely to become more adventurous, expanding their minds with study and travel. Whatever age they are, their spontaneity draws luck, success and admirers to them. Once they understand that life cannot always be sunshine and roses and that suffering is essential to psychological growth, their life can become infinitely more exciting and rewarding. Their destiny is to be a talking, walking inspiration of life lived fully in every moment to all those lucky enough to cross their path.

Potential: Spontaneous, inspirational

Dark side: Unreliable, superficial

Tarot card, lucky numbers, day, colors: The Lovers, 6, 7, Friday, lavender, blue

Born today: Thor Heyerdahl (explorer); Fannie Lou Hamer, Jazz Jennings (activists); Le Corbusier (architect)

October 7

The Birthday of Acquired Taste

"This is my way"

The life lesson:

is curtailing stubbornness.

The way forward: is to avoid confusing conviction with narrow-mindedness.

Luck maker: However strong your convictions, understand that there are always different viewpoints, each with valuable insights to offer.

People born on October 7 are furiously independent and strong-willed. They often have a reputation for speaking with deep-seated commitment about their beliefs. Reactions can be extreme—others either love or hate them—but whether people agree or disagree with them, they are generally impressed by their focus and determination. Although they may be "an acquired taste," they are not concerned about unsettling others, as they believe that progress can't be made without challenging the status quo. They prefer followers rather than enemies, but believe so strongly in their ideals and pioneering progress that they have the courage necessary to survive opposition or criticism along the way.

Born promoters, they may work independently or they may prefer to be an agent, spokesperson or lobbyist for social reform. They also have a gift for music, art and writing; journalism might be a meaningful occupation for them, as might technology, education, lecturing, publishing, advertising, counseling, negotiation, business, politics, religion and financial advice. They can be prone to comfort eating when they feel bored or stressed. Their key to wellbeing is regular exercise, going to bed and rising early, and avoiding long periods of isolation from loved ones. **For self-care**, wearing, meditating on and surrounding yourself with the color blue encourages you to be more objective, fair and open-minded.

Loners at heart, these people can benefit from loving companions. After 46 they become more optimistic, but whatever their age they need to keep their minds curious and to understand their way is not the only way. Once they can internalize their tremendous focus rather than externalize it in confrontational behavior, their destiny is to be among the world's truly brilliant and motivating innovators.

Potential: Influential, committed

Dark side: Stubborn, isolated

Tarot card, lucky numbers, days, colors: The Chariot, 7, 8, Friday, Monday, lavender, green

Born today: Niels Bohr (physicist); Desmond Tutu (archbishop); Simon Cowell (producer); Li Yundi (pianist)

October 8

The Birthday of the Liberated Spirit

"Come fly with me"

Those born on October 8 often feel a need to fly beyond existing knowledge. Their imagination is so creative that others see them either as highly original or slightly odd. But even those who struggle to relate to their wild creativity admit they are envious of their ability to free themselves from routine. They can appear flighty because they are easily distracted and lack common sense, but they have a powerful insight into what motivates others. Unfortunately, that insight doesn't extend to themselves, and because they have an experimental approach to life, they can find themselves forever searching for excitement and freedom. Although this makes them fascinating, until they are able to face the realities of life they feel restless and unsatisfied.

Born artists, they are creative and excel in performing, the arts and writing, but also in varied careers, such as politics, social reform, business, science, sport, coaching, counseling or technology. Because they tend to avoid facing their feelings, seeking counseling for themselves can be beneficial, as can mindfulness techniques to encourage them to live in the real world rather than an imaginary one. **For self-care,** spending more time in nature can encourage you to live in the moment and keep both your feet on the ground.

Commitment can be an issue, but the older these people get the more consistent they become. Before the age of 45 they have opportunities to discover more about themselves and what they want from life. Key to their success is their ability to be disciplined. After 45 they have an even greater desire to expand their horizons and take more risks. It's important they discover the excitement they crave within themselves, rather than relying on constant change. With their active imagination, excellent communication skills and love of life, they often find themselves at the forefront of new trends. But only when they are able to combine their emotions with willpower can they become a dynamic force for progress. When they have learned to commit to a worthy cause, their destiny is to inspire others with their idealism and ability to rise above any situation to see the bigger picture.

Potential: Visionary, exciting

Dark side: Odd, easily distracted

Tarot card, lucky numbers, days, colors: Strength, 8, 9, Friday, Saturday, lavender, brown

Born today: Sigourney Weaver, Matt Damon (actors); Bruno Mars (singer); R. L. Stine (author)

October 9

The Birthday of the Imaginative Psychologist

The life lesson: is tempering your eagerness to please.

The way forward: is to understand that people respect you more if you can say "no" when boundaries are crossed.

Luck maker: Listening to your intuition when things don't go as planned helps you stand up for yourself when others try to take advantage of you.

October 9-born are extraordinarily imaginative but also very observant, with the uncanny ability to accurately spot weaknesses or failings in others. However, because they are also extremely sensitive, their insights don't offend but inspire others. As natural psychologists, they love to observe everyone they meet and every new situation. Their personal life may be a different story though, because their perception and insight do not translate into self-awareness.

Born mentors, they may direct their energy toward teaching, psychiatry, the law, analysis, research, medicine, social work, life-coaching or even religious work, but whatever job they choose, they feel an urge to inform and inspire. Other careers that utilize their creativity include writing, music, art, sport, design, theater, modeling and the performing arts. It is important for these people to avoid holding grudges because they are prone to bouts of jealousy, anger and insecurity. Being able to forgive (not forget) and let go of negative thoughts promotes both emotional and physical health. Positive-thinking programs, such as cognitive behavioral therapy, are beneficial, as are yoga and meditation. They should avoid recreational drugs, alcohol and smoking, as they have addictive tendencies. **For self-care,** wearing the color red encourages you to be more assertive and have greater self-belief.

Those born on this day wear their hearts on their sleeve, and developing an identity outside their relationship is crucial to avoid co-dependency. Until the age of 44 they love change and they look outside themselves for a sense of purpose and identity, whether in their career or in their relationships. This is when their eagerness to please can overshadow their willpower, so it is vital for them to listen to and trust their powerful intuition. After 44 they reach a turning point when they become more adventurous and freedom-loving, and their genuine enjoyment of life shines through clearly. If they have learned to stand up for themselves and their dreams, these intelligent, intuitive and imaginative dreamers can turn their progressive visions into reality. Once they can examine themselves with the same insight they accord others, their destiny is to enlighten those around them.

Potential: Insightful, popular

Dark side: Needy, jealous

Tarot card, lucky numbers, days, colors: The Hermit, 1, 9, Friday, Tuesday, lavender, scarlet

Born today: John Lennon (singer); Mary Ann Shadd (activist); Bella Hadid (model); Guillermo del Toro (director)

October 10

The Birthday of the Overseer

The life lesson:

is asking for help.

The way forward: is to understand that asking for help is a sign of strength and self-belief, not weakness.

Luck maker: Follow your heart rather than your head, as sometimes greater joy can be found in giving than in receiving.

"Order is power"

People born on October 10 are happiest when they bring order and harmony to unproductive situations. It gives them more pleasure to make a process efficient than to see the end result. Their career is extremely important and they seek a vocation that is both fulfilling and meaningful. Their homes and personal lives are run as efficiently as their work. Although they can sometimes appear slightly serious, frugal and self-contained, they have an attractive sincerity that draws others to them. They are intelligent and articulate, but small talk is definitely not for them. These people need to find meaning in everything they think, say and do.

Born supervisors, they have natural authority and are well suited to being team leaders, business CEOs and executives. Their talents suit them to many careers, including technology, writing, the law, accounting, the civil service, education, administration, finance, editing, marketing, politics and community work. Their need for artistic expression may draw them to art and entertainment through the medium of music, film or theater. It is important for them to understand that health and wellbeing should be at the top of their priorities, above material wealth. Spending more time simply having fun can help them loosen up. **For self-care**, wearing, meditating on and surrounding yourself with the color orange encourages feelings of warmth, creativity and spontaneity.

Those born on this day may avoid emotional intimacy, fearing the loss of control love can bring, and need to understand that love can be a grounding force. Until the age of 43 they focus on personal growth and the first part of their lives can be the most challenging. They need to ensure their tendency to be logical does not overshadow their creativity and make them overly serious. After 43 the spotlight turns to travel and new experiences. Whatever age they are, the sooner they discover their free spirit within, and allow their heart sometimes to rule their head, the sooner they can become the inspired leaders they are born to be. Once they learn to be more spontaneous and to balance order and creativity, their destiny is to institute innovative, efficient and effortlessly productive strategies and systems.

Potential: Authoritative, constructive

Dark side: Unimaginative, overly serious

Tarot card, lucky numbers, days, colors: The Wheel of Fortune, 1, 2, Friday, Sunday, purple, orange

Born today: Giuseppe Verdi (composer); Clare Hollingworth (journalist); Harold Pinter (playwright); Chris Ofili (painter)

October 11

The Birthday of Cool Elegance

The life lesson:

is discovering and harnessing your ambition.

The way forward: is to understand that being popular does not bring fulfillment, but setting personal goals can help you achieve this.

Luck maker: Stop procrastinating—utilize self-discipline and take proactive steps to see dreams realized.

"Me and you both"

Those born on October 11 are often described by others as "cool." Attractive and popular, they are at their happiest and best at the center of a group or socializing. Their style is laid-back and elegant, and their likable, generous personality enables them to mix with all ages and walks of life. Others may envy the ease with which they strike up a conversation with a newcomer, advance up the career ladder and live what seems a charmed life. But underneath their graceful exterior, they can feel as if something important is missing: personal ambition. They can feel as if they have no control over their lives and their fear of challenge is damaging, because it is only through overcoming challenges that they can grow personally.

Born influencers, they may take a while to settle into a career and tend to change direction often. They can flourish in many professions, including writing, music, sport, social reform, sales, promotion, commerce, counseling, teaching, training, the law, politics, advertising, art, design, charity work and social media. They tend to be sedentary, so they need to incorporate activity, such as walking, into their daily lives. **For self-care,** meditation techniques help you strengthen your willpower, and writing down your goals encourages you to achieve them.

Sensual and pleasure-focused, these people must exercise discretion in their relationships and prize others for reasons other than looks and popularity. Until the age of 42 they focus on personal power and must grasp opportunities to challenge themselves, because this is key to their success. After 42 they seek inspiration through study, relationships or travel. Again, success comes from a willingness to take calculated risks and embrace challenge. When they discover a drive to achieve and the courage to avoid taking the safest route, their outstanding grace, humanity and intellect ensure that they won't just appear to be leading a charmed life—they can be living it. Once they find out what gives their lives meaning, and connect with their genuine desire to help and improve the lives of others, their destiny is to be a teacher and innovator in their chosen field.

Potential: Charming, cool

Dark side: Superficial, passive

Tarot card, lucky numbers, days, colors: Justice, 2, 3, Friday, Monday, purple, silver

Born today: Eleanor Roosevelt (US first lady); Cardi B (rapper); Joan Cusack (actor); Henry John Heinz (entrepreneur)

October 12

The Birthday of Effusive Complexity

The life lesson:

is getting over yourself.

The way forward: is to understand that although you may be the center of your own world, you are not at the center of everyone else's.

Luck maker: Turn the spotlight on someone else—by making someone else feel great, they are far more likely to want to help you.

"Here I am. Look at me"

October 12-born have larger-than-life personalities that make heads turn wherever they go. Determined to have their opinions heard, they may resort to outrageous tactics to get noticed. Although they are attention seekers, they have a heart as expansive as their head, and their tantrums are just as likely to be on behalf of others as themselves. It is this curious mixture of wholehearted generosity and extreme self-indulgence that makes them such complex individuals. They express their complexity in endless fascinating ways, but common to them all is their appetite for life, and their desire to inspire and invigorate others by their own passionate example.

Born performers, these people may excel in acting, dancing or singing, or in social-media influencing, teaching, research, psychology, the law, business, politics, journalism, writing, architecture, design, the media and publishing. They love life, and their appetite for its pleasures is huge, so they need to beware of excess when it comes to food, drink and sex, because this can lead to weight and health problems. Their wellbeing mantra should always be "less is more." **For self-care**, wearing, meditating on and surrounding yourself with shades of blue encourages you to be more disciplined, organized and objective.

These people make passionate, warm, giving companions and friends, but expect the same level of intensity in return, becoming moody and aggressive if they don't get enough attention. Until the age of 41 they concentrate on personal growth, and their chances of success improve significantly if they can become less addicted to attention and more focused on their goals. After 41 they may expand their perspective with study or travel. Whatever age they are, the key to their psychological growth and fulfillment is their ability to consider others' feelings. When they have found a balance between giving and taking, they provoke respect, and in some cases awe. Once they understand that they are not the only one who matters or the only voice that needs to be heard, their destiny is to be a pioneering and flamboyant innovator in their chosen field.

Potential: Dramatic, warm-hearted

Dark side: Attention-seeking, selfish

Tarot card, lucky numbers, days, colors: The Hanged Man, 3, 4, Friday, Thursday, pink, silver

Born today: Luciano Pavarotti (opera singer); Hugh Jackman (actor); Jean Nidetch (entrepreneur); Dick Gregory (comedian)

October 13

The Birthday of the Polished Diamond

is learning to relax.

The way forward: is to understand that regular time out gives you the perspective you need to make better judgments.

Luck maker: People with a sense of humor tend to be happier than those who are more serious—shaking up routine with laughter increases productivity, creativity, joy and luck.

"I am not for turning"

People born on October 13 are natural leaders. Their total focus on their goals, their polished performance and uncompromising strength inspire either devotion and awe, or tension, even fear, in others. They are serious people, not to be fooled around with. When they set their minds on something, nothing, including their own wellbeing, stands in their way. Their sharp minds can come up with ingenious solutions. Unsurprisingly, they are perfectionists; the near impossible expectations they place on themselves can make it difficult for them—and those close to them—to relax. They need to remind themselves that they are human and have emotions just like everyone else.

Born leaders, they have the vision, communication skills and determination to excel in many careers, but they make great lawyers, politicians, advisors, psychologists, social and charity workers, activists, campaigners, orators, business managers and teachers. Other career options that may appeal include advertising, marketing, business, journalism, performance and research. It is important for their health that they learn to relax and take time out. Regular breaks are essential, as is a good night's sleep. **For self-care,** mind–body techniques such as yoga and meditation help you become more self-aware.

Those born on this day find it hard to express their feelings and neglect their relationships for work. Until the age of 40 the focus is on personal motivation, and this is when they are unrelenting in the pursuit of their goals, yet happiness is elusive. After 40 they have a more optimistic and freedom-loving perspective. They may expand their mind through study, travel or new interests. If they can learn to be less critical and follow their inner voice rather than pressure to perform, these are the years when they can really come into their own. They have the potential to bring about progressive benefits for others and, once they have softened their rough edges, to earn their natural place in the spotlight. When they become less critical and more tolerant, their destiny is to inspire and contribute powerfully to the common good with their courage, clarity and determination.

Potential: Powerful, focused

Dark side: Stressed, cold

Tarot card, lucky numbers, days, colors: Death, 4, 5, Friday, Sunday, pink, turquoise

Born today: Margaret Thatcher (British prime minister); Alexandria Ocasio-Cortez (US politician); Joshua Wang (activist); Ashanti (singer)

October 14

The Birthday of the Middle Path

"Neither too much nor too little"

The life lesson:

is putting yourself on the line.

The way forward: is to understand that if you don't ever take a risk, face fears and challenge yourself, you deprive yourself of opportunities for psychological growth and success.

Luck maker: Learn from the past, but then let it go and look forward to a positive future.

Those born on October 14 are the steady rocks others cling to in a crisis. They have a wonderfully calming influence and their ability to counter extreme situations with practicality often propels them into positions of authority. Striving to achieve moderation and balance, doing the right thing in whatever situation they find themselves in is the driving force of these people. They usually find the middle way, giving everyone around them a feeling of security and structure. Although they are often the clear voice of reason, sometimes their common-sense approach stops them from taking any risks at all.

Born reporters, they are inquisitive, with an interest in social and ethical issues, and may find themselves attracted to journalism, filmmaking, politics, the law, education or art and design, while a deep desire to make a difference may draw them toward medicine and the healing, caring professions or the performing arts. As others rely heavily on them, they can be prone to stress and fatigue. Getting a good night's sleep is key, as is a healthy diet and regular exercise and time to relax. **For self-care**, wearing, meditating on and surrounding yourself with the color orange or yellow boosts your energy levels, and carrying a carnelian crystal helps counteract feelings of lethargy and despondency.

Those born on this day tend to seek calm, centered people but they need others in their lives who can keep them emotionally and mentally challenged. Until the age of 39 they concentrate on personal power and transformation. During these years they need to listen to their intuition as well as their common sense and let go of the past. After 39 they may expand their horizons through new experiences, study and travel. Whatever age they are, if they can learn to look ahead with positive expectancy and trust their gut more, they have the potential to become inspirational managers teaching moderation in all things. Their destiny is to be original agents of progress and messengers of healing tolerance.

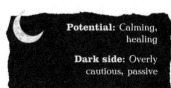

Potential: Calming, healing

Dark side: Overly cautious, passive

Tarot card, lucky numbers, days, colors: Temperance, 5, 6, Friday, Wednesday, pink, yellow

Born today: Dwight D. Eisenhower (US president); Ralph Lauren (designer); Cliff Richard, Usher (singers)

October 15

The Birthday of the Provocative Role Model

"This is me"

October 15-born have a seductive power and the key to their success is the way they use this provocative influence. If they use it positively, they can help others develop a sense of their own identity and power; if they use it recklessly, they can upset or provoke others. They are highly individualistic and nonconformist and don't want to restrain their ideas or behavior for anyone or anything, but their greatest wish is to make a positive contribution to the world. Being multitalented, with innovative ideas, their potential for success is great and they almost certainly make their mark, but they do need to watch that they don't become overconfident. They like to have things their own way, but working cooperatively as part of a team boosts their already strong chances of success.

Born philosophers, they are mentally restless and thrive in careers that give autonomy and offer intellectual challenge, such as writing, influencing, publishing, education, promotion, management, music, acting, the law, sales, information technology, engineering, social work, psychology and the healing professions. They need regular exercise, as they tend to be more sedentary than is usual. **For self-care**, pausing and reflecting before you speak encourages you to think carefully about how your words and behavior affect yourself and influence others.

These people have no problems attracting admirers, but long-term commitment poses a threat to their need for autonomy. Until the age of 38 there is a growing emphasis on emotional maturity, and these are the years for them to study psychology to help them answer questions about themselves. After 38 they are likely to expand their mental perspective and become more adventurous. If they can learn to moderate their constant urge to act as an independent agent and remember that others look to them for guidance and inspiration, they can become not just a positive role model but also a powerful agent of progress. Once they have experienced the joys of synergy, their destiny is to inform and educate others in a profound, potentially life-changing way.

413

October 16

The Birthday of the Breakthrough

"The truth shall set us free"

People born on October 16 are perceptive and intelligent. They observe and study everything and everyone they encounter, and human behavior provides them with endless material. Their greatest talent is their critical ability to expose failings with objective and, sometimes, brutal honesty. They enjoy the company of others, but their wit, independence and tendency to judge people from a distance, for example in writing, videos or blogging, can set them apart. They love to enlighten or inform, but the accuracy of their observations and the brusque way they express them may offend and alienate. When they get their own way—which they frequently do—they are models of charm, but when ignored they can become moody.

Born psychiatrists and critics, they are drawn to the academic world, where they can be excellent researchers, analysts, teachers or lecturers. Other choices include the law, accounting, podcasting, broadcasting, film, writing, commerce, advertising, TV, publishing, sports, community or charity work, as well as humanitarian reform. They push themselves hard at work, and can be prone to stress-related disorders such as fatigue, insomnia, anxiety and headaches. They need to take time out to recharge their batteries, and avoid alcohol dependence. **For self-care**, you are advised to go to bed before midnight and stick to a routine of waking up at the same time each morning.

These people give much of themselves to those they love, but can become controlling. Until the age of 37 they focus on emotional growth and this is when they are most stubborn in the face of opposition. After 37 they are likely to expand their horizons through travel, study and new adventures. They should work cooperatively with others, as this will attract good fortune their way. Their brilliant and unconventional minds and ability to cut to the core of any subject eventually leads them toward self-analysis, and this is when they make the most important and empowering breakthrough of all. Once they learn to be more sensitive to others and speak their mind tactfully, their destiny is to instigate positive reform by shining a spotlight on the honest truth.

Potential: Insightful, fair

Dark side: Demanding, moody

Tarot card, lucky numbers, days, colors: The Tower, 7, 8, Friday, Monday, pink, sea green

Born today: Oscar Wilde, Günter Grass (authors); Angela Lansbury, Tim Robbins (actors)

October 17

The Birthday of
the Lucky Escape

The life lesson:

is to overcome a tendency to embellish.

The way forward: is to understand that embellishing makes you appear needy and attention-seeking.

Luck maker: Get to know yourself—the fundamental rule of luck-making is to be true to yourself.

"Have no fear"

Those born on October 17 are supremely resilient, with the enviable ability to pick themselves up when things don't work out and start again without complaint. Although they know how to be responsible, taking chances is a way of life, with lucky escapes or risk-taking the order of the day. Their fearlessness and the constant air of excitement that surrounds them inspires respect and admiration from others, which they love. They are not above embellishing the truth if they feel it will get them the attention they deserve, but although this never fails to entertain others, it can be dangerous for their emotional wellbeing, as they risk losing touch with what is fact and what is fantasy in their lives. Once they are able to reveal their true self, they find their life takes on a whole new positive meaning and direction.

Born educators, they often feel compelled to further human knowledge, and may be drawn to careers in teaching, and scientific or technical research. Other choices might include translation, the media, writing, acting, publishing, travel, emergency services, stunt work, community work, psychology and counseling. The greatest risk to their health is their attraction to risk-taking and apparent lack of fear. They would benefit from cognitive behavioral therapy and meditation techniques, as these help them control their impulses. **For self-care**, wearing, meditating on and surrounding yourself with shades of blue encourages you to be less image conscious, and calmer and more cautious.

Those born on this day have an adventurous personal life to match their professional life, and it is important they are honest with those close to them to avoid conflicts. In their early thirties they may experience an intense longing to find deeper meaning, and this can induce them either to take greater risks or gain greater self-awareness. Typically, in their forties, they finally find a balance between their impulsive and cautious natures, and as long as they stay positive, and learn the value of patience and tolerance, they can achieve success and true happiness. Their destiny is to anchor their adventurousness and, by so doing, entertain, educate and enlighten humanity.

Potential: Resilient, courageous

Dark side: Reckless, dishonest

Tarot card, lucky numbers, days, colors: The Star, 8, 9, Friday, Saturday, pink, burgundy

Born today: Eminem (rapper); Arthur Miller (playwright); Evel Knievel (daredevil); Mae Jemison (astronaut)

October 18

The Birthday of Vulnerable Expectation

The life lesson:

is believing in yourself.

The way forward: is to understand that self-belief is your birthright—look at any baby.

Luck maker: Respect yourself enough to say "no" when the demands of others are not in your best interests.

"Liking me is easy"

October 18-born are dignified and determined. Their curiosity and intellect help them seek out opportunities and people who can assist them, but although they long to make their mark on the world and present a confident and strong persona, part of them longs to run away and hide. With all the imagination and talent to blaze exciting trails in life, they can still have a deep-seated craving for others' approval that can limit their potential. It is therefore vital for their psychological growth that they work on rebuilding their vulnerable self-esteem. If they don't, they are like reeds blown in the wind, flying high and strong when others applaud but falling down when the praise or support isn't there.

Born translators, they may be drawn to creative means of expression such as art, writing, acting and music, but they may also put their imaginative talents to good use in education, coaching, sales, promotion, advertising and social reform, and their determination to impress others bodes well for sporting excellence. A gift for communication and language may draw them to careers in interpreting, travel or work in different countries. They need lots of physical activity, not just because they have a lot of energy but also because it helps boost their self-esteem. **For self-care**, meditation, visualization techniques and carrying a tiger's eye crystal help boost your confidence.

These charming and kind people tend to give more than they take in relationships and they must learn to stand up for themselves. Until the age of 35 the focus is on emotional development, and these are the years that they need to start saying "no" to those who take advantage of them. Once they realize their own worth, there is nothing they cannot achieve. When they approach their forties and beyond, they become more adventurous, and need to leave self-doubt aside. When they finally see what others have always seen and realize how creative, courageous and inspirational they are, they have the potential to be an inspirational force for the common good. Their destiny is to further their quest for knowledge, and benefit and inspire others with their fascinating skills and discoveries.

Potential: Inspirational, kind

Dark side: Needy, self-sacrificing

Tarot card, lucky numbers, days, colors: The Moon, 1, 9, Friday, Tuesday, pink, lavender

Born today: Jean-Claude Van Damme, Zac Efron (actors); Martina Navratilova (tennis player); Mike Ditka (football coach)

October 19

The Birthday of the Peaceful Activist

"Show me, tell me"

The life lesson: is coping with routine.

The way forward: is to understand that looking within rather than outside yourself for excitement is the recipe for a happy and fulfilled life.

Luck maker: See heaven in a grain of sand—find magic in the ordinary and the everyday.

People born on October 19 appear peace-loving and conventional, but underneath the surface is a great deal of independence and originality. Rarely seen without a smile on their face, they work long and hard to support and help others in a team, but when conflict arises, their passion can shock even those who know them well. Indeed, it is during difficult times that they stand out, revealing their strength of character and the best and the worst of themselves. Deep down, they are warriors and just need a battle to expose their crusading spirit. Once this is revealed, others never underestimate them again. Fortunately, their chosen weapon is gentle persuasion and the logical presentation of their ideas, but if pushed in a corner, they can lash out furiously.

Born crisis managers, they are natural innovators and may be drawn to careers in science, research, sport, art or technology. Photography, writing, journalism, sales, promotion, fashion, education, the emergency services, the military, crime-fighting, campaigning, social reform and counseling may also appeal. Multitalented, they need a career that offers variety and opportunities to stand strong in a crisis. They suffer from boredom and need to find healthy ways to generate excitement and passion without relying on external circumstances. **For self-care**, wearing, meditating on and surrounding yourself with the color orange can energize you during peaceful times, while blue will help you to be more objective during stressful times.

Intimacy is therapeutic for these people, but they tend to run hot and cold in relationships. Until their mid-thirties they have opportunities for emotional growth and transformation. Injecting enthusiasm into their life without conflict as a stimulus is invaluable to their psychological growth. After 40 and beyond they may become more adventurous, desiring to travel or study. Once they direct their inspiring energy, conviction and courage toward a worthy cause, and realize that true adventure lies within, they have the potential to discover, shed light on and reverse injustices. Their destiny is to benefit others with their progressive and original discoveries and bring the world closer to its natural peace-loving state.

Potential: Courageous, energetic

Dark side: Tactless, easily bored

Tarot card, lucky numbers, days, colors: The Sun, 1, 2, Friday, Sunday, pink, orange

Born today: James Bevel, Amy Carter (activists); Evander Holyfield (boxer); John Lithgow (actor)

October 20

The Birthday of the Double Life

The life lesson:

is understanding yourself.

The way forward: is to appreciate that self-knowledge is the beginning of wisdom and to be human is to be complex and to constantly surprise yourself and others.

Luck maker: Admit your mistakes, learn from them and use that knowledge to move forward and generate new opportunities.

"If you don't know me by now ..."

Those born on October 20 are complicated, but in an intriguing way. There are typically two distinct sides to them: one is practical, authoritative and a lover of harmony and collaboration, while the other is utterly unpredictable but appreciative of sensuality, beauty and creativity. Generally, these people manage to integrate both sides, perhaps by pursuing a quiet career that pays the bills and then having an outside passion, or by having an adrenaline-fueled professional life and a very peaceful home life. Either way their complexity expresses itself somehow in their distinctive personal appearance, clothing and hairstyle choices. Sometimes the tension between the two sides creates conflict and they make the mistake of trying to fully identify with one side while denying their other side.

Born publishers, these multitalented people are suited to a variety of professions, from science to politics, business, art, building, design, technology and entertainment. Possible careers include writing, blogging, sales, public relations, education, editing, journalism, counseling, therapy, medicine, business and management. It is important for them to remember that their health and wellbeing should always come before anything else. **For self-care**, spending time in nature and natural settings as well as wearing, meditating on and surrounding yourself with the color green helps you find greater balance and harmony.

The double life of those born on this day shows up in their relationships, in that they are extremely giving, but their originality is so powerful they find it impossible to subordinate their own needs for too long. In their twenties they may struggle to express themselves creatively, but from their late thirties onward they become more adventurous. These are the years when it is crucial for them to find ways to reconcile their rational side with their creative impulses. If they can achieve this delicate balance, they can continue to lead a double life, but this time it feels completely natural and fulfilling. Their destiny is then to produce progressive, visionary and utterly unique work.

Potential: Creative, original

Dark side: Conflicted, unfulfilled

Tarot card, lucky numbers, days, colors: Judgment, 2, 3, Friday, Monday, pink, silver

Born today: Christopher Wren (architect); Arthur Rimbaud (poet); Kamala Harris (politician); Snoop Dogg (rapper)

October 21

The Birthday of Eloquent Charm

is managing emotions.

The way forward: is to step outside yourself and understand that you, not your anger, fear or sadness, are in charge of the way you feel.

Luck maker: Instead of making hasty, on-the-spot decisions, wait until you feel you have examined every angle so that you make better judgments.

"My words are my power"

October 21-born are often charming, creative and multitalented, but, first and foremost, they are communicators and their eloquence, whether expressed verbally or visually, is one of their greatest assets—used wisely it can help them win friends and influence important people. As well as being emotionally expressive, they are natural entertainers; people find themselves magnetically drawn to their spontaneous and upbeat personality. They love being center stage as the approval of others means a great deal, but they are more than just social butterflies. Far more important to them than their own popularity is using their considerable influence to improve the injustices of the world.

Born presenters and influencers, they can be inspirational writers, artists, musicians and actors, but they may also be drawn to teaching, the media, film, public relations, journalism, business, commerce, fashion, politics, advertising and sales, or to making their mark in campaigning, charity work, life-coaching, science, engineering and medicine. Impulsive and sensitive, they need to make sure during times of loneliness or anxiety that they don't seek relief in addictions. Regular exercise is highly beneficial, as is counseling to help them understand themselves better. **For self-care**, meditation techniques and wearing and surrounding yourself with calming shades of blue encourages you to take a step back whenever you want to rush forward.

Because they follow their heart and have many admirers, it can take those born on this day time to find someone special, but when they do, they are extremely loyal. Before the age of 32 they may lack self-confidence and be conservative in their approach to life, but after 32 they reach a turning point when they become more adventurous, confident and freedom-loving. It is important for them to realize that although acting on impulse is exciting, it can also be dangerous. Whatever age they are, these dynamic but eloquent and expressive individuals find fulfillment when they dedicate their talents to justice, healing and a spiritual perspective. Once they find a balance between their need to express themselves and to help others, their destiny is to use their infinite creativity and eloquence to make a lasting contribution to the greater good.

Potential: Articulate, influential

Dark side: Addictive, unfulfilled

Tarot card, lucky numbers, days, colors: The World, 3, 4, Friday, Thursday, pink, blue

Born today: Samuel Taylor Coleridge (poet); Carrie Fisher (actor); Ursula K. Le Guin (author); Alfred Nobel (chemist)

October 22

The Birthday of the Golden Aura

"Follow my lead"

The life lesson:

is coping when things are out of control.

The way forward: is to understand that sometimes going with the flow is the most empowering choice.

Luck maker: When others give to you, say thank you, as this not only makes you feel good about yourself but also makes the person who is giving feel appreciated.

People born on October 22 could not fade into the background if they tried, so compelling is their seductive power. Throughout their lives all eyes are glued to their golden aura. Although they bask in the attention, a part of them longs to be recognized for their skills rather than for their appearance or their desirability. Indeed, they have hidden talents, including intelligence, intuition, deep empathy and compassion, but they often don't get enough opportunities to express them. Not being taken seriously can be a problem, and they feel that they have to work twice as hard as anyone else to prove themselves. They can sometimes compensate by projecting their talents onto others and becoming controlling in the process, so they need to use these powers wisely.

Born performers with their powerful sense of justice, they may be drawn to the law, politics, charity, humanitarian work and the personal growth professions, but being multitalented and creative they can thrive in any career they choose, whether it be art, interior design, writing, music, acting, fundraising, engineering, health and beauty, social reform or diplomacy. Image matters a lot for them and they should focus on the way they feel, because beauty and style really do come from the inside. Stretching routines encourage flexibility in both mind and body. **For self-care**, spending more time doing what you love and thinking about how you can help others in some way nourishes your heart and soul.

These people are extremely giving, but less comfortable with receiving in their close relationships. As they often experience intense attractions, long-term commitment can be a problem. Before the age of 30 they tend to manipulate others emotionally, but after 30 they are likely to become less controlling and more open-minded and adventurous. This is when they can really come into their own. When directed positively, their golden aura, combined with their inner strength, finally manifests itself as healing or creative ability, as well as the urge to create a fairer world. Their destiny is to defend and represent the interests of those less fortunate.

Potential: Seductive, exciting

Dark side: Manipulative, superficial

Tarot card, lucky numbers, days, colors: The Fool, 4, 5, Friday, Sunday, lavender, electric blue

Born today: Jeff Goldblum (actor); Franz Liszt (composer); Shaggy (musician); Deepak Chopra (author)

SCORPIO

THE SCORPION
(OCTOBER 23–NOVEMBER 21)

✳ **Element:** Water

✳ **Ruling planets:** Mars, the warrior, and Pluto, the destroyer

✳ **Tarot card:** Death (Regeneration)

✳ **Lucky numbers:** 8, 9

✳ **Favorable colors:** Red, black, purple

✳ **Driving force:** Transformation

✳ **Personal statement:** I reinvent and renew myself

✳ **Chinese astrology counterpart:** The Pig

Scorpio is the sign of rebirth and renewal. Their main traits are a relentless, restless and intense energy that can wear anyone and anything down, in either a positive or a negative way, with its persistence. At their best, Scorpios are dynamic and unforgettable achievers but, if they can't get what or who they want, or if their incredible energy is blocked or restricted in some way, they will display their worst characteristics: jealousy, resentfulness, negativity and stinging sarcasm.

Personality potential

Of all the signs of the zodiac, Scorpios are probably the one with the most negative connotations, because the self-destructive traits of their symbol, the scorpion, are so obvious. But these connotations simply are not true. It's just that the creativity and energy associated with this sign can sometimes be so strong that they seem overpowering and over-intense. However, once they find a way to express their creativity and utilize their energy positively and productively, they have the potential to achieve outstanding things.

There are many sides to a Scorpio and every day new sides of their personality reveal themselves, but two aspects of their personality are showcased most frequently. First, there is the silent-but-deadly scorpion that takes delight in catching a person off-guard; then, there is the phoenix, the magical and mystical bird that dies but is reborn with renewed strength, wisdom, and potential to start again. It's no coincidence that the Tarot card linked to the sun-sign Scorpio is the card of Death. This card often scares people the most in a reading, but if they take the time to look beneath the surface they will discover that although death does mean endings, it also symbolizes new beginnings, and all the promise and potential of a new life or fresh start. It's not surprising, either, that the sign of Scorpio rules the genitals—the organs of reproduction— and that the planet Mars, the warrior, and Pluto, the planet

of rebirth, transformation and hidden knowledge, are also a strong influence over those born under this sign.

Scorpios are fascinated by the unknown and the unanswered mysteries of life. **Their intense stare seems to look right into another person's soul,** and their astute, original mind has the ability to combine logic with intuition so that they can immediately get right to the heart of the matter or the root of a problem. They are often magnetic personalities and excellent strategists who seem to be able to hypnotize other people to do whatever they want. Wherever or however they choose to direct their awesome energy, they have enormous resilience and staying power, as well as the potential to overcome obstacles and attract good fortune into their lives.

> " **Their intense stare seems to look right into another person's soul** "

Personality pitfalls

Jealousy, sarcasm, vindictiveness, possessiveness and stubbornness are words sometimes associated with this sign. There is no denying that the potential for these negative personality traits lies deep within them, like a sting in the tail. The most curious thing, though, is that Scorpios are often the first to admit these ugly traits in themselves but, instead of taking control of them, they frequently allow them to dominate or drive them. In other words, they can sting themselves in the tail with their compulsiveness and obsessiveness and are therefore their own worst enemies. There is also a masochistic side to them that can hurt them far harder than any criticism or rejection by other people.

Scorpios can be relentlessly self-critical and their suspicious personality will often dwell on past hurts, allowing resentments and negativity to build up. They also tend to judge the present by past experiences and, if they have been hurt in the past, they can be very reluctant to trust again. Often their feelings of insecurity can be masked by arrogant, dismissive behavior. And if they have been hurt or betrayed, they are the zodiac sign most likely neither to forgive nor forget. Their explosive temper is legendary.

Scorpios are also the master manipulators of the zodiac and they will never hesitate to use the knowledge they have gained with their probing insight and their dangerous charm to help them get to where they want. Perhaps their most self-destructive personality pitfall, though, is their deep and dark jealousy. Scorpios can smolder with resentment and eat themselves up with negative feelings if they think others have more or are doing better than they are.

Symbol

The scorpion is a dangerous, dark, silent and terrifying creature with a lethal sting in its tail. When cornered, the scorpion will sting itself to death rather than face defeat or humiliation. Like the scorpion, those born under this sun sign have the potential to destroy anyone or anything that obstructs their path. They also have great potential for self-sabotage when they feel that their life isn't going according to plan.

Darkest secret

The darkest secrets of Scorpios will typically remain a mystery, because their nature is to keep things about themselves hidden. Unwilling to open up emotionally, they can often feel incredibly isolated and alone—as if they are an observer rather than an active participant in their own lives. Within every Scorpio there's a deep need to be loved and accepted, but if they can't find ways to understand and love themselves better, they may find that this need goes unfulfilled.

Love

There's a secretive air about those born under this sun sign, which can make them extremely difficult to get to know, but their intuitive personality never has a problem understanding other people. As a result, they will have plenty of acquaintances and admirers, but only a few select people will know a Scorpio really well—and even fewer, if any, will get really close to them emotionally. This isn't to say that it's impossible for a Scorpio to fall in love. They are capable of deep love, but all too often they mistake passion and sex for love. The real test for a Scorpio's heart is after the honeymoon period. When things settle more into a routine, they may struggle to transform a sexual relationship into something deep and longer lasting. Whatever their relationship status, satisfying sex—and lots of it—is likely to be high on their list of priorities.

If there is a Scorpio in your life, they will almost certainly try to control you in some way, and if they see you confiding in anyone else their insecurity will be awakened. Many of the problems Scorpios face in their lives revolve around their intense emotions, in particular, love and jealousy. Prone to bouts of lovesickness, infatuation and impulse, it's often the case that common sense, reason and logic disappear, and reckless and self-destructive behavior takes their place.

Love matches:

Virgo, Capricorn Cancer, and Pisces.

The Scorpio woman

Magnetic, proud, confident, mysterious and deep are key words for the Scorpio woman. The chances are she will also be attractive and seductive, but, as stunning as she is, the Scorpio woman harbors a silent resentment. In her mind, being a woman brings its joys but also its restrictions. She may, for example, find the role of being a girlfriend challenging. She'll want to be the one making the move, and if it comes to marriage, she'll be the one who wants to pop the question. Then, if children come on the scene, although she can make a wonderful mother, she will struggle with the limitations that having a family might make on her career.

Sexy and sassy, the Scorpio female longs for more freedom and a life without limitation. She'll be the woman pushing the boundaries at work and when it comes to relationships, she has no time for mind games—she will cut to the chase. She does, however, know how to play the games of life well and will often disguise her true intentions behind a mysterious exterior. She has refined the art of getting people to do exactly what she wants without them even realizing it. Before you know it, you will be caught in her web. This woman is many things, but she is most often hypnotic and powerful.

Being so strong, a Scorpio woman can't stand weakness in others. In her relationships she will look for a partner who is ambitious and intelligent, like she is. She's deeply passionate and sexual, and, when times are tough, her calm inner strength will shine through. Although she is often touchingly honest in her affections and can be endearingly sweet, her partner will never feel they completely understand her—which is part of her magic.

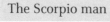

The Scorpio man

On the surface a Scorpio man can often appear calm, confident and in control, but if there is only one word to sum up a Scorpio man, that word would be "passion." Not just passion in the bedroom, but passionate intensity about everything and everyone involved in his life. If you find emotional intensity unsettling, then a relationship with a Scorpio man isn't ideal for you.

People tend to either love or dislike Scorpio men. It's impossible to be neutral about them and they will always make an impression with their hypnotic intensity. They are an enigma in every sense of the word and can be passionate one moment but

full of common sense the next; philosophical one day and earthy and sensual the day after. Full of surprises, they are impossible to second guess, and that suits them fine. They delight in unsettling people and encouraging them to let down their guard. Then, once that guard is down, they will either move in for the kill or scuttle away in search of another conquest.

Coming second is not in the Scorpio man's vocabulary. Losing is not only painful for him; it can kill a part of him. He doesn't just want to win in life; he *has* to win; and it's the same in relationships. He wants to control you and if he catches his partner's eyes wandering, his jealousy knows no bounds. However, he has a completely different set of rules for himself. You've got to give him space. You'll have to put up with his flirtations. Although this sounds very unfair, the fact is that you need to be extremely brave and strong to fall in love with a Scorpio. Once he's hypnotized you, however, you'll soar higher and further with him in physical, emotional and intellectual expression than you would ever have thought possible.

Family

Scorpio children often have a reputation for being sulky and moody. Instead of shouting and screaming when they don't get what they want, they may just go quiet and refuse to participate. It's extremely important for parents or carers to encourage their little Scorpio to talk about what is bothering them, because if opening up about themselves can be learned early in life, it will save them a lot of grief and unhappiness later on.

Intelligent and curious, these children also need to have plenty of interests and hobbies to keep them stimulated, because, if they get bored, they can become restless physically and volatile emotionally. Their curiosity can sometimes lead them to explore or want to talk about areas of life that their parents feel uncomfortable discussing, such as death, sex, drugs and disease. Instead of telling them they are not old enough—which will simply make them more curious—parents should try to find ways to openly discuss taboo subjects in a safe way.

Scorpio children often have endless supplies of energy and should be encouraged to use this up through active participation in sports, dance and regular exercise. There will always be a secretive aspect to their personality; they may, for example, keep a secret diary or have a secret place where they like to go when the world feels overwhelming. Parents should be aware of their child's need for secrecy and should monitor it to make sure they are safe, but they should not try to invade their space.

Scorpio parents are often fairly strict and set high standards for their children—sometimes too high. They may frequently try to encourage their child to follow the same road in life as themselves, but they need to learn to let go if a child wants to follow a different path. Their children's development is fascinating to them, but they need to ensure that they don't get obsessive about knowing everything their child is doing, thinking and feeling. Children have a need for space and freedom. As far as disciplining their children is concerned, Scorpio parents must understand that being strict and authoritarian has its merits, but that most children thrive better when rules guide rather than dictate their lives.

Career

Work matters more to Scorpios for a sense of personal fulfillment than for perhaps any other sign. They are willing to work extremely hard and long to carve themselves a career that will give them both emotional and financial security. Periods of unemployment, career confusion or sudden retirement can be deeply unsettling for them because there is no outlet for their energy. Others may tell them to relax, unwind and enjoy the time for themselves, but Scorpios are far happier when they are *doing*; for this reason, they may often seek out unpaid work rather than not working at all. **The reason work is so essential for Scorpios is that they always need to feel challenged.** They must have something to do that pressures them in some way.

> **The reason work is so essential for Scorpios is that they always need to feel challenged.**

Once Scorpios set their mind on a career there is little to stop them from succeeding—and they can often be found excelling in leadership roles—but they are particularly well suited to careers that involve research and detection. They make great criminologists, spies, detectives, researchers and journalists. They may also be drawn to jobs that allow them to take things apart and study them, such as being a mechanic or scientist. Other varied career options may include: surgery, pathology, psychology, psychiatry, stockbroking or market analysis, banking, politics, undertaking, insurance, therapy, computing, technology, diving, law enforcement, business, flying or space travel. For Scorpio—the sky really *isn't* the limit.

Health and wellbeing

Scorpios have a tendency toward self-indulgence as far as food and drink is concerned, and this can often lead to digestive upsets or constipation. It's especially important therefore that they aim for a balanced diet with the emphasis on moderation in all things. As far as alcohol, smoking, drugs and gambling are concerned, they should avoid them at all costs, given the extreme tendencies of this sun sign. They have seemingly endless reserves of energy, so regular exercise is a must, but they must be careful not to overdo it, as over-training can lead to injuries and strain. Often highly sexed, Scorpios can be extremely promiscuous, so if they are not in a committed relationship they need to ensure they practice safe sex.

Although Scorpios do need to slow down when they start pushing themselves too long and too hard, doing nothing neither suits them nor is healthy for them. Whether they are eight or eighty, those born under this sun sign need a compelling interest or lots of activities to keep them challenged, motivated and active, both physically and mentally. Leisure activities that particularly attract Scorpios are likely to include martial arts, jogging and anything to do with water, such as swimming, diving, snorkeling and water sports. The thrill-seeking aspect of their personality may be drawn to speed racing, extreme sports and mystery thrillers, and the intense side of their personality may be attracted to the occult arts, as well as the mysteries of metaphysics and self-improvement courses. Because they can find it hard to open up emotionally to others, Scorpios often bottle up their feelings. This can have a damaging effect, so, if they have no friends or family in whom to confide, counseling or therapy is advised.

Wearing, meditating on and surrounding themselves with the color **blue** will encourage them to keep a sense of perspective in life and be more calm, cool and collected when their emotions start to overwhelm them.

Born between October 23 and 31

Determination is the key word for people born between these dates. Some may regard them as insensitive and obsessive because they push forward so single-mindedly, but for them there are no half-measures in life. They want to be the best and they won't let anything stand in the way.

Born between November 1 and 10

People born in the first couple of weeks of November are not afraid of obstacles or challenges in any way. In fact, they positively thrive on them and love nothing better than trying to prove that no one can stop them—and as a result, more often than not, no one can.

Born between November 11 and 21

If these people are cornered or put in a compromising situation, they won't give in until they get what they want. Born fighters and seekers of justice, they know how to crush their opposition and do what they do best—win.

Life lessons

Deep, emotional and intense, Scorpios know what motivates others, but it isn't so easy to know what exactly motivates them. Their drive in life is to connect with others—and in their close relationships this can manifest in controlling behavior—but underneath this drive to connect there's often a deep-seated fear of being abandoned and left alone. Perhaps the most important life lesson is to learn to let go of their fear of abandonment and urge to control others. They need to learn that love requires surrender and trust. Just because people need space or want to express their independence in some way does not necessarily mean that they are distancing themselves.

Scorpios are obsessed with finding out secrets and they need to learn the value of privacy and trust in a relationship. One reason they may find trusting others so hard is that they find it hard to trust themselves. The first step for them must therefore be to learn to get a handle on their own insecurities. They need to learn to forgive themselves when they mess up and to take charge of negative emotions, such as jealousy, anger and fear, rather than let them take over. Once Scorpios discover that their emotions and thoughts do not control them and that it is they, themselves, rather than other people who make them feel a certain way, life will get much easier for them. This is because they will be in the driving seat of their lives rather than at the mercy or the whims and inconsistencies of others.

Fellow Scorpios can highlight the dangers of personal insecurity and how this can sometimes result in self-destructive behavior. Gaining emotional confidence is a tough lesson to learn, but in Scorpios' journey toward fulfillment and happiness in life, the other signs can point the way. The earth signs—Taurus, Capricorn and Virgo—can teach them the importance of self-care and the value of some kind of routine and structure in life. Aquarians have the inner calm and emotional self-control many Scorpios lack and Geminis the ability to see different points of view. Arians and Sagittarians can encourage them to express their emotions honestly, and Cancerians and Pisceans to open up to others rather than bottling things up. Leos can teach them to be warm and open-hearted rather than secretive and suspicious, and Libras can help them discover the priceless contentment that comes whenever they can find a balance in their life between giving and receiving, holding tight and surrendering.

Chinese astrology counterpart: The Pig

The Chinese Pig and Western Scorpio can both be drawn to the deeper and darker side of life, as well as simple earthly pleasures. They are also extremely focused and unstoppable once they have decided on a course of action, even if it's something everybody else disagrees with and isn't perhaps in their best interests. They want to be the ones to decide what is best and to experiment with different options to discover the truth for themselves.

As well as having a passion for personal growth and transformation, these people often possess a high sex drive and a lust for acquiring power and wealth, and more and more power and wealth. They can be moody and intensely dark at times, and, although they are confident and brave, they can also be selfish to the extreme, disrespecting the opinions and needs of others. Despite their pleasure-seeking approach to life, they are also idealistic and drawn to the spiritual. Seldom dishonest, these responsible, determined, generous, deep and utterly original and intense people rarely fail to make their mark or leave a lasting impression.

Note: Scorpios have an affinity with Pig-sign characteristics, but be sure to check which Chinese sign corresponds to your **year** of birth (see page xxi), to read about the characteristics associated with it, too.

October 23

The Birthday of the Tornado

"Always in the thick of it"

Those born on October 23 are exciting people who run on high-octane energy. There is always a tornado of energy and excitement around whatever they do. Others admire their lively charm, intelligence and courage, but feel frustrated by the confusion they cause. Their boredom threshold is very low and they may seek conflict simply to challenge themselves. Others find this need to stir things up inexplicable, but for these individuals, life lived in a comfortable routine isn't a life well lived. They need to be constantly active and during times of crisis they really come into their own.

Born entrepreneurs and influencers, they have the energy to excel in many professions. They may be drawn to artistic or sporting careers, but they also make excellent entrepreneurs and social-media influencers. Other choices include the emergency services, crime-fighting, the law, lobbying, social reform, education, writing, business, information technology, entertainment, health and leisure, advertising, sales and filmmaking. They lead very active lives and may spend a lot of their time in conversation or on their phones, so it is important they take regular time out to unplug and relax. **For self-care**, calming mind–body therapies, such as yoga and meditation, are beneficial, and listening to classical music can have a therapeutic effect.

Those born on this day are never short of fans, but they tend to think and talk about the power of love, rather than live it. Before the age of 30 they are likely to concentrate on personal power and they need to make sure this does not go to their head. After 30 they reach a turning point when they are likely to try to expand their horizons. Finding a balance between challenging themselves and their need to seek stability is key. Whatever path in life they choose, change is always a feature. Once they understand that they don't need a crisis to feel alive, their ability to respond instantly to stimulating opportunities for growth makes them among the most independent, progressive and compassionate individuals of the year. Their desire is to pioneer ground-breaking advances to benefit or inspire others.

Potential: Exciting, inspiring

Dark side: Restless, superficial

Tarot card, lucky numbers, days, colors: The Hierophant, 5, 6, Tuesday, Wednesday, red, green

Born today: Emilia Clarke, Ryan Reynolds (actors); Anita Roddick (entrepreneur); Pelé (soccer player)

October 24

The Birthday of Irresistible Intensity

is going with the flow.

The way forward: is to understand that certain things can't be controlled, so sometimes it's best to leave things alone.

Luck maker: When unforeseen circumstances derail or slow you down, you must be flexible, adapt and look for different ways to reach the same goal.

"Let's get serious"

October 24-born often have a compelling energy and intensity about them. Ruled by extreme emotions that they battle to control, one of their greatest strengths is that they can play it cool, even when they feel insecure or out of control on the inside. They get absorbed in the details of their work and love to present their findings at any opportunity. This doesn't mean they are show-offs, just that they take their work extremely seriously and pride themselves on their accomplishments. The upside of their great intensity is that it helps propel them to the top of their careers. The downside is that they can neglect their emotional life for their work. They can also become controlling, jealous and interfering, which can alienate them from those who give them a much-needed sense of perspective.

Born researchers, they are likely to thrive because of the strength of their dedication, laser-like focus and perfectionist attention to detail. They find themselves drawn to leadership positions in accounting, finance, the law, engineering, administration, public relations, sales, publishing, promotion, music and show business, education, science, the healing and caring professions, and the sport and leisure industries. Prone to stress and tension, regular time out and relaxing with loved ones is important to keep a sense of balance and perspective. **For self-care**, walking in green fields or among trees is extremely beneficial because wearing, meditating on and surrounding yourself with the color green has a calming and balancing effect on your mind.

Commitment can be a problem, but once they fall in love, they fall passionately to the exclusion of all else. Around the age of 29 they reach a turning point, which highlights a need for freedom and broadening their horizons through further education and travel. They should never stop devoting themselves to their work because, when this is balanced with greater tolerance and open-mindedness, they have outstanding potential to realize their ambitions and enjoy the fruits of success. Once they learn to *do* less and *be* more, their destiny is to lead and inspire others with their focused and dedicated example.

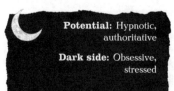

Potential: Hypnotic, authoritative

Dark side: Obsessive, stressed

Tarot card, lucky numbers, days, colors: The Lovers, 6, 7, Tuesday, Friday, red, pink

Born today: Kevin Kline (actor); Antonie van Leeuwenhoek (chemist); Robert Mundell (economist); Drake (rapper)

October 25

The Birthday of Tangible Results

"Show, don't tell"

People born on October 25 are driven by an intense desire to translate their progressive dreams into reality. They are articulate and intelligent, and don't have much time for small talk. Results matter to them and "Actions speak louder than words" is their motto. Others may accuse them of not being visionary enough, but this is not true. They have dreams and visions, and respect others' dreams, but they don't value ideas that can't be actioned or realized. Results-focused and no-nonsense, they can be a comforting and reassuring presence, but they are not the most caring and sharing individuals. Instead, they are a role model of self-discipline and determination. Unfortunately, they can be critical and intolerant at times, and this can earn them enemies.

Born producers and manufacturers, they bring much-needed order and structure to any career with their detailed, result-orientated approach, and are capable of outstanding achievement. Science, politics, education, design, architecture, farming, as well as art, drama, music, management, the law, crafts or inventing and working for yourself, may well appeal. They have perfectionist, workaholic tendencies and need to watch for warning signs of stress and burnout. Regular time to unplug and relax, as well as a healthy diet, exercise and sleep routines, are beneficial. **For self-care**, reading spiritual books is therapeutic, as is wearing, meditating on and surrounding yourself with the color pink to encourage you to be more loving, open and giving.

Never short of admirers, these people need to ensure they do more than simply take in relationships. From their early thirties onward, they become more expansive and may explore the meaning of life through philosophy, study or travel. Any opportunity to open their heart and spread their wings is good for them and helps rather than hinders their goal of producing progressive results not just in their own lives but in the lives of others too. Once they learn to be more tolerant, to give as well as receive and to focus and unwind in equal measures, their destiny is to express their truly visionary ideas in a practical and productive way.

Potential: Reassuring, focused

Dark side: Workaholic, intolerant

Tarot card, lucky numbers, days, colors: The Chariot, 7, 8, Tuesday, Monday, red, sea green

Born today: Katy Perry, Ciara (singers); Georges Bizet (composer); Pablo Picasso (artist)

October 26

The Birthday of the Powerful Planner

"My power is a force for good"

Those born on October 26 are goal-orientated and perhaps the most self-controlled and hard-working individuals of the year. They are both doers and planners and hugely ambitious and conscientious, but their motivation isn't money or success, it is power and they are at their finest when managing others. They may have natural authority but they are not power-crazed. They simply believe that organizing people to work collectively is the most effective way to achieve positive reform, making them progressive managers and leaders whose dedication and authority inspire tremendous trust and respect.

Born conductors and managers, they are suited to careers in business, politics, community work, accounting, finance, banking and social events organization, as well as the law, science, medicine, social reform, the caring professions, administration, life-coaching, careers advisory and the world of music and theater. They may have body-image issues; tossing away the scales and relying on common sense and their clothes size as a weight guide would be far more beneficial. Opening their minds and hearts with volunteer work encourages them to be more tolerant and giving. **For self-care**, training your intuition by paying attention to the meaning of dreams, signs, coincidences and gut feelings can help you with decision-making.

A lot of these people's energy is spent trying to get others to think the same as them. If others agree with them, their affectionate qualities surface; the opposite is true if others disagree. After the age of 26 they leave any shyness behind, grow in confidence and self-belief, and become more optimistic and expansive in their thinking. Whatever path they choose, they often find themselves successfully coordinating and directing others. To ensure this magic extends to their personal life, they need to trust their intuition more and stop suppressing originality—and that includes their own. Once they become more tolerant and able to embrace their own wonderful individuality as well as the individuality of others, their destiny is to organize, coordinate and inspire others toward a collective goal.

Potential: Focused, authoritative

Dark side: Obsessive, narrow-minded

Tarot card, lucky numbers, days, colors: Strength, 8, 9, Tuesday, Saturday, red, black

Born today: Leon Trotsky (Soviet revolutionary); Hillary Clinton (US politician); Charles-François Dupuis (astronomer); Bob Hoskins (actor)

October 27

The Birthday of the Inspirer

"Life is infinite possibility"

October 27-born are intensely idealistic and emotional individuals. They tend to react spontaneously to anyone or anything they encounter, and their ability to excite others and be a galvanizing force gives them outstanding potential to motivate and light up others' lives. Their decisions and opinions may be heart-centered, but they also have the intellect and practical skills to see their goals realized. Once their heart has been touched, they are an unstoppable force. Given their impulsive nature, it is not surprising they are prone to mood swings, and they often have a vulnerable side too. Getting the approval of others can matter too much to them, so they need to build their self-esteem, listen more to their intuition and take care of their own emotional needs before trying to inspire those around them.

Born musicians, they flourish in careers involving imparting their knowledge, such as teaching or journalism, but may also thrive as actors, composers, entertainers and writers. Other career options include broadcasting, life-coaching, promotion, sales, media, advertising, and the caring and healing professions. They can take longer to recover from disappointments and setbacks than others, so they need to ensure they take every opportunity to rest and recharge. **For self-care**, brisk walking by yourself is recommended to boost your mood and quieten your mind.

Love can be scary for these people despite their emotional nature, but is the easier option for them than the anxiety of avoiding it. After the age of 26 they likely become less emotional and sensitive, and more independent and adventurous. However, they always follow their heart rather than their head, and they feel things more deeply than other people. The key to their happiness is to direct that emotional intensity positively and to work on lighting themselves up as well as others. Once they recognize their own value and learn to calmly reflect before they speak and act, their destiny is to play a truly inspiring educational and directorial role in life.

Potential: Exciting, inspirational

Dark side: Reckless, insecure

Tarot card, lucky numbers, day, colors: The Hermit, 1, 9, Tuesday, scarlet, orange

Born today: James Cook (explorer); Theodore Roosevelt (US president); John Cleese (comedian); Sylvia Plath (author)

October 28

The Birthday of Preparation

"I live to work"

The life lesson:

is taking a risk.

The way forward: is to understand that a calculated risk is not reckless, but a way to move forward with your life.

Luck maker: Break the rules now and again or use your creativity and originality to work your way around them.

People born on October 28 tend to define themselves by their career. For them it is a vocation rather than work and the choice of career is of utmost importance to them. They may take a while to find their vocation, but once they do, they generally rise to the top because of their extraordinary self-discipline and eye for detail. They are extremely inquisitive, with an insatiable desire to explore, and when this is combined with their organizational skills, it gives them pioneering potential. They can, however, become so absorbed in their work that they don't have much of a life outside. Although this means they will succeed in their chosen field—which more often than not is dedicated to improving, entertaining or educating others—it can also mean they become overly serious, and in some cases emotionally isolated figures.

Born scientists, they may be attracted to research, finance, engineering and technology, but their desire to benefit others may also draw them to medicine, education, writing, blogging, life-coaching, acting, social and humanitarian reform, and community or charity work. They may lead sedentary lives due to long hours at a desk or computer, and regular exercise is highly beneficial, as are dance or yoga classes that teach correct breathing and posture. **For self-care**, keeping a mood journal and wearing, meditating on and surrounding yourself with the color orange encourages feelings of warmth and security.

It can take those born on this day a while to open up in relationships, but when they do so they can surprise themselves with their passion. Until the age of 25 they are at their most serious and intense, but after this age they crave freedom. They should grasp opportunities for travel, further education or study, because these offer the chance to become more fulfilled outside their career. If they can expend as much energy discovering and preparing themselves for the wonderful adventure life has to offer outside work, they can make their distinctive mark and create lasting connections with the world. Their destiny is to dedicate themselves to their vocation and inspire everyone else to prepare for and ensure clear progress is made.

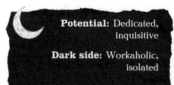

Potential: Dedicated, inquisitive

Dark side: Workaholic, isolated

Tarot card, lucky numbers, days, colors: The Magician, 1, 2, Tuesday, Monday, red, yellow

Born today: Bill Gates (entrepreneur); Joaquin Phoenix, Julia Roberts (actors); Howard Hanson (composer)

October 29

The Birthday of the Chess Master

"The law of surprise"

The life lesson:

is letting others know where you stand.

The way forward: is to understand that although secrecy can be extremely effective for professional success, the same is not true in your personal life.

Luck maker: People like to help those who show real passion, because it means you are alive and vibrant, and helping you makes them feel that way, too.

October 29-born are highly accomplished tacticians and strategists, but they are in no way predictable. They are extremely authoritative and innovative individuals, bursting with new ideas and energy. One of the reasons they invest so much energy in preparing and planning for potential outcomes is that, like a chess master, they appreciate the element of surprise and the benefits of keeping others in the dark about their true intentions. They tend to be secretive, and others never understand what makes them tick and are surprised by their sudden changes of direction. This only makes sense when the bigger picture of their lives is taken into account, because it includes a pronounced desire to direct others toward their personal goals or ideals. To some this may appear manipulative, but unpredictability is their empowering tactic.

Born criminologists, they are multitalented and likely to thrive in whatever career they choose. They may find themselves drawn to research, crime-fighting, forensics, psychology, science, the military, politics, the law or commerce. Publishing, marketing, writing, music, healing, social reform and charity work may also appeal. They thrive in tidy and orderly environments and if their homes or workspaces are messy, they can feel stressed. Clearing away clutter helps clear their mind. **For self-care**, plants in your home or office can lift your mood, as can playing uplifting music as you work or do your chores.

Game-playing may be effective in these people's professional life, but in their personal life they fail to see that close and loving relationships might be the checkmate they need. After the age of 24 they come out of their shells and start to be more adventurous emotionally. Whatever age they are, they should make a huge effort to reveal more of themselves to others, because although outstanding professional accomplishments are assured, personal success is more elusive until they can connect more honestly and openly. Once they are able to let go and trust their intuition more, their destiny is to take truly visionary and innovative action in their chosen field.

Potential: Masterful, innovative

Dark side: Devious, detached

Tarot card, lucky numbers, days, colors: The High Priestess, 2, 4, Tuesday, Thursday, red, silver

Born today: Winona Ryder, Kate Jackson, Richard Dreyfuss (actors); Carl Djerassi (chemist)

October 30

The Birthday of the Deep-sea Diver

"Bigger than me"

People born on October 30 involve themselves deeply in whatever project, situation or relationship captures their imagination. Like deep-sea divers, they jump in at the deep end and their whole world is taken over by their current interest or concern. The upside of this total absorption is that it gives them great potential for career success. The downside is that as well as neglecting other important areas of their lives, when the novelty wears off what they are focusing on, they tend to lose interest. This can leave their disillusioned followers without a motivated leader.

Born swimmers, they thrive in careers offering variety, such as sports, politics, the performing arts, teaching, publishing, medicine, self-help and the caring and healing professions. Their magnetism helps them when dealing with people or teams in public relations, advertising, travel, tourism and retail work, and their talent for words draws them to writing, the media and journalism. They can get so absorbed in work that they forget to pay attention to their health and wellbeing. Keeping well hydrated and paying attention to their posture are vital. **For self-care**, wearing or meditating on the color green brings you a more balanced perspective on life.

Prone to falling head over heels in love, those born on this day tend to struggle to keep the intensity alive and end relationships prematurely instead of investing energy into reigniting them. Before the age of 23 they may seem rather intense and serious. After 23 their emphasis switches to opportunities to study, travel and expand their horizons. Whatever age they are, these fascinating and sincere individuals always have a strong spirit of enterprise. When they are able to diversify their life from a one-dimensional to a multidimensional focus, they can fulfill their potential as inspirational leaders, and come out of the water and breathe. Once they can immerse themselves in the journey within as well as outside themselves and find the right balance between their personal and professional life, their destiny is to devote their overwhelming energy to the education, growth and development of others.

Potential: Charismatic, fascinating

Dark side: Obsessive, unpredictable

Tarot card, lucky numbers, days, colors: The Empress, 3, 4, Tuesday, Thursday, red, royal blue

Born today: Ashley Graham (model); John Adams (US president); Ezra Pound (poet); Diego Maradona (soccer player)

October 31

The Birthday of the Indominable Accommodator

is asserting yourself.

The way forward: is to understand that assertion is different from aggression and when you respect yourself it is easier for others to respect you.

Luck maker: Pay attention to details, but you should never let them obscure the bigger picture or end goal.

"The whole is greater than the sum of the parts"

Those born on October 31 have the talent and creativity to excel in whatever field they choose, but their natural modesty often prevents them from stepping forward. They much prefer to guide and praise others; as a result, people tend to rely on them for support, comfort and inspiration. Although they are generally accommodating, when they sense that injustice has been done, their true fire and fighting spirit can emerge, surprising those who may have wrongly labeled them as gentle, unassuming souls. They give their all to anyone or anything they believe in, and when their indomitable will and desire to support others combines with their excellent communication and organizational skills, they are a real force to be reckoned with. Their Achilles' heel is they can get bogged down with details, which can lead to confusion. It's important for them to always keep their ultimate goal in mind and not get sidetracked.

Born constructors, they are suited to careers in which they can contribute toward the common good, such as architecture, social work, the caring professions, the law, politics, law enforcement, social reform, and humanitarian and charity work. Education, counseling, medicine, psychology, writing, literature, filmmaking and performing also offer opportunities to create something of lasting value. Paying close attention to their physical health and emotional wellbeing helps them feel more confident. **For self-care**, martial arts, such as karate, can help you discover the warrior within, while wearing the color red can encourage you to become more assertive.

These caring souls crave harmony in their relationships, but, if they don't set boundaries, they attract toxic people who take advantage of them. After the age of 22 they focus on expanding their horizons through further education, travel and new experiences. They work better when they have a plan for what they want to achieve, and if they can stick to it, they can satisfy their strong desire to contribute something valuable to the world. Once they learn to be more proactive and stand up and be counted, their destiny is to make a lasting contribution toward the greater or common good.

Potential: Resilient, compassionate

Dark side: Self-effacing, passive

Tarot card, lucky numbers, days, colors: The Emperor, 4, 5, Tuesday, Thursday, red, silver

Born today: Johannes Vermeer (painter); John Keats (poet); Juliette Gordon Low (activist); Peter Jackson (director)

November 1

The Birthday of the Striker

The life lesson:

is self-knowledge.

The way forward: is to take the time to reflect and look within to increase self-awareness.

Luck maker: Thinking about how your behavior affects others increases the chances of attracting good fortune.

"Bring it on"

November 1-born fear a life without variety and challenge. They despise inaction and are energized by progressive, even radical concepts. Doers rather than thinkers, as soon as they have completed one project they speed ahead with great conviction to the next. They really thrive on challenge because the uncertainty of taxing situations makes them feel alive. If they find a way to satisfy their hunger for adventure and stimulation, their boundless energy gives them the power and potential to make things happen. If, however, they find themselves in an environment where they do not need to be in battle mode, they can sink into despondency, even depression. These people tend to be outspoken, willing to offer their opinion on anything, but can on occasion take dangerous risks or underestimate or misinterpret people and situations.

Born entrepreneurs, they need plenty of variety and may want to work for themselves in artistic, inventive, business, legal and scientific fields. Their constant need for challenge may lead them to leadership positions in the world of design, sport, acting, music and writing, and sales, banking, the stock market, tourism, education, medicine and social work. They naturally drift toward competitive activities, in particular soccer, rugby, baseball and basketball, as well as martial arts, boxing and mountain climbing. **For self-care**, carrying a small malachite crystal and meditating on and surrounding yourself with soothing shades of blue brings calmness into your life.

Those born on this day have high expectations in relationships and need to love people for who they are, not for what they could be. Until the age of 21 they may be intense and serious, but after 21 their adventurous nature shines through. Whatever age they are, their courageous spirit and expansive outlook give them potential to extend human knowledge. But to become the inspirational and influential force they are destined to be, self-knowledge, common sense and good judgment are crucial. Their destiny is to explore and develop exciting new ideas and to inspire others to do the same.

Potential: Energetic, exciting

Dark side: Unaware, restless

Tarot card, lucky numbers, days, colors: The Magician, 1, 3, Tuesday, Sunday, red, hunter green

Born today: Tim Cook (Apple CEO); Gary Player (golfer); Jim Steinman (songwriter); Aishwarya Rai (actor)

November 2

The Birthday of Regeneration

"Every day I am born anew"

is resisting the temptation to interfere.

The way forward: is to understand that change for its own sake only unsettles and confuses both you and others.

Luck maker: Good judgment isn't just about saying and doing the right thing, it's about sensing when to say and do the right thing—at the right time.

People born on November 2 often seem in the process of rebirth or renewal. Nothing gets them more excited than a new start. However, it is important for them to guard against change for its own sake. Ironically, they can sometimes be surprisingly resistant to change within themselves because, instead of focusing on their inner life, they tend to direct their energy outward to transforming the world around them. It's only when they learn to listen to the quiet voice within that they realize that too much change is counterproductive.

Born life coaches, they need constant variety and are well suited to careers in tourism, aviation, finance, sales, the law, public relations, psychology, education, charity work, arbitration, counseling, lobbying and campaigning, and the media. Alternatively, they may express their creativity in music, acting, blogging or social-media influencing. Work involving sport and leisure can also be good outlets for their energy and ambition. These people don't tend to have addictive personalities, but alcohol and smoking can become health problems if left unchecked. They have an active and inquisitive mind, so all forms of study, reading and intellectual challenge are beneficial. **For self-care,** meditation techniques help you search within for answers, and wearing the color purple encourages you to focus on higher things.

Never short of admirers, those born on this day may find that their taste for adventure leads them into short-lived relationships rather than enduring ones. After the age of 20, they focus on expansion and adventure in their lives through study, education or travel. After 50, they reach a turning point, which introduces more structure and realism. For their outstanding creative potential to be unlocked, they need to understand that, although regeneration is essential for psychological growth, it is a process rather than a goal in itself. Once they leave materialism behind, learn that the most important changes take place within, and get in touch with their feelings and motivations, their destiny is to inspire others to open their minds and broaden their horizons.

Potential: Energizing, influential

Dark side: Scattered, unaware

Tarot card, lucky numbers, days, colors: The High Priestess, 2, 4, Tuesday, Monday, red, silver

Born today: Shahrukh Khan, David Schwimmer (actors); Daniel Boone (explorer); k.d. lang (singer)

November 3

The Birthday of the Marathon Runner

The life lesson:

is coping with failure.

The way forward: is to understand that people learn more about themselves during times of disappointment than in times of victory.

Luck maker: When things don't work out, you should learn from the situation and forgive (but not forget), so you can release negative emotions and move on.

"In it to win it"

Those born on November 3 have the stamina of a long-distance runner. They are ambitious and energetic, and with their ability to keep calm under pressure, they can be labeled ruthless. The one thing that can unsettle their self-control is defeat or failure. They are terrible losers, and instead of trying to find better solutions, they focus on blaming others or themselves. They can be overwhelmingly negative at times, but when things go well, they can be very charismatic. In good times they also have a deep understanding of others and great compassion, but they lack similar insight into themselves. They must look within to understand why their need to win and their perfectionist drive can overpower their need to be happy.

Born designers and brokers, they are drawn to professions where they can exert influence over others, such as fashion, financial advice, the stock market, education, business management, the civil service, administration, social-media influencing, music and entertainment. Other careers include negotiation, writing, editing and the healing or caring professions. Habitually hiding their emotions and true intentions, these people can be prone to stress and depression. Cognitive behavioral techniques to reprogram their thoughts from negative to positive can be extremely beneficial, as can counseling or psychotherapy. For self-care, carrying a small malachite crystal brings a sense of calmness, as does meditating on and wearing the color orange.

Idealistic and romantic, those born on this day avoid half-hearted relationships and long to find someone with whom to fully share their lives—and they usually succeed. Despite being moody teenagers, after the age of 20 they are more optimistic, leading to a broadening of their horizons through travel or study. After 49, financial and greater emotional stability take center stage. They always remain highly competitive, but once they understand that the only battle worth winning is the one with themselves, they can apply their sharp intellect, superb communication skills and almost superhuman endurance to the winning cause of furthering the common good. When they become more forgiving and tolerant, their destiny is to transform their progressive ambitions into a reality that benefits all.

Potential: Focused, progressive

Dark side: Ruthless, negative

Tarot card, lucky numbers, days, colors: The Empress, 3, 5, Tuesday, Thursday, red, green

Born today: Lucian (poet); Amartya Sen (economist); Anna Wintour (editor); David Ho (researcher)

November 4

The Birthday of the Icebreaker

"Right to the heart of the matter"

Those born on November 4 appear reserved and sincere, but as soon as they start interacting with others, their provocative nature shines through. They have a talent for uncovering hidden weaknesses, and for luring everyone they meet into their web of controversy. They are extremely persuasive, with a great sense of humor, and believe they can convince everyone of their viewpoint. However, they are not manipulative but principled and honest, and believe they always know the truth. Above all, they are icebreakers, able to articulate the unspoken or unacceptable in such a way that they influence others to agree with them or review their own position. Sometimes their tactics can work against them and they may unintentionally offend others.

Born reformers, they may be drawn to social media, writing, journalism, art, teaching, tourism and performing, or politics and social reform. Other options include leadership or freelance positions in marketing, advertising, business, commerce, medicine, religion or spirituality. They need to become aware of the powerful link between their physical and emotional or mental health. When they are feeling run down, the chances are that a period of stress was the trigger. **For self-care**, regular long walks in the park or countryside can help you gain balance and perspective. Wearing, meditating on and surrounding yourself with the color green brings greater harmony and hope.

Once those born on this day learn to love themselves, their potential to attract loving people into their lives is great and they can be wonderfully giving and supportive. After the age of 19, their shyness recedes and is replaced by a need for freedom, study and travel. After 48, the emphasis is on financial and emotional security. Whatever age they are, the key to success is to use common sense and become aware how their approach affects people, including themselves. When greater self-awareness and self-discipline are combined with their intuitive perception and natural leadership, they can achieve truly spectacular results. And when they learn to have a more balanced perspective and tone down their enthusiasm so that it supports not offends, their destiny is to help open minds and instigate reform.

Potential: Exciting, sincere

Dark side: Provocative, overwhelming

Tarot card, lucky numbers, days, colors: The Emperor, 4, 6, Tuesday, Sunday, red, silver

Born today: Matthew McConaughey, Will Rogers (actors); Puff Daddy (rapper); Walter Cronkite (journalist)

November 5

The Birthday of the Spokesperson

"In the know"

November 5-born like to be at the center of things. They are the ones others turn to if they want to be in the know, because they end up being the official or unofficial spokesperson of whatever social group or cause they support. As information gatherers, they keep up to date with what is current, because they spot cutting-edge trends before anyone else. Sometimes they suffer from information overload, but despite their occasional absent-mindedness they are determined powerhouses who get things done. Their realism refuses to let their idealism get in the way of practical considerations.

Born spokespeople, the fields of sociology, promotion, sales, advertising, writing, singing, speaking and acting could be ideal, but they may also be drawn to negotiation, arbitration, public relations, lobbying, science, technology and business. They tend to be reactive rather than proactive—greater self-knowledge and control in their responses to people and situations are crucial for their emotional health. They may need time alone, perhaps even therapy or counseling, to discover who they are and what they want out of life. **For self-care**, carrying a small rose-quartz crystal encourages you to be as fascinated with your own heart and life as you are with those of others.

Sensitive and honest, these people fear losing themselves in close relationships, so it is important that they are not the one doing all the giving. After the age of 18 they gradually become more confident and outgoing; after 48 they become more organized and industrious, with a greater understanding of their goals. The key to their success, whatever their age, is not their ability to adapt to what is going on, but their capacity to control and direct it. When they become more self-aware, they not only find greater happiness, but also use their incredible insight and knowledge to benefit others. And when they take charge of their lives rather than allowing others or circumstances to set the tone, their destiny is to uncover and reveal insights that can truly enlighten others.

Potential: Inquisitive, determined

Dark side: Unaware, absent-minded

Tarot card, lucky numbers, days, colors: The Hierophant, 5, 7, Tuesday, Wednesday, red, green

Born today: Bryan Adams, Art Garfunkel (singers); Ella Wilcox (author); Will Durant (historian)

November 6

The Birthday of the Overachiever

"Over and above"

People born on November 6 are vibrant. They have the ability to inject enthusiasm wherever they go, motivating others with their endless energy. Driven and ambitious, with a can-do attitude, they refuse to be sidetracked from their goals by obstacles. Although this gives them incredible potential, they can become too confident of success without the necessary backup plans, and they need to inject realism into their lives by listening to dissenting voices too. A realistic outlook is not negative, but it takes into account both the upsides and the downsides of a situation. And toning down their energy to suit different audiences is key to avoid unintentionally offending.

Born speculators, they may be drawn to planning, marketing, sales, entertainment, international business, tourism, the leisure and sports industries, and teaching or coaching. They may also thrive in technology, science, politics, the law, medicine and the emergency services, while music, dance or writing are also attractive options. Blessed with limitless energy, they can overreach themselves. Fatigue and burnout are a real concern, so it is important for them to pace themselves. Regular vacations and plenty of time to relax and unwind, as well as quality sleep, are essential. **For self-care,** mind–body techniques such as yoga and meditation can encourage you to slow down, as can spending more time in nature or natural settings.

Those born on this day tend to be attracted to unattainable people and need to understand that, while this is their way of protecting themselves, it can damage them. After the age of 16, they start to develop their characteristic enthusiasm and drive, and develop through an expansive choice of education, career and travel. After 46, the focus shifts to becoming more realistic and organized. Realism is an important ingredient for their psychological growth, so this is when they are likely to realize there are always positive and negative outcomes in life. Once they have learned how to grow from setbacks, their destiny is to be inspired leaders and to follow their instinct to enlighten others and promote the common good with their innovative visions.

Potential: Uplifting, energetic

Dark side: Overconfident, despondent

Tarot card, lucky numbers, days, colors: The Lovers, 6, 8, Tuesday, Friday, red, lavender

Born today: Sally Field, Emma Stone (actors); John Philip Sousa (composer); Jerry Yang (entrepreneur)

November 7

The Birthday of the Curious Adventurer

"Live to explore"

Those born on November 7 are inquisitive, with an adventurous, pioneering spirit. They seize any opportunity to learn and discover something new, and to challenge themselves. Their curiosity is limitless and they love being able to figure out what makes someone tick or how something works. They are also ambitious and thrive on variety and change—being stuck in a routine is their personal nightmare. Although their potential for success is remarkable, their lack of focus can be problematic. In some ways their greatest strength—their inquisitive spirit—is also their greatest weakness, because their constant need to struggle, learn and challenge can stop them from setting achievable goals.

Born explorers, these multitalented people have the potential to thrive in any career. Possible options include social reform, sporting or artistic careers, and scientific research and innovation, but they may also be drawn to writing, education, research, politics, spirituality, tourism and entertainment. Alternatively, they may work for themselves. Fatigue, both intellectual and physical, can be a problem, and to make sure they don't suffer from energy slumps, they need plenty of quality sleep and a healthy diet and exercise routine. **For self-care,** making your bed every morning helps set an organized tone for the day ahead, and wearing or meditating on the color blue encourages you to be more goal-orientated.

Although light-hearted at the onset, they can become controlling in their long-term relationships. They must give those they love the same freedom they give themselves. Until the age of 45, they are likely to be restless and may have a burning urge to study, travel and expand their horizons. After 45, they need more order and structure, and they can build on the incredible knowledge and experience they have gained previously and use it as a launching pad to work practically toward realizing their goals. Typically, these goals are of benefit not just to themselves and those close to them, but also to the wider world. Once they have learned to focus, their destiny is to inspire and educate others with their upbeat and enthusiastic attitude.

Potential: Inquisitive, pioneering

Dark side: Restless, disorganized

Tarot card, lucky numbers, days, colors: The Chariot, 7, 9, Tuesday, Monday, red, sapphire

Born today: Marie Curie (scientist); Albert Camus (author); Joni Mitchell, Lorde (singers)

November 8

The Birthday of Deep Fascination

The life lesson:

is learning to laugh more.

The way forward: is to understand that taking yourself too seriously means a loss of the perspective and objectivity you need to make good judgments.

Luck maker: Connect with your inner child to help you be happy and spontaneous, and remember what is important in life.

"Still waters run deep"

November 8-born are blessed with imaginative and progressive minds, but can appear serious or intense. They are often attracted to deep or peculiar subjects. Brilliant at concentrating their energy on achieving their goals, their courage and ambition augur well for professional success. Many rise to the top and achieve a comfortable standard of living. Sometimes the desire to achieve materially can be overpowering, so it's important for them to remember what is truly important in life. Their curiosity can sometimes pull them to explore the darker aspects of the world, as they love to push the boundaries of knowledge and experience. If they remain objective they can become real innovators, but, if not, they risk becoming identified with the shadow side of life.

Born criminologists, they are suited to careers where they can be creative and curious. They make superb detectives, psychologists, writers, musicians, or pioneering scientists and engineers. Other areas that appeal include finance, real estate, administration, education, counseling, the law, journalism, or philosophical or spiritual occupations. They tend to love spending and need to ensure this doesn't get out of hand. Above all, they should spend more time relaxing and having fun to keep a sense of perspective and be less intense. **For self-care**, yoga and tai chi can encourage your mind and body to become more flexible.

These people may appear reserved, but they are deeply passionate. Tempted to seek out unusual types, they can benefit from being with more grounded individuals. Until the age of 33, the urge to explore the unconventional is at its strongest and they need to remember they can also learn much from what is routine. After 33 they become more practical, disciplined and goal-orientated. The key to their success lies in their ability to confront their inner fears. When they can do this, their hunger to explore the meaning of life inevitably draws them away from the darkness into the light. Once they have balanced the light and dark within them, their destiny is to explore the unconventional and expand the frontiers of human knowledge and experience.

Potential: Deep, inquisitive

Dark side: Overly serious, obsessive

Tarot card, lucky numbers, days, colors: Strength, 1, 8, Tuesday, Saturday, red, indigo

Born today: Edmond Halley (astronomer); Bram Stoker (author); Jack Kilby (engineer); Gordon Ramsay (chef)

November 9

The Birthday of Enticement

"Right here, right now"

People born on November 9 are passionate and courageous, but often find themselves in situations that challenge their resolve. Materialism and pleasure-seeking are powerful drives. Fortunately, they usually find a balance between satisfying their urges and doing the right thing, but occasionally they can behave questionably. They are well-intentioned, but can get so caught up in the moment that they lose their sense of right and wrong. They are also risk-takers, and while this can lead to success, they are not good at dealing with rejection and tend to isolate themselves with resentment and self-pity if rebuffed. Learning to become more resilient by tapping into their inner strength is essential for their psychological growth.

Born forensic experts, they may be drawn to detective work, the law, psychology, research and medicine. The limitless possibilities of art, science, technology, engineering and design have obvious appeal. They have a natural talent for writing and lecturing, and may also excel in tourism, business, commerce, sales, promotion and negotiation, as well as show business and politics. Because their lives tend to be stressful, ensuring they eat a balanced diet, get plenty of exercise and a good night's sleep keeps them grounded. **For self-care**, meditation and yoga can help you get in touch with your thoughts and feelings, as can interpreting your dreams. Surrounding yourself with the colors white and silver encourages you to examine situations carefully and make the right choices.

Those born on this day can be extraordinarily seductive and never lack admirers, but some may choose solitude or keep their distance in close relationships. Until the age of 42, they are most likely to expand their horizons, take risks and seek out challenges. After 42 they become industrious and practical, needing a strong sense of order and structure. Making sure that the spiritual side of their life is not neglected is absolutely crucial, because whenever they connect with their inner wisdom, they can resist the temptations that block good fortune and achieve remarkable success. Once they can look beyond the present and have an awareness of the consequences of their actions, their destiny is to inspire others to uncover the fascinating truth about themselves and their lives.

Potential: Interesting, seductive

Dark side: Materialistic, dubious

Tarot card, lucky numbers, day, colors: The Hermit, 2, 9, Tuesday, red, white

Born today: Imre Kertész (author); Mary Travers, Nick Lachey (singers); Katharine Hepburn (actor)

November 10

The Birthday of Awareness

"Self-knowledge is the beginning of wisdom"

is developing self-confidence.

The way forward: is to understand that you are as confident as you believe yourself to be.

Luck maker: Acting confidently—even when you don't feel that way—can trick your brain into believing you are indeed confident, and makes you more appealing to others.

Those born on November 10 are among the most self-aware people of the year. From an early age they know their strengths and weaknesses and have a realistic idea of their own potential. This self-knowledge gives them a huge advantage in the game of life, and when combined with their curiosity, intelligence and creativity, their potential for success is considerable. They also have a natural understanding of how objects, strategies or methods function and are often the fixers and menders in life. The only area they lack understanding of is other people. Individual and group dynamics are a mystery to them, so when it comes to socializing and networking they may feel out of their depth.

Born academics, careers that offer them regular periods alone appeal and they may be drawn to academia, technology, technical work, writing, the arts and science, or to freelancing. Other career choices include campaigning, psychology, investigative work, education, philosophy, tourism, entertainment, broadcasting, and spiritual growth and development. They tend to bottle up their emotions, and this can lead to stress and poor health. It is important for them to learn to open up and to be more trusting; counseling and therapy can be beneficial. **For self-care,** wearing and meditating on the color orange increases feelings of warmth, physical enjoyment, security and sexuality, and wearing the color red boosts confidence.

In relationships those born on this day can be intense and passionate, but tend to attract toxic or co-dependent people. Working on their self-confidence can change this dynamic. Until the age of 42 they have opportunities to reach out to others, which they may find frightening, but if they don't take them they risk becoming unhealthily self-absorbed. After 42 they become more practical, disciplined and goal-orientated. If they can overcome their shyness and resist the temptation to hold back, they can make the most of their creative potential and achieve just about anything. Once they have learned to reach out confidently, their destiny is to enlighten, inspire and help others either practically or with their progressive ideas.

Potential: Self-aware, creative

Dark side: Shy, self-absorbed

Tarot card, lucky numbers, days, colors: The Wheel of Fortune, 1, 3, Tuesday, Sunday, red, yellow

Born today: Ennio Morricone (composer), Tim Rice (lyricist); Mathis Wackernagel (activist); Martin Luther (theologian)

November  11

The Birthday of the Painted Veil

"You don't know me"

The life lesson:

is boosting your self-esteem.

The way forward: is to understand that until you like yourself enough, no amount of success can bring fulfillment.

Luck maker: Successful people make their good fortune look effortless, but to succeed you need to work hard, have self-discipline and, above all, believe in yourself.

November 11-born often appear carefree, with a youthful energy about them. But to those who know them better, their charm is often a veil masking a deeply complicated and intense personality. They know how to appeal to others and this is why they often get their own way, usually without others even knowing because they think hiding their ambition to succeed is the best way to win support. They are hugely creative and have the ability to surprise others with hidden depths. Unfortunately, they aren't always clear about what they want from life and this can cause them to procrastinate. Only when they can find the self-discipline to be proactive rather than reactive can their remarkable potential for success be unveiled.

Born creators and builders, they may lean toward careers that involve writing, acting, performing, design, research, building, repair or technical work. They may also make good psychologists, advisors, lecturers and teachers. Occupations connected to tourism may appeal, as may community or charity work. These people can be extremely concerned about their appearance and need to remind themselves that beauty comes from within. **For self-care**, regular meditation helps you to understand yourself, while wearing, meditating on and surrounding yourself with the color yellow promotes confidence.

Attractive, those born on this day rarely lack admirers, and may be drawn to older or nurturing figures who can offer support and guidance. Until the age of 40 there is a growing need for study, travel or a personal quest to discover meaning in life. If they become more assertive and resilient when setbacks occur, they can fulfill the promise shown from early days. After 40 they are likely to become more pragmatic and realistic and must not allow hidden insecurities to plunge them into procrastination. This would be a tragedy because, if they can summon the self-discipline and courage to believe in themselves, they are destined to lift their veil and shine by contributing their considerable talents to the greater good. Once they find a sense of direction, their destiny is to assist, direct or inspire others with their energetic and inspiring example.

Potential: Inspiring, enthusiastic

Dark side: Insecure, unaware

Tarot card, lucky numbers, days, colors: Justice, 2, 4, Tuesday, Monday, red, silver

Born today: Emma González (campaigner); Leonardo DiCaprio, Demi Moore (actors); Fyodor Dostoevsky (novelist)

November 12

The Birthday of the Mesmerizing Prerogative

The life lesson:

is taking responsibility.

The way forward: is to understand that until you acknowledge your own role in shaping your life, it may feel out of control.

Luck maker: Think of yourself as an inspiring role model, then your behavior will soon catch up and attract success.

"I bring light"

People born on November 12 have a golden aura and an ability to bring hope into the world. They feel it is their right to get whatever they want from life. With such powerful expectations, their chances of success are strong and they have the potential to be among the most mesmerizing people of the year. However, in some cases, although their boldness and imagination are outstanding, they aren't the positive force they were destined to be from an early age. They tend to flout convention to get what they want, so their ultimate success depends on how subtle they are in bending the rules, and how considerate and kind they are toward others.

Born gurus, they invest a great deal of energy in guiding people, which may lead to careers such as teaching, the healing or caring professions, psychology, medicine, the law, art, science, the emergency services, and social and charity work. They have an aptitude for business, promotion and sales, or may choose to become actors, directors, writers or musicians. They need to remember that what they think about tends to manifest in their lives, so negative thoughts attract negative people and situations. Learning to choose their thoughts carefully is therefore essential for success, as well as their holistic wellbeing. **For self-care**, meditation, yoga and the study of spirituality are beneficial, and wearing and meditating on the color purple encourages you to think of higher things.

Charming and sensual, these people attract others easily, but they can have problems believing they are loved, which can cause tension. Until the age of 39, they focus on adventure and freedom through study or travel. After 39, they take a more disciplined and practical approach. The key to their success is to prioritize their emotional wellbeing and learn to love themselves. When they are able to do that, happiness and success are not just their prerogative, but become their reality. Learning that it is not only *their* right but everyone's to be happy and fulfilled ensures that they carry out their destiny to bestow an illuminating gift on humanity.

Potential: Illuminating, magnetic

Dark side: Troubled, selfish

Tarot card, lucky numbers, days, colors: The Hanged Man, 3, 5, Tuesday, Thursday, red, purple

Born today: Elizabeth Cady Stanton (activist); Auguste Rodin (sculptor); Grace Kelly, Anne Hathaway (actors)

November 13

The Birthday of Transformation

"Now I see clearly"

The life lesson:

is changing your mind.

The way forward: is to understand that refusing to acknowledge alternative viewpoints or possibilities blocks change and progress.

Luck maker: Keep an open and curious mind, because if you are narrow-minded you can be so wrapped up in your familiar beliefs that you miss wonderful opportunities.

Those born on November 13 have strong and passionate convictions. At some point they are likely to experience a dramatic transformation that influences all their beliefs and opinions. This is not necessarily religious—it could be a new devotion to a cause—but whatever it is, they gather information to support their beliefs rather than the other way around. This means that they can be so dedicated to the version of the truth based on their beliefs that they don't acknowledge there can be other valid versions. Finding a cause or belief system worthy of their fierce energy, deep intellect and insight is therefore key to their success.

Born politicians, they may be drawn to campaigning, promotion, scientific or technical careers, or jobs that let them instruct or inspire, such as teaching, journalism, politics, acting, personal growth, life-coaching and religion. Other work options include writing, the law, psychology, research, lecturing, broadcasting and the medical and healing professions. These people often live fast-paced lives and can become unhappy and exhausted if they don't give themselves enough time to relax and unwind. **For self-care**, music can be a great healer, in particular classical music; also spending time in the countryside observing the natural rhythms of nature is beneficial.

Those born on this day are attracted to people who share their mindset, but may benefit from surrounding themselves with different beliefs. Until the age of 38, they are at their most zealous, with a strong emphasis on idealism. It is extremely important that they don't become inflexible and that they make a real effort to take on board what people say to them. After 38, they become even more determined and disciplined. During these years it's crucial they don't allow their idealism to slip into dogmatism. Getting to know themselves better helps them see that having strong opinions does not give them a sense of self. Once they can open their mind to other viewpoints and be more flexible and objective, their destiny is to inform, support and enlighten others with their passion and dedication to a truly worthy cause or set of beliefs.

Potential: Passionate, inspiring

Dark side: Narrow-minded, deluded

Tarot card, lucky numbers, days, colors: Death, 4, 6, Tuesday, Sunday, red, electric blue

Born today: Robert Louis Stevenson (author); Whoopi Goldberg, Gerard Butler (actors); Jimmy Kimmel (comedian)

November 14

The Birthday of the Guide

The life lesson:

is to avoid unnecessary meddling.

The way forward: is to understand that sometimes the best way you can help others is to let them learn from their mistakes.

Luck maker: Develop a strong handshake that signifies energy, trust and strength, as this can impress people and make them want to offer you their support.

"My sincere desire is to serve the greater good"

November 14-born appear intense and earnest, and others instantly sense their conviction. They are driven by a genuine desire to be of service or to help, improve and guide others. They have the ability to observe others objectively and offer spot-on insights and advice. But sometimes they can be a little meddling. They need to understand that there are situations in which their advice is not welcome and occasions when their judgments are not appreciated. They see themselves as teachers or guides and have the passion, integrity and intellect to be a positive force. However, until they can acknowledge their own need to shine in their own right, it is difficult for them to be a truly effective support for others.

Born advisors, they have natural affinity with social work, therapy, the medical professions, counseling, therapy, life-coaching and teaching. Their inquisitive minds may be drawn toward writing, blogging, design, science, art, research and psychology, as well as politics, campaigning and social and humanitarian reform. Theater, music and the arts may also appeal. They may visit their doctor once too often for minor ailments and should have more faith in their body's ability to heal itself; studying naturopathy can be beneficial. **For self-care,** carrying a small rose-quartz crystal reminds you to nurture yourself.

The relationships of those born on this day are intense and it can take time for them to trust anyone, but once they do, they remain loyal. Until the age of 37, they have opportunities to expand their outlook, and because they connect on an intellectual rather than an emotional level, they should try to integrate more with others. After 37, they become more realistic, seeking structure and order. Once they find what gives their own life meaning, they can then assist others, becoming not just the important guide and role model they were destined to be, but an inspirational person in their own right. When they learn to balance their own needs with those of others', their destiny is to offer potentially life-changing practical and emotional support, guidance and enlightenment to those they live and work with, potentially the world.

Potential: Insightful, helpful

Dark side: Interfering, directionless

Tarot card, lucky numbers, days, colors: Temperance, 5, 7, Tuesday, Wednesday, dark blue, deep red

Born today: Claude Monet (artist); Prince Charles (British royal); Aaron Copland (composer); Condoleezza Rice (politician)

November 15

The Birthday of the Cobra

"You never know"

People born on November 15 have an air of the unexpected. Smooth and slick, they can strike out suddenly and unexpectedly with the deadly accuracy of a cobra. Their life appears to be a series of unforeseen encounters, challenges or confrontations, but instead of crumbling under this friction, they thrive on it. They are brilliant at defending themselves and finding the Achilles' heel in their opponent's arguments or situation, as well as the right time to hit—they are enemies to be truly feared. They can be suspicious when they don't need to be and this can alienate others unnecessarily. Sometimes, their love of challenge makes them create conflict for the sake of it to enjoy the "excitement" it generates.

Born spies, they seek roles that offer constant challenge and careers involving travel and change. The secret service, detective work, emergency services and the military may appeal, as might being a bodyguard or working in scientific research or art. Business, politics, social reform and the law are other options, as are writing, acting and music. These people can expend a lot of energy on protecting themselves from real and imagined threats, but their greatest enemy is themselves. They need to learn to trust and be more open, recognizing that sometimes the greatest strength is gentleness. Swimming and martial arts can help them safely release pent-up energy. **For self-care**, wearing, meditating on and surrounding yourself with the color orange will encourage you to be more spontaneous, trusting and open.

In close relationships, those born on this day generally prefer to keep their feelings to themselves, but they can also be seductive and affectionate. Until the age of 36, their risk-taking tendencies are at their most intense, with mixed results. After 36, they become more disciplined and realistic, injecting a healthy dose of optimism and pure self-belief to balance out their hidden insecurities. This can give them sufficient confidence and trust to put down their sword, so that their heart of gold, and potential for happiness, success and fulfillment, can finally reveal themselves. Once they become less suspicious, their destiny is to help others prepare for the unexpected and keep the spirit of adventure alive.

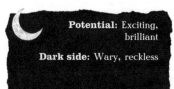

Potential: Exciting, brilliant

Dark side: Wary, reckless

Tarot card, lucky numbers, days, colors: The Devil, 6, 8, Tuesday, Friday, deep red, lavender

Born today: William Herschel (astronomer); Sam Waterston, Shailene Woodley (actors); Roberto Cavalli (designer)

November 16

The Birthday of
Dominion

"With all due respect"

People born on November 16 tend to command respect wherever they go, and because they are such highly perceptive and purposeful people, others instinctively follow their lead. Thankfully, they usually consider the greater good and are tactful. Fiercely independent, they love to challenge the status quo in their youth, but, over time, they come to understand that they can be more effective agents for change if they work within the system. Their natural authority suits them to leadership roles, though at times their compulsion to influence is so strong that their behavior becomes controlling and they refuse to acknowledge any other way forward.

Born managers, they are often drawn to teaching, coaching or mentoring, as well as to art and sport. Other options include self-employment, writing, research, politics, social reform, the law, advertising, philosophy, psychology, sales, water sports, diving, acting and online influencing. In business they are likely to assume management or directorship roles. They often feel attuned to water, and spending time by rivers, lakes or the ocean can help relax and calm them. Swimming is a fantastic way for them to exercise. **For self-care**, relaxing herbal teas and foot massages are music to your soul.

These people love to give to and support others, but can have problems accepting help, advice, or even loving themselves. Learning to trust and be more open is crucial for their happiness. Until the age of 35 they like to expand their horizons through study or travel. After 35, they take a more practical, ordered and realistic approach to life. Whatever age they are, it is important for them to ensure they use their authority wisely and don't abuse the position of trust they earn. If they can remember to respect others' rights to hold different opinions, and ensure there is give and take in all their relationships, not only can they exercise unquestionable authority over their chosen dominion, they can also use their creativity to become a voice of deep wisdom and inspiration. Their destiny is to extend the boundaries of human knowledge and endeavor.

Potential: Influential, understanding

Dark side: Controlling, self-involved

Tarot card, lucky numbers, days, colors: The Tower, 7, 9, Tuesday, Monday, deep red, sea green

Born today: Sanna Marin (Finnish prime minister); W. C. Handy (composer); Frank Bruno (boxer); Maggie Gyllenhaal (actor)

November 17

The Birthday of the Facilitator

"We're all in this together"

The life lesson: is self-care.

The way forward: is to understand that you need to nurture yourself before nurturing and helping others.

Luck maker: Set yourself personal goals and remind yourself often why achieving them matters.

Those born on November 17 tend to be deeply sensitive, with a powerful urge to promote the wellbeing of others. They often find themselves in the role of facilitator. They can effortlessly encourage others to work harder and better, and ensure everything runs smoothly, because they understand the importance of compromise. Whatever the nature of the compromise, they convince themselves that it's better to put the interests of others above their own. This generosity of spirit rightfully earns them great respect, but the downside is that others take advantage of them and they may have no idea what their own goals and concerns are.

Born interviewers, they do well in careers that involve teamwork and cooperation, but they can also thrive in the health and caring professions, teaching, media, sales, marketing, broadcasting and journalism. Their creativity may find expression in technology and engineering, as well as design, fashion, retail, filmmaking, acting and show business. Their spirits suffer if they don't give themselves time to pursue their own interests and time alone to become more self-aware. **For self-care,** carrying a tiger's eye crystal promotes confidence and courage, as will wearing the color red.

Charming, perceptive and with a sense of humor, these people never lack admirers, but need to ensure they don't get into unequal relationships where they do all the giving. They tend to over-relate to others, neglecting their own needs, so they need to prioritize self-love. Until the age of 34 they are likely to take chances; after this they become more progressive, determined and serious. Whatever age they are, they should not over-identify with the role of facilitator. As valuable and important as that role is, nothing is more important for their psychological growth—and for their ability to unlock their outstanding potential for success and happiness—than their acknowledgment of and willingness to express their own creativity and independence of spirit. Once they learn it really is fine to speak up for themselves and be creative, their destiny is to follow their hearts and encourage others to do the same.

Potential: Charming, generous

Dark side: Self-sacrificing, unfocused

Tarot card, lucky numbers, days, colors: The Star, 1, 8, Tuesday, Saturday, deep red, brown

Born today: Rem Koolhaas (architect); Martin Scorsese (director); Danny DeVito (actor); RuPaul (drag queen)

November 18

The Birthday of Sensitive Exuberance

is believing in
yourself.

*The way
forward:* is to
understand that
how successful
you are in life
is often directly
related to how
much you believe
in yourself.

Luck maker:
Consider what you
want to happen,
not what others
expect when
making decisions.
Tuning into your
own feelings
makes decision-
making a whole
lot easier.

"Shall we let the sunlight in?"

November 18-born can be likened to a ray of warm sunshine. Refreshingly upbeat in their approach to life, unsurprisingly their company is much sought after. They enjoy being admired and are honest and open about their fierce ambitions, making them natural candidates for leadership. However, underneath their upbeat persona lies uncertainty and conflict. This is because they are unusually and sometimes overly sensitive and empathetic to others' feelings. As a result, despite their clear potential to be winners or innovators, they can waste time feeling confused. If they can find a way to balance their sensitivity toward others with their own ambitions, their success is virtually assured.

Born innovators, they may be drawn to careers in science, research or technology, as well as in art or writing. Other work options include counseling, life-coaching, therapy, self-help, sports, business, teaching, lecturing, politics, music and the world of entertainment. Boosting their self-esteem so they rely more on their own intuition than on the attention of others is crucial to both their physical and emotional health. Cognitive behavioral therapy techniques may help them reprogram their thoughts from negative to positive, as can spending more time with upbeat, supportive people. **For self-care**, placing a tiger's eye crystal beside your bed at night has a calming effect, promoting confidence and courage.

Those born on this day can be wonderfully sexy and romantic, but if their partner or friends don't constantly reassure them of their devotion, they can lapse into moodiness. Until the age of 33, their emphasis is on freedom, adventure and expansion, so they may study, travel or experiment with their career. After the age of 33, they become more responsible, precise and practical, seeking structure and order. Whatever age they are, they need to use their sharp and probing mind and powerful intuition to investigate their own power and potential. With greater self-awareness and belief in their star potential, these vivacious individuals can achieve almost anything. Once they learn to believe in themselves and their own creativity, their destiny is to attain or point the way to great progress.

Potential: Innovative, vivacious

Dark side: Moody, confused

Tarot card, lucky numbers, day, colors: The Moon, 2, 9, Tuesday, all shades of red

Born today: Louis Daguerre (photographer); Sojourner Truth (feminist); Owen Wilson (actor); Alan Shepard (astronaut)

November 19

The Birthday of the Crusader

The life lesson:

is to think before you act.

The way forward: is to sleep on it, let some time pass, and your confident patience may maximize your chances of success.

Luck maker: When things don't go according to plan, learn from your mistakes, try a different approach and believe there must be something better in store.

"I can fly"

People born on November 19 have progressive goals. Born reformers, they are at their happiest and best when they can be a crusader or the representative of a revolutionary cause. From an early age they probably felt they were destined to make a significant contribution; there is something about them that makes people stop and stare. While others look to them for motivation and guidance, their confidence can work against them because their self-belief can be so powerful that they close their minds to alternative viewpoints. They should weigh up the pros and cons and listen to others' advice before making decisions because they are not, and never can be, superhuman.

Born VIPs, whatever career they choose, they have the conviction and energy to go to the top. Work options that might appeal include business, management, social reform, promotion, charity work, humanitarian concerns, politics, teaching, the law, sales, public relations, lecturing, engineering, design, sports, acting, counseling and the media. Health-wise, fatigue can be a problem due to dieting or eating fast food. They must ensure they get enough nutrients, especially vitamin B12 if they are vegetarians. **For self-care**, you will benefit from meditation, yoga, tai chi or any mind–body therapy that encourages you to be more objective and patient. Wearing, meditating on and surrounding yourself with the color blue helps you to stay cool emotionally and mentally.

Never short of admirers, these people would rather be alone than invest energy in superficial relationships. Until the age of 32 they may extend their horizons through study and travel, but after 32 they become more responsible, precise and hard-working. Whatever age they are, if they can slow down, take on board the advice of others and never allow pride to get in the way, they can not only make a significant contribution to the world, but also play a vital part in changing it for the better. Once they learn to look before they leap, their destiny is to champion and encourage others to embrace their progressive convictions.

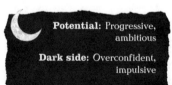

Potential: Progressive, ambitious

Dark side: Overconfident, impulsive

Tarot card, lucky numbers, days, colors: The Sun, 1, 3, Tuesday, Monday, red, gold

Born today: Meg Ryan, Jodie Foster (actors); Hiram Bingham III (archaeologist); Calvin Klein (designer)

November 20

The Birthday of the Wrestler

The life lesson:

is not to take yourself so seriously.

The way forward: is to understand that sometimes a light-hearted, subtler approach can have just as much impact as a forceful, direct one.

Luck maker: Treat everyone with respect, no matter what their qualifications, background or status, because you may need their help in the future.

"Struggle is progress"

Those born on November 20 are truly courageous and idealistic souls. Battle tends to be a theme—they are not afraid of standing up for what is right, even if that means standing alone. Because they are so driven, they have the potential to blaze a pioneering trail through life, inspiring others along the way. However, the conflict is more likely to be expressed emotionally. Indeed, their lives are often ruled by their ever-changing emotions: one moment they are optimistic and sensitive, the next they are bitterly disillusioned and lashing out. Their intensity and seriousness of purpose undoubtedly attract considerable success and respect. But if they don't pay attention to their wrestling emotions and learn how to manage them more effectively, fulfillment and happiness can elude them.

Born leaders, they excel in business-related careers, but their dramatic sense also helps them succeed in politics, entertainment or the arts. Other work options include education, writing, sales, city planning, environmental issues, self-help and charity work. They have an impulsive side and this can make them accident- and injury-prone, and they may benefit from anger-management techniques. **For self-care**, wearing, meditating on and surrounding yourself with the color blue helps you to keep calm during times of crisis and uncertainty.

Generous and sincere at first, over time those born on this day can be possessive and moody in their relationships. They may also chase unattainable people and be prone to lovesickness, so working on self-love is important. Before the age of 31, they move forward in a spirit of optimism, and this is when they are most likely to take risks. After 31 they gradually become more practical, ambitious and realistic, desiring order and structure. If they can learn to manage their emotions, they really come into their own now, but whatever age they are, emotional intelligence is key to their success, particularly anger management. This gives them the mental advantage they need to triumph over almost any obstacle, challenge or opponent standing in their way. Once they understand that their emotions are teachers, not guides, their destiny is to lead so that others can follow.

Potential: Idealistic, courageous

Dark side: Overly serious, volatile

Tarot card, lucky numbers, days, colors: Judgment, 2, 4, Tuesday, Monday, red, silver

Born today: Selma Lagerlöf (author); Edwin Hubble (astronomer); Joe Biden (US president); Bo Derek (actor)

November 21

The Birthday of Finesse

The life lesson: is intimacy.

The way forward: is to understand that opening yourself up to someone else is not a sign of weakness, but a sign you are human.

Luck maker: If you are expressive and open, people can relate to you, and this makes them more likely to offer you support and help.

"Diamonds are made under pressure"

November 21-born live by their own rules, but they also have a strong sense of justice and a wish to change the world. Often regal and refined, they are naturally empathetic leaders who like to work with the best, and more often than not, they *are* the best. They bring a quality touch to everything they do, and a major theme in their lives is refinement and surrounding themselves with excellence. This finesse can manifest itself in their bewitchingly stylish appearance or lifestyle, or internally in fine-tuning of their ideas. They are constantly improving and refining themselves, and, in the process, attracting success and respect. The only downside with this approach is that they can become too serious and risk losing their sense of humor and spontaneity.

Born literary agents and editors, they are hard-working and adaptable, tending to rise to positions of power and prominence. They may be drawn to business, advertising, publishing, technology and the media, or excel in politics, sport, charity work, science, medicine and the healing professions. They may also express their creativity in teaching, philosophy, writing or the arts. Prone to mood swings and bouts of self-pity, they need to understand that not everyone has their perfectionist drive. **For self-care**, regular social forms of exercise, such as aerobics or dance classes, can boost your mood and energy.

These people's search for perfection can isolate them from others and they need to beware of denying themselves the happiness of close relationships. Until the age of 30, they may find they want to experiment and broaden their horizons. After 30, they are likely to take a more disciplined, determined and serious approach to life. As long as they don't get too cautious, this is when they come into their own. Once they get in touch with their own feelings and are more sensitive to others, they have the ability to rise above difficult situations and solve problems with their inspired thinking. When they find the courage to be vulnerable and express their inner child and fun side more, their destiny is to inspire others to fine-tune their lives and make positive changes.

Potential: Elegant, disciplined

Dark side: Perfectionist, aloof

Tarot card, lucky numbers, days, colors: Judgment, 2, 4, Tuesday, Monday, red, silver

Born today: Voltaire (philosopher); William Beaumont (physician); Björk (singer); Goldie Hawn (actor)

SAGITTARIUS

THE ARCHER
(NOVEMBER 22–DECEMBER 21)

* **Element:** Fire
* **Ruling planet:** Jupiter, the philosopher
* **Tarot card:** Temperance (moderation)
* **Lucky numbers:** 3, 9
* **Favorable colors:** Rich purple, dark blue, yellow, white
* **Driving force:** Expansion
* **Personal statement:** I want to be challenged
* **Chinese astrology counterpart:** The Rat

Those born under the sign of Sagittarius are usually hungry for new experiences and they thrive on challenges, both physical and mental. They view the future with optimism and excitement. Sometimes, in their restless urgency to speed on to the next challenge, they don't see their current projects through to the end, but, even when they make mistakes, their natural enthusiasm and zest for life not only helps them bounce back but is highly contagious.

Personality potential

Sagittarians are the restless seekers of the zodiac whose thirst for knowledge and adventure is often insatiable. They always want to be learning something new. Freedom-loving, they can't bear to be confined or pinned down by conformity or routine, and their need for personal space is very strong. Like the other two fire signs, Aries and Leo, they are courageous risk-takers who radiate warmth and optimism, but because they are the last fire sign, their passion tends to be more focused.

Dependable, friendly, honest and lively, people born under this energetic sign are ruled by the planet Jupiter, the planet of hope and expansion. This means that they naturally bring enthusiasm, optimism, hope and excitement to any situation or relationship they are in. They are also incredibly open-minded and flexible in their thinking; this gives them great versatility, and they are often multitalented and capable of mastering almost any task if they set their mind to it. This sign is also blessed with a philosopher's mind, and their breadth of vision can be quite astonishing.

Bright, chatty, cheerful and a lot of fun, Sagittarians have a reputation for being rather charming. They like to be stimulated by new faces and new places, and are almost always on the move. Even if they settle in one place, they are likely to travel extensively or to have dozens of activities and interests. They rarely book or plan ahead, however, for their adventures and approach to life are very much spontaneous and last minute.

Sagittarians bring enormous creativity to any project they are involved in. They are generally well-liked people who enjoy significant personal power, both socially and individually, simply through being themselves. Although they do tend to exaggerate the truth from time to time, or put a positive spin on everything, for the most part they are honest personalities, and mind games don't appeal or make sense to them. With their enthusiasm and positivity always leading the way, it's hardly surprising that **Sagittarians often have a definite knack for being in the right place at the right time** and for attracting good fortune through their undeniable capacity for hard work.

> **"Sagittarians often have a definite knack for being in the right place at the right time"**

Personality pitfalls

Subtlety isn't a strong point for people born under this sign. Don't ask a Sagittarian their opinion unless you want a brutally honest answer. Although you can count on them to be right most of the time, they will often say the right thing at completely the wrong moment or the right thing in totally the wrong way; this can cause problems for them. In addition, their optimism about new projects, ventures or relationships can easily become over-optimism and an inability to face difficult truths. They may, for example, continue blindly in a situation for years, not wanting to deal with problems that are unpleasant or painful. Some may think of this approach to life as brave, but others might regard it as deluded. There's nothing sadder than seeing a Sagittarian's wonderful energy and intellect burned out and their opportunities wasted by battling on for years in a relationship or career to which they aren't suited.

Freedom and personal space are important issues for Sagittarians, and this can make them come across as fickle, irresponsible or emotionally distant in relationships. They can often be reluctant to commit to long-term plans and are prone to bouts of illogical panic; this means that instead of staying and facing their panic, they may simply respond by packing their bags and moving to somewhere new to start again. And, finally, although their risk-taking and love of danger make them exciting people to be around, they can also be reckless and may live to regret their hasty decisions and actions.

Darkest secret

Sagittarians hate rules and regulations more than any other sign of the zodiac, but deep down it's not the constraints themselves that they fear, but the fact that rules and regulations are sometimes necessary. Without these, life would descend into chaos and injustice and, although Sagittarians believe in the power of optimism, they find it incredibly painful to admit to themselves that sometimes optimism and smiling your way through adversity isn't enough to change people's lives or situations for the better.

Symbol

The symbol of Sagittarius is an archer with their bow poised to shoot. The arrow destined to fly through the air symbolizes the endless quest for knowledge that drives this sign, as well as their love of projecting their thoughts and energy to a future destination or target. Often the archer is represented in the shape of a centaur; this is a mythical creature that is half-human and half-beast, suggesting the dual nature of this sign that joins instinct with intellect.

Love

It may seem surprising, given that the Sagittarian is typically such a jovial, fun-loving and sociable individual, but people born under this sun sign are often more capable of living happily alone than many of the other signs of the zodiac. This is because they can often find being in committed relationships restrictive and they love the idea of being able to leave at a moment's notice—which, of course, they can't do so easily if they have a partner or a family to consider. However, if they do settle into a relationship, they are generous, interested and helpful partners, and will try harder than any other sign to make a relationship work, even if it's in deep trouble.

As a rule, Sagittarians have extremely high moral and personal standards, and they expect the same high standards from the people with whom they spend their time. This upstanding aspect of their personality can make them very unforgiving, not just of themselves but of others. These people don't forgive or forget easily if someone close to them transgresses the bounds of decency and civilized behavior. They may even decide to sever all ties completely with that person. In addition to sharing the same standards of decency and morality, the ideal partner for a Sagittarian is someone who is fun-loving, a great listener, adventurous and willing to share but not dominate the limelight with them.

Love matches:
Aries, Leo, Aquarius and Sagittarius.

The Sagittarian woman

Sagittarian women are often the most shockingly frank women of the entire zodiac. They see the world exactly as it is and will rarely, if ever, lie. Fortunately, they often reveal their brutal honesty in such a charming, intelligent and optimistic manner that it's hard to take offense. Extremely independent in their thinking, these women are capable of living happily alone, sometimes even when they are in a relationship. They may commit to a long-term relationship later than expected or be fairly reluctant to commit when there is talk of taking a relationship to the next stage. The reason is not that they don't ever want to commit to one person but that they always think of a partnership as something they will get round to in the future. Right now, there is so much they want to learn, see and do, and so many places they want to go, that they feel they can't make a commitment.

The Sagittarian woman is typically sociable and popular, but she can sometimes mistake friendship for love and vice versa, which can cause both herself and the other person involved confusion and heartache. Her affectionate nature and carefree, unconventional approach to relationships can cause a lot of misunderstandings and hurt feelings. At times she may appear over-casual in her approach to relationships, but this isn't an accurate assessment. When she eventually meets the person who can challenge her intellectually and who matches her optimism, she is capable of strong commitment and emotional connection. As long as she doesn't feel tied down and is allowed to make her own decisions, a Sagittarian woman can be unequaled in a relationship when it comes to loyalty, trust, affection and honesty; there will also be plenty of excitement and enough idealism to last a lifetime.

The Sagittarian man

There is likely to be a gathering of people surrounding a Sagittarian man, or, if he is alone, his phone will constantly be pinging. He won't be easy to pin down. His idealism, exuberance and curiosity are endearing and infectious, and although his innocent enthusiasm can sometimes get out of hand with reckless and careless behavior, his boundless optimism never fails to draw others to him. Although you may have to work through a lot of other people or messages to get to a Sagittarian man, the effort is worth it. His splendid

imagination, optimism and creativity can quite literally move mountains and there will rarely be a dull moment: There may, however, be a number of tense or difficult situations when his brutal honesty is nothing less than hurtful in its bluntness. So, as well as being optimistic, energetic and adventurous, potential partners of a Sagittarian need to develop a thick skin. However, when it comes to affairs of the heart, this man's frankness and openness is very refreshing. There are no mind games or falsehoods, and when he says he wants to spend the rest of his life with you, you can be sure he means it.

Once in a relationship, freedom is absolutely essential to a Sagittarian man—freedom to explore and freedom to dream. A possessive, suspicious or jealous partner does not last long; the independent spirit of a Sagittarian man won't tolerate a restriction. Many of the dreams and plans a Sagittarian has won't be as wise or as well thought out as they could be; this is because he doesn't just think with his mind, he also thinks with his heart. But somehow this doesn't matter, because the love of a Sagittarian man is truly special—a love that is honest, genuine and pure.

Family

The Sagittarian child is a bundle of enthusiasm and generosity. Sometimes exuberance can turn into boisterousness, so it's important for parents of Sagittarian children to find a channel for their child's incredible energy. They should be encouraged, for example, to have as many hobbies and interests as possible. Parents of Sagittarian children had better get used to plenty of those "why" questions, and honesty is always the best policy when attempting to answer them. Sagittarians of all ages can quickly spot bluffing or dishonesty. At school they are independent and can be counted on to make any newcomer to the group feel welcome. There is huge potential here for success both in and out of the classroom, but the secret is to ensure that their potential is properly guided. In other words, these children should not be left to progress at their own rate. Having said that, Sagittarian children can struggle with rules and regulations, so it is important that parents, carers and teachers offer them guidance and support rather than inflexible regulations. They will naturally choose the best option if it is presented to them in a way they can understand.

Sagittarian parents are often worshipped by their children for their lively, sometimes eccentric approach to life. They encourage their children to develop their talents through interests and hobbies and take an active part in seeing that these interests are progressing well. There may be times when Sagittarian parents feel restricted by their parenting role and it's therefore important, especially for Sagittarian mothers, that they don't allow their own interests to fall by the wayside when children arrive on the scene. These women should definitely try to set aside time for themselves because, as rewarding as motherhood is, the conversations and activities involved in bringing up a child are not enough for them to feel truly fulfilled.

Career

With their love of freedom, travel and intellectual stimulation, Sagittarians are rarely happy in careers that don't offer them these opportunities. Jobs that may suit this sign include travel-guiding, teaching, law, lecturing, piloting, consulting, interpreting, writing, publishing and therapy. The worlds of entertainment and performance, and media, may also have strong appeal, as these people simply love being in the limelight

Sagittarians with sporting ability may enjoy working in the field of health, fitness or personal training. Some Sagittarians may even do well as stunt people or explorers.

Whatever career they choose, the most important thing for a Sagittarian is challenge; repetitive jobs should be avoided, as should work that has a daily routine that rarely changes. They also don't tend to thrive in offices. **Their spirit of adventure needs work that takes them out into the world** around them to meet new people. Although they often do well in their careers, Sagittarians are not always ambitious as far as money or status are concerned. What matters more to them is that they are being challenged, learning and experiencing something new and, above all, making their own decisions.

> **"Their spirit of adventure needs work that takes them out into the world"**

Health and wellbeing

Their abundant energy means that it's hardly surprising that many Sagittarians often have a hearty appetite. In many cases they are so active in their daily lives that they burn off the calories right away, but they do need to be careful with their diet and avoid over-indulgence. They are often tempted by fast food but should try as much as possible to avoid convenience meals that have had all the goodness refined and processed out of them. One of the reasons Sagittarians tend to eat so much fast food is that, when they are hungry, they want something immediately to boost their energy levels; because of this they need to ensure they carry around with them plenty of healthy snacks, such as fruits, nuts, seeds and raisins, for when temptation strikes.

As far as exercise goes most people born under this sign will already be extremely active, but they do need to be careful that they don't overdo it, and that their daredevil nature doesn't cause them to suffer injuries, especially to their legs. It's also important for them to remember that they need to

modify the way they exercise as they get older—what worked in their twenties, for example, may not work in their fifties.

When it comes to leisure interests, many Sagittarians enjoy the challenge of outdoor activities such as hiking, horse riding, mountain climbing and camping, as well as team sports. Archery is also a popular pastime, and they may find satisfaction and mental challenge in learning a language, writing and the study of philosophy. Retirement offers them exciting opportunities for physical and intellectual travel and many Sagittarians think of this time as the most rewarding in their lives because they finally have the freedom they have always longed for to stretch both their mind and their body. There is always a tendency for Sagittarians to overdo things, so they would also benefit from regular yoga and relaxation. A mantra they should repeat to themselves every day is "moderation in all things." Wearing or meditating on the color **blue** will encourage them to be more consistent, moderate and disciplined in their approach to life.

Born between November 22 and December 1

People born between these dates are perhaps the most positive of the entire zodiac. They see the possibilities life offers as endless and never take no for an answer. Their cup is typically half full, not half empty, and—with their strong desire to travel and seek out new experiences—adventure is their middle name.

Born between December 2 and 10

These Sagittarians need plenty of stimulation and variety. They also love freedom, and this applies to relationships, family and work. They hate being tied down and, like Peter Pan, seem youthful, exuberant, adventurous and free whatever their age.

Born between December 11 and 21

Bold and dramatic, with action-packed lives and a mind brimming with ideas, these people are often life's gamblers. Luck seems to follow them around. Even when they lose, which they do from time to time, they always seem to land on their feet.

Life lessons

As long as they feel free and unrestricted, Sagittarians are refreshing people to have around because they are so energetic and positive. They never tire of learning something new, but if restrictions, responsibilities and expectations start to pile up, as they often tend to do in life, Sagittarians may lose some of their spark. They have the mistaken idea that commitment somehow reduces their freedom, so it's extremely important for them to learn that, although responsibility and freedom are two separate things, they are not necessarily mutually exclusive. They also need to understand that loyalty is an essential ingredient for success in relationships.

There is no doubt that the mind of a Sagittarian is astute, but they do have this tendency to be painfully blunt in the expression of what they perceive to be the truth. They need to learn to think before they speak, avoid self-righteousness and be more tactful in their approach to others. They also need to understand that sometimes it's better to be cautious about speaking their mind because other people may not be ready to hear the truth. Sagittarians tend to be risk-takers but, like their tendency to be too blunt or to argue for argument's sake, their risk-taking can sometimes be for its own sake, rather than for any actual benefit or particular outcome. They should avoid gambling. The only things that Sagittarians need to focus on for their own sake are love and kindness. In addition, taking unnecessary risks for the sake of it can prove disastrous and it would benefit Sagittarians enormously if they learned to look before they leap.

Fellow Sagittarians can encourage each other to be even more adventurous, which can be positive, but most people born under this sign don't need pushing to be more experimental than they already are. Other signs of the zodiac have more to teach Sagittarians. They can learn caution, self-restraint and careful analysis to determine a course of action from Virgos and Librans. Capricorns can show them that sometimes sticking to the rules can bring its own rewards. Cancerians and Pisceans can help them to be more compassionate and empathetic in their search for knowledge. Although Sagittarians are great listeners, they don't necessarily make great comforters, because they listen to learn more rather than to help others or make them feel better. Leos and Taureans can teach Sagittarians to relax more and fidget less. Arians can encourage them to take the lead and Scorpios can help them become more aware of the impact of their honesty on others.

Considered the luckiest sign in Chinese astrology, the Rat shares the adventurous, sociable, cheerful and outgoing spirit of its Western counterpart, Sagittarius. Both signs are alert, curious and hungry for knowledge and life experience. They are quick to learn and adapt to any situation, and don't hesitate to take advantage of any opportunities that appear.

Whereas child-like Aries begins the Western zodiac year, in Chinese astrology it is the Rat that comes first and, according to ancient stories, this is because the Rat used its speed and cunning to overtake all the other animals and win the race. And winning is what the Rat loves to do. In their desire to win at all costs, they will happily accept assistance from others, and share in their success to give themselves a head start or advantage. Their versatile, optimistic and energetic nature ensures their popularity and always seems to attract good fortune their way.

Note: Sagittarians have an affinity with Rat-sign characteristics, but be sure to check which Chinese sign corresponds to your **year** of birth (see page xxi), and to read about the characteristics associated with it, too.

13th sign?

According to recent NASA reports the 13th sign of the zodiac is called Ophiuchus and anyone born between November 29 and December 17 would be an Ophiuchus. However, astronomy is not astrology. Astrologers have known about the Ophiuchus constellation for thousands of years but chose to leave Ophiuchus out of the equation and correspond the zodiac with the 12 months of the year. Perhaps this was because Ophiuchus shares characteristics typically associated with Sagittarius, such as being a light bearer, healer and dreamer.

November 22

The Birthday of Wild Inspiration

"Follow me, if you can keep up"

is recognizing that you are not indispensable.

The way forward: is to remind yourself that as unique and important as you are, the world will continue to spin without you.

Luck maker: Too much passion or intensity can make people squirm, so when you are an outsider in a new situation, interact with people gently to win them over.

People born on November 22 will have felt from an early age that they think differently from others. They are always one step ahead, with a strong desire to free themselves from authority or conventional thinking. They make their own rules and don't care what others think. Although these liberated and intense people, with their wonderful insight and conviction, are refreshing and exciting, their wild instincts can cause problems. It is important they learn to be more tactful and choose the appropriate level of intensity. In the right environment they can be a powerful force for good, coming up with creative and innovative solutions to improve the welfare of those around them.

Born freelancers, they are not typically suited to careers in a structured or disciplined environment. They may be drawn to the media, show business, music, publishing, advertising, online influencing, management, the leisure, sport and beauty industries, and politics. Alternatively, they can excel in teaching or the arts, or as a counselor in the humanitarian, caring or healing professions. They need to ensure that they can enjoy the quieter side of life despite their wild nature, and they may find it hard to grow old gracefully. Sex is extremely important to them and they could have addictive tendencies that counseling or therapy can address. **For self-care**, as well as daily meditation or yoga, wearing, meditating on and surrounding yourself with the color blue helps you keep your cool.

Exciting and romantic in their relationships, those born on this day should guard against becoming controlling. Until the age of 29 they expand their horizons through new ventures, study or travel. After 29 there is a turning point when they become more practical and realistic; this is when they most likely realize their professional goals. The key to their success is their ability to set themselves new goals to challenge and reinvent themselves. If they can do this, they can unlock their outstanding potential for personal fulfillment and happiness. Their destiny is to profoundly inspire and excite others with their originality and creativity.

Potential: Innovative, liberated

Dark side: Wild, frustrated

Tarot card, lucky numbers, days, colors: The Fool, 4, 6, Thursday, Sunday, blue, purple

Born today: Scarlett Johansson, Jamie Lee Curtis (actors); George Eliot (author); Billie Jean King (tennis player)

November 23

The Birthday of Sweet Confrontation

The life lesson:

is to avoid confrontation.

The way forward: is to understand that stepping back from situations helps you develop the objectivity you need to deal more effectively with them and see the bigger picture.

Luck maker: The desire to retaliate is a natural reaction, but if you can learn to harness your anger and transform it into resolve, you greatly improve your chances of success.

"Like a moth to a flame"

Those born on November 23 have remarkably nimble, visionary minds, and their wit and grace make them much sought after. They seem to know exactly the right thing to say at the right time to the right person. However, they also have an edgy side that draws them irresistibly to confrontations and become the catalyst for making sparks fly. Sometimes this works because the truth is exposed and everyone feels lighter. But if they are not careful, tension can become a constant theme, which can be an extremely negative and difficult pattern to break.

Born politicians and business leaders, they have leadership potential but also need freedom. They may work for themselves or in education, coaching, technology, journalism, broadcasting, podcasting, the law, science, writing, self-help and personal growth, entertainment, acting or music. They benefit from time spent outside in the fresh air, and doing gentle breathing exercises brings greater balance into their lives. Easily hurt, they may also be prone to bouts of reactive depression and feelings of being alone. Learning not to take everything so personally helps them develop a thicker skin. **For self-care**, studying and practicing spiritual disciplines such as meditation and yoga helps you stay calm in the face of adversity.

Seductive, these people can sweet-talk anyone, but if their relationships are to remain fulfilling, they need to avoid confusing conflict with passion. Until the age of 28 they focus on expanding their horizons through study or travel, but after 28 they become more pragmatic, orderly and structured and prioritize their professional goals. If they want to avoid obstacles to success, they must learn to stop engaging in conflict for the sake of it. When they finally learn to choose their battles wisely, they can save their intelligent energy for what really matters: developing their outstanding potential for becoming authoritative and truly motivational role models. Once they become more objective, take control of their emotions and exercise good judgment, their destiny is to devise innovative changes and bring progress.

Potential: Charming, visionary

Dark side: Argumentative, isolated

Tarot card, lucky numbers, days, colors: The Hierophant, 5, 7, Thursday, Wednesday, purple, blue

Born today: Miley Cyrus (singer); Boris Karloff (actor); Harpo Marx (comedian); Sai Baba (guru)

November 24

The Birthday of Intrigue

"On the edge of mystery"

November 24-born are spirited individuals. They are at their best when debating issues or troubleshooting for a solution. People find themselves irresistibly drawn to their courageous spirit and thrilling ideas, plus their air of mystery. It doesn't matter how settled their lives appear, intrigue is never far behind. Whether this manifests in complicated situations or relationships or all-absorbing internal conflicts, there is always a question mark in their lives, and the outcome never appears certain. Rarely, if ever, boring, they are an endless topic of conversation for others, but sometimes they feel overwhelmed by feelings of uncertainty.

Born psychiatrists and psychologists, they have the communication and people skills to succeed in any job, but they are drawn to the caring professions, counseling, therapy, social reform, teaching, writing, sports, philosophy, research, music and entertainment, as well as the study of metaphysics and spirituality. If their lives settle into too much of a routine, they may suffer from fatigue and mood swings. They need to understand, however, that the answer does not lie in making outward changes, but within themselves. Cognitive behavioral therapy techniques are beneficial, as they can help them make these internal changes by altering the way they think about themselves. **For self-care**, interpreting your dreams and wearing, surrounding yourself with and meditating on the color purple encourages you to look within for inspiration.

These people tend to be drawn into complicated relationships or love triangles, and it is important they seek balance, simplicity and honesty in their relationships. Until the age of 27 they seek to expand their horizons through enterprising ventures, study and travel. After 27 they become more practical, goal-orientated and realistic, but after 58 expressing their individuality matters more to them. Whatever their age, they have opportunities to develop their original and ambitious plans, but their key to success is to simply accept themselves for who they are—highly creative and courageous individuals who can never fit into the mold because their destiny is to break it. By so doing, they encourage others to follow their exciting example and uncover the mysteries of their own lives.

Potential: Insightful, magnetic

Dark side: Unaware, complicated

Tarot card, lucky numbers, days, colors: The Lovers, 6, 8, Thursday, Friday, purple, pink

Born today: Stephen Merchant, Billy Connolly (comedians); Scott Joplin (composer); Arundhati Roy (author)

November 25

The Birthday of Global Concern

"The world is in our hands"

People born on November 25 are capable, logical and quietly progressive individuals, who are willing to take the time needed to complete a project perfectly. Their motivation is a benevolent urge to achieve excellence and make a real difference, rather than gain power and money. This gives them the determination to make things happen and the humility to support others. Indeed, social concern and taking responsibility for others' wellbeing is an important theme. Although their desire for independence is strong, their fulfillment is often found in inspiring people. Their perfectionist drive can lean toward intolerance and inflexibility, so establishing an identity for themselves outside of their job or cause, and learning to work with those holding alternative views, are essential for their psychological growth.

Born teachers, they gravitate toward education, coaching, science, politics, promotion, lobbying, spirituality, sociology, environmental and humanitarian concerns, the healthcare, healing and caring professions, as well as social care and charity. Their need for self-expression may express itself in writing, music, art or entertainment. They have workaholic tendencies and can be strict about their health. It's important that they ensure their concern to eat only the best does not rob them of the joy of eating; likewise, that their fierce desire for fitness never takes away the joy of movement. **For self-care**, meditating on and surrounding yourself with the color green encourages you to be more tolerant and accepting.

In their relationships those born on this day can have impossibly high expectations and need to learn that simply being happy is enough. Until the age of 26 they should expand their horizons through study or travel. After 26 they have a more pragmatic, ordered approach to life. Whatever stage they are at, they should find the courage to strike out on their own and direct their creative concern and sense of responsibility toward others. When they can do this, they unlock their outstanding potential for making a positive difference to the world by nurturing and strengthening connections rather than differences. Their destiny is to assist, educate and inspire others.

Potential: Accomplished, supportive

Dark side: Workaholic, inflexible

Tarot card, lucky numbers, days, colors: The Chariot, 7, 9, Thursday, Monday, purple, sea green

Born today: Andrew Carnegie (industrialist); Karl Benz (inventor); Joe DiMaggio (baseball player); Christina Applegate (actor)

November 26

The Birthday of Multitalented Uniqueness

"I am everything and nothing"

The life lesson: is emotional closeness.

The way forward: is to understand that the more comfortable you are with yourself, the more comfortable you will be with others.

Luck maker: People judge others on what they do rather than what they say, so impress them with your actions rather than your words.

Those born on November 26 are exciting, creative thinkers, with the world at their feet. Not only are they charismatic and intelligent, they are also multitalented and can excel in any profession. Despite their incredible potential, they can sometimes feel lonely—as if they don't belong. This is because they have so many talents and such an inquisitive mind that too many paths are open to them and choosing one becomes daunting. It can be a struggle to reconcile their practical, logical side with their highly creative part. At various points in life, they lurch between these two extremes, but the key to fulfillment lies in finding a balance between the two. Success-orientated, when they are not working toward a goal, these people feel restless and unsatisfied, so the sooner they find their path in life, the better.

Born creators and online influencers, their work options include education, research, technology, gaming, social media, philosophy, writing, engineering, IT, toy manufacturing, design, or any career or lifestyle, such as entrepreneurship, that allows them to be creative and innovative. The biggest risk to their emotional health is their tendency to withdraw or to isolate themselves, so staying in touch with friends and family or owning a pet benefits them enormously. **For self-care,** every night before bed you should write a to-do list for the next day. The following evening you can enjoy the satisfaction of ticking off items you have done.

Unwilling to sacrifice their freedom in relationships, those born on this day need partners and friends who are not co-dependent or controlling. Up to the age of 25, they may experiment with various careers as they focus on adventure, creativity and opportunity. However, after 25 they become more practical, goal-orientated and realistic. The key to their success is to make full use of their multitalented uniqueness rather than try to hide it—there is and never will be anybody quite like them, with their creativity, courage and determination to achieve their exciting and expansive goals. Once they can look within themselves and love what they see, their destiny is to make an outstandingly original contribution to society.

Potential: Innovative, talented

Dark side: Indecisive, unfocused

Tarot card, lucky numbers, days, colors: Strength, 1, 8, Thursday, Saturday, purple, brown

Born today: Charles Schulz (cartoonist); Rita Ora, Tina Turner (singers); Willis Carrier (engineer)

November 27

The Birthday of the Vortex

"I feel, therefore I am"

November 27-born are like a vortex of energy, enthusiasm and excitement. Fiercely individualistic, they go where their imagination leads them. The only trouble is that they often have no idea where they are heading, and their enthusiasm overwhelms their common sense. They need to learn to distinguish between intuition and wishful thinking, and the only way to do that is to understand themselves better and take a more realistic view of situations before they throw themselves in at the deep end. Although they encounter setbacks, they are remarkably resilient.

Born rock stars, these people thrive in any career in which they can pursue their quest for knowledge, and may be drawn to music, art, entertainment and sport. Their desire to benefit others may incline them toward science, research, technology, politics, education, social reform, while writing, tourism, advertising and working for themselves may also appeal. Impatient and highly strung, they often live life in the fast lane and would benefit from regular periods of calm to avoid burnout. Chewing their food thoroughly is beneficial, as is dining at the table rather than eating on the go. **For self-care,** swimming and yoga can help soothe your mind and bring you a sense of inner peace.

Those born on this day tend to idolize others and rush into relationships. Although they are capable of commitment, freedom is important to them and they rarely fall completely in love, preferring to jump from relationship to relationship. Until the age of 24 they experiment, travel or study to broaden their horizons. After 24 they become more pragmatic, orderly and focused on their goals. The secret to unlocking their infinite potential is their ability to control the powerful energy within and direct it to a worthy cause. Once they are able to do that, they can still be vortexes of dynamic energy and originality, but this time they know where they are heading, and that is usually to the very top. Their destiny is to enlighten, inspire and invigorate all those fortunate enough to cross their path.

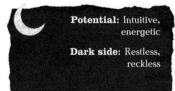

Potential: Intuitive, energetic

Dark side: Restless, reckless

Tarot card, lucky numbers, days, colors: The Hermit, 2, 9, Thursday, Tuesday, purple, orange

Born today: Kathryn Bigelow (director); Bruce Lee (martial artist); Jimi Hendrix, Parov Stelar (musicians)

November 28

The Birthday of Curious Impulsiveness

The life lesson:

is making realistic plans.

The way forward: is to set short-term goals that you can easily reach, then set more so that you move ahead.

Luck maker: Call on self-discipline, be willing to do things you don't always like and see things through to the end.

"Heaven in a grain of sand"

People born on November 28 are natural philosophers with open minds and a sense of infinite possibility. Bursting with curiosity for everything, they tend to overextend themselves in both thinking and actions. They can flirt with ideas as well as people, tending to be intensely enthusiastic at the start of new endeavors but then losing interest as things progress. Despite their sparkling wit and apparent flightiness, they are not superficial. Too honest to hide their feelings, whether disillusionment or boredom sets in, they can offend people along the way. Learning to think before they speak, and, most importantly, taking charge of their emotions, is key to their success. Others may criticize their moodiness and messiness, but they don't sulk for long and their mess is always creative and innovative. If they want, though, to achieve the success and recognition their expansive mind deserves, they must combine their creativity with dedication and discipline.

Born journalists, they are drawn to careers involving travel, communication and creativity. They prefer intellectually demanding work that benefits others, such as publishing, the law, medicine, social reform, politics, writing, blogging, broadcasting or the arts. Once they get serious about their responsibilities, they can do well in business or humanitarian projects. The more time they spend outdoors in natural surroundings the better, because this has a calming and balancing influence. **For self-care**, making your bed every morning when you wake up, and wearing and surrounding yourself with soothing shades of blue, encourages you to be more consistent and disciplined.

Those born on this day need to learn that commitment and freedom don't have to be mutually exclusive in relationships. As they can be loners, people who give them plenty of liberty are ideal. But the only way to attract self-sufficient souls into their lives is to love themselves enough first. After the age of 24, they focus on responsibility and achieving their goals. They should seize any opportunities, trust their powerful intuition and express their creativity in a disciplined and goal-orientated way. Their destiny is to motivate others to expand their horizons and, by so doing, be an inspirational force in the world.

Potential: Spontaneous, creative

Dark side: Restless, untidy

Tarot card, lucky numbers, days, colors: The Magician, 1, 3, Thursday, Sunday, blue, purple

Born today: William Blake (poet); Henry Bacon (architect); Berry Gordy (Motown owner); Ed Harris (actor)

November 29

The Birthday of Dynamic Controversy

"Way outside the box"

The life lesson:

is learning to listen.

The way forward: is to think like a mirror—this doesn't judge or give advice, just reflects back what the person is saying.

Luck maker: Your commitment to following through on agreed changes makes all the difference to your credibility and attracts more opportunities your way.

Those born on November 29 bring an air of excitement and possibility. They are optimistic and imaginative, stimulated by a desire to move forward. Their dynamism can encourage others to be more courageous, but they have a habit of stirring up controversy, because they think outside the box. They love to express their opinions, and it doesn't matter to them if they get a negative response—what they want is a reaction, and a negative one is better than none. Sometimes, however, their provocative manner oversteps the mark and they need to ensure they don't highlight emotional vulnerabilities in others for no reason other than to demonstrate their power.

Born reporters, they may gravitate toward careers in science, teaching or the arts, but they also make excellent debaters, media correspondents, film directors, journalists, and literary critics or commentators. Other work options include the law, politics, campaigning, sports, sociology, business, medicine, administration, design, architecture, charity and community work, as well as the self-help industry. They need to find ways to amuse or occupy themselves rather than always relying on the company of others to feel alive. Once they are more self-sufficient, they discover that stress and depression lift and life becomes much more fulfilling. **For self-care**, daily walks are beneficial because they give you much-needed time alone with your thoughts.

Often surrounded by admirers, they should learn the joys of solitude and finding happiness in their own company. Up to the age of 21 they may want to expand their opportunities through enterprising ventures, study or travel, but after 23 they become more realistic and goal-orientated in their approach and bring more order and structure into their lives. They are always a catalyst for change. If they can make sure that this is a positive change that can encourage progress both for themselves and for others, they have the potential to become truly inspired thinkers. Once they learn to listen and take on board different opinions and tap into their powerful intuition, their destiny is to inspire others to make significant progress in everything they do.

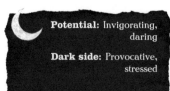

Potential: Invigorating, daring

Dark side: Provocative, stressed

Tarot card, lucky numbers, days, colors: The High Priestess, 2, 4, Thursday, Monday, blue, silver

Born today: Louisa May Alcott, C. S. Lewis (authors); Christian Doppler (physicist); Russell Wilson (football player)

November 30

The Birthday of Piercing Composure

is being spontaneous.

The way forward: is to understand that sometimes your best response to a situation is to trust your instincts and go with the flow.

Luck maker: Rediscover your inner child and develop the habit of looking at things as if for the first time.

"Busy is best"

November 30-born often feel there simply aren't enough hours in the day or years in their life to accomplish all their ambitions. They have so many talents that it can be hard to know where to invest their energy. Once they settle on a chosen course, they are extremely thorough in their approach, their attention to detail being second to none. As a result, they are well prepared for virtually any situation, and because they never leave anything to the last minute, they are typically composed, calm and convincing. In the unlikely event that they can't influence others—which they almost invariably can—they find it very hard to accept that someone can say no to or fail to be impressed by them.

Born editors, they are eloquent and detail-focused, and excel in writing, publishing, sales, politics, music, acting, art and filmmaking. Other career choices include leadership or planning positions in teaching, the law, business, science, research, design and administration. They should travel more to open their mind to other ways of looking at the world. Depression is a real threat, especially when their plans go wrong. They need to understand that they can't control everything but they can always control how they react. **For self-care**, wearing, meditating on and surrounding yourself with the color orange encourages you to be more spontaneous. You also benefit from time spent in the countryside in green surroundings.

These people make generous and supportive partners, but to find real love, they need to put their accomplishments aside and focus on making others feel loved. After the age of 22, they crave more order and structure. They tend to be highly controlled and lacking in spontaneity, so it is vital that they get in touch with their intuition, take themselves and others less seriously, and incorporate more fun and laughter into their lives. The sooner they loosen up and trust their heart and intuition as much as their rational side, the sooner they can maximize their potential for success. Once they understand that some situations simply can't be controlled, their destiny is to advance with well-thought-out and often hugely influential strategies and plans.

Potential: Convincing, multitalented

Dark side: Reactive, gloomy

Tarot card, lucky numbers, day, colors: The Empress, 3, 5, Thursday, purple, blue

Born today: Winston Churchill (British prime minister); Helané Wahbeh (scientist); Billy Idol (singer); Mark Twain (author)

December 1

The Birthday of Outrageous Charm

"Let me entertain you"

People born on December 1 are outrageously charming and vital. Unhindered by convention, they express themselves freely and delight in surprising and seducing others with their sparkling wit. Any attempts to censure their freedom simply have the effect of renewing their energy. They may lack tact or diplomacy, but their engaging charm still draws others to them, even when their words or actions are shocking. Underneath their larger-than-life personality, however, they are deep and complex; sometimes they don't know what motivates them at all and their vibrant front is simply their way of coping with inner confusion.

Born entertainers, they work well when they can be independent and original. Although they can be team players, they are natural leaders and enjoy being self-employed. They are well suited to the performance, sporting or artistic fields, as well as acting, music, film, the media, advertising, comedy, broadcasting and show business. They are often vigorous and athletic in their youth, but as they get older they tend to overindulge and live an increasingly sedentary lifestyle, so a healthy diet and exercise plan is key. **For self-care**, cognitive behavioral therapy is beneficial to help you become aware of how your thoughts are influencing your moods, and carrying a titanium crystal can help you find your true path in life.

These people tend to leave any shyness behind and emerge in their thirties as charismatic, supportive and much sought-after friends and lovers. Before the age of 50 they have many opportunities to become more pragmatic, orderly and structured, and to focus on their career, which is an important creative outlet for their energy and talents. After 50, they have a growing need for independence and for sharing their progressive ideas. They are free spirits, but if they can learn to be a little more diplomatic, cautious and self-aware, they can blaze their own highly original trail through life. Their destiny is to bring enlightenment and joy to the lives of others.

Potential: Entertaining, energetic

Dark side: Tactless, confused

Tarot card, lucky numbers, days, colors: The Magician, 1, 4, Thursday, Sunday, purple, blue

Born today: Woody Allen (director); Bette Midler (singer); Sarah Silverman (actor); Richard Pryor (comedian)

December 2

The Birthday of the Kaleidoscope

"Music to my soul"

December 2-born tend to be strikingly dramatic and colorful. It's impossible not to notice them. They wear their heart on their sleeve and are so spontaneous that the whole kaleidoscope of their emotions is displayed. Their emotional honesty is refreshing, and their drive and determination make them inspiring leaders. The effect they can have on others is striking, but it could be life-changing if they learned to balance their directness with a little tact, stepping back to examine what their emotions are saying before speaking or lashing out.

Born singers, they can make significant contributions to society, perhaps as pioneering scientists, or as inspirational inventors, designers, researchers, artists, musicians and performers. They may change career several times, but may also be drawn to education, sales, the law, publishing, the media, social media, blogging, writing, charity work, and the tourist and leisure industries. Music can help clear their mind and encourage them to see patterns and connections instead of confusion or fantasy. They should listen to classical music to enhance their creativity and language skills, as well as the logical, analytical side of their brain. **For self-care**, time spent reading and studying spiritual disciplines or mastering the techniques of meditation are beneficial.

Those born on this day can't help being terrible flirts, so potential partners and friends need to adjust to their shifting personality. After the age of 20 they more practical, goal-orientated and realistic. They need order and structure in their life, because too many changes of direction can lead to confusion and uncertainty. After 50, they seek more independence and to become more humanitarian. Charismatic individuals, they are also problem-solvers looking for a deeper meaning to their life. Once they find a way to work with their inner sensitivity, not only can they intuitively know what is best for them, but they can take charge of their emotions, find a cause worthy of their visionary, creative talents, and create the magical pattern of peace and happiness they so richly deserve. Their destiny is to make an inspirational or pioneering mark on the world.

Potential: Inspirational, visionary

Dark side: Unaware, inconsistent

Tarot card, lucky numbers, days, colors: The High Priestess, 2, 5, Thursday, Monday, purple, silver

Born today: Maria Callas, Britney Spears (singers); Gianni Versace (designer); Shiva Ayyadurai (inventor)

December 3

The Birthday of Progressive Expertise

"Let me concentrate"

People born on December 3 are at their best when formulating plans to educate, inspire or bring about improvements. Although their ideas are original and sometimes unorthodox, they are thorough, with formidable organizational and technical skills, and this rare combination gives them stunning expertise in their field. Not surprisingly, given their perfectionist nature, work plays a huge part in their lives and they often dedicate themselves wholeheartedly to their career. They tend to seek out those with similar driven mindsets, and while others respect their focus and admire their success, these people can be hard to get to know. Progressive and busy, they have little time for socializing.

Born engineers, they combine their ingenuity with their technical skills to excel in careers such as research, the law, science, psychology and technology, as well as sport. Other work options include sales, advertising, public relations, promotion, education and charity work, and expressing their originality through art, music, writing and drama. They lose themselves in work, and need to remind themselves to take pleasure in simple things such as gardening, walking in the countryside and talking to friends, which are essential for their wellbeing. **For self-care**, wearing, meditating on and surrounding yourself with the color orange encourages you to be more spontaneous and expressive.

Intense and independent, these people often need time alone, unaware that they have a host of admirers silently waiting. The driven aspects of their personality don't emerge until their twenties but give them a determination second to none. After 50, they focus on creating a happy life outside work. They need to be freer and more open with others, as this helps them understand that their ambition is driven by a desire for professional excellence and to play an inspirational role in people's lives. As long as they ensure that they prioritize their own emotional needs, they have the innovative potential to become truly dynamic vehicles of progress. Once they learn to balance their professional and personal life, their destiny is to profoundly influence others with their tremendous expertise and progressive ideas.

Potential: Innovative, ambitious

Dark side: Workaholic, withdrawn

Tarot card, lucky numbers, day, colors: The Emperor, 3, 6, Thursday, purple, blue

Born today: John Wallis (mathematician); Joseph Conrad (author); Daryl Hannah, Julianne Moore (actors)

December 4

The Birthday of the Captain

"I chart the course"

The life lesson: is coping with not being listened to.

The way forward: is to balance your leadership skills with a genuine concern for the welfare of others.

Luck maker: When you offer others recognition, you become an energy source for people who then want to keep you center stage and provide new opportunities for you.

Those born on December 4 are ambitious and resilient, with remarkable self-control. They have the rare ability to take charge of their emotions without losing their creativity, which gives them self-confidence and authority. They are like a daring but highly skilled ship's captain with the courage and ingenuity to successfully steer their vessel through uncharted waters to previously undiscovered lands. Although they are rebels, ironically they impose their radical ideas on others, sometimes forcefully, which can make them seem hypocritical. Fortunately, most of the time they are genuinely concerned for the wellbeing of others and their natural sense of justice propels them toward activities that benefit everyone rather than themselves.

Born sailors, pilots and natural leaders, they may be drawn to politics, campaigning, conservation, aviation, shipping, agriculture, research, archaeology, travel, tourism, the arts or entrepreneurship. Other career choices include business, commerce, advertising, sport, management, health and the caring professions, fashion, the media and entertainment. These people need to master the art of delegation, as letting others help them not only eases their workload, but also earns the loyalty of their colleagues and allows them to develop more outside interests. Spending more time in nature or natural settings, and meditation techniques to quieten their minds, are highly beneficial. **For self-care**, wearing, meditating on and surrounding yourself with the color purple brings a sense of inner harmony, peace and balance.

Those born on this day have no problem attracting admirers, but close relationships may be elusive until they learn to give and take in relationships. Their leadership skills emerge in their early twenties, and over the years these individuals become more practical, goal-orientated and realistic. After 48, there is a growing need for freedom, new ideas and expressing their individuality. If they can find a middle way between nobility and ambition, love and success, compassion and power, independence and the need to compromise, they can not only show inspired leadership, but might just become the visionaries of their generation. Their destiny is simple: to set and steer a course that advances the greater good.

Potential: Powerful, inspirational

Dark side: Authoritarian, hypocritical

Tarot card, lucky numbers, days, colors: The Emperor, 4, 7, Thursday, Sunday, blue, silver

Born today: Thomas Carlyle (historian); Edith Cavell (nurse); Jay-Z (rapper); Tyra Banks (model)

December 5

The Birthday of the Assured Adventurer

The life lesson:

is taking others' advice.

The way forward: is to understand that others always bring different perspectives and that you should listen to them as you may learn something useful.

Luck maker: Although positive thinking gets you far, being overconfident does not, and humility is an important part of the luck equation.

"If I can dream it, I can make it so"

December 5-born reach for the skies and somehow manage to get to where they want—or at least, close to it. From an early age they often display unusual self-confidence and courage. If they don't, they may have experienced knocks to dent their confidence, but sooner or later their characteristic optimism emerges. They believe anything is possible, and throughout their lives are a shining example of what self-belief can achieve. However, sometimes they can be overconfident and unwilling to listen to the advice of others, which can lead to avoidable mistakes. Although they should never lose their idealism and optimism, they need to ensure that the goals they set are realistic and achievable.

Born designers, they thrive in careers that provide constant stimulation. They may be drawn to art, writing, music, fashion, filmmaking, entertainment, education, research, science, social reform, politics, charity work or entrepreneurship. Regular exercise to boost their mood, keep their bones strong and muscles toned is beneficial, as is spending time with loved ones. **For self-care**, sprinkling a few drops of rose, clary sage or frankincense essential oil on a handkerchief to breathe in helps produce feelings of inner security and self-acceptance.

Hard to ignore or dislike, these people are generally accepted and admired, despite sometimes being overly ambitious. From their late teens onward, they are determined to make their distinctive mark on the world. Listening to the advice of experts could be key to unlocking their potential. After 47 they become more progressive and original in their ideas, and if they have managed to learn from past experience and make a realistic assessment of themselves and their situation, this is when they come into their own. They have a real desire to make a positive contribution to society, and once they can direct their determination, focus and willpower to a worthy cause, they can find ways to benefit the greater good. Their destiny is to open minds to visionary possibilities, and to introduce and promote innovation.

Potential: Confident, daring

Dark side: Arrogant, foolish

Tarot card, lucky numbers, days, colors: The Hierophant, 5, 8, Thursday, Wednesday, blue, orange

Born today: Walt Disney (animator); Werner Heisenberg, C. F. Powell (physicists); Little Richard (singer)

December 6

The Birthday of the Developer

is resisting the urge to interfere.

The way forward: is to understand that sometimes the best way you can help others grow is to let them learn from their own mistakes.

Luck maker: The more you give selflessly and without condition, the more people remember and wish to repay you.

"Let's sort it out"

People born on December 6 are practical and clear-sighted, with a real talent for management. They are often found organizing others and trying to develop plans or ideas so that they produce better results. Everyone turns to them first when things aren't working, and others value their rational and perceptive conclusions as well as the tactful way they present them. Lacking any hidden agenda, they are honest and to the point in both their professional and personal life. They can immediately see the flaws in a situation, and how to fix them and achieve the best possible result. Although others are often grateful for their advice, occasionally their desire to intervene can seem like meddling.

Born managers, they thrive in careers that let them organize and implement improvements. Options include science, research, publishing, advertising, sales, business, commerce, accounting, administration, the law, social reform and education, while they may also be drawn to music, filmmaking, entertainment and the arts, as well as to personal and spiritual development. They have workaholic tendencies and need to avoid stimulants such as caffeine and nicotine. Burning candles with aromatic scents is beneficial: ginger helps boost concentration, and lavender or sandalwood combats stress. **For self-care,** wearing, meditating on or surrounding yourself with the color purple encourages you to connect with your intuition and creativity.

Those born on this day love interesting conversations, and others are drawn to them for advice and guidance. They should choose who they help carefully and avoid toxic or needy people. Until the age of 45 they have a need for order and structure in their lives, and they concentrate on practical issues. During these years, evaluating concepts and systems, and devising strategies to improve them, are top of their agenda. After 45, they desire more independence, but this is also when they are likely to enlist others' support. Their highly developed clear thinking and objectivity make them natural leaders, with the potential to achieve results that enhance everyone's lives. Once they learn to leave others alone when their advice isn't required, their destiny is to spearhead remarkable progress.

Potential: Supportive, perceptive

Dark side: Interfering, unimaginative

Tarot card, lucky numbers, days, colors: The Lovers, 6, 9, Thursday, Friday, blue, pink

Born today: Judd Apatow (director); Steven Wright (comedian); Giannis Antetokounmpo (basketball player)

December 7

The Birthday of the Dreamer

"I dreamed a dream"

Those born on December 7 often feel they have a special purpose in life. They dare to be different and, as original and creative thinkers, they stand apart from the crowd. Although they have a thirst for adventure, they are first and foremost visionaries, and their minds take them to places others don't have the imagination to go. They can become trendsetters, and their freethinking, pioneering style both startles and delights. Their conversation is always interesting, but they tend to talk more than they act and others may dismiss them as dreamers, not doers.

Born philosophers and architects, they are suited to careers that involve independence and experimenting. Options include design, education, publishing, writing, the law, politics, commerce, sales, promotion and negotiation, and their need for creative self-expression may lead them to sport, music, art or drama. The more they escape into the countryside the better, because nature has a calming and uplifting effect on them. **For self-care,** classical music is highly therapeutic when you are suffering from bouts of stress and anxiety.

Those born on this day tend to put people they admire on pedestals and to be overly generous in their relationships, which can lead to disappointment if they don't set boundaries. Mixing with people who are positive and focused encourages them to find a sense of purpose and direction. Until the age of 44, they need to be practical and realistic in their approach to their goals, otherwise their tendency to flit from job to job or to stick with one they are clearly unsuited for can cause them great unhappiness. After 44, their desire to express their individuality is stronger than ever. If they haven't found their vocation by then, it's time to seek advice from experts about retraining for a new career. Alternatively, they may seek fulfillment outside work, as these people need to find what makes their heart sing. It would be a tragedy if the world did not benefit from their unique and magical creativity. Their destiny is to use their imagination to educate, inform and enlighten others.

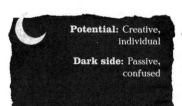

Potential: Creative, individual

Dark side: Passive, confused

Tarot card, lucky numbers, days, colors: The Chariot, 1, 7, Thursday, Monday, blue, sea green

Born today: Marie Tussaud (artist); Willa Cather (author); Noam Chomsky (philosopher); Larry Bird (basketball player)

December 8

The Birthday of Passion

The life lesson:

is being responsible.

The way forward: is to understand that you can be both responsible and passionate at the same time, and the combination of these qualities can put you on the winning team.

Luck maker: Take steps to reduce the number of mistakes you make by learning about the issues involved and listening to knowledgeable people before you act.

"I'm all in"

December 8-born often sparkle and their charisma attracts attention wherever they go. Intensely emotional and sensual, their passionate and spontaneous approach to life is their defining feature. They can't see the point of being half-hearted—their nature is to give one hundred percent. True idealists, they strive for fulfillment in all areas of their busy lives, but they need to understand that imperfection is the natural human state and what they seek can only be found within and not outside them.

Born dancers, they go where their heart leads, and their passionate intensity means their potential for success is strong whatever career they choose. They love to inspire others, so they excel as campaigners, social workers, writers, dancers, actors, singers, artists, musicians and performers. Business and self-employment are appealing to them, as is working for large enterprises with opportunities for advancement, change and travel. They tend to be owls rather than larks and should ensure they are in bed by midnight, as this is optimum for their health. They should also beware of recreational drugs and alcohol, because they have addictive tendencies. **For self-care**, wearing, meditating on and surrounding yourself with the color blue encourages you to be more objective and responsible.

These people are attracted to tempestuous relationships and must learn not to confuse tension with passion. Until the age of 43, they need order or structure, which can help prevent them from plunging into toxic relationships or situations. After 43, they may feel a growing need to become more self-aware and to develop their individuality. Whatever age they are, the key to their happiness and success is to be more cautious and not let their passionate intensity overpower their common sense. With a little more realism added to their stunning creativity and idealism, they will find much of the fulfilling passion they have been searching for and discover their destiny, which is to bring great hope and much-needed joy into the world.

Potential: Charismatic, passionate

Dark side: Irresponsible, unfulfilled

Tarot card, lucky numbers, days, colors: Strength, 2, 8, Thursday, Saturday, purple, brown

Born today: Horace (poet); Jim Morrison, Sinéad O'Connor (singers); Mary Queen of Scots (monarch)

December 9

The Birthday of the Gallant Hero

is patience.

The way forward: is to understand that sometimes you can't force progress—the best approach is to simply bide your time.

Luck maker: Give others credit and share their success, because recognizing and crediting them makes them more likely to respect you and steer opportunities your way.

"Never fear"

People born on December 9 are blessed with a fertile imagination. From an early age they think of themselves as a gallant hero swooping in to save the day and astonishing everyone with acts of daring. Their urge to make inspirational contributions to the world is strong, and with their dynamic energy and adventurous spirit they possess outstanding pioneering potential. Born leaders, their biggest challenge is patience. They can easily snap when things aren't going exactly the way they want them to or when people aren't listening. They need to learn when to promote their ideals and when to just let things unfold.

Born lawyers, they may be drawn to the political, legal or scientific spheres, or to artistic media such as music, writing, literature or drama. They love to help or enlighten others, so they favor education, business, journalism, social reform, politics, counseling and entertainment. They tend to live and eat fast. This can cause digestive problems, so they need to slow down, sit and chew their food carefully. Regular vigorous exercise, running in particular, is beneficial, as it can release pent-up tension. **For self-care**, wearing, meditating on and surrounding yourself with shades of the color blue helps you understand that you control your emotions and not the other way around.

These people are romantic and ardent lovers, but struggle when their relationships become routine, so they need to learn to appreciate the simpler things in life. By the time they reach their twenties, they start to come out of their shell; if they struggle to be assertive, developing their self-confidence is crucial, because they were born to be in the limelight. After 43 they may desire to be more independent and to express their individuality. They always have an all-encompassing, albeit occasionally self-centered urge to play a leading role in the lives of those around them. If they can learn to be cooler and take charge of their emotions, their destiny is to save the day and make not just an imaginative but a progressive and lasting contribution to the world.

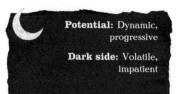

Potential: Dynamic, progressive

Dark side: Volatile, impatient

Tarot card, lucky numbers, day, colors: The Hermit, 3, 9, Thursday, blue, red

Born today: Kirk Douglas, John Malkovich, Judi Dench (actors); John Milton (poet)

December 10

The Birthday of Calm Intensity

"Got to have faith"

Those born on December 10 are defined by their strength of spirit and determination to achieve their goals. Profound thinkers, they long to further human knowledge or instigate beneficial reform. Blessed with an inner calm, their organizational skills and potential for success are outstanding. They have leadership potential, and when they find a cause they have faith in, they devote themselves wholly to it. The key word here is faith, because if they don't believe in what they are doing, they won't just go through the motions. Their choice of career frequently has a vocational element, as they need to feel they are serving a higher cause. They often ponder the meaning and purpose of life and can come across as detached.

Born directors, they find fulfilling careers in people or event management, politics, community service, or charity or humanitarian work. They are drawn to academia, religion, self-help, spiritual and personal development. Other career options include writing, promotion, sales, therapy, art, film, drama, design and architecture. These people need to ensure they don't become isolated and should reach out to others to boost their wellbeing. They must also guard against relying on one person to support and uplift them. **For self-care**, wearing, meditating on and surrounding yourself with the color orange increases feelings of warmth, enjoyment and security.

Those born on this day should follow their heart but must not let romantic idealism destroy their chances of finding happiness. They need to love people for who they are, not for what they could be. Until the age of 41, they strive to be practical and bring order and structure into their lives. This helps them develop a thicker skin and be resilient in the face of adversity. After 41 they need more independence. When they finally find a cause they feel passionate about, they discover they have the self-discipline, responsibility and sense of meaning they need to live up to their exceptional potential as gifted and progressive leaders. Their destiny is to formulate effective plans that serve the common good and significantly benefit all.

Potential: Determined, profound

Dark side: Isolated, fragile

Tarot card, lucky numbers, day, colors: The Wheel of Fortune, 1, 4, Thursday, Sunday, blue, yellow

Born today: Emily Dickinson, Nelly Sachs (poets); Kenneth Branagh (actor); Ada Lovelace (mathematician)

December 11

The Birthday of Profound Purpose

The life lesson:

is having fun.

The way forward: is to understand that the ability to take yourself less seriously is one of the most powerful ways to influence people and get your point across.

Luck maker: Believing there is plenty of luck to go around brings you a higher level of life satisfaction than those who don't believe this.

December 11-born have always felt there was a solemn and profound purpose to their lives. Whatever profession they choose, they are notable for their energy and determination. As perfectionists they demand as high a level of commitment and dedication from others as they demand from themselves. They excel professionally, but they can sometimes exhaust everyone, including themselves. Nor is there any let-up in intensity in their personal and social life, as they are influential and persuasive individuals who win over—or in some cases wear down—others with their charming persistence.

Born scientists, they excel in medicine, research, engineering, technology, mechanics, or may be drawn to emergency services, debating, the law, teaching, art and writing, as well as social and humanitarian reform. Executive or management positions in business may also appeal. They would benefit greatly from a more spiritual outlook on life and regular time spent alone with their phones switched to silent, reflecting on their real priorities. **For self-care**, interpreting your dreams helps you focus on your inner life, and wearing, meditating on and surrounding yourself with the color purple encourages you to think of higher things.

Charming and seductive, these people find that few can resist their spell, but they are drawn to ambitious individuals like themselves and feel happier with a more relaxed and spontaneous approach to relationships and life. Until the age of 40, a running theme is the need for a more practical and realistic approach to achieving their goals, but they should ensure that their single-minded approach does not make them manipulative or too materialistic. After 40, they desire to express their individuality and independence, and may become more involved with social issues and establishing a life outside work. It would benefit them to look within for meaning, and to consider more the impact of their behavior and words on others. Once they discover a higher spiritual purpose to balance their materialistic inclinations, they find that their uplifting destiny is to become an outstanding human being capable of improving or inspiring the lives of all around them—and in some cases humanity as a whole.

Potential: Charming, determined

Dark side: Materialistic, selfish

Tarot card, lucky numbers, days, colors: Justice, 2, 5, Thursday, Monday, blue, silver

Born today: Emmanuelle Charpentier (microbiologist); Eben Alexander (author); Annie Cannon (astronomer); Nikki Sixx (musician)

December 12

The Birthday of the Outspoken Teacher

"My life is my message"

People born on December 12 feel they have something important to say to the world. Alongside their desire to communicate their ideas, they also long to broaden their mind through study and travel. Others often admire their mental dexterity and their effortless ability to immediately pinpoint areas in need of improvement. They possess a tremendous amount of willpower and, although it can take a while for them to find a worthy cause or goal, they have all the ambition, talent and likability to be a huge success in all areas of their lives.

Born advisors and teachers, they are drawn to careers that let them impart knowledge, such as lecturing, education, writing, blogging, broadcasting, counseling, advising, politics, the law, coaching, and training. They may also be attracted to marketing, social-media influencing, promotion, advertising, sales—especially the promoting of innovative new products—the media, publishing, the theater and the arts. They tend to focus on their physical appearance, but once they understand the connection between their eating, sleeping and lifestyle habits and their looks and health, they often make positive changes. **For self-care**, you benefit greatly from grounding and calming activities such as tai chi and yoga, and mental disciplines such as meditation.

Dramatic and seductive, those born on this day usually have many relationships unless they decide to commit themselves fully to someone. Until the age of 39, they focus on the need for order and structure. This is when they are most likely to feel boxed in or tied down, and the struggle between their desire to establish themselves and their thirst for adventure can be confusing. After 39, they become even more experimental, and the drive toward greater freedom and making changes is particularly strong. If they can channel energy away from materialism toward looking within to develop their intuition, they can draw on their extensive knowledge and experience to realize their ambition of delivering a message of hope and progress to the world. Once they add a spiritual or deeper dimension to their lives, their destiny is to educate, advise and inspire others.

December 13

The Birthday of Erratic Precision

is letting go.

The way forward: is to understand that you can't control everything in your life.

Luck maker: Be ready to grab luck and seize the moment, even if it comes along before you are fully prepared.

"Through the eye of a needle"

Those born on December 13 bring confidence, resourcefulness, determination and stunning creativity to everything they do, plus a precise attention to the smallest detail. Although this rare combination bodes well for success in the long term, sometimes their careful approach can become overcautious and hesitant, and their procrastination can mean they miss out on opportunities. Also, while with their eye for detail they can be incredibly observant and perceptive of others, when it comes to themselves, they may lack similar awareness.

Born coders and programmers, they thrive in careers where patience and attention to detail are essential, and they may be drawn toward technology, engineering, computing, restorative work, architecture, accounting, the law, science, art, writing, research, forensics, detective work, sport, decorating, design, modeling, acting, music and archaeology. Careers involving travel, variety and creativity also suit. Cultivating interests outside work is also important for their wellbeing. **For self-care,** interpreting your dreams encourages you to be more expansive in your thinking, and cognitive behavioral therapy can help you recognize unhelpful thought and behavior patterns.

These people are romantic and know how to make their loved ones feel cherished, but they do need to beware of putting others on a pedestal and then being disappointed when they don't live up to their high expectations. Once they understand that no one is perfect, they usually get their priorities right and place love at the top. Until the age of 38 they pursue a practical and realistic approach, but this is when they must avoid focusing on the details and losing sight of the bigger picture. After 38 they are wont to express their individuality more and they can put their creative stamp firmly on the success they have already built. When they can step back and look at the impressive picture they are painting with their lives, they realize that they have much to be grateful for and to look forward to. Once they have learned to move on when situations can't be fixed or their point has been made, their destiny is to create highly ingenious and effective technical and creative advances.

Potential: Thorough, perceptive

Dark side: Exacting, hesitant

Tarot card, lucky numbers, days, colors: Death, 4, 7, Thursday, Sunday, purple, electric blue

Born today: Christopher Plummer, Dick Van Dyke, Jamie Foxx (actors); Werner Siemens (inventor); Taylor Swift (singer)

December 14

The Birthday of the Flamboyant Philosopher

The life lesson:

is getting your priorities right.

The way forward: is to reflect on what makes you happy, because until you understand what really matters to you, your life will lack direction.

Luck maker: If you want more success, start with the way you think and feel about yourself. If you don't feel good about yourself, how can you expect others to?

"Never stop learning and growing"

December 14-born struggle to merge into the crowd. They are very private people, but their flamboyant tastes, original ideas, high energy and enthusiasm, organizational skills and fierce determination set them apart. As natural philosophers, finding their own truth rather than conforming to the rules is important to them. Their provocative nature often outrages, but can also stimulate others, encouraging them to think outside the box. Their fulfillment lies in the quest for discovery and progress, and part of them longs to shut out all outside distractions so they can pursue their personal goals undisturbed. They prefer only to step into the limelight when they are ready to reveal the fruits of their labor.

Born philosophers, their decisiveness and perceptiveness make them natural leaders, but they thrive in careers where they can operate independently, and where research, manufacturing, invention and development play a key role. Choices include science, catering, technology, engineering, education, acting, philosophy, writing, advertising, publishing and sport. These people can suffer from low self-esteem, so taking care of their mind, body, heart and soul is crucial. Only when these four aspects of their life are nurtured daily does their life feel balanced and their self-esteem soar. **For self-care**, meditation and mindfulness techniques are beneficial for their calming effects, and carrying a small rose-quartz crystal attracts the energy of self-love.

If those born on this day have been hurt by someone they cared for deeply, work may take center stage and it can be hard for them to trust again. Until the age of 38 they focus on practical order and structure, which makes them more goal-orientated and responsible. After the age of 38 they become more concerned with expressing their individuality and making a mark on the world. Their keys to success are their ability to find a work–life balance and their willingness to develop their diplomatic skills, so that they can motivate others. Once they consider the impact of their words and actions, their destiny is to inspire others by example to look in the direction of discovery and progress.

Potential: Original, dramatic

Dark side: Workaholic, lonely

Tarot card, lucky numbers, days, colors: Temperance, 5, 8, Thursday, Wednesday, purple, orange

Born today: Nostradamus (astrologer); Tycho Brahe (astronomer); Miranda Hart (comedian); Vanessa Hudgens (actor)

December 15

The Birthday of the Optimist

People born on December 15 have the potential to be among the most upbeat individuals of the year. Once they set their sights on something, they truly believe they can attain it. This positive, can-do and can-have attitude tends to attract the success their many talents deserve. As well as being expansive and optimistic, they are blessed with an insatiable curiosity. They delight in discovering new information and in sharing this with others. Although their energy is infectious, they need to consider whether their plans are unrealistic or—worse still—foolish, and their influence on others irresponsible.

Born promoters, they can excel in social-media influencing, business, technology and management, but they may also be drawn to sales, marketing, promotion, campaigning, design, writing, teaching, music, the media, advertising, acting and performing. Whatever career they choose, variety is key to their motivation. They tend to take their health for granted and should pay closer attention to their diet and exercise routine. They are advised to breakfast like a king, lunch like a prince and supper like a pauper, because planning their food intake can give their digestive system a rest while they sleep. **For self-care,** wearing, meditating on and surrounding yourself with the colors blue or indigo encourages you to be more realistic in your approach to life.

Sensual and flirtatious, they rarely lack admirers, but until they learn self-control, quality relationships prove elusive. Until the age of 35, they have opportunities to develop a more practical and realistic approach. After 35, they feel a growing need to express their individuality. During these years it's vital for them to listen to others' advice, weighing up the pros and cons of a situation before jumping in over their heads. The key to success is their ability to recognize and leave behind unproductive situations, so that they can invest their outstanding potential in progressing, while motivating others with their creativity and can-do attitude. Once they learn to be more realistic, their destiny is to enlighten, educate and inspire others and make their upbeat mark on society.

Potential: Inspirational, energizing

Dark side: Foolish, reckless

Tarot card, lucky numbers, days, colors: The Devil, 6, 9, Thursday, Friday, purple, pink

Born today: Gustave Eiffel (architect); Antoine Henri Becquerel (physicist); Chico Mendes (activist); Michelle Dockery (actor)

December 16

The Birthday of the Creative Anthropologist

The life lesson:

is resisting the impulse to criticize.

The way forward: is to understand that sometimes your best approach is to focus on the solution, not the problem.

Luck maker: Don't isolate yourself to satisfy your career or personal goals, or you risk cutting yourself off from one of the biggest sources of luck in life: other people.

"Reason can serve passion"

Those born on December 16 are blessed with a soaring imagination, but they have a logical side that keeps them from running away with the fairies. They observe everyone and everything with the inquisitive detachment of an anthropologist. Nothing escapes the scrutiny of these sharp-witted people, and when their analytical mind combines with visionary imagination, they have the potential to create far-reaching innovations. Once they have settled on their objectives, they pursue them with dogged determination, and although this dramatically enhances their potential for professional success, their single-minded focus on their career can isolate them emotionally from others.

Born psychologists, they feel stifled within corporate structures and may prefer to work for themselves. They are well suited to research, sociology, anthropology, science, music, technology, management and software development. Other careers include social-media influencing, education, writing, blogging, politics, strategic planning, art, acting, filmmaking and broadcasting. Prone to fatigue and digestive disorders, those born on this day may find they have more stress in their lives than they think. Getting plenty of fresh air and mood-boosting daylight is beneficial. **For self-care**, wearing, meditating on and surrounding yourself with the color violet helps you get in touch with your intuition.

Until the age of 35 they take a practical and realistic approach to life, and often lose themselves in their career. Establishing a work–life balance and becoming more sensitive to the feelings of others are vital. After 35 they strive for independence and to express their individuality. Gradually, they start to experience life less as a research lab and more on a deeper, intuitive level where life should be experienced rather than examined. They also realize that the key to outstanding achievement is to keep their daily lives as grounded as possible, so that they are relaxed and receptive enough to tune into their powerful intuition and fulfill their destiny, which is to pioneer far-reaching and lasting innovations and ideals.

Potential: Perceptive, visionary

Dark side: Isolated, stressed

Tarot card, lucky numbers, days, colors: The Tower, 1, 7, Thursday, Monday, all shades of blue

Born today: Jane Austen, Noël Coward, Arthur C. Clarke (authors); Margaret Mead (anthropologist)

December 17

The Birthday of the Vital Realist

The life lesson:

is seeing the lighter side.

The way forward: is to understand that one of the quickest ways to improve your life satisfaction is to take everything and everyone less seriously.

Luck maker: Carry a lucky charm to activate your sense of wonder and inspire a positive expectation of good fortune.

"I am what I do"

December 17-born tend to say exactly what they mean and they expect others to do the same. Success to them can be measured in concrete terms and, as a practical realist, they garner responsibility and a reputation for honesty and hard work. With the courage and vitality to achieve almost any goal they set, these people are doers rather than thinkers. What interests them is facts, results and actions, not dreams, debates or theories. Everything is focused on what can be achieved or produced right now; this ability to concentrate only on what is before their eyes means they can achieve spectacular results. They can be overly serious at times and don't understand the importance of small talk and a sense of humor; they need to smile more and recognize that emotions sometimes can't be explained or categorized.

Born managers, they are drawn to business, retail, commerce, administration, accounting, the law and sales, but may also excel in education, writing, science, sport or research. Their artistic side may pull them toward music, acting or other creative pursuits. Their lifestyles can be sedentary, so regular exercise and paying attention to their posture helps them feel fitter and more upbeat. **For self-care**, wearing, meditating on and surrounding yourself with the color orange encourages you to be more spontaneous.

Although others value these people's earthy sensuality and sincerity, real intimacy requires them to lighten up a little. Until the age of 34 they focus on practical issues and a need for order and structure. They already tend to be pragmatic and realistic, so it is important they don't also become too materialistic. After 34 they become more experimental. The key to their success and happiness is their ability to introduce a spiritual dimension to their lives, because this will give them the sense of certainty, truth, order and wonder that they have been seeking. Once they are more self-aware and in touch with their emotions, their destiny is to pioneer wonderfully creative action plans.

Potential: Honest, capable

Dark side: Prosaic, materialistic

Tarot card, lucky numbers, days, colors: The Star, 2, 8, Thursday, Saturday, blue, brown

Born today: John Greenleaf Whittier (activist); Rian Johnson (director); Sarah Paulson (actor); Manny Pacquiao (boxer)

December 18

The Birthday of Possibility

"I believe I can fly"

The life lesson:

is enjoying solitude and silence.

The way forward: is to understand that stillness and solitude are empowering forces for enlightenment, change and progress.

Luck maker: Trust yourself and follow your intuition when making decisions.

People born on December 18 are daydreamers and are often dismissed or ridiculed by those who are less imaginative. Their determination to translate their expansive dreams into reality is, however, so powerful that they can withstand almost any criticism. Typically, they are quick learners, soaking up information and mastering skills long before others; and when all their knowledge and enthusiasm is added to their incredible creativity, anything is possible. These people think in the long term, not the short, and although progress may initially appear slow to others, they are carefully and steadily climbing their way to the top.

Born directors, they thrive in careers that let them act independently in pursuit of their creative visions, and may be drawn to science, technology, art, filmmaking, music, entertainment, the media or sport. Other options include business, writing, sales, publishing, teaching, charity work, fundraising, politics, and social reform. Although they are extremely productive, this can mean that they rarely take time out to relax, so they need to know their limits and not overdo things, because they are prone to stress and burnout. **For self-care**, spending more time in nature is beneficial, as are meditation and breathing techniques to help you find the space and stillness within.

Although these people are sensual and romantic, they tend to bury themselves in work and selfishly only emerge when they want attention or support. Until the age of 33 the emphasis is on developing a practical and realistic approach to life. They should accept assistance when it is offered, to simplify their workload and avoid exhaustion and alienation. After 33 they may become more individualistic. The key to their success is their ability to set themselves realistic goals and their willingness to pause and connect with their intuition or the silence within. This inside-out approach helps them see that the sense of wonder, discovery and possibility they long to create in the world around them already exists within them—all they need to do is find it. Their destiny is, by their example, to inspire others to follow their dreams.

Potential: Intelligent, creative

Dark side: Preoccupied, selfish

Tarot card, lucky numbers, days, colors: The Moon, 3, 9, Thursday, purple, red

Born today: Joseph Grimaldi (clown); Steven Spielberg (director); Billie Eilish, Keith Richards, Christina Aguilera (singers)

December 19

The Birthday of Touching Honesty

"My heart is right here on my sleeve"

Those born on December 19 often seem sensitive souls, but this conceals their remarkable hidden strength. They are not afraid to express themselves freely and they are honest enough to reveal their true feelings when people upset them. Fiercely individualistic, they are unlikely to thrive in environments where they need to conform. They have a strong need to question norms and generate original alternatives. Although their honesty can work against them, others respect them for their genuineness. When faced with professional challenges, they reveal their fighting spirit, but they seem unable to do the same in their personal life. If they can get a grip on their negativity and discover the same spirit within as they display to the outside world, no mountain is too high for them to climb.

Born mime artists and performers, they often share their knowledge through writing and teaching, but they may also be drawn to music, acting, the media, publishing, journalism, advertising, the healing professions, art and entrepreneurship. To help avoid negativity, they should remind themselves that they are in charge of their feelings and not the other way around. They should steer clear of drugs and limit alcohol, because when under the influence, their lack of control can have potentially damaging consequences. **For self-care,** laughing more, keeping a mood diary, and developing interests and hobbies outside work are beneficial.

The appealing personality of those born on this day attracts others easily, but they need to avoid negative company and seek out positive and upbeat people. Until the age of 32 they focus on practical issues and the need for order. Around the age of 32 they have a growing desire for more personal freedom and experimentation. If they can learn to think before they act and to redirect their thoughts positively when they spiral into negativity, they can show their commitment to making a valuable contribution to the greater good. Once they can accept and manage their emotions, their destiny is to educate and enlighten others with their touching honesty.

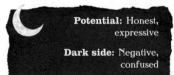

Potential: Honest, expressive

Dark side: Negative, confused

Tarot card, lucky numbers, days, colors: The Sun, 1, 4, Thursday, Sunday, purple, gold

Born today: Ralph Richardson, Jake Gyllenhaal, Jennifer Beals (actors); Édith Piaf (singer)

December 20

The Birthday of the Producer

"Let me illuminate"

December 20-born are magnetic and skilled problem-solvers with a marked talent for motivating and organizing others. Born leaders, they are at their best generating ideas and initiating projects. Once a project has got off the ground, however, they prefer to move on and put others at the helm, content in their role of producer and creator. Their impulse to keep moving forward is strong, and because they are also efficient, their output and achievements are often remarkable. They can, however, become frustrated and impatient with those who simply can't keep up or match their output. Despite their concern for the welfare of others and their intense desire to make the world a better place, their interpersonal skills often need attention.

Born agents, they are suited to careers where they can be the creator, leader or guide, and may excel as politics, teaching, the arts or science. Other choices include business, public relations, promotions, sales, writing, music, the entertainment business, alternative healing, charity work and sport. They need to make sure they don't run themselves down with too many activities and too much pressure. Burning essential oil of frankincense in an oil burner while working or relaxing is particularly beneficial if they suffer from depression caused by lack of natural sunlight. **For self-care**, wearing, meditating on and surrounding yourself with the color green helps you seek balance in your life.

Others are drawn to the charisma and can-do approach of these people, but those born on this day can be impatient and this can threaten their relationships. Until they reach 31 their practical, realistic and results-orientated approach draws as much praise as it does criticism from those who feel they are too hasty. After 31 they feel more independent and put their individual stamp on things. Developing their latent creative powers and rediscovering their joyful child-like spirit gives them the ability to both generate innovative ideas and really enjoy their life. Once they regard their mistakes as learning opportunities and take on board advice, their destiny is to play a guiding, inspirational role in the lives of others.

December 21

The Birthday of the Secret

The life lesson:

is trusting and sharing.

The way forward: is to understand that everything in life, including relationships, involves a certain amount of risk-taking.

Luck maker: Let go of hidden resentments and forgive (but not necessarily forget) to attract positive people and good fortune.

"Less is more"

People born on December 21 tend to be highly talented and strong-willed, but it can be hard to know what they are thinking and feeling, as they are by nature secretive. Less is more is their mantra and they prefer to express themselves with actions rather than words. Their powerful, quiet presence can be inscrutable even to those closest to them. Even though they are mysterious, they are not passive but fiercely proactive and driven. Others may feel that they are like a dormant volcano, quiet on the outside but with a burning intensity on the inside. They are surprisingly vulnerable beneath the self-confident "cool" exterior, although they would never let others know this. They should understand that although they can easily gain admiration, what they really need to feel fulfilled is affection; this can only be earned when they learn to love themselves first and find the courage to share their true feelings with others.

Born entrepreneurs, they can often be found in science, politics, business, sport, the arts, promotion, campaigning, social reform, acting and entertainment. They may also work for themselves and become high-flying entrepreneurs. Counseling or therapy is beneficial if they find it hard to open up and share with loved ones. Plenty of exercise, preferably of the social kind such as dancing, aerobics or team sports, is also recommended. **For self-care**, wearing, meditating on and surrounding yourself with the color orange encourages you to be more spontaneous and expressive.

These people are attractive but at times unsettling companions because, although they like to do their own thing, they are controlling and aren't comfortable with others doing theirs. Around the age of 32, they focus less on proving themselves and more on discovering their inner strength. If they can open their hearts to the magical potential hidden within them, they will discover the secret not only of their own happiness but of everyone else's, too. Once they understand that they are in charge of who or what they attract into their lives, their destiny is to combine their authority with self-awareness and compassion and, by so doing, become outstanding leaders in their chosen field.

Potential: Authoritative, intriguing

Dark side: Controlling, insecure

Tarot card, lucky numbers, day, colors: The World, 3, 6, Thursday, purple, blue

Born today: Jane Fonda, Samuel L. Jackson, Kiefer Sutherland (actors); Emmanuel Macron, Benjamin Disraeli (politicians)

CAPRICORN

THE GOAT
(DECEMBER 22–JANUARY 19)

* **Element:** Earth

* **Ruling planet:** Saturn, the teacher

* **Tarot card:** The Devil (materialism)

* **Lucky numbers:** 1, 8

* **Favorable colors:** Dark green, brown, gray, black

* **Driving force:** Determination

* **Personal statement:** I am ambitious and responsible

* **Chinese astrology counterpart:** The Ox

Whether they are shy and retiring or outgoing and comfortable in the limelight, all Capricorns have one thing in common and that is their determination. They take themselves seriously and expect others to do the same. Responsible and dependable, their dogmatic, black-and-white approach to life can sometimes make them seem overly serious, but, despite this, their hard-working attitude often transforms them into winners.

Personality potential

Capricorns are ruled by the planet Saturn, which is the planet of responsibility, discipline and education, and Capricorn is perhaps the most ambitious, disciplined, enduring and dependable sign of the entire zodiac. As the final earth sign—after Taurus and Virgo—it represents the richness and fertility of the earth. Associated with this sign are the many fulfilling rewards and benefits of hard work.

Although Capricorns are ambitious, the secret of their success is that they are also highly responsible; when in positions of power, they never abuse it. They are extremely disciplined, and with that discipline comes patience, wisdom and the practicality to keep their feet firmly on the ground. With their dogged persistence and realism they are likely to rise to the top of their field or profession, and they are more than capable of handling the loneliness and responsibility of power. They can also be very helpful and generous to those starting out and in need of their help and advice. Capricorns do take life seriously and have a cautious and steady approach, but this isn't to say they don't know how to laugh. They may appear serious, but those who know them better will often discover their wicked and unexpected sense of humor. They also seem to get younger with age, in that they are typically mature and serious children and young adults, and more playful and relaxed the older they get.

Capricorns have a strong sense of justice. **They find it impossible to stand back and observe any kind of unfairness**, and will do their best to correct unjust situations. They aren't hypocrites either, and apply the same strict sense of what is right and wrong to their own motives and behavior; in fact, they are often far harder on themselves than on anyone else. Above all, determination and a will to progress are hallmarks of this sign. They are never afraid of hard work, and their natural ability to be industrious means that the path of steady advancement is their preferred route. They also have the courage and drive to achieve any challenge that is worthy of them. No surprise then that all this focus and diligence tends to bring plenty of good fortune and success their way.

> **They find it impossible to stand back and observe any kind of unfairness**

Personality pitfalls

Warning words for Capricorns include narrow-mindedness, pessimism, rigidity and mean-spiritedness. They can also lack confidence in themselves, and this inner dissatisfaction creates a driving need for success in the outside world. Low self-esteem not only means that they judge people according to their status and what they can do to help them achieve their goals; it can also stop them from taking risks. Their tendency to always err on the side of caution can make them overly cautious and hesitant when action is required, leading to frequently missed opportunities. In addition, their lack of confidence in their own appeal can lead to behavior that is people-pleasing, and this can keep them from forming deep and lasting connections with others.

The ambitious streak in every Capricorn can run the risk of turning them into cold and calculating workaholics. They need to be constantly reminded of the importance of a work–life balance. Being a determined sign but one that lacks self-confidence, they also need to avoid falling into the trap of always being the second in command or the person behind someone else's success.

Capricorns are sometimes prone to bouts of gloom and cynicism. Their presence can be an incredibly heavy one, and when they are in one of their low moods, they are often guilty of putting the dampers on everyone else's enthusiasm. Another weakness is that they can be control freaks, and their controlling personality often views the world in narrow-minded terms, imposing rules and endless "shoulds" on themselves and others.

Darkest secret

Capricorns are incredibly insightful and see the world as it really is, but they aren't really as cool and detached as they appear. Their clear perception of what's going on around them can often cause them a lot of pain and distress. In addition, inside every Capricorn is a secret desire to let themselves go, run wild and join in the fun with everyone else, but all too often, fear of looking foolish holds them back.

Symbol

The symbol for Capricorn is the goat and, just like the mountain goat, Capricorns persevere until they have climbed the mountain of success and reach the very top. As well as being dogged and determined, mountain goats are also loners, and Capricorns often have a sense of reserve and detachment about them. In addition, the symbol of the goat suggests stability and conformity as embodied by the mythical sea goat (half-goat, half-fish) associated with this sign, which rose up to bring civilization to the world.

Love

Kind-hearted, dependable and honest, Capricorns often make appealing lovers and friends. When they are content in a relationship they are loving, affectionate, faithful and protective partners who can be depended on fully. In fact, finding and keeping the right relationship is often an essential ingredient for a Capricorn's success in life because it gives them the respite and strength they need when life overwhelms. They should try to seek partners who are receptive to change and a little more willing (but not too much) to take risks than they are, because such partners help balance out their overcautious streak. They also need to seek partners who are not intimidated by their strong self-discipline.

Although a solid relationship is a key ingredient for their fulfillment, many Capricorns may postpone committing themselves to someone else until they feel they have established their career or have financial security. This is a sensible approach but it isn't always the best thing to do, and, later in life, Capricorns may regret that they didn't act sooner to follow their heart. Their ambition may also drive them to marry for money or social status rather than love. Alternatively, some may make the mistake of marrying for love and then risking their relationship by devoting all their time and energy to their career.

Love matches:

Taurus, Scorpio, Pisces, Virgo.

The Capricorn woman

It's not easy to describe a typical Capricorn as she has so many sides to her personality, but whatever guise she appears in there will always be one thing in common: she will be ruled by the disciplined and determined planet Saturn. A great many Capricorn women reach career highs, but they can be equally happy in the role of homemaker. They need to feel challenged, but also secure and respected by others, whatever role they devote their energy to in life.

The Capricorn woman often appears calm and collected, but she is less even-tempered and emotionally steady than she appears. In fact, she is prone to really black moods and is capable of deep despondency. Her gloom may be triggered by disappointments or setbacks, but it's often far more deep rooted than that and tied up with her feelings of insecurity and inadequacy. Despite being incredibly capable, deep down she never feels quite good enough and her gloom will only disappear when she starts to truly believe in herself and her tremendous talents. The older she gets the more likely it is that her self-confidence will blossom. Capricorn girls are often mature beyond their years, but with this maturity there is often deep anxiety about doing the right thing. Capricorn women tend to lose their inhibitions and feel happier about themselves and their lives with age.

Rest and relaxation don't come easy to a Capricorn woman because she always needs to feel that she is working hard or climbing the ladder to success; if she isn't working for herself or her family, she'll work for a cause or a charity. She needs a partner who can lovingly help her believe in herself. In return, she'll give a deep and earthy love that is lasting and real.

The Capricorn man

The Capricorn man tends to come across as the strong and silent type, but it's a mistake to think that he prefers to be alone, because he doesn't. He may not be the life and soul of the party, but deep down the Capricorn man craves admiration. He also craves the spontaneity of love and romance; however, the practical, stern and disciplined part of his personality simply won't allow it. Sometimes, though, his yearnings will break through and you'll get flashes of humor and unexpected passion from him.

Capricorn men say they can live without romance, compliments and attention, but the way to the heart of this strong, independent, trustworthy, modest but ambitious man is to pay him compliments; then, when the relationship gets more intimate, give him plenty of affection. He needs to be encouraged to venture out of his self-imposed restrictions so the world can see more of this wonderful man.

Like F. Scott Fitzgerald's famous character Benjamin Button, more often than not a Capricorn man will grow younger with age. He will be incredibly serious in his teens and twenties, but then, as he approaches mid-life and beyond, he may start to relax and have more fun. He's unlikely to be unfaithful, though, as his strict moral sense and desire to do the right thing rarely lapse. When he's busy building his career, or at the height of it, he may have a tendency to stick to routines in his schedules, even when it comes to love-making. He may also seem constantly preoccupied with work; this lack of spontaneity can take its toll on any relationship. Fortunately, the older he gets, the less likely this is to be the case.

Although he may not be the most romantic of lovers, the Capricorn man will always be that strong man with a gentle heart throughout his life. And once he has given someone his heart, he will typically protect and provide for them and stand by them through the years, whether times are good or bad.

Family

Capricorn children are often wise beyond their years. Highly conventional and with a need for a secure, disciplined

upbringing, these old-soul children frequently surprise their parents with the insight they show about the world they live in. As sensible and grown up as they appear, however, these children are in real need of reassurance and encouragement so that the Capricorn Achilles' heel of low self-confidence does not become a habit from early in life. A child is still a child even when that child is a Capricorn child, and parents should remember that all children are prey to irrational fears and need unconditional love and constant encouragement. Their sense of fun and spontaneity should also be encouraged if they are to avoid becoming too serious and old before their time. At school, they are unlikely to be the most popular child in the class, but they will tend to have a select few friends—friends they often keep in touch with for decades afterwards. Their progress is slow and steady, and their quiet ambition ensures that their final grades are highly respectable. They also often excel at getting prizes, awards and certificates.

Capricorn parents are likely to encourage their children to be hard workers, just like they themselves are. Discipline is strong, especially moral discipline, but it's important for them to ensure they don't get too heavy-handed and strict

They should also make sure they give their children plenty of love and affection, and, just as important, plenty of their time. Capricorn parents can be so ambitious and fixated on giving their children financial security and the best education that they miss out on actually spending time with their children.

Career

Capricorns are ambitious and, whatever career they choose, they are sure to climb the ladder of success. They have natural authority and make good bosses, managers and CEOs, and are often associated with jobs related to education, bureaucracy and government. Roles to which they are well suited include civil servant, government employee, teacher, bank manager, accountant, chief executive officer and town planner. They may also be drawn to medical careers, as this sign is linked to the skeleton, so they may perhaps work as chiropractors, osteopaths and dentists. Many Capricorns can be found as architects and builders, and their love of logic, patterns and structure may also reflect in career choices that include mathematics, engineering and science. Finally, they are a good fit for careers in the legal and teaching professions, which is not surprising given that this sign is ruled by Saturn, the teacher.

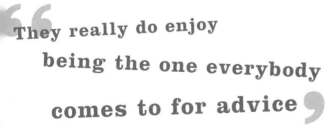

Other signs may find the responsibilities and loneliness of being at the top at work daunting, but Capricorns thrive on it. **They really do enjoy being the one everybody comes to for advice** and, in most cases, the advice they give is sound. Although they are destined to succeed, they tend to do it slowly and carefully. However wealthy or successful they become, their attitude to money is responsible and they rarely lack the finances to retire in comfort.

> **They really do enjoy being the one everybody comes to for advice**

Health and wellbeing

Self-discipline is strong for people born under this sun sign, so Capricorns are likely to be sensible about their diet and their lifestyle. They understand the importance of eating nutritious food, and overindulging is simply not in their nature, although they may be prone to comfort eating during bouts of low self-esteem. The best thing they can do for their health and wellbeing is to exercise regularly, but unfortunately this is usually the thing on which they tend to compromise because they are so busy working. They often spend a lot of time at their desk or at work in a job that is fairly sedentary, and this can lead to joint pain, weight gain and stress. Regular, moderate exercise for at least 30 minutes a day helps boost their mood and keep their joints, heart and weight healthy.

Bones, teeth and skin are areas of special concern for Capricorns. In addition to regular aerobic exercise, such as brisk walking and jogging, they should do some toning and weight training to keep their bones strong. Twice-daily flossing and brushing are also essential for healthy teeth, as are regular visits to the dentist, however busy things get at work.

As far as leisure interests are concerned, Capricorns are sometimes drawn to the world of music, in which they may display remarkable talent. They should make sure they get plenty of fresh air outside in the daylight, especially if their jobs keep them indoors for most of the day. Hill-walking, rambling and forest-bathing are excellent pursuits for Capricorns. The sooner people born under this sun sign learn to play as hard as they work, the better their lives will get, because unwinding and having fun can give them the balance and perspective they need to find the sense of fulfillment and security they long for. Wearing, meditating on and surrounding themselves with the color **orange** will encourage them to be more open, spontaneous, creative and fun-loving.

Born between December 22 and January 1

People born between these dates are often stoical, with an incredible capacity to withstand the blows of life. Their resilience and dedication are second to none and, like the steel under the blacksmith's hammer, they get stronger and more powerful with each blow.

Born between January 2 and 10

These Capricorns are more than capable of reaching the heights of any mountain. Their success is likely to occur later

in life, but, when it does come, they are generous and love to share their good fortune with others.

Born between January 11 and 19

They may come across as modest and unassuming, but these people are often excellent communicators with a knack for attracting success. If they accept a responsibility, they give it their full commitment. Dependable and strong, they demand the same level of integrity from everyone they deal with, both in the workplace and at home.

Life lessons

There is a tendency for Capricorns to become narrow-minded in their approach to life, so it's essential for them to learn to see things from the point of view of others. They also need to find their own inner voice, as they tend to get their opinions from those in authority over them, especially when they are in their twenties and thirties, rather than think for themselves. Another challenge for Capricorns is to express their spiritual side. With all their energy expended on career and material gain, they can lose sight of the deeper, more meaningful and fulfilling aspects of life. Although this sign is the most ambitious and self-disciplined of the zodiac, they often neglect the importance of things money can't buy—such as love, relaxation, fun and laughter. In addition, their journey to the top may sometimes become quite meaningless because they often want to get there simply for the status and recognition it can bring. But status and recognition are not good enough reasons to want to do anything, and Capricorns could benefit from contributing more to the greater good rather than selfishly focusing their talents on progressing in their career.

Perfectionist by nature, Capricorns are often terrified of making mistakes and, when this is combined with their stern self-discipline, it can make them overly tense and serious. Capricorns must learn to lighten up and not see one tiny mistake as a catastrophe. If they are in a position of authority they should avoid becoming a perfectionist obsessed with the details. It's absolutely vital for Capricorns to give themselves and others room for error. They must also stop being so obsessive about what people think when they make a mistake, because in most cases others are understanding or simply

don't even notice. If Capricorns can be less rigid in their thinking, they have the potential to produce inspired work and to be inspirations to others.

Fellow Capricorns can reveal the strength and focus of this sign but also the limitations when stubbornness takes over. Other signs can offer Capricorns more help and inspiration. Arians can teach them to move on quickly from disappointment and to do things to the best of their ability rather than perfectly. Taureans can encourage them to focus more on self-care, Scorpios can help them look for inspiration and direction from within; Cancerians to value loved ones more than their career; and Geminis to be more curious. Sagittarians can teach them to be more adventurous and inquisitive in their approach to life, and Librans can show them how to take a more balanced view when they make mistakes, as well as being more subtle and kind when it comes to getting their point of view across. Virgos remind them of the importance of logic and organization. Leos can bring sunshine and laughter into their lives, while Aquarians and Pisceans can help them focus more on the bigger picture than the details.

Chinese astrology counterpart: The Ox

The Chinese Ox shares the ambition, determination and strength of purpose of its Western counterpart—Capricorn. These people are hard-working, practical, efficient and responsible. They work to the best of their abilities and tend to achieve or acquire whatever they decide to focus their considerable energies on.

Material wealth and security is their primary concern and they can be extremely driven in pursuit of success. They often end up in leadership positions and tend to be respected for their integrity, reliability and formidable work ethic. At times they can be fiercely stubborn and cranky, and they can often frustrate others with their desire to follow all the rules or take things slowly, but their extraordinary determination and honesty usually end up winning the trust, admiration and support of others.

Note: Capricorns have an affinity with Ox-sign characteristics, but be sure to check which Chinese sign corresponds to your **year** of birth (see page xxi), and to read about the characteristics associated with it, too.

December 22

The Birthday of Enduring Poise

"I can see for miles and miles"

Those born on December 22 are life planners. At various stages they set long-term goals and create a master plan. They know what they want and how they are going to achieve it, and their thorough preparedness augurs well for success. Understanding the importance of discipline and patience, they are willing to bide their time and work steadily. Their remarkable poise is the result of an absolute faith that eventual success is their birthright and their self-belief can be a great role model for others. The danger is complacency—remaining for years in a lifestyle that doesn't challenge them. The secret of their success is to keep learning, fine-tuning their skills and testing themselves, so that they can live up to their own promise.

Born architects, these people flourish in careers offering them long-term goals and progression. Options include finance, stockbroking, accounting, administration, craftsmanship, manufacturing, management, writing, reporting, research, science, community work or self-employment. Alternatively, they may explore their creativity in acting, design, building and construction, art or music. Flexibility in mind and body is the key to help boost their wellbeing. A new course of study or learning a language is stimulating, while exercise such as yoga encourages them to be supple. **For self-care**, wearing, meditating on and surrounding yourself with the color orange encourages you to be more open, spontaneous and fun-loving.

Those born on this day can be passionate and loyal, but they take a while to let down their guard in relationships. Until the age of 29 they are goal-orientated and practical. But at 30 they feel a growing need for freedom and expressing their creativity. After the age of 60, they reach another turning point and focus on their emotional receptivity and intuition. They need to find a balance between self-belief and humility, long-term planning and spontaneity. As soon as they find this middle way, they can maintain it with their characteristic poise to find success and fulfillment. Once they understand that life is a series of challenges and they will never stop learning and growing, their destiny is to put their innovative plans into action so that others can benefit.

Potential: Dignified, self-confident

Dark side: Narrow-minded, complacent

Tarot card, lucky numbers, days, colors: The Fool, 4, 7, Thursday, Sunday, indigo, yellow

Born today: Giacomo Puccini (composer); Diane Sawyer (journalist); Maurice and Robin Gibb (musicians)

December 23

The Birthday of the Composed Revolutionary

"The tortoise wins the race"

December 23-born are quietly ambitious individuals who are at their best when they can identify areas of improvement and formulate original, practical solutions. Gifted and responsible and supremely organized, they prefer to plan way ahead and then carefully prepare and move slowly but surely toward lasting improvement. They often distrust sudden change and feel uncomfortable when it is thrust upon them, as it upsets their plans for steady progress. In fact, when they assume positions of power—which more often than not they do—they can be resistant to change. They can become controlling when challenged, and when offered alternative viewpoints they become defensive.

Born judges, they are suited to careers in the legal profession, law enforcement, social reform, the civil service, business management, finance, accounting, administration, retail and commerce, as well as entrepreneurship, science, art, writing, music, drama, design and spirituality. They are careful with their health and have a high chance of living to a ripe old age as long as they don't worry excessively and overwork, which can make them prone to stress and mood swings. Reading, studying and regular travel are beneficial and keep opening their minds to new ideas. **For self-care**, wearing, meditating on and surrounding yourself with the color red encourages you to be more passionate and impulsive.

Charming and dynamic, these people rarely lack admirers but can be quite cold when it comes to relationships. Before the age of 28 they may have shown a responsibility beyond their years. But after 28 they need to be more carefree and independent, and to express their individuality. After 60 they become more sensitive. When they start to be more spontaneous and to share their compassion, creativity and curiosity with others, they discover that they have the ability to lead and inspire others to follow them along the optimum path to progress. Once they are able to go more with the flow, their destiny is to advance the greater good.

Potential: Responsible, innovative

Dark side: Complacent, inflexible

Tarot card, lucky numbers, day, colors: The Hierophant, 5, 8, Thursday, purple, green

Born today: Richard Arkwright (inventor); Donna Tartt (author); Madam C. J. Walker (entrepreneur); Eddie Vedder (musician)

December 24

The Birthday of Exciting Far Sight

The life lesson:

is learning from your mistakes.

The way forward: is to learn from the past, not repeat it.

Luck maker: Learn to love yourself—believe you are enough and that you don't need other people or things to complete you.

"I knew that"

People born on December 24 seem born to live complicated, uncertain but exciting lives. Nothing is straightforward or stress-free for them. One of the reasons for complications is that they can be too blunt and aren't good at learning from their mistakes. They have a rare gift for seeing into the future, or for knowing what the most likely outcome will be, even when evidence points to the contrary. In this respect they are visionary, but unfortunately it takes a while to recognize and appreciate their gift of far-sightedness. Until that recognition comes, people wonder why they keep overcomplicating things.

Born innovators, they often choose to work as technical, manufacturing, political or educational specialists, or they may become leaders in the arts, writing, acting, broadcasting or entertainment. They may also be attracted to studying philosophy, metaphysics or mysticism. Their emotional lives can be complicated and they may be prone to anxiety and depression. Learning to accept and manage their emotions is crucial, because once they understand that they control their feelings and their emotions do not control them, their lives can improve immeasurably. They should be careful not to attract toxic people and they need to avoid recreational drugs. **For self-care**, meditating on the color pink and carrying a small rose-quartz crystal with you attracts the energy of self-love.

Highly sensual and appealing, those born on this day find hugs and affection bring much-needed calm into their action-packed days. Until the age of 27 they place practical considerations, order and security first, but after 27 they need more independence and to express their individuality. After 58, they focus on emotional receptivity, and their intuitive potential may even develop into precognitive ability. The key to their success is their ability to learn from their mistakes and be more sensitive and tactful with others. Add a dose of self-confidence and not only do they understand the people around them better, but life feels easier and more rewarding. When this comes together, they can finally see their own visionary potential and attract success and happiness into their lives. Their destiny is to better themselves, achieve great things and become an inspiring light for progress.

Potential: Visionary, dynamic

Dark side: Blunt, confusing

Tarot card, lucky numbers, days, colors: The Lovers, 6, 9, Saturday, Friday, indigo, pink

Born today: Howard Hughes (entrepreneur); Ricky Martin (singer); Stephenie Meyer (author); Stephanie Ruhle (journalist)

December 25

The Birthday of Ecstasy

"Follow our bliss"

The life lesson:

is being realistic.

The way forward: is to understand that setting goals or ideals that are unattainable isn't uplifting but the path to disillusionment and unhappiness.

Luck maker: Be self-aware enough to know who you are and what you believe in, but also open to increasing your potential for success through alternative information, feedback and experience.

Those born on December 25 struggle with the mundane aspects of life and are constantly searching for a state of heightened awareness where they can transcend the everyday. Others may dismiss them as unrealistic dreamers, but may secretly admire the wonder, energy and strength of will they bring to everything, as well as a willingness to push things further than others dare. It's possible that a contributing factor to their need to make their life experience extraordinary is that they generally receive less attention on their birthday than other people do because it's Christmas Day. Their lack of a separate or special birthday may make them more determined to stand out.

Born philanthropists, they are often drawn to science, business, politics or the arts. Other choices include design, architecture, social reform, humanitarian or charity work, the healing professions, teaching, writing, music, astronomy, chemistry and biology. Their love of metaphysics may also inspire them to study or teach philosophy, astrology, religion and spirituality. Regular rather than sporadic exercise not only boosts their self-esteem but helps them feel more connected to their body, as they tend to be detached at times. **For self-care**, wearing, meditating on and surrounding yourself with the color green helps keep you grounded and focused.

The infectious charm of these people attracts many admirers, but they need to ensure they do not flit from one person to another in search of constant bliss. Before the age of 26 they have a goal-orientated approach to life, but after 26 they need to experiment and express their individuality. They always place spiritual aspirations above material ones, which doesn't just set them apart but puts them ahead of others. As long as they can find ways to increase their chances of success by injecting realism into their idealistic visions, they are capable not only of great happiness and fulfillment, but of making lasting contributions to the greater good. Once they discover the intensity and joy of living in the present and finding the extraordinary in the ordinary, their destiny is to inspire others with their idealism.

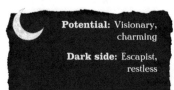

Potential: Visionary, charming

Dark side: Escapist, restless

Tarot card, lucky numbers, days, colors: The Chariot, 1, 7, Saturday, Monday, indigo, sea green

Born today: Isaac Newton (physicist); Clara Barton (nurse); Justin Trudeau (Canadian prime minister); Annie Lennox (singer)

December 26

The Birthday of the Vantage Point

The life lesson:

is admitting when you are wrong.

The way forward: is to understand that until you acknowledge you may have been wrong, you cannot move on and improve.

Luck maker: Seek out new experiences and information—the more inquisitive and alert you are, the more likely it is you will get lucky breaks.

"The view up here is spectacular"

December 26-born are never afraid to push themselves forward, and with their high energy and determination they often achieve whatever they strive for. Once they reach the top, however, they no longer strive to move forward but simply sustain their vantage point. They are therefore a curious mixture of ambition and a need for stability. The danger with this combination, even though it does attract considerable success, is that they can become too mechanical or unfeeling, so it's vital for their psychological growth that they get in touch with their emotions and avoid being overly serious and tough.

Born publishers, they are drawn to technology, politics, social services and the media. Possible work choices include big business, advertising, promotion, marketing, writing, acting and films. Whatever career they choose, they need plenty of diversity and challenge. They often suffer from tension, headaches and fatigue, and should perform exercise such as dance, swimming or aerobics to expend pent-up energy and encourage flexibility. **For self-care**, keeping a mood diary, interpreting your dreams, and wearing, meditating on and surrounding yourself with the color orange encourages you to be spontaneous and warm.

Dynamic and sensual, once those born on this day set their sights on someone, they tend to get them. They can be controlling and they need to give others the same freedom they expect for themselves. Until the age of 25 they desire order and structure, and they prioritize practical considerations. The key to their success is to learn to compromise and take others' feelings into consideration. After 25 their focus shifts to expressing their individuality and then, a few decades later, to promoting their emotional and spiritual growth. They should avoid clinging to what they know, or becoming too complacent. Once they understand that true progress requires taking risks and exploring unfamiliar territory, they have the potential to make things happen on a grand scale and to inspire others to do the same. If they can keep an open heart, their destiny is to make radical changes that can dramatically improve not just their own lives but those of others as well.

Potential: Inspirational, methodical

Dark side: Rigid, stern

Tarot card, lucky numbers, day, colors: Strength, 2, 8, Saturday, indigo, burgundy

Born today: Jared Leto, Kit Harington (actors); Charles Babbage (inventor); Alexander Wang (designer)

December 27
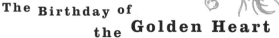

The Birthday of the Golden Heart

The life lesson: is saying "no."

The way forward: is to understand that saying "no" to others is saying "yes" to yourself.

Luck maker: Receiving may make you feel vulnerable, but to create luck you must be willing to gratefully accept help when it is offered.

"To be good is noble"

People born on December 27 have a heart of pure gold. Although they can be stubborn at times, they are life's givers, not takers. They also have a noble side and are often the first to offer their support or help, priding themselves on being kind and doing the right thing. However, because their compassion can make it hard for them to refuse any request, they may become drained by others' problems. Their generosity and good-natured charm win them many admirers, but underneath they can often be plagued by self-doubts. They can feel torn between strong feelings of responsibility to others and the need to take care of themselves.

Born counselors, whatever career they choose they make a healing difference. They may be drawn to teaching, nursing, medicine, the caring professions, public relations, human resources, the civil service, counseling, charity work, the emergency services, the leisure and beauty industries, sport or social reform, or to technology, design, writing, performing or working for themselves. They may be prone to anxiety, due to their giving nature and others taking advantage, but low self-esteem is also a cause. They need to learn to accept praise and to put their own happiness before others'. **For self-care**, wearing, meditating on and surrounding yourself with the color red boosts your confidence.

In relationships those born on this day may be drawn to their opposites—those who are selfish and ruthless—so it's important they learn to take as well as give. After the age of 25 they move from a goal-focused approach to a need to develop their individuality. Only when they can reconcile their drive to help others with their desire to find personal fulfillment can they unlock their remarkable potential to bring healing and light to the world. If they can strike out on their own and pay attention to what they want in life, they can rise to the top of their career, achieving long-lasting success and much-deserved happiness. Once they are able to take as well as give, their destiny is to be an inspirational role model and show others the importance of compassion, kindness and understanding in this world.

Potential: Generous, noble

Dark side: Self-sacrificing, frustrated

Tarot card, lucky numbers, days, colors: The Hermit, 3, 9, Saturday, Tuesday, dark green, red

Born today: Louis Pasteur (biologist); Johannes Kepler (astronomer); Marlene Dietrich (singer); Gérard Depardieu (actor)

528

December 28

The Birthday of the Shining Example

"Let me bring light"

Those born on December 28 typically impress others greatly with their verve, steady character and focus. They are a shining example of calmness, self-assurance and dependability and, not surprisingly, others often turn to them for support or advice. They would be almost perfect if they didn't find it incredibly hard to deal with rejection or challenges—instead of fighting back, they often slump into uncertainty. Although the image they present is one of capable sophistication, this competent exterior often masks an intensely felt but carefully hidden desire to find a deeper meaning in their lives.

Born mentors, they are often attracted to fields where they can inspire others, and may choose careers in education, research, publishing, counseling, the arts, the media, fashion, communications, writing, journalism, blogging, acting, singing, charity work, social reform or the healing and caring professions. Listening to music can be a great morale booster, and owning a pet, in particular a dog, may be beneficial as it brings out their playful, spontaneous side. **For self-care**, wearing, meditating on and surrounding yourself with the color orange encourage you to be more spontaneous.

These people have cool heads and warm hearts, and although they are not flirts, their charisma ensures they have many admirers. Their concern for the wellbeing of others can make them neglect their own needs and damage their chances of finding happiness. After the age of 24 they become less concerned about the image they present to the world and more interested in expressing their individuality. Once they have recognized that personal fulfillment and being of service to others are not incompatible needs, they can unlock their potential to be shining and inspirational role models. Their destiny is to inform and enlighten others and become the guiding light they were born to be.

Potential: Inspiring, confident

Dark side: Uncertain, serious

Tarot card, lucky numbers, days, colors: The Magician, 1, 4, Saturday, Sunday, dark green, yellow

Born today: Denzel Washington, Maggie Smith (actors); Lili Elbe (painter); John Legend (musician)

December 29

The Birthday of the Cool Commander

The life lesson:

is getting out of your comfort zone.

The way forward: is to understand that you need to discover the courage within to put yourself on the line, because that is how you learn and grow.

Luck maker: Tune into your feelings and learn to trust your first instincts, because more often than not they are right.

"Words of wisdom, or humor"

December 29-born are in great demand. It's not surprising others seek them out, given their responsible character and the delight they take in helping or advising others. They are not ruthless, but often find themselves in positions of responsibility. Although they can appear laid-back and others often describe them as "cool," they are extremely hard-working behind the scenes. Their greatest strength is their facility for commanding or controlling people and situations without appearing domineering. Part of the reason they do this so successfully is that they have superb communication skills, and their deadpan persona can mask a wonderful dry humor. They can hypnotize audiences with their intelligent and perceptive observations, and frequently use irony to get their message across effectively without others feeling offended or criticized.

Born interpreters, they are suited to roles offering guidance and support, such as in translation, counseling, teaching, coaching, social work, finance or politics, or where they can advance knowledge, such as science, technology or engineering. Other choices include writing, blogging, lecturing, research, music, acting and social-media influencing. They can lead sedentary lives and should make exercise an integral part of their daily routine. **For self-care**, wearing, meditating on and surrounding yourself with the color yellow encourages you to believe in yourself more.

These people have a strong need for companionship, but once committed to a relationship should keep the spark of passion alive by staying as spontaneous as possible. After the age of 23 they become less influenced by rules and traditions and more willing to develop their own perspective. At 53 they focus on their emotional life, dreams and developing an intuitive understanding of others. The key to their success is to stop doubting themselves, because they are bursting with creativity and have all the talent they need to make pioneering innovations. In short, they have the potential; they just need to step up, shake off negativity or anxiety about what others think, and become the great and very cool leader or pioneer they are destined to be.

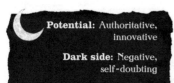

Potential: Authoritative, innovative

Dark side: Negative, self-doubting

Tarot card, lucky numbers, days, colors: The High Priestess, 2, 5, Saturday, Monday, indigo, silver

Born today: Mary Tyler Moore, Jude Law (actors); Charles Goodyear (chemist); Marianne Faithfull (singer)

December 30

The Birthday of the Choreographer

The life lesson:

is expressing yourself.

The way forward: is to understand that explaining yourself to others is not a waste of time because it builds bridges of understanding.

Luck maker: Tell yourself that luck is coming your way and, with this attitude of positive expectancy, the chances are it will.

"Treat triumph and disaster just the same"

People born on December 30 are at their best when they are bringing order to confusion. They can swiftly identify what doesn't work or needs improving, and have the creativity and vision to initiate and implement changes. In many ways they are like choreographers who can direct and coordinate the steps, with the bigger picture in mind. At times their intentions may seem unclear, but everything always seems to come together perfectly. Their ability to motivate and inspire those around them to perform at their best makes them successful leaders. They can occasionally be prone to a glass-half-empty approach to life, but this doesn't mean they don't know how to have fun. People of few words, when they do speak, others are often stunned by their perceptiveness. But working on their communication skills can be beneficial.

Born officers and commanders, they flourish in business or commercial ventures, but are also drawn to politics, diplomacy, teaching, sports, coaching, training, the military, business, community work, writing, poetry, dance, music, conducting and other positions that require coordinating large numbers of people. They are prone to bouts of negativity and depression, and are sensitive to stress. Cognitive behavioral therapy techniques can help them to reprogram their thoughts more positively. **For self-care**, wearing, meditating on and surrounding yourself with the color orange encourages you to be more spontaneous and positive.

Those born on this day attract attention because they have a solemn charisma, but they do need to be careful that fear of putting their hearts on the line does not mean they miss out on lasting love. Before the age of 21 they are cautious in their approach to life, but after 21 they become more adventurous, independent and less influenced by others. Once they realize just how creative and capable they can be, their self-confidence flowers and they attract all the success and happiness they richly deserve. When they can reprogram their thoughts to take into account both positive and negative outcomes, and be more flexible and forgiving when things don't go to plan, their destiny is to be a much-needed bringer of harmony, cooperation and synergy.

Potential: Commanding, inspiring

Dark side: Inflexible, negative

Tarot card, lucky numbers, days, colors: The Empress, 3, 6, Saturday, Thursday, dark green, purple

Born today: LeBron James (basketball player); Tiger Woods (golfer); Rudyard Kipling (author); Davy Jones (singer)

December 31

The Birthday of the Connoisseur

The life lesson:

is accepting you are not always right.

The way forward: is to understand we are all unique and what is right for you may not necessarily be right for someone else.

Luck maker: Demonstrating a willingness to learn draws others to you because people like to help those who help themselves.

"My beautiful design"

Those born on December 31 pride themselves on their immaculate taste, and their charisma draws admirers to them wherever they go. They are on a mission to reform and refine and make the world a more appealing place. They set high standards, but what makes them such gifted leaders is that they never expect more from others than from themselves. They tend to impose their own standards of what is beautiful or correct, and dismiss others' opinions or visions. This can make them narrow-minded and intolerant, and they need to remind themselves that beauty lies in the eye of the beholder.

Born team-builders, they are suited to careers where they can create harmony, such as business management, strategic planning and events organization, education, lecturing, community work and interior design, or where they can express their creativity such as in fashion, retail, the theater, opera, film or art. Worry, pessimism and overwork tend to be their downfall. They need to look within for self-confidence and fulfillment. Their appearance matters greatly to them, so they generally eat well and get plenty of exercise. **For self-care**, interpreting your dreams, listening more to your feelings, and holding a moonstone to meditate upon help strengthen your intuition, your capacity to decide what you want out of life and your ability to recognize the beauty that lies within.

These people have a flair for the dramatic and may give the impression of being a free spirit, but they have a deep need for security and affection in their relationships. Before the age of 20 they may come across as artistic yet disciplined, but after 21 they become less influenced by tradition and others, and more independent. After 51 they focus on developing their sensitivity and a strong inner life. At any age, getting in touch with their intuition can show them that harmony isn't just important in the outside world—first and foremost it must be created within. Once they understand that everyone has their own idea of beauty, their destiny is to bring a much-needed touch of harmony and grace into the world.

Potential: Tasteful, charismatic

Dark side: Opinionated, materialistic

Tarot card, lucky numbers, days, colors: The Emperor, 4, 7, Saturday, Sunday, dark green, silver

Born today: Henri Matisse (painter); Anthony Hopkins, Ben Kingsley, Val Kilmer (actors)

The Best and Worst of Days

"All we have to do is decide what to do with the time that is given us."

J. R. R. Tolkien

So, are there better days to be born than others?

According to a number of scientific studies, the day you were born and the month it falls in are associated with an increased or decreased risk of certain diseases and also of depression, with September- and October-born leading the way in the good health stakes. However, this isn't written in stone, as the conclusions differ from study to study. Also, as the risk is associated with early exposure to sunlight, this will vary dramatically depending on whether you are born in the northern or southern hemisphere.

Perhaps more convincing than health and birthdays research are surveys that link birth month with potential career path. These findings are fascinating as they suggest a small but significant correlation between certain careers and the month a person is born. Here's what was discovered:

Born in January:
A higher proportion of doctors and finance professionals

Born in February:
Artistic people and entrepreneurs

Born in March:
An increased number of pilots and airline staff

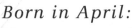

Born in April:
More managers and leaders

Born in May:
People taking up a variety of different careers

Born in June:
Business leaders and CEOs

Born in July:
More manual workers and artists

Born in August:
Politicians and people less interested in school or university

Born in September:
Those most likely to be drawn to university education

Born in October:
Sportsmen and sportswomen, politicians and finance professionals

Born in November:
People working in caring and teaching professions

Born in December:
Dentists

Of course, this is not written in stone, but it is fascinating all the same that statistics showed a mild association between certain jobs and birth months.

Other interesting studies indicate months when more people are born than others. It seems that September is a common birthday month, with the last week in September being the most popular. For obvious reasons February 29 is the least common day on which to be born.

A recent study boldly suggested that June 6 was the best day of the year to be born given the number of successful or highly influential people born that day. Other research points to certain days that indicate a potential Oscar winner or president, but such research is deeply flawed as there will always be exceptions. For example, December 16 has been flagged up as perhaps the worst day to be born, but how can it be when both Jane Austen and Noël Coward were born on that day?

Hopefully, this book has proved loud and clear that the choice to fulfill your personality potential is always your own. Every single one of the 366 birthdays has infinite potential to become the best day of the year to be born. And every day is a truly special and happy, happy day to be born and to be alive!

Reach for Your Stars

"We turn not older with years, but newer every day."

Emily Dickinson

The Pirahã from Brazil have been described as among the happiest and most fulfilled people on earth. They are a simple people, but what makes them most remarkable is their attitude toward sleep. They get very little of it. Instead they choose to nap for half an hour or so whenever they feel sleepy rather than sleeping through the night. They believe sleeping for longer than that is a risk, because it would stop them protecting themselves from deadly snakes while asleep. This makes sense in their indigenous culture but not in our very different lifestyle.

I'm in no way suggesting here that you should cut back on your sleep, as a good night's sleep is vital for your health and wellbeing. I am referencing the Pirahã and their approach to sleep because they have an absolutely fascinating belief about what happens to your personality when you sleep.

They believe that if you sleep for more than a few hours you actually wake up a different or new person. You are no longer "you" anymore. Pirahã who sleep longer than a few hours may even change their names, because they believe the person they were yesterday before they fell asleep has "died" and is not the same person who wakes up in the morning. They even refer to the person they were yesterday as "him" or "her"—in other words, a previous version of themselves.

The Pirahã may be on to something deeply real here. Science proves that when you fall asleep, your body isn't just resting—it is regenerating. Your cells repair and renew, your brain also recalibrates. In this way you do wake up every morning renewed and different from the person you were the day before. Each night when you fall asleep, the person you were that day "dies." You are born anew and rejuvenated physically and psychologically every time you wake up.

So, in this sense every single day of the year truly is your "birthday."

Make Every Day Count

This book can help you make every day count. In the morning before your day begins be sure to slowly read the birthday profile for that day. Then, spend a few moments meditating on the wisdom offered there. Let the day's insight guide and inform the choices you make. Allow it to help you become a more aware and evolved version of yourself than you were yesterday. The more you learn about yourself during the day, the more you will store and process while you are sleeping.

Wake up filled with gratitude for the new day and the opportunities to fulfill your potential that lie ahead, and end your day with similar feelings of gratitude. Those twice-daily twilight moments between sleeping and waking, and waking and sleeping, are powerful ones because that is when your brain is most receptive to reprogramming. Let your brain know you are truly grateful for all that you are and all you can be.

In essence, this book isn't just about discovering your infinite birthday potential, it's about making the most of every single day of your life. It's a daily reminder that every new dawn is a special and glorious miracle, a once-in-a-lifetime opportunity to be born anew and reach as high as you can for your sun, moon and stars.

About the Author

Theresa Cheung was born on April 8 (Buddha's birthday) into a family of astrologers and mystics. Since leaving King's College, Cambridge, with a degree in Theology and English, she has written numerous bestselling New Age titles, including two *Sunday Times* top-10 books and *The Dream Dictionary A to Z*. Her books have been translated into dozens of languages all over the world and been featured in national newspapers. She has also been interviewed about New Age topics by Piers Morgan on *GMB* and Russell Brand on *Under the Skin*. She works closely with scientists studying consciousness. Her website is www.theresacheung.com. You can contact Theresa via her email: angeltalk710@aol.com.